SUPERVISION

CONCEPTS AND PRACTICES OF MANAGEMENT

6TH EDITION

Raymond L. Hilgert
Professor of Management and Industrial Relations
John M. Olin School of Business
Washington University

Edwin C. Leonard, Jr.
Professor of Business Administration
School of Business and Management Sciences
Indiana University-Purdue University at Fort Wayne

Theo Haimann
The Mary Louise Murray Professor of Management Sciences
School of Business and Administration
St. Louis University

SOUTH-WESTERN College Publishing

An International Thomson Publishing Company

Sponsoring Editor: Randy G. Haubner
Developmental Editor: Cinci Stowell
Production Editors: Rebecca Roby, Eric Carlson, Shelley Brewer
Production House: WordCrafters Editorial Services, Inc.
Designer: Craig LaGesse Ramsdell
Photo Researcher: Feldman and Associates
Photo Editor: Jennifer Mayhall
Marketing Manager: Scott D. Person

GZ94FA
Copyright © 1995
by South-Western College Publishing
Cincinnati, Ohio

Library of Congress Cataloging-in-Publication Data

Hilgert, Raymond L.
    Supervision : concepts and practices of management / Raymond L.
Hilgert, Edwin C. Leonard. — 6th ed.
        p.   cm.
    Includes bibliographical references and index.
    ISBN 0-538-83689-X (alk. paper)
    1. Supervision of employees.   2. Personnel management.
I. Leonard, Edwin C.   II. Title.
HF5549.12.H55   1995
658.3'02—dc20   94-15555
                                                             CIP

International Thomson Publishing
South-Western College Publishing is an ITP Company. The ITP trademark is used under
license.

2 3 4 5 6 7 8 9 PR 3 2 1 0 9 8 7 6 5
Printed in the United States of America

PREFACE

TO THE INSTRUCTOR

If there is one constant in today's business world, it is change. Wholesale changes in technologies, in organizational and competitive structure, in the social, economic, and political environments—all seem to be accelerating more rapidly than ever before. To operate successfully in this changing environment, organizations need supervisors with the managerial skills and creativity to turn uncertainty into opportunity. We prepared this sixth edition of *Supervision: Concepts and Practices of Management* to equip students with the skills they need to thrive as supervisors in the present and future business world.

A TEXT THAT IS SKILLS-FOCUSED

The 6th edition has been revised significantly from its predecessor, while retaining its thrust as a comprehensive single source and leading textbook on supervisory management. We have focused the text on helping students develop supervisory skills they can really use. While learning important supervisory management concepts, they will also learn how to be supervisors—how to apply the principles of management in the real world.

The text is introductory in that it assumes no previous management knowledge. However, it presents challenging material in language that students can understand. The concepts are presented in direct, practical terms. It is not intended as a book for academic theoreticians.

A major goal of the book is to help the student, the potential supervisor, or the newly appointed supervisor analyze the many problems that confront supervisors, and the book offers practical advice for their solutions. For experienced supervisors, the text is intended to refresh their thinking, widen their horizons, and challenge them to examine how they are relating to employees, other supervisors, and higher management.

Materials for this text have been drawn from writings and research of scholars in management and the behavioral sciences and from reported experiences of many supervisors, managers, and administrators. In addition to the authors' own experiences in management, the text reflects our backgrounds in teaching supervisory management courses, in participating in many stimulating discussions in supervisory development programs, and in consulting for numerous organizations.

TEXT FEATURES

Current Topics/New Concepts

All chapters have undergone major revisions and updating. In particular, we have extensively updated material on organizational concepts, motivation and styles of supervisory management, coaching and discipline, supervision of protected-group employees, performance appraisal, and group dynamics and work teams. Among the many current topics discussed in the 6th edition are:

- strategic management
- organizational restructuring
- personal and positional power of supervisors
- employee empowerment
- total quality management (TQM)
- participative management
- work teams
- cultural diversity
- sexual harassment
- the effect of the Americans with Disabilities Act and the Family and Medical Leave Act on supervision
- alternative forms of conflict resolution
- performance and skilled-based pay systems
- inventory and statistical control systems
- accounting and financial tools for supervisors

An Integrated Teaching and Testing System

We have organized the text and supplements around the learning objectives to create a comprehensive teaching and testing system. Each text chapter begins with a series of learning objectives covering the key concepts. The objectives then appear in the text margins, identifying where each objective is fulfilled. The key concepts are again reinforced at the end of the chapter, where they are summarized under their learning objectives.

The integrated system creates a close tie between the text and supplements. Since they are organized around the learning objectives, you can customize your lectures and exams to emphasize the concepts that you feel your students need most. The extensive lecture outlines in the Instructor's Manual identify the materials that fulfill each objective, so that you can be sure your lectures cover the key concepts. Students using the Study Guide can find the material they need to review by simply locating the learning objectives in the text margins that correspond to those of the study guide questions they found difficult.

"You Make The Call" Opening Problems

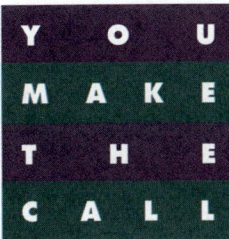

To grab student interest, we begin each chapter with an opening scenario entitled "You Make The Call." Each scenario presents a real-world supervisory situation that students will learn to handle from studying the chapter. These case-like scenarios, written in the second person, draw students personally into a problem situation and ask them to decide what to do. At the conclusion of the chapter, a section entitled "What Call Did You Make?" appears just before the chapter summary. Here we show students how to approach the problem in the scenario, using the concepts they just learned in the chapter. Students can then compare their own approaches and decisions to those suggested by the authors and perhaps also by you, their instructor. By applying chapter concepts to these opening problems and then comparing their results to those provided, students are also learning how to tackle the end-of-part cases.

Contemporary Issues Boxes

To make a smooth transition into the business world, students need to understand the issues facing supervisors now and in the future. In our "Contemporary Issues" boxes within each chapter, we present selected issues surrounding such current supervisory topics as:

- management by wandering around as a means of communication (Chapter 3)
- cooperative efforts between employees, unions, and management in a competitive environment (Chapter 6)
- the virtual corporation in an age of agility (Chapter 9)
- electronic meetings: their uses and shortcomings (Chapter 11)
- new directions in labor union organizing (Chapter 12)
- problems in implementing participative management (Chapter 16)
- opportunities and apprehensions in complying with the Americans with Disabilities Act (Chapter 18)

These contemporary issues tend to be controversial, providing a source of debate concerning application of supervisory principles in current business practice. Most of these boxes cite specific company examples.

Skills Applications

To develop skills, students need practice. Therefore—new for the 6th edition—we have provided three skills applications projects at the end of each chapter. These are hands-on tasks which require students to apply what they have learned. Some projects ask students to compare their own experiences with those of practicing supervisors. Others provide opportunities for small group work within or outside of class, or require self-assessment, library research, interviews with practicing supervisors, and other interesting applications.

Cases

Instructors all over the country have told us that our case studies are excellent tools for teaching supervisory skills. In response to this enthusiasm, we have increased the number of cases in the 6th edition to 50. Because the cases involve concepts from more than one chapter, they appear at the end of each major text part. To help you identify when to use each case, the lecture outlines in the Instructor's Manual suggest case choices next to the chapter coverage where they most apply.

We intentionally kept the cases short—many are less than a page each—so that they could be challenging without being overwhelming for students. All cases are based on actual experiences of supervisors in numerous work environments. The case discussion questions help students focus their thinking. For this 6th edition, we have expanded our commentaries on the case questions in the Instructor's Manual to provide you with even more guidance in implementing the cases and evaluating student responses.

You can use the cases in several ways: as fuel for class or seminar discussions, as written homework assignments, or as examinations. Case assignments are an excellent way for students to practice their skills on real supervisory problems and for you to assess their ability to apply what they have learned.

Video Cases

Today's students like the stimulation of visual presentations. To meet this need in the 6th edition, for each part we have added video cases about actual companies. These cases, developed by Professor Edward White of Danville Community College, are based upon broadcasts on the CNBC cable news network. The CNBC video segments are combined on one easy-to-use video tape, which is available free to adopters. Each video segment is short—only a few minutes each—so they make excellent discussion-starters without taking up too much class time. The Instructor's Manual contains a complete description of each segment, including the running time, plus all the information you need to integrate the video cases into your class presentation.

Other Pedagogical Features

In addition to the features described above, the text provides a number of other features to enhance student learning. Among these are:

Marginal Definitions. In an introductory supervision course, students need to learn the language of business. Therefore—new for the 6th edition—we have placed concise definitions of all key terms in the margins of the text where they are first introduced. The key terms and their definitions are also compiled in a glossary at the end of the book for quick reference.

Summary Points. The major chapter concepts are summarized at the ends of the chapters, organized around the learning objectives. By reviewing these summaries, students can quickly identify areas where they need further review. Then, using the learning objectives in the text margins, they can easily locate the discussion of the concepts they want to review.

Questions for Discussion. The end-of-chapter discussion questions are designed to help students check their understanding of chapter materials.

Key Terms. All key terms are listed at the end of the chapter, with page numbers to make the explanations of the terms easy to find.

SUPPLEMENTS TO EASE YOUR TEACHING LOAD

Instructor's Manual

Instructors always have more to do than there are hours in a day. To make your class preparations easier, we have greatly expanded the Instructor's Manual. New to the 6th edition are extensive lecture outlines, which form the core of the integrated teaching system. These outlines provide everything you need for faster and easier lecture preparations. They contain references to all supplementary materials right next to the chapter concepts to which they apply. You will be advised when to show each transparency, use the cases, bring in the discussion of the chapter's boxed features, and more—all organized around the learning objectives. The outlines also contain discussion suggestions for the transparencies, "You Make The Call" features, and "Contemporary Issues" boxes.

In addition to the lecture outlines, the new, comprehensive Instructor's Manual includes:

- A test bank expanded by over 200 questions beyond the previous edition, including many new application questions, all keyed to the learning objectives.
- Summaries of key concepts by learning objective.
- Commentaries on all cases, which will help you guide discussions or evaluate students' written analyses.

- Commentaries on the Video Cases.
- Commentaries on all Skills Applications, including suggested solutions and follow-up approaches.
- Solution guidelines for all end-of-chapter discussion questions.
- A bibliography of additional published resources.

Acetate Transparencies

New, and free to adopters, is a set of 66 colorful acetate transparencies, all closely correlated to the text presentation, but all originals—not simply reproductions of text illustrations. All were carefully designed to be attractive to students as well as easy to read.

Study Guide

Students told us that they want a Study Guide that will enhance their learning and help raise their test scores. With this goal in mind, Professor Taggart Smith of Purdue University developed the new Study Guide in close association with Elizabeth Elam of Bernard M. Baruch College, who wrote the test questions, to make sure that the style and difficulty level of the Study Guide questions closely parallel those of the test bank.

ACKNOWLEDGMENTS

In developing this text and supplementary materials, we are indebted to so many individuals that it is impossible to give all of them credit. Special thanks goes to those organizations, supervisors, and managers who provided materials for the cases, exercises, applications projects, and certain illustrations. We appreciate the contributions of the following professors who reviewed the text and offered numerous helpful suggestions and comments:

Raymond F. Balcerzak, Jr.
Ferris State University

Lorraine P. Bassette
Prince George's Community College

Jerry E. Boles
Community College of Western Kentucky University

Steve Byrd
Southeast Missouri State University

Michael A. Cardinale
Palomar College

Win Chesney
St. Louis Community College-Meramec

Kent Curtis
Northern Kentucky University

Michael Dougherty
Milwaukee Area Technical College

Ben G. Dunn
York Technical College

Mary E. Falkey
Prince George's Community College

Roger S. Gilbert, Jr.
Santa Fe Community College

Tommy Gilbreath
University of Texas-Tyler

John B. Horton
Southern Illinois University

Charles Lamb
Northwestern University

Kenneth L. Lehmann
Forsyth Technical College

Sharon Pinebrook
University of Houston

William Recker
Northern Kentucky University

James H. Riley
Langston University-University Center at Tulsa

H. Giles Schmid
Winona State University

Bob F. Thomas
Roane State Community College

We particularly want to thank Professor Edward White of Danville Community College for his excellent work in preparing the video cases. We are extremely grateful to Professor Taggart Smith of Purdue University and to Elizabeth Elam, who teaches at Bernard M. Baruch College, for their excellent supplementary materials.

We express our appreciation to Karen Pressel and Karen Broyles, graduate students at Washington University, who assisted in developing some of the cases and case instructional materials. We gratefully acknowledge the word-processing services of Leslie Stroker and Karen Busch of the Washington University staff and of Louise Pruse of the staff at Indiana University/Purdue University at Fort Wayne.

Finally, we note the passing of the co-author of previous editions of this text, Dr. Theo Haimann. His prior contributions are gratefully acknowledged, and he will long be remembered by his many colleagues, former students, and friends.

Raymond L. Hilgert

Edwin C. Leonard, Jr.

ABOUT THE AUTHORS

Dr. Raymond L. Hilgert currently is Professor of Management and Industrial Relations at the Olin School of Business of Washington University. He graduated from Westminster College, Fulton, Missouri, with a Bachelor of Arts Degree, and received his Master's and Doctor's degrees from Washington University. His business experience includes management positions at Southwestern Bell Telephone Company and a market research position with an advertising company. Dr. Hilgert has taught at Washington University for over 30 years, and he has served as an Assistant Dean and Director of Management Development Programs. He has published some 80 articles in management, business, and academic journals and has co-authored five books on human resources management, supervision, and collective bargaining, three of which are in their third, sixth, and seventh editions.

Dr. Hilgert is a member of the Academy of Management, the Industrial Relations Research Association, the Society for Human Resource Management, and the American Management Association. He has participated in or directed numerous management, supervisory, and business ethics programs and seminars. Dr. Hilgert is an arbitrator certified by the Federal Mediation and Conciliation Service and the American Arbitration Association, and he holds the Senior Professional in Human Resources (SPHR) accreditation from the Personnel Accreditation Institute. He has received a number of teaching awards from students at Washington University.

Dr. Edwin C. Leonard, Jr. currently is Professor of Business Administration at Indiana University/Purdue University at Fort Wayne. He received his Bachelor's, Master's, and Doctor's degrees from Purdue University. Since joining the faculty over 25 years ago, he has held a variety of faculty and administrative positions, including serving as chair of the Management and Marketing Department in the School of Business and Management Sciences. Dr. Leonard has designed and conducted workshops and seminars for thousands of supervisors and managers. These programs often are customized to meet specific organizational needs. Dr. Leonard also is associated with a major full-service training and consulting firm.

Dr. Leonard's primary research interests are in the areas of employee involvement, teaming, organizational climate and leadership, human resource management interventions, and case development. He has published in a variety of academic and professional journals, instructional supplement manuals, and proceedings. His professional memberships include the Midwest Academy of Management, the American Evaluation Association, the Midwest Society for Human Resources/Industrial Relations, the Society for Case Research, the Business and Health Administration Association, the Indiana Academy of the Social Sciences, and the Society for Human Resource Management.

Dr. Leonard was the recipient of the National University Continuing Education Association's Service Award for Continuing Education for the Professions, and he has received the Award of Teaching Excellence from the Indiana University School of Continuing Studies.

BRIEF CONTENTS

Contents

PART 4
STAFFING

PART 6
CONTROLLING

Chapter 21 Fundamentals of Controlling   574

Chapter 22 Financial Reports, Budgets, and Other Controls   595

APPENDIX I

APPENDIX II

PART 1

SUPERVISORY MANAGEMENT OVERVIEW

1

The Supervisory Challenge

LEARNING OBJECTIVES

After studying this chapter, you will be able to:

1 Explain why someone might want to become a supervisor.

2 Describe the contributions of four schools of management thought.

3 Identify and discuss the major demographic and societal trends that will affect supervisors.

4 Discuss the leadership component of supervision.

5 Explain why supervisors must continually grow and develop as professionals.

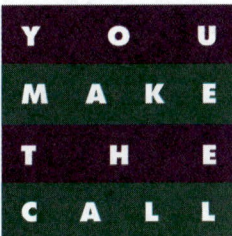

YOU MAKE THE CALL

Every chapter in this text will begin with a section titled "You Make the Call." As you read each chapter, think about how the concepts apply to the opening problem. After you finish each chapter, check the "calls" you made against the suggestions in the section called "What Call Did You Make?". This section will appear just before the summary for each chapter.

You are Randy Harber, a 36-year-old construction crew chief employed by one of the largest mechanical contractors in the country. Your employer currently operates in 44 states and 14 foreign countries. You and your spouse, Eileen, have two children, aged seven and three. Eileen is a registered nurse and works part time in a family practice office.

You began your career in the construction field by entering the apprenticeship program immediately after completing high school. You rose through the trade union ranks, served as an officer in the local union, and became a crew chief three years ago. Your technical skills rank among the best. During the past two years, you have taken evening courses at the local community college to enhance your supervisory skills. You desire to become a field superintendent. However, the construction industry has enjoyed no real growth, and opportunities for advancement are slim. During the past winter, you and others suffered reduced work weeks and had your use of the company truck severely restricted. Kevin Cook, vice president of field operations, calls you into his office.

Kevin: Randy, you know that our revenues are down about 25 percent from last year.

You: Yes (while thinking to yourself, "Here it comes, I'm going to get laid off").

Kevin: We've been trying to expand our base of operations and have bid on contracts all over the world. I think we have the opportunity of a lifetime, and you figure to be one of our key players. The United Methodist Church is collaborating in a joint venture in Liberia to build a hospital on the outskirts of Monrovia, the capital city. They have had a medical missionary program there, and this hospital is a 23-million-dollar project. The general contractor will be out of Milan, Italy, and we got the mechanical portion of the contract.

You: That's great! We can use the work.

Kevin: This project will give us a strategic advantage in the European-African corridor. The top-level managers have talked it over, and we would like you to be our field superintendent on this project. Not only is this a great opportunity for us, but it will also give you valuable experience. In addition, your salary would almost double. All of the people on this project will be our very best. You'd be leaving in three weeks, and we'd expect you to be on site for 14 months. What do you think?

You: Gee, that sounds fascinating. How soon do you need an answer?

Kevin: Go home, think it over, talk to Eileen, and let's get back together tomorrow afternoon about 3:00.

What are you going to do?
YOU MAKE THE CALL.

WHY WOULD ANYONE WANT TO BE A SUPERVISOR?

1 Explain why someone might want to become a supervisor.

Supervisor
First-level manager in charge of entry-level and other departmental employees.

Virtually every aspect of contemporary life has undergone major changes during the past several decades. There is little doubt that major changes will continue to take place in our society during coming years, and continuing change will be a challenge to every organization. Like all aspects of modern life, organizational concepts and managerial practices are also undergoing major changes, as illustrated in the Contemporary Issue box. Managers at all levels will be at the forefront of planning and coping with trends, factors, and problems requiring attention and more effective management if they and their organizations are to survive. This book will focus primarily on the first tier of management, which generally is referred to as the supervisory level, or supervisory management. **Supervisors** are first-level managers who are in charge of entry-level and other departmental employees.

From an economic, political, geographical, and sociological perspective, the last decade stands as a time of turbulence in U.S. business. Current critical commen-

CONTEMPORARY ISSUE
The Organization Is Changing

Supervisor/worker; manager/employee; the company/the union; us/them: That is the way the workplace has been organized in the United States since the turn of the century, and until recently we have taken the system for granted. Owners and managers expect to run the corporate show; employees expect to do what they are told. It is us versus them.

Point: A new mindset is needed. The marketplace has changed dramatically in the last 20 years, and now the old thinking no longer works. It is evident in the sorry state of so many companies in the United States

and in managers' frenzy to try out employee empowerment, total quality management, and the other hot-off-the-presses managerial techniques. They are creating a whole different mindset about business and a different way of organizing work—one in which there is no room for "us" and "them."

Counterpoint: Is there a need for supervisors? Tom Peters suggests that corporate structures should be changed. His suggestions leave the question of what to do with first-line supervisors, of whom 90 percent are redundant, unanswered.

Source: Adapted from John P. Case, "A Company of Business People," *Inc.* (Volume 15, Number 4, April 1993), pp. 79–93; and Tom Peters, *Thriving on Chaos* (New York: Alfred A. Knopf, 1987), p. 263.

taries on the U.S. business system indicate that the traditional notions of getting a job done through power and positional authority are no longer effective. Today's managers and supervisors, whether they are in factories, nursing care units, business offices, retail stores, or government agencies, must realize that reliance on authoritarian direction and close control will not bring about the desired results. Managers everywhere will continue to expect supervisors to obtain better productivity from all of their human resources. In some organizations the role of the supervisor may change drastically. The term "supervisor" may even be eliminated from the company vocabulary. It will be replaced by terms such as "team leader," "facilitator," or "coach."

Supervisory work has become more complex, sophisticated, and demanding, and it requires professional and interpersonal skills. As depicted in Figure 1-1, the job of the supervisor is both rewarding and stressful. The ideas presented are not all inclusive, but they give a feel for the functions and activities of the supervisor.

Although the first-line supervisory position is one of the three levels on the management hierarchy (see Figure 1-2), it is the level in which most people obtain their first management experience. By this stage of your career, you have probably developed a picture of what supervisory management is all about. Your past experiences as a child, student, employee, and/or supervisor have allowed you to observe some of the prevailing supervisory practices. In all likelihood, your observations made you aware that there are distinct differences in how the concepts are applied.

In the past, many managers achieved their positions on the basis of practical experience they obtained in the first-level supervisory position. Today, the study of management has become more formalized, and many prospective supervisors learn management concepts and principles in a classroom setting. Although the system-

FIGURE 1-1
The Trials and
Tribulations of a
Supervisor

POINT: THE SUPERVISOR'S JOB IS REWARDING

- A supervisor can find great personal satisfaction in helping employees reach their full potential.
- The accomplishment of various tasks is rewarding, particularly when others thought it was not possible.
- A supervisor gains satisfaction from the opportunity to use a wide variety of skills and gain valuable experiences.
- The opportunity to make decisions and be held accountable for those decisions is satisfying. Increased involvement in decision making is a positive benefit to many supervisors.
- Supervisory experience provides learning. The so-called "school of hard knocks" provides experiences that no textbook can provide.
- Supervisors who constantly look for the good in other people will uncover some strengths in themselves. The supervisors can then build on those strengths.

COUNTER POINT: THE SUPERVISOR'S JOB IS CHALLENGING

- Supervisors work long hours. The number of hours worked tends to increase as a person climbs the organizational ladder.
- A supervisor's work is fragmented; episodes are brief. Given supervisors' high activity level, they have little time to devote to any single activity. Interruptions, crises, and problems are the rule.
- Information is the basic ingredient of the supervisor's work. Supervisors spend much of their time obtaining, interpreting, and giving information.
- The supervisor is constantly juggling the needs of the organization (completion of task) and the needs of the employees. The need to recognize both concepts and establish priorities is essential.
- A supervisor, particularly one promoted from within, is no longer one of the group. In many organizations the us-versus-them mentality develops. The newly promoted supervisor is now one of "them." Therefore, the supervisor needs to develop a professional rather than a personal relationship with employees.
- The growth of the human resources department, coupled with the movement toward more employee participation, is perceived by some as an erosion of the supervisor's authority. At the same time, it has been suggested that 90 percent of the supervisory positions in U.S. corporations are redundant. These notions are threatening to many supervisors.

Source: Adapted with permission from Morgan W. McCall, Jr., Ann M. Morrison, and Robert L. Hannan, *Studies of Managerial Work: Results and Methods* (Technical Report No. 9) (Greensboro, NC: Center for Creative Leadership, 1978), pp. 6–18; and from E. C. Leonard, Jr., presentation to Fastener and Vulcraft Divisions, Nucor Corporation, St. Joe, Indiana, September 20, 1993.

atic study of management is a 20th-century phenomenon, the authors believe that a better knowledge of the past will lead to a more productive future. While it is not our intent to provide an in-depth analysis of the past, we feel that prospective supervisors need to understand the historical perspective of management.

FIGURE 1-2
The supervisory position is where most people begin their management careers.

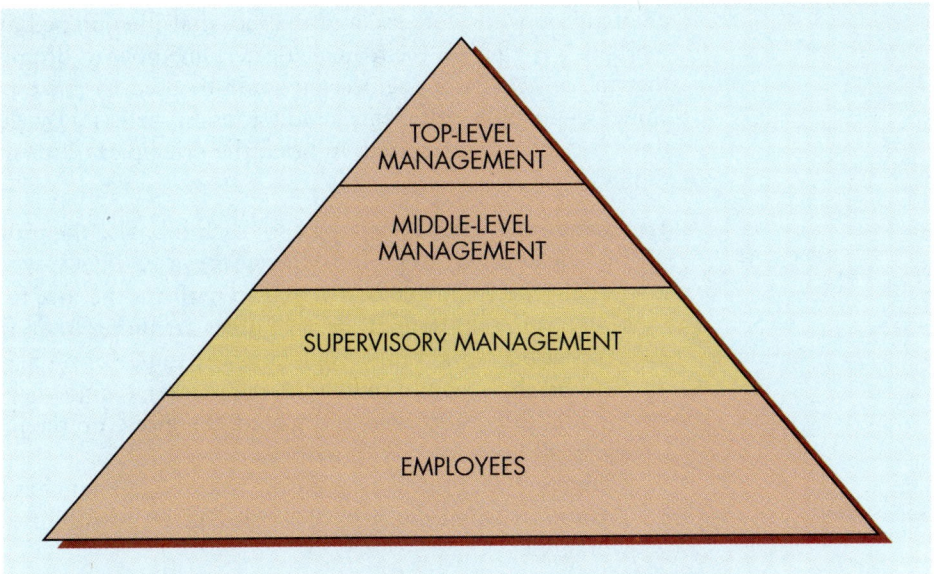

TOP-LEVEL
MANAGEMENT

MIDDLE-LEVEL
MANAGEMENT

SUPERVISORY MANAGEMENT

EMPLOYEES

HISTORICAL PERSPECTIVE[1]

2 Describe the contributions of four schools of management thought.

Management practices can be traced throughout history, beginning with the Bible. The Great Wall of China, the Pyramids of Egypt, the Roman Coliseum, the Eiffel Tower, and the Statue of Liberty all resulted from the application of management principles. While there is no universally accepted theory of management, there is a common thread among the various theories: Each attempts to answer the question "What is the best way to manage the task at hand?" Many of the early schools of thought still influence the way people approach the supervisory task. While there is little agreement on the exact number and nomenclature of the various management theories, we believe that four are deserving of mention here.

Scientific Management

Scientific management approach
School of management thought that focuses on the "one best way" to achieve production efficiency.

One of the first approaches to the study of management was the **scientific management approach**, designed to determine the "one best way" to do a job. Frederick Winslow Taylor, the father of scientific management, believed that the manager should plan what, when, where, and how employees should produce the product; that is, the manager's job was to perform the mental tasks. The employees' job would be to perform the physical tasks. To this end, Taylor developed certain principles to increase productivity. It should be noted that everyone plans; the essential difference is that the manager plans the work of others.

Taylor believed that workers did not put forth their best efforts and that, as a result, production suffered. As a manager at Midvale Steel Works in Philadelphia, Taylor was shocked at the lack of systematic procedures, the output restriction among groups of workers, and the fact that ill-equipped and inadequately trained workers were left on their own to determine how to do their jobs. Taylor believed that the principles of engineering could be used to make people as much like machines as possible—efficient, mindless, and repetitive. By eliminating choice, operations could be standardized. In brief, the principles of scientific management are as follows:

1. Analyze the tasks associated with each job. Use the principles of science to find the one best way to perform the work.
2. Recruit the employee best suited to perform the job; that is, choose the person who has the skills, aptitude, and other attributes to do the job.
3. Instruct the worker in the one best way to perform the job.
4. Reward the accomplishment of the worker. Taylor believed that workers were economically motivated and would, therefore, do the job the way they were instructed if rewarded with money.
5. Cooperate with workers to ensure that the job matches plans and principles.
6. Ensure an equal division of work and responsibility between managers and workers.

Figure 1-3 suggests how Taylor believed in separating planning from doing; that is, the manager should do the research, the planning, and the instructing while the worker should do the actual work.

Frank and Lillian Gilbreth concentrated on motion study. They identified 17 basic on-the-job motions, which helped in studying how to accomplish work more efficiently. Taylor, the Gilbreths, and others laid the foundation for the field of industrial engineering.

The Functional Approach

Henri Fayol, a French industrialist, identified 14 principles of management that he believed could be applied universally. Several of the more widely accepted principles will be introduced in subsequent chapters. In general, Fayol believed that authority should be equal to responsibility, unity of command, and unity of direction.

Functional approach
School of management thought that asserts that managers apply various functions in doing their jobs, e.g., planning, organizing, staffing, leading, and controlling.

More important, Fayol introduced the **functional approach** to the study of management. This approach defined the manager's role and proposed that managers do their jobs by performing various functions. He identified five functions as being critical for managerial effectiveness:

1. Planning: setting down a course of action.
2. Organizing: designing a structure, with tasks and authority clearly defined.
3. Commanding: directing subordinates in what to do.
4. Coordinating: pulling the organizational elements together toward common objectives.
5. Controlling: ascertaining that plans are carried out.

Other writers have built upon these ideas. This textbook is organized around the more current version of the functional approach to the study of management: planning, organizing, staffing, leading, and controlling.

FIGURE 1-3
Separate planning
from doing.

Frederick W. Taylor's story about a mythical worker, Schmidt, reveals the idea behind scientific management.

The worker was to carry a "pig," a 92-pound block of iron, up an incline and drop it into an open rail car. The average worker handled about 12½ tons in a 10-hour day while being paid about $1.15 per day. Taylor selected Schmidt for the job and asked him whether he wanted to be a "first-class" pig-iron handler. After being told that a "first-class" pig-iron handler would be properly instructed in techniques of lifting and carrying, would follow the foreman's instructions explicitly, and would be paid about $1.85 per day, Schmidt was most interested in the "new way." Using this approach, Schmidt was able to increase his daily output to 47 tons per day. While this approach made work more efficient, it also made many jobs highly routine and monotonous. The problem with this, of course, is that some people who are bored with their jobs tend to lose their attentiveness, stay away from work, or seek employment elsewhere.

Human Relations/Behavioral School

The works of Taylor and others gave rise to the notion that (1) if managers would use the principles of scientific management, worker efficiency would increase and, thus, productivity increases would follow; and (2) if managers would strive to improve working conditions, then productivity increases would follow. The studies at the Hawthorne plant of Western Electric provided some of the most interesting and controversial results in the study of management.

Elton Mayo and Fritz Roethlisberger, leaders of a Harvard research team, conducted a series of experiments from 1924 to 1932. In the Illumination Experiments they hypothesized that if lighting improved, then productivity would increase. Contrary to expectations, productivity rose in both the control group (no changes made in working conditions) and the experimental group (working conditions varied). Numerous variations in working conditions were introduced, and no matter what change was introduced, productivity continued to rise until it stabilized at a relatively high level. The researchers concluded that the workers performed differently than they normally did because the researchers were observing them. This reaction is known as the **Hawthorne effect**. Other phases of the Hawthorne studies are discussed in Chapter 17.

The experiments at the Hawthorne plant gave rise to what was known as the **human relations movement**, and later as the **behavioral science approach**, which focused study on the behavior of people in organizations. Chapter 5 discusses various causes of individual behavior and the impact of supervisory practice on employee motivation.

Quantitative Approach

While it is beyond the scope of this text, the **quantitative approach** to management had its origins in the operations research approach developed by the British during

Hawthorne effect
The mere fact that interest is shown in people causes them to behave differently.

Human relations movement/behavioral science approach
Approach to management that focuses on the behavior of people in the work environment.

Quantitative approach
Field of management that uses mathematical modeling as a foundation.

World War II. This approach relies heavily on mathematical modeling. Interest in this approach has increased with the development of the computer, which enables easy manipulation of large quantities of data. This approach is generally used by large organizations. For example, sales, cost, and production data are analyzed. Then mathematical modeling is used to build "what if" situations—What would be the effect on sales if the price rose 10 percent, 20 percent, and so forth? Several of the planning concepts introduced in Chapter 7 rely heavily on this approach.

FACTORS AND TRENDS AFFECTING THE ROLE OF THE SUPERVISOR

3 Identify and discuss the major demographic and societal trends that will affect supervisors.

Throughout the foreseeable future, supervisors will have to understand and deal with many complex environmental factors and trends. Therefore, we will examine some major demographic and societal factors and trends that are likely to affect the supervisory management position. Figure 1-4 illustrates many of the challenges faced by a supervisor.

While every supervisor is responsible for managing numerous resources, unquestionably the most important, overriding aspect of supervision is the management of people. Therefore, the nature of the workforce should be of vital concern to the supervisor who plans for the future. Finding and developing qualified people have always been among the most important supervisory responsibilities. However, the traditional challenges of attracting and retaining the most qualified employees may be superseded by the more acute challenge to supervisors of leading and motivating an increasingly changing workforce. The most significant characteristic of this changing workforce will be its **diversity**. Work groups will be composed of employees who differ on cultural, ethnic, gender, age, educational level, racial, and life-style characteristics. The supervisor will need to get people from many different cultures to work together.

Diversity
The cultural, ethnic, gender, age, educational level, racial, and life-style differences among employees.

Population and Workforce Growth[2]

Despite the rather low birth rates of recent decades, both the population and the workforce are growing. It is estimated that the U.S. population will grow at a modest rate from a 1990 level of about 250 million people to nearly 270 million people by the year 2000. The workforce is also projected to increase by 20 million during the same time period. It can be seen from these estimates that a somewhat higher percentage of the total population will be employed in the workforce—a continuation of a trend that has existed over the previous two decades. It is expected that the workforce growth will be buoyed by an increase in immigration.[3] The growth in new immigrants may create interracial and intercultural disputes that will test the supervisor's conflict-resolution skills.

While managing a diverse workforce presents many difficulties, our intent in the following sections is to create an awareness of differences, that is, to accomplish some "consciousness raising." First, supervisors must understand the rights of

FIGURE 1-4
Effective supervisors must be adaptable and be able to maintain their perspective in the face of rapidly changing conditions.

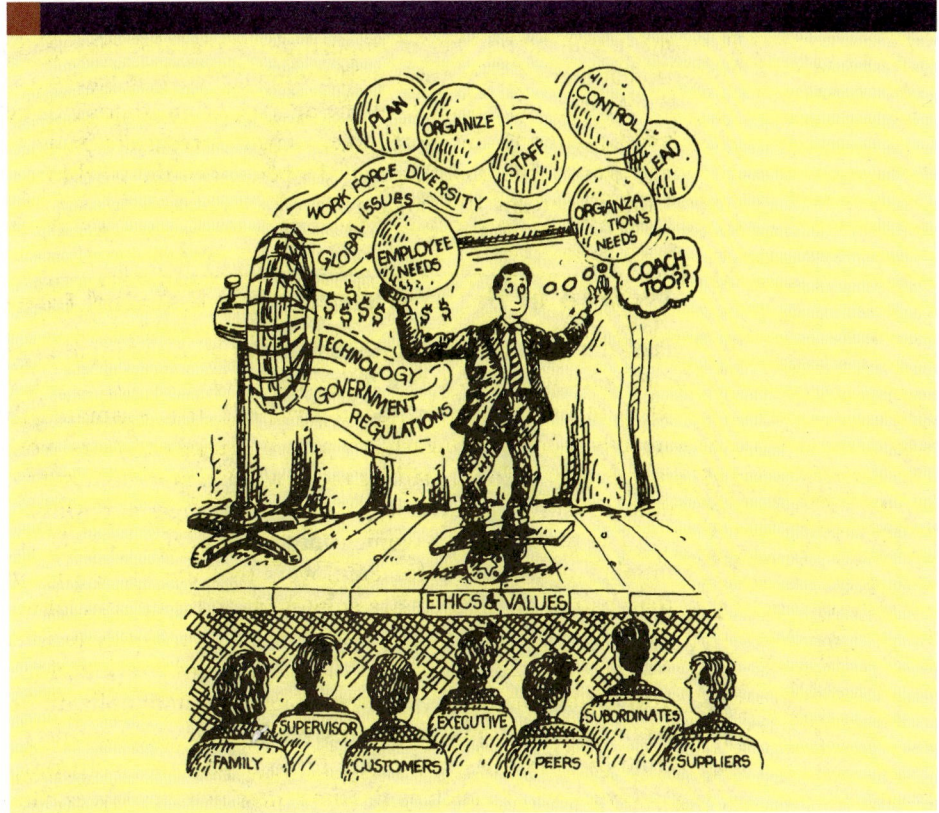

employees as well as the obligation of the employer. Second, supervisors will need to recognize the value of a diverse workforce and their own need to become more adaptable. And finally, perhaps more than ever before, supervisors will have to strive to be scrupulously fair in supervising diverse groups of employees through nondiscriminatory and progressive actions.

The Aging of America

Both the population and workforce are getting older. For example, in 1990 about 40 percent of the workforce was between 35 and 54 years of age; this age group will comprise about 50 percent of the workforce by the year 2000. Since this age group normally provides the highest percentage of people who are promotable to supervisory and other management positions, in the future more people will be available to fill these positions. Thus, the competition for supervisory positions will be keen.

Furthermore, these older workers have years of experience and generally occupy supervisory or managerial positions. If they stay on for an additional five or ten years, there may be a glut of younger employees waiting for opportunities to develop. These mismatches between the number of employees desiring advancement and the number of opportunities available may lead to increased dissatisfaction and greater turnover as the younger workers leave to seek positions elsewhere.

At the opposite end of the age spectrum, there will be relatively fewer young people entering the workforce. Census forecasters project that the 16- to 24-year age group will constitute only 16 percent of the workforce in the year 2000, down from 20 percent 10 years earlier.

Women in the Workforce and Related Issues

Probably the most dramatic change has been the rapid increase in both the number and percentage of women in the U.S. workforce. In 1990, women comprised about 45 percent of the workforce. By 2000, it is estimated that this percentage will steadily increase to nearly 50 percent. In recent years women have assumed many jobs formerly dominated by men. Women now hold over one-third of the nation's administrative, supervisory, and other managerial positions.

The movement of women into the workforce, however, has brought with it a number of problems for employers that are likely to continue. Currently, more than half of all mothers are employed, and a substantial number of those are single working mothers. Employees may bring their family problems to work. Supervisors will need to understand that their employees' work performance may be negatively affected by this conflict between job and family obligations. In order to attract and retain the most qualified employees, employers may need to provide high-quality child-care facilities and continue to experiment with different types of workdays and work weeks, such as **flextime** (in which employees choose their work schedules within certain limits), **job sharing** (in which two or more employees share a job position), **telecommuting** (in which the employee works at home and is linked to the office by computer and modem), and the four-day, 10-hour-a-day work week. Given the increasing numbers of single working parents and the concern over the quality of child-care services, firms are likely to implement these types of working arrangements. Efforts to help employees balance the responsibilities of home and job will require better supervisory coordination and planning skills.

Another major challenge for supervisors will be to ensure that sexual harassment does not occur in the work environment. Sexual harassment has been perpetrated against both men and women, but media attention has focused on the latter. Recent court decisions have reiterated the implications for supervisors. They must take action to prevent harassment, and they must take steps to remedy reported incidents of harassment. The topic of sexual harassment will be explored in greater detail in Chapter 18.

Flextime
Policy that allows employees to choose their work hours within stated limits.

Job sharing
Policy that allows two or more employees to perform a job normally done by one full-time employee.

Telecommuting
Receiving and sending work to the office from home via a computer and modem.

Growth of Racial Minorities in the Workforce

In the future, racial minorities will enter the workforce in much greater numbers than ever before. It is projected that the principal minority groups—African

Women in the workforce hold a substantial number of managerial positions.

Americans, Hispanics, and Asians—will comprise 12 percent, 10 percent, and 4 percent, respectively, of the workforce by the year 2000.

Census data reveal that one out of seven residents of the United States speak a language other than English at home. In New York City, students are being taught in 82 languages, and in Los Angles County, only 54.6 percent of students aged 5 years and older speak English at home. Winston Churchill once said, "It is a good thing for an uneducated man to read books of quotations. . . . The gift of a common tongue is a priceless inheritance, and it may well someday become the foundation of a common citizenship."[4] It will be common for supervisors to find that their employees are natives of different countries and that the common tongue has disappeared. The challenges for supervisors will be to learn about the cultural, racial, and language differences and develop strategies for promoting cooperation among the diverse groups.

Equal Opportunity for Women and Minorities

Progress in upgrading the status of women and minorities has been slow. Some firms still seem to relegate women and minorities to the lower-skilled and lower-paying jobs and have not fully utilized the potential contributions that many have to offer. In reality, many organizations have not opened the doors of equal opportunity to women or minorities. While positive strides have been made, many women and minorities are limited to the lower-level jobs. There appears to be an invisible barrier—a "**glass ceiling**," that limits advancement. To compound the problem, many organizations have segregated women and minority employees into certain occupations such as human resources, customer service, and so forth. These "**glass walls**" that segment employees deny them the opportunity to develop the variety of skills necessary for advancement. Negative stereotypes and the lack of mentors have been identified as two reasons why women have not cracked the glass ceiling.[5] We suspect that the same is true for minorities.

Minority and women employees will continue to need an effective combination of educational and job-related experiences to provide them with opportunities to develop their talents. Organizations will be expected to design programs to attract and develop women and minority employees and provide them with the full range of opportunities open to everyone else.

Educational Preparation

Accompanying the changes in the racial and ethnic composition of the workforce are educational preparation factors that also will challenge supervisors in the future. More people than ever before have some college education. Nearly two-thirds of high school graduates go on to college. Currently, over 14 million students are enrolled in colleges and universities, and of these, about 20 percent are pursuing graduate degrees.

The college enrollment boom has been spurred by nontraditional students—part-timers, who comprise nearly 45 percent of the student body, and women, who comprise 55 percent. Nearly 2.5 million college students are over 35 years of age. Going to school part time while working is exhausting enough. Add to this the fact that many also must maintain a household, and the potential for stress increases. Something may have to give. Often, the job, school, and family all suffer, and the employee becomes overstressed. The supervisor will need to directly address the effect on work performance and perhaps lend a sympathetic ear. Many organizations have instituted programs to assist their employees with their personal problems. Chapter 17 will provide more in-depth coverage of this topic.

Some forecasters believe that we may soon encounter problems with an overeducated workforce. That is, more and more college-trained employees will compete for jobs that do not necessarily require a college education to perform. It has been reported that at least 35 percent of recent graduates now take jobs that don't require college degrees.[6] The intense competition for jobs and the increase in lower level service industry jobs will create underemployment. **Underemployment** occurs when employees bring a certain amount of skill, knowledge, and ability (**SKAs**) to the workplace and find that the job lacks meaning and/or the opportunity to fully utilize their SKAs. The challenge for supervisors will be to create a workplace environment that stimulates the underemployed. The current glut of college graduates gives corporate recruiters a distinct advantage—the opportunity to pick the best.

Yet we must keep in mind the other side of the picture; namely, that millions of young workers entering the workforce will not have completed a secondary school

---

Glass ceiling
Invisible barrier that limits advancement of women and minorities.

Glass walls
Invisible barriers that compartmentalize or segregate women and minorities into certain occupational classes.

Underemployment
Situation in which people are in jobs that do not utilize their skills, knowledge, and abilities (SKAs).

SKAs
Skills, knowledge, and abilities that a person has.

education. Of those who complete high school, many will receive an inferior education because their schools do not offer the variety or quality of classes that other schools offer. Thousands more will not have completed grade school and thus will not be educationally prepared to compete for better jobs. In addition, many individuals entering the workforce will have had considerable formal education, but this education will not have prepared them with specific skills that are directly applicable to the job market. All of these factors will put pressure on firms to provide employment and training opportunities for people who are unprepared and unskilled and then to train and develop those whose specific skills are limited—despite their level of formal education—but who are motivated to work.[7]

Occupational and Industry Trends

Occupational and industry forecasts project that there will be a steady need for more people in business-related services such as computer services, retail trade, health-care services, transportation, and banking and financial services well into the 21st century. The forecasts for federal, state, and local government employment opportunities are mixed at best. President Clinton has speculated that government needs to be "reinvented"; some infer this to mean a reduction in size. At best, increased employment opportunities will be in selected job categories. Nevertheless, all levels of government will compete with private industry for competent and qualified employees, particularly those who have the requisite education and skills.

On the negative side, the nation's largest industrial corporations have eliminated an average of 400,000 jobs annually since 1982. The staff reductions by General Motors, Sears, and IBM, as well as those of other corporations, are well documented. No job class has been immune from dismissals. There will be fewer positions available in manufacturing firms in part because of changing technology, which increasingly aims at substituting mechanization for labor, and in part because of international competition, relocation of facilities outside of the United States, and foreign imports. Chapter 9 will discuss staff reductions, called "downsizing," more fully.

While the popular press focuses on Big Business, small businesses and mid-sized firms are expected to create most of the job growth in the foreseeable future. Currently, only 15 percent of the workforce is employed in firms that have 1,000 or more employees. More than half of the workforce work in enterprises that employ fewer than 100 employees. We believe that a strong small business provides a unique employment opportunity for the new graduate. Generally, supervisors in small firms can gain broader and more diverse experiences than those in larger firms.

Changing Technology and Business Conditions

Many business organizations have been completely revamped because of technological advances, computers, robotics, automation, changing markets, and other competitive influences that demand both internal and external adaptations. Although corporate buyouts, mergers, and acquisitions will probably be slower in the future as compared to the 1980s, they nevertheless will continue to occur as many companies attempt to cope with the intensive pressures of domestic and foreign competition. Firms will form **strategic alliances**—agreements to join forces to accomplish mutual objectives more efficiently than either could do alone. Both large and small firms will ally in order to build on each other's strengths and ultimately gain competitive advantage. These redesigned organizations are expected to do a better job of meeting customers' needs. The net result will be fewer full-time employees. In addition, movements of plants, offices, and personnel will be constant and commonplace, influencing job positions, management policies, and supervisory practices.

As illustrated in Figure 1-5, the "Computer Revolution" will continue to be apparent throughout most organizations. It is conceivable that supervisors will have high-powered notebook-style computers. Advances in hardware, software, and communication technology require supervisors to learn how to operate computers as part of their day-to-day responsibilities.

Since it is difficult to forecast specifically when and how technological change will impact a supervisor's position, every supervisor will have to continue to be broadly educated. Supervisors will have to prepare themselves and their employees, both technologically and psychologically, for anticipated changes. Supervisors who keep up to date with all of the changes unquestionably will be more valuable to their organizations.

Strategic alliances
Cooperative ventures between different organizations to build on each other's strengths to accomplish mutual objectives more efficiently.

Global Challenges

Global challenges will continue to impact the supervisor. Substantial investment has been made in U.S. firms by the British, Germans, Swiss, Canadians, Japanese, and others. Identifying the various cultural/value system and work ethic differences is beyond the scope of this text. However, the supervisor must recognize that management practices differ culturally and structurally in these firms compared to U.S.-owned and -operated firms.

The production facilities of numerous U.S. firms may be drawn to Eastern Europe, Korea, South America, Africa, Mexico, or other locations by the attraction of low wages and other factors that can be used to gain a competitive advantage. While these countries have a wage rate advantage, their workers may not be as well prepared as American employees, nor will they have as many skilled supervisors to lead employees. Offshore opportunities for technically competent American supervisors such as Randy Harber, in the opening You Make the Call section, will increase. However, transplanted American supervisors will need to learn about cultural differences and find ways to adapt to nontraditional management styles.

Work Scheduling and Employment Conditions

General working conditions are changing rapidly and will continue to evolve. Restructured companies will employ more part-time employees. The average work week has shrunk to 34.5 hours, due in part to the rise in part timers. Projections are that by the year 2000, the average work week will be only 4 days, or 32 hours.

FIGURE 1-5
The "Computer Revolution" will continue to impact supervisory responsibilities.

More employers will expand the use of such workers in the future in their efforts to reduce wage and benefit costs associated with full-time employees.[8]

Current business conditions have caused many companies to employ **contract employees**—sometimes called "employee leasing" (more permanent) or "temporary help" (less permanent). For a fee, agencies supply qualified employees to the firm. The firm does not incur recruiting costs, training costs, or other costs associated with long-term employment. But the per-hour cost of contract labor is usually higher than that of regular employees. When a project is finished or business necessity dictates (e.g., orders decline), the contract employees leave.

Another thorny issue is that of the **two-tier wage system**, which is a company policy to pay inexperienced workers a lower wage than more experienced workers. In 1993, the United Auto Workers (UAW) and Ford Motor Company negotiated a contract that provides for a two-tier wage system. With the use of contract employees or a two-tier wage system, the supervisor will be challenged to motivate a workforce that includes employees that are compensated differently for doing essentially the same work.

Many displaced employees have had to take lower-paying, part-time or temporary jobs. This has meant wage erosion. The displaced workers have had to scramble to replace lost income by working more hours and longer work weeks, moonlighting, or having spouses enter the workforce. Moreover, losing a job or seeing another person experience job loss leads an individual to conclude that job security is no longer relevant. Many research studies support the position that employees are much less loyal to their employers than they were in the past. How will the supervisor motivate employees who consider themselves, at best, transient—that is, just working at the present firm until something better comes along? Numerous studies have indicated that lower productivity and increased accidents occur when employees are not fully committed to their jobs. Motivating employees who are not fully committed will be another supervisory challenge.

Contract employees
Workers supplied by an external agency for a specified period of time and for a fee.

Two-tier wage system
Paying new employees at a lower rate than more senior employees.

Ethical Issues and Corporate Culture

Corporate culture
Set of shared purposes, values, and beliefs that employees hold about their organization.

Corporate culture is the set of shared purposes, values, and beliefs that employees have about their organization. Top-level management creates the overall vision and philosophy for the firm. For example, when Hewlett-Packard was formed, David Packard and William R. Hewlett formulated a vision that was later stated in the Hewlett-Packard (HP) Statement of Corporate Objectives:

The achievements of an organization are the result of the combined efforts of each individual in the organization working toward common objectives. These objectives should be realistic, should be clearly understood by everyone in the organization, and should reflect the organization's basic character and personality.

Bill Hewlett frequently described the "HP Way" as follows: "I feel that in general terms it is the policies and actions that flow from the belief that men and women want to do a good job, a creative job, and that if they are provided the proper environment they will do so." This philosophy has been prominently communicated to every employee and as such becomes a way of life at Hewlett-Packard.[9]

Supervisors can influence the culture within their departments. They have a profound role to play in informing, educating, and setting an example of ethical behavior. The concern for ethical behavior has become one of the most challenging issues confronting U.S. business. The daily news is filled with information regarding the misuse of business power and the contention that corrupt business practices are the primary way to profits. Examples from the government sector, the savings and loan debacle of the 1980s, and numerous recent examples cause employees to wonder what is right. The value systems of some employees allow them to advocate that it is acceptable to do something questionable, as long as they do not get caught.

Ethical behavior and fair dealing have always been foundations for good management. The personal ethics that the supervisor holds are a guide for making decisions. Supervisors are often confronted with situations involving ethics in the workplace. Chapter 6 discusses further the wide range of ethical standards that can serve as guides to decision making.

Other Governmental and Societal Issues

Other governmental and societal issues will continue to emerge that will complicate the supervisory management position in the future. For example, numerous environmental concerns remain as serious long-term problems for business, government, and the general public. Energy availability and costs may be determined by international and domestic political and economic changes. These types of issues and societal pressures often become part of business planning and operations.

A list of federal legislation that affects the supervisor's job is found in Appendix A at the end of the book. In addition, state and local governments have laws and regulations that impact businesses. The effect of such legislation can be quite costly, and organizations may be required to change their methods of operation in order to comply.

Supervisors are influenced both directly and indirectly by such governmental requirements, and they must continue to stay abreast of any legislation that may influence their operations. Furthermore, supervisors must be sensitive to pressures exerted by special-interest groups. Consumer groups, in particular, have demanded better products and services from business, labor, and government. Environmentalists seek to influence business decisions that may have an adverse environmental impact. Some employees (especially parents of young children or employees who have elderly parents) will demand that their employers provide day-care facilities so that they can combine their family and job responsibilities better. It seems likely that numerous other permanent and temporary special-interest groups will continue to place community and political demands on firms in ways that will affect how supervisors will operate in the future.

All indications are that these pressures will remain intense. A utility company supervisor said recently, "I have to be more of a lawyer and political scientist these days than a manager!" Although a bit overstated, this supervisor's comment reflects a realistic aspect of every supervisor's contemporary role.

Shifting Employee Values and Expectations

Employee values and expectations will continue to vex employers in the future. During periods of economic recession, employees typically are content to hold their jobs in order to survive economically. But over the long run, particularly when economic conditions are favorable, most individuals have higher employment aspirations. In all periods of economic activity, it is expected that employees will be scrambling—scrambling for available work, for better jobs, for enhanced opportunity, or for job security.

Employees spend most of their waking hours going to, being at, and coming home from work. More and more employees will question what they want work to do for them. Many employees, however, do not find personal satisfaction in their jobs. For example, assembly-line workers and employees who perform other types of unskilled, routine, or repetitive jobs tend to find their daily work boring and unrewarding, even though they may be highly paid. When highly skilled people are placed in routine, monotonous jobs—whether in the factory or in the office— stresses develop that can become more serious over time. Younger employees, in particular, expect their employment to contribute to their development as individuals, and they expect personal involvement in their jobs.

Empowerment and Employee Participation in Decision Making

Employees will continue to expect to have a greater voice in workplace decision making. Whether or not a labor union or employee association represents employees in an organization, many employees will want more from their jobs and will demand a voice in decisions that concern their employment. This does not have to be objectionable to a supervisor. In fact, once supervisors realize that their employees have something to contribute, they will welcome employee participation in decisions rather than fear it.

Many companies already have accepted the premise that employee participation can improve an organization's performance. Terms such as "empowerment," "employee involvement groups," "total quality management (TQM)," and "continuous improvement" have become the "buzz words" of the 1990s. These concepts and appropriate approaches will be discussed in more detail in Chapters 5, 7, and 17.

Empowerment
Giving employees the authority and responsibility to accomplish organizational objectives.

Empowerment means giving employees the authority and responsibility to achieve. Opportunities to make suggestions and participate in decisions affecting their jobs can and should be supported. However, some supervisors become worried when workers challenge what has traditionally been management rights, and they prefer to think that certain areas should be beyond employee challenge. Many quality circles and other participatory management approaches of the last decade failed, in part, because managers failed to listen to the suggestions of employees, did not act upon those suggestions in a timely fashion, or felt threatened by those suggestions. Nevertheless, there will continue to be pressure from employees, labor unions, minorities, and other groups for more influence in decisions pertaining to the workplace.

Participative management
Allowing employees to be involved in organizational decision making.

Many supervisors have become accustomed to the practice of **participatory management**, which essentially means a willingness to permit employees to influence or share in managerial decisions. If supervisors learn to react to this in a positive way, it should improve their own and their company's performance. We will discuss employee participation in Chapters 4, 10, and 16.

Although forecasts are always precarious, experienced supervisors will recognize that these trends have already begun. Supervisors must understand and plan for them.

LEADERSHIP: THE CORE OF SUPERVISORY MANAGEMENT

4 Discuss the leadership component of supervision.

Although many supervisors are aware of the importance of motivation, there still is considerable misunderstanding concerning the supervisor's leadership role in influencing employee motivation and performance. This misunderstanding often stems from a misconception regarding the meaning of leadership itself. Occupying a position of responsibility and authority does not necessarily make someone a leader that subordinates will follow.

The Test of Supervisory Leadership

Actually, it is not the supervisor's position alone that defines the supervisor as a leader. "Leadership" is the ability to guide and influence the opinions, attitudes, and behavior of others. This means that anyone who is able to direct or influence others toward objectives can function as a leader, no matter what position that person holds.

In the workplace, members of the work group often assume leadership roles. The direction of informal employee leadership can be supportive of or contrary to the direction the supervisor desires. For example, employee resistance to changes in work arrangements, work rules, or procedures is a common phenomenon. Such resistance usually is the result of some informal leadership within the work group itself.

Thus, leadership in the general sense is a process rather than just a positional relationship. Leadership includes what the followers think and do, not just what the supervisor does. *The real test of supervisory leadership is whether subordinates follow* (see Figure 1-6). Leadership resides in a supervisor's ability to obtain the work group's willingness to follow, a willingness based on commonly shared goals and a mutual effort to achieve them.

Leadership Can Be Developed

Supervisors often believe that any definition of leadership should include "basic traits" possessed by a leader. That is, they consider effective leadership as some special qualities possessed by the leader, and they point to certain successful supervisors as being representative of outstanding leadership.

Are certain natural qualities necessary to become an effective leader? Generally, the ability to lead is something that can be learned: Leaders are made, not born. Many studies have shown that there is no significant relationship between one's ability to lead and characteristics such as age, height, weight, sex, race, and other physical attributes. Although there are indications that successful supervisors tend to be somewhat more intelligent than the average subordinate, they are not so superior in intelligence that they cannot be understood. Intelligence is partially hereditary, but for the most part it depends on environmental factors such as amount of formal education and diversity of experiences. Successful supervisors do tend to be well rounded in their interests and aptitudes; they are good communicators; they are mentally and emotionally mature; and they possess a strong inner drive. Most important, they tend to rely on their supervisory skills to a greater extent than on their technical skills. These are essentially learned characteristics, rather than innate qualities.

Putting this in perspective, supervisory leadership is something that an individual supervisor can develop if the supervisor has a real desire to be a leader and not just someone in charge of a group of people. Most supervisors can become more effective leaders if they earnestly strive to develop their managerial and human relations capacities and skills.

Effective Supervisory Leadership as a Dynamic Process

Effective supervisory leadership is a dynamic process that takes place among the supervisor, the work group, and various situations confronting the supervisor. Good communication is the foundation of effective leadership. The ability to communicate well, to keep the lines of communication open at all times, and to communicate in a way that meets workers' expectations and needs is essential for any supervisor to be a leader.

The nature of the work environment, the size of the work group, and the type of people involved also are important. Generally, the larger the work group, the more important it is for the supervisor to be an effective planner, organizer, and coordinator of activities. The larger the work group, the more the supervisor will have to delegate authority. The smaller the work group and the closer the supervisor's physical location is to the employees, the more he or she must deal with the individual needs of those in the group.

Understanding the expectations of employees is vital in effective supervision. As discussed previously, today's employees want to participate in decisions concerning their jobs. However, sometimes a supervisor must exercise authority and make decisions that may not be popular with the work group. The ability to assess employee expectations and the demands of the job situation and then act appropriately is a skill that can be developed with experience and practice.

Although many such studies have been made, one of the most famous series of studies focusing upon employees' needs and expectations, supervisory leadership, and productivity was conducted by behavioral science researchers from the University of Michigan.[10] In studies made of office employees, railroad workers, and factory employees, it was established that a similar type of supervisory leadership pattern consistently was associated with high productivity and a high degree of job satisfaction experienced by work-group members. This effective supervisory leadership pattern included the following significant characteristics:

1. General supervision rather than close, detailed supervision of employees.
2. More time devoted to supervisory activities than to doing work normally assigned to employees.
3. Much attention to planning of work and special tasks.
4. A willingness to permit employees to participate in the decision-making process.
5. An approach to the job that is "employee centered" (i.e., showing a sincere interest in the needs and problems of employees as individuals), as well as production oriented.

SUPERVISION: A PROFESSIONAL PERSPECTIVE

5 Explain why supervisors must continually grow and develop as professionals.

Supervisors' primary responsibility is to manage their firm's most important resource—the human resource. It is the human resource upon which any organization ultimately depends. Managing people starts with selection and training to fill job openings, and it continues with ongoing development, motivation, and leadership and with preparing employees for promotion.

Thus, supervisors will have to become true professionals with a growing professional perspective. Supervisors will have to develop as innovators and idea people. They must look to the future with a professional awareness of the trends influencing human behavior and observe how these trends impact the management of people in a complex society.

In all of this, there is an imperative to take the professional perspective, which recognizes the need for constant self-improvement and self-renewal. No amount of formal or informal education can ever be enough to fulfill a supervisor's personal program of self-improvement. Supervisors must recognize that they, too, can become obsolete unless they constantly take measures to update their own skills and knowledge through a program of continuous self-development.

Supervisors who master the managerial concepts and skills discussed in this textbook should make considerable progress in terms of personal development, but just knowing concepts and approaches is not enough. They must constantly seek new ways to apply this knowledge in the challenging, complex, and dynamic situations they will encounter.

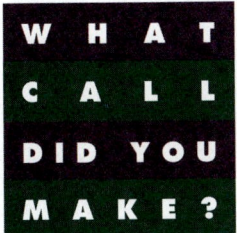

WHAT CALL DID YOU MAKE?

Every chapter in this textbook will end with a section called "What Call Did You Make?". This section refers back to the problem posed in the section called "You Make the Call" at the beginning of the chapter. In this concluding section, we will help you compare your analysis with ours.

As Randy Harber in the chapter-opening vignette, you must avoid making a hasty decision. You must consider your commitment to the organization that currently employs you, your commitment to your family, and your commitment to yourself. As you compare your "call" with that of other students, you may find that for some students family goals are more important than organizational goals. How will you reconcile this conflict? To what extent will your need for personal and professional growth influence the decision? This call is based on your personal preference. Most important, your call should be made only after you collect additional information. Where exactly is Liberia? What are the political, economic, and sociological conditions there? Will you be able to take your family? If not, how often can you return home? What are your family's needs and concerns, and to what extent should they be in-

volved in this decision? What type of employees will you be supervising? How diverse will they be? What will your duties and responsibilities be? How much authority will you have? Can you effectively coordinate the efforts of a diverse group of employees? Will your experiences on this project enable you to upgrade your leadership skills? If you turn down this assignment, will other chances to become a superintendent arise?

You should recognize that you have more options than just the "go"/"no go" alternative. Pause for a second and ask yourself what information you need to make an intelligent decision. Where can you get that information? After collecting the information, reflect on how it can help you make the decision. For most people, this is not an easy call to make.

SUMMARY

1 Explain why someone might want to become a supervisor.

Supervisors are the first tier of management. They manage entry-level and other departmental employees. New ways of managing employees will be the supervisor's challenge. In the face of a contemporary mindset and an environment that is rapidly changing, the success of the supervisor will rest in the ability to balance the requirements for high work performance with the diverse needs of the workforce.

Supervisory management focuses primarily on the management of people. For many people, being a supervisor provides a variety of satisfying experiences. What one person sees as an opportunity and a reason for accepting the supervisory challenge, others see as a negative. Among these are the challenge of getting diverse people to work together, the increased responsibility that comes with climbing the management hierarchy, the unpredictable nature of the job, and the sense of accomplishment from doing a job well. Conversely, there are reasons why people avoid supervisory responsibility. Being a supervisor is a full-time job, and many people want to avoid conflict. A supervisor must reconcile the needs of the organization and the needs of employees. These are delicate problems.

In addition, major environmental factors impact everything the organization does. These factors are not static; the whole world is changing rapidly, and some people do not want to deal with change.

2 Describe the contributions of four schools of management thought.

There is no one universal school of management thought. The scientific management approach attempts to find the "one best way." The manager's primary function is to plan the work. Time and motion study and the other principles of industrial engineering are used to analyze the work to be performed. The functional approach assumes that there are a series of functions that managers should perform. The human relations/behavioral science approach emphasizes that managers need to understand what causes employees to behave the way they do. This approach began with the Hawthorne studies at Western Electric Company. The quantitative approach applies mathematical models to help solve organization problems. An understanding of the various schools of thought gives supervisors a foundation upon which to build their own supervisory philosophy.

3 Identify and discuss the major demographic and societal trends that will affect supervisors.

Many factors and trends surrounding the workforce will have an impact on how most organizations operate. The workforce will grow at a somewhat faster rate than the overall population, and the age composition of the workforce will change drastically. Women and minorities will continue to enter the workforce in increasing numbers, and they will be utilized more fully than they have been in the past, including further advancement in supervisory and management positions. Substantial numbers of part-time employees and contract employees will be found in the workplace. The more diverse workforce will create numerous problems (e.g., multicultural and multilingual problems, family obligation versus job obligation, etc.).

The workforce generally will consist of more college graduates, but millions of people will not be prepared educationally to qualify for many of the employment opportunities available.

Occupational and industry trends, changing technology and business conditions, and the competition from the global marketplace will be major influences on supervisory management.

Government laws and regulations will continue to have a major impact on the policies and activities of most organizations.

Supervisors will have to be sensitive to existing and expected employee trends. For example, more employees than ever before will expect their jobs to have greater personal meaning to them as individuals. It is likely that supervisors will have to be somewhat flexible in their approaches to managing. Employees will continue to expect a greater voice in workplace decision making. Employees will expect to be empowered.

4 Discuss the leadership component of supervision.

Effective supervisory management means that supervisors must become leaders in the true sense of the word. Supervisory leadership primarily resides in the ability of a supervisor to influence the opinions, attitudes, and performance of employees toward accomplishing company goals. The test of supervisory leadership is whether subordinates follow willingly.

5 Explain why supervisors must continually grow and develop as professionals.

The habits of highly effective people can be developed. Supervisors who want to be more effective will put themselves into situations in which they can practice those techniques. Finally, supervisors who aspire to become more effective leaders need to have a professional outlook and must recognize the necessity for a personal program of continuous self-development.

KEY TERMS

Supervisor (page 4)
Scientific management approach (page 7)
Functional approach (page 8)
Hawthorne effect (page 9)
Human relations movement/behavioral science approach (page 9)
Quantitative approach (page 9)
Diversity (page 10)
Flextime (page 12)
Job sharing (page 12)
Telecommuting (page 12)

Glass ceiling (page 14)
Glass walls (page 14)
Underemployment (page 14)
SKAs (page 14)
Strategic alliances (page 16)
Contract employees (page 17)
Two-tier wage system (page 17)
Corporate culture (page 18)
Empowerment (page 20)
Participative management (page 20)

QUESTIONS FOR DISCUSSION

1. What are some of the advantages of being a supervisor?

2. How would you respond to someone who suggests that the principles and functions of management apply to all organizations? Justify your response.

3. From the standpoint of the prospective supervisor, what is the significance of the following: Taylor's scientific management, Fayol's functions of management, and the Hawthorne studies?

4. Of those factors or trends projected to reshape the workplace, which will create the greatest challenge for supervisors? Why do you think so?

5. From your point of view, analyze how the shifting workforce values toward work and expectations will influence a supervisor's planning and functioning in the future.

6. Some people have postulated that the "hand of government should be invisible" in the marketplace. What are some arguments for having the federal government regulate business?

7. Do you look forward to working in a more diverse workforce? Why or why not? What adjustments will you have to make?

8. Define "corporate culture" and discuss how an organization's culture might affect its ability to compete more effectively in the marketplace.

9. Discuss the factors involved in effective supervisory leadership. Why is the concept of blending organizational (supervisory) objectives with the employees' needs and objectives at the heart of effective supervisory leadership?

10. Why is continuous self-development vital to the supervisory role?

SKILLS APPLICATIONS

Skills Application 1-1: Career Choice Checklist

Review the You Make the Call section at the beginning of the chapter. Then make a complete list of all the reasons why you should take the assignment in Liberia. Make a complete list of all the reasons why you should not take the assignment. Prioritize the items on each list. Compare your list with that of a classmate. Why are certain items similar? Why are certain items different? What are the critical factors that would cause you to accept or reject a supervisory assignment?

Skills Application 1-2: Ethical Dilemmas

Write a definition of business ethics. Find an illustration from the local newspaper, *The Wall Street Journal*, *Business Week*, or some other business publication that points out unethical behavior. Ask yourself what you would have done in that situation. Would you have behaved according to your definition of business ethics? Why or why not?

Skills Application 1-3: Cultivating Diversity

Analyze the workforce of the organization where you work. (If you do not work, select the organization of a friend.)

1.   What percentage of the workforce is women or minorities?

2.   How do these figures match with those of the local community?

3.   What approach should the company take to increase the cultural diversity of its workforce?

4.   Make a list of the advantages of having a diverse workforce.

ENDNOTES

1.   For a discussion of the problems of developing universal agreement on management approaches, see H. Koontz, "The Management Theory Jungle Revisited," *Academy of Management Review* (Volume 5, 1980), pp. 175–188. An overview of the evolution of management thought is provided in J. Baughman, *The History of American Management* (Englewood Cliffs, N.J.: Prentice-Hall, 1969); C. George, *The History of Management Thought* (Englewood Cliffs, N.J.: Prentice-Hall, 1972); and Allen C. Bluedorn, eds., "A Special Book Review Section on the Classics of Management," *Academy of Management Review* (Volume 11, April 1986).

The principles of scientific management are described in Frederick W. Taylor, *Shop Management* (New York: Harper & Brothers, 1911); Frank G. Gilbreth and Lillian M. Gilbreth, *Applied Motion Study* (New York: Sturgis & Walton, 1917); Frank B. Copely, *Frederick W. Taylor, The Father of Scientific Management* (New York: Harper & Brothers, 1923); Edna Yost, *Frank and Lillian Gilbreth* (New Brunswick, N.J.: Rutgers University Press, 1949); and Edwin A. Locke, "The Ideas of Frederick W. Taylor: An Evaluation," *Academy of Management Review* (Volume 7, January 1982), pp. 22–23.

See Henri Fayol, *General and Industrial Management*, trans. Constance Storrs (London: Pitman Publishing Corp., 1949).

Additional information on the human relations/behavioral science school of thought can be found in E. Mayo, *The Human Problems of Industrial Civilization* (New York: Macmillan, 1933); Fritz J. Roethlisberger and W. J. Dickson, *Management and the Worker* (Boston: Harvard University Press, 1939); A. Maslow, "A Theory of Human Motivation," *Psychological Review* (Volume 50, July 1943), pp. 370–396; D. McGregor, *The Human Side of Enterprise* (New York: McGraw-Hill, 1960); and J. A. Sonnenfeld, "Shedding Light on the Hawthorne Studies," *Journal of Occupational Behavior* (Volume 6, 1985), pp. 111–130.

2.   The statistics and projections included in this and other sections are drawn from various U.S. government publications: U.S. Bureau of the Census, *Statistical Abstract of the United States*, 1992, (Washington, D.C.: U.S. Government Printing Office); U.S. Department of Labor, Bureau of Labor Statistics; *Employment and Earnings*; U.S.

Department of Labor, Bureau of Labor Statistics; *Occupational Projections and Training Data, A Statistical and Research Supplement to the 1992–93 Occupational Outlook Handbook, Monthly Labor Review*; and *Survey of Current Business*. Also see Robert Goddard, "Workforce 2000," *Personnel Journal* (February 1989), pp. 64–71; and Gary S. Becker, "Illegal Immigration: How to Turn the Tide," *Business Week* (February 22, 1992), p. 23. For an in-depth look at trends and projections, see "Reinventing America: Meeting the Challenges of a Global Economy," *Business Week 1992 Special Bonus Issue*. For a definitive work on diversity, see Lee Gardenswarz and Anita Rowe, *Managing Diversity: A Complete Desk Reference and Planning Guide* (Homewood, IL: Business One Irwin, 1993).

3.   "Labor Letter: A Special News Report on People and Their Jobs in Offices, Fields, and Factories." *The Wall Street Journal* (August 14, 1990), p. 1A.

4.   Winston Churchill, *My Early Life* (1930) Reprint. (New York: Charles Scribner's Sons, 1987), chapter 9.

5.   Jacklyn Fierman, "Why Women Still Don't Hit the Top," *Fortune* (July 30, 1990), pp. 40–60.

6.   See Julie A. Lopez, "College Class of '93 Learns Hard Lesson: Career Prospects are Worst in Decades," *The Wall Street Journal* (May 20, 1993), pp. B1–B12; and Joan E. Rigdon, "Glut of Graduates Lets Recruiters," *The Wall Street Journal* (May 20, 1993), p. B1.

7.   See Amanda Bennett, "Firms Become a Crucial Agent of Social Change," *The Wall Street Journal Centennial Edition* (June 23, 1989) p. A22.; and Ronald Henkoff, "Companies That Train Best," *Fortune* (March 22, 1993) pp. 62–74.

8.   See Gene Koretz, "Taking Stock of the Flexible Work Force," *Business Week* (July 24, 1989) p. 12; and Juliet Schor, *The Overworked American: The Unexpected Decline of Leisure* (New York: Basic Books, 1991).

9.   Adapted from *Hewlett-Packard Statement of Corporate Objectives and Annual Reports*. Also, see "Hewlett-Packard: Where Slower Growth Is Smarter Management," *Business Week* (July 9, 1975), pp. 50–58. The statement was first put in writing in 1957, has been modified occasionally since then, and has been a significant part of the "HP Way."

10.   For a review of these studies as well as a review of other research findings concerning supervisory style, productivity, and employee job satisfaction, see Rensis Likert, *New Patterns of Management* (New York: McGraw-Hill, 1967), pp. 13–46; J. Trempe, A. J. Rigny, and R. R. Haccoun, "Subordinate Satisfaction with Male and Female Managers: Role of Perceived Supervisory Influence," *Journal of Applied Psychology* (Volume 70, 1985), pp. 44–47; and G. Pascal Zachary and Bob Ortega, "Age of Angst: Workplace Revolution Boosts Productivity at Cost of Job Security," *The Wall Street Journal*, (March 10, 1993), pp. 1A–8A.

2

The

Managerial

Functions

LEARNING OBJECTIVES

After reading this chapter, you will be able to:

1 Summarize the difficulties supervisors face in fulfilling managerial roles.

2 Explain why effective supervisors should possess a variety of skills.

3 Define management and discuss how the primary managerial functions are interrelated.

4 Discuss the concept of authority as a requirement of any managerial position.

5 Explain the need for coordination and cooperation and how these depend on the proper performance of the managerial functions.

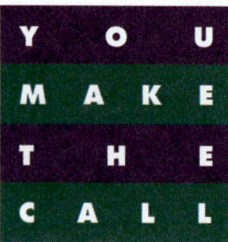

You are Carol Reeves, supervisor of Kincaid Pharmacy's State Street store. The pharmacist has responsibility for the pharmacy operations, while you have total responsibility for the rest of the store. You report to Donald Kincaid, manager of operations for the 16-store chain. The firm's philosophy emphasizes, "Customer service is your number one job. Do whatever is necessary to exceed the needs of the customer!"

Kelly, one of your cashiers, is a single parent with one preschool-aged child. She has exhausted her vacation hours for the year and has no personal time left. On a day she is scheduled to work, her daughter develops a high temperature and seems very ill. Even though the sitter is willing to take her, she would prefer not to. Kelly knows that she needs the money to make ends meet and that she has no paid leave time. Fifteen minutes before store opening, Kelly calls the store.

Kelly: Carol, I'm not feeling well this morning. I think it might be that new strain of flu, and I'd hate to spread it to anyone else. I'll call you later in the day and let you know how I'm feeling, because I'm scheduled to work tomorrow also.

You know that it will be difficult to get coverage at that late hour and that the pharmacy's staffing is lean to begin with.

You: I'm sorry that you are not feeling well, Kelly. Take good care of yourself and get it under control. Please let me know as soon as possible regarding tomorrow.

Kelly: Thanks for your understanding. I really appreciate it.

You contemplate the work ahead. You call several employees, and none is available to fill in for Kelly until later in the day. You wonder how you will get through the day. What will you do to alleviate the situation? **YOU MAKE THE CALL.**

THE PERSON IN THE MIDDLE

1 Summarize the difficulties supervisors face in fulfilling managerial roles.

The supervisory position is a difficult and demanding role. Supervisors are "people in the middle"—the principal link between higher-level managers and employees. A supervisor is a first-level manager, that is, a manager in charge of entry-level and other departmental employees. Every organization, whether a retail store, a manufacturing firm, a hospital, or a government agency, has someone who fills this role.

Throughout this textbook we use the terms "worker," "employee," and "subordinate" interchangeably to refer to individuals who report to supervisors or managers. An increasing number of companies are using the term "associate" instead of "employee." Regardless of the term used, employees may view their supervisor as the management of the organization; the supervisor is their primary contact with management. Employees expect a supervisor to be technically competent and to be a good leader who can show them how to get the job done.

But the supervisor also must be a competent subordinate to higher-level managers. In this role the supervisor must be a good follower. Moreover, the supervisor is expected to maintain satisfactory relationships with supervisors in other departments. Thus, a supervisor's relationship to other supervisors is that of a colleague who must cooperate and must coordinate his or her department's efforts with those of others in order to reach the overall goals of the organization.

In general, the position of any supervisor has two main requirements. First, the supervisor must have a good working knowledge of the jobs to be performed. Second—and more significant—the supervisor must be able to manage, that is, run the department. It is the managerial competence of a supervisor that usually determines the effectiveness of his or her performance.

MANAGERIAL SKILLS MAKE THE DIFFERENCE

2 Explain why effective supervisors should possess a variety of skills.

In most organizations some supervisors appear to be under constant pressure and continuously do the same work their subordinates do. They are getting by, although they feel overburdened. These supervisors endure long hours, may be very devoted to their jobs, and are willing to do everything themselves. They want to be effective, although they seldom have enough time to actually supervise. Other supervisors appear to be on top of their jobs, and their departments function in a smooth and orderly manner. These supervisors find time to sit at their desks at least part of the day, and they are able to keep their paperwork up to date. What is the difference?

Of course, some supervisors are more capable than others, just as some mechanics are better than others. If we compare two maintenance supervisors who are equally good mechanics, have similar equipment under their care, and operate under approximately the same conditions, why might one be more effective than the other? The answer is that effective supervisors manage their departments in a manner that gets the job done through their people instead of doing the work themselves. The difference between a good supervisor and a poor one, assuming that their technical skills are similar, is the difference in their managerial skills.

The managerial aspects of the supervisor's position too often have been neglected in the selection and development of supervisors. Typically people are selected for supervisory positions on the basis of their technical competence, their seniority or past performance, and their willingness to work hard. When appointed supervisors, they are expected to assume responsibilities of management, even though their previous job did not involve these skills. New supervisors must make a conscious effort to develop their managerial skills by learning from their own manager, through company training programs, or by any other avenues available to them.

Traditionally, some writers have grouped the managerial skills needed by supervisors into the following four major classifications:

Conceptual skills
The ability to obtain, interpret, and apply information.

Human relations skills
The ability to work with and through people.

Administrative skills
The ability to plan, organize, and coordinate activities.

Technical skills
The ability to do the job.

Political skills
The ability to understand how things get done outside of formal channels.

1. **Conceptual skills:** the ability to obtain, interpret, and apply the information necessary to make sound decisions.
2. **Human relations skills:** the ability to work with and through people.
3. **Administrative skills:** the ability to plan, organize, and coordinate the activities of a work group.
4. **Technical skills:** the ability to perform the actual jobs within the supervisor's area of responsibility.

In recent years, many observers have added **political skills**—the savvy to ascertain the hidden rules of the organizational game and to recognize the roles that various people play in getting things done outside of formal organizational channels. Anyone who has worked in an organization knows that informal relationships among people have a lot to do with what happens within the organization. All of these skills are important to a supervisor's performance. Technical skills alone are not sufficient.

The Need for Technical Competence in Supervision

A competent supervisor must thoroughly understand the specific, technical aspects of the department's operations. Perhaps the supervisor actually is the most skilled person within the department and is able to do a quicker, more efficient job than most of the subordinates. Yet, the supervisor must learn to avoid stepping in and personally doing the employees' jobs except for the purpose of instruction or in short-handed or emergency situations. In some companies a union contract may restrict supervisors from performing employees' work. The responsibility of a supervisor as a manager is to see that the employees do their jobs and do them properly. As a manager, the supervisor must plan, guide, and supervise.

In some organizations supervisors are considered to be "working supervisors," or "lead persons," whose responsibilities include performing certain jobs within their departments. Supervisors of very small departments, for example, often are expected to perform a share of the workload assigned to their units. Similarly, supervisors in retail stores and in many service occupations typically work along with their employees to accomplish the work. Nevertheless, whenever a supervisor is occupied with a job that could be performed by an employee, the supervisor's managerial functions necessarily are neglected.

At the other extreme, some departments are involved in varied and complex operations in which individual jobs may be quite diversified and even specialized. In these situations it would be impossible for a supervisor to comprehend the exact details of each job. However, it remains important for the supervisor to at least understand the broad technical aspects of each job under his or her supervision—and to know where to get help when needed.

Managerial Skills Can Be Learned and Developed

Many people believe that good managers, like good athletes, are born, not made. Much research has indicated that this belief is generally incorrect, even though it is true that people are born with different potential and that, to some degree, heredity does play a role in intelligence. An athlete who is not endowed with natural physical advantages is not likely to run 100 yards in record time. On the other hand, many individuals who are so-called "natural athletes" have not come close to that goal either.

Most superior athletes have developed their natural endowments into mature skills by practice, learning, effort, and experience. The same holds true for a good manager. The skills involved in managing are as learnable as the skills used in playing golf. It does take time, effort, and determination for a supervisor to develop managerial skills. Supervisors will make some mistakes, but people learn from mistakes as well as from successes. By applying the principles discussed in this textbook, the supervisor can develop the skills that make the supervisory job a challenging and satisfying career.

Simply talking about supervisory management is somewhat like Mark Twain's comment about the weather: "Everybody talks about it, but no one does anything about it." Therefore, throughout the textbook there are various activities designed to reinforce the concepts presented. There is no guarantee of supervisory success. Jack Nicklaus, one of the greatest golfers of all time, wrote *Golf My Way*. If you wanted to learn to play golf, we could give you a copy of the book to read, but we would also have to provide you with the proper tools (clubs) and a time to practice (learn from your mistakes and make corrections). The challenge for supervisors is to stay on the path of continuous improvement.

Benefits from Better Supervisory Management

You may recall from Figure 1-1 in Chapter 1 that there are many benefits accruing to the effective supervisor. A supervisor has daily opportunities to apply managerial principles on the job. Proper application of the principles will contribute to a smoother-functioning department in which the work gets done on time and the workers contribute toward stated objectives more willingly and enthusiastically. Thus, the supervisor will be on top of the job, instead of being consumed by it. Supervisors who manage well are able to make suggestions to higher-level managers and to other supervisors. Effective supervisors become aware of the needs and objectives of other departments as well as the interrelationships between those other departments and their own. They seek to work in closer harmony with colleagues who supervise other departments. Briefly, better supervisory management means doing a more effective job with much less effort.

In addition to direct benefits, there are indirect benefits. The supervisor who manages well will become capable of handling larger and more complicated assignments, which could lead to more responsible and higher-paying positions within the managerial hierarchy. Managerial skills are applicable in any organization and at all managerial levels, regardless of where a supervisor's future career may lead.

FUNCTIONS OF MANAGEMENT

3 Define management and discuss how the primary managerial functions are interrelated.

Management
Getting objectives accomplished with and through people.

The term "management" has been defined in many ways. Figure 2-1 contains a sampling of definitions provided by academicians and management scholars.[1] In general, **management** is the process of getting things accomplished with and through people by guiding and motivating their efforts toward common objectives.

In most endeavors one person can accomplish relatively little. Therefore, individuals join forces with others to attain mutual goals. In a business, top-level managers are responsible for achieving the goals of the organization, but this requires the efforts of all subordinate managers and employees. Those who hold supervisory positions significantly influence the effectiveness with which people work together and utilize the resources available to attain stated goals. In short, the managerial role of a supervisor is to make sure that assigned tasks are accomplished with and through the help of employees. Thus, the better the supervisor manages, the better will be the departmental results.

The Managerial Functions Are the Same in All Managerial Positions

The managerial functions of a supervisory position are similar, whether they involve supervision of a production line, a sales force, a laboratory, or a small office.

FIGURE 2-1
Definitions of
Management

- Boone and Kurtz: "Management is the achievement of organizational objectives through people and other resources. The manager's job is to combine human and technical resources in the best way possible to achieve these objectives."
- Cunningham, Aldag, and Block: "Management is the art of getting things done through people."
- Drucker: "Management is a liberal art. 'Liberal' because it deals with the fundamentals of knowledge, self-knowledge, wisdom, and leadership; 'art' because it is practice and application."
- Gitman and McDaniel: "Management is the process of coordinating a firm's human and other resources to accomplish its goals."
- Peters: "Managers are people who do things right and leaders are people who do the right thing."
- Wagner and Hollenbeck: "Management is a process of planning, organizing, directing, and controlling organizational behaviors in order to accomplish a mission through division of labor."

See Endnote 1 on page 49 for citations.

Moreover, the primary managerial functions are the same regardless of the level within the hierarchy of management. It does not matter whether one is a first-level supervisor, a middle-level manager, or part of top-level management. Nor does the kind of organization matter. Managerial functions are the same whether the supervisor is working in a profit-making firm, a nonprofit organization, or a government office. Supervisors, as well as other managers, perform the same basic managerial functions in all organizations. In this textbook we classify these functions under the major categories of planning, organizing, staffing, leading, and controlling. The following description of these functions is general and brief, since most of the book is devoted to discussing their application— particularly at the supervisory level.

Planning. The initial managerial function—determining what should be done in the future—is called **planning**. It consists of setting goals, objectives, policies, procedures, and other plans needed to achieve the purposes of the organization. In planning, the manager decides a course of action from various alternative courses that are available. Planning is primarily conceptual in nature. It means thinking before acting, looking ahead and preparing for the future, laying out in advance the road to be followed, and thinking about what and how the job should be done. It includes collecting and sorting information from numerous sources to make decisions. Not only does planning include deciding what, how, when, and by whom work is to be done, but it must also include the development of "what if" scenarios. A word of caution: Regardless of how well a supervisor like Carol Reeves ("You Make the Call") plans, crises will happen, and supervisors need to anticipate them, considering what they will do if this or that happens.

Many supervisors find that they are constantly confronted with one crisis after

Planning
Determining what
should be done in the
future.

another. The probable reason for this is that they neglect to plan; they do not look much beyond the day's events. It is every supervisor's responsibility to plan, and this cannot be delegated to someone else. Certain specialists, such as a budget officer, a production scheduler, or an engineer, may provide the supervisor with assistance in planning. But it is up to each supervisor, as the manager of a department, to make specific departmental plans that coincide with the general objectives established by higher-level management.

Planning is the managerial function that comes first, and, as the supervisor proceeds with other managerial functions, planning continues, previous plans are revised, and different alternatives are chosen as the need arises. This is particularly true as a supervisor evaluates the results of previous plans and adjusts future plans accordingly.

Organizing. Once plans have been made, the organizing function primarily answers the question, "How will the work be divided and accomplished?" This means that the supervisor defines the various job duties, and groups these activities into distinct areas, sections, units, or teams. The supervisor must specify the duties required, assign them, and, at the same time, provide subordinates with the authority needed to carry out their tasks. **Organizing** means arranging and distributing work among members of the work group to accomplish the organization's goals.

Organizing
Arranging and distributing work among members of the work group to accomplish the organization's goals.

Staffing. The managerial tasks of recruiting, selecting, orienting, and training employees may be grouped within the function called **staffing**. This function includes appraising the performance of employees, promoting employees where appropriate, and providing them with further opportunities for development. In addition, staffing includes devising an equitable compensation system and rates of pay. Some activities involved in the staffing function are handled by the human resources (or personnel) department in many companies. For example, the human resources department and top-level managers establish the compensation system. Supervisors do not perform this task. However, day-to-day responsibility for essential aspects of the staffing function remains with the supervisor.

Staffing
The tasks of recruiting, selecting, orienting, training, appraising, and evaluating employees.

Leading. **Leading** means guiding the activities of employees toward accomplishing objectives. The leading function of management involves guiding, teaching, and supervising subordinates. This includes developing the abilities of employees to their maximum potential by directing and coaching them effectively. It is not sufficient for a supervisor just to plan, organize, and have enough employees available. The supervisor must attempt to motivate them as they go about their work. Leading is the day-to-day process around which all supervisory performance revolves. Leading is also known as directing, motivating, or influencing, since it plays a major role in employee morale, job satisfaction, productivity, and communication. It is through this function that the supervisor seeks to create a climate that is conducive to employee satisfaction and at the same time achieves the objectives of the department. Finding ways to satisfy the needs of a diverse employee workforce is a significant challenge. In fact, probably most of a supervisor's time is spent on

Leading
Guiding the employees' activities toward accomplishing organizational objectives.

Among the activities of leading are teaching, coaching, and motivating employees to perform their jobs effectively.

this function, since it is the function around which departmental performance revolves.

Controlling
Ensuring that actual performance is in line with intended performance and taking corrective action.

Controlling. The managerial function of **controlling** involves ensuring that actual performance is in line with intended performance and taking corrective action as necessary. Here, too, the importance of planning as the first function of management should be obvious. It would not be possible for a supervisor to determine whether work was proceeding properly if there were no plans against which to check. If plans or standards are superficial or poorly conceived, the controlling function is limited. Thus, controlling means not only making sure that objectives are achieved, but also taking corrective action in case of failure to achieve planned objectives. It also means revising plans if circumstances require it.

The Continuous Flow of Managerial Functions

The five managerial functions can be viewed as a circular, continuous movement. If we view the managerial process as a circular flow consisting of the five functions (Figure 2-2), we can see that the functions flow into each other and that each af-

FIGURE 2-2
The circular concept il-
lustrates the close and
continuous relationship
between the manager-
ial functions.

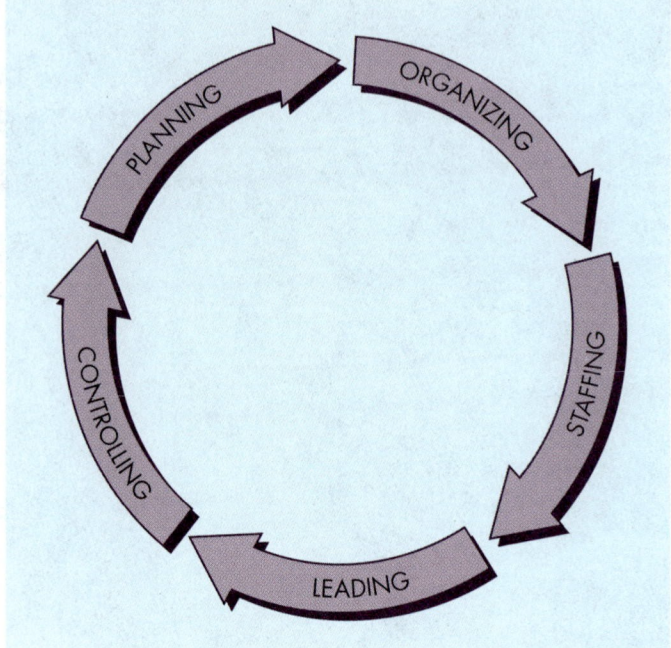

fects the performance of the others. At times there is no clear line to mark where
one function ends and the other begins. Also, it is not possible for a supervisor to
set aside a certain amount of time for one or another function, since the effort
spent in each function will vary as conditions and circumstances change. But there
is no doubt that planning must come first. Without plans, the supervisor cannot organize, staff, lead, or control.

Managerial Functions Relative to Time and Position

As previously stated, managerial functions essentially are the same for all managers,
whether they are board chairpersons, top-level executives, middle-level managers,
or supervisors. However, the time and effort devoted to each of these functions will
vary depending on a person's level within the management hierarchy. Various studies indicate that top-level executives spend most time planning and controlling and
less time organizing, staffing, and leading. Typically, the supervisors spend more
time leading and controlling and less time planning, organizing, and staffing.

Because the operating environment changes so quickly, long-term planning cy-
cles have been shortened. Today, the chief executive may plan for at least one year
ahead, or for three or even five years ahead. The supervisor normally makes plans
for much shorter periods. There are times when the supervisor will plan for only
the next few weeks, the present week, the present day, or even the present shift.
Thus, both the span and the magnitude of the first-line supervisor's plans will be
smaller than those of high-level managers. For example, an executive may plan to

FIGURE 2-3
The time and scope involved in managerial functions vary with a person's position in the management hierarchy.

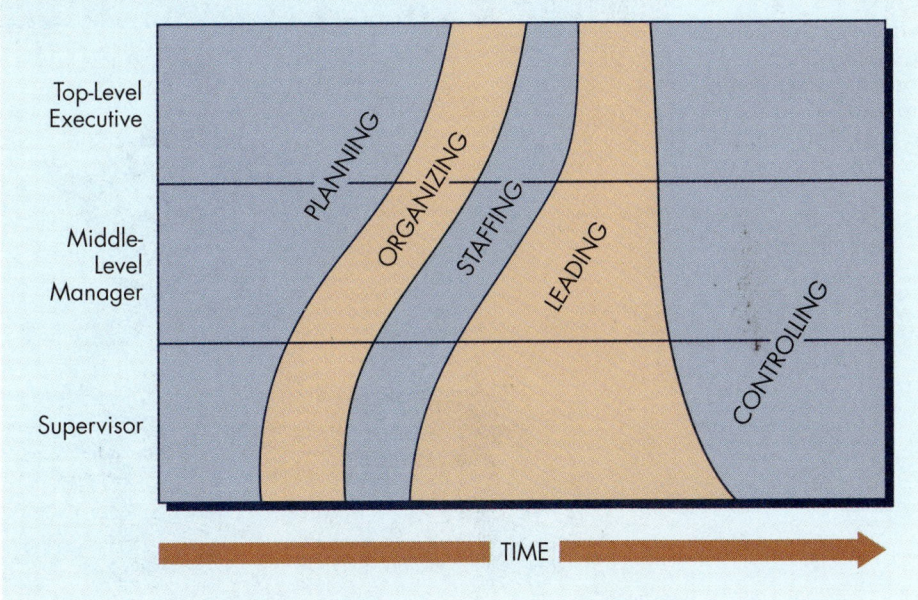

buy equipment involving millions of dollars and affecting the entire organization. By comparison, the supervisor typically plans for the use of employees, equipment, and material for a short period of time and involving restricted amounts of money and resources.

The same is true for the leading function. The top-level executive, who delegates and depends on subordinate managers to carry out assignments, normally spends a minimum of time in direct supervision. The first-line supervisor, however, is concerned with getting the job done each day and has to spend considerable time leading the efforts of subordinates.

To summarize: All managers perform the same managerial functions, regardless of their level in the hierarchy. The time and effort involved in each of these functions will vary, depending on the rung of the management ladder the manager occupies. This concept is illustrated in Figure 2-3.

MANAGERIAL AUTHORITY

4 Discuss the concept of authority as a requirement of any managerial position.

Authority
The legitimate right to lead others.

Does the individual possess the authority to perform the managerial functions? If the answer is no, the individual cannot perform well as a manager (see Figure 2-4). **Authority** is the legitimate or rightful power to lead others, the right to order and to act.[2] It is the power by which a manager can require subordinates to do or not to do a certain thing that the manager deems necessary to achieve objectives. Managerial authority is not granted to an individual but rather to the position the individual holds at the time. When the individual leaves the job or is replaced, he

or she ceases to have that authority. When a successor takes over the position, that person will then have the authority.

Having managerial authority means that the supervisor has the power and right to issue directives in order to accomplish the tasks that have been assigned to the department. This authority includes the power and right to reward and discipline, if necessary. If a subordinate performs well, then the supervisor has the power to give a raise or other reward to the subordinate, within company guidelines. If a worker refuses to carry out a directive, the supervisor's authority includes the power and right to take disciplinary action, even to the extent of discharging the subordinate. Of course, this power, like all authority, has limitations. For example, a union contract and legal restrictions may require that certain conditions be fulfilled before a worker can be discharged. Also, upper-level managers establish guidelines for the size of raises supervisors may give employees, based on performance level.

Avoiding Reliance on Managerial Authority

Most successful supervisors know that to motivate workers to perform their required duties it usually is best not to rely on their formal managerial authority but to employ other approaches. Generally, it is better for a supervisor not to display power and formal authority, and in practice many supervisors prefer not even to speak about their authority. They prefer to speak of their "responsibility," "tasks," or "duties," instead of stating that they possess authority. Some supervisors consider it better to say that they have responsibility for certain activities, instead of saying that they have authority within that area. Using the words "responsibility," "tasks," and "duties" in this sense—although these certainly are not the same as

CONTEMPORARY ISSUE
How Would You Like to Work for This Boss?

In an era of endless restructuring, cutting heads like Robespierre on a rampage is just average behavior for many managers. These leaders inflict pain by messing with your mind as well. The following describe how some people view their manager(s):

1. Uses intimidation to get what he or she thinks is right.

2. Has an inhuman drive for perfection that can burn out even the most motivated worker.
3. Is a screamer who's not above swearing like a trooper.
4. Plays good and bad cop to keep people off balance.
5. Has an intimidating military style.
6. Is cold, calculating, and mean . . . hot-tempered.

Source: Adapted with permission from Brian Dumaine, "America's Toughest Bosses," *Fortune* (October 18, 1993), pp. 39–50. © Time Inc. All rights reserved.

authority—helps the supervisor to avoid showing the "club" of authority. See this chapter's "Contemporary Issue" for examples of how employees view managers who use their authority to an extreme.

Research shows that approaches that foster mutual trust and respect between supervisor and subordinate generally result in increased job satisfaction and higher productivity. We contend that employees are likely to perform better if they understand why the task needs to be done and have a voice in how to do it, rather than simply being told to do it. Regardless of how a supervisor applies authority, the point to remember is that the supervisory position must have it. Without managerial authority, a supervisor cannot perform well as a manager.

Delegating Authority

Delegation
The process of entrusting duties and related authority to subordinates.

Included within positional managerial authority are the right and duty to delegate authority. **Delegation** of authority is the process by which the supervisor receives authority from a higher-level manager and, in turn, makes job assignments and entrusts related authority to subordinates. Just as the possession of authority is a required component of any managerial position, the process of delegating authority to lower levels within the hierarchy is required for an organization to have effective managers, supervisors, and employees. Chapter 4 and Chapter 9 discuss in detail the concepts of authority, responsibility, and the delegation of authority.

COORDINATION

5 Explain the need for coordination and cooperation and how these depend on the proper performance of the managerial functions.

"Management" was generally defined as a process of getting things done through and with the help of people by directing their efforts toward common objectives. In a sense, all levels of management could be broadly visualized as involving the coordination of efforts of all the members and resources of an organization toward overall objectives. Some writers, therefore, have included the concept of coordination as a separate managerial function.

Coordination
The synchronization of employees' efforts and the organization's resources toward achieving goals.

Coordination is the orderly synchronization (or putting together) of efforts of the members and resources of an organization to accomplish the organization's objectives. Coordination is not a separate managerial function; it is an implicit, interrelated aspect of the five major managerial functions previously cited. That is, coordination is fostered whenever a manager performs any of the managerial functions of planning, organizing, staffing, leading, and controlling. In a sense, coordination can best be understood as being a direct result of good management, rather than as a managerial function in itself. The ability to communicate clearly and concisely is essential for coordination.

Achieving coordination typically is more difficult at the executive level than at the supervisory level. The chief executive officer has to synchronize the use of resources and human efforts throughout the entire organization, that is, throughout numerous departments and levels. A supervisor of one department has the responsibility to achieve coordination primarily within the department. However, this, too, can be difficult to achieve, especially during periods of rapid change.

Cooperation As Related to Coordination

Cooperation
The willingness of individuals to work with and help one another.

Cooperation is individuals' willingness to work with and help each other. It primarily involves the attitudes of a group of people.

Coordination is more than the mere desire and willingness of participants. For example, consider a group of workers attempting to move a heavy object. They are sufficient in number, willing and eager to cooperate with each other, and trying their best to move the object. They are also fully aware of their common purpose. However, in all likelihood their efforts will be of little avail until one of them—the supervisor—gives the proper orders to apply the right amount of effort at the right place at the right time. Then they can move the object. It is possible that by sheer coincidence mere cooperation could have brought about the desired result in this instance; but no supervisor can afford to rely upon such a coincidental occurrence. Although cooperation is helpful and the lack of it could impede progress, its presence alone will not necessarily get the job done. Efforts must be coordinated toward the common goal.

Attaining Coordination

Coordination is not easily attained, and the task of achieving coordination is becoming more complex. As an organization grows, coordinating the many activities of various departments becomes an increasingly complicated problem for higher-level managers. At the supervisory level, as the number and types of positions within a department increase, the need for coordination to obtain desired results similarly increases. On the other hand, organizational downsizing may force supervisors to be even more effective in coordination (see Chapter 9).

Complexities of human nature present additional problems of coordination. Many employees understandably are preoccupied with their own work because, in the final analysis, they are evaluated primarily on how they do their jobs.

Therefore, they tend not to become involved in other areas, and often they are indifferent to the fact that their activities may affect other departments.

Supervisors can achieve coordination by building networks focused on attaining common objectives. According to the dictionary, a network is a "fabric or structure of cords or wires that cross at regular intervals and are knotted or secured at the crossings." This visual image is helpful in conceiving of a network from a supervisor's perspective. A supervisor should think of a network as any number of individuals or groups linked together by a commitment to shared purpose and values. **Networking** is the process by which supervisors become connected with other individuals or groups to achieve particular goals. Simply stated, networking is people connecting with people, linking ideas, resources, and work effort. Carol Reeves, supervisor of the Kincaid Pharmacy ("You Make the Call"), should develop networks with others, both inside and outside the pharmacy. Also, she must understand that the network runs on both sides of the street. When Carol has a need, she contacts another person in her network who might have a resource, and vice versa. Networking enables Carol to maintain a balance between autonomy on one hand and dependence on the other. Networking facilitates the flow of ideas across organizational barriers and thereby eases the coordination effort.

Networking
Individuals or groups linked together by a commitment to shared purpose.

Coordination as Part of the Managerial Functions.

While performing the managerial functions, the supervisor should recognize that coordination is a desired result of effective management. Proper attention to coordination within each of the five managerial functions contributes to overall coordination.

The planning stage is an important time for fostering coordination, since a supervisor must see to it that the various plans within the department are properly interrelated. For example, a supervisor may wish to discuss departmental job assignments with the workers who are to carry them out. In this way they have the opportunity to express their opinions or objections, which need to be reconciled in advance. Furthermore, employees may be encouraged to make suggestions and to participate in discussing the merits of proposed plans and alternatives. If employees are involved in departmental planning at the initial stages, the supervisor's chances for achieving coordination usually will be improved.

The concern for coordination must be prevalent when a supervisor organizes. The purpose of establishing who is to do what, when, where, and how is to achieve coordination. For example, whenever a new job is to be done, a supervisor assigns it to the unit that has employees best suited to accomplish the work. Thus, whenever a supervisor groups activities and assigns subordinates to them, coordination should be uppermost in the supervisor's mind. Achieving coordination also should be of concern as a supervisor establishes authority relationships within the department and among employees. Clear statements as to specific duties and reporting relationships in the department will foster coordination and prevent duplication of efforts and confusion.

Similarly, coordination should be a high priority when a supervisor performs the staffing function. There must be the right number of workers possessing the proper skills in all of the positions to ensure the group's effective performance. The supervisor must see to it that employees have the abilities and job training they need to contribute to the coordination of their efforts.

When leading, the supervisor is significantly involved in coordination. The essence of giving instructions is to coordinate the activities of employees in such a manner that the overall objectives will be reached in the most efficient way possible. In addition, a supervisor must assess and reward the performance of employees to maintain a harmonious work group.

The supervisor is also concerned with coordination when performing the controlling function. By checking, monitoring, and observing, the supervisor makes certain that activities conform to established plans. If there are any discrepancies, the supervisor should take immediate action to reprioritize or reassign tasks and, in so doing, may achieve coordination at least from then on. The very nature of the controlling process contributes to coordination and keeps the organization moving toward its objectives.

Coordination with Other Departments. Not only must supervisors be concerned with coordination within their own departments, but they also must coordinate the efforts of their departments with those of others. For example, a production department supervisor must meet with supervisors of scheduling, quality control, maintenance, and shipping to coordinate various activities. Similarly, an accounting supervisor typically meets with supervisors from production, sales, and shipping to coordinate cost accounting, inventory records, and billing. Achieving coordination is an essential component of the supervisory management position.

Cooperation and Coordination—Easier Said Than Done. A group of employees becomes a team when its members possess shared values and a shared purpose. How well the objectives are achieved depends on the supervisor's coordination and team-building skills. The move toward increased employee participation, broader spans of control, and fewer managerial levels will result in a greater need for coordination skills. Meanwhile, many supervisors have higher aspirations: They want to be promoted eventually to positions of increased responsibility. Referring back to the opening "You Make the Call" section, you will notice that there is less opportunity as a person moves up the organization. As Carol Reeves, one of the 16 store supervisors at Kincaid Pharmacy, you, in all likelihood, will be competing with the other 15 store supervisors for the position of operations manager. The challenge for the organization is to get people to cooperate and work together when in reality the structure of the organization may impede cooperation.

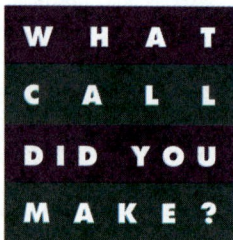

WHAT CALL DID YOU MAKE?

As Carol Reeves, you have legitimate or positional authority because of the supervisory position you hold. You have adequately performed all of the functions outlined in this chapter. Unfortunately, a situation arises over which you have little control. Your best-laid plans have gone awry. You must develop a contingency plan at the last minute to provide coverage to meet customer needs. You had a plan, and, since the future did not develop as predicted, you must respond quickly. Remember that plans must be flexible.

Kincaid Pharmacy places a high value on customer service, and you must do whatever it takes to fulfill that expectation. Since none of the State Street store employees can come in on short notice, perhaps one of the other stores has someone who can fill in on his or her day off. Hopefully, as the supervisor, you have previously developed networks to help you with your current need. Your previous networking and cooperative efforts with the other store supervisors may pay off, and they will assist you in finding someone to provide coverage. Perhaps the human resources department can help you by recommending a temporary help service or other options. If they cannot help you, you should get back to the person who said he or she could come in later in the day.

In all likelihood, you will have to roll up your sleeves and fill in where needed. You have the technical skills, and periodically you will have to use them. You will need to communicate to the other employees that Kelly's absence will necessitate an extra effort on their part. Generally, the employees you ask to provide extra coverage are likely to perform better if they understand why the task needs to be done and have a voice in how to do it. Unfortunately, time is not on your side, because the store opens in a few minutes.

Your coordination skills will be taxed. You might have to spread your existing staff to cover the work. Conflicts may arise, and your ability to perform the leading function will make the task less difficult. Can you prevent the problem from recurring? The answer is no, but you can learn from this experience and develop contingency plans for when it happens again.

A word of caution: Often employees who show up for work regularly are punished when someone like Kelly does not show up on her scheduled work day. They will be asked to pick up the slack, and some may resent it. As the supervisor, you need to find ways to reward employees who give extra effort during a crisis.

SUMMARY

1 Summarize the difficulties supervisors face in fulfilling managerial roles.

Supervisors are the "people in the middle." Employees see their supervisors as being management, but supervisors are subordinates to their own managers at higher levels. Toward supervisors of other departments, they are colleagues who must cooperate with each other. Supervisors must have good working knowledge of the jobs being performed in their department and the ability to manage.

2 Explain why effective supervisors should possess a variety of skills.

The effective supervisor needs to possess administrative, conceptual, human relations, and technical skills. The supervisor must understand the technical aspects of the work being performed. While attempting to manage job performance, understanding employee needs is essential. The "people skills" help the supervisor accomplish objectives with and through people. It is equally important for the supervisor to possess an understanding of the dynamics of the organization and to recognize organizational politics.

The skills are important to all levels of management. Most supervisors come to the job equipped with some of the skills. Supervisors have daily opportunities to apply managerial skills and must continually strive to develop those skills. Effective application of the skills will contribute to the accomplishment of organizational objectives and will allow the supervisor to stay on top of the job. Supervisors who effectively apply the skills will be able to contribute suggestions to higher-level managers, and will be able to work in harmony with their colleagues. In short, the skilled supervisor will be a candidate for advancement and additional job responsibilities.

3 Define management and discuss how the primary managerial functions are interrelated.

While there are numerous definitions of management, we have defined management as the process of getting things accomplished through people by guiding and motivating their efforts toward common objectives.

The five major managerial functions are planning, organizing, staffing, leading, and controlling. The functions are viewed as a continuous flow—that is, the functions flow into each other, and each affects the performance of the others.

Planning is the first function of management, and the performance of all other managerial functions depends upon it. The five managerial functions are universal, regardless of the job environment, the activity involved, or a person's position in the management hierarchy. Typically, supervisors spend most of their time leading and controlling. A supervisor's planning will cover a much shorter time and narrower focus than that of a top-level executive.

4 Discuss the concept of authority as a requirement of any managerial position.

A supervisor must possess authority in order to perform well as a manager. Authority is the legitimate or rightful power to lead others. Authority is delegated from top-level managers through middle-level managers to supervisors, who, in turn, delegate to their employees. All supervisors must be delegated appropriate authority to manage their departments. Most supervisors, rather than relying primarily on formal managerial authority, prefer to use other approaches for enhancing employee performance.

5 Explain the need for coordination and cooperation and how these depend on the proper performance of the managerial functions.

Coordination is the orderly synchronization of efforts of the members and resources of an organization toward the attainment of stated objectives. Cooperation—as distinguished from coordination—is the willingness of individuals to work with and help each other. While cooperation is helpful, it cannot itself get the job done. Efforts must also be coordinated. Both coordination and cooperation are attainable through good management practices.

KEY TERMS

Conceptual skills (page 32)   Administrative skills (page 32)
Human relations skills (page 32)   Technical skills (page 32)

QUESTIONS FOR DISCUSSION

1. Identify four major managerial skills needed by every supervisor. Why are these important? Do you consider political skills to be as important? Why or why not?

2. How would you respond to someone who says, "I really get along well with everyone. I think I would be a good manager."

3. Does managerial ability really make the major difference between a good supervisor and a poor supervisor? Discuss.

4. Evaluate the definitions of management given in the text. Develop your own definition based on what you have learned.

5. Define each of the five managerial functions. What effect do hierarchical differences have on these functions? Are these functions adequate to describe the complexities of a managerial position? Discuss.

6. It is often said that planning is the most important managerial function. Do you agree? Why or why not?

7. Define authority and discuss its importance.

8. What is coordination? Some writers prefer to consider coordination as a separate managerial function. Explain why coordination can be considered an integral part of all managerial functions.

9. Define the concept of cooperation. How are coordination and cooperation interrelated?

10. Is networking essential for a college student's survival? Why or why not?

SKILLS APPLICATIONS

Skills Application 2-1: Attributes of a Successful Manager

Think of the most successful manager you have ever known or heard about. Write a paragraph describing what that manager does to be described as successful. Compare your paragraph with that of a classmate. Are there skills, knowledge, or abilities common to both? Why do you think there are common items?

Skills Application 2-2: Self-Assessment of Supervisory Skills

1. From the following list select the six items that you believe are most critical to supervisory success.

2. Select the six items that are the least critical. Select *only* six items for either most critical or least critical.

3. Weight each category as follows: Most critical item = 3, least critical item = 1, all others = 2.

4. Rate your abilities on each of these items as follows: major strength = 3, minor strength = 2, minor weakness = 1, major weakness = 0.

5. Multiply the weight of each item by your assessed strength.

6. Sum the strength ratings.

Item	Weight (×)	Rating =	Strength Rating
Ability to develop contingency plans	___	___	___
Technical competency	___	___	___
Follows direction from above	___	___	___
Ability to obtain needed information	___	___	___
Ability to make sound decisions	___	___	___
Leads by example	___	___	___
Ability to plan	___	___	___
Ability to coordinate activities of others	___	___	___
Ability to get things done through others	___	___	___
Ability to delegate	___	___	___
Ability to empower employees	___	___	___
Ability to listen actively	___	___	___
Ability to work under pressure	___	___	___
Anticipates crises	___	___	___
Keeps up to date on work-related matters	___	___	___
Ability to give effective instructions	___	___	___
Accepts responsibility for the results of others	___	___	___
Uses praise for job well done	___	___	___
Ability to get diverse people to function as a team	___	___	___
Ability to establish priorities	___	___	___
Provides feedback on performance	___	___	___
Ability to train and develop employees	___	___	___
Provides employees with a vision	___	___	___
Ability to select employees with potential	___	___	___
Ability to evaluate employees fairly	___	___	___
Total Strength Rating			___

To derive your total supervisory strength rating, add the strength rating for each item. If your score is less than 110, you need to focus your attention on those critical items where improvement is most needed.

Skills Application 2-3: Sell Yourself

The following advertisement appeared in the local paper:

SUPERVISOR

Mid-size high-volume plastics mfg. facility needs a self-starter with communication and teaching skills to lead and coordinate the production activities of 30-plus employees. Primary responsibilities will include fostering a work environment consistent with company philosophy and objectives while managing production to quality, safety, quantity, cost, and profit standards.

Demonstrated ability to lead, motivate, select, and train personnel is a must. Related associate degree is preferred. We offer competitive pay and benefits and a team-oriented environment. Submit résumé with salary history to:

E.R.M
Stevens Packaging
P.O. Box 5226
Fort Wayne, IN 46895-5226

Write a letter outlining your interest in the position. Develop a list of questions that you would ask the company if you were selected for an interview. Compare these questions with those developed by others in the class.

ENDNOTES

1.   There is no universal definition of management, as the list in Figure 2-1 shows. Citations for each of the definitions listed are as follows: Louis E. Boone and David L. Kurtz, *Contemporary Business* (7th ed.; Hinsdale, Ill.: The Dryden Press, 1993), p. 214; William Cunningham, Ramon Aldag, and Stanley Block, *Business in a Changing World* (3d ed.; Cincinnati: South-Western Publishing Co., 1993), p. 746; Peter F. Drucker, *The New Realities* (New York: HarperCollins Publishers, 1989), p. 22; Lawrence Gitman and Carl McDaniel, *The World of Business* (Cincinnati: South-Western Publishing Co., 1992), p. 759; Tom Peters and Nancy Austin, *A Passion for Excellence: The Leadership Difference* (New York: Random House, 1985), p. 333; and John A. Wagner, III and John R. Hollenbeck, *Management of Organizational Behavior* (Englewood Cliffs, N.J.: Prentice-Hall, 1992), p. 24.

2.   One of Fayol's 14 principles of management included authority and responsibility. He defined formal authority as the "right to give orders." Henri Fayol, *General and Industrial Management,* trans. Constance Storrs (London: Sir Isaac Pitman & Sons, 1949), pp. 19–43. Also, see Jack J. Phillips, "Authority: It Just Doesn't Come with Your Job," *Management Solutions* (Volume 31, August 1986), pp. 35–37, for a perspective on informal authority.

3

Communication: The Vital Link in Supervisory Management

LEARNING OBJECTIVES

After studying this chapter, you will be able to:

1 Define communication and discuss its implications for effective supervisory management.

2 Discuss the major channels of communication available to the supervisor.

3 Explain the benefits of the various methods of communication.

4 Identify and discuss barriers to effective communication.

5 Describe ways to overcome the communication barriers.

6 Contrast five conflict resolution styles.

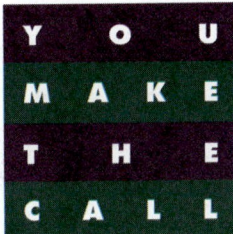

You are Ed, area supervisor for Clark Quik Stops. Four months earlier, Clark acquired eight Citgo Convenience Shops. You were given four of these stores to add to the eight already in your area. Two months ago, the decision was made by top-level management to close six stores, two of which were in your area. As a result of the reorganization your workload has grown tremendously.

A friend took you to a meeting at the local college where a professor of management expounded on some ideas that caught your attention. The professor said that management is a "universal" function, that all managers, regardless of level, perform basically the same managerial functions. The professor stated that the more effective managers do a better job of communicating. You thought back on the past two months. Until you heard the professor's presentation, you had been feeling pretty confident about the job you had done in reorganizing your area. You wondered whether you could have done a better job of communicating the bad news to the employees you had to let go.

A few hours ago, there was a meeting of the area supervisors for a preliminary discussion on the yearly planning and budget period coming up. Each area is to operate as a profit center. You know that this could result in the closing of several more stores in your area. Upon returning to your office, you find Louise Abbott, an assistant store supervisor, waiting.

Louise: I need to talk with you right now. Employee resistance to change has delayed training and implementation of the new computer scanning and inventory system. I need your help.

You (sarcastically): Look, I really don't have time to discuss that right now. I just returned from a meeting downtown. We've got to cut some additional overhead costs, and you have to have the system operational within 10 days. You were given the responsibility because you have more computer knowledge than anyone else.

Louise: You haven't listened to anything I've said during the past two months. You know that I'm over my head with this project. I'm only an assistant supervisor,

and I have no leverage with those store managers. Someone at your level has to become involved to help me carry this out.

You: Wait just a minute. I've had lots of anguish with the reorganization, and now before I even get my coat off you're on my case. That system should have been operational before now.

Louise (bitterly): Well, with the way you've been acting lately, I didn't think you'd be any help.

Louise turns in a huff and heads out the door. You know that you had better do something and do it quickly. What will you do?
YOU MAKE THE CALL.

THE NEED FOR EFFECTIVE COMMUNICATION

1 Define communication and discuss its implications for effective supervisory management.

Communication
The process of transmitting information and understanding.

Communication is the process of transmitting information and understanding from one person to another. Effective communication means that there is a successful transfer of information, meaning, and understanding from a sender to a receiver. In other words, communication is the process of imparting ideas and making oneself understood by others. While it is not necessary to have agreement, there must be a mutual understanding for the exchange of ideas to be successful.

Most supervisory activities involve interaction with others, and each interaction requires skillful handling of the information process. The ability to communicate effectively is a key to supervisory success. Communication is the process that links all managerial functions. There is no managerial function that a supervisor can fulfill without communicating. In managing their departments, supervisors must explain the arrangement of work. They must instruct employees, describe what is expected of them, and counsel them. Supervisors must also report to their managers, both orally and in writing, and discuss plans with other supervisors. All of these activities require communication.

Studies have indicated that supervisors generally spend between 70 and 90 percent of their time sending and receiving information. With the advent of electronic forms of communication and other convenient means of information flow, it seems that communication problems should be diminishing. Yet, supervisors still see communication difficulties as their most persistent challenge. As one frustrated su-

FIGURE 3-1
Communication does not take place unless the message is received and understood.

pervisor expressed it, "There are more messages now being sent and received, but, frankly, I think we communicate with each other more poorly than ever before!"

Effective Communication Requires a Two-Way Exchange

Communication was defined as a process of transmitting information and understanding from one person to another. The significant point is that communication always involves at least two people, a sender and a receiver. For example, a supervisor who is alone in a room and verbally states a set of instructions does not communicate, because there are no receivers present. While the lack of communication is obvious in this case, it may not be so obvious to a supervisor who sends a letter. Once the letter has been mailed, the supervisor may believe that communication has taken place. However, this supervisor has not really communicated until and unless the letter has been received and information and understanding have been transferred successfully to the receiver (see Figure 3-1).

It cannot be emphasized too strongly that effective communication includes both sending and receiving information. A listener may hear a speaker, because the listener has ears, but the listener may not understand what the speaker means. Understanding is a personal matter between people. If the idea received has the same meaning as the one intended, then we can say that effective communication has taken place. But if the idea received by a listener or reader is not the one intended, then effective communication has not been accomplished. The sender has merely transmitted spoken or written words. This does not mean that the sender and receiver must agree on a particular message or issue; it is possible to communicate and yet not agree.

Effective Communication Means Better Supervision

Some supervisors are more effective as communicators than others. Usually these supervisors recognize that communication is vital, and they give it their major attention. Unfortunately, many supervisors simply assume that they know how to communicate, and they do not work at developing their communication skills. Yet a supervisor's effectiveness will depend greatly on the ability to transfer information or ideas to employees. The employees must understand the supervisor's instructions to achieve their objectives. Similarly, the supervisor must know how to receive information and understand the messages sent by employees, other supervisors, and higher-level managers. Fortunately, the skills of effective communication can be developed. By becoming a more effective communicator, a supervisor will also become a more effective manager.

CHANNELS OF THE COMMUNICATION NETWORK

2 Discuss the major channels of communication available to the supervisor.

In every organization the communication network has two primary and equally important channels: the formal, or official, channels of communication and the informal channels, usually called the "grapevine." Both channels carry messages from one person or group to another in organizations, downward, upward, and horizontally.

Formal Channels

Formal communication channels are established primarily by the organizational structure. The vertical formal channels can be visualized by following the lines of authority from the top-level executive down through the organization to supervisors and lower-level employees.

Downward Communication. The concept of a downward formal channel of communication suggests that someone at the top issues instructions or disseminates information that managers at the next level in the hierarchy pass on to their subordinates, and so on down the line. The downward direction is the channel most frequently used by higher-level managers for communication. Downward communication helps to tie different levels together and is important for coordination. It is used by managers to start action by subordinates and to communicate instructions, objectives, policies, procedures, and other information to them. Generally, downward communication is mostly of an informative and directive nature and requires action on the part of subordinates. Downward communication from a supervisor involves giving instructions, explaining information and procedures, training employees, and engaging in other types of activities designed to guide employees in performing their work.

Upward Communication. Upward is an equally important direction of communication in the official network. Supervisors who have managerial authority accept an obligation to keep their superiors informed and to contribute their own ideas to management. Similarly, employees should feel free to convey their ideas to

CONTEMPORARY ISSUE
Management By Wandering Around (MBWA) Improves Upward Communication

The most effective leaders, from Mohandas Gandhi to Sam Walton, of Wal-Mart, have always led from the front line, where the action is. Today, any leader, at any level, who hopes for even limited success must likewise lead from the trenches. . . . Getting out and about (commonly known as Management by Wandering Around, or MBWA) . . . deals with . . . gathering the information necessary for decision-making, with making a vision concrete, with engendering commitment and risk-taking, with caring about people. . . .[1]

William Malec, chief financial officer of the Tennessee Valley Authority (TVA), spends one day a month doing the job of one of his employees. This might mean scrubbing the toilets at midnight, sorting mail with the couriers at 5:00 a.m., or any one of a variety of jobs.

During the past five years, TVA had eliminated 18 thousand jobs company wide. Malec decided on the MBWA approach as a way to facilitate upward communication and build morale. He said that when he worked side by side with employees, they told him things he would not normally hear. He heard complaints about having to fill out multipage forms accepted only at certain local stores just to buy a mop. Consequently, he gave plant managers credit cards that could be used anywhere. This procedure saved an estimated $1.3 million a year in purchasing costs.[2]

As Malec's experience shows, upward communication can be very valuable. No one knows the problems—and possible solutions—better than the employees who are actually doing the job. To tap into this important source of information, supervisors must develop a good rapport with their employees—and then really listen to them.

Sources: [1] Tom Peters, *Thriving on Chaos* (New York: Alfred A. Knopf, 1987), pp. 423–424. [2] Adapted from Todd Gutner, "Meeting the Boss," *Forbes* (Volume 151, Number 5, March 1, 1993), p. 126.

their supervisors and to report on activities related to their work. Managers and supervisors should encourage a free flow of upward communication.

Upward communication usually is of an informing and reporting nature, including questions, suggestions, and complaints. This is a vital means by which managers can determine whether proper actions are taking place and obtain valuable employee insights about problems facing a unit. For example, employees may report production results and also present ideas for increasing production in the future.

Supervisors should encourage upward communication among employees and give ample attention to the information transmitted. Supervisors must show that they want employee suggestions as well as the facts and then must evaluate them promptly. As discussed in Chapter 5, participative-type supervisors convey a genuine desire to obtain and use the ideas suggested by employees. This chapter's Contemporary Issue illustrates one way to encourage upward communication.

Most supervisors will agree that it is often easier for them to converse with subordinates than to speak with their own manager. This is particularly true if they have ever had to tell their manager that they did not meet a schedule or made a mistake. Nevertheless, it is a supervisory duty to advise the manager whenever there are significant developments and to do this as soon as possible, either before or after such events occur. It is quite embarrassing to a manager to learn important news elsewhere; this can be interpreted to mean that the supervisor is not on top of his or her responsibilities.

Higher-level managers need to have complete information, because they retain overall responsibility for organizational performance. Of course, this does not mean that supervisors need to pass upward every bit of trivial information. Rather, it means that supervisors should mentally place themselves in their managers' position and consider what information their managers need to perform their own jobs properly.

A supervisor's upward communication should be sent on time and in a form that will enable the manager to take necessary action. The supervisor should assemble and check the facts before passing them on. This may be quite difficult at times. A natural inclination is to "soften" the information a bit so that things will not look quite as bad in the manager's eyes as they actually are. When difficulties arise, it is best to tell the manager what is really going on, even if this means admitting mistakes. Higher-level managers depend on the supervisor for reliable upward communication, just as the supervisor depends on his or her employees for the upward flow of information.

Horizontal Communication. There is a third direction of formal communication that is essential for the efficient functioning of an organization. This is lateral, or horizontal, communication, which is concerned mainly with communication between departments or people at the same levels but in charge of different functions. A free flow of horizontal communication is needed to coordinate functions among various departments.

Horizontal communication typically involves discussions and meetings to accomplish tasks that cross departmental lines. For example, a production manager may have to contact managers of the marketing and shipping departments to ascertain progress on a delivery schedule for a product. Or someone from the human resources department may have a meeting with a number of supervisors to discuss how a new medical leave policy is to be implemented at the departmental level. Still another example is the cashier who pages the stock clerk to inquire when a particular item will be available. Without effective horizontal communication, any organization would find it virtually impossible to coordinate specialized departmental efforts toward common goals.

Informal Channels—The Grapevine

Grapevine
The informal, unofficial communication channel.

Informal communication channels, commonly referred to as the **grapevine,** are a normal outgrowth of informal and casual groupings of people on the job, of their social interactions, and of their understandable desire to communicate with one another. Every organization has its grapevine. This is a perfectly natural activity, since it fulfills the employees' desires to know the latest information and to socialize with other people. The grapevine offers members of an organization an outlet for their imaginations and an opportunity to express their apprehensions in the form of rumors.

The grapevine offers employees an opportunity to learn the latest information and socialize with others.

Understanding the Grapevine. The grapevine can offer considerable insight into what employees think and feel. An alert supervisor acknowledges the grapevine's presence and tries to take advantage of it whenever possible. The grapevine often carries factual information, but sometimes it carries half-truths, rumors, private interpretations, suspicions, and other bits of distorted or inaccurate information. Research indicates that many employees have more faith and confidence in the grapevine than in what their supervisors tell them.[3] In part, this reflects a natural human tendency to trust one's peers to a greater degree than one trusts people in authority, such as supervisors or parents.

The grapevine has no definite patterns or stable membership. Its workings cannot be predicted, since the path followed yesterday is not necessarily the same as today or tomorrow. The vast majority of employees hear information through the grapevine, but some do not pass it along. Any person within an organization may become active in the grapevine on occasion, although some individuals tend to be more active than others. They feel that their prestige is enhanced by providing the latest news, and they do not hesitate to spread and embellish upon the news. The rumors they pass on serve in part as a release for their emotions, providing an opportunity to remain anonymous and say what they please without the danger of being held accountable.

The grapevine sometimes helps clarify and supplement formal communications, and it often spreads information that could not be disseminated as well or as rapidly through official channels.

The Supervisor and the Grapevine. The supervisor should accept the fact that it is not possible to eliminate the grapevine. It is unrealistic to expect that all rumors can be stamped out, and the grapevine is certain to flourish in every organization. To cope with it, supervisors should tune in on the grapevine and learn what it is saying. They should determine who its leaders are and who is likely to spread information.

Many rumors begin in the wishful-thinking stage of employee anticipation. If employees want something badly enough, they may start passing the word along to each other. For instance, if secretaries want a raise, they may start the rumor that management will offer an across-the-board raise. Nobody knows for certain where or how it started, but the story spreads rapidly because everyone wants to believe it. Of course, morale will suffer when hopes are built up in anticipation of something that does not happen. If such a story is spreading and the supervisor realizes it will lead to disappointment, the supervisor ought to move quickly to refute it by presenting the facts. The best cure for rumors is to expose the true facts to all employees and to give a straight answer to all questions whenever possible.

Other frequent causes of rumors are uncertainty and fear. If business is slack and management is forced to lay off some employees, stories multiply quickly, as illustrated by Figure 3-2. During periods of insecurity and anxiety, the grapevine becomes more active than at other times. Often the rumors are far worse than what actually will happen. If the supervisor does not disclose the actual facts to the employees, they will make up their own "facts," which may be worse than reality. Thus, much of the fear caused by uncertainty can be eliminated or reduced if the truth of what will happen is disclosed. Continuing rumors and uncertainty may be more demoralizing than even the saddest facts presented openly.

Rumors also arise out of dislike, anger, or distrust. Again, the best prescription is to state the facts openly and honestly. If the supervisor does not have all the necessary information available, he or she should frankly admit this and then try to find out what the situation actually is and report it to the employees. One of the best ways to stop a rumor is to expose its untruthfulness. The supervisor should bear in mind that the receptiveness of a group of employees to rumors is directly related to the quality of the supervisor's communications and leadership. If employees believe that their supervisor is concerned about them and will make every effort to keep them informed, they will tend to disregard rumors and look to the supervisor for proper answers to their questions.

As stated before, there is no way to eliminate the grapevine, even with the best efforts made through all formal channels of communication. The supervisor, therefore, should listen to the grapevine and develop skills in dealing with it. For example, an alert supervisor might know that certain events will cause undue anxiety. In this case, the supervisor should explain immediately why such events will take place. When emergencies occur, changes are introduced, and policies are modified, the supervisor should explain why and answer all employee questions as openly as possible. Otherwise, employees will make up their own explanations, and often these will be incorrect. There are situations, however, when the supervisor does not have the facts either. Here the supervisor should seek out the appropriate higher-level manager, to explain what is bothering the employees and to ask for specific

FIGURE 3-2
Especially during periods of economic uncertainty, the grapevine carries bits of distorted information that flow quickly through the organization.

instructions as to what information may be given, how much may be told, and when. Also, when something happens that might cause rumors, it is helpful for supervisors to meet with their most influential employees to give them the real story. Then the employees can spread the facts before anyone else can spread the rumors.[4]

METHODS OF COMMUNICATION

3 Explain the benefits of the various methods of communication.

The preceding section described the various communication flows or channels of communication. The effective supervisor must be concerned with not only the content of communication directed at others but also the context of communication. The following sections explore various methods for delivering a message.

Behavior Is Communication

Body language
All observable actions of either the sender or the receiver.

Supervisors should realize that their behavior as managers on the job is an important form of communication to their subordinates. **Body language** is the observable actions of either the sender or the receiver. The supervisor's body language communicates something to employees, whether it is intended to do so or not. Gestures, a handshake, a shrug of the shoulder, a smile, even silence—all of these have meaning and may be interpreted differently by different people. For example, a supervisor's warm smile and posture slightly bent toward employees can send out positive signals to the employees. Conversely, a frown on a supervisor's face may communicate more than 10 minutes of oral discussion or a printed page (see Figure 3-3).

FIGURE 3-3
Body language com-
municates more than
words.

A word of caution: Body language does not have universal meaning. The message sent by different expressions or postures varies from situation to situation and particularly from culture to culture. Touching, as illustrated by the traditional "pat on the back," may be perceived differently by different people. Studies report that women distinguish between touching for the purpose of conveying warmth and friendship and touching to convey sexual attraction, while men may not.[5] A male supervisor must recognize that misinterpretation of his touching female employees may generate resentment or even charges of sexual harassment.

A supervisor's inaction is a way of communicating, just as unexplained action may communicate a meaning that was not intended. For example, a supervisor arranged to have some equipment removed from the production floor without telling the employees that the equipment was removed because it needed mechanical modifications. To the employees, who feared a threatened shutdown, this unexplained action communicated a message that the supervisor had no intention of sending.

Oral and Written Communication

Spoken and written words are the most widely used forms of communication in any organization. They also constitute a challenge to every supervisor who wishes to communicate effectively. Words can be tricky. Instructions that mean one thing to one employee may have a different meaning to someone else. There is a story about a collection agency supervisor who told a new employee, "Get tough with Mr. Stump. His account is two months overdue." Upon checking an hour later, the supervisor found that the new employee had started foreclosure proceedings against Mr. Stump. Obviously, instructions like "get tough" can be interpreted in several different ways!

Since words are the essence of oral and written communication, supervisors should constantly try to improve their skills in speaking, listening, writing, and reading. Although most messages are delivered orally, a well-balanced communication system uses both written and oral media. Supervisors do not have as many occasions to use the written medium, since a high proportion of supervisory communication takes place by word of mouth.

Oral communication generally is superior to written communication, because it facilitates better understanding and takes less time. This is true both with telephone and face-to-face communication. Face-to-face discussion between a supervisor and employees is the principal method of two-way communication. Employees like to see and hear the supervisor in person, and no written communication can be as effective as an interpersonal discussion. In a face-to-face discussion, both employees and supervisors can draw meaning from body language as well as the oral message. Another reason for the greater effectiveness of oral communication is that most people can express themselves more easily and completely by voice than by a letter or memo.

Probably the greatest single advantage of oral communication is that it can provide an immediate opportunity for determining whether or not effective communication has been accomplished between the sender and receiver. Although the response may be only an expression on the receiver's face, the sender can judge how the receiver is reacting to what is being said. Oral communication enables the sender to find out immediately what the receiver hears and does not hear. Oral communication enables the receiver to ask questions immediately if the meaning is not clear, and the sender can clarify. The human voice can impart a message with meaning and shading that pages of written words cannot convey. Body language and tone of voice help convey the message.

The principal problem with oral communication is that usually there is no permanent record of it, and, over time, speakers' and listeners' memories will blur the meaning of what was conveyed. This is why many supervisors follow up certain meetings and discussions with some type of memorandum or document, to have a written basis for recalling what was discussed.

To reiterate, a supervisor must always remember that effective communication takes place only when the meaning received by the listener is the same as that which the sender intended to send. Supervisors who are effective communicators know how to speak clearly and be aware of the listener. They are sensitive to the many barriers to effective communication that can distort communication lines. They know how to overcome these barriers, how to "clear the pipelines." Such supervisors recognize that a speaker and a listener are unique individuals who live in different worlds and that many factors can interfere with messages that pass between them.

A Picture Is Worth a Thousand Words

The power of visual media in conveying meaning to people should never be underestimated. As shown in Figure 3-4, pictures, charts, cartoons, and symbols can be effective visual aids, and the supervisor should employ them where appropriate. They are particularly effective if used in connection with well-chosen words to complete a message. Businesses make extensive use of visual aids such as blue-

FIGURE 3-4
Pictures, charts, cartoons, and symbols can be effective visual aids.

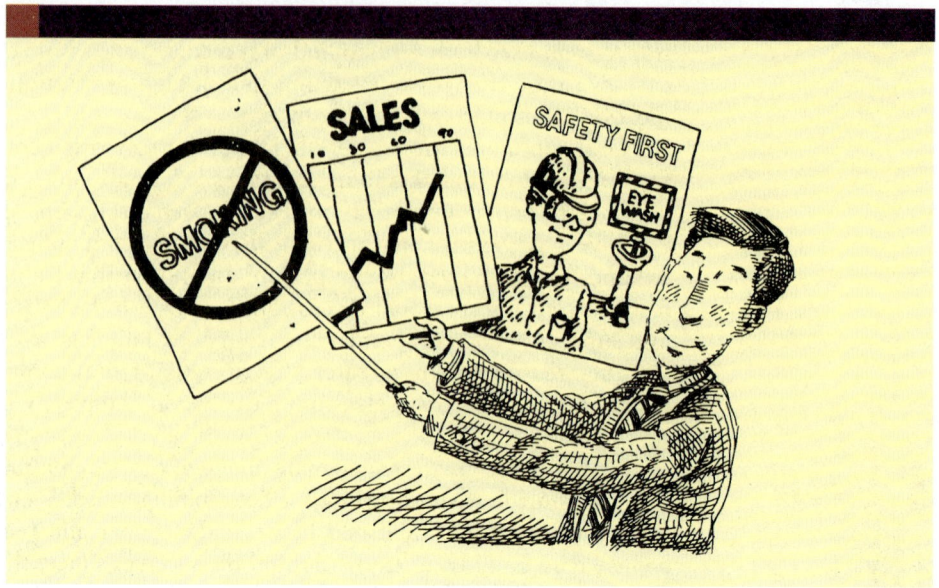

prints, charts, drafts, models, and posters to communicate information. Movies, videos, and comic strips demonstrate the power of visual media in communicating.

BARRIERS TO EFFECTIVE COMMUNICATION

4 Identify and discuss barriers to effective communication.

Noise
Obstacles that distort messages between people.

Human differences and organizational conditions can create obstacles that distort messages between people. These obstacles can be referred to as **noise.** Misunderstandings and conflicts can develop when communication breaks down. These breakdowns not only are costly in terms of money but also create dilemmas that hurt teamwork and morale. Many supervisory human relations problems are traceable to faulty communication, since the way a supervisor communicates with subordinates constitutes the essence of their relationships.

Language and Vocabulary Differences

Jargon
The use of words that are peculiar to a particular occupation or specialty.

People vary greatly in their ability to convey meaning that others understand. For example, words in themselves can be confusing, even though language is the principal vehicle people use to communicate with each other. People at different levels or in different departments sometimes seem to speak in different "languages," even though they are actually speaking English.[6] For example, an accounting department supervisor may use specialized words that may be meaningless when conversing with the plant manager. Similarly, if the plant manager uses highly technical engineering terms when conversing with the accounting supervisor, the latter will probably be confused. This is the communication problem known as **jargon,** or the use of words that are peculiar to a person's particular background or specialty.

Another communication problem lies in the multiple meanings of words,

Semantics
The multiple meanings
of words.

known as **semantics.** Words can mean different things to different people, particularly in the English language, which is one of the most difficult in the world. The way some words are used in sentences can cause people to interpret messages in a manner other than the way that was intended. *Roget's Thesaurus,* a dictionary of synonyms, identifies the numerous meanings that commonly used words can have. For example, the word "smart" can be used in several ways. We speak of a "smart" person in the sense that the person is intelligent; a "smart aleck" is someone who is difficult to get along with; a person who dresses "smartly" is someone who dresses fashionably; and a "smarting" pain means a stinging or sharp pain. Many other words can also be used in many different ways. Where a word can have multiple meanings, the meaning intended must be clarified, since listeners tend to interpret words based on their own perceptions, past experiences, and cultural backgrounds.

There are instances in which a frustrating conversation between a supervisor and employee ends with, "We are not talking the same language," even though both have been conversing in English. To avoid such breakdowns, supervisors should use words to which the employees are accustomed and which they can understand. The question is not whether the employee *ought to* understand the words; it is whether the employee *does* understand. Therefore, supervisors should strive to use plain, direct words in brief, uncomplicated statements. If necessary, they should restate messages in several ways to clarify the proper (semantic) meaning or context that was intended.

Status and Position

Status
Attitudes toward a person based on the position he or she occupies.

The organization's structure, with its several levels in the managerial hierarchy, creates a number of status levels among members of the organization. **Status** refers to the attitudes that are held toward a position and its occupant by the members of the organization. There is a recognized status difference between an executive level and a supervisory level and between supervisors and employees. Differences in status and position become apparent as one level tries to communicate with another. For example, a supervisor who tries to convey enthusiasm to an employee about higher production and profits for the company may find that the employee is indifferent to these types of company goals. The employee may be primarily concerned with achieving higher personal wages and security. Thus, the supervisor and the employee may represent different points of view merely by virtue of their positions in the company, and this may present a serious obstacle to understanding each other.

When employees listen to a message from the supervisor, several other factors become operative. They evaluate the supervisor's words in light of their own backgrounds and experiences. They also take into account the supervisor's personality and position. It is difficult for employees to separate a message from the feelings that they have about the supervisor who sends the message. Therefore, the employees may infer nonexistent motives in the message. For example, union members may be inclined to interpret a management statement in very uncomplimentary terms if they are convinced that management is trying to weaken the union.

Obstacles due to status and position also can distort the upward flow of communication when subordinates are anxious to impress management. Employees may screen information passed up the line; they may tell the supervisor only what they think the latter likes to hear and omit or soften the unpleasant details. This problem is known as **filtering.** By the same token, supervisors are also anxious to make a favorable impression when talking to managers in higher positions. They may fail to pass on important information to their managers because they believe that the information would reflect unfavorably on their own supervisory abilities.

Filtering
The process of omitting or softening unpleasant details.

Resistance to Change or New Ideas

Many people prefer things as they are, and they do not welcome changes in their working situation. If a message is intended to convey a change or new idea to employees—something that will upset their work assignments, positions, or part of their daily routine—the natural inclination is for the employees to resist the message. It is normal for people to prefer that their existing environment remain the status quo. Consequently, a message that will change this equilibrium may be greeted with suspicion. The employees' receiving apparatus works just like a screen, rejecting new ideas if they conflict with a currently comfortable situation.

In the same fashion, most listeners are likely to receive that portion of a message which confirms their present beliefs and will tend to ignore whatever conflicts with those beliefs. Sometimes beliefs are so fixed that the listeners do not hear anything at all. Even if they hear a statement, they will either reject it as false or find a convenient way of twisting its meaning to fit their own perceptions.

Receivers usually hear what they wish to hear. If they are insecure or fearful in their positions, this barrier becomes even more difficult to overcome. Supervisors often are confronted with situations in which their employees do not fully attend to what is being said. Employees become so preoccupied with their own thoughts that they give attention only to those ideas they want to hear and select only those parts of the total message that they can accept. Bits of information that they do not like, or that are irreconcilable to their biases are brushed aside, not heard at all, or easily explained away. Supervisors must be aware of these possibilities, particularly when a message intends to convey some change that may interfere with the normal routine or customary working environment.

Perceptual Barriers

A message is often misunderstood because we all see the world differently. Thus, perception is one of the major barriers to effective communication. Some barriers arise from deep-rooted personal feelings, prejudice, and physical conditions.

Bias is a major barrier, as illustrated by the following example:

Research indicated that aging employees got poorer performance ratings from their supervisors despite doing a better job. The researchers concluded that supervisors biased their appraisals.[7]

Undoubtedly, the bias leads to ineffective communication between the older employee and the supervisor. The perception that all people in a certain group share common attitudes, values, and beliefs is called **stereotyping.** Stereotyping influences how people respond to others. It becomes a barrier to effective communication as people are categorized into certain groups because of their gender, age, or race instead of being treated as unique individuals. Managers need to be aware of stereotyping, because it can adversely affect communication.

Stereotyping
The perception that all people in a certain group share common attitudes, values, and beliefs.

Insensitive Words and Poor Timing

Sometimes, one party or the other uses so-called "killer phrases" in a conversation. Comments such as "That's the stupidest idea I've ever heard!" "You do understand, don't you?" or "Do you really know what you're talking about?" can kill conversation. Often, the result is that the receiver of the "killer phrase" becomes silent and indifferent to the sender. Sometimes, the receiver takes offense and directs anger back to the sender. Insensitive, offensive language or impetuous responses can cause difficulty in understanding. It is not difficult to think of many workplace illustrations of these occurrences. Often, the conflict that results impedes the accomplishment of organizational goals.

Another barrier to effective communication is the timing factor. Employees come to the workplace with extra "baggage"—that is, they sometimes carry to work events that have happened off the job. From personal experience, you can understand why it is hard to pay attention to someone else when you are anticipating an upcoming test. You pretend to listen politely, but you probably are not listening carefully. Under these circumstances your attentiveness and responsiveness to information will not be as the other party expected.

Since barriers to effective communication are numerous and diverse, supervisors should not assume that the messages they send will be received as they were intended. In fact, supervisors may want to assume that most of the messages they send are likely to be distorted. If supervisors operate from this premise, they more likely will do everything within their power to overcome these barriers and improve the chances for mutual understanding.

OVERCOMING BARRIERS TO EFFECTIVE COMMUNICATION

5 Describe ways to overcome the communication barriers.

Most techniques for overcoming communication barriers are relatively easy and straightforward. Supervisors will recognize them as techniques that they use sometimes but not as frequently as they should. A supervisor once remarked, "Most of these are just common sense." The reply to this comment was simply, "Yes, but have you ever observed how uncommon common sense sometimes is?"

Preparation and Planning

A first major step toward becoming a better communicator is to avoid speaking or writing until the message to be communicated has been thought through to the point that it is clear in the sender's mind. Only if supervisors can express their ideas in an organized fashion can they hope for others to understand. Therefore, before communicating, supervisors should know what they want and should plan the sequence of steps necessary to attain their objectives. The old cliché "Count to ten or pause and think before speaking" is essential for the supervisor. Rare is the activity that requires an instantaneous response.

For example, if supervisors want to make a job assignment, they should first analyze the job thoroughly so as to be able to describe it properly. If supervisors want to explain the solution to a problem, they should study the problem until it is so clear in their minds that they will have little difficulty explaining the solution. When researching the facts, supervisors should determine in advance what information they need so that they can ask intelligent, pertinent, and precise questions. If a communication is to involve a disciplinary action, supervisors should have sufficiently investigated the case and compiled all relevant information before issuing a penalty. In other words, communication should not begin until supervisors know what they ought to say in relation to what they want achieved.

Using Feedback

Feedback
The receiver's verbal or nonverbal response to a message.

Among the methods available to improve communication, feedback is by far the most important. In communication, **feedback** is the receiver's verbal or nonverbal response to a message. Feedback can be used to determine whether or not the receiver understood the message and to get the receiver's reaction to it. To obtain feedback, the sender can initiate feedback by using questions, discussion, signals, or clues. Merely asking the receiver, "Do you understand?" and receiving a "Yes" as an answer may not be enough feedback. More information than this is usually required to make sure that a message was actually received as it was intended.

A simple way to do this is to observe the receiver and to judge that person's responses by nonverbal clues such as an expression of bewilderment or understanding, a raised eyebrow, a frown, or the direction or movement of eyes. Of course, this kind of feedback is possible only in face-to-face communication, and this is one of the major advantages of this form of communication.

Perhaps the best feedback technique is for the sender to ask the receiver to restate or "play back" the information just received. This is much more satisfactory than merely asking whether the instructions are clear. If the receiver states the content of the message, then the sender will know what the receiver has heard and understood. At that time the receiver may ask additional questions and request comments, which the sender can provide immediately. This technique probably is the most direct and immediate approach to make certain that a message has been understood.

The feedback technique also is applicable when a supervisor is on the receiving end of a message from an employee or a higher-level manager. To clear up possible misunderstandings, a supervisor can say, "Just to make sure I understand what you want, let me repeat in my own words that message you gave me." An employee or a manager will appreciate this initiative to improve the accuracy of communication.

The feedback technique just discussed is most applicable in face-to-face communication. Feedback can also be helpful when written communication is involved. Before sending a written message, the supervisor can have someone else—perhaps a colleague—read the message for comprehension. Most writing can be improved. It may be necessary to develop several drafts of a written message and have various people provide feedback as to which draft is the most clearly stated and readily interpreted.

Similarly, after sending a memo or letter, it often is desirable to discuss the written correspondence over the telephone to make sure that the receiver understands it. When a supervisor receives a written message from someone else, and if there is any doubt about the meaning of the message, the supervisor should contact the sender to discuss the message and clarify it as necessary.

Direct and Clear Language

Another sound approach for attaining effective communication is to use words that are understandable and as clear as possible. Supervisors should avoid long, technical, and complicated words. They should use language that the receivers will be able to understand without difficulty. Jargon or "shop talk" should be used only if the receiver is comfortable with it. The old "KISS" approach is usually a good motto to remember: KISS stands for "Keep It Short and Simple."

A Calm Atmosphere

Tension and anxiety were mentioned previously as being serious barriers to effective communication. If a supervisor tries to communicate with an employee who is visibly upset, chances for mutual understanding are minimal. It is much better to communicate when both parties are calm and not burdened by unusual tension or stress. One of the best ways for a supervisor to ensure the proper atmosphere for communicating or discussing a problem with an employee is to set an appointed time for a meeting in a quiet room. This usually enables both parties to prepare to discuss the problem in a calm and unhurried fashion. Similarly, if supervisors want to discuss something with their managers, they should arrange for an appointment at a time and place that is mutually conducive to having a good, uninterrupted discussion.

Taking Time and Effort to Listen

Another approach for overcoming barriers to communication is for both the sender and the receiver to take more time to listen, that is, to give the other person full op-

FIGURE 3-5
The Do's and Don'ts of
Effective Listening

DO'S FOR LISTENING

1. Do adopt the attitude that you will always have something to learn.
2. Do take time to listen, give the speaker your full attention, and hear the speaker out.
3. Do withhold judgment until the speaker is finished. Strive to locate the main ideas of the message.
4. Do try to determine the word meanings within the context of the speaker's background. Listen for what is being implied as well as what is being said.
5. Do establish eye contact with the speaker. Read body language. Smile, nod, and give an encouraging sign when the speaker hesitates.
6. Do ask questions at appropriate times to be sure that you understand the speaker's message.
7. Do restate the speaker's idea at appropriate moments to make sure that you have it correctly.

DON'TS FOR LISTENING

1. Don't listen with only half an ear by "tuning out" the speaker and pretending that you are listening.
2. Don't unnecessarily interrupt the speaker or finish the speaker's statement because of impatience or wanting to respond immediately.
3. Don't fidget or doodle while listening. Don't let other distractions bother you and the speaker.
4. Don't confuse facts with opinions.
5. Don't show disapproval or insensitivity to the speaker's feelings.
6. Don't respond until the speaker has said what he or she wants to say.
7. Don't become defensive.

portunity to express what is on his or her mind. The supervisor who listens to what the employee is saying will learn more about the employee's values and attitudes toward the working environment. The supervisor should provide feedback by restating the employee's message from time to time and asking, "Is this what you mean?" A supervisor should always patiently listen to what the employee has to say. Intensive listening helps to reduce misunderstandings, and by listening the supervisor will be better able to respond in ways that are appropriate to the concerns of the employee.

One of the worst things supervisors can do is to sit with faked attention while their minds are on mental excursions. The supervisor can avoid this situation by politely stating, "Right now is not a convenient time for us to have this discussion. It needs my full attention, and if we can reschedule this meeting for 10:00 in the morning, you will have my undivided attention." Attentiveness to the speaker will go a long way toward building a climate of trust. Figure 3-5 contains some practical do's and don'ts for effective listening.

Listening is a very important part of the supervisor's job, whether in one-on-one conversations or in meetings. Ability to listen is critical to success as a super-

FIGURE 3-6
A supervisor communicates by actions as much as by words.

visor. Therefore, supervisors should work to develop their listening skills every chance they get.

Repetition of Messages

It is often helpful to repeat a message several times, preferably using different words, or different methods. For instance, a new medical insurance claim process might be mentioned in a staff meeting, the subject of an article in the company newsletter, posted on the bulletin board, and maintained in a policy file available for employee use. The degree of repetition will depend largely on the content of the message and the experience and background of the employees or other people involved in the communication. However, the message should not be repeated so much that it gets ignored because it sounds too familiar or boring. In case of doubt, some repetition probably is safer than none.

Reinforcing Words with Action

To succeed as communicators, supervisors need to complement their words with appropriate and consistent actions. Supervisors communicate much by what they do, that is, by their actions; and as the cliché goes, actions speak louder than words (see Figure 3-6). Therefore, one of the best ways to give meaning to messages is to act accordingly. If verbal announcements are backed up by action, the supervisor's credibility will be enhanced. However, if the supervisor says one thing but does another, sooner or later the employees will be influenced primarily by what the supervisor does.

COMMUNICATION: THE KEY TO RESOLVING CONFLICT[8]

6 Contrast five conflict resolution styles.

Sometimes supervisors have to act like referees in resolving conflicts that occur in the workplace. They must guard against losing their own temper and getting themselves in deeper. Most supervisors do not like conflict, because they are drawn into the fray as a third party. Imagine that you are the parent of two children who are arguing over the last piece of strawberry pie. Their argument grows louder and louder, and suddenly you find yourself involved. There are a number of ways to handle the situation. Often, regardless of what you do, both children end up angry—at you. For this reason, most of us view conflict as dysfunctional—that is, not contributing to the overall objectives.

There are many events in the workplace that trigger conflict. Communication breakdowns, competition over scarce resources, unclear job boundaries ("That isn't my responsibility"), inconsistent application of policy ("You didn't punish Joe when he was late"), unrealized expectations ("I didn't know that you expected me to do that"), and time pressures ("You didn't give us enough notice") are common events in the workplace that lead to conflict. As a general rule, it is a good idea to diagnose a conflict situation before taking action.

Because many companies are facing dramatic changes and great uncertainty, it is important for supervisors to be aware of the styles of conflict resolution. These styles are also referred to as "negotiation styles." It is generally agreed that there are five conflict resolution styles, as depicted in Figure 3-7.

The horizontal axis, degree of cooperativeness, ranges from low to high. A high degree of cooperativeness implies that one desires a long-term, harmonious relationship with the other party. A customer tells a sales supervisor that a competitor can provide the same services for a substantially lower price. The price is just slightly above the supervisor's break-even point. A conflict arises between what the supervisor is willing to sell the product for and what the customer is willing to pay. If the customer is a long-time purchaser of large quantities of the product, the supervisor would be "high" on the cooperativeness scale. On the other hand, if the customer purchased very little and only when others could not fill his or her orders, the supervisor might rate a moderate to low score on the scale. A final question serves as a guide: When you have a conflict with someone else, ask yourself whether the relationship is worth saving. If the answer is yes, then you are at a higher position on the horizontal axis than if the answer were no.

Low to high concern for self, or degree of assertiveness, is found on the vertical axis. To determine location on this scale, the supervisor must ask: "What is really important to me?" Numerous supervisors have expressed that product quality is number one and is equally as important as employee safety. In other words, they are willing to go to the wall for quality and safety.

Various combinations of these concerns yield five conflict resolution styles:

- *Withdraw/avoid:* This approach may be appropriate when the issue is perceived to be minor and the costs of solving the problem are greater than the benefits derived. For example, as you leave class, you see an altercation in the parking

FIGURE 3-7
Conflict Resolution
Styles

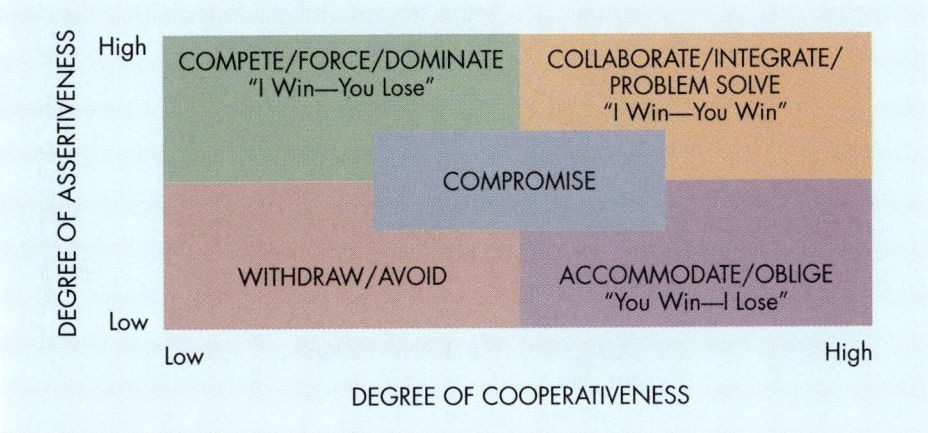

lot. Two students unknown to you are arguing. Withdrawal is probably the best strategy. The potential costs to you outweigh the potential benefits. However, workplace conflict between two employees must be addressed. If left alone, conflicts have a tendency to fester. Thus, the supervisor needs to address the conflict because the costs in terms of declining performance are potentially great.

- *Accommodate/oblige:* The primary strength of this style is that it encourages cooperation. You go home this evening and the very special person in your life says, "I thought we'd go out for dinner tonight. I would really like to go to the Olive Garden." You had your heart set on having a candlelight dinner at home. But you sacrifice your own needs to preserve the relationship over the long term. Often, this style is thought of as "You win–I lose." No one wants to lose all the time. Therefore, this style implies the rule of reciprocity—that is, you give up something now to eventually get something of value in return.

- *Compromise:* This style is referred to as "Win some–lose some." Compromise styles can be traced throughout history, beginning with the story of King Solomon in the Bible. Labor-management negotiations often use a compromise technique. Unfortunately, if one party knows that the other always compromises—that is, splits the difference—then they bring inflated demands to the bargaining table. Thus, valuable time is wasted trying to sort out what really are the issues.

- *Compete/force/dominate:* This style is characterized as "I win–You lose." This style may be appropriate in resolving the following type of conflict: Employees have not been wearing their safety glasses, because in the humid weather they are uncomfortable. The supervisor could force a decision upon the employees, because the potential safety factor is deemed more important than their personal feelings. The observant student should question why the supervisor had to force the solution on the subordinates. If the organization supported an open and participatory climate, then the effective supervisor would use good communication skills to gain understanding rather than manage by edict. The forcing style may foster resentment and cause long-term harm.

- *Collaborate/integrate/problem solve:* This time-consuming style is best characterized as "Win–Win." As Herb Cohen, an expert on negotiation, stated, "Successful collaborative negotiation lies in finding out what the other side really wants and showing them a way to get it, while you get what you want."[9] This style gives the supervisor an opportunity to ask questions of the other parties to ascertain their interests and needs. Joint problem solving leads all parties to understand the issues, interests, and needs. Solutions are developed collaboratively. Mutual trust and respect can be the primary gain of this style.

One of the first lessons you learned in school was that you do not have to shout. However, suppose that a production worker comes to you and is really angry that the material handler let some inferior-quality material get through. The angry production employee is shouting. To defuse the employee's anger and to gain control of the situation, some communication experts advocate the following: Get the employee's attention by shouting right back: "You have every right to be angry and I'm as angry as you are." Then continue in a normal tone of voice: "Now that we both agree this is a serious problem, what can we do about it and how can we prevent it from happening again?" This approach has put the employee back on track by focusing on the issues. The objectives of the organization and the needs of the employee can both be met through collaborative problem solving.

In all of this, it should be apparent that the most effective communication will take place when people try to share common perspectives. If employees are on the same team and want to do a good job—and if supervisors are clear in their objectives and are working toward improving the human relations atmosphere—there is a better chance of making the organizational climate conducive to effective communication.

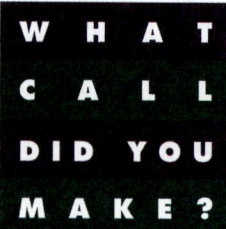

Communication is a two-way street. It is easy to tell the other person what to do, but it takes real skill to listen to what the person is really saying. Skillful communication depends not only on what you say, but on how you say it, and sometimes even when you say it. It is very easy for supervisors to get so wrapped up in the pressures of their work that they allow their personal relationships with others to deteriorate.

This "You Make the Call" situation exemplifies the problems that occur when people allow the barriers to effective communication to prevent understanding. While Ed is more wrong, both parties must share culpability for the events that occurred. Louise needs to be more sensitive to the timing of her message. Also, what is it she really wants Ed to do? Prior planning is essential. On the other hand, Ed violated most of the principles of effective communication. It appears that he did not adequately instruct her in what needed to be done and, more important, was not readily available for assistance. This may not have been a convenient time for him, but he needed to listen attentively to her concerns. He should have determined a mutual time to explore the problem fully. Both Ed and Louise could have paused and asked probing questions of the other party, but they did not.

Ed's supervisory image is tarnished by his ineffective use of communication skills. The fundamental question to ask in making the call is whether or not the working relationship is worth saving. If it is, then Ed, after developing a communication plan, should approach Louise and ask whether this is a convenient time to talk. A sincere apology goes a long way toward opening channels for communication. Based on the insensitivity that occurred, the channel may only be slightly open. Moreover, it can be safely assumed that the grapevine contains information regarding the conflict.

Remember that successful collaborative negotiation lies in finding out what the other party really wants and showing that person a way to get it while you get what you want. Conflict resolution involves getting the heads of both parties going in the same direction. Ed and Louise could agree that they both want the computerized scanning system to be operational.

Accommodation might work in the short term, but the long-term interests of all are served if they can engage in the collaborative approach. All of the techniques of effective communication come into play if the "win-win" solution is developed.

SUMMARY

1 Define communication and discuss its implications for effective supervisory management.

Effective communication means that a successful transfer of information and understanding takes place between a sender and a receiver. The ability to communicate effectively is one of the most important qualities leading to supervisory success.

Communication is a two-way process. Communication is only successful if the receiver understands the message. The receiver need not agree with the message, just understand it as the sender intended.

2 Discuss the major channels of communication available to the supervisor.

Formal channels of communication operate downward, upward, and horizontally. These communication channels primarily serve to link people and departments in order to accomplish organizational objectives. Supervisors communicate downward to their employees. Equally important is the supervisor's duty to communicate upward to management and horizontally with supervisors in other departments. In addition to formal channels, every company has informal channels, called the "grapevine." The grapevine can carry rumors as well as facts. Supervisors should stay in touch with what is being transmitted on the grapevine and counteract rumors with facts where necessary.

3 Explain the benefits of the various methods of communication.

Methods of communication range from oral, written, and visual to the unspoken body language. Spoken and written words are the most important means of communication. However, body language—a person's actions, gestures, posture, and so forth—also communicate, often in more powerful ways than words themselves. Oral communication is generally superior because it enables face-to-face interaction. Feedback is instantaneous. Written words and visuals are often preferred because of their permanency. Visual aids, such as pictures, charts, and videos, can be powerful tools in conveying meaning.

4 Identify and discuss barriers to effective communication.

Human differences and organizational conditions can create obstacles, called "noise," which distort messages between people. The use of jargon that the receiver does not understand can impede communication. Also, words have different meanings, so the sender must make sure that the receiver understood the intended meaning.

People who have different status or position levels within an organization bring different points of view to an interaction, which can distort meaning. People may "filter out" unpleasant information going up to their managers. Also, people's natural resistance to change can cause them to avoid "hearing" messages that upset the status quo or conflict with their own beliefs.

Individuals perceive the world from the context of their own backgrounds and prejudices. Perceptual barriers between sender and receiver, such as biases and stereotyping, can impede communication, as can conversation-killing phrases and poor timing.

5 Describe ways to overcome the communication barriers.

To overcome communication barriers, supervisors should adequately prepare what they wish to communicate. During face-to-face communication, the receiver's verbal and nonverbal responses, called "feedback," can help the supervisor determine whether or not the receiver understood the message. Asking the receiver to restate the message is one feedback technique that helps verify understanding. For written communication, the supervisor can obtain feedback by asking a colleague to comment on the message before it is sent and by discussing it with receivers after it is sent to check understanding.

Using clear, direct language that the receiver can understand will facilitate communication. Also, both parties should agree on a time to talk when both parties will not be overly stressed and will have time to really listen to each other. Repeating the message in various words and formats can improve understanding, if not done to excess. Also, to be effective, words must be reinforced by consistent actions.

6 Contrast five conflict resolution styles.

An understanding of the five conflict resolution (negotiation) styles can help supervisors facilitate organizational goals. The styles are withdraw/avoid, compromise, accommodate/oblige, compete/force/dominate, and collaborate/integrate/problem solve. Changes in the workplace make it necessary for supervisors to be able to use all of these styles. However, the collaborative style is preferred, in that a "win–win" mentality is developed. This style aids in developing a climate of mutual trust and respect that is essential for the attainment of organizational objectives.

KEY TERMS

Communication (page 52)
Grapevine (page 56)
Body language (page 59)
Noise (page 62)
Jargon (page 62)

Semantics (page 63)
Status (page 63)
Filtering (page 64)
Stereotyping (page 65)
Feedback (page 66)

QUESTIONS FOR DISCUSSION

1. What is meant by effective communication? Why is mutual understanding at the heart of any definition of effective communication?

2. In the electronic age, it appears that there is more communication and less understanding. What can the effective supervisor do to ensure that this is not the case?

3. Why should the supervisor be able to use all the communication channels?

4. Why is the upward flow of communication important for management?

5. Discuss the techniques by which a supervisor can cope with the grapevine effectively.

6. Discuss the various methods of communication used in an organization. Why is the old cliché that "actions speak louder than words" applicable to the supervisory position?

7. Barriers hinder the supervisor's attempts to communicate. What can the supervisor do to overcome communication barriers?

8. What specific steps do you need to take to improve your listening skills?

9. Describe a conflict you are familiar with. How can you use conflict resolution techniques and good communication skills to resolve the conflict?

10. Discuss the following statement: "Good supervisory practices and effective communication tend to go hand in hand."

SKILLS APPLICATIONS

Skills Application 3-1: Role-Play Exercise

Assume that you have been asked to role play the "You Make the Call" situation at the beginning of this chapter.

1. Plan your communication with Louise. Make a list of all the questions that you will ask her. Anticipate at least two extreme responses (the "best-case response" and the "worst-case response") to each of your questions. Develop a list of your responses to these responses.

2. Now put yourself into Louise's shoes. She is an assistant supervisor and has been asked to coordinate the computer installation for all stores in your district. How does this information affect your planning and preparation?

3. Pair up with a classmate and decide which of you will be Ed and which will play Louise. Pick up the action from where the "You Make the Call" leaves off. Try to be realistic.

4. Are you pleased with your follow-up to the situation? What did you do well? What could you have done more effectively?

Skills Application 3-2: Which Message Do You Prefer?

Communication skills are important to all managers. Effective use of communication skills enables supervisors to lead, motivate, and make changes in the organization.

Consider the following statements:

Statement A: "When I disagree with someone, I make sure I am heard. I never back down. I want the other person to hear my position before they make a decision."

Statement B: "When I hear someone voice an opinion that's different from mine, I first try to understand why and how the person could possibly think that. I look for common areas of interest."

Statement C: "I find it easier to give in rather than try to change the other person's point of view. If the other person gets emotional, I find it easier to agree with his or her point."

Statement D: "When someone offers an opinion, I like to take the contrary position. I try to find flaws and weak points in the position. I enjoy a good argument."

Statement E: "I learn a lot from listening to people explain what leads them to think the way they do. I'm prepared to make changes if they are."

1.   Which of these statements most closely describes the person you are? Why?

2.   Which statement most closely reflects the person you would like to be? Is there a difference? If so, what accounts for the difference?

3.   Which statement reflects the type of person you would rather talk with? Why?

4.   Tell yourself: I am going to practice my listening skills today by listening as carefully as I can to other people. I will even listen to myself and become more aware of my communication.

Skills Application 3-3: Develop a "Bad News" Plan

You have been supervising a special project team developing a product for a major customer. The project is nearing completion. Due to a work stoppage (labor contract dispute) at one of your suppliers, you will be seven days late on delivery of the prototype to the customer. Everyone was assured that you would be able to meet the deadline. Develop a plan for communicating this bad news to your immediate supervisor.

ENDNOTES

1.   Tom Peters has strongly advised that managers need to become highly visible and do a better job of listening to subordinates. We could not agree more. For additional information on the information contained in the Contemporary Issue, see Tom Peters, *Thriving on Chaos* (New York: Alfred A. Knopf, 1988), pp. 423–440.

2.   Tom Horton, president of the American Management Association, selected Management By Wandering Around as his nomination for the most ridiculous recent management fad; see "The Hazards of Business Fads," *Detroit News* (January 12, 1987). Nevertheless, it appears that some managers have found this an effective way to enhance communication.

3.   The grapevine cuts across the formal channels of communication. See Stanley J. Modic, "Grapevine Rated Most Believable," *Industry Week* (Volume 238, May 15, 1989), pp. 11, 14; and Walter Kiechel III, "In Praise of Office Gossip," *Fortune* (August 19, 1985), pp. 253, 254, 256. The classic article on the subject is Keith Davis's "Management Communication and the Grapevine," *Harvard Business Review* (September–October 1953), pp. 43–49.

4.   For further discussion of informal channels of communication and the grapevine, see Jerald Greenberg and Robert A. Baron, *Behavior in Organizations* (4th ed.; Boston: Allyn and Bacon, 1993), pp. 506–509, 525; and Stephen R. Axley, "Managerial and Organizational Communication in Terms of the Conduit Metaphor," *Academy of Management Review* (July 1984), pp. 428–437.

5.   Brenda Major, "Gender Patterns in Touching Behavior," in *Gender and Non-Verbal Behavior,* ed. Nancy M. Henley (New York: Springer-Verlag, 1981).

6.   The English language is estimated to contain some 750,000 words, but the vocabulary of the average person is only in the range of 20,000 to 40,000 words. While English is generally recognized as the world's primary language, not all employees will understand the "common tongue."

7.   David A. Waldman and Bruce J. Avolio, "A Meta-Analysis of Age Differences in Job Performance," *Journal of Applied Psychology* (February 1986), p. 36.

8.   For additional details on conflict resolution, see M. Afzalur Rahim, "A Measure of Styles of Handling Interpersonal Conflict," *Academy of Management Journal* (June 1983), pp. 368–376; Robert A. Baron, "Reducing Organizational Conflict: An Incompatible Response Approach," *Journal of Applied Psychology* (May 1984), pp. 272–279; and Stephen P. Robbins, *Training in Interpersonal Skills* (Englewood Cliffs, N.J.: Prentice-Hall, 1989), pp. 214–232.

9.   Herb Cohen, *You Can Negotiate Anything* (New York: Bantam Books, 1980), p. 162.

4

Delegation: The Supervisor's Strategy for Getting Work Done

LEARNING OBJECTIVES

After studying this chapter, you will be able to:

1 Explain the importance of authority to supervisory management.

2 Describe the types of power potentially available to the supervisor.

3 Discuss the delegation process and define the three major components.

4 Explain various organizational approaches to delegation.

5 Discuss why some supervisors do not delegate and describe some benefits of delegation.

6 Compare the autocratic approach with the general approach to supervision.

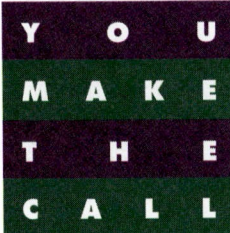

Y O U
M A K E
T H E
C A L L

You are Anita Mathews. You have worked in the Accounting and Data Services Department of the Concord Community Bank for 10 years, and recently you were promoted to supervisor of a data processing section that sends bank statements to depositors. Due to an unusually large number of absences caused by the flu, your department has fallen behind in its scheduled operations. Since you used to do this work, you decided to help in order to alleviate the situation. You spent between two and four hours a day operating one of the machines to help get the statements out. You did not neglect any of your supervisory duties. Of course, while you were operating the machine, you were doing nothing else.

Art Roberts, your supervisor, returned from an out-of-town trip and found you operating a machine and not in your office. Roberts had been looking for you because he wanted to discuss some problems with you. He became annoyed with you because of what you were doing, and he asked you into his office. He proceeded to lecture you, stating that it was a supervisor's job to get things done through and with people and that did not mean doing the work of the employees, even when the department was shorthanded. You listened patiently to Roberts's statements and pondered your response. **YOU MAKE THE CALL.**

UNDERSTANDING MANAGERIAL AUTHORITY

Explain the importance of authority to supervisory management.

In training personnel, the military employs two major principles embodied in the following statements:

- In order to learn how to give an order, you must first learn how to take an order.
- If you give people a job to do, give them the authority they need to carry out their responsibilities.

These statements are as relevant to a civilian supervisor as they are to a military person. They focus on the importance of delegating authority along with responsibility. As you learned in Chapter 2, delegation of authority means entrusting job duties and related authority to subordinates, so that they can perform within prescribed limits.

A supervisor must be a good subordinate and follower in relation to his or her own manager. Supervisors are delegated a certain amount of authority from their managers in order to manage their departments. In turn, supervisors must learn to delegate authority to their employees if the objectives of the department are to be accomplished. In Chapter 1, we defined "empowerment" as giving employees the authority and responsibility to accomplish organizational objectives. Delegation, as the title of this chapter suggests, is the strategy by which effective supervisors achieve desired results through others. In other words, delegation empowers employees to make decisions.

Since having authority is a necessary characteristic of being a manager, it is essential for supervisors to know what authority means and how to use it. The way a supervisor uses authority usually makes the difference between subordinates' grudging compliance or willing acceptance of supervisory directives. Although most competent supervisors find it unnecessary to make a show of their authority when giving instructions, firm leadership is sometimes needed. For supervisors to apply their managerial authority appropriately, they must first understand where their authority comes from.

Origin of Formal Authority

Every supervisor has been delegated formal authority directly by an immediate superior. The supervisor receives authority, for example, from a middle-level manager who in turn receives authority from a higher-level manager, who in turn traces authority directly back to the chief executive. In a small company such as a bicycle shop, there are fewer management layers, but the principle is the same. The store owner grants authority to the department supervisors, who pass on to the sales clerks and repair specialists the authority they need to do their jobs. This is the traditional, or formal, way of looking at the origin of authority, which arises from the recognition of private property rights. It has been said humorously that this is a version of the "Golden Rule"—that is, "Those who have the gold make the rules!"

Although it is difficult to generalize for not-for-profit organizations such as governmental entities, educational institutions, and hospitals, it can be said that formal authority resides in boards of directors, who in turn appoint or elect executives to manage the resources of the organization. From the chief executive position, authority flows down through the chain of command until it reaches the lowest level of the organization.

The Acceptance Theory of Authority

A supervisor should not rely solely on formal authority in day-to-day relations with employees, as the following story illustrates. An argument occurred between a supervisor and a worker concerning a directive. When the argument intensified, the supervisor finally shouted, "Jack, unless you do what I tell you, you're fired!" Jack, in the same heated manner, replied, "You can't fire me ... I quit!" Jack walked off the job because he chose to lose his job rather than accept the supervisor's authority. His remark, "You can't fire me ... I quit," illustrates why a supervisor should be concerned about other strategies and not depend solely on the sheer weight of formal authority.

Acceptance theory of authority

Theory that holds that the manager only possesses authority when the employee accepts it.

The **acceptance theory of authority** states that a manager does not possess any authority until and unless the subordinate accepts it. For example, a supervisor may instruct an employee to carry out a certain work assignment. The employee has several alternatives from which to choose. Although such a response is not likely, the employee can refuse to obey, thereby rejecting the supervisor's authority and becoming exposed to possible disciplinary action. Alternatively, the employee may only grudgingly accept the supervisor's direction and carry out the assignment in a mediocre fashion. Or the employee may accept the order and carry it out with varying degrees of performance and enthusiasm. For example, the employee may go well beyond the requirements of the supervisor and do far more than was expected. Thus, the degree to which the employee accepts the supervisor's authority—or the amount of "upward authority" granted the supervisor—is an important part of the employee's choice of alternatives. The acceptance theory states that unless employees accept managerial authority, the supervisor actually does not possess such authority. Of course, employees sometimes have little choice between accepting authority and not accepting it; the other alternative they obviously have is to leave the job. Since this is not a desirable choice, there is merit in considering authority as something that must be accepted by the employees if exercise of authority is to bring about the desired results.

Briefly stated, then, the origin of authority can be considered from two viewpoints: (a) the formal way of looking at authority as something that originates with ownership rights—formally handed from the top all the way down to the lowest-level employee; and (b) the consideration of authority as something that subordinates confer on a supervisor by the degree of willingness with which they accept or respond to the supervisor's direction.

There is some validity in each point of view. A supervisor should consider both approaches, since in reality each weighs heavily in the practice of supervision. Few supervisors rely solely on the weight of formal authority to motivate workers to

The manner in which the supervisor applies formal authority can make the difference between being accepted or resented.

perform their jobs, although there are some occasions when supervisors have to resort to it. Even when a supervisor has to invoke formal authority, the manner in which it is applied is critical in determining whether the authority is resented or accepted. There are supervisory decisions that the employee dislikes but cannot be avoided at the time. The manner in which the supervisor invokes authority can make the difference between being resented or being accepted as a fair supervisor.

Limitations to Authority

There are definite limitations to authority—both explicit and implicit, external and internal. Over a period of time many political, legal, ethical, moral, social, and economic considerations place limitations on the exercise of authority. For example, many organizations have adopted policies of nondiscrimination in employment, in part because they recognize that these policies are socially and ethically desirable, but also because they are required to do so by law. An organization's articles of incorporation may limit the authority of the chief executive, and the bylaws may present further restrictions. Many laws and contracts clearly limit the authority of managers. For example, wage and hour laws require employers to pay certain minimum wages and overtime rates and restrict the use of child labor. Union contracts limit a manager's freedom to take various actions, for example, in disciplining employees. In addition, every manager is subject to the specific limitations stemming from the assignment of duties and delegation of authority.

Generally, the scope of authority is more limited the farther one descends in the management hierarchy. Usually, the lower the level at which supervisors are located in the management hierarchy, the more restrictions are placed on their authority. First-line supervisors, for example, usually find that there are definite limits placed on their authority to utilize resources and to make certain types of managerial decisions. A supervisor should not resent this, since it is a natural part of the process of delegating authority in any organization.

POWER—THE ABILITY TO INFLUENCE OTHERS

2 Describe the types of power potentially available to the supervisor.

Position power
Power derived from the formal rank a person holds in the chain of command.

Personal power
Power derived from a person's skill, knowledge, or ability and how others perceive them.

Among the most confused terms in management are "authority" and "power." Chapter 2 defined "authority" as the legitimate right to lead others. The effective supervisor must understand the difference between authority and power. Some behavioral scientists contend that a manager's power comes from two sources: position power and personal power.[1] **Position power** comes from the organizational position the person occupies. For example, the department manager has more position power than the first-line supervisor. **Personal power,** on the other hand, emanates from the relationship that the supervisor has with other people. A supervisor's personal power depends to a greater extent on the perceptions of his or her followers.

Other theorists, such as French and Raven, purport that power arises from the following five sources:

1. Reward power: A supervisor has reward power if he or she has the ability to grant rewards.
2. Coercive power: The supervisor who uses threats of punishment and discipline is using coercive power.
3. Legitimate power: Some supervisors gain compliance by relying on their position or rank.
4. Expert power: Knowledge or valuable information gives a person expert power over those who need such information.
5. Referent or charismatic power: People are often influenced by others because of some tangible or intangible aspect of the others' personality.[2]

Effective supervisors need to understand the effect their power has on others. Research indicates that reward power, coercive power, and legitimate power often force employees to comply with directives but do not get their commitment to organizational objectives. Accordingly, supervisors who use expert power and referent power effectively have the greatest potential for achieving organizational goals.[3]

The acceptance theory of authority also has relevance for the application of power. For example, you can be an expert in computer applications, but if others do not need that knowledge, you will have very little influence over them. Therefore, two supervisors can hold the same title, occupy the same level in the hierarchy, and have equal authority, yet have different degrees of power, depending on their abilities and how others perceive them.

THE PROCESS OF DELEGATION

3 Discuss the delegation process and define its three major components.

Just as authority is a major component of the managerial job, so the delegation of authority is essential to the creation and operation of an organization. In the broadest sense, delegation gives employees a greater voice in how the job is to be done; the employee is empowered to make decisions. Unfortunately, some managers view delegation as a means to lighten their own workload. They assign unpleasant tasks to employees and subsequently find that the employees are not motivated to complete those tasks. The manager must look at delegation as a tool to develop employees' skills and abilities, rather than a way to get rid of unpleasant tasks.

The subordinate manager receives authority from a higher-level manager through the process of delegation, but this does not mean that the higher-level manager surrenders all accountability. **Accountability** is the expectation that employees will accept credit or blame for the results achieved in performing assigned tasks. When a manager delegates, he or she is still ultimately accountable for successful completion of the work.

Accountability
The expectation that employees will accept credit or blame for the results achieved in performing assigned tasks.

Delegation is a supervisor's strategy for accomplishing objectives. It consists of the following three components, all of which must be present:

1. Assigning duties to immediate subordinates.
2. Granting permission (authority) to make commitments, use resources, and take all actions necessary to perform these duties.
3. Creating an obligation (responsibility) on the part of each employee to perform the duties satisfactorily.

Unless all three components are present, the delegation process is incomplete. They are inseparably related in such a manner that a change in one will require adjustment of the other two.

Assigning Duties

Each employee must be assigned a specific job or task to perform. Job descriptions may provide a general framework through which the supervisor can examine duties in the department to see which to assign to each employee. Routine duties usually can be assigned to almost any employee, but there are other functions that the supervisor can assign only to employees who are qualified to perform them. There are also some functions that a supervisor cannot delegate—those which the supervisor must do. The assignment of job duties to employees is of great significance, and much of the supervisor's success will depend on it.

Granting Authority

The granting of authority means that the supervisor confers upon employees the right and power to act, to utilize certain resources, and to make decisions within prescribed limits. Of course, the supervisor must determine the scope of authority that is to be delegated. How much authority can be delegated depends in part on the amount of authority the supervisor possesses. The degree of authority is also related to the employees and jobs to be done. For example, if a sales clerk is responsible for processing items returned to the store, that clerk must have the authority to give the customer's money back, with the understanding (limit) that the clerk should alert the supervisor if the returned item was obviously abused in some way. In every instance, enough authority must be granted to the employee to enable the employee to perform assigned tasks adequately and successfully. There is no need for the amount of authority to be larger than the tasks assigned, but the authority granted must be sufficient to meet the employee's obligations.

Defining Limitations.
A supervisor must be specific in telling employees what authority they have and what they can or cannot do. It is uncomfortable for employees to have to guess how far their authority extends. For example, an employee may be expected to order certain materials as a regular part of the job. This employee must know the limits within which materials can be ordered, perhaps in terms of time and costs, and when permission from the supervisor is needed before ordering additional materials. If the supervisor does not state this clearly, the employee probably will be forced to test the limits and to learn by trial and error. If it becomes necessary to change an employee's job assignment, the degree of authority should be checked to make certain that the authority delegated is still appropriate. If it is less (or more) than needed, it should be adjusted.

Unity-of-Command Principle.
Throughout the process of delegation, employees must be reassured that their orders and authority will come from their immediate supervisor. The **unity-of-command principle** holds that each employee should report directly to only one supervisor. That supervisor is usually the only person who delegates authority to the employee.

Situations sometimes occur in which two supervisors give orders and delegate authority to the same employees. Chapter 9 describes matrix organizational structure and the use of functional staff authority, which are examples of employees' legitimately receiving authority from more than one source. Similarly, the use of task forces, project groups, and committees to handle certain types of assignments may blur the unity-of-command concept. Committees and problem-solving groups are discussed in Chapter 11.

Since Biblical times, at least, it has been recognized that it is difficult, if not impossible, to serve two masters. Having more than one supervisor usually leads to unsatisfactory performance by the employee due to confusion of authority. When the basic principle of unity of command is violated, conflicts usually result. Therefore, a supervisor should make certain that—unless there is a valid reason against it—only one supervisor gives directives to an employee.

Unity-of-command principle
Principle that holds that each employee should report to only one supervisor.

Creating Responsibility

The third component of the process of delegation is the creation of an obligation on the part of the employee toward the supervisor to perform the assigned duties satisfactorily. Acceptance of this obligation creates responsibility; without responsibility, delegation is not complete.

The terms "responsibility" and "authority" are closely related. Like the concept of authority, responsibility is often misunderstood. Supervisors commonly use expressions such as "keeping subordinates responsible," "delegating responsibilities," and "carrying out responsibilities." Simply stated, however, responsibility is the obligation of a subordinate to perform duties as required by the supervisor. By accepting a job position or accepting an obligation to perform assigned duties, the employee implies acceptance of responsibility. Responsibility recognizes an implied agreement in which the employee agrees to perform duties in return for rewards such as a paycheck. The most important facet of the definition is that responsibility is something that a subordinate must recognize and accept if delegation is to succeed.

Supervisory Accountability Cannot Be Delegated

Although a supervisor must delegate authority to employees to accomplish specific jobs, the supervisor's own personal accountability cannot be delegated. Assigning duties to employees does not relieve the supervisor of the responsibility for these duties. Thus, when delegating assignments to employees, the supervisor still remains accountable for the actions of the employees in carrying out these assignments.

To reiterate, responsibility includes (a) the subordinate's obligation to perform assigned tasks, and (b) the supervisor's obligation to his or her own manager, or accountability. Thus, for example, when a higher-level manager asks a supervisor to explain performance within the department, the supervisor cannot plead as a defense that the responsibility for performance has been delegated to employees in the group. The supervisor remains accountable and must answer to the manager. Regardless of the extent to which a supervisor creates an obligation on the part of employees to perform satisfactorily, the supervisor retains the ultimate responsibility, along with the authority, that is part of the supervisor's departmental position. As illustrated in Figure 4-1, effective delegation requires an appropriate mix of the assignment of tasks and the authority and responsibility needed to carry out those tasks.

The fact that accountability cannot be delegated may be a worrisome thought for some supervisors, but the fact remains that responsibility for the work of others goes with the supervisory position. Delegation is necessary for jobs to be accomplished. Although a supervisor may use sound managerial practices, employees will not always use the best judgment or perform in a superior fashion. Therefore, allowances must be made for errors. Although accountability remains with supervisors, supervisors must depend on their employees. If employees fail to carry out

FIGURE 4-1
Effective delegation
requires an
appropriate mix of
task assignments and
the authority and
responsibility to
accomplish the tasks.

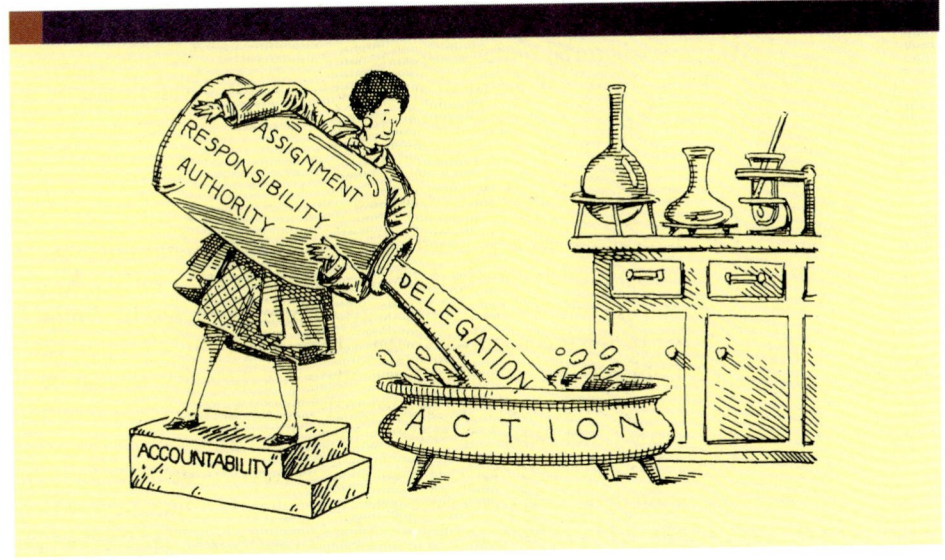

their assigned tasks, they are accountable to the supervisor, who must then redirect
the employees as appropriate. When appraising a supervisor's performance, higher-
level managers usually take into consideration how much care the supervisor has
taken in selecting employees, training them, supervising them, and controlling their
activities.

Implied in the accountability concept is the notion that punishments or rewards
will follow, depending on how well the duties are performed. However, the ultimate accountability to top-level managers lies with the supervisor who is doing the
delegating. Supervisors are responsible and accountable not only for their own actions, but also for the actions of their subordinates.

ORGANIZATIONAL APPROACHES TO DELEGATION

4 Explain various
organizational
approaches to
delegation.

We have stated that an essential characteristic for the supervisor is the ability to
delegate authority effectively. If authority has not been delegated, we can hardly
speak of an organization in the true sense of the word. The overall approach to
delegation chosen by top-level managers generally determines much of the culture
of the enterprise and the constraints under which subordinate managers and supervisors operate.

For example, many small companies are one-person organizations. There is little, if any, delegation of authority from the president or owner of the company to
anyone else. The consequences are usually disastrous to this type of company when
the key person becomes incapacitated, dies, or for some other reason leaves the

scene. Since there is no real organization, the company usually collapses or must be restructured under someone else.

However, in most organizations the question is not whether authority will be delegated, but how much and to whom.

Centralized Authority

Centralized authority
The organizational approach to delegation that places most decision-making responsibility with upper-level managers.

The extent to which authority is delegated determines the degree to which an organization is centralized or decentralized. **Centralized authority** means that upper-level managers retain most decision-making responsibility. Variations in the degree of delegated authority can range from the completely centralized organization (which in reality is not delegating) to the organization in which authority has been delegated broadly to the lowest level. At the one extreme the chief executive is in close touch with all operations, makes all or most decisions, and gives all or most of the instructions. Little or no authority is delegated. Some refer to this as "micro-managing." Managers refuse to let go; they make every decision, including those at the most remote levels of the organization. Many small businesses operate along these lines. Of course, it is understandable that the owner of a small company may have no desire or may be in no position to delegate authority, especially at the beginning of the undertaking.

Limited Decentralized Authority

Many organizations delegate authority to a limited degree. In these organizations top-level managers establish major policies and procedures. They then delegate application of policies and procedures in day-to-day operations and planning, along with limited authority, to first-line supervisors. This organizational approach often is found in medium-sized companies. It has the advantage of limiting the number of supervisors that the top-level manager must hire. Moreover, it can be advantageous in that the top-level manager's knowledge and good judgment can be applied rather quickly and directly.

Broadly Decentralized Authority

Decentralized authority
The organizational approach to delegation that disperses authority and decision making to the lowest feasible level in the organization.

At the other end of the spectrum are organizations that delegate authority to the broadest extent possible and to all levels of management, including first-line supervisors. This approach is called **decentralized authority**. More and more organizations, particularly large ones and others whose operations are complex or widely dispersed, are practicing broad decentralization.

To determine how decentralized an organization is, we must study what kind of authority has been delegated, how far down the organization it has been delegated, and how consistently it has been delegated. The criteria for delegation usually can be found in answers to the following questions: "How significant a decision can the manager make?" and "How far down within the managerial hierarchy can the decision be made?" The answers to these questions usually indicate whether an organization's management has delegated authority to a limited or broad extent.

Although centralized authority or limited decentralized authority is logical in the early stages of an organization, top-level managers sooner or later must delegate more if the organization is to grow. Decentralization becomes necessary when top-level managers become so preoccupied with routine decision making that they do not have enough time to plan or maintain a long-range point of view. As an organization grows, usually it will move gradually toward decentralization.

DELEGATION BY THE SUPERVISOR

5 Discuss why some supervisors do not delegate and describe some benefits of delegation.

Although few supervisors at the departmental level will have an opportunity to practice broad decentralization of formal authority, every supervisor must delegate some authority to employees. This assumes, of course, that the employees are capable and willing to accept the authority delegated to them. Yet many employees complain that their supervisors make all of the decisions and constantly watch their work closely because they do not trust the employees to carry out assignments. These types of complaints usually describe a supervisor who is unable or unwilling to delegate except to a minimal extent.

Reasons for Lack of Supervisory Delegation

A supervisor may be reluctant to delegate for several reasons—some valid, some not.

Shortage of Qualified Employees. Some supervisors cite a lack of qualified employees as an excuse for not delegating authority. Actually, such supervisors feel that their employees are not capable of handling authority or are not willing to accept it. If these supervisors refuse to delegate, employees will have little opportunity to obtain the experience they need to improve their judgment and enable them to handle broadened assignments. Supervisors must always bear in mind that, unless they make a beginning somewhere, they probably will never have enough employees who are capable and willing to accept more authority with commensurate responsibility.

Fear of Making Mistakes. Some supervisors think it best to make most decisions themselves because, in the final analysis, they retain overall responsibility. Out of fear of mistakes, such supervisors are unwilling to delegate, and, as a result, they continue to overburden themselves. However, indecision and delay often are costlier than the mistakes they hoped to avoid by refusing to delegate. Also, these supervisors may make mistakes by not drawing on employees for assistance in decision making.

The "Do-It-Myself" Mentality. The old stereotype of a good supervisor was that of one who pitched in and worked alongside the employees, thereby setting an example by personal effort. Even today, this type of supervision often occurs when a supervisor has been promoted through the ranks and the supervisory position is a reward for hard work and technical competence. By being placed in a supervisory position without having managerial training, this type of supervisor is faced with new problems that are difficult to comprehend. The supervisor therefore resorts to a pattern in which he or she feels secure by working alongside the employees. There are occasions when the supervisor *should* pitch in—for example, when the job is particularly difficult or when an emergency arises. With the trend toward eliminating management levels and consolidating operations, people will have to work together more closely. Under these conditions the supervisor should be close to the job to offer help. Aside from emergencies and unusual situations, however, the supervisor should be supervising and the employees should be doing their assigned tasks. Normally, it is the supervisor's job not to do, but to get things done.

Frequently supervisors complain that if they want something done right they have to do it themselves. They believe that it is easier to do the job personally than to correct an employee's mistakes. Or they may simply prefer to correct an employee's mistakes rather than to clearly explain what should have been done. Such supervisors may even feel that they can do the job better than any of the employees, and this may be true. But these attitudes interfere with a supervisor's prime responsibility to supervise others to get the job done.

A good supervisor occasionally shows how a job can be done more efficiently, promptly, courteously, and so forth. However, an employee who does the job almost as well will save the supervisor time for more important jobs—for innovative thinking, planning, and more delegating. Thus, the effective supervisor strives to see to it that each employee, with each additional job, becomes more competent. After a period of time, the employee's performance on the job should be as good as or better than what the supervisor would have done.

Other Factors. Ineffective supervisors insist on handling all of the details themselves. They are afraid to let go. Supervisors may fear that if they share their knowledge with employees and allow them to participate in decision making, the employees will become so proficient at making good decisions that the supervisor will be unnecessary. The fear of not being needed can be partially overcome if the supervisor cannot be promoted unless someone has been prepared to take his or her place.

Not everyone wants to take the responsibility for making decisions. The supervisor needs to identify those employees who need the opportunity to grow and who want to be empowered. Employees may be reluctant to accept delegation because of their own insecurity or fear of failure, or they may think that the supervisor will not be available for guidance.

It is difficult for supervisors to create an environment of employee involvement and freedom to make decisions when their own managers do not allow them the same opportunity. An environment for delegation and empowerment must be part of the organization's culture. Upper-level managers must advocate delegation at all levels.

Benefits from Supervisory Delegation

Can supervisors realize benefits from delegation if they have only a small number of employees and there is no real need to create subunits within a department? This is the kind of situation that many supervisors face. Is delegation in this type of working situation worth the trouble and risks that it entails? In general, the answer to this question is a strong yes.

The supervisor who delegates expects employees to make more decisions on their own. This does not mean that the supervisor is not available for advice. It means that the supervisor encourages the employees to make many of their own decisions and to develop their self-confidence in doing so. This in turn should mean that the supervisor will have more time to concentrate on managing. Effective delegation should result in employees' being able to perform an increasing number of jobs and recommending solutions that are workable and contribute to good performance. As the supervisor's confidence in employees expands, the employees' commitment to better performance should also grow. This may take time, and the degree of delegation may vary with each employee and with each department. However, in most situations, a supervisor's goal should be one of delegating more authority to employees whenever feasible. This goal contributes to employee motivation and better job performance.

Despite the positive results of empowerment, there is substantial evidence that many managers do not delegate. This chapter's "Contemporary Issue" presents some thoughts on delegation.

There are some supervisory areas that cannot be delegated. For example, it remains with the supervisor to formulate certain policies and objectives, to give general directions for the work unit, to appraise employee performance, to take necessary disciplinary action, and to promote employees. Aside from these types of supervisory management responsibilities, however, the employees should be doing most of the departmental work themselves.

GENERAL VERSUS AUTOCRATIC SUPERVISION

6 Compare the autocratic approach with the general approach to supervision.

Most employees accept work as a normal part of life. In their jobs they seek satisfaction that wages alone cannot provide. Most employees probably would prefer to be their own bosses, or at least have a degree of freedom to make decisions that pertain to their own work. The question arises as to whether this is possible if an individual works for someone else. Can a degree of freedom be granted to employees if they are to contribute their share toward the achievement of organizational objectives? This is where the delegation of authority can help. The desire for free-

CONTEMPORARY ISSUE
Delegation or Empowerment?—Another View

Delegating is a high-performance leadership style that produces long-term results. It is defined as sharing special projects with others and empowering them to complete these correctly with a minimum of interference.

Delegation often forces subordinates to eliminate work that has little benefit to the organization and delegate some of their work to others.

Empowerment takes on a stronger meaning than simple delegation; the [authority] to change a process

is permanently given to the person at the lowest level possible. Without empowerment, the odds of an employee remaining committed over the long term are slim.

It is apparent that "empowerment" and "delegation" may be viewed differently in every company. Nevertheless, their effectiveness lies as much in their application as in the belief that employees want to do a good job and participate in decision making.

Sources: Adapted from Richard S. Johnson, "TQM: Leadership for the Quality Transformation (Part 4)," *Quality Progress* (Volume 26, Number 4, April 1993), pp. 47–49; and "TQM: Leadership for the Quality Transformation (Part 3)," *Quality Progress* (Volume 26, Number 3, March 1993), pp. 91–94.

dom and being one's own boss can be enhanced by delegation, which in the daily routine essentially means giving directions in broad, general terms. It means that the supervisor, instead of watching every detail of the employees' activities, is primarily interested in the results they achieve and is willing to give them considerable latitude in deciding how to achieve these results.

General Supervision

General supervision
The style of supervision in which the supervisor sets goals and limits but allows employees to decide how to achieve the goals.

The delegation process can be promoted through general supervision. **General supervision** means that the supervisor sets the goals, discusses them with employees, and fixes the limits within which the work has to be done. Within this established framework, the employees have considerable freedom to decide how to achieve their targets. In a more advanced form of general supervision, the supervisor may even encourage employees to establish their own approaches and objectives within the framework of the department's goals. If properly carried out, this can be one of the most positive approaches for increasing employee motivation. This approach is a version of management by objectives, which is discussed in Chapters 5 and 7. General supervision is discussed further in Chapter 16.

As an example of general supervision, an office supervisor may discuss with employees the various projects that must be completed by the end of the week. The supervisor outlines which items have top priority but avoids stating exactly how the work is to be done or in what order (see Figure 4-2). Thus the supervisor demonstrates confidence that the employees will complete the work on time and in the proper fashion. The employees are trusted to figure out how to allocate the available time efficiently.

FIGURE 4-2
In general supervision,
the supervisor
discusses with
employees the
objectives to be
accomplished.

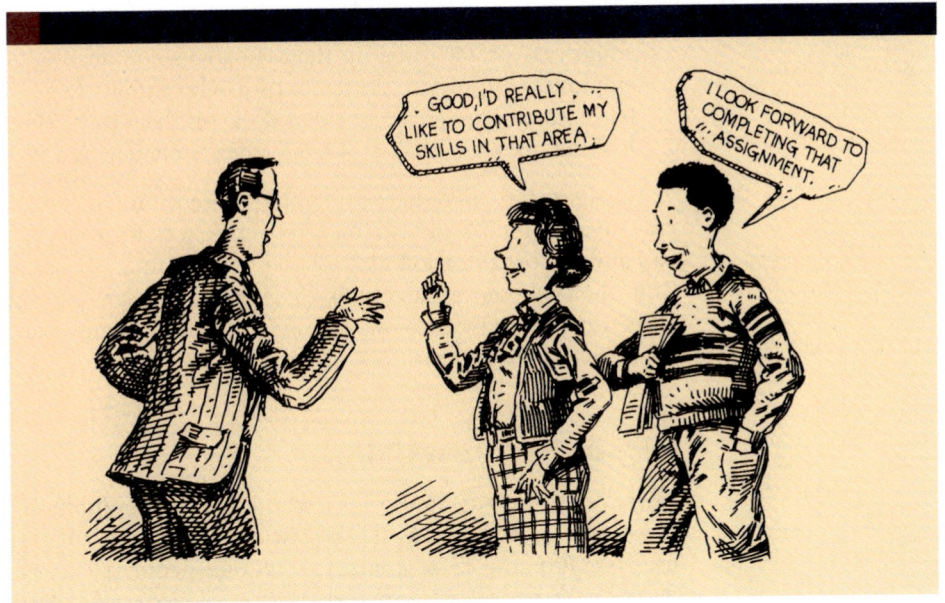

FIGURE 4-2 In general supervision, the supervisor discusses with employees the objectives to be accomplished.

Advantages of General Supervision

General supervision has several advantages for supervisors as well as employees.

1. It allows the supervisor more time to be a manager. General supervision frees the supervisor from many details, which allows time to plan, organize, and control. This leadership style should also give the supervisor more time to assume additional responsibility. By contrast, the supervisor who tries to make almost every decision personally soon becomes exhausted physically and mentally. In addition, such a supervisor can irritate employees and make them less productive.

2. It provides employees with a chance to develop their talents and abilities by making on-the-job decisions themselves. At times the supervisor will have to be away from the department. By practicing general supervision, the supervisor can be more confident that employees will carry out the work and develop suitable approaches to making decisions on the job. It is difficult to instruct employees in decision making; they can learn it only by practice.

   Related to this advantage is the fact that a supervisor's decisions on work details may not be as good as the decisions made by the employees, who are closest to these details. Moreover, there is no guarantee that mistakes will not happen when the supervisor specifies all the details of every job. By getting practice in making decisions and using their own judgment, employees can become more independent and competent.

3. It motivates employees to take pride in the results of their own decisions. Most employees prefer to be on their own to some degree. Surveys have shown that employees appreciate the supervisor who shows them how to do a job and then trusts them enough to let them do it on their own. By participating in decision making, they feel that they have a better chance to advance to higher positions.

In summary, there is considerable evidence to support the conclusion that general supervision usually is a more effective way to manage for supervisors, employees, and the organization as a whole. By pursuing a broad, general kind of supervision, many of the satisfactions that employees seek on the job—and that money alone does not provide—may be fulfilled. More important, general supervision is conducive to better work performance.

Autocratic Supervision

Autocratic supervision
The supervisory style that relies on formal authority, threats, pressure, and close control.

There are still many supervisors who believe that emphasis on formal authority, or **autocratic supervision,** is the best way to obtain results. A supervisor of this type uses pressure and close control to require people to work and may even threaten disciplinary action, including discharge, if employees do not perform as ordered. An autocratic supervisor may even assume that most employees are lazy, that the primary reason they work is to earn money and benefits, that they work because they fear losing their jobs, and that they try to get away with doing as little as possible. This belief is similar to the "Theory X" managerial assumptions discussed in Chapter 5. Because of these assumptions, this type of supervisor feels a need to tell the workers precisely what to do without allowing them to use their own judgment. Such supervisors also believe that they must be strong and that delegation would be a sign of weakness.

However, the totally autocratic approach to supervision has lost the majority of its followers. Most employees expect not only economic satisfaction from a job, but also personal satisfactions. In addition, our educational system has had a significant influence on attitudes. Many years ago, children were accustomed to the requirement of strict obedience to their elders. Now teachers and parents emphasize freedom and self-expression. Therefore, younger employees tend to resent autocratic supervision on the job. The presence of labor unions and protective legislation have also made it more difficult for supervisors to discipline or discharge employees for below-average performance.

Those who believe in the sheer weight of authority and the "be strong" form of supervision tend to discount the fact that workers may react in ways that were not intended by the supervisor. Employees who strongly resent autocratic supervision may become frustrated, rather than find satisfaction in their daily work. Such frustration can lead to arguments and other forms of discontent.

The excessive autocratic approach provides little incentive for employees to work harder than the minimum required to avoid punishment and discharge. Under such conditions, and where employee antagonism toward autocratic supervision is severe, employees—even if they are not unionized—may engage in slowdowns or sabotage. Supervisors will likely react to such actions by watching the workers even more closely. This, in turn, encourages employees to try to "out-smart" management. Thus, a vicious circle may begin, with new restraints being imposed by supervisors and new methods for evading them being devised by employees.

The Proper Balance of Delegation

Although we have stressed the advantages of delegation that can be realized through general supervision, it is important to recognize that the process of delegation is delicate. It is not easy for a supervisor to part with some authority and still be left with the responsibility for the performance and decisions made by workers. Proper delegation requires sound judgment and skill. The supervisor must achieve a balance among too much, too little, and the right amount in order to delegate enough without losing control. There are situations in which supervisors have to resort to their formal authority to attain the objectives of the department and get the job done. Supervisors at times have to make decisions that are distasteful to employees. Delegation does not mean that a supervisor should manage a department by consensus or by taking a vote on every issue.

How and when a supervisor should delegate depends on many factors. To a large degree, however, the answer is closely related to understanding employee motivation and alternative leadership approaches that supervisors can implement. These will be discussed in Chapter 5.

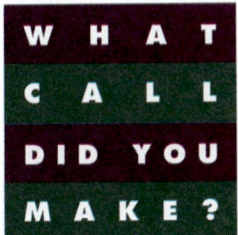

WHAT CALL DID YOU MAKE?

As Anita Mathews, in the opening vignette, you need to plan your communication carefully. Art Roberts may be upset at more than the fact that you are doing the work of employees. You need to try to understand what the real issue is. Does he understand that the department is shorthanded? Before you respond, think back to earlier conversations between yourself and Art. Has he communicated clearly what he expects from you? Have you felt free to disagree with Art when you talk? Is he aware of the problems you have in doing your job? What will the repercussions be if customers get their statements late?

You have fallen into one of the most common traps of supervision. When supervisors are asked the question, "What is the easiest and quickest way to get a job done?" they usually respond, "Do it myself!" It is natural to help out when you are needed. You feel comfortable doing the work, and in all likelihood you believe that your efforts in helping to get the work out on time will be appreciated. However, your supervisor, Art Roberts, does not like what you are doing and believes that you should not do any of the work of the employees, or that a supervisor should step in and do the work only in extreme emergency situations.

Ideally, you would have recognized the work backlog and talked to the employees about the problem. They could help you establish priorities and suggest that you work alongside them for a period of time. You also thought about calling in temporary help to ease the backlog. However, you are uncertain about your authority. Do you have the authority to call in temporaries? What budgetary authority do you really have? These are issues that need to be clarified. It is your responsibility to clarify what is expected from you and what authority you have to get things done.

On the other hand, maybe Art is trying to teach you something. Remember from Chapter 2 that we defined management as getting things done through others. Maybe he wants you to discover other ways to get the job done or to rejuggle priorities for your people.

Nevertheless, you will be uneasy telling Art how you feel since you are relatively new to the supervisory ranks. Pause and plan before you begin your discussion with Art. You want him to clarify his expectations. Ask specific questions that will elicit the answers needed to do the job. Recognize that perhaps now is not the best time to continue this discussion.

When you and Art discuss this issue, emphasize the importance of the customers and their expectation that their statements will be on time. Ask him what he would have done in similar circumstances. Clarify your authority. Above all, avoid conflict that could strain your long-term relationship with Art.

SUMMARY

1 Explain the importance of authority to supervisory management.

Managerial authority is a necessary component of any manager's position, and delegating authority is the means of making the managerial process throughout the organization a reality. Generally, supervisors must first learn how to take an order before they can learn how to give an order. Supervisors assign job duties and authority to employees so they can perform within prescribed limits. In essence, delegation of authority means empowering employees to make decisions.

The formal way of looking at managerial authority is that it originates from the top and is delegated through a chain of command from the top-level executive down to the lowest-ranking employee. However, the acceptance theory of authority suggests that supervisors have authority only if and when their subordinates accept it. In reality, an employee's choice between accepting or not accepting a supervisor's authority may be the choice between staying in the job and quitting. But the degree of acceptance will affect the quality and quantity of the employee's work and the enthusiasm with which the employee performs the job.

Most first-line supervisors have definite limits placed on their authority.

2 Describe the types of power potentially available to the supervisor.

Supervisors have power because of the position they occupy. Position power increases as a person advances up the organization hierarchy. The supervisor derives personal power from his or her relationship with others. Subordinates' perceptions of the supervisor's skill, knowledge, and ability play an integral role in the supervisor's ability to influence them.

Theorists French and Raven identify five sources of power: reward, coercive, legitimate, expert, and referent or charismatic. Research indicates that supervisors who use expert power and referent power effectively have the greatest potential for achieving organizational goals. The power that a supervisor has is based, for the most part, on the willingness of the employee to accept it.

3 Discuss the delegation process and define its three major components.

The process of delegation is made up of three components: assigning a job or duties, granting authority, and creating responsibility. For delegation to succeed, supervisors must give employees enough authority and responsibility to carry out their assigned duties. All three components are interdependent, in that a change in one requires a corresponding change in the other two.

The supervisor must be specific in telling employees what authority they have and what they can or cannot do. The unity-of-command principle holds that each employee should report directly to only one supervisor and—unless there is a valid reason—only one supervisor gives directives to an employee. The supervisor delegates authority to employees to accomplish specific jobs, but the supervisor's own personal accountability cannot be delegated.

4 Explain various organizational approaches to delegation.

The extent to which authority is delegated determines the degree to which an organization is centralized or decentralized. The question is not whether management will delegate authority, but how much and to whom. In a centralized organization, managers micromanage—they make most decisions. Small companies are often centralized. On the other hand, if much authority is delegated through the ranks, then the organization is decentralized. As an organization grows, usually it moves gradually toward greater decentralization.

5 Discuss why some supervisors do not delegate and describe some benefits of delegation.

Included among the many reasons supervisors are reluctant to delegate are shortage of qualified employees, fear of making mistakes, the "do-it-myself" mentality, fear of not being needed, reluctant employees, and lack of managerial support for delegation.

Effective supervisors see the benefits of delegation. Employees become more involved and gain knowledge and confidence in their skills. The supervisor benefits from greater flexibility, better decisions, higher employee morale, and better job performance.

6 Compare the autocratic approach with the general approach to supervision.

General supervision promotes delegation because it provides employees with considerable freedom in making decisions and in doing their jobs to meet departmental objectives. General supervision offers many advantages to supervisors as well as employees. The supervisor saves time in the long term. By giving employees practice in making decisions and using their own judgment, the supervisor encourages them to become more competent and more promotable.

Some supervisors still believe that autocratic supervision is more likely to get results from employees than general supervision. There are occasions when supervisors have to rely on their managerial authority. For the most part, however, these should be the exceptions, rather than the rule.

The extent to which a supervisor uses the autocratic or general approach requires a delicate balance. The advantages of delegation are realized through general supervision. However, at times supervisors have to resort to their formal authority to attain departmental objectives.

KEY TERMS

Acceptance theory of authority (page 81)   Centralized authority (page 88)
Position power (page 83)   Decentralized authority (page 88)
Personal power (page 83)   General supervision (page 92)
Accountability (page 84)   Autocratic supervision (page 94)
Unity-of-command principle (page 85)

QUESTIONS FOR DISCUSSION

1. Define managerial authority. Discuss the following issues related to the concept of authority:
    a.   The origin of formal authority.
    b.   The difference between power and authority.
    c.   The acceptance theory of authority.
    d.   Limits to a supervisor's authority.
2. What does delegation of authority mean? Why is delegation essential if an organization is to operate efficiently and grow?
3. Define responsibility. Why are the concepts of responsibility, authority, and accountability closely related? Why can a supervisor's personal accountability not be delegated?
4. Define and discuss the three major components of the process of delegation.
5. Define the unity-of-command principle.
6. Does the arrangement whereby Anita (in the "You Make the Call" section) occasionally helps out create serious long-term problems for the organization? Explain your rationale.
7. What are meant by the terms "centralized" and "decentralized" authority? How do organizations vary in terms of applying these concepts?
8. Why are many supervisors reluctant to delegate? What benefits typically accrue to a supervisor who learns how to delegate?
9. Define general supervision. Will this approach work with every employee? How can a supervisor know how and when to implement general supervision? Discuss.
10. Is autocratic supervision always inappropriate? Are there situations in which a supervisor will have to rely on authority in order to receive proper employee performance? Discuss.

SKILLS APPLICATIONS

Skills Application 4-1: Delegation Practice
The following are some guidelines for effective delegation:

1. Make a list of your duties and responsibilities (tasks).
2. Identify regular tasks that could be delegated.
3. Make a list of your employees. Indicate their major strengths and weaknesses. What training opportunities do they need?
4. Match each task to the employee's abilities and needs.
5. Plan the communication; spell out specific objectives.
6. Provide training, coaching, and guidance as necessary.
7. Give employees freedom to do the task their way.
8. Monitor performance. Be available for assistance.
9. Make adjustments as necessary.
10. Provide reinforcement.

Your assignment:

Step 1

a. Review what needs to be done for the next two weeks. Check those items you can assign or delegate to someone else.

b. Develop a plan for assigning one of the tasks to someone else. (Note: this person may be a family member, roommate, or member of a group to which you belong.)

c. Make a list of the important information that must be communicated to the other person.

d. Determine how often and in what form you want progress reports.

e. Practice by giving someone the assignment.

Step 2

Critique your approach. What could you have done better?

Skills Application 4-2: Delegating or Dumping?

The store manager stumbles upon a card game in the employee lounge during the lunch hour. The employees are obviously playing for money. The store manager storms into the supervisor's office and bawls him out for letting this go on. "I don't care how you do it, but I want it stopped."

1. Is the store manager delegating or dumping? Explain your response.

2. Develop a way for the store manager to better handle the situation.

3. Compare your responses with those of an experienced supervisor and with other student responses.

4. What good ideas did you have that others did not? What ideas did others have that you would adopt?

Skills Application 4-3: The Delegating Professor

You are scheduled to take a course titled "Team Building for Total Quality Management." The first day of class, the professor states: "There is no syllabus for the course, no assigned textbooks, and no formal structure. This is the first time I have taught the course. I expect you to understand how the supervisor can help employees become empowered team players in the pursuit of a total quality effort! Your job is to come to class next time with a list of how you plan on achieving that objective. In addition, I want you to determine how I should reward or punish (grade) your efforts. See you next time."

1. How would you like this approach? Why?

2. Is the professor delegating or abdicating? Why?

3. Make a list of ways you would gain the information necessary for accomplishing the professor's wishes.

4. Is it important for the employees (students) to know how they will be rewarded/punished? Why?

ENDNOTES

1.   Much has been written about power. For additional information on position power and personal power, see Amitai Etzioni, *A Comparative Analysis of Complex Organizations* (New York: Free Press, 1961), pp. 4–6; John P. Kotter, "Power, Dependence, and Effective Management," *Harvard Business Review* (July–August 1977), pp. 131–136; and Henry Mintzberg, *Power in and Around Organizations* (Englewood Cliffs, N.J.: Prentice-Hall). Also see Allan R. Cohen and David L. Bradford, *Influence Without Authority* (New York: John Wiley & Sons, 1990).

2.   John R. P. French and Bertram Raven, "The Bases of Social Power," in *Studies in Social Power*, ed. Dorwin Cartwright (Ann Arbor: University of Michigan Press, 1959), pp. 150–167. Also see A. J. Stahelski, D. E. Frost, and M. E. Patch, "Uses of Socially Dependent Bases of Power: French and Raven's Theory Applied to Workgroup Leadership," *Journal of Applied Social Psychology* (March 1989), pp. 283–297.

3.   See Timothy R. Hinkin and Chester A. Schriesheim, "Relationships Between Subordinate Perceptions and Supervisor Influence Tactics and Attributed Bases of Supervisory Power," *Human Relations* (March 1990), pp. 221–237.

5

Motivation and Supervisory Management Styles

LEARNING OBJECTIVES

After studying this chapter, you will be able to:

1 Discuss reasons why people may behave the way they do.

2 Compare various motivation theories and explain their importance for understanding employee behavior.

3 Compare the styles of supervisory management under Theory X and Theory Y assumptions with the management styles identified by Blake and Mouton.

4 Discuss supervisory approaches for stimulating employee motivation—especially contingency style leadership, broadened job tasks, job redesign, and participative management.

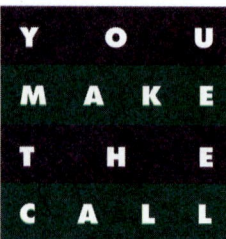

You are John Jackson, production supervisor for Amity Cable and Wire Products, located in Indiana. You supervise 28 assembly-line production workers. About a year ago, the Illinois facility was closed and six of the workers from that site were transferred into your group. Jim Collins, the plant manager, has been greatly concerned because production has remained constant but quality has varied greatly. The wire products produced by your group are used in the auto industry, and your prime customer, Ford Motor Company, has said that you must improve your quality or the work will go to other suppliers. You know that the loss of Ford as a customer would result in massive layoffs.

Several of the younger employees have you baffled. Sandy Hall and Tony Aquirre appear to speak for the group and are the informal leaders. They set the pace for the group, but on occasion they have a tendency to loaf on the job. When they slow down, everyone else slows down, seeming to think it is the social hour. Sandy loves to tell stories, and when she does, she has the attention of all employees. The trouble is that although their output quantity is better than most, on occasion their reject rate approaches an unacceptable 10 percent. A discussion with the two did not go the way you expected.

"You must be crazy," Tony said. "I've always wondered why you expect us to work so hard. We make the same money—and not much of it, at that! The way I figure it, why bust your tail? Chances are that it will only lead to a layoff."

Sandy added, "Yeah, like what happened over at Carter Products.

They started a quality improvement program, and before long they didn't need as many employees. Look, I like what I'm doing, and it's important to me to do a good job. But that's all I want to do, no more, no less."

Tony said, "I've seen too many people—my dad, for example—sweat their whole life away, and what did it get them? My dad's plant closed several years ago and left him high and dry. Sandy's right. You know we'll keep up our end of production, but it's impossible to meet those quality standards Ford imposes. Only Superman could do it right all the time."

You know that you will have to do something and quickly. But what will you do?

YOU MAKE THE CALL.

DETERMINANTS OF HUMAN BEHAVIOR

1 Discuss reasons why people may behave the way they do.

In Chapter 2, we defined "management" as getting things accomplished with and through people by guiding and motivating their efforts toward common objectives. To manage effectively, as this definition suggests, supervisors must understand employee motivation and develop approaches that encourage employees to work to the full extent of their capabilities.

Human beings constitute a resource that is quite different from any other the supervisor is asked to manage. Our society places great value on the worth of human beings. Human beings have values, attitudes, needs, and expectations that significantly influence their behavior on the job. The feelings people have toward their supervisors, their job environment, their personal problems, and numerous other factors are often difficult to ascertain. Yet they have a tremendous impact on employee motivation and work performance.

What causes employees to behave the way they do? This question is difficult to answer, because each individual is unique. The behavior of people as individuals and in groups at work is often rational, consistent, and predictable. However, at times, people's behavior may seem irrational, inconsistent, and unpredictable. When an employee's behavior is not consistent with the organization's expectations, problems arise for the supervisor. Behavior is influenced by many forces, making it difficult for the supervisor to formulate simple principles that apply to every situation.

The forces that stimulate human behavior come from within individuals and from their environment. To illustrate, think about why parents' behavior changes when they become grandparents. One answer might be that the parents are now older (perhaps more mature or experienced). They have received feedback on their earlier parenting efforts and have taken corrective action. Many grandparents have extra income to spend or more time to devote to grandparenting. Also, they can always send the grandchildren home to their parents; their duties and responsibilities have changed. All of these factors acting in combination may lead to a behavioral change.

Determinants of Personality[1]

Every individual is the product of many factors, and it is the unique combination of these factors that results in an individual human personality. **Personality** is the complex mix of knowledge, attitudes, and attributes that distinguish one person from all others.

Many people use the word "personality" to describe what they observe in another person. However, the real substance of human personality goes far beyond external behavior. The essence of an individual's personality includes the person's attitudes, values, and ways of interpreting the environment, as well as many internal and external influences that contribute to his or her behavior patterns. There are several major schools of personality study that can help us comprehend the complexity of human beings. We will first discuss the primary determinants of personality and then describe how some major theories relate these factors to employee motivation.

Physiological (Biological) Factors. One major influence on human personality is a person's physiological (or biological) makeup. Such factors as sex, age, race, height, weight, and physique can affect how a person sees the world. Intelligence, which is at least partially inherited, is another. Most biological characteristics are apparent to others, and they may affect the way in which a person is perceived. For example, a person who is tall is sometimes considered to possess more leadership ability than a shorter person. One research study showed that tall male job applicants usually were offered higher starting salaries than were shorter male applicants. While physiological characteristics should not be the basis for evaluating an employee's capabilities, they do exert considerable influence on an individual's personality as well as define certain physical abilities and limitations.

Early Childhood Influences. Many psychologists feel that the very early years of a person's life are crucial in that individual's development. The manner in which a child is trained, shown affection, and disciplined will have a lifelong influence. In *The Managerial Woman*, Hennig and Jardim's portraits of the personal and professional lives of 25 women who made it to the top identify the early childhood influences that were conducive to their success:

For each of the twenty-five their "typical" mother provided a warm, caring and socially sanctioned feminine model. . ., while their fathers supported them and confirmed them in believing that these were not binding models of behavior but a matter of choice and option. . . .

As little girls they were free to take part in activities usually reserved for little boys. . . . their fathers confirmed their freedom to be more. . . .[2]

Parents who encourage autonomy, independence, exploration, and the ability to deal with risk while instilling an awareness to work with others provide the child with valuable lessons. Various biographies illustrate that an individual's ability to cope with problems and work in harmony with others may be determined partly through the influences to which that individual was subjected as a child.

Personality
The knowledge, attitudes, and attributes that combine to make up the unique human being.

Environmental (Situational) Factors. Sociologists and social psychologists emphasize the immediate situation or environment as being the most important determinant of adult personality. Such factors as education, income, employment, home, and many other experiences that confront an individual throughout life will influence what that person is and eventually becomes.

Every day's experiences contribute to an individual's makeup. This is particularly true in terms of the immediate working environment. For example, the personality of the blue-collar worker performing routine, manual labor on an assembly line is affected by this type of work in a different manner than the personality of a professional white-collar person who performs primarily mental work involving thought and judgment. Stating this another way, what a supervisor does in a work situation affects the personalities of the people being supervised.

Cultural (Societal) Values. The broader culture also influences personality. In the United States such values as competition, rewards for accomplishment, equal opportunities, and similar concepts are part of a democratic society. Individuals are educated, trained, and encouraged to think for themselves and to strive for the achievement of worthwhile goals. However, some cultural values are changing. For example, for many years the workforce in the United States was relatively homogeneous and the cultural values of the majority of workers tended to be similar. In recent decades, however, the workforce has become increasingly diversified, reflecting many different subcultures and subgroups. As the diversity of the workforce has increased, so has the effect of different cultural norms and values on the workplace. In particular, the values of certain ethnic, age, and other minority groups may be quite different from the values of the majority. By recognizing and respecting different cultural values, supervisors should become more adept in dealing effectively with people unlike themselves.

Recognizing Human Differences and Similarities

The many complexities of human personality have been discussed here only briefly, because there are an infinite number of factors that cause personality to adapt and change over time. Ideally, supervisors should get to know their employees so well that they can tailor their supervisory approaches to the uniqueness of each individual's personality. Realistically, however, it is impossible to understand all the unique characteristics of a person's personality.

Fortunately, behavioral studies have demonstrated that people tend to be more alike than different in their basic motivational needs and their reasons for behavior. Supervisors can implement managerial techniques that emphasize the similarities rather than the differences among people. This does not mean that unique differences in people should be overlooked. Supervisors can understand the unique needs and personality makeup of individual employees enough to adapt general approaches to individuals to some extent. But a consistent supervisory approach based on similarities rather than differences is a practical way to lead a group of employees toward achieving company goals.

UNDERSTANDING MOTIVATION AND HUMAN BEHAVIOR

Too often motivation is viewed as something that one person can give to or do for another. Supervisors sometimes talk in terms of giving a worker a "shot" of motivation or of having to "motivate their employees." However, motivating employees is not that easily accomplished, since the concept of human motivation really refers to an inner drive or an impulse. Motivation cannot be poured down another's throat or injected intravenously! In the final analysis, it comes from within a person. **Motivation** is a willingness to exert effort toward achieving a goal, stimulated by the effort's ability to fulfill an individual need. In other words, employees are more willing to do what the organization wants if they believe that doing so will result in a meaningful reward. The supervisor's challenge is to stimulate that willingness by making sure that achievement of organizational goals results in rewards that employees want. The rewards need not always be money; they can be anything employees value. For example, praise and recognition can be powerful motivators.

Since employee motivation is crucial to organizational success, it is a subject about which there has been much research. The theories presented in this chapter are fundamental, and much more has been written elsewhere. However, most theories emphasize the similarities, rather than differences, in the needs of human beings.

The Hierarchy of Needs (Maslow)

Most psychologists who study human behavior and personality generally are convinced that all behavior is caused, goal oriented, and motivated. Stating this another way, there is a reason for everything that a person does, assuming that the person is rational, sane, and not out of control (e.g., not under the influence of drugs or alcohol). People constantly are striving to attain something that has meaning to them in terms of their own particular needs and in relation to how they see themselves and the environment in which they live. Often we may not be aware of why we behave in a certain manner, but we all have subconscious motives that govern the way we behave in different situations.

One of the most widely accepted theories of human behavior is that people are motivated to satisfy certain well-defined and more or less predictable needs. Psychologist Abraham H. Maslow formulated the concept of a **hierarchy** (or priority) **of needs**.[3] He maintained that these needs range from lower-level needs to higher-level needs in an ascending priority (see Figure 5-1). These needs actually overlap and are interrelated, and it may be preferable to consider them as existing along a continuum, rather than as being separate and distinct from one another.

Maslow's theory of a hierarchy of human needs implies that people attempt to satisfy these needs in the order in which they are arranged in the hierarchy. Until the lowest-level or most basic needs are reasonably satisfied, a person will not be motivated strongly by the other levels. As one level of needs is satisfied to some extent, the individual focuses on the next level, which then becomes the stronger mo-

Compare various motivation theories and explain their importance for understanding employee behavior.

Motivation A willingness to exert effort toward achieving a goal, stimulated by the effort's ability to fulfill an individual need.

Hierarchy of needs Maslow's theory of motivation, which suggests that employee needs are arranged in priority order such that lower-order needs must be satisfied before higher-order needs become motivating.

FIGURE 5-1
Hierarchy of Needs

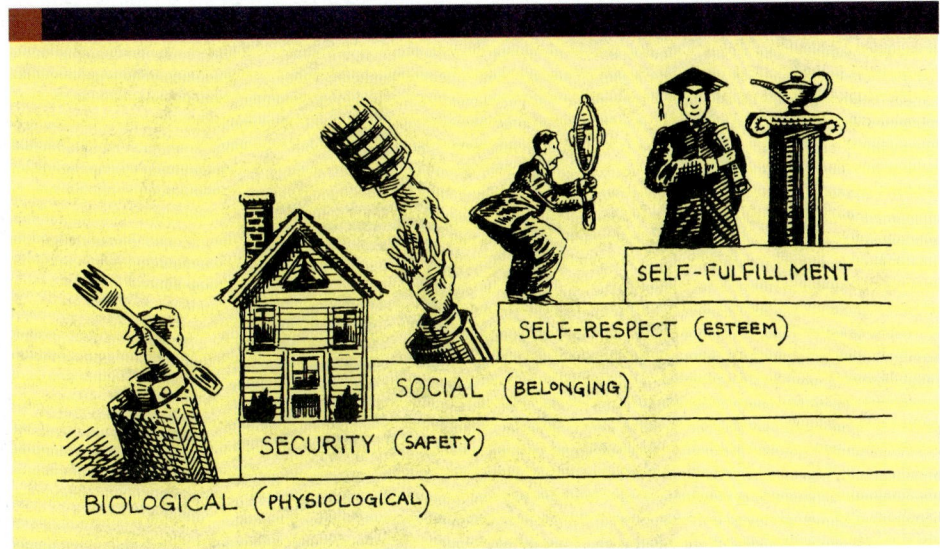

tivator of behavior. Maslow even suggested that once a lower level of needs was reasonably satisfied, it no longer would motivate behavior, at least in the short term.

Biological (Physiological) Needs. At the first level are the **biological** (or physiological) **needs**. These are needs that everyone has for food, shelter, rest, recreation, and other physical necessities. Virtually every employee views work as being a means for taking care of these fundamental needs. The paycheck enables a person to purchase the necessities vital to survival, as well as the comforts of life.

Biological needs
The basic physical needs, such as food, rest, shelter, and recreation.

Security (Safety) Needs. Once a person's physiological needs are reasonably satisfied, other needs become important. The **security** (or safety) **needs** include the needs to protect ourselves against danger and to guard against the uncertainties of life. Most employees want some sense of security or control over their future. In order to satisfy such expectations, many employers offer a variety of supplementary benefits. For example, medical, retirement, hospitalization, disability, and life insurance plans are designed to protect employees against various uncertainties and their possible serious consequences. Wage and benefit packages are designed to satisfy employees' physiological and safety needs. By fulfilling these basic needs, organizations hope to attract and retain competent personnel.

Security needs
Desire for protection against danger and life's, uncertainties.

Social (Belonging) Needs. Some supervisors believe that good wages and ample benefits are sufficient to motivate employees. These supervisors do not understand the importance of the higher-level needs of human beings, beginning with social (or belonging) needs. **Social needs** are those that people have for attention,

Social needs
Desire for love and affection and affiliation with something worthwhile.

Providing athletic facilities to employees can help satisfy their recreational needs and social needs.

for being part of a group, for being accepted by their peers, and for love. Many studies have shown that group motivation can be a powerful influence on employee behavior at work in either a negative or a positive direction. For example, some employees may deliberately perform in a manner contrary to organizational goals in order to feel that they are an accepted part of an informal group. On the other hand, if informal group goals are in line with organizational goals, the group can influence individuals toward exceptional performance. Some employers provide off-the-job social and athletic opportunities for their employees as a means of helping them satisfy their social needs and to build loyalty to the organization as a whole.

Self-respect needs
Desire for recognition, achievement, status, and a sense of accomplishment.

Self-Respect (Esteem) Needs. Closely related to social needs are **self-respect** (or esteem or ego) **needs.** These are needs that everyone has for recognition, achievement, status, and a sense of accomplishment. Self-respect needs are very powerful, because they relate to personal feelings of self-worth and importance. Supervisors should look for ways by which these internal needs may be satisfied, such as providing variety and challenge in work tasks and recognizing good performance. Something as simple as saying "good job" to someone can keep that person doing good work.

Self-fulfillment needs
Desire to use one's abilities to the fullest extent.

Self-Fulfillment Needs. At the highest level of human needs are **self-fulfillment** (or self-realization) **needs**—the desire to use one's capabilities to the fullest.

People want to be creative and to achieve within the limits of their capacities. Presumably, these highest-level needs are not satisfied until a person reaches his or her own full potential. As such, they persist throughout the person's life and probably can never be completely satisfied.

Many jobs frustrate rather than fulfill this level of human needs. For example, many factory and office jobs are routine and monotonous, and workers must seek self-fulfillment in pursuits off the job and in family relationships. However, supervisors can provide opportunities for self-fulfillment on the job by assigning tasks that challenge employees to use their abilities more fully.

Application of the Needs Theories to Supervisory Management

Supervisors can use the model of a hierarchy of human needs as a framework to visualize the kinds of needs that people have and to assess their relative importance in motivating individuals in the work group. The supervisor's problem is to make individual fulfillment a result of doing a good job. For example, if the supervisor senses that an employee's most influential motivator at the time is social needs, then the employee is most likely to do a good job if he or she is assigned to work with a group and the whole group is rewarded for doing the job well. If an employee seems to be seeking self-respect, then to influence this employee toward good performance the supervisor might provide visible signs of recognition, such as a trophy or praise in front of the employee's peers at a departmental meeting. The key for the supervisor is to recognize where each employee is in the hierarchy, so that the supervisor can determine what needs are currently driving the employee.

As mentioned previously, many supervisors believe that motivation is something they do to get a response from their employees. However, the essence of motivation is what individuals feel and do in relation to their own particular needs. Ultimately, all motivation is self-motivation. Thus, a good supervisor structures the work situation and reward systems in such a manner that employees are motivated to perform well because good work performance leads to satisfaction of their particular needs. The "Contemporary Issue" box depicts how a manager used these concepts to help an employee balance personal needs with job needs.

On the other hand, job security has become increasingly important to many employees. Whether due to natural economic trends, the North American Free Trade Agreement (NAFTA), or other factors, almost half of all major U. S. companies downsized during 1993. According to a recent survey conducted by Wyatt Company, "reducing or freezing employees' pay rather than creating incentives to work has not given the required results. Companies still think that all they need to do is cut heads."[4]

Yet, it is normal for employees to expect good wages and generous benefit plans. The key to longer-term, positive motivation of employees resides in better satisfying their higher-level needs (social, self-respect, and self-fulfillment). Supervisors should recognize that just giving employees more money, better benefits, and better working conditions will not bring about excellent work performance.

CONTEMPORARY ISSUE
Fulfilling an Employee's Needs

Consider the case of Josephine C. Pigg, a clerk with U.S. West Inc. in Grand Junction, Colorado. She was 14 months from retirement when her daughter was diagnosed with cancer. The prognosis was not good, and Pigg decided to stay in Denver with her daughter rather than travel 250 miles back and forth. Her supervisor, Penny Larson Hubbard, figured out a way to keep Pigg working. With the help of a human resources manager, Hubbard found Pigg a job with U.S. West in Denver. Hubbard said, "Jo is valuable to our company. If our employees have done a good job, we try and accommodate their situation."

Supervisors such as Hubbard aren't typical. However, if organizations want to succeed, they will have to change in this respect. By accommodating Pigg's needs, Hubbard undoubtedly gained a larger, longer-term payoff. Other U. S. West employees observed that the organization cared about their needs and could be flexible in devising ways to fulfill them. Effective supervisors embrace the general concept that this is the best way to manage people. Supervisors who want to obtain better performance from all employees must be flexible in helping employees fulfill personal needs through their jobs.

Source: Adapted from Michele Galen, "Work and Family: How Companies Are Starting to Respond to Workers' Needs—And Gain from It," *Business Week* (June 28, 1993), pp. 80–88.

For many employees, these items may play a secondary role in day-to-day motivation.

Negative Employee Motivation and Frustration

Conditions that do not bring about the fulfillment of a person's needs will ultimately result in dissatisfaction and frustration. Thus, when their needs are not satisfied on the job, many employees resort to behavior patterns that are detrimental to their job performance and to the organization. A typical approach for frustrated employees is to resign themselves to just getting by on the job. This means that they simply go through the motions and put in time without trying to perform in other than an average or marginal manner. They look for personal satisfaction off the job and are content to do just enough to draw a paycheck.

Some employees constantly find things that distract them from doing the job, and at times they even try to beat the system. They often are absent or tardy, or they break the rules as a way of trying to get back at situations that they find frustrating.

Still other employees who are dissatisfied adopt aggressive behavior, which ultimately may cause them to leave the job. Examples of aggressive behavior are poor attitudes, vandalism, theft, fighting, and temper outbursts. When the situation becomes intolerable, they quit or almost force their supervisors to fire them.

These types of reactions to job situations are undesirable and should be prevented. Costs of employee turnover, absenteeism, tardiness, poor performance, and other unsatisfactory conduct on the job can be extremely high to an organization. Rather than just accepting an employee's behavior, a supervisor should endeavor to relieve frustration by providing more opportunities for need fulfillment.

Motivation-Hygiene Theory

Motivation-hygiene
theory
Herzberg's theory that
factors in the work
environment only
influence the degree of
job dissatisfaction,
while job content
factors influence the
amount of job
satisfaction.

Another theory of motivation is the **motivation-hygiene theory**, sometimes called the two-factor theory or the dual-factor theory, developed by Frederick Herzberg.[5] Herzberg's research has demonstrated that some factors in the work environment that traditionally were believed to motivate people actually serve primarily to reduce their dissatisfaction rather than motivate them positively.

Herzberg and others have conducted numerous studies in which people were asked to describe events that made them feel particularly good or bad about their jobs. Other questions were designed to determine the depth of their feelings, the duration for which these feelings persisted, and the types of situations that made employees feel motivated or frustrated. These studies were made of employees in various organizations and industries, including personnel at all levels and from different technical and job specialties. Interestingly, the general pattern of results was fairly consistent. It revealed a clear distinction between factors that tend to motivate employees (motivation factors) and those that, while expected by workers, are not likely to motivate them (hygiene factors).

Motivation factors
Elements intrinsic in
the job that promote
job performance.

Motivation Factors. Herzberg identified the **motivation factors** as elements intrinsic in the job that promote job performance. Among the most frequently identified motivation factors are the following:

- Opportunity for growth and advancement.
- Achievement or accomplishment.
- Recognition for accomplishments.
- Challenging or interesting work.
- Responsibility for work.

Stating this another way, job factors that tend to motivate people positively are primarily related to their higher-level needs and aspirations. These factors are all related to outcomes associated with the content of the job being performed. Opportunity for advancement, greater responsibility, recognition, growth, achievement, and interesting work are consistently identified as the major factors that make work motivating and meaningful. The absence of these factors can be frustrating and nonmotivating. These motivation factors are not easily measured, and they may be difficult to find in certain types of jobs.

Hygiene factors
Elements in the work
environment that, if
positive, reduce
dissatisfaction but do
not tend to motivate.

Hygiene Factors. Also referred to as the "dissatisfiers," **hygiene factors** are elements in the work environment that, if positive, reduce dissatisfaction but do not tend to motivate. Herzberg identified the following hygiene factors:

- Working conditions.
- Money, status, and security.
- Interpersonal relationships.
- Supervision.
- Company policies and administration.

The factors that employees complained about the most were conditions in the work environment: poor company policies and administrative practices; lack of good supervision in both a technical and a human relations sense; poor working conditions; and inadequate wages and benefits. Herzberg concluded that these job-context factors tend to dissatisfy rather than motivate. Where these factors are negative or inadequate, employees will be unhappy. However, where these factors are adequate or even excellent, they do not, by themselves, promote better job performance. This does not mean that hygiene factors are unimportant. They are very important, but they serve primarily to maintain a reasonable level of job motivation, not to increase it.

Application of Herzberg's Theory to Supervision

Herzberg's theory suggests that, to obtain better performance, the supervisor should implement strategies that target the motivation factors—that is, those that contribute to the satisfaction of employees' social, self-respect, and self-fulfillment needs. As seen in Figure 5-2, one of the supervisor's strategies should be to "catch people doing something right" and "give them credit when credit is due." A note of caution: praise and other forms of recognition must be highly individualized and genuinely deserved in order to be effective. A key element in effective supervision is to give employees an opportunity to fulfill their needs as a result of good job performance.

The supervisor should not conclude from Herzberg's work that hygiene factors such as money, benefits, good working conditions, and the like are unimportant. These factors are extremely important, and organizations must strive continuously to be competitive in these areas. However, employees often take such factors for granted, especially when job opportunities are plentiful. Positive employee motivation is more related to people's higher-level needs.

Expectancy Theory

Expectancy theory
Theory of motivation that holds that employees will perform better if they believe such efforts will lead to desired rewards.

Another interesting and practical way of looking at employee motivation is provided by expectancy theory.[6] **Expectancy theory** is based on the worker's perception of the relationships among effort, performance, and reward. According to expectancy theory, workers will be motivated to work harder if they believe that their greater efforts will actually result in improved performance and that such improved performance will then lead to rewards they desire. The expectancy theory model is illustrated in Figure 5-3.

Expectancy theory is based on worker perceptions and on relationships referred to as "linkages." Employee motivation is dependent on the workers' being able to perceive an effort-performance linkage as well as a performance-reward linkage. If an employee cannot recognize that such linkages clearly exist, he or she will not be highly motivated.

For example, if computer operators have not received adequate training, they will probably not be able to perceive a relationship between their effort and perfor-

FIGURE 5-2
A bit of sincere,
genuine praise goes a
long way.

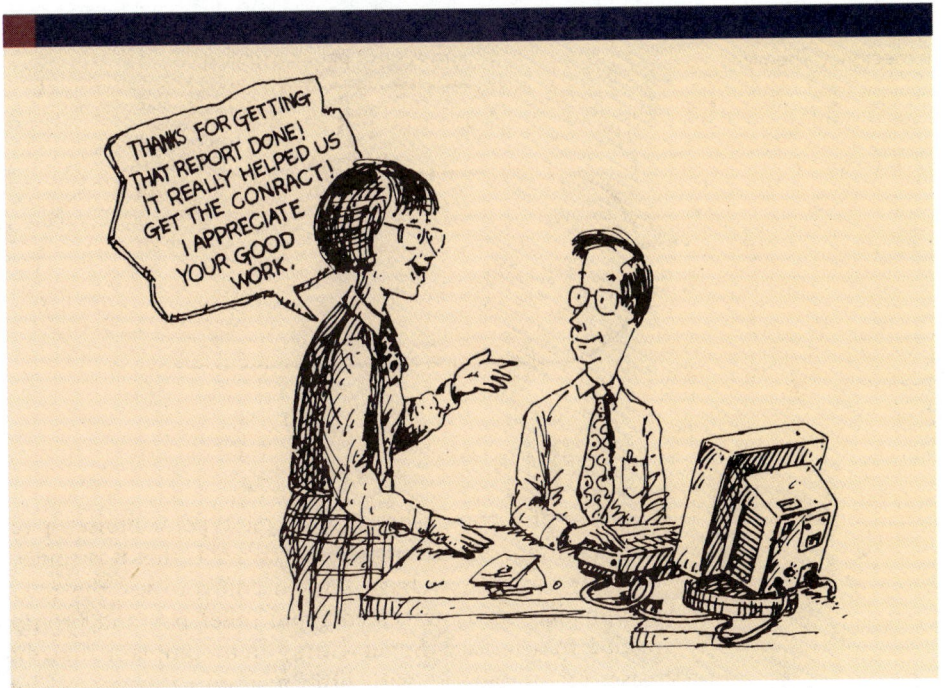

mance. Instead they will conclude that no matter how much effort they expend, there will be no significant improvement in their job performance. Similarly, if nurses' aides in a hospital perceive that their high-performing co-workers are not being rewarded any more than the average or even substandard performers, they will not believe that there is a performance-reward relationship, so they will not be motivated toward good performance.

Supervisors may believe that their organization rewards high-quality work. However, such a belief may be based on management's perception of the reward system. Supervisors should try to verify whether the workers perceive the linkages. Supervisors and employees often do not view reward systems in the same way. For example, on his last day on the job, an assembly-line employee in a manufacturing plant participated in an exit interview. When the interviewer asked him why he was leaving, the worker said that he had become extremely frustrated waiting for work to come to his workstation. The worker said that he became fed up with coming to work every day knowing that no matter how hard he worked, it would not be visible on the production chart.

It does not matter how clearly supervisors view the linkages among effort, performance, and rewards. If the workers cannot see them, the linkages might just as well not be there. Supervisors should strive to show employees that increased effort will lead to improved work performance, which in turn will result in increased rewards. Rewards may be extrinsic, in the form of additional pay, or intrinsic, such

FIGURE 5-3
Expectancy Theory

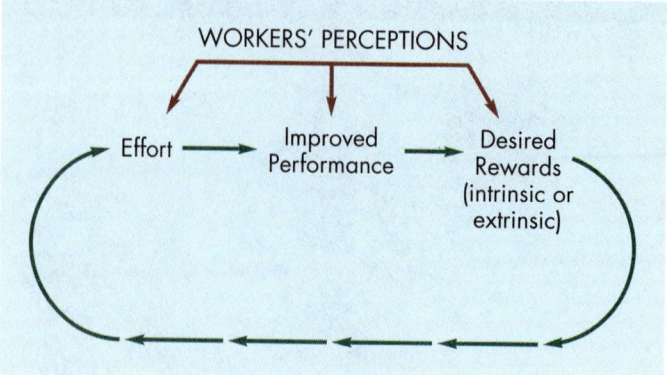

as a sense of accomplishment or some type of praise or recognition. Probably the most important characteristic of a reward is that it is something the person desires.

A supervisor may have limited control over the rewards that are available. Union-management agreements and other pay and promotional systems typically are tied to seniority. Supervisors often complain that many employee wage increases are automatic, with little relation to merit and job performance. Even in these types of situations, however, there are approaches available to supervisors that can yield motivational results.

SUPERVISORY MANAGEMENT STYLES

3 Compare the styles of supervisory management under Theory X and Theory Y assumptions with the management styles identified by Blake and Mouton.

A continuous (and unresolved) question that often confronts supervisors is what general approach, or style, will best contribute to positive employee motivation. This age-old dilemma typically focuses on the degree to which supervisory approaches should be based on satisfying employees' lower-level and higher-level needs. This often becomes an issue of the degree to which supervisors should rely on their authority and position as compared with trying to utilize human relations practices that may provide greater opportunities for employee motivation.

Research concerning supervisory management styles is replete with many findings and some contradictions. Here we review only a few of the significant findings.

McGregor's Theory X and Theory Y

In his book *The Human Side of Enterprise*, Douglas McGregor noted that individual supervisory approaches usually relate to each supervisor's perceptions concerning what people are all about. That is, each supervisor manages employees according to his or her own attitudes and ideas about people's needs and motivations.

For purposes of comparison, McGregor stated that the extremes in attitudes among managers could be classified as Theory X and Theory Y.

The basic assumptions of Theory X and Theory Y as stated by McGregor are as follows:[7]

Theory X
Assumption that employees dislike work, avoid responsibility, and must be coerced to do the job.

Theory Y
Assumption that employees enjoy work, seek responsibility, and are capable of self-direction.

Theory X: The assumption that employees dislike work, avoid responsibility, and must be coerced to work hard.

Theory Y: The assumption that employees enjoy work, seek responsibility, and are capable of self-direction.

Supervisors who are Theory X oriented have a limited view of employees' capabilities and motivation. They feel that employees must be strictly controlled; closely supervised; and motivated on the basis of money, discipline, and authority. Theory X supervisors believe that the key to motivation is in the proper implementation of approaches designed to satisfy employees' lower-level needs.

Theory Y supervisors have a much higher opinion of employees' capabilities. They feel that if the proper approaches and conditions can be implemented, employees will exercise self-direction and self-control toward the accomplishment of worthwhile objectives. According to this view, management's objectives should fit into the scheme of each employee's particular set of needs. Therefore, Theory Y managers believe that the higher-level needs of employees are more important in terms of each employee's own personality and self-development.

The two approaches described by McGregor represent extremes in supervisory styles (as illustrated in Figure 5-4). Realistically, most supervisors are somewhere between Theory X and Theory Y. Neither of these approaches is wrong in and of itself, for the appropriateness of a given approach will depend on the needs of the individuals involved and the demands of the situation. In practice, supervisors may on occasion take an approach that is contrary to their preferred one. For example, even the strongest Theory Y supervisor may revert to Theory X in a time of crisis, such as when the department is shorthanded, when there is an equipment failure, when a serious disciplinary problem has occurred, or when a few employees need firm direction.

Advantages and Limitations of Theory X. Supervisors who adopt the Theory X style typically find that in the short term a job is accomplished faster. Since the questioning of orders is not encouraged, it may appear that the workers are competent and knowledgeable and that work groups are well-organized, efficient, and disciplined.

A major disadvantage of the Theory X approach is that there is little opportunity for employees' personal growth. Since supervision is close and constant, employees are unlikely to develop initiative and independence. Moreover, most workers resent Theory X supervision, and this may breed negative motivation. Traditionally, supervisors who advocated the Theory X approach could get employees to do what they wanted by using the "carrot-and-stick" approach ("Do what I want you to do and you will be rewarded!"). Punishments were applied when the job was not done. This approach is still used by many. However, employ-

ees may rebel when confronted with the stick, and supervisors may not have suffi-cient rewards to get employees to subject themselves to this tight control.

Advantages and Limitations of Theory Y. An overriding advantage of Theory Y supervision is that it promotes individual growth. Since workers are given opportunities to assume some responsibility on their own and are encouraged to contribute their ideas in accomplishing their tasks, it is possible for them to par-tially satisfy their higher-level needs on the job.

Although the Theory Y approach is often viewed as more desirable, it is not without some disadvantages. Theory Y can be time consuming in practice, espe-cially in the short term. Since personal development is emphasized, supervisors must become instructors and coaches if they are to help their employees move to-ward the simultaneous attainment of organizational and personal goals. Some su-pervisors find the extreme application of Theory Y to be more idealistic than prac-tical, since some employees expect firm direction from their supervisors.

The Managerial Grid®

Another approach to analyzing leadership styles has been described by Robert R. Blake and Jane S. Mouton. They developed a Managerial Grid, which identifies five types of managerial leadership based on concern for production coupled with concern for people. The Grid, republished in 1991 as The Leadership Grid®, has a

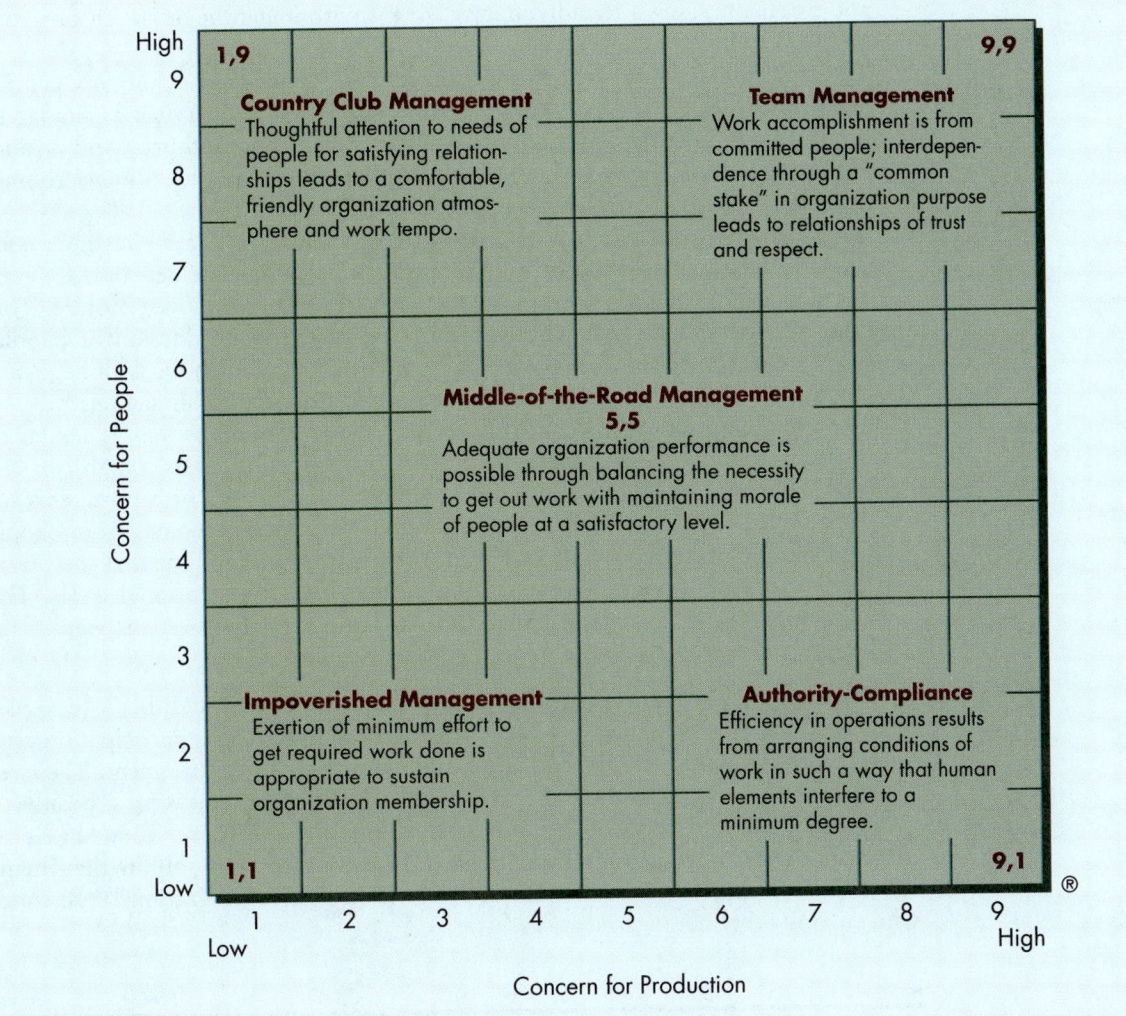

High

9   **1,9**   **9,9**

Country Club Management   **Team Management**
Thoughtful attention to needs of   Work accomplishment is from
people for satisfying relation-   committed people; interdepen-
8   ships leads to a comfortable,   dence through a "common
friendly organization atmos-   stake" in organization purpose
phere and work tempo.   leads to relationships of trust
and respect.
7

6   **Middle-of-the-Road Management**
5,5
5   Adequate organization performance is
possible through balancing the necessity
to get out work with maintaining morale
4   of people at a satisfactory level.

3
Impoverished Management   **Authority-Compliance**
Exertion of minimum effort to   Efficiency in operations results
2   get required work done is   from arranging conditions of
appropriate to sustain   work in such a way that human
organization membership.   elements interfere to a
1   **1,1**   minimum degree.   **9,1**

Low

1   2   3   4   5   6   7   8   9
Low   High

Concern for Production

Concern for People *(vertical axis label)*

Source: The Leadership Grid® Figure from *Leadership Dilemmas–Grid Solutions*, by Robert R. Blake and Anne Adams McCanse (formerly The Managerial Grid Figure by Robert R. Blake and Jane S. Mouton) Houston: Gulf Publishing Company, p. 29. Copyright © 1991, by Scientific Methods, Inc. Reproduced by permission of the owners.

FIGURE 5-5
The Leadship Grid®
Figure

nine-unit scale on both the vertical and horizontal axes, as shown in Figure 5-5. (See Appendix II for an expanded view of the Leadership Grid.) The five managerial styles identified by Blake and Mouton are as follows:

1. The impoverished manager (1,1—low concern for production and for people on the grid) is more or less withdrawn. This supervisor does little either to stimulate employees or to get work out; he or she is primarily interested in getting by and surviving.
2. The country club manager (1,9—low concern for production but high concern for people) believes that by taking care of the human relations needs of people

and by encouraging a friendly, happy work environment, he or she ensures that the work will get done in some way.

3. The authority-compliance, or task manager (9,1—high production, low people) has primary concern for getting the work done. This supervisor is similar to those who follow Theory X, emphasizing efficiency and authority and arranging the work in such a way as to ensure that human elements interfere only minimally.

4. The organization person, or middle-of-the-road manager (5,5—medium concern for production and people) is one who tries to balance demands for production against human factors, particularly those of employee morale. This type of supervisor is not wholly committed to either production or people. Often he or she adopts a political role of getting just enough work done to satisfy superiors, but at the same time giving some attention to human needs.

5. The team manager (9,9—high concern for production and people) is similar to one who follows the Theory Y style. The team supervisor has a high concern for both getting the work out and developing the capacities of people. This supervisor believes that the best organizational performance comes from people who are committed to the objectives of the organization and see that their own needs can best be served by pursuing worthwhile organizational goals. The team supervisor has a high concern for bringing out the best in people and helping them grow and develop in the organization.

Although they recognize that the team manager style may be difficult to implement in some work situations, Blake and Mouton advocate this participation-centered teamwork approach as being applicable in any work environment. Their research has led them to conclude that this approach is the one that is most positively associated with high productivity, job satisfaction, and creativity. They have also found that team types of supervisors tend to be evaluated favorably by their managers and typically advance at a faster rate within their organizations than those who employ other managerial styles.[8]

SUPERVISORY APPROACHES FOR ATTAINING POSITIVE EMPLOYEE MOTIVATION

4 Discuss supervisory approaches for stimulating employee motivation—especially contingency style leadership, broadened job tasks, job redesign, and participative management.

Having reviewed several prominent theories of employee motivation and management styles, the next question is: Which of these theories is the most meaningful? There is no simple set of do's and don'ts that a supervisor can implement to achieve high motivation and excellent performance. Human beings are much too complex for that. Although leadership skills can be learned and developed, no one formula will apply in all situations and with all people.

Contingency-Style Leadership

Behavioral scientists have proposed various models and approaches, which have been described under the general headings of "contingency-style leadership" and

Contingency-style leadership
Models that hold that no one leadership style is best; the appropriate style depends on the situation.

"situational management." Essentially, the **contingency-style leadership** models emphasize that no one supervisory management approach is universally applicable and that the proper approach depends on numerous factors in any given situation. These include considerations involving the supervisor, the organization, the type of work, the employees involved, time pressures, and other factors.

Fiedler developed a contingency-style leadership effectiveness model that presumes that the performance of the work group depends on the interaction of leadership style and situation.[9] Fiedler's controversial model rests on two important questions:

1. To what extent does the situation provide the supervisor with the power and influence needed to be effective? In other words, from the perspective of the supervisor, how favorable are the situational factors?
2. To what extent can the supervisor predict the effects of his or her style on employees' work performance?

Consider the situation of John Jackson, the production supervisor in the opening "You Make the Call" section. Suppose for the sake of illustration that Jackson believes strongly in the concept of employee participation. However, the exploratory discussion with Sandy Hall and Tony Aquirre did not yield the desired results. Two elements in the situation have changed: Ford Motor Company has said that quality must improve and Sandy and Tony have rebuffed his efforts at participative management. The current situation does not appear to provide Jackson with the power and influence he needs to be effective. Thus, the situation is unfavorable, and when a situation is very unfavorable, the leader—according to Fiedler's contingency model—must strongly emphasize the need for task accomplishment.[10] Earlier in this chapter, the authority-obedience or task supervisor was introduced as one who has primary concern for getting the work done. Even though this is not Jackson's preferred style of supervision, contingency theory would propose that this is the appropriate style for the current situation.

Of the various theories, Hersey and Blanchard's situational style of leadership appears to be the most widely accepted managerial approach. It is easy to understand, offers suggestions for changing leadership style, and shows leaders what to do and when to do it. It focuses on the need for flexibility in adapting leadership style to employees and situation.[11] Critics of contingency and situational models contend that these models are inconclusive and may even lead supervisors to believe that they should not be consistent in supervisory management approaches with their people. A detailed discussion of the various models is beyond the scope of this textbook, since they are rather complex and theoretical.[12]

While there is no one best supervisory approach, some approaches work better than others in promoting good job performance. In general, these approaches are consistent with Theory Y or the team management position on the Managerial Grid. The premises and approaches suggested here are in concert with what is known about people, their needs, and their motivations. There is widespread evidence that, when implemented sensibly and consistently, these approaches do work to influence employee motivation and job performance in a positive way. These approaches are further developed throughout this book, particularly in Part 5.

Broadening the Scope and Importance of Each Job

There are ways to give employees new tasks and new work experiences by which the basic nature of the job can be broadened in scope and importance. Variety and challenge can keep jobs from becoming monotonous and can fulfill employee needs.

Job rotation
The process of switching job tasks among employees in the work group.

Job Rotation. Switching job tasks among employees in the work group on a scheduled basis is known as **job rotation**. This is a process that most supervisors can implement, and it often is accompanied by higher levels of job performance and increased employee interest. Job rotation not only helps to relieve employees' boredom, but also enhances their job knowledge. Although the different tasks may require the same skill level, learning different jobs prepares employees for promotion in the future. A major side benefit to the supervisor is that job rotation results in a more flexible workforce, which can be advantageous during periods of employee absence. Moreover, job rotation should mean that employees share both pleasant and unpopular tasks, so work assignments are perceived as fair.

Job enlargement
Increasing the number of tasks an individual performs.

Job Enlargement. Another motivational strategy is **job enlargement**, which means expanding an employee's job with a greater variety of tasks to perform. For example, tasks that previously were handled by several employees may be combined or consolidated within one or two enlarged jobs.

Some employees respond positively to job enlargement, and this is reflected in their performance and in increased job satisfaction. In one furniture factory, for example, a number of routine jobs were changed so that each job required five or six operations, rather than just one constantly repeated operation. Employees were supportive of the change. Such comments as, "My job seems more important now" and "My work is less monotonous now" were common reactions.

There can be problems in implementing job enlargement. Union work rules and job jurisdictional lines may limit the supervisor's authority to change job assignments. Attitudes toward the idea of job enlargement may also present significant difficulties. Some employees, for example, object to the idea of being given expanded duties because they are content with their present jobs and pay. Usually they will not object if at least a small increase in pay comes with the enlarged job.

Job enrichment
Job design that helps fulfill employees' higher-level needs by giving them more challenging tasks and more decision-making responsibility for their jobs.

Job Enrichment. A motivational approach that is increasingly advocated is **job enrichment**, which means assigning more challenging tasks and giving employees more decision-making responsibility for their jobs. Job enrichment goes beyond job rotation and job enlargement in an effort to appeal to the higher-level needs of employees. To enrich jobs, the supervisor should assign everyone in a department a fair share of the challenging as well as the routine jobs and give employees more autonomy in accomplishing the tasks. Unfortunately, many supervisors prefer to assign the difficult, challenging jobs only to their best employees and the dull jobs to the weaker employees. This can be defeating in the long term. The supervisor should provide opportunities for all employees to find challenging and interesting work experiences within the realistic framework of the department's operations. Sometimes job enrichment can be accomplished by committee assignments, special problem-solving tasks, and other unusual job experiences that go beyond the routine performance of day-to-day work. In its most developed form, job enrichment may involve restructuring jobs in such a way that employees are given direct control and responsibility for what they do.

Supervisors may be uncomfortable with job enrichment at first. It may require them to relinquish some control and delegate some planning and decision making. But if job enrichment is practiced sincerely, subordinates usually assume an active role in making or participating in decisions about their jobs over time. The result can be better decisions and a more satisfied and motivated workforce. For example, one supervisor enriched the jobs of machine operators by giving them a greater role in scheduling work and devising their own work rules for the group. The result was a schedule that better met their needs and rules that they were willing to follow, since they helped create them.

In a sense, job enrichment involves the employees' assumption of some of the supervisor's everyday responsibilities. The supervisor remains accountable, however, for the satisfactory fulfillment of these obligations. Therein lies a major risk inherent in job enrichment; yet, despite the risk, many supervisors endorse job enrichment because it works.

Comparing the Approaches to Job Enhancement. The differences among job enrichment, job enlargement, and job rotation are a matter of degree. Each is an attempt to diversify work and make it more meaningful to employees. Job enrichment adds a vertical dimension, or greater depth, to the task, so that employees can satisfy their higher-level needs through their work. Job enlargement emphasizes the horizontal dimension of the task, since it gives employees more duties. Job rotation moves an employee from one job to another on a periodic basis with the intent of reducing boredom and increasing employee interest and breadth of knowledge. These three job design strategies are similar in the sense that each attempts to increase employee performance by improving job satisfaction.

Job Redesign

It is generally believed that well-designed jobs lead to increased motivation, higher-quality performance, higher satisfaction, and lower absenteeism and turnover. These desirable outcomes occur when employees experience three critical psychological states:

1. They believe that they are doing something meaningful because their work is important to other people.
2. They feel personally responsible for how the work turns out.
3. They learn how well they performed their jobs.

Many job redesign programs are based on the model developed by Professors Hackman and Oldham (see Figure 5-6). Their model says that the higher the expe-

FIGURE 5-6
The Job Characteristics
Model

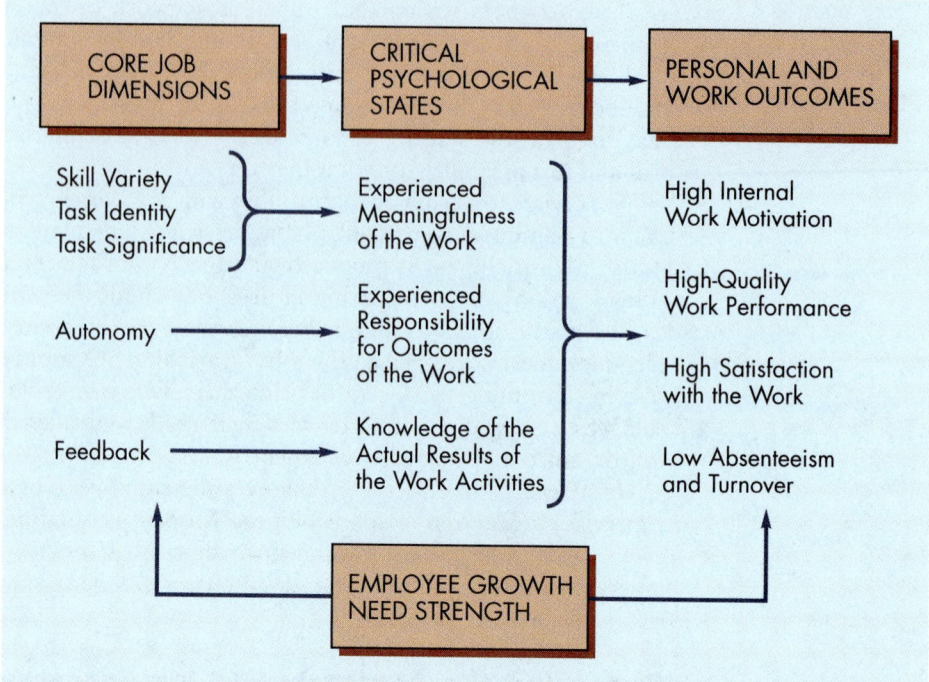

Source: J. Richard Hackman and Greg R. Oldham, *Work Redesign* (Figure 4.6 and Appendix A), © 1980 by Addison-Wesley Publishing Company, Inc. Reprinted by permission of the publisher.

rienced meaningfulness of work, responsibility for the work performed, and knowledge of the results, the more positive the work-related benefits will be. According to this model, any job can be described in terms of the following five core job dimensions:

1. Skill variety: the degree to which an employee has an opportunity to do various tasks and to use a number of different skills and abilities.
2. Task identity: the completion of a whole, identifiable piece of work.
3. Task significance: the degree to which the job impacts the lives or work of others.
4. Autonomy: the amount of independence, freedom, and discretion that an employee has in making decisions about the work to be done.
5. Feedback: the amount of information an employee receives on job performance.[13]

The instrument contained in Skill Application 5-3 can be used to evaluate your own job to determine the extent to which each of these characteristics is present.

With this instrument it is possible to calculate a "motivating potential score" (MPS) for the specific job. Low scores indicate that the individual will not experience high internal motivation from the job. Such a job is a prime candidate for job redesign. Suppose that close examination reveals that the task significance score is relatively low. The supervisor could, for example, assign workers in a typing pool to specific departments as opposed to letting the typing pool serve the company as a whole. This approach could increase both skill variety and task significance scores, thereby increasing the job's motivating potential.[14]

On the other hand, high scores indicate that the job is currently stimulating high internal motivation. According to Hackman and Oldham's theory, internal motivation occurs because the employee is "turned on to [his or her] work because of the positive internal feelings that are generated by doing well, rather than being dependent on external factors (such as incentive pay, job security, or praise from the supervisor) for the motivation to work effectively."[15]

Participative Management

One of the most effective ways to build a sense of employee pride, teamwork, and motivation is for the supervisor to seek advice, suggestions, and information from employees concerning ways in which work should be performed and problems solved. This supervisory approach, in which employees have an active role in decision making, is known as **participative management**. Studies in group behavior have shown that work groups can help the supervisor improve decision making. As discussed in Chapter 4, delegation is important to building positive motivation among employees. This does not mean turning over all decisions to employees, nor does it mean just making employees believe that they are participating in decisions. Rather, it means that the supervisor should earnestly seek employees' opinions whenever possible and be willing to be influenced by their suggestions and even by their criticisms. When employees feel that they are part of a team and that they can have an influence on the decisions that affect them, they are more likely to accept the decisions and seek new solutions to future problems. Supervisors who practice participative management properly are aware of the importance of prompt feedback. They know that it is vital to respond fully to subordinates' suggestions as soon as they have had sufficient time to consider them.

The major advantages of participative management are that decisions tend to be of higher quality and that employees are more willing to accept them. One disadvantage is that this approach can be time consuming. Also, participation makes it easier for employees to criticize, which some supervisors find threatening. On balance, however, participative management is widely recognized as an effective motivational strategy; its advantages outweigh its disadvantages.

Some organizations have found that formal suggestion systems are helpful. Suggestion systems provide monetary rewards to employees for suggestions that are received and accepted.[16] The monetary reward is only part of the employee's overall compensation. Employees like to have their suggestions heard and answered. To some employees, the fact that a suggestion has been accepted may mean more than the monetary award.

Employee Involvement Programs. In recent years, many companies have adopted employee involvement programs in both unionized and nonunionized situ-

---

Participative management
Supervisory approach that gives employees an active role in making decisions about their jobs.

ations. These types of programs often are known by other labels, such as "problem-solving teams," "quality circles (QCs)," "labor-management participation teams," "semiautonomous work teams," "quality-of-work-life (QWL) programs," and the like. Regardless of what they are called, they stem from a common emphasis on using participative management as an ongoing, recognized activity.

During the past decade much attention was focused on quality circles. QCs usually involve six to twelve employees and one or more supervisors—all from the same or similar work areas—who voluntarily meet regularly to discuss production and quality problems. These groups try to identify job-related problems and develop feasible solutions, which then can be implemented realistically. Employees within a QC often come up with excellent ideas, and the QC also helps promote a flow of open, two-way communication between employees and supervisors.

Quality-of-work-life (QWL) programs are even more ambitious than quality circles. "QWL" refers to "a philosophy of management that enhances the dignity of all workers; introduces changes in an organization's culture; and improves the physical and emotional well-being of employees (e.g., providing opportunities for growth and development)."[17] Jac Fitz-enz, president of Saratoga Industries, cites the example of Tandem Computers, which has done a good job of dealing with poor productivity, spiraling benefit costs, and poor quality. He states that, at Tandem, "the critical difference seems to be trust.... Tandem has paid attention to the personal and social situation of each employee."[18] The belief that people should have a stake in their work situation and that the work environment should be structured to meet the employees' needs underlies QWL programs.

The following comprehensive definition of QWL involving union-management environments was developed by the American Center for the Quality of Working Life:

Quality of Work Life improvements are defined as any activity which seeks greater organizational effectiveness through the enhancement of human dignity and growth . . . a process through which the stakeholders in the organization—management, union(s), and employees—learn how to work together better . . . to determine for themselves what actions, changes, and improvements are desirable and workable in order to achieve the twin and simultaneous goals of an improved quality of life at work for all members of the organization, and greater effectiveness for both the company and the unions.[19]

Various work team concepts have evolved from quality circles and QWL programs. Additional information on task teams is given in Chapter 17. Any employee involvement effort must be based on the beliefs that employees want to contribute to the long-term success of the organization and that managers have a strong commitment to participative management as a way of organizational life.

Supervising with a Management-by-Objectives Emphasis. Another well-known motivational approach that has been widely adopted is called "management by objectives" (MBO), or "management by results." Stated simply, **management by objectives** involves (a) having individual employees set or participate in

Margin notes

Quality-of-work-life (QWL) programs
Management philosophy that enhances employee dignity, introduces cultural change, and provides opportunity for employee development.

Management by objectives (MBO)
A process in which the supervisor and employee jointly set the employee's objectives, and the employee receives rewards based on achievement of these objectives.

setting their own performance targets within certain limits (rather than having the targets unilaterally set by supervisors or higher-level managers) and (b) having employees initially appraise themselves in the context of their own objectives. Some organizations have elaborate MBO systems that extend from top-level managers all the way down to entry-level employees.

MBO will not work with everyone, and it is not a cure-all for supervisory problems. However, it does offer an approach by which the burden of certain aspects of planning and performance appraisal is placed on the employee rather than on the supervisor. This in itself should make it attractive to supervisors. Chapter 7 describes a step-by-step outline of the MBO process in greater detail.

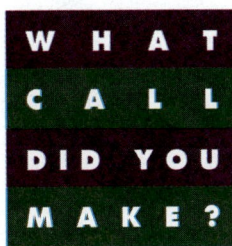

WHAT CALL DID YOU MAKE?

Motivating employees is central to the challenge facing John Jackson. Currently the goals of the employees are not consistent with organizational expectations.

As John Jackson, you must facilitate motivation by taking supportive actions. You will need to strive to understand your employees and their needs. Remember: Each employee is unique. Therefore, the next time you discuss productivity with Sandy and Tony, do it individually. You might learn more about their personal values, attitudes, needs, and expectations that way.

You will need to establish and clarify desired behavior patterns for the employees. Ask yourself this question: What happens when employees do the job right? Are they being appropriately recognized for achievement? You will need to develop a reward system for reinforcing employee accomplishments. The reward system for performing the job well must be consistent with employees' individual needs.

Good communication is essential to your success. You must listen and observe to assess your employees' needs, and you must communicate your expectations. Quality is one of the most important accomplishments of an organization. Therefore, you must constantly stress its importance. You might consider allowing small groups of employees to interact directly with the major client, Ford, to fully appreciate the importance of doing the job right the first time. This would elevate the task significance aspect of their jobs. You might arrange to have teams of Ford employees visit your facility or allow your informal leaders to visit the Ford facility.

There are other strategies you might use to increase the meaningfulness of employees' jobs. The self-reporting questionnaire presented in Skills Application 5-3 could be used to assess the motivating potential of these jobs. If scores are low, you can attempt to discover which of the core job characteristics is causing the problem. If the scores are high, you will need to look for other factors that are causing the dissatisfaction.

In addition, it may be appropriate to use management by objectives or one of the other employee participation programs cited in the chapter. However, if the comments by Sandy and Tony are reflective of the feelings of the majority, then you will have to deal with these feelings of inequity and frustration before you can begin an employee participation program.

Discipline may be appropriate if performance does not improve. Ultimately, if quality does not improve substantially, Amity may lose its major customer, and many employees may lose their jobs.

SUMMARY

1 *Discuss reasons why people may behave the way they do.*

This is difficult because each individual is unique. Behavior is influenced by many factors within both the individual and the environment. Personality is the complex mix of knowledge, attitudes, and attributes that distinguish one person from another.

Prominent factors that interact to form the personality of each individual include physiological makeup, early childhood experiences, the immediate and continuing environment through life, and cultural values. Among the almost infinite number of influences that become part of an employee's personality is the working environment.

Supervisors need to be sensitive to individual differences and similarities among human beings. A consistent supervisory approach based on similarities is a practical way to lead employees.

2 *Compare various motivation theories and explain their importance for understanding employee behavior.*

Motivation is a willingness to exert effort toward achieving a goal, stimulated by the effort's ability to fulfill an individual need. According to Maslow, needs in ascending order of importance are biological, security, social, self-respect, and self-fulfillment. When a lower-level need is fulfilled, higher-level needs emerge that influence one's motivation.

It is important for supervisors to recognize the different need levels. Supervisors can influence employee motivation in a positive way if they rely on supervisory approaches that promote higher-level need fulfillment. When employee needs are not satisfied on the job, job performance usually suffers. Some employees express their dissatisfaction through absenteeism; others may display aggressive and disruptive behavior; still others quit. The result is that the organization suffers from a decrease in production and a loss of quality.

Herzberg's motivation-hygiene research studies indicate that hygiene factors such as money, management policies, working conditions, and certain aspects of supervision must be adequate to maintain a reasonable level of motivation. Forces that stimulate good performance, called "motivation factors," are intrinsic to the job—for example, such as the employees' needs for achievement, opportunity for advancement, challenging work, promotion, growth, and recognition. Effective supervisors implement strategies that target motivation factors to promote good job performance.

Expectancy theory suggests that employees will be motivated if they perceive links between their efforts and performance and between their performance and rewards. Supervisors must clarify such relationships for the workers or strive to develop them.

3 *Compare the styles of supervisory management under Theory X and Theory Y assumptions with the management styles identified by Blake and Mouton.*

The Theory X (authority-obedience) supervisor believes primarily in autocratic techniques, which relate to the lower-level human needs. The Theory X approach implies the use of a "carrot-and-stick" approach to fulfill the most basic needs. The Theory Y (team) supervisor prefers to build motivation by appealing to employees' higher-level needs.

Blake and Mouton's five leadership styles are based on the degree of a manager's concern for people and concern for task. The team manager effectively blends both concerns. The country club manager exhibits high concern for people, while the task manager exhibits little concern for people and very high concern for task. The middle-of-the-road style is moderately high on both concerns. The impoverished manager shows little concern for either people or task. The team manager emphasizes both a people orientation and a task orientation.

Blake and Mouton contend that the team manager approach, which correlates to Theory Y, is the one most positively associated with high productivity, job satisfaction, and the creativity of people involved.

4 *Discuss supervisory approaches for stimulating employee motivation—especially contingency style leadership, broadened job tasks, job redesign, and participative management.*

The contingency models stress that the proper approach is contingent on the factors in any given situation—the supervisor, the organization, the type of work, the subordinates, time pressures, and so forth. Fiedler contends that one situation factor is the amount of power and influence the supervisor has. Although no one supervisory management style is universally applicable, a number of approaches are in harmony with modern theories of motivation.

The major approaches to job design include job rotation, job enlargement, and job enrichment. The job characteristics model has been used to guide job redesign efforts.

The advantages of participative management are that decisions tend to be higher quality and that employees are more willing to accept decisions. Employee participation programs are widely used and varied in application. Delegation strategies, suggestion programs, quality circles, quality-of-work-life programs, and management by objectives are approaches that emphasize employee involvement.

Getting people at all levels of the organization involved in objective setting and problem solving, rearranging duties and responsibilities, and creating ways to reward people for their accomplishments are the essence of the approaches to motivate employee performance. The supervisor must learn to implement different supervisory approaches as appropriate to different people and settings.

KEY TERMS

Personality (page 104)
Motivation (page 106)
Hierarchy of needs (Maslow) (page 106)
Biological needs (page 107)
Security needs (page 107)

Social needs (page 107)
Self-respect needs (page 108)
Self-fulfillment needs (page 108)
Motivation-hygiene theory (Herzberg) (page 111)

Motivation factors (page 111)

Hygiene factors (page 111)

Expectancy theory (page 112)

Theory X (page 115)

Theory Y (page 115)

Contingency-style leadership (page 119)

Job rotation (page 120)

Job enlargement (page 120)

Job enrichment (page 120)

Participative management (page 123)

Quality-of-work-life (QWL) programs (page 124)

Management by objectives (MBO) (page 124)

QUESTIONS FOR DISCUSSION

1. Why are human beings a type of resource different from any other that a supervisor must manage?

2. Discuss four determinants of human personality. Which of these can be influenced or controlled to the greatest degree by the supervisor?

3. From the aspect of practical application, what are the benefits of each of the motivational theories discussed in the chapter?

4. What are the basic elements of Theory X and Theory Y? Should these be considered as "right" and "wrong," "good" and "bad"? Can you think of any reasons why Theory Y should not be appropriate for every supervisor?

5. Discuss the leadership styles described within the Managerial Grid.

6. How could a supervisor's effort to treat employees equally lead to problems? Explain your rationale.

7. Why might an employee not respond positively to the supervisor's efforts to enrich his or her job?

8. Why does a supervisor need to be well versed in the various motivational theories?

9. How might the concepts of the job characteristics model be used to increase the internal motivation of Sandy and Tony in the "You Make the Call" section?

10. Compare quality-of-work-life (QWL) programs with management by objectives (MBO), job rotation, job enlargement, and quality circles.

SKILLS APPLICATIONS

Skills Application 5-1: Using Motivation Concepts

1. Identify from the chapter a list of what you believe to be the most important motivational application concepts that you, as John Jackson in "You Make the Call," should apply in order to motivate employees such as Sandy and Tony.

2. Next, think of the most effective supervisor you have known or heard about. To what degree did that person practice the applications you listed?

3. How would you explain the similarities and differences among the applications you listed?

Skills Application 5-2: Satisfying Attributes of the Job

1. Think of a time you felt especially good about your job. Write a paragraph describing what caused you to feel that way. Set your paragraph aside for a day. Then reread it in order to identify the specific factors that caused satisfaction.

2. Ask at least three people who are employed in different organizations what caused them to feel especially good about their jobs.

3. Compare your satisfying factors with those of other people you interviewed. Are they similar to what you expected?

4. Finally, compare your lists with the factors identified by Herzberg. Why are there commonalities among the factors?

Skills Application 5-3: Job Diagnostic Survey

Hackman and Oldham developed a self-report instrument for managers to use in diagnosing their work environment. The first step in calculating the "motivating potential score" (MPS) of your job is to complete the following questionnaire.

Instructions:

1. Use the scales below to indicate whether each statement is an accurate or inadequate description of your present or most recent job. After completing the instrument, use the scoring key to compute a total score for each of the core job characteristics.

5 = Very descriptive   2 = Mostly nondescription
4 = Mostly descriptive   1 = Very nondescriptive
3 = Somewhat descriptive

_____ 1. I have almost complete responsibility for deciding how and when the work is to be done.

_____ 2. I have a chance to do a number of different tasks, using a wide variety of different skills and talents.

_____ 3. I do a complete task from start to finish. The results of my efforts are clearly visible and identifiable.

_____ 4. What I do affects the well-being of other people in very important ways.

_____ 5. My manager provides me with constant feedback about how I am doing.

_____ 6. The work itself provides me with information about how well I am doing.

_____ 7. I make insignificant contributions to the final product or service.

_____ 8. I get to use a number of complex skills on this job.

_____ 9. I have very little freedom in deciding how the work is to be done.

_____ 10. Just doing the work provides me with opportunities to figure out how well I am doing.

_____ 11. The job is quite simple and repetitive.

_____ 12. My supervisors or co-workers rarely give me feedback on how well I am doing the job.

_____ 13. What I do is of little consequence to anyone else.

_____ 14. My job involves doing a number of different tasks.

_____ 15. Supervisors let us know how well they think we are doing.

_____ 16. My job is arranged so that I do not have a chance to do an entire piece of work from beginning to end.

_____ 17. My job does not allow me an opportunity to use discretion or participate in decision making.

_____ 18. The demands of my job are highly routine and predictable.

_____ 19. My job provides few clues about whether I'm performing adequately.

_____ 20. My job is not very important to the company's survival.

_____ 21. My job gives me considerable freedom in doing the work.

_____ 22. My job provides me with the chance to finish completely any work I start.

_____ 23. Many people are affected by the job I do.

2. Scoring Key:

Skill variety (SV) (items # 2, 8, 11*, 14, 18*) = _____ /5 = _____

Task identity (TI) (items # 3, 7*, 16*, 22) = _____ /4 = _____

Task significance (TS) (items # 4, 13*, 20*, 23) = _____ /4 = _____

Autonomy (AU) (items # 1, 9*, 17*, 21) = _____ /4 = _____

Feedback (FB) (items # 5, 6, 10, 12*, 15, 19*) = _____ /6 = _____

(*Note*: For the items with asterisks, subtract your score from 6.)

Total the numbers for each characteristic and divide by the number of items to get an average score.

3. Now you are ready to calculate the MPS by using the following formula:

$$\text{Motivating Potential Score (MPS)} = \frac{\text{SV+TI+TS}}{3} \times \text{AU} \times \text{FB}$$

MPS scores range from 1 to 125.

4. You can compare your job characteristics with those of a fellow classmate or with norms that your instructor has. Is the MPS of your job high, average, or low?

5. What could be done to increase the motivating potential of your job?

Source: J. Richard Hackman and Greg R. Oldham, *Work Redesign* (Figure 4.6 and Appendix A), © 1980 by Addison-Wesley Publishing Company, Inc. Reprinted by permission of the publisher.

ENDNOTES

1. Many companies rely in part on personality assessment programs to evaluate employees. One of the more widely recognized approaches to the identification of individual differences is the Myers-Briggs Type Indicators. If your college has available the Myers-Briggs test, use it to identify your basic personality type. You can also use it to identify those personality types that do not complement your style.

2. Margaret Hennig and Anne Jardim, *The Managerial Woman* (New York: Anchor Press/Doubleday, 1977), p. 82.

3. See Abraham H. Maslow, *Motivation and Personality* (2d ed.; New York: Harper & Row Publishers, 1970), Chapter 4.

4.   Gilbert Fuchsberg, "Why Shake-ups Work for Some," *The Wall Street Journal* (October 1, 1993), pp. B1, B4.

5.   The complete dual factor theory is well explained in Frederick Herzberg, Bernard Mausner, and Barbara Bloch Snyderman, *The Motivation to Work* (2d ed.; New York: John Wiley & Sons, 1967); and in Herzberg's classic article, "One More Time: How Do You Motivate Your Employees?" *Harvard Business Review* (Volume 46, January–February 1968), pp. 53–62.

6.   For a discussion of expectancy theory, see Victor H. Vroom, *Work and Motivation* (New York: John Wiley & Sons, 1964); and Terence R. Mitchell, "Expectancy Models of Job Satisfaction, Occupational Preference and Effort: A Theoretical, Methodological, and Empirical Appraisal," *Psychological Bulletin* (Volume 81, 1974), pp. 1053–1077.

7.   Douglas McGregor, *The Human Side of Enterprise* (New York: McGraw-Hill, 1960), pp. 33–43 and 45–57.

8.   Robert R. Blake and Jane S. Mouton, *The Managerial Grid III* (Houston: Gulf Publishing Company, 1985), p. 13 and pp. 95–96; and Blake and Anne Adams McCanse, *Leadership Dilemmas—Grid Solutions* (Houston: Gulf Publishing Company, 1991).

9.   Fred E. Fiedler, *A Theory of Leadership Effectiveness* (New York: McGraw-Hill, 1967).

10.   See Fred E. Fiedler and Martin M. Chemers, *Improving Leadership Effectiveness: The Leader Match Concepts* (rev. ed.; New York: John Wiley & Sons, 1976), pp. 134–137; and Arthur G. Jago, "Leadership: Perspectives in Theory and Research," *Management Science* (Volume 28, 1982), p. 324.

11.   See Paul Hersey and Kenneth H. Blanchard, *Management of Organizational Behavior: Utilizing Human Resources* (5th ed.; Englewood Cliffs, N.J.: Prentice-Hall, 1988). Situational Leadership is a registered trademark of Leadership Studies, Inc. Also see Paul Hersey, *The Situational Leader—The Other 59 Minutes*; *Lead Instrument Self/Other*, a diagnostic instrument to evaluate an individual's leadership style. (Available from Pfeiffer and Company, 8517 Production Avenue, San Diego, CA 92121-2280.)

12.   For additional information and discussion on the contingency theory, see Fred E. Fiedler, "The Contingency Model and the Dynamics of the Leadership Process," *Advances in Experimental Social Psychology* (Volume 11, New York: Academic Press, 1978); James M. Kouzes and Barry Z. Posner, *The Leadership Challenge: How to Get Extraordinary Things Done in Organizations* (San Francisco: Jossey-Bass, 1990); and David A. Nadler and Michael L. Tushman, "Beyond the Charismatic Leader: Leadership and Organizational Change," *California Management Review* (Winter 1990), pp. 7–97.

13.   J. Richard Hackman, Greg R. Oldham, Robert Janson, and Kenneth Purdy, "A New Strategy for Job Enrichment," *California Management Review* (Summer 1975), pp. 51–71; J. R. Hackman and G. R. Oldham, "Development of the Job Diagnostic Survey," *Journal of Applied Psychology* (Volume 60, 1975), pp. 159–170; J. R. Hackman and G. R. Oldham, *Work Redesign* (Reading, MA: Addison-Wesley, 1980); and Carol T. Kulik, Greg R. Oldham, and Paul H. Langner, "Measurement of Job Characteristics: Comparison of the Original and the Revised Job Diagnostic Survey," *Journal of Applied Psychology* (August 1988), pp. 462–466.

14.   Ibid., p. 58.

15.   Ibid.

16.   According to 1992 data from the Employee Involvement Association, the average American employee submitted .17 suggestions per year and about one-third were adopted. The projected net savings of each adopted suggestion was $7,102. In comparing the U.S. and Japanese suggestion systems, it was found that the average Japanese employee submitted 32 suggestions per year, 87 percent were adopted, and the net savings was only $129 per adopted suggestion. See Michael A. Verespej, "Suggestion Systems Gain New Lustre," *Industry Week* (Volume 24, November 16, 1992), pp. 11–18. Several techniques outlined in this and the previous chapter can be adopted to increase employee involvement.

17.   Richard E. Kopelman, "Job Redesign and Productivity: A Review of the Evidence," *National Productivity Review* (Summer 1985), p. 239.

18.   Jac Fitz-enz, "Getting and Keeping Good Employees," *Personnel* (Volume 67, August 1990), p. 28.

19.   Lee M. Ozley and Judith S. Ball, "Quality of Worklife: Initiating Successful Efforts in Labor-Management Organizations," *Personnel Administrator* (May 1982), p. 27.

CASE 1-1
The Socializing Supervisor

Tiffany Miles recently was promoted to the supervisory position in the word processing department of a savings and loan association. She had been chosen for this position by the operations manager, Roy Callahan, who felt that Miles was the ideal candidate for the supervisory position. Miles had been hired five years previously as a word processor, and she had accrued more seniority than any other employee in the department. Her job ratings had been superior, and she seemed to be well liked by her colleagues and others who knew her.

When Callahan told Miles that she was to become supervisor of the word processing department, she asked him how she should handle the problem that her former fellow employees now would be her subordinates. Callahan told her not to be concerned about this and that her former associates would soon accept the transition. Callahan also told Miles that the company would send her to a supervisory management training program sponsored by a local financial services association just as soon as time became available for her to be sent to the program.

After several months, however, Callahan was getting the impression that Miles was not making the adjustment to her new position. Callahan particularly was concerned that he had observed Miles socializing with her employees during lunch breaks, coffee breaks, car pools, and the like. Callahan had received reports that Miles often socialized with several of her employees after work, including going on double-dates and parties arranged by these employees.

Furthermore, Callahan had received a number of reports from supervisors of other departments that the word processing services were not being performed as efficiently as they should be. Several supervisors in the company told Callahan that the word processing department employees spent too much time away from their work in exceeding breaks, lunch periods, and the like. One supervisor even told Callahan, "Since Miles became supervisor of word processing, there is little discipline in the department, and it's just a big social group that reluctantly does a little work."

Callahan realized that Miles had not made a good adjustment to supervising employees in her department. He wondered how much of this was attributable to her lack of experience as a supervisor and worried that her former colleagues might be taking advantage of her. At the same time, Callahan was concerned that Miles perhaps did not have the desire to disassociate herself from socializing and being a "buddy" to her employees. Callahan wondered what his next step should be.

Questions for Discussion

1. Evaluate the decision to promote Tiffany Miles to supervisor. Discuss the problems inherent in promoting anyone to supervisor over his or her former fellow employees.

2. Besides sending Miles to a supervisory training program, what other actions could Callahan and Miles have taken to prepare Miles for the transition to the supervisory role?

3. Why is it dangerous for a supervisor to socialize with direct-reporting employees? Why does this leave a supervisor open to criticism, as exemplified in this case?

4. At the end of the case, what should Roy Callahan do? Consider alternatives that may be open.

CASE 1-2
Long Hours for Supervisors

All supervisors of the Westside Manufacturing Company were employed with the understanding that they were expected to do everything within their capabilities to achieve the goals of the company and to get production out regardless of the hours they had to work. Supervisors were paid on a straight weekly salary basis. In addition, a certain percentage of the net profits was set aside for these supervisors each year and distributed among them as bonuses. For a number of years, these bonuses typically had amounted to several thousand dollars per supervisor. However, the amount of the bonuses had decreased in the last two years because of a general economic downturn. Expectations for the current year were not good, since the company was just about breaking even. The major reason for this was the depressed state of the economy, not a lack of employee productivity.

During the fall of the current year, the company received an unusually large number of orders. The workforce put in one hour of overtime daily and worked on Saturdays, but even this did not alleviate the need for more output. The manufacturing manager informed the supervisors that the plant would have to work seven days a week. Supervisors, in turn, were to inform the employees that this seven-day schedule would be necessary for the next month.

The workers were delighted, since this meant double pay for Sunday work; therefore, all of them reported for work. However, five of the twenty supervisors did not show up on the first Sunday. In each case they telephoned to explain their absence with various excuses. On the next Sunday seven supervisors were absent, although all the workers were on the job. The plant manager wondered what should be done about the supervisors' absences.

Questions for Discussion

1. Was the bonus system for the supervisors an aid or a deterrent to motivating them? Discuss.

2. Should supervisors be expected to work overtime and weekends without any direct additional compensation for their efforts? Discuss.

3. What should the plant manager do? Consider various alternatives open at this point.

CASE 1-3
Supervisory Humor

Don Wilmes, supervisor of customer service at Software-n-More, was articulate and possessed a dry sense of humor. He could be counted on for occasional practical jokes, and he was not discriminating in his selection of targets.

Software-n-More was a major computer software, supplies, and services firm. The company had recently experienced some tough financial times. As a result, there had been layoffs of employees, several supervisors, and one middle-level manager. This restructuring had resulted in a consolidation of positions. The surviving supervisors were assigned additional employees and duties. Virtually everyone felt stressed from seeing colleagues depart and having more to do in the same amount of time.

Wilmes decided that he would write a humorous news item to try to boost morale. He wrote and posted on several employee bulletin boards a one-page memorandum titled "The Chopping Block." A few excerpts follow:

Question: Rich, what is your reaction to the loss of your beloved supervisor, Karen Kates?

Response: Ding Dong, the Witch is Gone!!

Question: Jackie, how do you like taking on the responsibilities of the parts department while continuing to supervise the testing lab?

Response: My boss, Dave Kohenski, gave me a half-hour pep talk, and I was up to speed and on top of things at the end of the morning.

Question: Employees, how do you feel about our fearless leader's new motto, "Do More with Less!"?

Response: We feel that our president, Bob Swan, can teach us the true meaning of this motto, since he has lived it since birth.

Wilmes also printed copies of this memorandum and put it on virtually everyone's desk. One copy somehow made it to the executive suite. It was the talk of the company, and everyone was laughing—that is, everyone but the company president, Bob Swan.

Swan contacted Jean Mane, director of human resources, and asked her to arrange a meeting with Don Wilmes and his boss, Bernie Collins. Swan told Mane that he was deeply concerned over the offensive remarks in the bulletin. He stressed that this type of so-called humor was not acceptable. If carried to extremes, it could result in lawsuits by individuals who felt they were being ridiculed or defamed.

Later that day Don Wilmes was summoned to Jean Mane's office. Bernie Collins already was present when Wilmes arrived. Mane said, "Don, your behavior was unprofessional and inappropriate." He replied, "It was just a joke. Company management needs to lighten up. Everyone is so uptight here that my little memo will be forgotten quickly." Mane replied, "Don, this is serious. You didn't exercise good supervisory judgment. Other supervisors and employees have been fired for less than this." However, Bernie Collins told Jean Mane that if Wilmes was disciplined, it would alienate all of the other supervisors. He felt that the humor was "a bit sarcastic, but everyone is saying the same things in private."

When the meeting ended, Jean Manes pondered what her recommendation to Bob Swan should be.

Questions for Discussion

1.   Was Don Wilmes's memorandum just a bit of humor to improve morale, or was it a serious breach of a supervisor's responsibilities? Discuss.
2.   Evaluate the general positions as stated by each individual in this case. Which of these do you find the most and which the least credible?
3.   If you were Jean Manes, what would you recommend, and why?

CASE 1-4
Romance on the Assembly Line

Louise Nance had been working on the assembly line of the Jackson Manufacturing Company for about six months. During recent weeks, her supervisor, Ben Miller, noticed that her production had gone down to such an extent that she could not keep up with the pace, and she had caused serious delays. When Miller called this to her attention, Nance told him about the difficulties she was having at home. Her husband had recently left her without any explanation. Miller replied that her personal affairs were of no interest to him and that he was concerned only with her work. He warned her that unless her production improved she would be separated from the company.

A few days thereafter, Ben Miller was promoted to a higher-level management position. His place was filled by Jack Armstrong, who had recently joined the company. Armstrong immediately took a liking to Louise Nance and started dating her. Although she told him about her marital difficulties, he kept seeing her. When she remarked to him one day that her car needed some repairs, he offered to see whether he could fix it for her.

On the following Saturday, Nance's estranged husband appeared and found Armstrong repairing her car, which was parked on the street in front of her apartment. The two men got into a fight on the street, and police were called to separate them. The local newspapers carried a short report about the incident, mentioning the fact that Nance and Armstrong were employed at the Jackson Manufacturing Company.

A few days later, Jack Armstrong was called into the office of Kay McCaslin, the human resources director, who had read the newspaper reports. McCaslin advised Armstrong to stop seeing Louise Nance or he might be fired. McCaslin reminded Armstrong that informal company policy discouraged close fraternization between supervisors and employees, since this tended to weaken a supervisor's authority in dealing with employees. Moreover, publicity of this sort would undoubtedly hurt the company's image in the community. Armstrong replied that this was none of the company's business and that he could spend his time away from the plant any way he chose. He stated that a threat of discharge was totally improper, since his private life was his own and not subject to company regulations. Furthermore, Nance's work record had improved under his supervision, and it was now about the same as the records of most of the other people on the line. Armstrong left McCaslin's office with the comment that he would continue to date Louise Nance, since they were very much in love.

Kay McCaslin wondered whether she should drop the matter or discuss it with higher-level management—including Ben Miller, who now was Jack Armstrong's superior.

Questions for Discussion

1. Is the informal company policy that discourages close fraternization between supervisors and employees sound? Why or why not?

2. What alternatives are open to Kay McCaslin, the human resources director? What should she do?

3. Should Jack Armstrong's own supervisor, Ben Miller, be called into the situation?

4. If you were Jack Armstrong, what would you do?

5. If you were Louise Nance, what would you do?

CASE 1-5
Should the Supervisor Have Authorized Overtime?

The supervisor of the shipping department of the Zeltins Corporation, Tina Leeming, had been given strict instructions that all permissions for overtime had to come from her boss, the plant manager. In previous years the department supervisors had possessed the authority to have employees work overtime at time-and-a-half rates whenever they considered it absolutely necessary. The supervisors generally had not taken advantage of this privilege. However, when a recent fiscal report showed a decline in profits and a substantial increase in labor costs, the company president issued directives stating that all overtime had to be approved by the plant manager. For certain other activities, the president's permission was needed.

Leeming was now experiencing an increased workload. Due to employee absences, the shipping department was late in sending out a number of important orders. In fact, she knew that these orders might be canceled by the customers if they were not shipped before the week was over. Since Leeming was convinced that overtime work would help alleviate this situation, she tried to contact the plant manager. However, the plant manager was out of town at a convention and could not be reached. Leeming also had heard that some time ago a similar problem had occurred in the maintenance department and that the supervisor in charge had authorized overtime without the necessary permission of the plant manager. Although the maintenance department supervisor claimed that waiting for the plant manager's return the next day would have made the repair job more difficult and costly, he was severely disciplined for his unauthorized action.

Tina Leeming did not know what to do. If she authorized overtime, she would step beyond her area of authority. If she did not, some of the orders would not be shipped in time and would probably be canceled. Leeming thought about contacting the president of the company, but the president also was out of town. So Leeming decided to be on the safe side and did not ask her employees to work overtime. Most of the shipments, therefore, did not leave on time. Eventually, as she had feared, several major orders were canceled by unhappy customers. She wondered what she should do if this situation occurred again.

Questions for Discussion

1. Do you agree with Tina Leeming's decision not to work overtime under the circumstances of the case? Why or why not?

2. Why do both top-level managers and the company supervisors share in the blame for Leeming's decision dilemma?

3. What should Leeming do? Should she let the situation ride, or should she try to have the directives of the plant manager and president changed?

4. How can such a situation be prevented in the future?

CASE 1-6
The Troubled Technician

As part of its main office, Centaur Electric Company had a development engineering department. This department's work consisted of control and revision of old products and design of new products.

The chief development engineer and head of the department was Vincent Gabris. Assigned to Gabris were three development engineers and their technicians. In general, the development engineers did all the creative and design engineering work. The technicians worked closely with the engineers in mechanical and electrical testing, physical layouts, equipment and product plans, and on various other tasks as assigned.

The engineers scheduled the work of the technicians and were responsible for their training and performance. The engineers, however, did not determine the technicians' rate of pay. Development engineers were salaried, while technicians were paid hourly wages. In scheduling the workload of a technician, an engineer was responsible for the number of hours per day that the technician would work. However, Vincent Gabris often assigned projects to technicians; he was supposed to notify the development engineers when a technician was assigned to a different project or job.

The educational level of the engineers and the technicians differed by an average of about four years. Typically, development engineers had graduate degrees; none of the technicians had more than one year of college.

John Turner, a technician, had been working at Centaur for two years. He had no previous experience in this type of position. Turner had attended a local school of engineering for two semesters, dropped out, and gone to work as a factory laborer. On the basis of high scores on the firm's mechanical aptitude and intelligence tests, Turner was hired by Centaur for a technician's job. His training at Centaur was internal and informal. Turner, age 28, was married and had two children, and his wife was expecting another. Barbara Kurton, an engineer, was Turner's current supervisor. Kurton considered Turner to be conscientious, task oriented, and a perfectionist in his work. She also believed that he tried to learn from his work experiences.

However, in recent months Kurton had detected a serious drop-off in Turner's output. He seemed to wander about the work area, doing little and complaining that he had too many bosses. It had been a particularly trying month, with considerable overtime work, so Kurton thought little about it. But when the problem persisted the next month, Kurton started to investigate. She talked with Turner and learned that he felt that too many people were making too many demands on him—often all at the same time. He said that he had tried to please everyone but that there wasn't enough time to work for all. This frustration was the cause of his lowered output. Kurton immediately set to work to alleviate the demands on Turner by asking everyone to channel all work requests for him through her. This, she felt, would give Turner the impression, at least, that he had a lighter workload, because she could assign priorities to the work given. It also could actually stabilize Turner's workload and ease the tension.

After this system was put into effect, Turner's workload did level out considerably, but his output nevertheless dwindled steadily. It eventually reached the point where Kurton felt that discharging Turner was justified. Hoping to avert this, she had several long talks with him. From these talks came the revelation that Turner was thousands of dollars in short-term debt. This included what he owed on his mobile home and car. A problem with his car had triggered the conflict. When Turner had tried to sell the car, he found that he owed more on it than it was worth. With a new baby on the way, he was continually worried about the future and his money troubles. Kurton also learned that Turner had little understanding of financial matters or budgets.

Kurton pondered what she could do to help motivate this employee to return to his previous productive self or whether she should simply solve the problem by discharging him. She also wondered whether she should take the problem to her own boss, Vincent Gabris.

Questions for Discussion

1. Should a supervisor become involved in the personal problems of an employee?

2. Should Barbara Kurton try to work with John Turner to straighten out his personal life? Is Turner worth extra effort on the part of his supervisor?

3. Should Turner be discharged because his work has not been up to standard? How would such a discharge affect the other employees in the department? How would the other workers be affected if Kurton kept Turner despite his low productivity?

4. If you were Barbara Kurton, what would you do?

CASE 1-7
The Picnic Conversation

The annual picnic of the Mendoza Company was well attended as usual. It was a well-planned, day-long family affair for all the employees of the firm, giving them an opportunity to have an informal get-together. At the picnic, Charlene Knox, one of the supervisors, had a long chat with her boss, Jim Cross, the general manager. They spoke about many things, including some work problems. Cross put great emphasis on the need for cutting costs and a general "belt-tightening." He told Knox that he had already received a number of written suggestions and plans from some of the other supervisors. He highly praised their efforts as appropriate and helpful.

Three weeks after the picnic, Charlene Knox received a memo from her boss asking her why her "report in reference to cost-cutting had not yet arrived." At first she wondered what Jim Cross was referring to, and then she remembered their talk at the picnic. She realized that was the only time Cross had discussed with her the need to cut costs! Knox pondered what her response should be.

Questions for Discussion

1.   Is it appropriate for a supervisor to give a directive to a subordinate in a social, off-the-job setting? Why or why not?
2.   Was Charlene Knox at fault for not having understood what her boss told her at the picnic conversation? Was Jim Cross at fault? Were both managers at fault?
3.   What should Knox do?

CASE 1-8
Jerry Jones Talks About Owning and Managing "America's Team"

Asked to name the owners of most National Football League franchises, it is likely that even the most ardent fans could name only a few. Most, however, would know Jerral W. (Jerry) Jones, owner of the Dallas Cowboys. Jones bought the struggling Dallas Cowboy franchise from Bum Bright in 1989, immediately fired Tom Landry, the only coach the team had ever had, and hired his college teammate Jimmy Johnson, then coach of the University of Miami football team. He proceeded to trade away the team's star running back, Herschel Walker, and watched his team go through the year with just one win. At the end of the season most Cowboy fans were calling for Jones's head. However, there is nothing like success to turn doubters into followers, and the team of Jones and Johnson have provided just that, including Super Bowl Championships in 1993 and 1994.

Jones's management style is an interesting one in a profession that is characterized by big money and huge egos. Yet he says that "a (football) team is like any business. Nothing stands still. You shouldn't ever wait to make changes." Although he was once nicknamed "Jethro" by fans and media critics who likened him to the NFL equivalent of a Beverly Hillbilly, he made wholesale changes upon his arrival, totally disregarding the NFL's time-honored "how-to" manual, and with seeming disregard for his critics. Unlike most other NFL owners, Jones is also the team's general manager and is personally involved in all decisions except those made on the field. He evaluates talent, negotiates contracts, and makes all personnel decisions. He does, however, involve Coach Johnson in personnel decisions.

If the proof of a manager's success is measured by the bottom line, Jones has to be labeled extremely successful. After he bought the ailing Cowboys for $140 million, they lost $6 million in their first year, generating total revenues of $36.2 million. According to Jones, the 1992 total revenues exceeded $65 million. In just three years the Cowboys had attracted 20,000 new season-ticket holders with an average age of 30. When Jones bought the team, the average age of all season-ticket holders was 55. But Jones's success with the Cowboys has not been easy.

Although the fans are back as avidly as ever, there has been discontent among the players as well as the head coach.

At the beginning of the 1993 season, star running back Emmitt Smith was without a contract and announced that he would sit out a season rather than accept less than what he thought the self-proclaimed "best player at his position" should be paid. After the Cowboys started the season with a 1–2 won/lost record, including a defeat at the hands of the archrival Washington Redskins, Jones and Smith came to terms on a four-year contract that made him the highest paid runner in football history. The impact on the team was immediate, and the season was salvaged. Jones evidently decided not to have a repeat of the lesson learned with Smith, and he signed the team's quarterback, Troy Aikman, to a multiyear, multi-million-dollar contract before the end of the 1993 season.

Johnson's discontent with Jones is not about money; it involves two super-egos in conflict with each other. Johnson is a compulsive winner and accepts nothing less than perfection. He has been known to become violent, even after a team victory, if he felt that the team did not play up to its potential. A case in point is the 1992 27–14 win over the Chicago Bears. With the Cowboys leading 27–0 going into the fourth quarter, Jones marched onto the sidelines with Prince Bandar bin Sultan, Saudi Arabia's ambassador to the United States and one of the world's biggest Cowboy fans. Walking along the sidelines congratulating the players, Jones had invaded Johnson's territory, and Johnson became outraged. Watching backup running back Curvin Richards fumble twice, one of which was returned for a touchdown, then seeing Jones and Bandar celebrating on the sidelines was more than Johnson could stand. His postgame rage began with a tongue-lashing of the team for its sloppy play in the fourth quarter; continued with a short, yet testy press conference; and ended in Jones's office, where assistant coach Larry Lacewell intervened as Jones and Johnson literally engaged in a nose-to-nose debate. Johnson, often labeled as a long-time college friend and roommate of Jones, has on more than one occasion publicly denounced his boss and said that the stories of their friendship are greatly overstated. In fact, Johnson often sees Jones as a frustrated "wanna-be coach" who has no experience in an area where he (Johnson) has paid his dues. He also complains that Jones has cut scouting budgets and manpower unrealistically and that the coaching staff is underpaid.

Jones replies that one of the principles he learned while earning his masters degree in business is tolerance of ambiguity. "What this means is that some people work better when they don't know what's going to happen, and some don't work well unless they know exactly what's going to happen. I've known Jimmy Johnson for a long, long time, and he's fine as long as he knows exactly what the rules are. You tell him he has 60 players or he has 30 players and that's it; he'll accept it and go on. You tell him it's fourth-and-a-foot with the score 10–7 in the seventh game of the season, and he'll take a calculated risk and go for it. But he and I operate in different worlds. He has his thumb on everybody in his world. He completely controls it. I can't control my world. I make deals that often require a high tolerance for ambiguity, and I've been making them since I was 16 years old." Jones, like Johnson, seems to understand the world in which he lives and works, and especially the personalities of those who share that world with him and upon whom he must depend for success.

References

Graham Button, "The Cowboys Bounce Back," *Forbes* (October 12, 1992), p. 14.
Peter King, "Back in the Saddle," *Sports Illustrated* (September 27, 1993), pp. 30–31.
Patricia Sellers, "Turnaround Tips from Jerry Jones," *Fortune* (May 8, 1993), p. 16.
"Such Good Friends," *Sports Illustrated* (July 12, 1993), pp. 66–76, (excerpted from *The Boys* by Skip Bayless).

Questions for Discussion

1.   What do you think the supervisory challenge is for a person who has been as successful as Jerry Jones?

2.   Although Jones had never been involved with professional football and had no experience coaching or managing a football team at any level, when he bought the Dallas Cowboys he named himself the general manager. Why do you think he has been successful in this role, even though he does not have the technical experience that most general managers of professional sports teams possess?

3.   To be successful, supervisors must be able to communicate effectively with their subordinates. Do you think Jerry Jones is a good communicator? Why or why not? Give specific examples to explain your answer.

4.   For many of the members of the Dallas Cowboys, including Jerry Jones, money is not a motivator for wanting to win. Discuss the motivational factors that spur successful athletes as well as other successful people to continue to want to excel.

Epilogue

On March 29, 1994, at a major news conference, Jerry Jones and Jimmy Johnson announced a "mutual decision" that Johnson no longer would coach the Dallas Cowboys. This announcement followed several weeks of public bickering between them as reported in the media. Since Johnson had a number of years left on his coaching contract, speculation was that the buyout of his contract was in the several-million-dollar range.

Both Jones and Johnson indicated that some might describe their association as having been "rocky." However, they claimed that what they had accomplished in their five years together was a mutual, joint achievement, and that something about their relationship had worked. Despite their well-publicized disagreements, Johnson stated that "99 percent of every decision was made working together." Jones similarly commented, "We never had a disagreement when it came to football." Thus ended what Jerry Jones categorized as "one of the greatest stories ever told in sports."

Source: From an article in the *St. Louis Post Dispatch* (March 30, 1994), pp. 1D and 6D; based upon an article written by Tom Cowlishaw of the *Dallas Morning News* and other wire services.

PART 2

PLANNING

6

The Supervisor and Decision Making

LEARNING OBJECTIVES

After studying this chapter, you will be able to:

1 Explain the importance of decision-making skills in supervisory management.

2 Describe the types of decisions made in organizations.

3 Describe and apply the basic steps of the decision-making process.

4 Explain why a supervisor should not make hasty decisions.

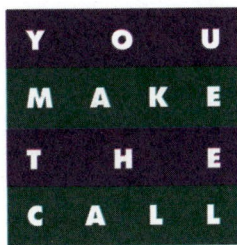

Y O U
M A K E
T H E
C A L L

You are Carol Reeves, supervisor of the Kincaid Pharmacy's State Street store. (Please refer back to the "You Make the Call" section in Chapter 2 for review of events leading up to the current situation.)

About one week after Kelly called in sick, David, a co-worker, asks to speak with you.

David: Carol, I need to speak with you. There is something that has really been bothering me. Remember last week when Kelly called in sick and you couldn't find anyone to cover for her?

You: Yes, I do, David. I really appreciated your help that day, and I think I expressed that appreciation to you, Sarah, and Annie. We wouldn't have made it without your giving 150 percent.

David: Well, I really hate to bring this up. As you know, I wasn't feeling particularly well either, but I showed up for work. Often, I have to miss some of my children's school activities, but I always work when I'm scheduled. Kelly never goes the extra mile. She always seems to take advantage of you and us.

You: What, specifically, do you mean?

David: I'm not the only one concerned about this. We're all working so hard, and it doesn't seem fair. Kelly's pay is almost the same as mine. What really burns me up is her lying. I overheard her talking to her babysitter. She wasn't really sick that day; it was her kid who was sick.

Kelly doesn't seem to think she has to obey the rules or do her fair share. I know one other time she called in sick when she really wasn't. I don't want to work with her, because if she lies about being sick, then what else will she do that is dishonest?

You: David, I can understand your anger over this, and I appreciate your sharing this with me. Now, to be fair to you and all the other employees, let me investigate this. I would appreciate it if you would keep this conversation between us until I can look into the matter fully.

You check with Kelly, and she admits lying about her illness. She is in clear violation of company policy. According to the Kincaid Pharmacy Employee Handbook, dishonesty may be cause for discharge. Firing someone is something you have never done. As a matter of fact, you have never had to deal with a problem of this nature. On the other hand, if David suspects that Kelly has been lying about some things, what do the other employees think? If you do not discipline Kelly, how will they feel? What should you do? **YOU MAKE THE CALL.**

THE IMPORTANCE OF DECISION-MAKING SKILLS TO SUPERVISORS

1 Explain the importance of decision-making skills in supervisory management.

Decision making
Making a choice between two or more alternatives.

All human activities involve decision making. Everyone has problems at home, at work, and in social groups for which decisions must be made. Thus, decision making is a normal human requirement that begins in childhood and continues throughout life.

Decision making can be defined as the process of choosing a course of action from among alternatives. Many of the problems that confront supervisors in their daily activities are recurring and familiar; for these problems, most supervisors have developed routine answers. But when supervisors are confronted with new and unfamiliar problems, many find it difficult to decide on a course of action.

Managers and supervisors at all levels are constantly required to find solutions to problems that are caused by changing situations and unusual circumstances. Regardless of their managerial level, they should use a similar, logical, and systematic process of decision making. Although decisions made at the executive level usually are of a wider scope and magnitude than decisions made at the supervisory level, the decision-making process fundamentally should be the same throughout the entire management hierarchy.

Of course, once a decision has been made, effective action is necessary. A good decision that no one implements is of little value. However, in this chapter we are not concerned with the problem of getting effective action. Here, we discuss the process that should lead to the best decision or solution before action is taken.

A decision maker often is depicted as an executive bent over some papers, with

FIGURE 6-1
To make a decision, you must first know the result you want to accomplish.

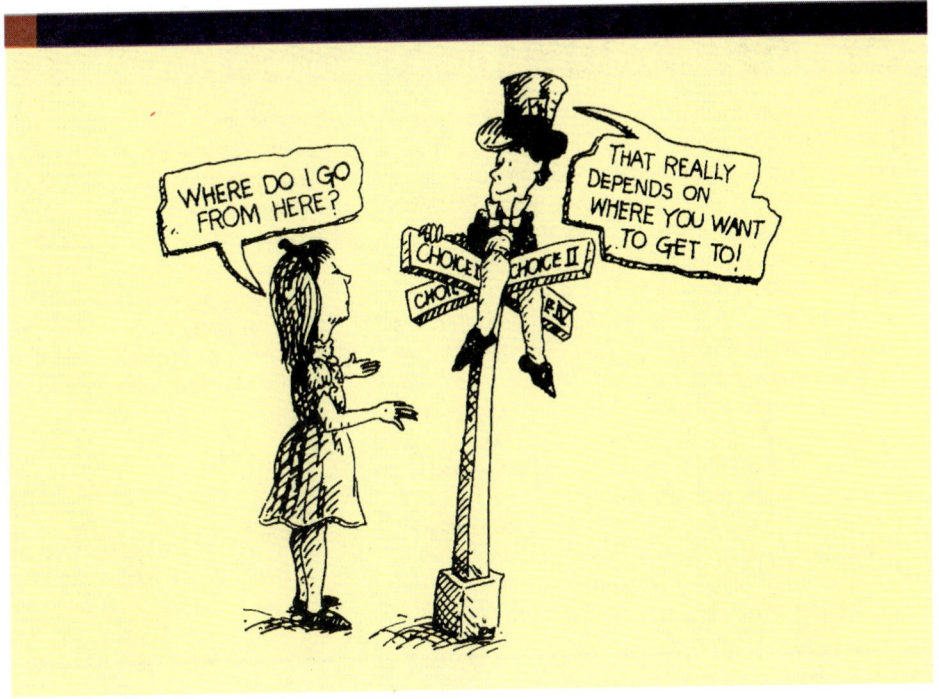

pen in hand, contemplating whether or not to sign on the dotted line. Or the image may be that of a manager in a meeting, raising an arm to vote a certain way. Both of these images have one thing in common: They portray decision makers as people at the moment of choice, ready to choose an alternative that leads them from the crossroads. Often, the supervisor, as seen in Figure 6-1, wants to know which direction to go, but she has not given a lot of thought to the end result. The supervisor needs to understand that information gathering, analysis, and other processes precede the final moment of selecting one alternative over the others.

Decision making is an important skill for supervisors. It is a skill that can be developed—just as the skills involved in playing golf are developed—by learning the steps, practicing, and exerting effort. By doing this, supervisors can learn how to make more thoughtful decisions and improve the quality of their decisions.

At the same time, supervisors should ensure that their employees learn to make their own decisions more effectively. A supervisor cannot make all the decisions necessary to run a department. Many daily decisions in a department are made by the employees who do the work. For example, what materials to use, how a job is to be done, when it is to be done, and how to achieve coordination with other departments are decisions that employees often have to make without their supervisor. As evidenced by this chapter's "Contemporary Issue" box, companies are giving employees a more active role in decision making. Therefore, training subor-

CONTEMPORARY ISSUE
Workplace of the Future or Erosion of Managerial Prerogatives?

AT&T and the Communications Workers of America (CWA) announced an agreement that may signal a new era in labor-management relations. To help protect employees' jobs, the company agreed to allow workers to have a voice in corporate decision making, implementing new technology, and job creation policies. In exchange, the union agreed to increase productivity and allow wage rates to be based partially on skills, performance, and unit profits.

This new arrangement does not flow from a new-found love between management and unions. It is forged out of necessity—perhaps even issues of survival—due in part to technological change and increased global competition.

According to Jeff Miller, a CWA spokesperson, "We got into it as a result of our rocky relationship. AT&T realized they had a morale problem and that poor labor relations is not a good thing." Burke

Stinson, an AT&T spokesperson, while disputing some points, essentially agreed and noted that limited partnerships with the CWA date back nearly 12 years.[1]

Increasingly, organizations are finding that employee participation in the decision-making process is the foundation of total quality management. The shift in thinking by the top-level managers of AT&T represents an effort to improve the company's performance. However, as organizations encourage employee participation in decision-making, two important issues arise:

1. A decision made today must be maintained tomorrow and, possibly, modified. Who has that responsibility?
2. As employees make more and more decisions, what will be the role of the first-line supervisor?

[1]Source: Adapted in part from *Labor Trends* (Volume 49, Number 13, April 3, 1993) pp. 1–2.

dinates in the process of making decisions should be a high priority for all supervisors.

TYPES OF DECISIONS

2 Describe the types of decisions made in organizations.

Programmed decisions
Solutions to repetitive and routine problems provided by existing policies, procedures, rules, etc.

Nonprogrammed decisions
Solutions to unique problems that require judgment, intuition, and creativity.

A prominent management decision-making theorist once suggested that all decisions can be classified as either programmed or nonprogrammed, with many decisions falling somewhere between these two extremes.[1]

Programmed decisions are solutions to problems that are repetitive, well structured, and routine. The term "programmed" is descriptive in the same sense that it is used in computer programming; there is a specific procedure, or program, that can be applied to the problem at hand. Many daily problems that confront supervisors are not difficult to solve, because a more or less "pat" answer is available. These problems usually are routine or repetitive, and fixed answers, methods, procedures, rules, and the like exist. Supervisors can delegate these kinds of decisions to subordinates and be confident that the decisions will be made in an acceptable and timely manner.

Nonprogrammed decisions occur when supervisors are confronted with new or unusual problems for which they must use their intelligent, adaptive problem-solving behavior. Such problems may be rare, unstructured, or unique, and they are typically one-time occurrences. There are no pat answers or guidelines for decision making in these situations. Nonprogrammed decisions tend to be more important, demanding, and strategic than programmed decisions. In nonprogrammed decision making, supervisors are called on to use good judgment, intuition, and creativity in attempting to solve problems. In these situations they should apply a decision-making process by which they can approach the problems in a consistent and logical, but adaptable, manner.[2] The remainder of this chapter will refer primarily to non-programmed decision making.

THE DECISION-MAKING PROCESS

3 Describe and apply the basic steps of the decision-making process.

Decision-making process
A systematic, step-by-step process to aid in choosing the best alternative.

In making nonprogrammed managerial decisions, supervisors should follow the steps of the **decision-making process** (see Figure 6-2). First, they must define the problem. Second, they must analyze the problem using available information. Third, they need to establish decision criteria—factors that will be used to evaluate the alternatives. Fourth, after thorough analysis, they should develop alternative solutions. Only after these steps have been taken should a supervisor evaluate the alternatives and select the solution that appears to be the best or most feasible under the circumstances. The concluding step in this process is follow-up and appraisal of the consequences of the decision.

Step One: Define the Problem

Before seeking answers, the supervisor first should identify what the real problem is. Nothing is as useless as the right answer to the wrong question. Defining the problem is not an easy task. What appears to be the problem might be merely a symptom that shows on the surface. It usually is necessary to delve deeper to locate the real problem and define it.

Consider the following scenario. Tom Engle, an office supervisor, believes that a problem of conflicting personalities exists within the department. Two employees, Diana and Stuart, are continually bickering and cannot get along together. Because of this lack of cooperation, the job is not being done in a timely manner. Engle needs to develop a clear, accurate problem statement. The problem statement should be brief, specific, and easily understood by others. A good problem statement should address the following key questions:

- What is the problem?
- How do you know there is a problem?
- Where has the problem occurred?
- When has it occurred?
- Who is involved in or affected by the problem?

Expressing a problem through a problem statement can help the supervisor understand it. A careful review of answers to the key questions can lead to a problem

FIGURE 6-2
The effective
supervisor follows the
steps of the decision-
making process.

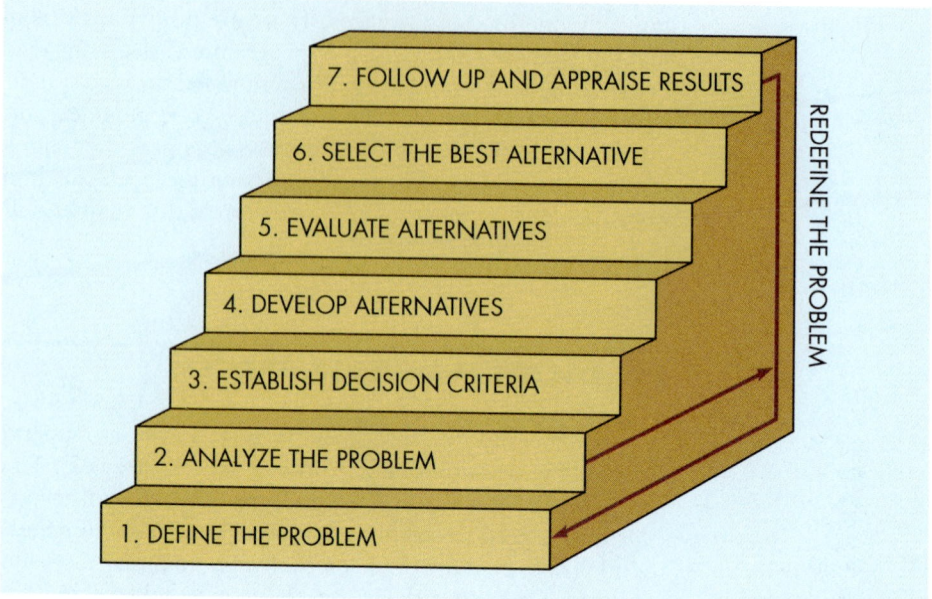

FIGURE 6-2
The effective
supervisor follows the
steps of the decision-
making process.

statement shown as Figure 6-3, which reveals that the major problem is that the work is not getting done in a timely manner. When checking into this situation, the supervisor should focus on why the work is not getting done.

Defining a problem is, in most circumstances, a time-consuming task, but it is time well spent. A supervisor should not go any further in the decision-making process until the problems relevant to the situation have been specifically determined. Remember, a problem exists when there is a difference between the way things are and the way they should be. The effective supervisor will use problem solving not only to take corrective action but also as a means to make improvements in the organization.

Step Two: Analyze the Problem: Gather Facts and Information

After the problem—not just the symptoms—has been defined, the next step is to analyze the problem. The supervisor begins by assembling facts and other pertinent information. This is sometimes viewed as being the first step in decision making, but until the real problem has been defined, the supervisor does not know what information is needed. Only after gaining a clear understanding of the problem can the supervisor decide how important certain data are and what additional information to seek.

Tom Engle, the office supervisor in the earlier scenario, needs to find out why the work is not getting done. When he gathers information, he finds out that he never clearly outlined the expectations for each employee—where their duties begin

FIGURE 6-3
Example of a Problem
Statement

> The bickering between Diana and Stuart detracts from the completion of work assignments. Last Monday and Tuesday, neither of them completed assigned customer callbacks. Customers, other department employees, and the shipping department are all affected.

and where they end. What appeared on the surface to be a problem of personality conflict was actually a problem caused by the supervisor. The chances are good that once the activities and responsibilities of the two employees are clarified the friction will end. Engle needs to monitor the situation closely to ensure that the work is being completed on time.

Being only human, a supervisor will find that personal opinion is likely to creep in to decision making. This is particularly true when employees are involved in the problem. For example, if a problem involves an employee who performs well, the supervisor may be inclined to show this person greater consideration than would be accorded a poor performer. Therefore, the supervisor should try to be as objective as possible in gathering and examining information.

Sometimes the supervisor does not know how far to go in searching for additional facts. A good practice is to observe reasonable time and cost limitations. This means gathering all the information that can be obtained without undue delay in time and without excessive costs.

In the process of analysis the supervisor should try to think of intangible factors that play a significant role. Some intangible factors are reputation, morale, discipline, and personal biases. It is difficult to be specific about these factors; nevertheless, they should be considered in the analysis of a problem. As a general rule, written and objective information is more reliable than opinions and hearsay.

Step Three: Establish Decision Criteria

Decision criteria
Standards to use in
evaluating alternatives.

Decision criteria are standards to use in evaluating alternatives. These standards are statements of what the supervisor wants to accomplish with the decision. These criteria can also be used to determine how well the implementation phase of the process is going—that is, whether the decision is doing what it was intended to do. To illustrate, suppose that Tom Engle's initial actions do not remedy the situation. It will be appropriate to establish decision criteria. Figure 6-4 provides examples of the decision criteria that can be used for evaluating other courses of action.

Once the decision criteria are established, the supervisor must determine which criteria are absolutely necessary and their order of priority. Because it is likely that no solution alternative will meet all the criteria, the supervisor needs to know which criteria are most important so that alternatives can be judged by how many of the important criteria they meet. The supervisor may want to consult with upper-level managers, peers, or employees to assist in prioritizing the criteria.

FIGURE 6-4
Examples of Decision
Criteria

The solution

- should result in the work assignments being completed on time.
- should incur no financial cost to implement.
- must not impede quality of service to the customer.
- should not put either Diana's or Stuart's job in jeopardy.
- should allow us to differentiate our product or service in the marketplace.
- should not have a negative impact upon other employees.
- must alleviate the problem within one week.

Step Four: Develop Alternatives

After the supervisor has defined and analyzed the problem and established decision criteria, the next step is to develop various alternative solutions. The supervisor should consider as many possible solutions as can reasonably be developed. By formulating many alternatives, the supervisor is less apt to overlook the best course of action. Stating this another way, a decision will only be as good as the best alternative that has been developed.

Almost all problem situations have a number of alternatives, not just "either this or that." The choices may not always be obvious, but supervisors must search for them. If they do not do this, they are likely to fall into the "either/or" kind of thinking. It is not enough for supervisors just to decide from among alternatives that employees have suggested, because there may be other alternatives to consider. Thus, supervisors must stretch their minds to develop additional alternatives, even in the most discouraging situations. None of the alternatives might be desirable, but at least the supervisor can choose one that is least undesirable.

Suppose that an office supervisor has been ordered to make a 20 percent reduction in employment because the firm is experiencing financial problems. After careful study, the supervisor develops the following feasible alternatives:

1. Lay off employees who have the least seniority, regardless of their jobs or performance, until the overall 20 percent reduction is reached.
2. Lay off employees who have the lowest performance ratings until the overall 20 percent reduction is reached.
3. Analyze department duties and decide which jobs are essential. Keep the employees who are best qualified to perform those jobs.
4. Without laying off anyone, develop a schedule of reduced work hours for every employee that would be equivalent to a 20 percent reduction.
5. Develop proactive alternatives to increase the firm's revenues so that no employee has to be laid off.

While alternative 5 is most attractive, it is not realistic, given the current economic situation. Although none of the other alternatives may be an ideal solution

Brainstorming can be an effective way to find creative solutions to problems facing the organization.

to this unpleasant problem, at least the office supervisor has considered several alternatives before making a decision. Unfortunately, these are "no-win" situations, but the illustration does portray the realities of organizational life.

Brainstorming and Creative Problem Solving. When enough time is available, a supervisor should get together with a group of other supervisors or employees to brainstorm solution alternatives to a perplexing problem. **Brainstorming** is a free flow of ideas within a group, with judgment suspended, in order to come up with as many alternatives as possible. Using this technique, the supervisor presents the problem and the participants offer as many alternative solutions as they can develop in the time available. It is understood that any idea is acceptable at this point—even those that may at first appear to be wild or unusual. Evaluation of ideas is suspended so that participants can give free rein to their creativity.

Brainstorming
A free flow of ideas within a group, while suspending judgment, aimed at developing many alternative solutions to a problem.

Alex Osborn, an authority on creativity and the brainstorming approach, has suggested the following four major guidelines for effective brainstorming:

1. Defer all judgment of ideas. During the brainstorming period, allow no criticism by anyone in the group. It is natural for people to suppress new ideas both consciously and unconsciously, and this tendency must be avoided. Even if an idea seems impractical and useless at first, it should not be rejected by quick initial judgments, because such rejection could inhibit the free flow of more ideas.

2. Seek quantity of ideas. Idea fluency is the key to creative problem solving, and fluency means quantity. The premise here is that the greater the number of ideas, the greater the likelihood that some of them will be viable solutions.
3. Encourage "free wheeling." Being creative calls for a free-flowing mental process in which all ideas, no matter how extreme, are welcome. Even the wildest idea may, on further analysis, have a germ of usefulness.
4. "Hitchhike" on existing ideas. Combining, adding to, and rearranging ideas often can produce new approaches that are superior to the original ideas. When creative thought processes slow or stop, review some of the ideas already produced and attempt to hitchhike on them with additions or revisions.[3]

Creative approaches and brainstorming meetings are particularly adaptable to nonprogrammed decisions, especially if the problem is new, important, or strategic in dimension. Even the supervisor who takes time to mentally brainstorm a problem alone is likely to develop more alternatives for solving the problem than one who does not brainstorm.

Ethical Considerations. Both in the development and the evaluation of alternatives, a supervisor should consider only those that are lawful and acceptable within the organization's ethical guidelines. In recent years, many firms have become concerned that their managers, supervisors, and employees make ethical decisions, because they recognize that, in the long term, good ethics is good business.[4] Consequently, many firms have developed handbooks, policies, and official statements that specify the ethical standards and practices expected. If a supervisor believes that a particular alternative is not lawful or might not be acceptable within the firm's ethical policies, the supervisor should consult with his or her manager— or with a staff specialist who is knowledgeable in the area—for guidance in how to proceed.

Step Five: Evaluate the Alternatives

The ultimate purpose of decision making is to choose the specific course of action that will provide the greatest number of wanted and the smallest number of unwanted consequences. After developing alternatives, supervisors can mentally test each of them by imagining that each has already been put into effect. They should try to foresee the probable desirable and undesirable consequences of each alternative. By thinking the alternatives through and appraising their consequences, supervisors will be in a position to compare the desirability of the various choices.

The easiest way to begin is to eliminate alternatives that do not meet the supervisor's previously established necessary decision criteria. After doing this, the supervisor should evaluate how many of the most important criteria each remaining alternative meets. The final choice is the one that meets the most criteria at the highest priority levels. More often than not, there is no clear choice.

Nonprogrammed decisions usually require the decision maker to choose a course of action without complete information about the situation. Because of this uncertainty, the chosen alternative may not yield the intended results. Thus, there is risk involved. Some supervisors will consider the degree of risk involved in each course of action. There is no such thing as a riskless decision; one alternative may simply involve less risk than the others.[5]

The issue of time may make one alternative preferable, particularly if there is a difference between how much time is available and how much time is required to carry out one alternative in comparison with another. The supervisor should also consider the facilities, records, tools, and other resources that are available. It is also critically important to judge different alternatives in terms of economy of effort and resources. In other words, which action will give the greatest benefits and results for the least cost and effort?

In cases in which one alternative clearly appears to provide a greater number of desirable consequences and fewer unwanted consequences than any other alternative, the decision is fairly easy. However, the best alternative is not always so obvious. At times, two or more alternatives may seem equally desirable. Here the choice may become a matter of personal preference. It is also possible that the supervisor may feel that no single alternative is significantly stronger than any other. In this case, it might be possible to combine the positive aspects of the better alternatives into a composite solution.

Sometimes none of the alternatives is satisfactory; all of them have too many undesirable effects, or none will bring about the desired results. In such a case, the supervisor should begin to think of new alternative solutions or perhaps even start all over again by attempting to redefine the problem.

Moreover, a situation might arise in which the undesirable consequences of all the alternatives appear to be so overwhelmingly unfavorable that the supervisor feels that the best available solution is to take no action at all. However, this may be self-deceiving, since taking no action will not solve the problem. Taking no action is as much a decision as is taking a specific action, even though the supervisor may believe that an unpleasant choice has been avoided. The supervisor should visualize the consequences that are likely to result from taking no action. Only if the consequences of taking no action are the most desirable should it be selected as the appropriate course.

Step Six: Select the Best Alternative

Optimizing
Selecting the best alternative.

Satisficing
Selecting the alternative that minimally meets the decision criteria.

Selecting the alternative that seems to be the best is known as **optimizing.** However, sometimes the supervisor makes a **satisficing** decision—selecting an alternative that minimally meets the decision criteria. Nobel laureate Herbert Simon likened the difference to the comparison between finding a needle in a haystack (satisficing) and finding the biggest, sharpest needle in the haystack (optimizing).[6] Nevertheless, after developing and evaluating alternatives, the supervisor needs to make a choice.

Among the most prominent bases for choosing the best alternative are experience, intuition, advice from others, experimentation, and statistical and quantitative decision making. Regardless of the process used, a supervisor will rarely make a decision that is equally pleasing to everyone (see Figure 6-5).

FIGURE 6-5
A manager rarely
makes a decision that
pleases everyone!

Experience. In making a selection from among various alternatives, the supervisor should be guided by experience. Chances are that certain situations will recur, and the old saying that "experience is the best teacher" does apply to a certain extent. A supervisor often can decide wisely based on personal experience or the experience of some other manager. Knowledge gained from experience is a helpful guide, and its importance should not be underestimated. On the other hand, it is dangerous to follow experience blindly.

When looking to experience as a basis for choosing among alternatives, the supervisor should examine the situation and the conditions that prevailed at the time of the earlier decision. It may be that conditions still are practically identical to those that prevailed on the previous occasion and that the decision should be similar to the one made then. More often than not, however, conditions have changed considerably and the underlying assumptions are no longer the same. Therefore, the new decision probably should not be identical to the earlier one.

Experience can be helpful in the event that the supervisor is called on to substantiate his or her reasons for making a particular decision. In part this may be a defensive approach, but there is no excuse for following experience in and of itself. Experience must always be viewed with the future in mind. The underlying circumstances of the past, the present, and the future must be considered realistically if experience is to be of assistance in selecting from among alternatives.

Intuition. Supervisors admit that at times they base their decisions on intuition. Some supervisors even appear to have an unusual ability to solve problems satisfactorily by subjective means.[7] However, a deeper search usually will disclose that the so-called "intuition" on which the supervisor appeared to have based a decision was really experience or knowledge that had been stored in the supervisor's memory. By recalling similar situations that occurred in the past, supervisors may better reach a decision even though they label it as "having a hunch."

Intuition may be particularly helpful in situations in which other alternatives have been tried previously with poor results. If the risks are not too great, a supervisor may choose a new alternative because of an intuitive feeling that a fresh approach might bring positive results. Even if the hunch does not work out well, the supervisor has tried something different. The supervisor will remember this as part of his or her experience and can draw upon it in reaching future decisions.

Advice from Others. Although a supervisor cannot shift personal responsibility for making decisions in the department, the burden of decision making often can be eased by seeking the advice of others. The ideas and suggestions of employees, other supervisors, staff experts, technical authorities, and the supervisor's own manager can be of great help in weighing facts and information. Seeking advice does not mean avoiding a decision, since the supervisor still must decide whether or not to accept the advice of others.

Many believe that two heads are better than one and that input from others will improve the decision process. The following four guidelines can help the supervisor decide whether groups should be included in the decision-making process:

1. If additional information would increase the quality of the decision, involve those who can provide that information.
2. If acceptance of the decision is critical, involve those whose acceptance is important.
3. If people's skills can be developed through participation, involve those who need the development opportunity.
4. If the situation is not life threatening and does not require immediate action, involve others in the process.[8]

Generally, the varied perspectives and experiences of others will add to the decision-making process.

Experimentation. In the scientific world, where many conclusions are based on tests in laboratories, experimentation is essential and accepted. In supervision, however, experimentation to see what happens often is too costly in terms of people, time, and money. Nevertheless, there are some instances in which a limited amount of testing and experimenting is advisable. For example, a supervisor may find it worthwhile to try several different locations for a new copy machine in the department to see which location employees prefer and which is most convenient for the work flow. There are also some instances in which a certain amount of testing is advisable in order to provide employees with an opportunity to try out new ideas or approaches, perhaps of their own design. While experimentation may be valid from a motivational standpoint, it can be a slow and relatively expensive method of reaching a decision.

Statistical and Quantitative Decision Making. Numerous techniques and models of quantitative decision making have received much attention in management literature and practice. Included among these techniques are linear programming, operations research, and statistical probability and simulation models. These tend to be sophisticated mathematical approaches, often used in connection with computers.[9] They require the decision maker to quantify most of the information that is relevant to a particular decision. For many supervisors, these quantitative decision-making techniques are rather remote. Yet, many large firms have management decision support systems that assist supervisors in making nonprogrammed decisions. One desirable feature of quantitative decision making is the ability of the user to perform "what if" scenarios—the simulation of a business situation over and over again using different data in each case for selected decision areas.

With the increasing use of desktop computers and networks, many firms are able to develop programs and information storage and retrieval systems that supervisors can use relatively easily for certain types of decisions, especially when historical and statistical databases are involved. For some types of problems, supervisors may be able to seek the help of mathematicians, engineers, statisticians, systems analysts, and computer specialists who can bring their tools to bear on relevant problems. This can be an involved and costly procedure, however, and decisions like those facing Carol Reeves in the "You Make the Call" section generally cannot be made from statistical or quantitative models.

Step Seven: Follow Up and Appraise the Results

After a decision has been made, specific actions are necessary to carry it out. Follow-up and appraisal of the outcome of a decision are actually part of the process of decision making.

Follow-up and appraisal of a decision can take many forms, depending on the nature of the decision, timing, costs, standards expected, personnel, and other factors. For example, a minor production scheduling decision could easily be evaluated on the basis of a short written report or perhaps even by the supervisor's observation or a discussion with employees. However, a major decision involving the installation of complex new equipment will require close and time-consuming follow-up by the supervisor, technical employees, and higher-level managers. This type of decision usually requires the supervisor to prepare numerous, detailed written reports of equipment performance under varying conditions, which are compared closely with plans or expected standards for the equipment.

The important point to recognize is that the task of decision making is not complete without some form of follow-up and appraisal of the actions taken. If the supervisor has established decision criteria or specific objectives that the decision should accomplish, it will be easier to evaluate the effects of the decision. If the consequences have turned out well, the supervisor can feel reasonably confident that the decision was sound.

If the follow-up and appraisal indicate that something has gone wrong or that the results have not been as anticipated, then the supervisor's decision-making process must begin all over again. This may even mean going back over each of the various steps of the decision-making process in detail. The supervisor's definition and analysis of the problem and the development of alternatives may have to be completely revised in view of new circumstances surrounding the problem. In other words, when follow-up and appraisal indicate that the problem has not been resolved satisfactorily, the supervisor will find it advisable to treat the situation as a brand new problem and go through the decision-making process from a completely fresh perspective.

TIME IMPACTS THE DECISION-MAKING PROCESS

4 Explain why a supervisor should not make hasty decisions.

Supervisors may feel they do not have time to go through the decision-making process outlined here. More often than not, a manager, a co-worker, or an employee comes up to the supervisor, says "Here's the problem," and looks to the supervisor for an immediate answer. However, supervisors cannot afford to make a decision without considering the steps outlined here. A problem rarely needs an immediate answer.

Often when an employee brings up a problem, the supervisor asks questions such as the following:

1. How extensive is the problem? Does it need an immediate response?
2. Who else is affected by the problem? Should they be involved in this discussion?
3. Have you (the employee) thought through the problem, and do you have an idea of what the end result should be?
4. What do you recommend? Why?

This supervisor is using a form of participative supervision, and, more important, is developing the employee's skills. The supervisor will then think through the problem, apply the decision-making steps, and make a decision.

Many supervisors get themselves into trouble by making hasty decisions without following the steps outlined in the decision-making process. A word of advice: If, during any stage of the process, supervisors tell other people that they will get back to them, the supervisors should state a specific time. If supervisors fail to make a decision by the stated time or give feedback to the other people, they run the risk of losing trust.

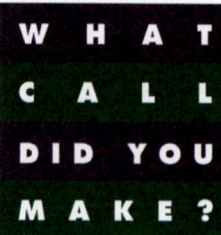

You must make a decision. This situation illustrates the point that supervisors rarely can make decisions that please everyone. Naturally, you feel for Kelly. You know that if she loses her job at Kincaid Pharmacy she will not find another easily.

Did you write a problem statement? A problem statement that addresses what, how, where, when, and who can help you better understand the problem. Your problem statement might resemble the following:

David reported that Kelly lied about being sick last week. Kelly verified that she had lied because she had used all her vacation days and the company's policy did not allow time off with pay for the illness of a family member. During Kelly's absence, David, Sarah, and Annie worked exceptionally hard to provide the level of service our customers expect.

Deficiencies in the store's policy put the employee in a situation in which lying about her health was the only option she saw available to her. You cannot condone lying, but to prevent the situation from recurring you should try to get the policy changed or modified.

On the other hand, Kelly was well informed by the employee handbook. She knew the rules. She lied about the situation. You need to ask what other information is needed to help make the decision. Who has the information? Your immediate supervisor should be able to help you with precedent (what has been done in similar cases). A review of Kelly's performance appraisals, work reports, and time logs may also reveal helpful information.

What decision criteria should you use to evaluate the alternatives? The morale of all employees, a sense of fairness (equity), long-term consequences of your actions on Kelly, and the fact that your actions will set a precedent, are some of the possible considerations. In addition, you may want to ask yourself whether Kelly is worth saving as an employee. If the answer is yes, then one of your criteria would be that Kelly remains as an employee. Finally, you must remember that Kelly's actions are a breach of ethical conduct. Most supervisors are going to consider this situation in the context of their own experience, company policies, Kelly's personal situation, her work history, and so forth, and they may arrive at a variety of conclusions. Some would contend that the employee should be fired after one lie. Others might recommend that Kelly be formally reprimanded and suspended for a short time without pay. Still others might contend that she also owes the company for the day's pay she got under false pretenses.

The ultimate evaluation of this situation is not based on the decision you make, but on the thought processes you used to get you there. Because we have not discussed various disciplinary procedures, we do not expect you to be able to decide whether to reprimand, suspend, or discharge Kelly. But you should be able to analyze the situation, define the problem, determine what information to collect, and establish decision criteria. Whatever call you made should be based on touching each of the steps in the decision-making process.

SUMMARY

1 Explain the importance of decision-making skills in supervisory management.

All supervisory activities involve decision making. Supervisors must find solutions for problems that are caused by changing situations and unusual circumstances. Decision making based on careful study of information and analysis of the various courses of action available is still the most generally approved avenue of selection from among alternatives. Decision making is a choice between two or more alternatives, and the decisions made by supervisors significantly affect departmental results

Decision making is a skill that can be learned. Organizations are giving employees a more active role in decision making today than they did in the past. A decision made today may set precedent for tomorrow.

2 Describe the types of decisions made in organizations.

Supervisors confront many decision situations, which can vary from the programmed type at one extreme to the nonprogrammed type at the other. Decisions for routine, repetitive-type problems are usually made easier by the use of policies, procedures, standard practices, and the like. However, nonprogrammable decisions are usually one-time, unusual, or unique problems that require sound judgment and systematic thinking.

3 Describe and apply the basic steps of the decision-making process.

Better decisions are more likely to occur when supervisors follow the steps of the decision-making process. These are as follows:

a.   Define the problem.
b.   Gather facts and information and analyze the problem.
c.   Establish decision criteria.
d.   Develop a sufficient number of alternatives.
e.   Evaluate alternatives by using the decision criteria or by thinking of them as if they had already been placed into action and considering their consequences.
f.   Select the alternative that has the greatest number of wanted and least number of unwanted consequences.
g.   Implement, follow up, and appraise the results.

If may be necessary to take corrective action if the decision is not achieving the desired objective.

The supervisor should develop a problem statement that answers the questions of what, how, where, when, and who. Proper problem definition clarifies the difference between the way things are and the way they should be.

After defining the problem, the supervisor must gather information. Decision criteria, or standards of what the supervisor wants to accomplish with the decision, should be specified. In developing alternatives, supervisors can use brainstorming and creative thinking techniques.

Only alternatives that are lawful and ethical within the organization's guidelines should be considered. In the process of evaluation and choice, a supervisor can be aided by personal experience, intuition, advice from others, experimentation, and quantitative methods.

Once the decision has been made, specific actions are necessary to carry it out. Follow-up and appraisal are essential.

4 Explain why a supervisor should not make hasty decisions.

Supervisors run the risk of getting themselves into trouble unless they follow the steps of the decision-making process. The process is time consuming. Most problems do not require an immediate answer. It is often valuable to allow subordinates to assist in the decision-making process. They may see the problem from a different perspective and they may have information that bears on the problem.

KEY TERMS

Decision making (page 146)   Decision criteria (page 151)
Programmed decisions (page 148)   Brainstorming (page 153)
Nonprogrammed decisions (page 148)   Optimizing (page 155)
Decision-making process (page 149)   Satisficing (page 155) .

QUESTIONS FOR DISCUSSION

1.   Think of a major decision you have made in your life. For example, why did you decide to go to college? Why did you decide upon the college you selected? Why did you decide upon your major? Explain how you applied the decision-making steps identified in this chapter. What factors should you have considered to make a better choice?

2.   Define decision making. Does the decision-making process vary depending on where a manager or supervisor is located in the managerial hierarchy? Discuss.

3.   Distinguish between programmed and nonprogrammed types of decisions. Enhance your answer by identifying a significant decision and an insignificant decision for each type.

4.   Why should supervisors write a problem statement to assist them in defining the problem?

5.   Review the steps of the decision-making process in their proper sequence. What pitfalls should the supervisor avoid at each step?

6.   Identify the major elements of the brainstorming approach.

7.   Describe a situation in which you would prefer to solve the problem in a group rather than by yourself. Why? What are the advantages of each approach? The limitations?

8.   Define and discuss the factors that a supervisor should consider in developing and evaluating alternatives in the decision-making process. To what degree should ethical issues be a consideration?

9.   Discuss how a decision to take no action concerning a problem can be a valid approach, rather than an attempt to avoid an issue.

10.   When deciding on a course of action, do you tend to rely more on past experiences or on the need to be creative? Cite an illustration to support your answer.

SKILLS APPLICATIONS

Skills Application 6-1: Identifying Supervisory Problems

1.   Interview at least three people in supervisory positions. Ask them to identify (a) the major problem they have in doing their job and (b) the major problem facing their organization.

2. Compare the problems identified by the supervisors. Did the supervisors state the problems in a way that makes them understandable to others? How serious are the problems? Can the problems identified in skills application 1(a) be solved by the supervisors, or do they need the assistance of others to solve them?

3. In your opinion, would the supervisors be better off solving the problems themselves or eliciting the input of others? Why?

Skills Application 6-2: Mastering the Registration Process

The notion of continuous improvement assumes that every process can be improved. Think back to the registration process at your college. Were you able to complete the registration process with a minimum of effort, or was the process cumbersome and inefficient?

1. Break into groups of seven or more people. Each student should consider the registration process from one of the following perspectives:

    a. The registrar (responsibility for scheduling classes and rooms).

    b. The business office (responsibility for collecting fees).

    c. The dean of students.

    d. The president of the college.

    e. The bookstore manager.

    f. A faculty member (responsibility for teaching a variety of courses at various times).

    g. Student (one or more).

2. As a group, formulate a clear problem statement for the problem.

3. Make a list of the information you feel you will need in order to solve the problem. Where will you get the information?

4. List the decision criteria that any solution must meet.

5. Brainstorm alternative solutions.

6. Suppose the college president says that the registrar has the responsibility for making the final decision. If the registrar solves the problem from his or her own perspective, does that person run the risk of creating greater problems for others? Explain.

Skills Application 6-3: An Exercise in Brainstorming

A long-term customer tells you that your competitor can provide the same service that you offer but at a significantly lower price. The customer wants to know whether you can meet or beat the price. You have the authority to reduce prices, but not to the extent the customer implies. The competitor's price is less than your breakeven point. You promise to give the matter some thought, check with others, and get back with an answer tomorrow afternoon.

1. Working alone, take a few minutes to make a list of at least three reasons the customer may have for wanting a price reduction.

2. Get together with three other people and brainstorm as many options as you can, other than cutting price, that might meet the customer's needs.

3. Analyze the brainstorming activity. Did the process take more time than working alone? Did the process enable you to see a variety of options? Did the group generate several options that you would not have thought of?

4. What did you conclude from this exercise about the benefits and limitations of brainstorming?

ENDNOTES

1.   Nobel laureate Herbert A. Simon distinguished among the types of decisions. See *The New Science of Management Decision* (New York: Harper & Row, 1960), pp. 5–6.

2.   For a more thorough discussion of this approach, see David A. Cowan, "Developing a Classification Structure for

Organizational Problems: An Empirical Investigation," *Academy of Management Journal* (June 1990), pp. 366–390. See also Jack Falvey, "Making Great Managers," *Small Business Reports* (February 1990), pp. 15–18 for a discussion of slowing down the process to train managers to be better decision makers. Also, see Jan Hermanns and Katy Clawson, *Problem Solving Leader's Guide* (Del Mar, Calif.: McGraw-Hill Training Systems, 1986), a practical application guide for using a systematic problem-solving approach.

3.   For more information on brainstorming, see Alexander F. Osborn, *Applied Imagination* (3d ed.; New York: Charles Scribners Sons, 1979).

4.   See Raymond L. Hilgert, "What Ever Happened to Ethics in Business and Business Schools?" *The Diary of Alpha Kappa Psi* (Volume 79, Number 1, April 1989), pp. 4–7; Rushworth M. Kidder, "A Yardstick for Business Ethics," *The Christian Science Monitor* (February 26, 1990), p. 14; Alan Weiss, "Seven Reasons to Examine Workplace Ethics," *HR Magazine* (Volume 36, Number 3, March 1991), pp. 69, 71–72, 74; T. M. Jones, "Ethical Decision Making by Individuals in Organizations: An Issue-Contingent Model," *Academy of Management Review* (April 1991), pp. 366–395; or *Corporate Ethics: A Prime Business Asset,* a special report published by The Business Roundtable (New York, February 1988).

5.   Most theorists now see uncertainty as the reason why a decision is risky. See Ted G. Eschenbach and George A. Geistauts, "A Delphi Forecast for Alaska," *Interfaces* (November–December 1985), pp. 100–109.

6.   See J. G. March and H. A. Simon, *Organizations* (John Wiley & Sons, 1958), pp. 10–12.

7.   See Russ Holloman, "The Light and Dark Sides of Decision Making," *Supervisory Management* (December 1989), pp. 33–34.

8.   The guidelines were adapted from Robert Kreitner and Angelo Kinicki, *Organizational Behavior* (2d ed.; Homewood, Ill: Richard D. Irwin, 1992), pp. 567–568.

9.   For a general overview of several quantitative approaches to decision making, see William Newman, E. Kirby Warren, and Andrew McGill, *The Process of Management* (6th ed.; Englewood Cliffs, N.J.: Prentice-Hall, 1987), pp. 135–151; or Leslie Rue and Lloyd Byars, *Management: Theory and Application* (4th ed.; Homewood, Ill.: Richard D. Irwin, 1986), pp. 168–187 and 582–595.

7

Managerial

Planning

LEARNING OBJECTIVES

After studying this chapter, you will be able to:

1 Define planning and clarify why all management functions depend on planning.

2 Explain the concept of visioning and its relationship to strategic planning.

3 Describe the supervisor's role in planning.

4 Identify the benefits of planning.

5 Explain the role of planning in quality improvement.

6 Discuss the need for well-defined organizational goals and objectives, particularly as they relate to the supervisor.

7 Explain management by objectives and describe how it is applied.

8 Identify the major types of standing plans and explain how these are helpful in supervisory decision making.

9 Discuss the principal types of single-use plans in which supervisors play an important role.

10 Discuss just-in-time inventory control systems and scheduling and planning tools.

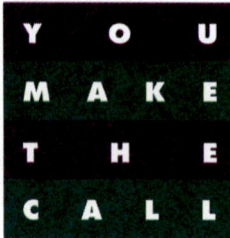

You are Shannon O'Neill, transportation supervisor for the Middletown School Corporation. Your basic responsibilities include hiring, training, and evaluating all employees in the department; scheduling bus utilization; purchasing all fuels and maintenance supplies; coordinating extracurricular activity transportation; and safely transporting 1,700 children to and from school each day. The school district covers over 400 square miles, and about half of the students walk to their neighborhood school.

You developed a computerized planning system to schedule transportation requirements and preventive maintenance. The Middletown School Corporation had substantially lower per-pupil transportation costs than other corporations and thus was able to use the savings to pro-

vide enrichment experiences for the district's children. You are frequently called upon to explain the benefits of your system to other school districts, and last year you were invited to address the School Administrators Association.

You are highly regarded as a supervisor. Employee turnover is minimal, and the list of people wanting to work for you is long. The employees meet each Thursday afternoon to review progress, identify potential problem areas, and make recommendations for improvement. Your department gets together informally once each month to celebrate accomplishments.

The foundation of your supervisory style was inherited from your father, whose favorite saying was "Plan your work, then work your plan!" Each evening before you leave work, you develop your "Plan for Tomorrow." You list all the things to be done the next day in order of priority. You list the time of day that each task should be done and who is responsible for its accomplishment. Your employees follow the same procedure. Each workday begins with an employee meeting to recap the accomplishments of the previous day, list expectations for the current day, and discuss problems and issues in common. The process has worked very well.

A new superintendent of schools arrived this fall and announced a program of continuous improvement. At the meeting this morning, all supervisors were strongly encouraged to question their current supervisory practices and find ways to improve them. Each supervisor is to develop a list of three strategies for improvement in his or her areas of responsibility and submit them within two weeks.

You believe that your style works very well and that your system for continuous improvement is well in place. How will you respond to the superintendent's request? **YOU MAKE THE CALL.**

MANAGEMENT FUNCTIONS BEGIN WITH PLANNING

1 Define planning and clarify why all management functions depend on planning.

Planning
Establishing objectives based on the current situation and forecasts of the future, and determining the actions needed to achieve the objectives.

There is some disagreement among management scholars and practitioners concerning the number and designation of managerial functions. However, there is general consensus that the first and probably most crucial managerial function is planning.

Planning means deciding in advance what is to be done in the future. It includes analyzing the situation, forecasting future events, establishing objectives, setting priorities, and deciding what actions are necessary to achieve those objectives. Planning logically precedes all other managerial functions, since every manager must project a framework and a course of action for the future before attempting to achieve desired results. For example, how could a supervisor organize the operations of a department without having a plan in mind? How could a supervisor effectively staff and lead employees without knowing which avenues to follow? How could a supervisor possibly control the activities of employees without having standards and objectives for comparison? Thus, all of the other managerial functions depend on planning.

Planning is a managerial function that every supervisor must perform every day. It should not be a process used only occasionally or when the supervisor is not too engrossed in daily chores. By planning, the supervisor realistically anticipates future problems and opportunities, analyzes them, anticipates the probable effects of various alternatives, and decides on the course of action that should lead to the most desirable results. Of course, plans alone do not bring about desired results. But without good planning, activities would become random, producing confusion and inefficiency.

VISIONING AND THE STRATEGIC-PLANNING PROCESS

2 Explain the
concept of visioning
and its relationship to
strategic planning.

Strategic planning
The process of making
decisions that will
enable an
organization to
achieve its long-term
objectives.

Turbulent and rapid changes in economic conditions and technology, coupled with increasing competition, have forced organizations to do a better job of planning. **Strategic planning** involves making decisions that will enable an organization to achieve its long-term objectives. Noted management scholar Peter Drucker says that every organization must think through its reason for being:

[Organizations must ask themselves] "What is our Business?" This leads to the setting of objectives, the development of strategies, and the making of today's decisions for tomorrow's results. This clearly must be done by a part of the organization that can see the entire business; that can balance objectives and the needs of today against the needs of tomorrow; and can allocate resources . . . to key results.[1]

In most organizations, top-level managers are responsible for the development and execution of the strategic plan. However, once the strategic goals and plans are identified, supervisors become the foundation of planning activities throughout the organization.[2] They plan their work unit activities toward achieving the organization's overall goals. A supervisor like Shannon O'Neill in the "You Make the Call" section will likely be involved in helping to develop the strategic plan for the school corporation—not in curriculum or other classroom matters, but in issues related directly to his department.

Many articles discussing the application of strategic planning principles to small business conclude that the lack of strategic-planning knowledge is a serious obstacle for many small-business owners and that the strategic-planning process in small firms is more informal. These same articles tout the benefits of strategic management in giving direction to the organization as a whole.[3] Regardless of the size of the organization, managers need to be involved more in strategy formulation, because their participation in the strategic-planning process is a key to gaining commitment for the chosen objectives and strategies.

Answering Drucker's question "What is our Business?" or "What is our mission?" is essential for effectively establishing objectives and formulating plans. Top-level management must answer this question and then articulate it throughout the organization. This point is well illustrated by Edward Thompson, who left Procter and Gamble to become president of Schneider Trucking Company:

We started the process with a rather structured approach. We picked a time period out three to four years to get us out of the influence of the pressures of the current state. We worked to make statements of what we would look like at that point— revenue levels, number of employees, equipment types, maintenance and support systems, technology and operating methods, desired customer base, and so on.

As we involved more people in the process the focus shifted and became more mature. For example, working through a lot of the human dimensions generated direction. We explored new ways to align and empower people. You know in service industries like ours over half our people touch the customer in some way each day. We really have some ideas on new ways to do the human side of trucking. The vision also grew as we pushed ourselves in areas like building in an ongoing change orientation and viewing ourselves as innovators in asset management. We kind of picture that this visioning will be an organic or ongoing part of our work. We are getting more and more of our people involved.[4]

Visioning is the process of developing a mental image of what the organization could become. For example, Disney's stated aim of "making people happy" has been critical to its success. It is not enough to articulate the vision to subordinates. The organization develops plans and aligns its structure accordingly to achieve its vision. Because the vision puts the day-to-day work activities in a new perspective, Disney employees see their jobs in relationship to the vision.

Visioning
Management's view of what the company is to become that sets the foundation for other activities.

Visioning answers a key question for every company, whether it be Disney, Schneider Trucking Company, or a local not-for-profit agency: What is it that distinguishes our organization from another? Father Theodore Hesburgh, former president of Notre Dame University, stated it well when he said, "The very essence of leadership is [that] you have to have vision. It's got to be a vision you articulated clearly and forcefully on every occasion. You can't blow an uncertain trumpet."[5] Says John F. (Jack) Welch, General Electric CEO, "Good business leaders create a vision, articulate the vision, passionately own the vision, and relentlessly drive it to completion."[6] This chapter's Contemporary Issue box illustrates the visioning process at one company.

Effective supervisors can use the process of visioning to shape their particular part of the organization. To illustrate, let us refer back to the "You Make the Call" section in the beginning of this chapter. The new superintendent of schools did not arrive in Middletown without giving much thought to the future. During the job interview, he or she was probably asked about past experiences and what could be done to revolutionize the school system. The new superintendent's ideas will be more welcome if Middletown has severe financial problems or is confronted with other operating challenges than if Middletown's school system is a model of excellence. In the latter case, ideas will face much opposition.

The superintendent probably created a mental image of what he or she expects the Middletown School Corporation to look like in the future. The superintendent's job is to see the school corporation not as it is, but as what it can become. The superintendent presented the concept of continuous improvement for each supervisor to identify with and to follow. Each supervisor was asked to develop three areas for improvement. Shannon O'Neill will have the opportunity to solicit ideas from his employees. Employee participation in the visioning process is crucial to future attainment of the vision.

ALL MANAGERIAL LEVELS PERFORM THE PLANNING FUNCTION

3 Describe the supervisor's role in planning.

Planning is the responsibility of every manager, whether chairperson of the board, president, division manager, or supervisor of a department. However, the magnitude of a manager's plans will depend on the level at which they are carried out. Planning at the top level is more far-reaching than it is at the supervisory level. The

CONTEMPORARY ISSUE
The Need for a Vision to Guide Planning

AlliedSignal was made up of the old Allied Chemical Company and parts of Bendix and Signal Companies. When chairman Lawrence A. Bossidy arrived, it had poor profit margins, too much debt, and negative cash flow. Bossidy says, "To inaugurate large-scale change, you may have to create a burning platform. You have to give people a reason to do something differently."[1] Organizational survival was the burning platform that stood as the foundation of the visioning process. Employees knew AlliedSignal would have to be successful to provide them with job security and growth opportunities.

According to chairman Bossidy, "We set about putting in a mechanism to focus on what AlliedSignal should be. We tried to analyze the business and the people leading it. We went into 1992 with three objectives: to make our numbers; to make Total Quality a reality, not just a slogan; and to make AlliedSignal a unified company."[2]

Part of AlliedSignal's plan to reach this vision is to have each employee, from janitor to chairman, attend a four-day training course where employees, organized in teams, analyze their business units, articulate their goals, and learn to resolve business problems.

Annual earnings growth of 13 to 17 percent is projected through 1995. Bossidy says, "The focus now is on ways to more quickly bring products to market and respond to customer orders, and to cut material costs." He emphasizes a "cultural change" moving the organization from being "internally focused" to "customer focused"; from being a "vertically organized" to a "horizontally organized" structure in which people with different duties work as a team; and from motivating employees to leading and motivating them.[3]

Sources: [1,2] Stratford Sherman, "A Master Class in Radical Change," *Fortune* (December 17, 1993), p. 84. [3]Amal Kumar Naj, "Allied Signal's Chairman Outlines Strategy for Growth," *The Wall Street Journal* (August 17, 1993), p. B4.

top-level executive is concerned with overall operations of the enterprise and long-range planning for new facilities and equipment, new products and services, new markets, and major investments. At the supervisory level, the scope is narrower and more detailed. The supervisor usually is concerned with day-to-day plans for accomplishing departmental tasks—for example, meeting production quotas for a particular day.

Although planning always involves looking to the future, an evaluation of what has happened in the past should be part of managerial planning. Every manager can learn to plan more effectively for the future by evaluating earlier plans and trying to benefit from past successes and failures.

In formulating plans, a supervisor may find that certain aspects of planning call for specialized help—for example, for implementing employment policies, computer and accounting procedures, or technical know-how. In such areas, the supervisor should consult with specialists within the organization to help carry out the required planning responsibilities. For example, a human resources staff specialist can offer useful advice concerning policies involving employees. A supervisor should utilize all of the available help within the organization to accomplish thorough and specific planning. This also means consulting with employees for their suggestions on how to proceed in certain situations. Employees like to be consulted, and their advice may help the supervisor develop day-to-day plans for running the department. In smaller firms, expertise may not be readily available, so the supervisor may want to draw upon personal contacts outside the firm. In the final analysis, however, it is each supervisor's personal responsibility to plan.

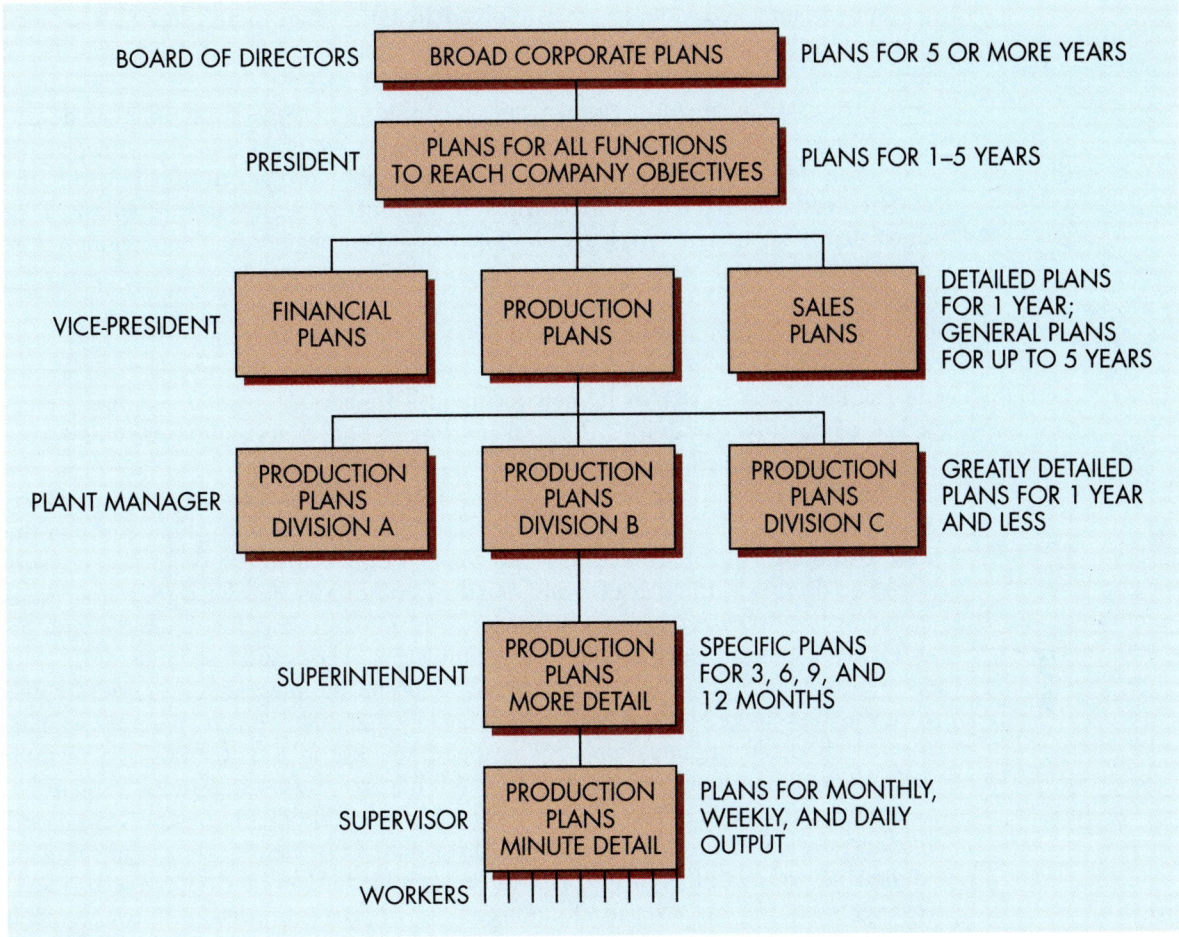

FIGURE 7-1
The Planning Flow

PLANNING PERIODS

For how long a period should a manager plan? Usually a distinction is made between long-range and short-range planning. The definitions of long-range and short-range planning will depend on the manager's level in the organizational hierarchy, the type of enterprise, and the kind of industry in which the organization is operating. Most managers define short-term planning as that which covers a period of less than one year. Long-term planning goes beyond a year and may involve a span of three, five, or ten years or even more. In some firms, planning for one to five years is known as intermediate planning. Figure 7-1 shows how the planning process might flow in a manufacturing firm from top-level management down through the supervisory level. Note how planning becomes more short range and detailed as it progresses down the organization chart.

Supervisors occasionally are involved in long-range planning. As the need arises, middle-level managers may discuss with supervisors the part they are to play in planning for the future. For example, a company may be considering a major restructuring, or an introduction of new technology may be contemplated due to competition and other developments. Supervisors might be asked to project the long-term trends of their particular activity, especially if it seems apparent that the activity will be affected by increasing mechanization, automation, robotics, or downsizing. Supervisors may also be asked for their suggestions about long-range plans, and they will have to stay informed and be ready to adapt as these plans are implemented.

Supervisors should also make longer-range plans. Long-range plans may indicate that (a) there is a need to reassign or retrain some employees; (b) people with new skills must be hired; or (c) new techniques are necessary due to changing market or competitive conditions. Thus, from time to time every supervisor will participate in long-range planning.

For the most part, however, supervisors give most of their attention to short-range planning. This means that a supervisor must take time to think through the nature and amount of work that is assigned to the department. Many supervisors prefer to do this at the end of a day or at the end of a week, when they can evaluate what has been accomplished in order to formulate plans for the immediate future. This is the very least amount of planning that every supervisor must do.

Short-range plans made by a supervisor should be integrated and coordinated with the long-range plans of higher-level management. Supervisors who are well informed about an organization's long-range plans are in a better position to integrate their short-range plans with the overall plans. All too often there is a gap between the knowledge of top-level managers and what middle- and supervisory-level managers are told about future plans. This often is justified by the claim that certain plans are confidential and cannot be divulged. However, effective top-level managers know that lower-level managers and supervisors need to know as much as possible about company plans in order to plan their groups' activities effectively.

Most of the time, a supervisor will plan for several months, one month, a week, or perhaps just one day or one shift. Very short-range planning is involved, for example, in scheduling a production line or scheduling departmental employees in a retail store. There are some activities for which the supervisor can plan for several months in advance, as, for example, in planning preventive maintenance.

Top-level, long-range plans should be communicated and fully explained to lower-level managers and supervisors as soon as possible so that they will be in a better position to formulate plans for their departments. By the same token, each supervisor should bear in mind that employees will be affected by the plans. Whenever possible, a supervisor should explain to employees in advance what is being planned for the department. The employees can contribute helpful ideas and begin preparing themselves for new skills they will need. At the very least, well-informed employees will appreciate the fact that they have not been kept uninformed or that they have not had to look to the grapevine for information about their future.

4 Identify the benefits of planning.

BETTER PLANNING MEANS BETTER RESOURCE UTILIZATION

Planning promotes efficiency and reduces waste and costs. Through thorough planning, haphazard approaches can be minimized and duplication avoided. The minimum time for completion of activities can be planned and scheduled, and facilities can be used to optimum advantage. Even in a small department or small firm, the total investment in physical and human resources may be substantial. Only by planning will the supervisor be able to employ resources, both human and physical, to their fullest potential.

PLANNING FOR QUALITY IMPROVEMENT

5 Explain the role of planning in quality improvement.

Total quality management
An organizational approach involving all employees in the continual improvement of goods and services.

Benchmarking
The process of identifying and improving upon the practices of the leaders.

The past decade has witnessed an emerging commitment to quality in successful firms. Many firms have turned to total quality management (TQM) and continuous improvement. In manufacturing firms, quality traditionally meant inspecting the product at the end of the production process. Today, the notion of **total quality management** means that the total organization is committed to quality—everyone is responsible for doing the job right the first time. TQM means planning for quality, preventing defects, correcting defects, and continuously building increased quality into goods and services as far as economically and competitively feasible.[7]

The increased emphasis on achieving higher product quality has led many firms to follow guidelines or criteria developed by others. The process of identifying and improving upon the best practices of the leaders is called **benchmarking.** Jack Welch, GE's CEO, says that a firm had better be as good as the best in the world. "If you can't meet a world standard of quality at the world's best price, you're not even in the game."[8] All of us have used benchmarking. When we evaluate the performance of our favorite sports team, we look to see how well it is doing in comparison with the team on top. We analyze the attributes of the players of the top team, the coaching styles, and so forth, and conclude that our team could be just as good—if not better—if the owners/managers would make the necessary changes and copy the successful practices of the leaders of the top team.

The essence of benchmarking is to be as good as or better than the best in the world. The steps in the benchmarking process are as follows:

1. Determine what to benchmark—quality, costs, customer service, employee development, compensation, or the like.
2. Identify comparable organizations both within the industry and outside.
3. Collect comparative performance data.
4. Identify performance gaps.
5. Determine the causes of the difference.
6. Ascertain the management practices of the "best."

Once these steps are completed, management can develop plans that will result in meeting or beating the "best in the world" standards.

FIGURE 7-2
Malcolm Baldrige
National Quality
Award Criteria

1. **Leadership:** the success of top-level managers in creating a vision for quality and building quality values into the way the firm operates.
2. **Information and analysis:** the effectiveness of the firm's collection and analysis of information for quality improvement and planning.
3. **Strategic quality planning:** the effectiveness of the firm's integration of customers' quality needs into its business plan.
4. **Human resources utilization:** the success of the firm's efforts to realize its workforce's full potential for quality.
5. **Quality assurance of products and services:** the effectiveness of the firm's systems for assuring quality control of all its operations and for integrating quality control with continuous quality improvement.
6. **Quality results:** the firm's improvements in quality and demonstration of excellence in quality on quantitative measures.
7. **Customer satisfaction:** the effectiveness of the firm's systems to determine customers' requirements and its demonstrated success in meeting them.

ISO 9000
A rigorous series of quality standards created by the International Organization for Standardization.

Only in recent years have firms begun to give serious attention to ways of achieving quality improvements. Adherence to the quality standards established by ISO 9000 and the Baldrige Quality Award are but two options available to firms that wish to compare themselves to the best. **ISO 9000** is a series of quality management and assurance standards that were originally developed for the manufacturing sector, although they can also be applied to service organizations.[9] ISO 9000 was created in 1987 by the International Organization for Standardization, of Geneva, Switzerland. ISO has nudged firms into creating more interchangeable parts by establishing a rigorous quality standard that focuses on the firm's overall plan for quality management—structure, responsibilities, processes, and resources. Firms that want to compete internationally will have to produce products and services that conform to quality standards that only the "best" will be able to meet.

In 1987, the U.S. Department of Commerce established the Malcolm Baldrige National Quality Award to recognize firms that exemplify world-class business quality as well as satisfy the needs of their customers. Many more firms than those applying for the Baldrige National Quality Award are subjecting themselves to the rigorous analysis of the effectiveness of their integration of customers' quality requirements into their business plans. Figure 7-2 lists the seven examination categories for the Baldrige Award.[10] The planning function plays a most important role in establishing, maintaining, and increasing product and service quality.

6 Discuss the need for well-defined organizational goals and objectives, particularly as they relate to the supervisor.

ORGANIZATIONAL GOALS AND OBJECTIVES

The first step in planning is to develop a general statement of goals and objectives that will identify the overall purposes and results toward which all plans and activities are directed. Setting overall goals is a function of top-level management, which

XYZ CORPORATION

XYZ Corporation's existence is dependent on having the respect and support of four groups—its customers, employees, shareholders, and the public, which includes the citizens of each country in which we do business. For us to have a satisfactory future, we must continuously earn the support, respect, and approval of all four groups. This requires that XYZ:

For customers	Be committed to total customer satisfaction and continuous quality improvements.
For employees	Offer stability of employment, fairness in promotion, and opportunity for individual growth.
For shareholders	Offer both security of principal and competitive return through a combination of increased value of stock and dividends.
For the public	Conduct all of its business affairs not only in a legal manner but in a morally acceptable manner. XYZ must be a good neighbor.

XYZ's long-term corporate objectives and its interim goals must meet all of the obligations imposed by each of the four groups.

Corporate Objectives

1. To achieve continuing long-term growth in earnings and a record of financial stability that attracts to XYZ the capital—equity and debt—required to support its growth.

2. To concentrate our efforts in business and product areas in which XYZ can realistically expect to achieve a leadership position and in which leadership will be rewarded.

3. To offer our products and services wherever in the world XYZ's operations can be consistent with its management principles and corporate benefits.

4. To have a working environment in which each individual is treated with fairness that encourages and rewards excellence and stimulates maximum growth of the individual.

5. To anticipate the needs of the future sufficiently well to develop the human talent necessary to remain and be a leader.

6. To be a responsible corporate citizen.

must define and communicate to all managers the primary purposes for which the business is organized. These overall goals usually define upper-level managers' vision for the firm concerning the production and distribution of products or services, obligations to the customer, being a good employer and responsible corporate citizen, profit as a just reward for taking risks, research and development, and legal and ethical obligations. Figure 7-3 is an example of a company's statement of its corporate goals and objectives.

While some firms make a distinction between the terms "goals" and "objectives," we will use these terms interchangeably. Some firms define a "goal" as any long-term target—that is, one that will take more than a year to achieve—and an "objective" as a short-term target—that is, one that will take less than a year to achieve. Other firms define these terms to mean exactly the opposite.

The goals formulated for an organization as a whole become the general framework for operations and lead to the formulation of more specific objectives for divisional and departmental managers and supervisors. Each division or department in turn must clearly set forth its own objectives as guidelines for operations. These objectives must be within the general framework of the overall goals, and they must contribute to the achievement of the organization's overall purposes. Sometimes these objectives are established on a contingency basis—that is, some may be dependent or contingent on the availability of certain resources or reflect changing priorities.

Objectives usually are stated in terms of what is to be accomplished and when. A department's "what by when" statements are generally more specific than the broadly stated objectives of the organization. While the higher-level goal may be "to provide quality maintenance services for the entire organization," the maintenance supervisor's objective might be "to reduce machine downtime by 12 percent by year end." While the supervisory level objectives are more specific than the broadly stated objectives of an organization, they are consistent with and give direction to departmental efforts toward organizational objectives.

Whenever possible, objectives should be stated in measurable or verifiable terms, such as "to reduce overtime by 5 percent during the month"; "to increase output per employee hour by 10 percent during the next quarter"; "to achieve a 10 percent increase in employee suggestions during the next year"; and so on. This enables a supervisor to evaluate performance against specific targets. This approach is an essential part of management by objectives programs, which have been implemented by many organizations as a system for planning and attaining results.[11]

MANAGEMENT BY OBJECTIVES—A SYSTEM FOR PARTICIPATIVE MANAGEMENT

7 Explain management by objectives and describe how it is applied.

Management by objectives (MBO)
A process in which supervisor and subordinate jointly determine what is to be done.

Management by objectives (MBO) is a management approach in which managers and employees jointly set goals against which performance is later evaluated. It is a management system—that is, a total approach to management—that involves participative management. Management by objectives requires full commitment to the objectives of the organization, which must start with top-level management and permeate throughout all levels.

As depicted in Figure 7-4, the effective MBO system has four major elements. The determination of specific and measurable objectives is the foundation. The other elements are the inputs, or the resources necessary for goal accomplishment; the activities and processes that must be carried out to accomplish the goal; and the results, which are evaluated against the objectives. While MBO emphasizes results

FIGURE 7-4
Elements of the
Management by
Objectives Approach

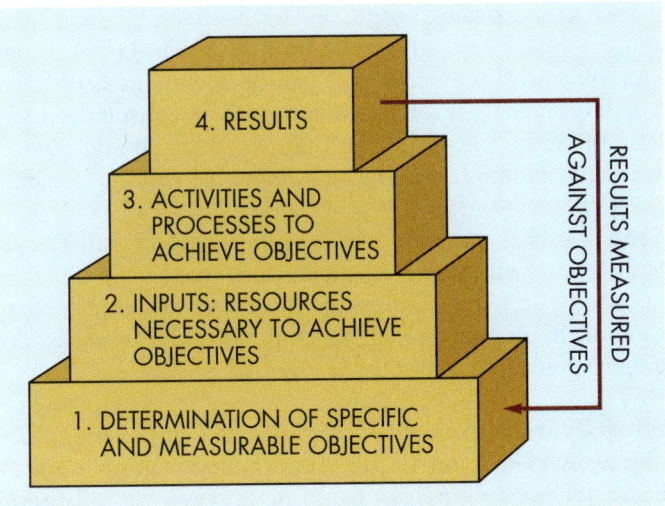

rather than the techniques used to achieve them, an effective system of MBO must be constructed in such a way that all of the aforementioned elements are integrated and support each other.

Why Use Management by Objectives?

There are many reasons why companies have adopted the management by objectives approach. The following are among the most important. First, MBO is results oriented. It requires thorough planning, organization, controls, communication, and dedication on the part of an organization. Properly implemented, MBO influences motivation and encourages commitment to results among all employees. It provides a sound means for appraising individuals' performance by its emphasis on objective criteria, rather than vague personality characteristics. In addition, it provides a more rational basis for sharing the rewards of an organization, particularly compensation and promotion based on merit.

A Step-by-Step Model

Any management by objectives system must be developed to meet the unique purposes and character of the organization. There is no such thing as a "pure" model that fits all situations and all places. The following, however, is a suggested step-by-step model that would apply in most organizational situations.

Step 1. Top-level managers identify the major goals of the organization for the coming period. Usually this is done at about the same time as the annual budget is prepared. Top-level managers determine the broad objectives for the coming period in such areas as sales, production levels, costs, profitability, employee development, and the like. Although corporate objectives may be broad, the more specifically they are stated, the better they can be communicated throughout the organization. Top-level managers develop these goals in consultation with managers at the next level of management. When finalized, there should be a consensus that the goals are challenging, yet realistic and attainable within the established time frame.

Step 2. The next step, which in some respects must be done in conjunction with Step 1, is for all managers, supervisors, and employees to review their job descriptions to be sure they understand their responsibilities and authority. A thorough review of the organizational structure will help to reveal gray areas where overlapping responsibilities need to be clarified.

Step 3. The crucial third step is for all employees to develop their own specific objectives in relation to the broader organizational and departmental objectives. Each individual prepares a list of objectives—typically about six to ten—that cover major results expected within their areas of responsibility. Objectives must be stated in terms that are measurable and verifiable, that is, with a number, ratio, due date, or some other specific criterion of accomplishment. It is important for employees to develop not only routine objectives for their normal areas of responsibility but also objectives that involve some elements of creativity and personal growth.

Step 4. A meeting must be arranged between each individual and his or her supervisor to discuss the employee's list of objectives. The final list of objectives should be negotiated to attain mutual agreement between supervisor and employee. Both parties should strive to agree on objectives that are challenging but realistic and attainable. Priorities must be established where appropriate.

Although it does not always happen, research results have shown that employees often stipulate more challenging objectives than their supervisors initially thought they were capable of attaining. Once the list of objectives is finalized, both the supervisor and the employee sign a copy, and this becomes the primary document on which the employee's performance will be judged.

Step 5. Employees and their supervisors periodically review progress toward accomplishment of the agreed-upon objectives. Some authorities suggest a quarterly review, during which objectives are compared with progress. During such reviews, objectives may be adjusted upward or downward as deemed appropriate.

Step 6. The next step is to compare results against objectives at the end of the period, usually a year. Performance appraisal and the appraisal meeting are discussed in greater depth in Chapter 15. A good approach is to have each individual do a self-evaluation of performance in terms of the objectives that were to be accomplished. Here, too, some employees will be more critical of their performance than their supervisors are.

The supervisor and employee then meet to discuss the employee's performance. They discuss such questions as the following: What was the employee's overall "batting average"? Were objectives accomplished (or not accomplished) due to the employee's performance or because of circumstances beyond anyone's control? What does the comparison of performance with objectives indicate about the employee's strengths and weaknesses? It is important to build on each individual's strengths and seek ways to improve areas of weakness. Step 6 in reality starts the cycle all over again, since setting the next period's objectives will flow logically from the analysis of the results achieved in the previous period.

Most MBO experts believe that salary adjustments should not be a part of the discussion described in Step 6. Of course, those who have performed well expect to be rewarded generously, while those who fail to meet most of their objectives should expect less reward. Thus, it is desirable to discuss salary several weeks after the discussion concerning performance results. Done properly, salary adjustments should reinforce the MBO program as a management system designed to reward most favorably those who have contributed the most.

MBO Facilitates Better Planning and Coordination of Efforts

The foregoing was a brief outline of the format of management by objectives. There are other considerations that any management team should be aware of before deciding whether or not to adopt an MBO program. It should not be looked upon as a panacea that will cure all management problems. However, some aspects of MBO already exist in most organizations of any appreciable size. Most managers, for example, have plans that revolve around production goals, sales targets, profit goals, cost containment, budgets, and the like. With or without MBO, effective higher-level managers recognize the importance of delegating authority along with responsibility to managers, supervisors, and employees if goals and objectives are to be achieved. The advantage of a formal MBO system is that it ties together many plans, establishes priorities, and coordinates activities that otherwise might be overlooked or handled loosely in the press of business operations. A sound MBO program encourages the contributions and commitment of people toward common goals and objectives.

STANDING PLANS

8 Identify the major types of standing plans and explain how these are helpful in supervisory decision making.

After setting major goals and objectives, all levels of management participate in the design and execution of additional plans for attaining desired objectives. In general, such plans can be broadly classified as (a) standing or repeat-use plans, which can be used over and over as the need arises, and (b) single-use plans, which focus on a single purpose or specific undertaking.

Many of a supervisor's day-to-day activities and decisions are guided by the use

Standing plans
Policies, procedures,
methods, and rules
that can be applied to
recurring situations.

of so-called **standing plans,** or "repeat-use plans." Although terminology varies, these types of plans typically are known as policies, procedures, methods, and rules. All of these should be designed to reinforce one another and should be directed toward the achievement of both organizational and work unit objectives. Top-level managers formulate company-wide standing plans, and supervisors formulate the necessary subsidiary standing plans for their work units.

Policies

Policy
A standing plan that
serves as a guide to
thinking in making
decisions.

A **policy** is a general guide to thinking when making decisions. Corporate policies are usually statements that channel the thinking of managers and supervisors in specified directions and define the limits within which they must stay as they make decisions.

Effective policies promote consistency of decision making throughout an enterprise. Once policies are set, managers find it easier to delegate authority, since the decisions a subordinate supervisor makes will be guided by the boundaries of the policies. Policies enable the supervisors to arrive at about the same decisions their managers would make or, at least, to be within acceptable parameters. While policies should be considered as guides for thinking, they do permit supervisors to use their own judgment in making decisions, as long as their decisions fall within the parameters of the policy.

For example, most companies have policies covering vacations with pay based on seniority. Depending on length of service with the company, an employee is entitled to one week, two weeks, three weeks, or more of vacation. All the supervisor has to do is ascertain an employee's years of service with the company in order to determine the length of that employee's vacation. However, the supervisor may have to develop a workable plan within the department concerning when each employee may take a vacation. The supervisor is likely to decide that the employee with the most seniority has first choice, the employee with the next highest seniority has second choice, and so on down the line. The supervisor may also limit the number of employees who can be on vacation at one time. In other words, the supervisor develops a departmental policy within the framework of the broader company policy. The supervisor's role in a leaves of absence policy is illustrated in Figure 7-5.

Origin of Policies. Major company-wide policies are originated by top-level managers, since policymaking is one of their important responsibilities. Top-level managers must develop and establish overall policies, which guide the thinking of subordinate managers so that organizational objectives can be achieved. Broad policies become the guides for specific policies developed within divisions and departments. Departmental policies established by supervisors must complement and coincide with the broader policies of the organization.

Smaller firms tend to have fewer policies. On one hand, the absence of policies gives the supervisor greater flexibility in dealing with situations as they occur. A survey of firms employing fewer than 100 people found that most did not have

FIGURE 7-5
Example of a Policy
Statement

LEAVES OF ABSENCE POLICY

Introduction

Leaves of absence for reasons other than for personal sickness or family leave may be authorized for hourly employees who are regularly employed and meet the conditions of eligibility as defined in the following policy. There are two general types of leave: leaves of absence with pay and leaves of absence without pay. This policy is established to provide fair and equitable treatment of all employees.

Department heads and/or supervisors are responsible for the administration of the leaves of absence policies and procedures, for the maintenance of employee records of absence, for arranging workloads, and for the continuance of normal operations, production, and service during periods of employee absence.

Leaves of Absence with Pay

Absence from work without loss of pay or creditable service and with continuance of coverage under group insurance plans is authorized for the following purposes:

Vacation: Hourly employees who are classified as regular employees and have completed three consecutive months of employment shall be eligible to take vacation with pay. Vacation periods must be scheduled at the convenience of the department and must be approved by the department head and/or supervisor.

Accrual and Allowance: Regular hourly employees shall accrue vacation hours in direct proportion to the hours paid and based upon completion of continuous employment on the following schedule:

During Year	Annual Vacation Days	Accrual Hours
1	5	40
2–5	10	80
6–10	12	100
11–20	15	120
21 + years	20	160

Regular employees who are employed less than full time shall accrue vacation hours in direct proportion to the hours paid. Vacation credits shall not be accrued for working overtime hours (hours in excess of 40 in any one week).

LEAVES OF ABSENCE WITHOUT PAY

Employees requesting leaves of absence without pay other than those covered by the Family Leave Act Policy shall make such a request in writing to the personnel office at least 14 days in advance of the leave. The human resources office, in consultation with the supervisor, will make a timely decision (within 24 working hours after receipt of the request) and notify the employee in writing on the disposition of the request.

policies for drug or alcohol use but handled problems on an individual basis as they arose. The absence of policies, on the other hand, may cause inconsistent supervisory practice and lead to charges of unfairness.

In addition to policies formulated by top-level managers, some policies are imposed on an organization by external forces, such as government, labor unions, trade groups, accrediting associations, and the like. The word "imposed" indicates compliance with an outside force that cannot be avoided. For example, in order to be accredited, schools, universities, hospitals, and other institutions must comply with regulations issued by the appropriate accrediting agency. Government regulations concerning minimum wages; pay for overtime work; and hiring of people without regard to race, age, and gender automatically become part of an organization's policies. Any policy imposed on the organization in such a manner is known as an "externally imposed policy," and everyone in the organization must comply with it.

Written Policy Statements Promote Consistency. Since policies are guides to decision making, they must be explicitly stated and communicated to those in the organization who are affected by them. Although there is no guarantee that policies always will be completely followed or understood, they are more likely to be followed consistently if they are written. Few organizations have all of their policies in written form, and some have few or no written policies, either because they simply never get around to writing them down or because they would rather not state their policies publicly. However, the benefits derived from clearly stated written policies usually outweigh the disadvantages. The process of writing policies requires managers to think through the issues more clearly and consistently. Supervisors and employees can refer to a written policy as often as they wish. The wording of a written policy cannot be changed by word of mouth, because if there is any doubt the written policy can be consulted. Furthermore, written policies are available to supervisors and employees who are new in the organization, so that they can quickly acquaint themselves with the policies. Every policy should be reviewed periodically and revised or discarded if conditions or circumstances warrant it.

Supervisory (Departmental) Policies. Supervisors seldom have to issue policies. If a department is extremely large or geographically dispersed, or if several subunits exist within the department, the supervisor may find it appropriate to write departmental policies. But for the most part, instead of writing policies the supervisor will be called on to apply existing policies in making decisions. That is, most of the time it is the supervisor's role to interpret, apply, and explain the meaning of policies. Since supervisors will be guided by policies in many daily decisions, they must understand the policies and learn how to interpret and apply them.

A supervisor may occasionally experience a situation for which no policy exists or seems applicable. For example, suppose a group of employees asks the supervisor for permission to visit the end user of their product in order to better understand how the product is used. To make an appropriate decision in this matter, the supervisor should be guided by a policy so that the decision will be in accord with other decisions regarding time away from work. If, upon investigation, the supervisor finds that higher-level management has never issued a formal policy to cover such a request, the supervisor needs guidance and should ask his or her manager to issue a policy—a guide for thinking—to be applied in this case as well as in the future, so that there is consistency not only within the supervisor's particular department but across the organization. After consulting with other supervisors who may have a stake in the issue, the supervisor may want to draft a suggested policy and present it to the manager. In large firms, it is not likely that many such instances will happen, since top-level management usually has covered the major areas where policies are needed. However, in small firms where fewer policies exist, supervisors will have to use good judgment in determining when to make decisions themselves and when they should consult their managers.

Procedures

Procedure
A standing plan that defines the sequence of activities to be performed to achieve objectives.

Procedures, like policies, are standing plans for achieving objectives. They are derived from policies but are more specific. Procedures essentially are guides to action, not guides to thinking. They define a chronological sequence of actions that will take employees toward their objectives. Procedures aim for consistency by defining steps to be taken and the sequence to be followed.

For example, a company may have a policy that requires supervisors to use the human resources department in the preliminary steps of hiring. This policy may contain several guidelines designed to meet nondiscriminatory hiring goals. To carry out this policy, management develops a procedure governing the selection process. For example, the procedures to be followed by a supervisor who wants to hire a word processor might include filling out a requisition form, specifying the job requirements, interviewing and testing potential candidates, and other such actions. Thus, the procedure lists in more detail exactly what a supervisor must do or not do in order to comply with the company's hiring policies. All supervisors must follow the same procedure.

At the department level, the supervisor often must develop procedures to determine how work is to be done. If a supervisor were fortunate and had only highly skilled employees to lead, he or she could depend on the employees to a great extent to select efficient paths of performance. But this is not common, and most employees look to the supervisor for instructions on how to proceed.

One advantage of preparing a procedure is that it requires an analysis of work to be done. Another advantage is that once a procedure is established, it promotes greater uniformity of action, reduces the need for much routine decision making, and encourages a predictable outcome. Procedures also provide the supervisor with a standard for appraising work done by employees. In order to realize these advantages, a supervisor should devote considerable time and effort to devising departmental procedures to cover as many phases of operations as practical, such as work operations and work flow, scheduling, and personnel assignments.

Methods

A **method** is also a standing plan for action, but it is even more detailed than a procedure. Whereas a procedure shows a series of steps to be taken, a method is concerned with a single operation—one particular step. It indicates exactly how that step is to be performed. For example, a departmental procedure may specify the chronological routing of work in the assembly of various components of a product. At each subassembly point, there should be a stated method for the work to be performed at each step in the total process.

For most jobs, there is usually a "best method," that is, the most efficient way for the job to be performed given existing technology and circumstances. Again, if a supervisor could rely on skilled workers, the workers might know the best method without having to be told. However, for the most part, the supervisor or someone in management must design the most efficient method for getting the job done. Much time should be spent in devising methods, since proper methods have all the advantages of procedures cited previously. In devising methods, the supervisor may utilize the know-how of a methods engineer or a motion-and-time-study specialist, if such individuals are available in the organization. These are specialists who have been trained in industrial engineering techniques to study jobs systematically with the objective of making them more efficient. Where such specialists are not available, the supervisor's experience and input from experienced employees actually doing the work should be sufficient to design work methods that are appropriate for the department.

In some activities, a supervisor need not be overly concerned with devising procedures and methods, because employees already have been trained in standard methods or standard procedures. For example, journeyman machinists are exposed to many years of education and training during which great emphasis is placed on proper procedures and methods of performing certain tasks. Similarly, in the supervision of a department in which highly skilled or professional employees work, the supervisor's main concern is to see to it that generally approved procedures and methods are carried out in professionally accepted ways. However, most supervisors have employees who are not well trained and for whom procedures and methods must be established.

Rules

A rule is different from a policy, procedure, or method, although it is also a standing plan that has been devised in order to attain objectives. A rule is not the same as a policy because it does not provide a guide to thinking, nor does it leave discretion to the parties involved. A rule is related to a procedure insofar as it is a guide to action and states what must or must not be done. However, it is not a procedure, because it does not provide for a time sequence or set of steps. A **rule** is a directive that must be applied and enforced consistently. When a rule is a specific guide for the behavior of employees in a department, the supervisor must follow it wherever it applies, without deviating from it. For example, "No possession or

All employees must be informed of organizational rules. Posting rules and regulations is a common way of communicating them.

consumption of alcoholic beverages on company premises" is commonly on the list of organizational rules. It means exactly what it says, and there are to be no exceptions.

There are occasions when supervisors have to devise their own rules or see to it that the rules defined by higher-level managers are obeyed. For example, rules concerning employee meal periods usually specify a certain amount of time that employees may be away from their jobs for meals. Usually these rules are developed by higher-level managers, but often a supervisor will have to formulate departmental rules concerning the actual scheduling of meal periods. Regardless of who develops the rules, it is each supervisor's duty to apply and enforce all rules uniformly as they relate to each area of responsibility.

9 Discuss the principal types of single-use plans in which supervisors play an important role.

Single-use plans
Plans developed to accomplish a specific objective that, once achieved, most likely will not recur.

SINGLE-USE PLANS

As discussed in the preceding sections, policies, procedures, methods, and rules are known as repeat-use, or standing, plans, because they are followed each time a given situation is encountered. Unless they are changed or modified, repeat-use plans are used again and again. In contrast to repeat-use plans are plans that are no longer needed, or are "used up" once the objective is accomplished or the time period of applicability is over. These are known as **single-use plans**. Single-use plans include budgets, programs, and projects. Major budgets, programs, and projects are usually the concern of higher-level managers, but supervisors also play a role in developing and implementing single-use plans at the departmental level.

Budgets

Budget
A plan that expresses anticipated results in numerical—typically financial—terms for a stated period of time.

Although budgets are generally part of the managerial controlling function, a budget is first and foremost a plan. A **budget** is a plan that expresses anticipated results in numerical terms, such as dollars and cents, employee hours, sales figures, or units to be produced. It serves as a plan for a stated period of time, usually one year. All budgets eventually are translated into monetary terms, and an overall financial budget is developed for the entire firm. After the stated period is over, the budget expires. It has served its usefulness and is no longer valid. This is why a budget is a single-use plan.

As a statement of expected results, a budget is associated with control. However, the preparation of a budget is planning, and this again is part of every manager's responsibilities. Since a budget is expressed in numerical terms, it has the advantage of being specific rather than general. There is a considerable difference between just making general forecasts and attaching numerical values to specific plans. The figures that the supervisor finds in a budget are actual plans, which become standards to be achieved.

The Supervisor's Role in Budgeting. Since supervisors have to function under a budget, they should have a part in its preparation. Supervisors should participate in what commonly is called "grass roots budgeting." What this means is that supervisors should have the opportunity either to propose detailed budgets for their departments or at least to participate in discussions with higher-level managers before final departmental budgets are established. Supervisors will have to substantiate their budget proposals in discussions with their managers and possibly with the financial manager when the final budgets are being set.

Supervisors usually are more committed to budgets if they have had a role in formulating them. Furthermore, supervisors are usually closest to the real needs of the department. This does not mean that the requests of the supervisor should always prevail. No budget should ever be accepted without careful analysis by both the supervisor and higher-level managers to be sure it is as accurate as possible. Differences between budget needs and estimates should be discussed and resolved carefully.

There are numerous types of budgets in which supervisors can play a part. For example, supervisors may design budgets in which they plan the work hours to be used for jobs within their departments. Supervisors also may prepare budgets for materials and supplies, wages, utility expenses, and other departmental expenditures.

Budget Review. Most organizations have interim monthly or quarterly reviews when the budget is compared to actual results. This is why a budget is also a control device. If necessary, the budget is revised to adjust to current results and revised forecasts. This topic is discussed further in Chapter 22.

Supervisors should study and analyze significant variations from the budget carefully to determine where and why plans went wrong, what and where adjustments need to be made, and what the revised budget should reflect, including new factors and any changes in the department. When an annual budget is about to expire, it becomes a guide for preparing the next year's budget. Thus the planning process continues from one budget period to the next in a closely related pattern.

Programs and Projects

Program
A comprehensive single-use plan designed to accomplish the organization's objectives.

A **program** is a single-use set of plans for a specific major undertaking related to the organization's overall goals and objectives. A major program may have its own policies, procedures, and budgets. The program may take several years to accomplish. Examples of major programs are the expansion of a manufacturing plant or the addition of new facilities in a hospital. Such expansion programs usually involve plans for the architectural design, new equipment or technology, financing, recruitment of employees, and publicity, all of which are part of the overall program. Once the expansion program is completed, its plans will not be used again. Thus, a program is a single-use plan.

Project
A single-use plan for accomplishing a specific nonrecurring activity.

Supervisors are typically more involved in planning projects. While a **project** may be part of an overall program, it is an undertaking that can be planned and fulfilled as a distinct entity, usually within a relatively short period of time. For example, the preparation of a publicity brochure by the public relations department to acquaint the public with new facilities as part of a hospital expansion program could be called a project. Arranging the necessary construction financing for the building expansion would be another project. Although connected with a major program, these projects can be handled separately by individuals designated to implement them.

An example of a project at the supervisory level is the design of a new inventory control system by a warehouse supervisor. Another example is a research project conducted by a marketing department supervisor to determine the effectiveness of a series of television commercials. Projects such as these are a constant part of the ongoing activities at the departmental level. The ability to plan and carry out projects is another component of every supervisor's managerial effectiveness.

PLANNING TOOLS

10 Discuss just-in-time inventory control systems and scheduling and planning tools.

While it is not our intent to go into great detail regarding techniques for developing procedures and methods, effective supervisors must become familiar with them, as they are readily adaptable to most organizations. The following are some planning tools that supervisors can use.

Planning Inventory

Maintaining large inventories of component parts and finished goods is costly. It requires warehouse space, which must be rented or bought, heated, and lit. It also requires workers to store and keep track of the materials. To reduce the costs of maintaining large inventories, many firms use inventory control techniques to better plan the inflow of materials needed for production.

Just-in-time (JIT) inventory control system
A system for scheduling materials to arrive precisely when they are needed in the production process.

A **just-in-time (JIT) inventory control system,** also called **kanban,** is a system for scheduling raw materials and components needed in the production process to arrive at the firm precisely when they are needed. This avoids having to keep large amounts of these items in stock. JIT requires close coordination between the firm and its suppliers. For the system to work, suppliers must be willing and able to supply parts on short notice and in small batches. Also, the firm must keep suppliers well informed about its projected needs for their products, so that suppliers can plan their production efficiently.[12]

Kanban
Another name for a just-in-time inventory control system.

Scheduling and Project Planning

Much time is spent planning various projects. Supervisors need to consider what needs to be accomplished, the necessary activities, the order in which they are to be done, who is to do each, and when they are to be completed. This process of planning activities and their sequence is called **scheduling.** Two well-known project planning tools are Gantt charts and PERT.

Scheduling
The process of developing a detailed list of activities, their sequence, and the required resources.

Gantt Charts. A **Gantt chart** is a graphic scheduling technique that shows the relationship between work planned and necessary completion dates.[13] Figure 7-6 depicts a simplified Gantt chart developed by a student for completing the college admission process. The student needs to decide what activities must be done to get admitted, the order in which they must be done, and the time that must be allocated to each activity. The project is broken down into separate major activities, and these are listed on the vertical axis. The time frame is indicated on the horizontal axis. The bar shows the duration and sequence of each activity. Each bar is shaded to indicate the actual progress. Thus, it is possible to assess progress at a glance. A review of Figure 7-6 shows that everything has been accomplished to date except getting teachers to write letters of recommendation. This is one month behind schedule. Given this information, the student needs to make a special effort to catch up and ensure that no further delays occur. Unless corrective action is taken, admission to college will be delayed.

Gantt Chart
A graphic scheduling technique that shows the activity to be scheduled on the vertical axis and necessary completion dates on the horizontal axis.

Gantt charts are helpful in projects in which the activities are independent of each other. However, if a large project such as a complex quality improvement program needs to be planned, PERT should be used.

PERT
A flowchart for managing large projects, showing the necessary activities with estimates of the time needed to complete each activity and the sequential relationship among them.

Program Evaluation and Review Technique (PERT). Successfully used in the production of the Polaris missile and the construction of the World Trade Center, **PERT** is a flowchart-like diagram showing the sequence of activities

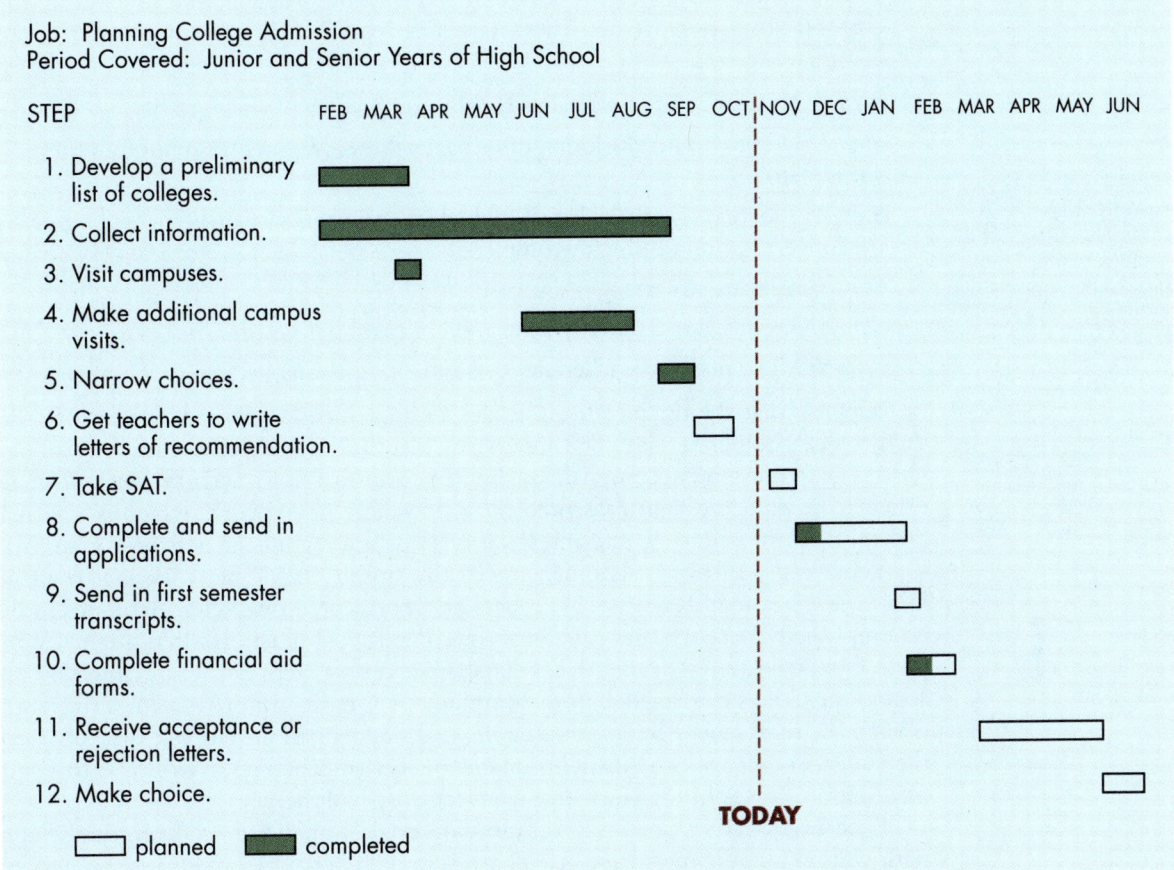

Job: Planning College Admission
Period Covered: Junior and Senior Years of High School

STEP   FEB MAR APR MAY JUN JUL AUG SEP OCT NOV DEC JAN FEB MAR APR MAY JUN

1. Develop a preliminary
   list of colleges.
2. Collect information.
3. Visit campuses.
4. Make additional campus
   visits.
5. Narrow choices.
6. Get teachers to write
   letters of recommendation.
7. Take SAT.
8. Complete and send in
   applications.
9. Send in first semester
   transcripts.
10. Complete financial aid
    forms.
11. Receive acceptance or
    rejection letters.
12. Make choice.

                                                            TODAY

        □ planned   ■ completed

FIGURE 7-6
Example of a Gantt
Chart

needed to complete a project and the time associated with each. PERT goes beyond Gantt charts by clarifying the interrelatedness of the various activities.

PERT helps a supervisor think strategically. A clear statement of goals serves as the focal point for the entire planning process. PERT begins with the supervisor defining the project not only in terms of the desired goal but also all the intermediate ones on which the ultimate goal depends. The construction of a PERT network includes the following steps:

Step 1: Determine the goal. For example, a firm may want to improve its customer service by improving delivery times.

PERT event
The beginning and/or ending of an activity.

Step 2: Clarify events. A **PERT event** is the beginning and/or ending of an activity. Receiving an order from a customer is an event. Thus, events are a particular point in time.

PERT activity
A specific task to be accomplished.

Step 3: Identify all activities that must be accomplished for the project and the sequence in which these activities should be performed. A **PERT activity** is a specific task to be accomplished. Contacting the customer, demonstrating how your product can provide a solution to a specific problem, and motivating the customer to action are activities. Activities require a certain amount of time to complete.

Step 4: Determine time estimates for the completion of each activity.

Step 5: Develop a network diagram that includes all the information in the previous steps.

Step 6: Identify the **critical path,** which is the sequence of activities requiring the longest period of time to complete.

Step 7: Allocate necessary resources.

Step 8: Record actual activity time and compare with estimates.

Step 9: Make necessary schedule revisions or adjustments.[14]

Critical path
The path of activities in the PERT network that will take the longest time to complete.

Suppose that the organization decides to implement a program to improve the quality of customer service. The supervisor identifies the PERT events, lists all activities that must be accomplished, and determines which activity must precede others. The data are then presented on a flowchart or network, which is a visual portrayal of the sequence and interrelationships among all the activities necessary for achieving improved customer service. A simple PERT network is shown in Figure 7-7. In the PERT network, events are represented by circles. Activities to be accomplished are represented by an arrow. Figure 7-7 illustrates that after "Complete Quality Audit" (Event A) has happened, certain activities represented by an arrow must be performed before "Implement Quality Improvement Program" (Event G), represented by another circle, can happen. In developing the network, the supervisor provides realistic estimates of how much time it will take to complete certain stages of the work and what the costs will be.

Each event-activity path to the ultimate goal is analyzed to determine which path will require the most time. This path is termed "critical" and is represented by thick arrows in Figure 7-7. Any delay in the activities on this path will also delay the project's completion. The total time to complete the project can be determined by adding the individual time units on the critical path. The project in Figure 7-7 will take 45 time units to complete.

The idea of a "critical path" is a very important concept. It can help the supervisor decide where and when to put forth extra effort, additional employees, or other resources to avoid delaying the entire project. The supervisor may be able to shorten the 45 total time units in Figure 7-7 by allocating additional resources to tasks on this path or making corrective adjustments. For example, if the amount of time required to benchmark could be shortened by 3 units, the project could be completed in less time.

PERT is a helpful planning tool because it requires systematic thinking and planning for large, nonroutine projects. The development of PERT networks by hand is time consuming. However, the use of Gantt charts and PERT is expected to increase because of the proliferation of commercially available computer software packages that can assist supervisors in planning, decision making, and controlling. Effective supervisors will become familiar with the various planning tools and apply them as the situation warrants.

FIGURE 7-7
Example of a PERT
Network for Quality
Improvement

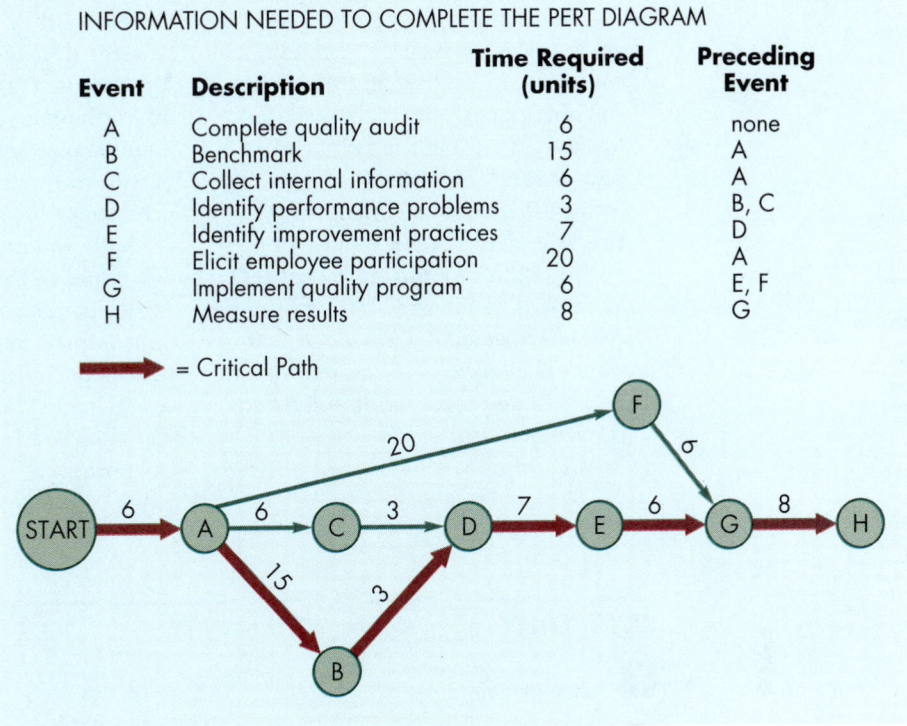

INFORMATION NEEDED TO COMPLETE THE PERT DIAGRAM

Event	Description	Time Required (units)	Preceding Event
A	Complete quality audit	6	none
B	Benchmark	15	A
C	Collect internal information	6	A
D	Identify performance problems	3	B, C
E	Identify improvement practices	7	D
F	Elicit employee participation	20	A
G	Implement quality program	6	E, F
H	Measure results	8	G

⟶ = Critical Path

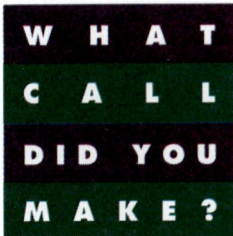

As Shannon O'Neill, you have a well-defined planning process in place. Your system is forward looking, involves employees in the process, and provides for immediate feedback on performance. Total quality management improves quality of service by involving everyone in the process. You do not appear to have a system to evaluate the students' or their parents' perceptions of quality. You may want to solicit input from them regarding their perceptions of the service provided.

However, before you spend too much time trying to determine what, exactly, the new superintendent wants, you should talk to your immediate supervisor. Before the various management levels can begin working on their plans for continuous improvement, the superintendent needs to share his or her vision for the school corporation.

There is no right or wrong answer for this scenario. Every process, procedure, and activity can be improved. The purpose of this "You Make the Call" section is to get you to think of ways that you can get ideas for improvement. While you travel around the country sharing your computerized transportation scheduling with others, maybe you can get some ideas on things that other districts do better than you do.

Employee involvement is the key to a system of total quality management and continuous improvement. Ask your employees to help you create a vision for their department, areas of responsibility, and so forth. Ask them questions such as the following: What will the taxpayers expect of the Middletown Schools' transportation department three to five years from now? What will they be willing to pay for those services? What will be the essential services we will be expected to provide at that time? The answers to these questions will help guide your continuous improvement efforts.

In addition, look at the policies, procedures, and methods currently in place. Are they needed? Should some be refined or discarded? You may want to use Gantt charts, PERT, and other planning techniques to improve maintenance scheduling. A review of inventory levels might reveal that the inventory of spare parts is too high or that a modification of the JIT system could be implemented.

Remember that whatever continuous improvement plan you and your department develop, it must complement the vision and strategic plans of the Middletown School Corporation.

SUMMARY

1 Define planning and clarify why all management functions depend on planning.
Planning is the managerial function that determines what is to be done in the future. It includes analyzing the situation, forecasting future events, establishing objectives, setting priorities, and deciding what actions are necessary to achieve objectives. It is a function of every manager from the top-level executive to the supervisor. Without planning there is no direction to the activities of the organization.

2 Explain the concept of visioning and its relationship to strategic planning.
Visioning is the process of developing a mental image of what the organization could become. Top-level management defines its vision and articulates it throughout the organization. The vision clarifies for all employees where the organization intends to be at some future time. Strategic planning involves making decisions that will enable the organization to achieve its long-term objectives. Visioning serves as the focal point for the establishment of objectives. The organization develops plans based upon the vision.

While top-level managers are responsible for the development and execution of the strategic plan, supervisors direct their work unit plans toward achieving the strategic goals. Effective supervisors create a mental image of what their department could become. Plans are developed that complement this vision. The vision, when shared with employees, gives meaning to their work.

3 Describe the supervisor's role in planning.
Planning is the responsibility of every manager. Often, the supervisor needs to consult with others to develop plans that are consistent with those of upper-level management. Supervisors devote most of their attention to short-term planning. The supervisor's short-term plans should be integrated and coordinated with the longer-term plans of upper-level

management. Supervisors need to communicate to employees in a timely fashion what is being planned.

4 Identify the benefits of planning.

Planning facilitates use of human and physical resources to their fullest potential. Planning how to best utilize the material, capital, and human resources of the firm is essential. The time and human resources needed to complete a particular activity can be utilized more effectively. Planning promotes efficiency.

5 Explain the role of planning in quality improvement.

Not surprisingly, various quality improvement concepts relate directly to planning. Total quality management means planning for quality, preventing defects, correcting defects, and continuously improving quality. Benchmarking—the process of identifying and improving upon the best practices of others—precedes the development of plans. Organizations that want to be as good as or better than the best in the world will want to conform to quality standards established in ISO 9000 or the Malcolm Baldrige National Quality Award. A review of the Baldridge criteria reveals that planning for effective human resources utilization and integrating the customer's quality needs into the business plan are two examination categories. Plans must be developed for establishing, maintaining, and increasing product and service quality. Quality improvement doesn't just happen; it has to be planned.

6 Discuss the need for well-defined organizational goals and objectives, particularly as they relate to the supervisor.

Setting objectives is the first step in planning. Although the overall goals and objectives are determined by top-level management, supervisors formulate their departmental objectives, which must be consistent with and direct employee efforts toward achieving organizational objectives. Objectives should state what should be done and when.

7 Explain management by objectives as a system of management and describe how it is applied.

Management by objectives (MBO) is an approach based on organizational objectives. The effective MBO system has four major elements. The development of specific and measurable objectives serves as the foundation for determining the necessary resources, the activities that must be carried out, and the results, which are evaluated against the objectives. MBO ties together planning, establishes priorities, and provides coordination of effort.

In practice, specific objectives are mutually agreed upon by employees and their supervisor. Periodic reviews are conducted to make sure that progress is being made. At the end of the appraisal period, results are evaluated against objectives, and rewards are based on this evaluation. Goals for the next period are then set, and the process begins again.

8 Identify the major types of standing plans and explain how these are helpful in supervisory decision making.

In order to attain objectives, standing plans must be devised. Top-level managers typically develop company-wide policies, procedures, methods, and rules, and each supervisor formulates the necessary subsidiary standing plans for his or her work unit.

Policies are guides to thinking for decision making, and most of them originate with higher-level management. The supervisor's concern with policies primarily is one of interpreting, applying, and staying within them when making decisions for the department. Policies are more likely to be followed consistently if they are written.

Procedures, like policies, are standing plans for achieving objectives. They specify a sequence of actions that will guide employees toward objectives. The supervisor often develops procedures to determine how work is to be done. The advantages of procedures are that they require analysis of what needs to be done, promote uniformity of action, and provide a means of appraising the work of employees.

In addition, the supervisor will be called on to design and follow methods and rules, which essentially are guides for action. They are more detailed than procedures. A rule is a directive that must be applied and enforced consistently.

9 Discuss the principal types of single-use plans in which supervisors play an important role.

Supervisors should participate in establishing budgets, which are single-use plans expressed in numerical terms. A budget serves as a control device that enables the supervisor to compare results achieved during the budget period against the budget plan. Supervisors at times play a role in organizational programs and projects, which are single-use plans designed to accomplish specific undertakings on a one-time basis.

10 Discuss just-in-time inventory control systems and scheduling and planning tools.

To reduce inventory costs and better plan for materials, just-in-time inventory control systems ensure that materials and components will arrive precisely when they are needed. Gantt charts and PERT networks are graphic tools to aid supervisors in planning, organizing, and controlling operations. Gantt charts require supervisors to identify various activities, determine their sequence, and specify the time spent on each activity. A visual check shows the progress of various activities. If the project is behind schedule, supervisors must develop plans for getting it back on schedule.

Program evaluation and review technique (PERT) is appropriate for scheduling and sequencing large, complex projects. PERT aids in planning because it forces the supervisor to estimate the time the project will take to complete. The development of PERT networks is time consuming. Computer software packages are available to assist in the development of PERT networks.

KEY TERMS

QUESTIONS FOR DISCUSSION

1. What is the importance of an organization's vision? Why should the vision that top-level managers have for the organization be shared with all employees? Discuss how supervisors may have occasion to become involved in developing the strategic plan.

2. Define planning. Why is planning primarily a mental activity rather than a "doing" type of function?

3. Distinguish between long-range planning and short-range planning. Relate these concepts to the planning period for top-level managers as compared with the planning period for first-line supervisors.

4. Why should a first-line supervisor understand the organization's objectives? Why is this knowledge important to planning?

5. Discuss the step-by-step model for management by objectives presented in the text. Explain why each step is crucial if MBO is to be implemented successfully.

6. Define and distinguish between each of the following:
- **a.** Policy
- **b.** Procedure
- **c.** Method
- **d.** Rule

7. If you were a supervisor in a small firm that had few policies and you believed that several employees were using illegal drugs, how would you go about developing a plan to handle the situation? Why would it be desirable to have the policy in written form?

8. Discuss the supervisor's role in the budgeting process.

9. List guidelines a supervisor could follow to develop a system of continuous improvement or total quality management (TQM).

10. Why do firms need to implement systems such as just-in-time inventory systems?

SKILLS APPLICATIONS

Skills Application 7-1: Planning Comparison

1. Interview two supervisors from diverse occupations (e.g., production, banking, health care, retail, etc.). Ask them the following questions:
- **a.** To what extent do you use planning in your daily work?
- **b.** What advantages do you gain from planning?
- **c.** What problems do you have in fulfilling your plans?
- **d.** What one tip can you give me as a prospective supervisor that would enable me to do a better job of planning?

2. Compare the answers of the two supervisors. What items are similar? Dissimilar?

3. Compare your one tip for better planning with those of other students.

4. Make a composite list of tips. Which of those do you currently use in your planning process? Which should you add to your toolbox of skills?

Skills Application 7-2: Need for a Vision

Someone once said, "Nothing is more exciting than venturing into the unknown. There is a need to plan effectively to reach the unknown."

1. Close your eyes for a few seconds. Visualize what you would like to be doing five years from today.

2. Write a paragraph describing your vision. Assume that this vision is an objective that you want to attain, so conclude by writing a specific objective ("what" by "when") statement (e.g., "Five years from today, I will . . .").

3. Briefly list the interim events that must be attained to reach your five-year vision.

4. Develop a timetable for achieving the things that will lead you to your vision.

5. Periodically check your process toward your objective, making necessary corrections and adjustments.

Skills Application 7-3: PERT Application

Think of a group project, either real or hypothetical, that you must complete by the end of term. The project must require the involvement of several other people.

1. Working backward from the end result (the due date), lay out the various activities required to complete the project.

2. Now estimate the amount of time required to complete each activity.

3. Follow the steps given in the chapter to draw a PERT diagram. Be sure to identify the critical path.

4. What difficulties did you have in developing your PERT diagram?

5. Summarize in a few words what you learned by using this planning tool.

ENDNOTES

1.   See Peter F. Drucker, *Management: Tasks, Responsibilities, and Practices* (New York: Harper & Row, 1974), p. 611. Also see Drucker, *The Practice of Management* (New York: Harper Brothers, 1954), pp. 62–65, 126–129; and Drucker, "Plan Now for the Future," *Modern Office Technology* 38 (March 1993), pp. 8–9.

2.   There are numerous books and articles on the subject of strategic management. See Gilbert Fuchsberg, "Visioning Missions Becomes Its Own Mission," *The Wall Street Journal* (January 7, 1994), pp. B1 and B4; William H. Newman, James P. Jogan, and W. Harvey Hegarty, *Strategy: A Multi-Level Integrative Approach* (Cincinnati: South-Western Publishing Co., 1989); M. Jill Austin, "Planning in Service Organizations," *SAM Advanced Management Journal* (Volume 55, Summer 1990), pp. 7-–12; and J. Gardner, R. Rachlin, and A. Sweeney, eds., *Handbook of Strategic Planning* (New York: John Wiley & Sons, 1986).

3.   Some of the articles include: R. Robinson, J. Pearce, G. Vozikis, and T. Mescon, "The Relationship Between Stage of Development and Small Firm Planning and Performance," *Journal of Small Business Management* (Volume 22, Number 2, April 1984), pp. 45–52; P. H. Thurston, "Should Smaller Companies Make Formal Plans?" *Harvard Business Review* (September–October 1983), pp. 162–188; and J. Bracker and J. Pearson, "Planning and Financial Performance of Small Mature Firms," *Strategic Management Journal* (Volume 7, 1986), pp. 503–522.

4.   Noel M. Tichy and Mary Anne Devanna, *The Transformational Leader* (New York: John Wiley & Sons, 1986), p. 127.

5.   Tom Peters, *Thriving on Chaos* (New York: Alfred A. Knopf, 1988), p. 399. [Quote originally appeared in *Time*, May 1987.]

6.   Noel M. Tichy and R. Charan, "Speed, Simplicity, Self-Confidence: An Interview with Jack Welch," *Harvard Business Review* (September–October 1989), p. 113.

7.   For additional information on TQM and continuous improvement, see H. M. Wadsworth, K. S. Stephens, and A. B. Godfrey, *Quality Control* (New York: John Wiley & Sons, 1986); W. E. Deming, *Out of the Crises* (Cambridge, Mass.: MIT Center for Advanced Engineering Study, 1986); H.S. Gitlow and S. J. Gitlow, *The Deming Guide to Quality and Competitive Position* (Englewood Cliffs, N.J.: Prentice-Hall, 1987); W. J. Duncan and J. G. Van Matre, "The Gospel According to Deming: Is It Really New?" *Business Horizons* (July–August 1990), pp. 3–9; and Vincent K. Omachonu and Joel E. Ross, *Principles of Total Quality* (Delray Beach, Fla.: St. Lucie Press, 1994).

8.   Stratford Sherman, "Are You as Good as the Best in the World?" *Fortune* (December 13, 1993), p. 95.

9.   *ISO 9000: Handbook of Quality Standards and Compliance* (Waterford, Conn.: Bureau of Business Practice, 1992). Also, see Frank Voehl, Peter Jackson, and David Ashton, *ISO 9000: An Implementation Guide for Small to Mid-Sized Businesses* (Delray Beach, Fla.: St. Lucie Press, 1994).

10. *1993 Application Guidelines: Malcolm Baldrige National Quality Award* (Washington, D.C.: United States

Department of Commerce, 1993). Also see Gilbert Fuchsberg, "Two Earn Baldriges As Winner's Circle Grows a Bit Tighter," *The Wall Street Journal* (October 19, 1993), p. A5; Ron Zemke, "Bashing the Baldrige," *Training* (Volume 28, February 1991), pp. 29–39; Jeremy Main, "How to Win the Baldrige Award," *Fortune* (April 23, 1990), pp. 101–116; and Donald S. Bacon, "How the Baldrige Winners Did It," *Nation's Business* (January 1989), pp. 32–34.

11. Surveys show that MBO is utilized in 80 percent of the Fortune 500, Forbes best managed, and Dun's list of best-managed companies. National Management Association Hall of Fame member and the leading proponent of MBO, George S. Odiorne, died in early 1992. See his last article, "MBO Means Having a Goal and a Plan—Not Just a Goal," *Manage* (Volume 44, Number 1, September 1992), pp. 8–11. Also, see Robert Rodgers and John E. Hunter, "Impact of Management By Objectives on Organizational Productivity," *Human Resource Management* (Volume 76, April 1991) pp. 322–336; and Odiorne, "MBO: A Backward Glance," *Business Horizons* (Volume 21, October 1978), pp. 14–24. Yet, not everyone is satisfied with MBO. See Ronald Starcher, "Mismatched Management Techniques," *Quality Progress* (Volume 25, Number 12, December 1992), pp. 49–52; and David Halpern and Stephen Osofsky, "A Dissenting View of MBO," *Public Personnel Management* (Volume 19, Fall 1990), pp. 59–62. For information about a firm that discarded MBO, see Larry Marion, "Changing the Culture at Teradyne," *Electronic Business* (Volume 19, Number 1, January 1993), pp. 28–32; and "Teradyne Inc., Zehntel Systems," *Quality Assurance: Blueprints for Action from 50 Leading Companies* (Waterford, Conn.: Bureau of Business Practice, 1991), pp. 109–110.

12. For information on just-in-time inventory systems and kanban, see Lloyd S. Morris, "Management Heads into the Next Decade," *Security Management* (Volume 36, Number 12, December 1992), pp. 20–21; and Caron H. St. John and Kirk C. Heriot, "Small Suppliers and JIT Purchasing," *International Journal of Purchasing & Materials Management* (Volume 29, Number 1, Winter 1993), pp. 11–16; and for empirical evidence of the effectiveness of kanban, see Lee J. Krajewski, Barry E. King, Larry P. Ritzman, and Danny S. Wong, "Kanban, MRP, and Shaping the Manufacturing Environment," *Management Science* (Volume 33, January 1987), pp. 39–57; R. Dave Garwood, "Explaining JIT, MRP II, Kanban," *P & IM Review and Apics News* (Volume 4, October 1984), pp. 66–68; Paul H. Zipkin, "Does Manufacturing Need a JIT Revolution?" *Harvard Business Review* (Volume 69, January–February 1991), pp. 40–50; and Satish Mehra and Anthony Inman, "Determining the Critical Elements of Just-In-Time Implementation," *Decision Sciences* (Volume 23, Number 1, January–February 1992), pp. 160–173. For a contrary opinion on JIT, see R. Anthony Inman and Larry D. Brandon, "An Undesirable Effect of JIT," *Production and Inventory Management Journal* (Volume 33, Number 1, First Quarter 1992), pp. 55–58; or Gene H. Johnson and James D. Stice, "Not Quite Just in Time Inventories," *National Public Accountant* (Volume 38, Number 3, March 1993), pp. 26–29.

13. For examples illustrating the use of Gantt charts, see H. L. Gantt, *Organizing for Work* (New York: Harcourt, Brace, and Howe, 1919), Chapter 8. Also see Mike Hack, "Harvard Project Manager Serves Pros, Casual Users," *InfoWorld* (January 30, 1989), pp. 54–55.

14. For additional information on PERT networks, see Li-Chih Wang and Wilbert E. Wilhelm, "A PERT-based Paradigm for Modeling Assembly Operations," *IIE Transactions* (Volume 25, Number 2, March 1993), pp. 88–103; Paul A. Strassman, "The Best-Laid Plans," *Inc.* (Volume 10, October 1988), pp. 135–138; and Edward A. Wasil and Arjang A. Assad, "Project Management on the PC: Software, Applications, and Trends," *Interfaces* (March–April 1988), pp. 75–84. Also see Donald W. Fogarty and Thomas R. Hoffmann, *Production and Operations Management* (Cincinnati: South-Western Publishing Co., 1989).

8

Supervisory Planning and Time Management

LEARNING OBJECTIVES

After studying this chapter, you will be able to:

1 Discuss forecasting at the supervisory level.

2 Describe some tactical strategies for gaining acceptance of plans.

3 Summarize major areas of supervisory planning for the effective and safe use of material and human resources.

4 Discuss the importance of time management and suggest techniques for supervisors to plan better use of their own time.

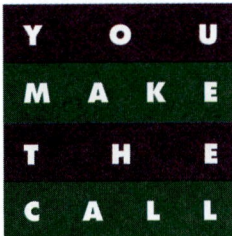
The rumors about the company's economic problems are at an all-time high. You are Phil Moore, a salaried maintenance supervisor for Paul's Home Center, a locally owned general merchandise store. Paul's Home Center has faced great competition since Wal-Mart, the nation's largest retailer, opened a store two miles down the road about three years ago.

You are 45 years old, married, with five children aged 9 to 18. Shortly after graduating from high school you were drafted into the Army and spent a tour of duty in Vietnam. Your military experience honed both your maintenance skills and your leadership skills. You returned home to marry your childhood sweetheart and have worked at the same job for the past 16 years. You are a working supervisor, and until three months ago you had four employees under your direction. When one of the younger employees quit to follow his spouse to another position out of state, Sally Paul, the sole owner of the store, decided not to allow you to fill the position.

You reflect on the events of the past several weeks: "This is not a dream or a newspaper story about someone else in another part of the country. This is happening here to us. I have to ask my people to do more, and I have been putting in 10- and 12-hour days to get the work done. The past two weeks have been unreal. The temperature set record highs almost every day, and the humidity hovered near 100 percent. Sally Paul has decided to face Wal-Mart head on. She purchased an adjacent building, added more parking space, lowered prices, and embarked on a customer service campaign that has employees bending over backward to give personal attention and greater service to customers."

You have been busy supervising the renovation of the adjacent building and the construction of the new parking lot. The past weekend should have been wonderful. Labor Day had always been a chance to put all the worries aside and relax at the in-laws' lakeside cottage. Historically, the store had always closed at 1:00 P.M. on Saturday, and old-man Paul would turn over in his grave if he could see all the changes.

Basically, the store is now open from 9:00 A.M. to 9:00 P.M. Monday through Saturday and from noon to 6:00 P.M. on Sundays. The additional hours have led to increased stress for all members of your department. You have not spent a day away from the business in over two months.

You know very well that you are shorthanded and that if things do not improve your remaining employees will leave. Surely something can be done to improve the situation. What can you do?
YOU MAKE THE CALL.

SUPERVISORY FORECASTING

1 Discuss forecasting at the supervisory level.

The survival and success of any organization depend in large measure on its managers' skills in forecasting and preparing for the future. Planning, as discussed in Chapter 7, means establishing objectives based on the current situation and forecasts of the future and determining the actions necessary to achieve objectives. Thus, managers must make certain assumptions about the future even if it is fraught with uncertainties.

Top-level executives must forecast the future in a more general and far-reaching manner than the supervisor. To identify potential growth opportunities or threats to the organization's success, top-level managers must make predictions about the competitive and general economic climate in which the organization will operate during future years. Demographic changes; resource availability and costs; and many other social, political, financial, and economic problems that influence business operations must be anticipated in the strategic planning process. However, our concern in this chapter is with planning at the supervisory level, where day-to-day planning is less likely to involve such global dimensions.

Forecasts
Predictions of future events.

Although they overlap to a certain degree, some distinction exists between planning and forecasting. **Forecasts** are an attempt to predict the future, but they do not spell out what actions to take. Forecasts are more like "building stones" on which plans are to be based. This means a supervisor has to look into the future and make forecasts in order to establish sound, realistic plans for the department.

Supervisory Concerns in Forecasting

Supervisors are responsible for forecasting future events that may affect departmental operations. In particular, supervisors should be familiar with recent developments in technology in their fields and be able to estimate how new technology might help their departments operate more efficiently. Supervisors can keep current by attending trade association meetings and exhibits and by reading journals and other appropriate literature. To some extent, supervisors can seek assistance from suppliers who are making new equipment that could be used in the department. Because technology is progressing so rapidly, in not too many years a department's technological functions may be significantly different from what they are now. They may be reduced or simplified, or they may grow, become more sophisticated, and take on greater prominence. The supervisor's technological projections should include some ideas about what types of equipment will be used in the department in both the short term and the long term and how such equipment will influence production, work flow, space allocations, material requirements, and other related factors.

The supervisor must also be prepared to forecast the number and types of employees who will be needed in the department. The supervisor may foresee a need for better or differently educated or more highly skilled employees, or for employees who possess skills that previously have not been required in the department or in the organization. Conversely, the supervisor might foresee that due to a projected increase in mechanization or computer assistance, fewer or less-skilled employees will be needed to perform departmental jobs.

Conceivably, it might appear to the supervisor that the department will diminish in importance or become obsolete due to new discoveries or new methods. Although this is not a pleasant thought, if it is looming on the horizon, it is better for the supervisor to recognize it early than to be confronted with such an event without being prepared for it. If obsolescence is threatening, the supervisor should inform higher-level management accordingly. Managers usually are willing to find a new position for any supervisor who is so farsighted, since such a person is recognized as being too valuable to lose. The supervisor can be just as capable of supervising another department, perhaps one that has not existed previously. In other words, farsighted supervisors who have the courage to suggest that their departments might eventually be eliminated are likely to survive and prosper themselves.

Only by making forecasts for the future will supervisors be able to clarify in their own minds the directions in which their departments must proceed. By forecasting, supervisors are in a position to formulate definite plans for implementation when and if the forecasted events occur.

Forecasting Means Readiness for Change

All forecasts contain certain assumptions, approximations, and estimates. At best, forecasting is an art, not an exact science. Forecasting accuracy, however, increases with supervisory experience. As time goes on, making estimates about the future becomes a normal activity. Supervisors should exchange forecasts, consult and check with each other, and share information whenever it is available. By so doing, a supervisor should become more accurate in forecasting. Even if some of the anticipated events do not occur exactly as anticipated, it still is better to have forecast them than to risk being confronted with unanticipated major changes and their consequences.

Having made needed forecasts, supervisors usually are in a better position to ready their departments to incorporate changes as they are needed. Although this may sound like a formidable task, all that really is required is to be alert to possible changes and trends. It is not uncommon for supervisors to review their years of work and, with hindsight, lament that they did not take seriously certain trends that had been visible earlier. If supervisors constantly estimate and anticipate the future, they will be more ready to implement necessary changes when those events do occur.

SUPERVISORY PLANNING: TACTICAL STRATEGIES

2 Describe some tactical strategies for gaining acceptance of plans.

Before making specific plans for the future, supervisors should consider a number of tactical strategies that may be crucial to a future plan. Planning cannot be done in a vacuum, nor can plans be implemented in a vacuum. Plans will have an impact on others, and they will elicit reactions from other supervisors, employees, the manager, and top-level management. Furthermore, implementation is critical to the success of a plan. A well-implemented average plan may be superior to a poorly implemented excellent plan. Therefore, effective planning should take into account certain tactical strategies that can help make a plan successful.

A supervisor should choose the strategies best suited for the problem. A few of the most commonly employed strategies will be suggested here, although they may not always be applicable. The application of these approaches will depend on the specific objective, the people involved, the urgency of the situation, the means available, and a number of other factors. By thinking through the strategy that is most appropriate for a particular plan, a supervisor will be in a much better position to make a plan become a reality and to minimize negative reactions.

Timing Alternatives

Timing is a critical factor in all planning. Thus, a supervisor may choose the planning strategy "strike while the iron is hot." This strategy advocates prompt action when the situation and time for action are advantageous. For example, this strategy might be employed when a supervisor finds that many orders in the department have been delayed and a number of customers have complained because their orders have fallen behind schedule. The supervisor might then ask for more employees, more equipment, or other resources that are necessary for the department over the long term.

On the other hand, the supervisor may decide to invoke the "time is a great healer" approach. This is not an endorsement of procrastination. However, it is often advisable to move slowly in a difficult situation, because some things take care of themselves after a short while. This is also referred to as the "wait and see" strategy, which suggests that it may be better to move a bit more cautiously than to propose a major change under duress or in a crisis. For example, the introduction of a new computerized customer checkout system in supermarkets typically causes numerous initial complaints from customers and employees. However, supermarket managers have found that with careful planning, ample communication, patience, and time, most of the initial complaints are mitigated. People eventually become accustomed to and accept the computerized system as an improvement in service.

Target Dates and Deadlines

The amount of time allotted for planning sets a constraint on a supervisor. Using the "do the best you can in the time available" strategy, a supervisor may ask the manager to impose some time limits. Without any time limitation, a supervisor may either give a plan little attention or waste much time in search of a "perfect" plan. Either extreme is undesirable. Given a time constraint of two days, for example, a supervisor will have to develop a plan that is the most feasible within the time limitations. The practicality of this approach was illustrated by the response one supervisor gave her manager, who asked whether the plan she submitted for a work layout renovation was the best possible one. She replied, "No, it is not. But it is the best recommendation I could make given the time available to me." Deadlines help motivate supervisors to accomplish the planning task.

Responses to Organizational Change

When major organizational changes are involved in plans, the supervisor may choose the strategy of the "mass concentrated offensive." This strategy advocates quick, radical, or complete action in order to make an immediate, favorable showing. For example, an office supervisor might believe that the performance of the office could be improved significantly by consolidating all word processing and other support services in a centralized location. To accomplish this plan, the supervisor might decide to make the change all at once in order to overcome potential opposition and to accomplish the objectives quickly.

On the other hand, the supervisor might prefer to use a different strategy, known as "get a foot in the door." This tactic advocates that it may be better to institute only a part of the planned change at the beginning, especially if it is of such magnitude that its total acceptance would be doubtful. In choosing this strategy, the office supervisor might consolidate only part of the word processing and other services at a centralized location on a trial basis to see how it works out before changing the entire office procedure.

Gaining Reciprocity

Sometimes a plan might advocate changes that could come about more easily if supervisors of other departments would participate in formulating and implementing the plan. A supervisor might find it advisable to have allies to promote the change by seeking strength in unity. For example, if a supervisor hopes to gain a budget increase for new departmental furniture, it may be expedient to have other supervisors join in making similar requests to higher-level management. This strategy is "you scratch my back and I will scratch yours." This tactic of reciprocity is well known in political circles and in the activities of sales representatives and purchasing agents. It simply means returning a favor for a favor. Reciprocity also is helpful in building more cooperative relationships among supervisors in carrying out other day-to-day obligations.

SUPERVISORY PLANNING FOR USE OF RESOURCES

3 Summarize major areas of supervisory planning for the effective and safe use of material and human resources.

Because supervisors are especially concerned with day-to-day planning, they must plan for the best utilization of all the resources at their disposal. These include both physical and human resources.

Utilization of Tools, Machinery, and Equipment

Supervisors must plan for efficient utilization of their departments' tools, machinery, and equipment, all of which represent a substantial investment. Tools, equipment, and machinery that are poorly maintained or are not efficient for the jobs to be done not only cause operating problems but also adversely affect employees' morale. A supervisor does not always have the most desirable or advanced equipment to work with, but the available equipment, when adapted and properly maintained, usually is sufficient to do the job. Therefore, before requesting new equipment, supervisors should first determine whether employees are using available tools and equipment properly. Many times when employees complain about poor equipment, investigation reveals that the equipment is being operated incorrectly. Thus, supervisors should periodically observe the employees using the equipment and ask them whether the equipment serves their purposes or needs improvement.

It is also the responsibility of the supervisor to work closely with the maintenance department in planning for periodic maintenance of tools, equipment, and machinery. Poorly maintained equipment may be blamed on the maintenance department in some cases, but the supervisor must share in the blame if he or she has not planned or scheduled needed maintenance with that department. The maintenance group can do only as good a job as other departments will allow them to do.

On occasion, the supervisor may decide that some equipment needs to be replaced. In making this request, the supervisor should also develop a plan to dispose of inefficient equipment and submit this plan to higher-level management. To determine when a change of tools, machinery, or equipment should take place, supervisors should review trade journals, listen to what salespeople have to say about new products, read literature circulated by distributors and associations, and generally keep up with developments in the field. A stronger argument can be advanced to higher-level managers if the supervisor has thoroughly studied the alternatives available and is prepared to make a recommendation based on several bids and models. Facts are more likely than emotional arguments to persuade higher-level managers to decide in favor of the supervisor's position.

Even though a supervisor has recommended a change that is supported with well-documented reasons, higher-level managers may turn it down on the basis that it is not economically feasible to replace the equipment at present. Although disappointed, the supervisor should support the decision and live with it. However, the supervisor should not hesitate to point out at any appropriate time the potential hazards in both production and morale of failing to replace the equipment in question.

In the long term, a supervisor's plans for replacement of equipment or purchase of new equipment probably will be accepted in some form. However, even when such requests are denied, the supervisor will be recognized as being on top of the job by planning for better equipment use in the department.

Improvement in Work Procedures and Methods

Supervisors often are so close to the job that they may not recognize when prevailing work methods need updating. However, each supervisor should periodically look at departmental operations as a stranger coming into the department for the first time might view them. By looking at each operation from a detached point of view, the supervisor can determine answers to questions such as the following: Is each operation really necessary? What is the reason for each operation? Can one operation be combined with another? Are the steps performed in the best sequence? Are there any avoidable delays? Is there unnecessary waste?

Methods improvement generally means any change in the way the department currently is doing something that will lead to an increase in production, lowered costs, or improvement in the quality of a product or service. Improvement in work procedures, methods, and processes usually makes the job of the supervisor easier. Besides personally looking for ways to improve operations, the supervisor should solicit ideas from employees. Employees usually know their jobs better than anyone else in the organization. Alternatively, the supervisor may be able to enlist the help of a specialist, such as an industrial engineer or a systems analyst, if this type of person is available within the organization.

When studying areas for methods improvement, a supervisor should concentrate on situations in which large numbers of employees are assigned; costs per unit are exceptionally high; or scrap figures, waste, or injury reports appear out of line. A good reason for concentrating on such areas is that it will be less difficult for the supervisor to convince both employees and higher-level managers that recommended changes will bring about considerable improvement, savings, or other benefits.

Organizations need to become more proactive in meeting the threat of increasing competition. Therefore, every supervisor should consider the benefits of a methods improvement program. In an earlier chapter we discussed employee suggestion programs. The supervisor must encourage employees to look for a better way to do the job.

Often, the supervisor can use sampling techniques to cut costs, save time, and increase employee efficiency. Broadly stated, sampling involves inspecting a small amount of typical work from an entire job to determine areas for improvement. Generally, work sampling techniques are the tools of the industrial engineer. However, in smaller firms the supervisor may have to wear the hat of the industrial engineer.[1] While work sampling is a useful tool, every effort must be made to ensure that the sample is typical of the whole it is intended to represent.

Safe Work Environment

Most managers and supervisors recognize that a safe work environment is one of their major responsibilities, since this is essential for the welfare and productivity of employees. Safety statistics have long indicated that employees themselves cause accidents more often than do faulty tools and equipment, because of carelessness, poor attitudes, inadequate training, and a host of other reasons. Yet the supervisor shares a major responsibility, both ethically and legally, to do everything possible to see to it that the safest possible work environment is maintained. Of course, there are some job categories that by their very nature are more hazardous than others. For example, supervisors in mining, construction, and heavy manufacturing face major challenges in working to reduce the potential for serious injuries and fatalities. By contrast, supervisors in the generally comfortable surroundings of an office usually do not have to worry about major injuries. Nevertheless, the potential for accidents exists in any situation if employees are not fully trained and reminded to follow safe work habits.

Observance of OSHA and Other Safety Regulations.
Since the passage of the Occupational Safety and Health Act of 1970 (OSHA), supervisors have been expected to devote major attention to reducing and preventing injuries and accidents on the job. OSHA has had a significant impact on the scope and administration of safety programs in many organizations. It has expanded the responsibility of the supervisor in planning for and bringing about a safer job environment.

The Occupational Safety and Health Act is a very complicated law.[2] Supervisors should have a general understanding of all safety requirements associated with the law as it affects departmental operations. Larger firms will have someone in management—typically in the human resources, safety, industrial engineering, or risk management department—who is familiar with the technical requirements of OSHA, as well as any other laws, court rulings, and industry-mandated safety regulations that must be observed. Regardless of the size of the firm, supervisors must plan to meet with managers, as well as with employees, union leaders, and even with government officials if necessary, to do everything possible to maintain compliance with all safety regulations.

Safety Committees and Safety Programs.
Many supervisors find it advisable to form employee safety committees, which are sometimes jointly spon-

Encouraging employee participation in accident prevention programs is an important part of a supervisor's responsibilities.

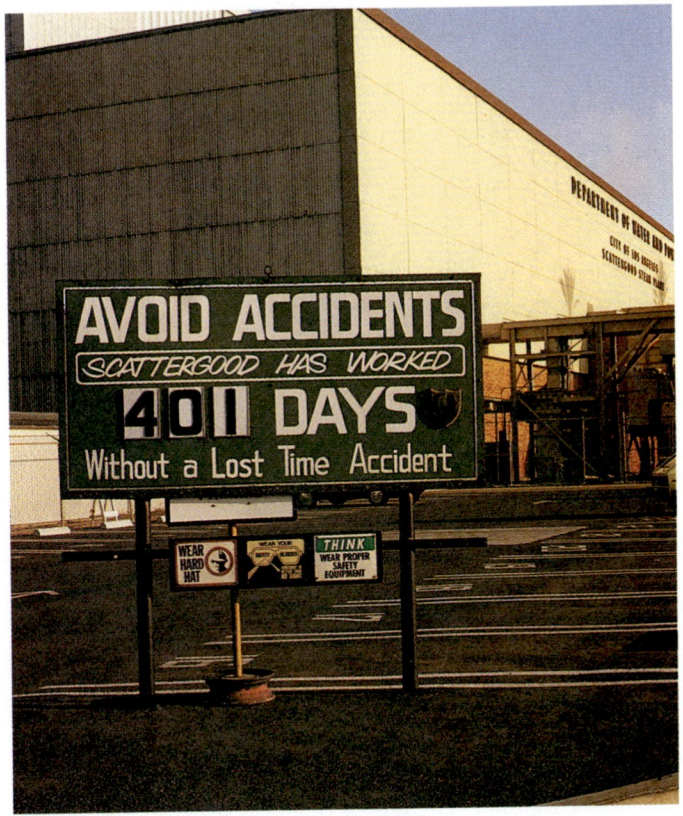

sored by both management and the union(s). The purpose of a safety committee is to assist the supervisor in developing safer work areas and enforcing safety regulations. The supervisor and safety committee can plan for periodic meetings and projects to communicate to employees the importance of safe work habits and attitudes.

A number of jobs require employees to repeat the same hand or arm motion for extended periods of time. For example, clerks who must use computer keyboards for hours at a time, day in and day out, may develop carpal tunnel syndrome (CTS). According to recent statistics compiled by the Department of Labor, repetitive motion injuries accounted for more than half of compensated workplace injuries. Such injuries cost businesses thousands of dollars in health care costs, downtime, and quality and productivity losses. A safety committee can be helpful in finding ways to redesign the clerk's workstation, for example, by changing the height of the keyboard, providing rests for the wrist, or finding other tasks to provide relief from the repetitive tasks.

The supervisor's constant attention to safety is mandatory if a safe work environment is to be maintained. Statistics show that well over three-fourths of all acci-

FIGURE 8-1
People are the most
common cause of
accidents.

dents on the job are caused primarily by human failure (see Figure 8-1). This means that the supervisor must emphasize safe work habits in daily instructions to employees and make sure that all equipment in the department is used properly and has ample protective devices. The supervisor should plan meetings throughout the year to emphasize safety themes. Supervisors will find that employees and higher-level managers usually are willing to assist in developing a strong safety program.

A commonly held half-truth is that a safety program is the responsibility of the safety department or safety engineers. However, without the full support of supervisors and diligent supervisory observance of employee work practices in every department, almost any safety program will be unsuccessful.

Efficient Use of Space

Supervisors must also plan for the allocation and utilization of space. This means that they should determine whether too much or too little space is assigned to the department and whether the space is used efficiently. Here, too, a supervisor may solicit industrial engineering help, if available.

In planning for use of space, a floor layout chart can be drawn and analyzed to determine whether there is sufficient space for the work to be performed and whether the space allocated has been laid out appropriately. If the chart indicates a need for additional space, the supervisor should include with the request a thorough analysis of how the current space is being allocated. Chances are that the supervisor has to compete with other departments that also would like to have more space. Unless the supervisor has planned thoroughly, the request for additional space has little chance of being granted. Even if the request is denied, the plans the supervisor has assembled will not have been prepared in vain. They will alert the supervisor to some of the conditions under which employees are working and where improvements might be feasible.

Use and Security of Materials, Supplies, and Merchandise

Another supervisory responsibility is to plan for the appropriate use, conservation, and security of materials, supplies, and merchandise. In most departments substantial quantities of materials and supplies are used and maintained in inventory. Even if each single item represents only a small value, the items add up to sizable dollar amounts in the total budget. Many employees do not realize the magnitude of the money tied up in materials and supplies, and sometimes they are careless in using these items. The supervisor should remind them that economical use of supplies ultimately is to their own advantage: Whatever is wasted cannot be used to raise wages or improve working conditions.

A major problem in recent years has been loss and theft of materials, supplies, merchandise, and other company property, sometimes carried out by employees themselves.[3] Supervisors must make sure that adequate security precautions are taken to discourage individuals from theft and to make it difficult for items to be lost or stolen. For example, many supplies can be kept locked up, with someone assigned the responsibility for distributing them as needed. If the firm has its own security force, the supervisor should meet with security personnel to plan and implement security devices and procedures that are suited to the department. In retail establishments, this may mean removing the opportunity for theft and training employees to pay attention to customers' bags, clothing, carts, boxes, and so forth. Increased attention can often deter a theft or a fraudulent return or exchange. A supervisor may even request such assistance from local police or a private security agency.

A supervisor's plans for utilization and security of materials, supplies, and merchandise cannot eliminate all waste and loss. But such planning usually will reduce waste and loss, and it will tend to promote a more efficient and conscientious work atmosphere among employees.

Employee Work Schedules

To plan effective work schedules for employees, supervisors should operate from the premise that most employees are willing to turn in a fair day's work. Supervisors should not expect all employees to work continuously at top speed. Rather, they should establish a work schedule based on an estimate of what constitutes a fair (rather than a maximum) output. Allowances must be made for fatigue, unavoidable delays, personal needs, and a certain amount of unproductive time during the workday. Some supervisors may be able to plan employee time with the help of a specialist, such as a motion and time analyst. Even without such help, most supervisors have a good idea as to what they can expect, and they are capable of planning reasonable performance requirements that their employees will accept as fair. Such estimates are based on normal rather than abnormal conditions. In this regard, it may not be advisable for a supervisor to schedule a department to operate at 100 percent capacity, because this would not leave any room for emergencies or changes in priorities and deadlines. Some flexibility is invariably needed to operate; thus, only short periods of 100 percent capacity should be scheduled. Also, several rest periods usually are a regular part of employee work scheduling.

Overtime and Absences. On occasion, supervisors find it necessary to plan for overtime, although overtime should be considered primarily as an exception or as an emergency measure. As a general rule, supervisors should anticipate a reduction of between 5 and 10 percent in productivity from employees when they work overtime. If a supervisor finds that excessive overtime is required regularly, then alternative methods of doing the work should be found or additional employees should be scheduled or hired.

Supervisors must also plan for employee absences. Of course, a supervisor cannot plan for every instance when an employee will be absent because of sickness, injury, or personal problems. However, the supervisor can plan for holidays, vacations, temporary layoffs, turnover, and other types of leaves or predictable absenteeism. Planning for anticipated absences will ensure the smooth functioning of the department.

Alternative and Part-Time Work Schedules. In recent years, many organizations have adopted alternative work schedules for their employees, such as part-time work, job sharing, working at home, and unconventional hours. As was discussed in Chapter 1, flextime is one form of alternative scheduling in which employees can choose—within certain limits—the hours they would like to work. Alternative work schedule plans are quite diverse. In some organizations, employees have the option to choose a four-day workweek—usually a four-day, 10-hour-per-day arrangement. Other companies have made it possible for employees to select different starting and ending times within a five-day workweek. Alternative work arrangements are becoming more commonplace, particularly in situations in which an employee's work is not closely interdependent or interrelated with that of other employees or departments. Figure 8-2 is an example of a statement from an insurance company employee manual regarding flexible working schedules and the role the supervisor plays in administering the schedule.

Supervisors have found that alternative work schedules create problems in maintaining coverage of all workstations or job positions, and that it may be difficult to exercise supervisory control at certain times of the workday. Nevertheless, supervisors who must cope with alternative work schedules learn to adapt within their departments and in their relations with other departments. In some situations, supervisors may be in charge of different work groups on different days and at dif-

FIGURE 8-2
Company Policy
Concerning Alternative
Work Scheduling

WORKWEEK

Your normal workweek is 38 hours and 45 minutes—7 hours and 45 minutes per day, Monday through Friday.

The normal work day begins at 8:15 a.m. and ends at 5:00 p.m. However under our "flextime" program, you may be given the choice, when possible, of working one of the following schedules:

> 7:00 a.m.–3:45 p.m.
> 7:15 a.m.–4:00 p.m.
> 7:30 a.m.–4:15 p.m.
> 7:45 a.m.–4:30 p.m.
> 8:00 a.m.–4:45 p.m.
> 8:15 a.m.–5:00 p.m.
> 8:30 a.m.–5:15 p.m.
> 8:45 a.m.–5:30 p.m.
> 9:00 a.m.–5:45 p.m.

We think you will like having the opportunity of choosing a work schedule which best suits your personal needs. Your supervisor will tell you which options are available in your department.

Many of our employees are required by law to have their work time recorded on time cards. If you are in this category, your supervisor keeps a weekly record showing time lost during the week and any overtime that was worked. You and the supervisor will review and sign the time card at the end of each week to show that both of you agree with the information recorded.

ferent times of the day as a result of flexible work scheduling. This, in turn, requires that supervisors on different shifts and in different departments coordinate their activities to achieve overall organizational effectiveness.

The use of part-time employees is increasing. Retailers, service establishments, and health-care centers, in particular, often have large numbers of part-time workers. Scheduling part-time employees requires considerable advance planning to match the needs of the department or business operation with the hours that the part-time people will be available.

Part-time work arrangements must be developed and monitored carefully if they are to be advantageous to both employees and management. Most studies of alternative work schedule plans have concluded that employees generally appreciate the opportunity to select their work schedule, and that flexible work schedules usually are associated with improvements in absenteeism rates, tardiness rates, retention, morale, and productivity.[4]

Full Utilization of Human Resources

Employees are the enterprise's most important resource. Planning for their full utilization always should be uppermost in every supervisor's mind. Full utilization of the workforce means getting employees to do their best. It means making plans for recruiting, selecting, and training employees; searching for better ways to group activities; training employees in proper and safe use of the materials associated with their jobs; supervising employees with an understanding of the complexities of human needs and motivation; communicating effectively with employees; appraising their performance; giving recognition; promoting the deserving; adequately compensating and rewarding them; and, if need be, taking just and fair disciplinary actions. All of these are ongoing aspects of a supervisor's plans for the full utilization of human resources.

Planning for the full utilization of employees is at the core of professional supervision. It is mentioned here again only briefly, since most chapters of this text are concerned in some way with this primary objective of supervisory management.

TIME MANAGEMENT

4 Discuss the importance of time management and suggest techniques for supervisors to plan better use of their own time.

To this point, we have emphasized the need for thorough planning for optimum use of physical and human resources. Another important resource that affects all other resources is the supervisor's own time.[5] The old saying that "time is money" applies with equal relevance to both the supervisor's time and the employees' time. A supervisor's time is a major resource that must be expended carefully. Like many other supervisors, Phil Moore (in the "You Make the Call" section) is experiencing days that are so full of demands that he feels as though he can never take care of all the matters that need attention. The days and weeks are too short; he would like to "buy" additional time somewhere. However, the supply of time is inflexible, and it cannot be renewed or stored. If supervisors want more time, they must make it themselves.

Most supervisors would welcome even a modest increase in their effectiveness. Given the many demands on them, supervisors who have a system for managing their time are far more likely to be effective than those supervisors who approach each day haphazardly. Although some supervisors insist that they need more time, what they really need is better use of the time they already have. One suggestion for using the time you have is to prepare each day for the day at hand. (See Figure 8-3).

Some supervisors put in extremely long days, but they are not on top of their jobs. Phil Moore (in the "You Make the Call" section) may be an example of a supervisor who equates long hours with devotion and effectiveness. Many times just the reverse is true. Such supervisors need to examine what effort is put into the hours worked and with what results, rather than looking only at the number of hours they have worked as a sign of their dedication. The key is to gain control over the workday rather than to be controlled by it. Time management, too, starts with careful planning.

FIGURE 8-3
There is no substitute for daily preparation!

Managing Time Means Reducing Stress

It is no consolation that our overworked supervisor, Phil Moore, like many others, does not have enough time to do all the things that must be done. Some supervisors work better under pressure, while others become less efficient under such conditions. While it is beyond the scope of this book to give broad coverage to techniques for managing stress, supervisors should understand the individualistic reactions that occur under stressful conditions. This chapter's "Contemporary Issue" box underscores the importance of managing time to reduce stress.

Most studies portray managers as members of high-stress groups. Increased stress has been tied to lower productivity, increased accidents, higher absenteeism, and alcohol and drug abuse. Stress is often looked upon as being bad, but a reasonable amount of stress can motivate people toward greater achievement.

Stress is directly related to the ability to cope with various time pressures and other pressures.[6] **External stressors** are causes of stress that come from outside the person, such as pressures of the job, family, and environmental conditions. The supervisory position by its very nature is pressure prone, since (as we discussed in Chapter 2) supervisors are barraged by many demands from managers, employees, and fellow supervisors. **Internal stressors** are pressures that people put on themselves, for example, by being ambitious, diligent, competitive, and aggressive.

Many courses teach people ways of coping with the pressures that induce stress. Some recommended stress control techniques are exercise, meditation, biofeedback training, and progressive relaxation. Typically, however, the suggested remedy is better time management, or as one author succinctly stated, "Managing stress means managing time. The two are so intertwined that controlling one can only help the other."[7] By employing better time management procedures, supervisors learn to prioritize duties and tasks, which in turn enables them to accomplish

External stressors
Causes of stress that arise from outside the individual, such as job pressures, responsibilities, and work itself.

Internal stressors
Pressures that people put on themselves, such as feeling a need to be perfect.

CONTEMPORARY ISSUE
The Need for Time Management[1]

Have you ever experienced any of the following? If so, you may not be alone.

1. *The stress of seeing your desk cluttered.* According to Daniel Stamp, founder of Priority Management Systems, the average worker has 36 hours worth of work on his or her desk and wastes three hours a week just searching for things.
2. *The pressure of being at the mercy of others.* According to Terrance Kotnour, senior management consultant, Dupont/Gemini Alliance Sodium Project, the time of a first-line maintenance supervisor is almost always at the mercy of others. How can one person handle all the demands placed on him or her and not go crazy?
3. *The feeling of being hurried.* Mismanagement of time may lead to a feeling of being hurried. The need to hurry is evidence of mismanagement of the specific and limited time available to managers. It means that their work is poorly done because they are trying to do too many things in too few hours. Hence, they are doing them badly and thus are *themselves* creating a vicious spiral of worry and emotional strains that can only end in physical troubles.

4. *The knowledge that you are your own worst enemy.* To quote Pogo, "We have met the enemy and he is us." Most of us fritter away time we could be putting to better use for work or for pleasure. There are managers who are so busy that they never get to see their families, or who develop health problems from pushing themselves too hard.
5. *Too much work to do and not enough people to do it.* In some of the understaffed offices of today, more may be demanded of people than they reasonably can accomplish. But jobs are so hard to come by that people do not dare quit, no matter how much they are exploited. People who operate under this sort of pressure do so by choice—or because they have not learned how to manage their time.

Time is a unique resource. *Everybody* has the same amount of it, so time is not our problem, but how we use it is!

Source: Adapted from (Point 1) Robert A. Mamis, "Undo Desk Clutter," *INC.* (Volume 15, November 3, March 1993), p. 46; (Point 2) Terrance J. Kotnour, "Time Management Helps First-Line Maintenance Supervisors Handle Pressures," *Industrial Engineering* (Volume 25, Number 3, March 1993), pp. 50–53; (Point 3) Ralph J. Cordiner, former GE president, cited in *The Work of a Professional Manager: Book III of Professional Management in General Electric* (New York: General Electric Company, 1954); and (Point 4) R. Alex Mackenzie, "How to Make the Most of Your Time," *U.S. News and World Report* (December 3, 1973), pp. 45–54.

more of what they really need to get done. Virtually by definition, better time management means increased accomplishment and reduced stress and frustration.

Classifying Duties with a Time-Use Chart

A first step toward better time management is for supervisors to analyze how they currently use time. A time-use chart, or time inventory, is an excellent tool to help supervisors examine how and where they currently are spending their time. Then they can begin to attack pockets of inefficiency.

Prior to constructing such a chart, supervisors should identify their primary job duties and daily activities and classify them as (a) routine duties, (b) regular duties, (c) special duties, or (d) innovative duties. They may wish to add another classification to cover time spent handling emergencies, although it is difficult to predict an emergency and the time needed to correct a crisis situation.

Routine duties are minor tasks that are done daily but make a limited contribution to the objectives of the department. Such work includes answering the tele-

Routine duties
Minor tasks, done daily, that make a minor contribution to achievement of objectives.

Regular duties
The essential components of a supervisor's job, such as giving directives and checking performance.

Special duties
Tasks not directly related to the core tasks of the department, such as meetings and committee work.

Innovative duties
Creative activities aimed at finding a better way to do something.

phone, reviewing the mail, chatting informally with others, cleaning up, and the like. Some of these tasks can be assigned to subordinates. **Regular duties** constitute the supervisory work most directly related to accomplishing the objectives of the department. Regular duties primarily involve the day-to-day activities that a supervisor must do personally and that are the essential components of the supervisor's responsibilities. Examples of these are giving directives, checking performance, writing reports, counseling employees, updating job descriptions, training new employees, and reviewing departmental operating procedures. **Special duties** consist of meetings, committee work, and special projects that are not directly related to core tasks of the department. **Innovative duties** are creative-thinking and improvement-oriented activities—for example, looking at new or improved work methods or finding better ways to communicate with employees.

Supervisors who are effective at managing their time do find time for innovative duties. Indeed, it is the innovative supervisor who usually stands out and is most often noticed by higher-level managers. This, of course, should not imply that a supervisor ought to work on innovative duties to the neglect of other duties. The amount of supervisory time spent on various duties will vary. Supervisors themselves must judge what are the appropriate proportions for their particular situations. One thing is clear, however: If a supervisor does not plan carefully, routine and special duties have a way of crowding out the time needed for regular and innovative duties.

A time-use chart is a useful technique for gathering information about how a supervisor is currently spending time. The supervisor can start by constructing a time-use chart similar to the one shown in Figure 8-4. Duties should be classified as routine, regular, special, or innovative. Then the supervisor should decide what amount of time should normally be allocated to duties under each category and correspondingly set goals for each day. Once these steps are taken, the supervisor should keep an ongoing record of the time that actually was spent on various duties. After a week or two of recording daily how time is actually spent, the supervisor should bring together the time-use sheets and total the amount of time spent in each of the categories. These totals should be compared with the original estimates or goals. The supervisor is then in a position to evaluate his or her use of time. With rare exceptions, the supervisor will be in for some surprises!

By analyzing the actual times versus the goals or estimates, the supervisor can determine whether appropriate amounts of time are being spent on various duties. For example, are some regular duties not getting done because too much time is devoted to routine duties or special projects? Could some tasks be eliminated altogether? Is there sufficient time for innovative work and planning? Answers to these and similar questions give the supervisor a better feel for what she or he ought to be working on, rather than simply tackling the problems that happen to come up first or seem most pleasant to work on at the moment.

Overcoming Time Wasters by Setting Priorities

Invariably, supervisors discover time wasters that have hampered their ability to work on important things in their department. Such time wasters as random activi-

FIGURE 8-4
Time-Use Chart

Goals for the Day	Estimated Time (in hours and fractions of hours)	Percentage (calculate)
Routine		
Regular		
Special		
Innovative		

Actual Time Use	Routine	Regular	Special	Innovative
		(Record the time spent in hours and fractions of hours)		
6:00–7:00				
7:01–8:00				
8:01–9:00				
9:01–10:00				
10:01–11:00				
11:01–12:00				
12:01–1:00				
1:01–2:00				
2:01–3:00				
3:01–4:00				
4:01–5:00				
5:01–6:00				
Totals				
Calculated Percentages				

Evaluation of Effectiveness_____

_____

ties, too much time on the telephone, too much time visiting or being visited, procrastination, unnecessary meetings, and lack of delegation may be revealed by a time inventory. The discovery and recognition of time wasters represent only one step. The supervisor must begin immediately to attack these old habits and build desirable ones. See Figure 8-5 for suggestions on improving time management.

Supervisory problems crop up continuously, often without an apparent sequence of priority. Therefore, supervisors must discipline themselves to decide between matters that they must handle personally and those that can be assigned to someone

FIGURE 8-5
Tips for Overcoming
Time Wasters.

"I waste time shuffling papers instead of dealing with an item until completed."

TIP: CONCENTRATE YOUR TIME AND ENERGY ON THE TASK AT HAND!

"I seem to be worn out by the time I get to the toughest tasks."

TIP: KNOW WHEN YOUR PEAK ENERGY TIME IS! WORK ON THE TOUGHEST TASKS—THE ONES REQUIRING THE MOST CONCENTRATION AND CREATIVITY—WHEN YOU ARE AT YOUR BEST.

"This is something I should be able to finish before I go home."

else. For every task delegated—particularly routine duties—a supervisor gains time for more important matters, such as regular and innovative duties. Doing this may be worthwhile even if the supervisor has to spend extra time training an employee in a particular task. The supervisor then should plan the remaining available time so that it is allocated properly among the duties that he or she alone must perform. These duties must be classified according to which are the most and the least urgent.

The "Pareto Principle," named after a famous 19th-century Italian economist, holds that many people, because they fail to set priorities, spend most of their time on minor, unimportant tasks. It has been estimated that some supervisors spend 80 percent of their time on duties that contribute to only 20 percent of the total job results. A supervisor who does not establish a priority of duties is inclined to pay equal attention to all matters at hand. This type of supervisor tends to handle each problem in the order it happens, and consequently, the most important matters may not receive the attention they deserve. When priorities are established, time is planned so that the most important things have sufficient space on the schedule. However, supervisors should leave some flexibility in their schedules, because not every event that occurs can be anticipated. Emergencies and changing priorities do occur, and supervisors must attend to them. Flexibility permits supervisors to take care of unanticipated problems without significantly disrupting their schedule of priorities.

Basic Tools of Time Management

Effective time utilization requires mental discipline. This means that supervisors should assign priorities to duties and stop trying to do everything brought to their attention. Once such a mental attitude is fixed, they can better use a number of common tools as aids in managing their time.

Every supervisor should use a pocket or desk calendar every day to note activities that need major attention, such as appointments, meetings, reports, and discussions. By scheduling such activities as far in advance as practicable and noting them on their calendars, supervisors are less likely to overlook them.

Another tool for effective time utilization is the weekly planning sheet (or, if preferred, a monthly planning sheet). Typically, a planning sheet for a week is prepared at the end of the previous week. The planning sheet shows the days of the week divided into mornings and afternoons and lists the items to be accomplished (see Figure 8-6). At a glance the supervisor can check what is planned for each morning and afternoon. As each task is accomplished, it is circled. Tasks that have been delayed must be rescheduled for another time. Tasks that are planned but not accomplished during the week remain uncircled and should be rescheduled for the following week. This record indicates how much of the original plan was carried out, and it provides information concerning how the supervisor's time was spent.

Another basic tool many supervisors find helpful is the "to-do" list, which can be used in conjunction with a desk calendar or weekly planning sheet. This is essentially an ongoing listing of things to do—both major and minor—to which a supervisor can refer as each day progresses. As an item is accomplished, it is crossed off the list. The supervisor must prioritize all items on the list and schedule and perform important tasks before attending to the minor items. Many supervisors find that the best time to review and reprioritize their to-do lists is at the beginning of the workday or at the end of the day before they leave.

There are other tools that supervisors can implement to accomplish better time management. Regardless of what tools they decide to use, however, it is their responsibility to plan and manage their time for each day and week and to have a system for recording tasks that were planned and those that were accomplished.

Time for Creative and Innovative Thinking

Every supervisor needs to leave some time open for creative and innovative thinking. Although a manager's evaluation of a supervisor will depend primarily on how effectively the department functions, the manager also will recognize the supervisor for innovative changes, new ideas, and progressive suggestions. Unless supervisors set some time aside for thinking about constructive improvements, they will find themselves bogged down with routine work and putting out fires.

SUNDAY 9/21	MONDAY 9/22	TUESDAY 9/23	WEDNESDAY 9/24	THURSDAY 9/25	FRIDAY 9/26	SATURDAY 9/27
AM	AM 7:30 (Staff Mtg.) (Monthly safety committee meeting)	AM (Discuss with human resources director interpretation of changes in policy)	AM (Talk to engineering about preventive maintenance plan)	AM (Turn in scrap report) 11AM (Staff Mtg.)	AM (Attend management seminar)	AM
PM	PM (Discuss direct labor cost figures with comptroller)	PM (Work on budget for next six months)	PM	PM (Check absentee, turnover, and accident rates)	PM (Meeting with Union Grievance Committee to discuss unresolved grievances)	PM

FIGURE 8-6
The Weekly Planning Sheet

One technique some supervisors find helpful in this regard is to develop a list of improvement projects or innovative ideas and write them on a special desk pad or wall chart. This list becomes a constant visual reminder of items that the supervisor would like to accomplish when time becomes available. When there are lulls in a day, or during slack periods, the supervisor can decide which of the innovative items on the list to tackle. Interestingly, the mere thought of having such a list can be a major incentive to attempt an improvement project that otherwise might not be attempted. When the improvement project is done, it is a good feeling to cross the item off the list and mark it as accomplished.

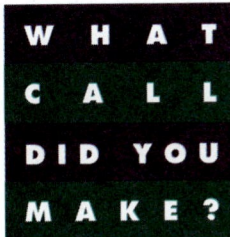

W H A T   C A L L   D I D   Y O U   M A K E ?

Some people work better under pressure, but a continuous diet of long hours with no end in sight is too much. Not only is Phil Moore feeling the stress, it appears that his staff is feeling it also, particularly since the firm is understaffed. Unfortunately, this situation may be fairly typical with the current trends of downsizing organizations and not filling positions when employees leave.

As Phil Moore, you do not appear to have time for creative or innovative thinking about how to handle the current situation. Nevertheless, you must make time.

For yourself and other members of the department, you need to prepare a time-use chart for a few days. "Know thyself," said Socrates. Evaluate how you are using the time you have. Perhaps you might want to seek anonymous assessments from others and compare their perceptions with your own. Analysis of the time-use charts should tell you whether your time allotments are going where they will do the most good. We suspect that you will find that you are not spending your time as wisely as you think. Many working supervisors tend to pay attention to all the little details instead of delegating them.

Depending on the analysis of the time-use chart, you may want to prepare a written list illustrating how the department's productivity is suffering and potentially affecting the entire organization. You could review the list with your staff before you present it to Sally Paul. You should also be prepared to propose solutions. If the current situation is unacceptable and you want to see a change soon, you will have to be assertive.

While Ms. Paul might allow you to add staff, you need to use the techniques presented in this chapter to help you make more efficient use of your employees' time and your own.

SUMMARY

1 Discuss forecasting at the supervisory level.

Planning means establishing objectives based on the current situation and forecasts of the future, and determining the actions needed to achieve the objectives. Top-level managers forecast the future in a more general and far-reaching manner. Supervisory forecasting is an effort to predict future events that may affect departmental operations. Thus, supervisors need to be alert to possible changes and trends.

Forecasts serve as "building stones" on which plans are based. Supervisors who realistically try to anticipate certain events will be in a better position to prepare for them. Supervisors need to be alert for new technologies that will enable their departments to operate more efficiently. Supervisors must also project human resources needs and forecast the skills employees will need in the future.

Forecasting helps supervisors anticipate possible changes and their consequences. Supervisors should share information with others. They also need to be concerned with the effects their forecasts may have on their employees and other members of the organization. In so doing, they will be prepared to incorporate needed changes.

2 Describe some tactical strategies for gaining acceptance of plans.

In making plans, supervisors should consider strategies that can be helpful in gaining acceptance of the plans by employees, higher-level managers, and/or other supervisors. The application of the strategy will depend on the specific objectives, the people involved, the urgency of the situation, the means available, and a number of other factors. The strategies include the following:

a. Choosing the best timing for proposing the plan, which may mean either taking prompt action when the situation and time for action are advantageous, or moving slowly and cautiously in difficult situations or when major changes are contemplated.

b. Establishing deadlines so that employees are motivated to complete the task within the preestablished time limit.

c. Making a major change all at once to reduce potential resistance to change and accomplish objectives quickly.

d. Instituting only part of the planned change to see how it works out.

e. Involving other supervisors in the introduction of change.

While there is no one best strategy, supervisors should choose a strategy that is most likely to result in successful implementation of their plans.

3 Summarize major areas of supervisory planning for the effective and safe use of material and human resources.

Supervisory planning typically focuses on short-term operational matters. Specifically, supervisors must plan for efficient utilization of the department's tools, machinery, and equipment. Effective planning requires close coordination with the maintenance department.

Planning for improvement in work procedures and methods means looking for more efficient ways to achieve objectives. Encouraging employees to look for a better way to do the job and periodic work sampling may result in substantial savings for the organization.

Supervisors should have a general understanding of all safety requirements. Safety committees and safety programs are helpful in planning for and bringing about a safe work environment.

A major problem has been loss and theft of materials, supplies, merchandise, and other company property. Supervisors must ensure that adequate security precautions are taken to discourage individuals from misusing or stealing items.

Planning work schedules for employees includes establishing reasonable performance requirements and anticipating overtime requirements and absences from the workplace. Many organizations are experimenting with various types of alternative and part-time work schedules. Planning for the full utilization of employees is at the core of professional supervision.

4 Discuss the importance of time management and suggest techniques for supervisors to plan better use of their own time.

Time is one of the supervisor's most valuable resources. Everybody has the same amount of it, so time is not the problem, but how we use it is. Therefore, supervisors must plan and manage their own time if they are to be effective. Supervisors are members of high-stress groups. Better time management means reduced stress.

Supervisors need to analyze and plan their schedules so as to maximize their time on regular and innovative duties and, by delegating and setting priorities, minimize their time spent on routine and other low-priority tasks.

Since supervisors never seem to have enough time to do all the things that must be done, they must screen their time-use charts to identify the time wasters that steal time from them. Some of the basic tools are pocket calendars, weekly or monthly planning sheets, and to-do lists. Establishing priorities, developing a plan, and working the plan are essential to better use of time.

KEY TERMS

Forecasts (page 200)   Regular duties (page 215)
External stressors (page 213)   Special duties (page 215)
Internal stressors (page 213)   Innovative duties (page 215)
Routine duties (page 214)

QUESTIONS FOR DISCUSSION

1.   Identify and discuss the most important factors a supervisor should consider in making departmental forecasts.

2.   Evaluate the following statement: "Plan your work—Work your plan!"

3.   Evaluate each of the tactical strategies that can be used in a supervisor's planning function. Then identify guidelines a supervisor should use in choosing which strategy (or combination of strategies) to use in planning.

4.   Discuss the supervisor's planning responsibilities for tools, machinery, and equipment and for work procedures and methods.

5.   Why has safety planning received more supervisory emphasis in recent years? Outline several steps supervisors can take to plan for a safer work environment.

6.   What techniques should a supervisor use to plan for better use and security of space, materials, supplies, and merchandise?

7.   Analyze the following statement: "Planning for the full utilization of employees is at the core of professional supervision."

8.   Discuss the major considerations supervisors should keep in mind when planning employee work schedules. Discuss the pros and cons of flexible and part-time work scheduling.

9.   Define each of the following types of supervisory duties in connection with a time-use chart:

   a.   Routine duties
   b.   Regular duties
   c.   Special duties
   d.   Innovative duties

10. List and explain what a supervisor like Phil Moore (in the "You Make the Call" section) can do to maximize the efforts of his employees. Discuss general and specific approaches supervisors can use to plan their own time more effectively.

SKILLS APPLICATIONS

Skills Application 8-1: Getting Control Over Time

1.   Ask a supervisor to identify factors that he or she personally regards as time wasters. From the list of time wasters, ask the supervisor to identify the one that has the most adverse impact.

2.   Ask the supervisor what he or she would do to minimize the impact of the time wasters.

3.   Compare your list with the time wasters discussed in this chapter. To what degree do they coincide and/or differ? How do you account for the differences?

Skills Application 8-2: Developing a Personal Time Budget

1.   Take one hour on Sunday evening as your personal weekly planning period. Develop a time plan for the forthcoming week. List all of the regular tasks that need to be done and estimate the time required for each.

2.   Keep a time-use chart for the week, listing all activities and the time spent on each. Compare your time plan with the chart. How well did you plan? Identify the activities (time wasters) that impeded your schedule.

Skills Application 8-3: Flextime Analysis

You have been given a special assignment by your supervisor. Your charge is to investigate the advantages and disadvantages of flexible work scheduling. Your report is due in one day, so you must do the best you can in the time available.

1.   Three things you would like to do are as follows:

   a.   Visit the local library and run a data search to find at least three current articles on the scope of flexible scheduling.

   b.   Develop a list of questions you would ask representatives of a firm about their use of flexible scheduling.

   c.   Identify a local firm that uses flexible scheduling and interview the human resources manager or staff support person, a supervisor, and an employee, using your previously prepared questions.

2.   Prepare a list of the other things you might do to complete the project. Estimate the time required for each activity. Are all of the tasks doable within your time limits?

3.   Prioritize your activities. If you cannot do everything in the time allotted, which tasks would you focus on first?

4.   How did the time limits reinforce the notion that a supervisor's time is a major resource that must be managed carefully?

ENDNOTES

1.   For information on work sampling techniques, see Richard F. Weaver, ed., *Brief Work-Factor* (Moorestown, N.J.: Science Management Corporation, 1976).

2.   For an OSHA overview beyond the scope of this text, see Arthur W. Sherman, Jr., and George W. Bohlander, *Managing Human Resources* (9th ed.; Cincinnati: South-Western Publishing Co., 1992), Chapter 13.

3.   Statistically, such losses to U.S. businesses have been estimated to be in the billions of dollars. Most experts agree that the United States has the highest rate of employee theft and dishonesty in the world. See Jill A. Fraser, "Preventing Employee Theft," *Inc.* (Volume 15, Number 2, February 1993), p. 39; Joseph T. Wells, "Internal Fraud and the Credit Business," *Credit World* (Volume 81, Number 3, January–February 1993), pp. 36–38; and Bruce Gathart, "Loss Prevention: Minimizing Risk, Maximizing Deterrents," *Discount Merchandiser* (Volume 33, Number 1, January 1993), pp. 58–59.

4.   For an introductory overview, see Sue Shellenbarger, "More Companies Experiment with Workers' Schedules," *The Wall Street Journal* (January 13, 1994), pp. B1 and B6; D. Keith Denton, "Using Flextime to Create a Competitive Workplace," *Industrial Management* (Volume 35, Number 1, January–February 1993), pp. 29–31; Hermine Zagat Levine, "Alternative Work Schedules: Do They Meet Workforce Needs? Part 1," *Personnel* (February 1987), pp. 57–92; Robert Golembiewski and Carl W. Proehl, Jr., "A Survey of the Empirical Literature on Flexible Workhours: Character and Consequences of a Major Innovation," *Academy of Management Review* (Volume 3, 1978), pp. 8837–8855; and Raymond L. Hilgert and John R. Hundley, III, "Supervision: The Weak Link in Flexible Work Scheduling," *The Personnel Administrator* (January 1975), pp. 24–26. For a counterpoint, see David A. Ralston, William P. Anthony, and David J. Gustafson, "Employees May Love Flextime, But What Does It Do to the Organization's Productivity?" *Journal of Applied Psychology* (Volume 70, May 1985), pp. 272–279.

5.   Excellent books on time management include those by R. Alex Mackenzie, renowned time-management consultant, *The Time Trap* (New York: McGraw-Hill/AMACOM, 1972) and *The Time Trap: The New Version of the 20-*

Year Classic on Time Management (New York: AMACOM, 1990). For an excellent practical application article on time management, see Terrance J. Kotnour, "Time Management Helps First-Line Maintenance Supervisors Handle Pressures," *Industrial Engineering* (Volume 25, Number 3, March 1993), pp. 50–53. Time management principles may not work for everyone; see Eleena De Lisser, "Some People Plan; Some People Pan the Rise of Planners," *The Wall Street Journal* (September 9, 1993), pp. A1 and A6.

6.   Much information has been provided on the bad side of stress. For a counterargument, see Dru Scott, *Stress That Motivates: Self-Talk Secrets for Success* (Los Altos, Calif.: Crisp Publications, 1992); or Peter G. Hanson, *The Joy of Stress* (self-published, 1985); and Hanson, *Stress for Success: How to Make Stress on the Job Work for You* (New York: Doubleday, 1989). The article by Patrick E. Connor and Charla Hart Worley, "Managing Organizational Stress," *Business Quarterly* (Volume 56, Number 1, Summer 1991), pp. 61–67, provides practical insights.

7.   From Randall S. Schuler, "Managing Stress Means Managing Time," *Personnel Journal* (December 1979), pp. 22–25. Also, see Stephen Ash, "What to Do If You Feel Overworked," *Manage* (Volume 43, Number 2, February 1992), pp. 4–5.

CASE 2-1
A Shortage of Policies

The Montclair Manufacturing Company produced a wide array of electronic gauges and employed about 250 people. Chuck Adams, the factory superintendent, was eating his lunch in the company cafeteria with Bill Whitaker and Gerry Parker, two supervisors on the assembly line; Mary Stoebeck, the purchasing agent; and Werner Koff, one of the district sales managers. Their conversation centered around a common complaint, namely, that the company had few written policies or guidelines and that this lack caused them unnecessary discomfort when they had to make decisions. Adams deplored the fact that some employees ate their lunches at the workbench, and he felt that there should be a policy forbidding this practice. Whitaker and Parker mentioned the need for a policy on granting employees leaves of absence. Stoebeck stated that she needed a clear policy specifying how to obtain bids from prospective suppliers. Koff was concerned that top-level management had not bothered to issue a policy regarding whether salespeople should wear informal sportswear or conventional business attire when making calls. In addition to these specific concerns, there were numerous other complaints that reflected a feeling of dissatisfaction among the company's managers.

The group concluded that the best way to attack this problem would be to confront the president of the company, Jay Montclair, with their questions and ask him to define policies in these and other areas. While they were deliberating this, May Murphy, the assistant to the president, joined them at lunch and listened to much of the conversation. Murphy asked, "Are these really matters for the president to decide, or should you supervisors be making these types of decisions for your own departments?"

Questions for Discussion

1. Analyze each of the individual problem situations mentioned in the case. For which areas should policies have come from top-level management, and for which areas should policies have been made by departmental supervisors?

2. Is there an appropriate dividing line between policies to be made by top-level management and policies that must be made at the departmental level? Discuss.

3. Should the group of supervisors confront the president of the company with a request for more clearly defined policies? What strategies might be suggested for the supervisors to bring their concerns to the company president?

CASE 2-2
Interpreting Funeral-Leave Policy

Joan Sutherland supervised a unit of 15 nurses who worked on the evening shift at a large hospital located in a midwestern city. She had recently been promoted to the position of supervisor after having worked as a registered nurse in another unit in the hospital for three years.

One day Sutherland received a telephone call from one of her employees, a licensed practical nurse named Betty Sherman who had been employed at the hospital for about four years. It was obvious from Sherman's voice that she was upset; she had difficulty in speaking without crying. She said, "My Aunt Frances passed away last night. She was my foster mother who helped raise me for several years during my teens, after my parents separated and my mother remarried. I will need several days off in order to attend the funeral. Aunt Frances lived in a small town about 50 miles away from here, and the rest of the family will be gathering there this afternoon."

Joan Sutherland replied, "I'm terribly sorry that you had this death in your family. Let me check the policy manual to see what you are entitled to." Quickly, she opened the policy manual to the section marked "Death in Family." The section read as follows:

In the event of death in your immediate family (spouse, child, parent, brother, sister, father-in-law, mother-in-law), if you are a permanent employee, you will be granted an excused absence with pay of up to 3½ successive days following the death.

Joan Sutherland said, "I'm not sure whether this policy provides time off for the death of a foster parent. I'll call the human resources department to see whether they have a ruling. Let me call you right back." With that she dialed the human resources department office, but she was informed by a secretary that the director of human resources would be out of town until the following week. The secretary did not know whether the hospital provided for funeral-leave benefits to employees who lost a foster parent.

As Joan Sutherland hung up the telephone, she wondered what she should say to Betty Sherman.

Questions for Discussion

1. Should the policy of the hospital be interpreted to include an employee's foster mother as part of the immediate family? Discuss.

2. What should Joan Sutherland do? Consider various alternatives that are open to her.

3. What are the precedent implications of this case?

CASE 2-3
The Snow Day Stir

It was mid-February in a midwestern city when a major snowstorm was predicted for the following day. The forecast was for 8 to 12 inches of snow. Weather conditions normally weren't a concern for the Wiess Products Company. However, in this situation management distributed a memorandum informing plant employees that if the plant was to be closed due to heavy snow, such a closing would be announced on local radio stations at 6:00 A.M.

On the morning of February 14 snow was falling, but it had only accumulated 1 to 2 inches by 6:00 A.M., and the plant wasn't closed. Virtually all the first-shift employees made it to work, and the snow continued to fall. At approximately 1:30 P.M., two hours before the end of the shift, the snow was still falling, and it already had accumulated to 8 inches. After consulting with the company president, the director of human resources, Dick Smear, announced that the plant was closing. The first-shift employees were sent home, and second-shift employees were contacted by telephone about the closing. Radio announcements to the same effect were broadcast by several local stations at 2:00 P.M.

On the following day, again after consulting with the company president, Dick Smear announced that all plant employees would receive eight hours' pay for February 14. Wiess was a nonunion plant, and there was no formal policy for this type of event since this was the first such occurrence. Because all supervisors were salaried, they, too, would be paid as usual, even though the second-shift supervisors had stayed home on February 14. In Smear's announcement, he said that the company felt that employees should not suffer a loss of income for circumstances beyond their control.

The announcement that all employees would receive eight hours' pay for February 14 created a stir on the shop floor. It was around 3:30 P.M. when the shifts were in the process of changing. The first-shift employees were loudly complaining that it wasn't fair that they had to work for six hours, and that second-shift employees didn't have to work at all but still received eight hours' pay. This stir escalated when Carla Peters, a first-shift operator, and David Carpenter, a second-shift operator, started debating the fairness of the issue. A heated argument ensued among them and several other employees.

A first-shift supervisor, Doug Beck, and a second-shift supervisor, Marta Tropp, heard the argument and went to the floor to check out the situation. When they found out what the argument was about, Beck told Tropp that he that agreed with Carla Peters. Beck said that it was "grossly unfair" that first-shift employees and supervisors who worked and had to contend with traveling in the snow were not treated any differently from the second-shift workers who had stayed comfortably at home. The conversation was going nowhere, so Beck and Tropp told the employees to "cool off" and that they would go see Dick Smear to review the matter further. Peters and Carpenter responded that the employees felt that the matter had been handled poorly and that the company managers should have consulted with the employees and supervisors before making such a decision.

Questions for Discussion

1.   Do you agree with the company managers' decision in this situation? Why or why not? If you disagree, what would you have done differently?
2.   Should the managers have consulted with any of the employees or supervisors before making the decision to pay everyone for the snow day? Discuss.
3.   If you were Dick Smear, what would you recommend to the company president, and why?

CASE 2-4
Objections to Free Coffee and Beverages

Alice Erickson was the administrative office manager of the Southern Oil Company. She was in charge of about 75 office employees. There were 10 departments within the office, and each was headed by a supervisor. This made for an average span of supervision of approximately 6 to 10 employees, although two departments handling routine work had 15 employees.

It had been customary for employees to go out of the building to a nearby restaurant for their morning and afternoon breaks. These breaks were so timed that only some of the employees were gone at any one time. Although 20 minutes had been allocated for this, employees usually were absent from their desks for about 30 minutes.

Erickson was about to send a suggestion to her boss, the vice-president of operations, to replace these outside breaks by sending a coffee cart through the departments twice a day. The company would provide coffee and other beverages free. Although this would entail some expense, the company would save money by having employees served at their desks instead of their being away for about 30 minutes.

Before submitting this recommendation for approval, Erickson thought she should discuss it with the 10 supervisors in the office. Much to her surprise, the offer for free coffee and beverages served from the coffee cart was not greeted with enthusiasm but rather with severe criticism and misgivings. Some of the major objections were that this would prevent the supervisors and employees from getting together informally. In addition, it would remove their chance to speak with personnel from other departments, with whom they often discussed company problems as well as personal matters. The supervisors felt that these outside breaks offered an important channel of communication, the loss of which would hurt the smooth functioning of the office.

After meeting with the supervisors, Alice Erickson pondered what she should do next.

Questions for Discussion

1. If you were one of the supervisors, what would you prefer?

2. Should Alice Erickson go ahead with her idea for free coffee and beverages to be served from a cart?

3. Do coffee breaks actually serve as a channel of communication that is important to the smooth functioning of an office? Does this depend upon the situation? Discuss.

4. Why should policies generally be enforced consistently, especially policies involving work schedules and break periods?

CASE 2-5
The Violator of the No-Smoking-in-the-Washroom Rule

"Tom, we're going to have to fire Charlie Fiedler. He's been goofing off, and I've had all of it I can take. Let's get him out of here," said Mike Walling over the telephone to Tom Keel, the director of human resources of the Giles Manufacturing Company.

"But Mike, I thought you rated Charlie Fiedler as one of your bright young employees who might be an apprentice toolmaker in a couple of years," responded Keel.

"Well, he seemed to be a good worker for a while; but ever since we got rid of those old lathes and I've had him on bench work, he's gone totally sour, and now he's a real troublemaker," retorted Walling.

"Okay, Mike, but I'd like to talk to him," said Keel. "What's the specific reason for the discharge?"

Walling responded, "Well, you can put it on the record that I found him smoking in the washroom three times. He was warned twice, and I just caught him the third time. Management has insisted that we enforce that no-smoking-in-the-washroom rule, and Charlie's the worst offender. I know he didn't like it when we took him off the lathes. We put in two high-speed machines and got rid of five old ones.

Others had seniority. There wasn't anything to do with Charlie but put him on bench work, and ever since he's been goofing off."

"Send him up to me, Mike," said Keel. "I'll tell him you're letting him go for breaking rules."

Tom Keel first reviewed Charlie Fiedler's employment record and noticed that he had been with the company for about three years. Fiedler was 24 years old, a high school graduate, and had been married for approximately six months. During his employment with the company, he had received five pay increases and "superior" ratings on three appraisal reviews. After his last two reviews, his record had been marked "promotable" by his foreman, Mike Walling.

Within a few minutes Charlie Fiedler was in the human resources office and seemed to be anxious to speak with Tom Keel. As soon as he was seated at Tom's desk he blurted out, "Is Mike going to fire me?"

"Well, Charlie," said Tom, "he's not exactly pleased with your work at this moment, and he says he thinks you ought to be discharged from the machine shop. Tell me, just what is your trouble with Mike?"

Fiedler: Things are terrible in the shop now. I used to think Mike was a great guy. He's an expert on every machine in the shop and he taught me a lot, but now I'm convinced he's a slave-driver. All he wants is work, work, work—it's impossible to please him. I've worked on drill presses, punch presses and small lathes, and when I was full time on bonus jobs I had no trouble. But this lousy bench work is getting me down. You're always shifted from one job to another—and you can't make standard on any of them. And then three or four bosses are always coming around telling me what to do, and Mike's the worst of the lot.

Keel: Didn't you expect a different kind of work when you were moved from the lathes to the benches?

Fiedler: Oh, that was a terrible deal. It must have been three months ago. I had been on lathes for a long time. In fact, I even told my wife that I had the best job in the world. I used to make $40 a week or more bonus. But I never knew Mike was going to get rid of the old lathes and get in those high-speed jobs. He never said a word to me about it, and then one Monday morning I come to work and find a dispatcher's table where my lathe should have been. When I tried to find my machine, he says, "You knew we were going to get rid of those old lathes. You're supposed to go over and work on the benches today." I've been doing this lousy bench work ever since.

Keel: But Charlie, didn't you realize that all of the old equipment throughout the shop was being replaced with new machinery?

Fiedler: Oh, I knew there were a lot of changes, but I never really thought it would put me out of machine work.

Keel: Well, Mike says the specific reason for letting you go is because you are always violating the no-smoking rule.

Fiedler: Mr. Keel, that rule is a big joke. Everyone goes into the washroom and has a smoke. There's no other place to go except outside the building, and we can't do that except on breaks or lunch hour. Anytime Mike wants to get someone in trouble, he waits until they've gone in the washroom and then nine times out of ten he can go in and catch them smoking. Sure, he caught me a couple of times. It's the way Mike does things—he's really sneaky, and I never realized it until lately. I really like the company, but I guess I ought to quit my job, because Mike has it in for me now.

Keel: Don't you work for a supervisor who reports to Mike? What do you think of him?

Fiedler: Yes, Bill Simpson supposedly is in charge of bench work. He's okay, but he doesn't have much to say. I guess you think there are seven or eight supervisors on the floor, but they only do set-up work. Simpson is just a "straw-boss" who does whatever Mike tells him to do. There are 150 people in the shop, and everyone takes orders from Mike. I guess I'm washed up around here, so I might as well tell you: That man is just another Hitler.

For several minutes, Tom Keel listened patiently to Charlie Fiedler's criticism of his foreman, Mike Walling. Keel realized that at one stage Fiedler's past performance had been extremely good and wondered whether something could be done to retain his services for the company. Keel concluded the interview by asking Fiedler to leave the plant and to return for another interview the following morning at 10 o'clock.

Questions for Discussion

1.   As a human resources staff person, what, if anything, should Tom Keel do to correct the management problems in the company and especially Mike Walling's department? Discuss possibilities.

2.   If the problems that Charlie Fiedler asserts have in fact existed for a long time, is it conceivable that Tom Keel has been lacking as a director of human resources? Why or why not?

3.   What should Tom Keel do in regard to Charlie Fiedler? Consider alternatives.

CASE 2-6
The Busy Manager

Paul Jackson, president of the Laclede Manufacturing Company, arrived at his desk and found a stack of papers on it, although he remembered that he had cleared everything away before he left at eight o'clock the previous night. He asked his secretary what these papers contained. She informed him that they had arrived in the mail late yesterday afternoon and that they were requisitions and letters for authorization from the Texas plant. Since she had read them, he asked her to tell him briefly what each request contained. He thought he could save time by doing this. The discussion went as follows:

Secretary: Request for approval for the purchase of five acres of land adjoining the Ft. Worth plant amounting to $195,000, as discussed while you were in Ft. Worth the last time.

Jackson: Okay, I'll sign it.

Secretary: Request for approval to purchase an additional computer and printer for word processing, $4,000.

Jackson: I know nothing about this. Please inquire why it is needed and who is supposed to get it.

Secretary: Requisition for a new sign at the entrance of the plant costing $900.

Jackson: Okay, I'll sign it.

Secretary: Request for approval to place an ad amounting to $100 as a contribution to the local Police Circus.

Jackson: Why not! I'll approve.

Secretary: Requisition to contribute $1,000 to the company's bowling league expenses.

Jackson: Absolutely not. Get some more information on this.

Secretary: This needs your approval, also. Some of the offices need painting, and the contractor's estimate is $2,800. (Jackson didn't answer, but put his signature on this paper.)

Secretary: Request for approval of the purchase of stationery and factory work tickets, totaling $650. (Again, Jackson signed the paper without comment.)

On and on it went. After more than an hour, Paul Jackson was finished with these requisitions, and all the other incoming mail from the morning was placed on his desk. As he started to read, he received numerous telephone calls. He was informed that five people were waiting in the anteroom to discuss some matters with him. While he was still reading the mail, his secretary informed him that the plant superintendent had an important problem on the factory floor and asked that he come to the plant at once. Jackson immediately left his desk and returned after half an hour, wondering to himself why the superintendent could not have solved the problem on his own. All day, things were piled up regardless of how many decisions he made and how many problems he solved.

On his way home late in the afternoon, Paul Jackson asked himself, "Why do I seem to be so terribly busy and yet, when the day is over, I don't know where all the hours have gone? The day passes all too quickly, and too little is accomplished. And there are so many people who think that being the president of a company is a soft job."

Questions for Discussion

1. What is the major problem apparent in this case?
2. What would you recommend to Paul Jackson to help him to manage personal time? Discuss.
3. How can a subordinate (e.g., the secretary or a supervisor) help his or her manager manage time more effectively?

CASE 2-7
Pepsi Proves It's Not to Be Tampered With

According to Earl Triplett, on June 9, 1993, after he and his wife, Mary, returned from their 61st wedding anniversary vacation in Alaska to their home near Tacoma, Washington, they found a syringe inside a can of Diet Pepsi. Mr. Triplett reported that the can had actually been opened the night before, and when he picked it up the next morning he heard the syringe rattling inside. The Tripletts called their lawyer, who called the press and local health officials, who notified the police. Within a matter of days more than 50 similar reports were received from Pepsi customers in 23 states.

Since the first two reports came from the Seattle, Washington, area, Pepsi decided to treat the incidents as a local issue. They responsed by making executives from their bottling corporation available to the media. But when reports of tampering began to be received from outside of the Seattle area, Pepsi executives began to prepare for national media attention. The actions that were taken have since been recognized as an example of decisive problem solving and decision making by the managers of Pepsi-Cola North America.

The first step they took was to assemble a crisis team of 12 executives to outline a plan of action. Pepsi decided to fight the media crisis with media and declared that the company would not recall any products. Craig Weatherup, president and chief executive officer of Pepsi-Cola North America, declared, "Our point of view was a recall would give credence to a problem that didn't exist." His decision was supported by FDA Commissioner David Kessler, who joined Pepsi in its attempt to determine the truth of the claims being made.

Weatherup took the lead in providing the media with information about the bottling process, making himself available for interviews, and supplying visuals and anything else that would show the public that the bottling process used by Pepsi is absolutely safe. "To make that statement, that the can is 99.9% safe, was our defense. We just tried to explain that in 50 ways," said Rebecca Maderia, vice-president for public affairs and a leader on the crisis team.

Dr. Kessler joined Craig Weatherup on ABC-TV's *Nightline* show and stressed that the maximum penalty for making false complaints is a $250,000 fine and five years in prison. He also advised consumers who were concerned about possible product tampering to pour canned drinks into a glass. "Having Dr. Kessler rolled into place was a stroke of genius," according to Tom Pirko, president of Bevmark, a consulting firm.

Although claims continued to mount for several days, Pepsi felt that the tide was beginning to turn when news stories began using the terms "copycat" and "hoax" in their reports. Pepsi's big break came when a Pepsi manager in Colorado learned that the retailer where a syringe reportedly had been found used a surveillance camera. Looking at the tape from the previous day, he discovered a clear picture of a woman shopper putting something into an open Diet Pepsi can. She then called the sales clerk's attention to the "found" object. Soon afterward, Dr. Kessler stated that "it is simply not logical to conclude that a nationwide tampering has occurred." By this time several people had been arrested for making false claims. The Pepsi crisis team began to breath a collective sigh of relief.

Wishing to put the incident behind them before the upcoming July 4th holiday, Pepsi executives ran a national newspaper ad on June 19 to June 21 stating, "Pepsi is pleased to announce . . . nothing." In addition, each of the 50,000 company and bottler employees was offered up to $50 in coupons, which they could give to their family and friends. Coupons were also run in newspaper ads saying simply, "Thanks America."

The actions taken worked. Any damage done to Pepsi's brand image and market share was short term and minimal. Craig Weatherup responded to the crisis, declaring, "I'd say there's a far greater probability that it's a plus than a minus. The most logical answer is that it didn't have an impact one way or another." Weatherup clearly sees the outcome as a victory.

References

Elizabeth Lesly and Laura Zinn, "The Right Moves Baby," *Business Week* (July 5, 1993), pp. 30–31.

Marcy Magiera, "The Pepsi Crisis: What Went Right," *Advertising Age* (July 19, 1993), pp. 14–15.

Marcy Magiera and Alice Cuneo, "Pepsi Weathers Tampering Hoaxes," *Advertising Age* (June 21, 1993), pp. 1 & 46.

Annetta Miller et al., "The Great Pepsi Panic," *Newsweek* (June 28, 1993), p. 32.

Julie Tilsner, "Jabbing Pepsi," *Business Week* (June 28, 1993), p. 41.

Anastasia Toufexis, "A Weird Case, Baby? Uh Huh!," *Time* (June 28, 1993), p. 41.

Questions for Discussion

1. In your opinion, did the managers of Pepsi properly employ the concepts of problem solving and decision making to deal with the claims of product tampering? Why or why not?

2. Once the crisis team had decided how it would deal with the tampering claims, what specific actions were taken and by whom? Were they successful?

3. Why do you think Pepsi offered coupons and other incentives to its customers after proving that Pepsi was not to blame for the product tampering? Is this type of action part of the decison-making process? Explain.

4. Why do you think Craig Weatherup concluded that the crisis presented a greater probability of being a plus than a minus?

5. Have Pepsi's actions indicated that the problem has been resolved satisfactorily? Why or why not?

PART 3

ORGANIZING

Principles of Organizing

LEARNING OBJECTIVES

After reading this chapter, you will be able to:

1 Identify the organizing function of management.

2 Explain the unity of command principle and its applications.

3 Define the span of management principle and the factors that influence its application.

4 Describe departmentation and alternative approaches for grouping activities and assigning work.

5 Explain the meaning of line and staff authority and how these relate to organizational structures.

6 Describe how functional authority may be granted to specialized staff for certain purposes.

7 Discuss applications of matrix-type organizational structure.

8 Define downsizing and its implications for organizational principles.

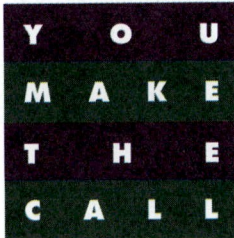
YOU MAKE THE CALL

You are Alice Austin, supervisor of the information services department of Gatewood Community College. You supervise about 15 word processors and administrative service employees. You report directly to the dean of administration, who in turn reports to the president of the college. However, your department is located in a different classroom building, since you provide services for faculty as well as for other administrative, operations, and maintenance departments.

Several problems facing you have grown in recent months. Although all work orders and requests are supposed to come directly through you, faculty members, supervisors, administrators, and others are bringing their work requests directly to individual employees in the department. The dean of administration and the college president or their secretaries have bypassed you on occasion by making direct work requests or demanding expedited services from selected employees. Several employees have told you that these requests or demands were impossible to meet, or that they required shifting other job requests or priorities that you had established. The matter came to a head this morning. While you were temporarily out of the office, two faculty members from the psychology department came into your office and gave instructions to two employees to have a major report typed by the next day. When your employees protested, the faculty members became vocal and angry and criticized them in front of other employees in the department. Hearing this report, you know that you will have to do something to remedy these problems.

What would you do?
YOU MAKE THE CALL.

ORGANIZING AS AN ESSENTIAL MANAGERIAL FUNCTION

1 Identify the organizing function of management.

As one of the five major functions of management, the organizing function requires that every manager be concerned with building, developing, and maintaining working relationships that will help achieve the organization's objectives. Although organizations may have a variety of objectives and may operate in many kinds of environments, the fundamental principles of organizing are universal.

Organizing
Designing a structure by grouping activities, assigning them to specific work units, and establishing authority and responsibility relationships.

A manager's **organizing** function consists of designing a structure—that is, grouping activities and assigning them to specific work units (e.g., departments, teams) to carry out as planned. Organizing includes establishment of formal authority and responsibility relationships among the various activities and departments. In order to make such a structure possible, management must delegate authority throughout the organization and establish and clarify authority relationships among the departments. We will use the term **organization** to refer to any type of group structured by management to carry out designated functions and accomplish certain objectives.

Organization
Group structured by management to carry out designated functions and accomplish certain objectives.

Management should design the structure and establish authority relationships based on sound principles and organizational concepts, such as delegation of authority, unity of command, span of supervision, division of work, departmentation, and line and staff authority.

Organizing the overall activities of the enterprise is the responsibility of the chief executive. However, eventually it becomes the responsibility of supervisors to organize their departments. Therefore, supervisors must understand what it means to organize. Although the range and magnitude of problems associated with the organizing function are broader at higher managerial levels than for supervisors, the principles to be applied are the same.

UNITY OF COMMAND AND AUTHORITY RELATIONSHIPS

2 Explain the unity of command principle and its applications.

The chief executive groups the activities of the organization into divisions, departments, services, teams, or units, and assigns duties accordingly. Upper-level management places managers and supervisors in charge of divisions and departments and defines their authority relationships. Supervisors must know exactly who their managers are and who their subordinates are. To arrange authority relationships in this fashion, management normally follows the principle of unity of command. As previously discussed, unity of command means that each employee has only one immediate supervisor, that is, only one person to whom the employee is directly accountable. Formal communications normally flow upward and downward through the chain of command, although there are exceptions such as the use of functional authority and matrix organizational structure, which are discussed later in this chapter.

FIGURE 9-1
A manager can
effectively supervise
only a certain number
of employees.

THE SPAN OF MANAGEMENT PRINCIPLE

3 Define the span of
management principle
and the factors that
influence its
application.

Span of management
The maximum number
of subordinates that a
supervisor can
manage effectively.

The establishment of departments and the creation of several managerial levels are
not ends in themselves; actually, they are the source of numerous difficulties.
Departments are expensive because they must be staffed by supervisors and employees. Moreover, as more departments and levels are created, communication
and coordination problems arise. Therefore, there must be valid reasons for creating levels and departments. The reasons are associated with the span of management principle. There is an upper limit to the number of employees a supervisor
can effectively manage. A supervisor's **span of management** is that maximum number. Often this principle is called "span of supervision," "span of managerial responsibility," "span of authority," or "span of control." (See Figure 9-1.)

Because no one can manage an unlimited number of people, top-level managers
must organize divisions and departments as separate operating units and place
middle-level managers and supervisors in charge. Top-level managers then delegate
authority to the middle-level managers, who in turn redelegate authority to supervisors, who in turn supervise the employees. If a manager could supervise 100 or
more employees effectively, each of the 100 would report directly to that manager
and their different activities would not have to be grouped into departments. Of
course, such a wide span of management is not practical.

The principle that a manager can effectively supervise a limited number of employees is as old as recorded history.[1] However, it is not possible to state a definite
figure as to how many subordinates a manager should have. It is only correct to
say that there is some upper limit to this number. In many industrial concerns, the

top-level executive will have from three to eight subordinate managers. But the span of management usually increases the farther down a person is within the managerial hierarchy. It is not unusual to find a span of management of from 15 to 25 employees at the first level of supervision.

Factors Influencing the Span of Management

The number of employees that one person can supervise effectively depends on a number of factors, such as the abilities of the supervisor, the types and amounts of staff assistance available, the employees' capabilities, the kinds of activities being performed within the space or physical layout, and the degree of objective performance standards in place.

Supervisory Abilities. Among the most significant factors that influence the span of management are the training, experience, and know-how that the supervisor has acquired—in other words, the supervisor's competence. Some supervisors are capable of handling more employees than others. Some are better acquainted with good management principles, have had more experience, and are better managers overall. For example, what the supervisor does during the time available is of major importance. The supervisor who must make individual decisions on every departmental problem takes more time than does the supervisor who has established policies, procedures, and rules that simplify decision making on routine problems. Comprehensive planning can reduce the number of decisions the supervisor has to make and hence increase the potential span of management. Thus, the number of employees a supervisor can supervise effectively depends to some degree on the supervisor's managerial competence.

Specialized Staff Assistance. Another factor on which the span of management depends is the availability of help from specialists within the organization. If numerous staff experts are available to provide specialized advice and service, then the span of management can be wider. For example, when a human resources department assists supervisors in recruiting, selecting, and training employees, supervisors have more time and energy available for their departments. But if supervisors themselves are obligated to do all or most of these activities, then they cannot devote that portion of time to otherwise managing their departments. Therefore, the amount and quality of staff assistance available influence the span of management.

Employee Abilities. How broad a span a supervisor can handle also depends on the abilities and knowledge of employees in the department. The greater the employees' capacities for self-direction, the broader the feasible span. Here, of course, the employees' training and experience are important. For example, the span of management could be greater with fully qualified mechanics than with inexperienced mechanics. However, the factor of employee competence may be offset to some degree by the nature of the activities being performed, as explained below.

Nature and Complexity of Activities. The amount, nature, complexity, and predictability of activities influence the span of management. The simpler, routine, and more uniform the work activities, the greater the number of people one supervisor can manage. If the tasks are repetitious, the span may be as broad as 25 or more employees. If the activities are varied or interdependent, or if errors would have serious consequences, the span might have to be as small as 3 to 5. In departments engaged in relatively unpredictable activities—for example, nurses in an intensive care unit in a hospital—the span will tend to be narrow. In departments concerned with fairly stable activities—such as an assembly line or a word processing center—the span can be broader.

Objective Performance Standards. Still another factor influencing the span of management is whether a department has ample objective standards for guiding and measuring employee performance. If each employee knows exactly what standards are expected—for example, a certain number of sales units each week, or the production of a specific amount each day—the supervisor will not need to have frequent discussions with employees about performance. Thus, good standards support a broader span of management.

Balancing the Factors

As stated previously, there is no set figure to identify the number of employees a supervisor can manage effectively. The principle of span of management indicates only that an upper limit exists. In most situations there must be a balancing of the factors just discussed to arrive at an appropriate span of management for each supervisor. Such a balancing of factors for the most part is the responsibility of higher-level management.

How Managerial Levels and Span of Management Are Related

If a higher-level manager concludes that the span of management for a certain activity or department is too broad, he or she may decide to divide the span into two or three groups and place someone in charge of each group. By narrowing the span to a smaller number of employees, the manager creates another organizational level, because a supervisor or "lead person" has to be placed over each of the smaller groups. A **lead person**, sometimes called a "working supervisor," usually is not considered to be part of management, especially in unionized firms. Nevertheless, these individuals perform most of the managerial functions, although their authority is somewhat limited, particularly in discipline of employees.

Lead person
Employee placed in charge of other employees who performs limited managerial functions but is not considered part of management.

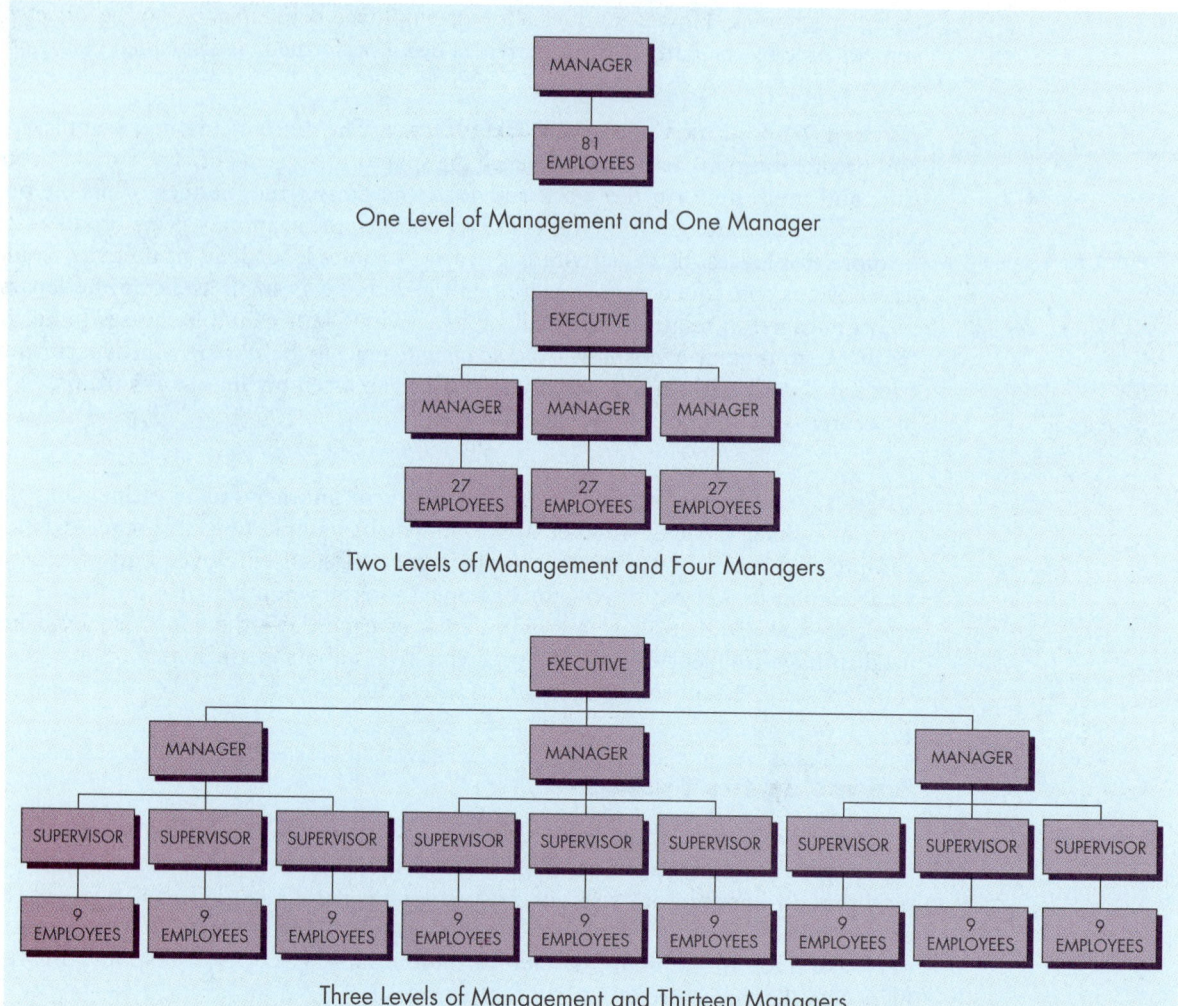

One Level of Management and One Manager

Two Levels of Management and Four Managers

Three Levels of Management and Thirteen Managers

FIGURE 9-2
How Span of
Management and
Organizational
Levels Are Related

Other things being equal, the narrower the span of management becomes, the more managerial levels have to be introduced into organizational design. Adding levels may not be desirable, since more levels are costly and also complicate communication and control. Thus, there is a trade-off between the width of the span and the number of levels. The managerial problem is: Which is best—a broad span with few levels, or a narrower span with more levels? (See Figure 9-2.) This is an important question, which often confronts higher management. A first-line supervisor normally does not directly confront this question, but supervisors should understand how it influences the design and structure of their organizations. It is an integral part of organizational downsizing, which is discussed later in this chapter.

DEPARTMENTATION

4 Describe departmentation and alternative approaches for grouping activities and assigning work.

Division of work (specialization)
Dividing work into smaller components and specialized tasks to improve efficiency and output.

Organizational structure is largely determined by the principle of **division of work** or **specialization**. This principle holds that jobs can be divided into smaller components and specialized tasks to achieve greater efficiency and output. Technological advances and increasing complexity have made it less possible for employees to know everything about their work fields. Dividing the work into smaller tasks allows employees to specialize in narrower areas within their fields. Employees can then master these smaller tasks and produce more efficiently. For example, as cars become more complex and diverse, it becomes more difficult for a mechanic to know how to fix everything on every type of car. Thus, specialty repair shops such as muffler shops, oil-change services, and foreign car specialists have sprung up. Even within shops that do many types of repairs, mechanics often specialize in certain repairs. By specializing, employees can become expert enough in their areas to produce efficiently.

Departmentation
The process of grouping activities and people into distinct organizational units.

Department
An organizational unit for which a supervisor has responsibility and authority.

Departmentation is the process of grouping activities and people into distinct organizational units, usually known as departments. A **department** is a designated set of activities and people over which a manager or supervisor has responsibility and authority. *Terminology used by organizations is quite varied. A department in one may be called a division, an office, a service, a unit, or some other term in another.* Most organizations have departments of some sort, since division of work and specialization contribute to efficiency and better results.

Approaches to Departmentation

Whereas major departments of an organization are established by top-level managers, supervisors primarily are concerned with activities within their own areas. Nevertheless, from time to time supervisors will be confronted with the need to departmentalize within their areas, and they should be familiar with the alternatives available for grouping activities. These are the same options available to top-level managers when they define the major departments. Departmentation is usually done according to function, products or services, territory, customer, process and equipment, or time.

Functional Departmentation. The most widely used form of departmentation is to group activities by function—the jobs to be done. Consistent with the idea of specialization and division of work, activities that are alike or similar are placed together in one department and under a single chain of command. For example, word processing, fax machine, and key-entering services may be grouped together into a clerical department or information processing center; sales and promotional activities into a marketing department; manufacturing assembly work into a production department; inspection and monitoring activities into a quality control department; and so on. As an enterprise undertakes additional activities, these new activities—for the most part—are simply added to the already existing departments.

Functional departmentation is a method that has been and still is successful in most organizations. It makes sense, since it is a natural and logical way of arranging activities of any enterprise. Grouping departments along functional lines takes advantage of occupational specialization by placing together jobs and tasks that are performed by people with the same kinds of training, experience, equipment, and facilities. Each supervisor is responsible primarily for one type of operation on which his or her energy and expertise can be concentrated. Functional departmentation also facilitates coordination, since a supervisor is in charge of one major area of activity. It is easier to achieve coordination this way than to have the same functions performed in different departments.

Product or Service Departmentation. Many companies utilize product or service departmentation. To departmentalize on a product basis means to establish each major product (or group of closely related products) in a product line as a relatively independent unit within the overall framework of the enterprise. For example, a food products company may choose to divide its operations into a frozen food department, a dairy products department, a produce department, and the like. Product departmentation can also be a useful guide for grouping activities in service businesses. For example, most banks have separate departments for commercial loans, installment loans, savings accounts, and checking accounts. Many home maintenance firms have separate departments for carpentry, heating, and air-conditioning services.

Geographic (Territorial, Locational) Departmentation. Another way to departmentalize is by geographical considerations. This approach to departmentation is important for organizations with physically dispersed activities. Large-scale enterprises often have divisions by territories, states, and cities. Increasingly, many companies also have international divisions. Where units of an organization are physically dispersed or where functions are to be performed in different locations—even different buildings—geographic departmentation may be desirable. Locational considerations may be significant even if all activities are performed in one building but on different floors. An advantage of territorial departmentation is that decision-making authority can be placed close to where the work is being done.

Customer Departmentation. Many organizations find it advisable to group activities based on customer considerations. The paramount concern here is to service the differing needs and characteristics of different customers. For example, a university that offers evening programs in addition to day programs attempts to comply with the requests and special needs of part-time and full-time students. Companies may have special departments to handle the particular requirements of wholesale and retail customers. Major department stores may attempt to reach different segments of the buying public, such as customers for a "bargain basement" or lower-priced division at the one extreme and an exclusive high-priced fashion division at the other extreme. Most large hospitals have separate units for outpatient services.

When employees need training and expertise to operate specialized equipment, they may be grouped into a separate department based on process and equipment.

Process and Equipment Departmentation. Activities also can be grouped according to the process involved or equipment used. Since a certain amount of training and expertise are required to handle complicated processes and operate complex equipment, activities that involve the use of specialized equipment may be grouped into a separate department. This form of departmentation often is similar to functional departmentation. For example, in a machine-shop department, specialized equipment is used but only certain functions are performed; function and equipment become closely allied. A data processing department utilizing a mainframe computer may serve the processing requirements of a number of operations and departmental needs throughout an organization.

Time Departmentation. Another way to departmentalize is to group activities according to the period of time during which work is performed. Many organizations are engaged in round-the-clock operations and departmentalize on the basis of time by having work shifts. Activities are departmentalized by time (day, afternoon, night shift), although the work operations of all the shifts for the most part may be the same. Here, too, there may be an overlap in the departmentation process. Where time is a partial basis for departmentation, it is likely that other factors will be involved. For example, a maintenance division—based on function and services—may be further departmentalized by shifts, such as the maintenance night shift. Shift departmentation can create organizational questions of how self-contained each shift should be and what relationships should exist between regular day-shift supervisors and the off-shift supervisors.

Mixed Departmentation. In order to achieve the most effective structure, a supervisor may have to apply several types of departmentation at the same time. This is referred to as "mixed" departmentation. For example, there may be an inventory control clerk (functional) on the third floor (geographic) during the night shift (time). In practice, many organizations have a composite departmental structure involving functional departmentation, geographic departmentation, and other forms. All of these alternatives may be available to supervisors to facilitate the grouping of activities in their departments.

There are some departments in which additional subgroupings are not needed. However, supervisors of departments of considerable size may find it necessary to divide various jobs and skills into different groups under a lead person or foreman, who in turn will report to the supervisor. Whatever structure is chosen, the purpose of departmentation is not to have a beautiful, well-drawn organization chart. The purpose is to have a sound departmental structure that will best achieve the objectives of the department and the entire organization.

Work Assignments and Organizational Stability

The problem of how and to whom to assign work confronts a supervisor much more frequently than does the problem of how to organize departments. This problem always involves differences of opinion. Nevertheless, the assignment of work should be justifiable and explainable on the basis of good management, rather than on personal likes and dislikes or hunch and intuition. The supervisor is subject to pressures from different directions. Some employees are willing and want to assume more work, while others believe that they should not be burdened with additional duties. One of the supervisor's most important responsibilities is to assign work so that everybody has a fair share and all employees do their parts equitably and satisfactorily.

Supervisors often are inclined to assign heavier and more difficult tasks to the capable employees who are most experienced. However, in the long term it is advantageous to train and develop the less experienced employees so that they, too, can perform the difficult jobs. If supervisors rely too much on one person or a few people, a department will be weakened if the top performers are absent, are promoted, or leave the enterprise. The **principle of organizational stability** advocates that no organization should become overly dependent on one or several key "indispensable" individuals whose absence or departure would seriously disrupt the organization. Organizations need a sufficient number of employees who have been trained well and have flexible skills. One way to develop a flexible workforce is to assign certain employees to different jobs within the department on a temporary basis as, for example, during vacation periods or employee absences. In this way there will usually be someone available to take over any job if the need arises. As emphasized previously, a supervisor's problem of assigning departmental work will be minimized if the supervisor consistently utilizes the strengths and experience of all employees.

FIGURE 9-3
The assignment of work should be based on good management, not on personal likes or dislikes.

LINE AND STAFF AUTHORITY RELATIONSHIPS AND ORGANIZATIONAL STRUCTURES

5 Explain the meaning of line and staff authority and how these relate to organizational structures.

Once management establishes departments, it must then establish and clarify authority relationships among and within the departments. In Chapter 4, we discussed the meaning of managerial authority and the process of delegation. Here we will discuss how most organizations establish authority relationships, beginning with an explanation of line and staff organization—the most commonly used arrangement.

Line and Staff as Authority Relationships

In many large organizations it is common to speak of the sales staff, the human resources staff, the nursing staff, the administrative staff, and other staff designations. In such a context, the word "staff" is used to identify groups of people or departments who are engaged primarily in one activity or several related activities or jobs. However, in most books and other writings about formal organizational structure, the meaning of the word "staff" is quite different. In this text—consistent with other management literature—*the terms "line," "staff," and "functional" represent different types of authority relationships within an organization.*

Much has been written and said about line and staff, and few aspects of management have evoked as much debate as these concepts. Yet many of the difficulties and frictions encountered by today's supervisors are due to line and staff problems. Misconceptions and lack of understanding of what constitutes line and staff can be the source of confrontation, personality conflicts, disunity, duplication of effort, waste, and lost efficiency.

All supervisors should know whether they are part of the organization in a line or a staff capacity, and what these words imply in terms of their positions and in relation to other departments. Supervisors should consult their job descriptions or organizational manuals. If necessary, they should ask higher-level managers for clarification, because it is top-level management that confers line or staff authority on a department.

In previous chapters, we referred to managerial authority as an essential component of the managerial job, and we defined it as the legitimate managerial right to direct the activities of subordinates. Technically this is line authority. Here we will add to and further clarify the meaning of authority.

Line-Type Organizational Structure

Line authority
The right to direct others and to require them to conform to decisions, policies, rules, and objectives.

In every organization there is a vertical, direct line of authority, which can be traced from the chief executive to the departmental employee level. **Line authority** (also referred to as "scalar authority") provides the right to direct others and require them to conform to decisions, policies, rules, and objectives. Line authority establishes who can direct whom throughout the organization. A primary purpose of line authority is to make the organization work smoothly.

Line-type organizational structure
A structure that consists entirely of line authority arrangements with a direct chain of authority relationships.

Some organizations consist entirely of line authority arrangements (see Figure 9-4). Usually these organizations are fairly small, both in operations and in number of employees. A **line-type organizational structure** enables managers to know exactly to whom they can give directives and whose orders they have to carry out. Throughout, there is unity of command, which can be traced in a direct line (or chain) of authority relationships. With a line-type organizational structure, decisions can usually be made and carried out more quickly as compared to other structures. It is particularly appropriate for small organizations, such as a sole proprietorship.

Many small companies essentially are line-type organizations, built around one or several key people who also may own the firm. These owner/managers serve as "Jacks of all trades," making most of the decisions necessary to carry out business operations. When they need special assistance, they usually go outside the firm to request assistance or pay consultants or others for services. Many small companies are built around such key individuals, who must have knowledge in a wide range of business areas. These types of enterprises can be successful as long as the business remains relatively small and operations focus on a limited range of activities. As a small business grows, it can outgrow its owner/manager's expertise. Then more specialists are hired into the company to fill gaps in the owner/manager's knowledge.

Line-and-Staff Type Organizational Structure

Staff authority
The right to provide counsel, advice, support, and service in a person's areas of expertise.

As organizations grow, activities become more specialized and complicated. Managers cannot be expected to direct subordinates adequately and expertly in all phases of operations without some assistance. Line managers, in order to perform their managerial functions, need the assistance of specialists who have been granted staff authority. **Staff authority** is the right and duty to provide counsel, advice, sup-

FIGURE 9-4
Line Type of
Organizational
Structure

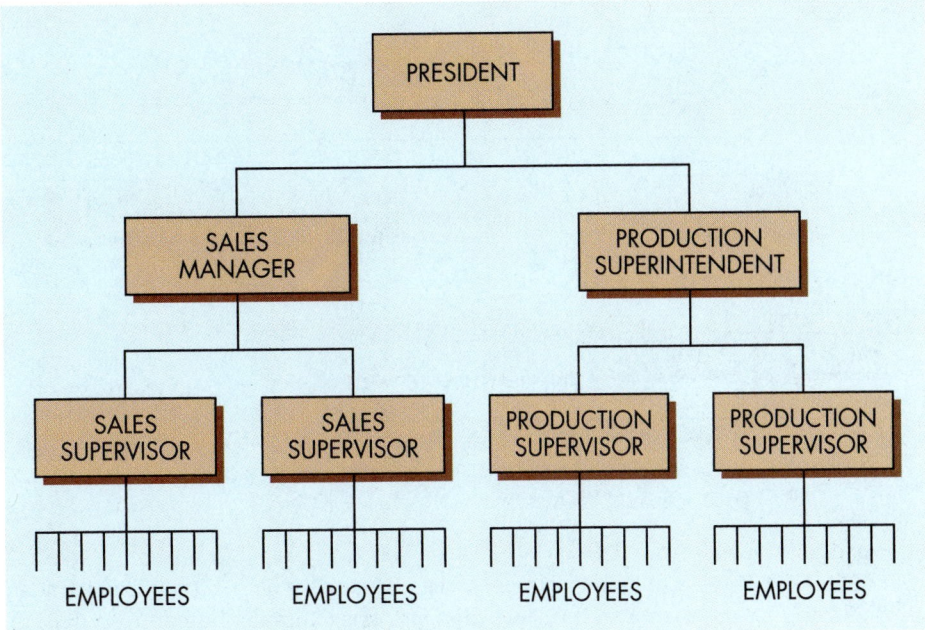

port, and service in regard to policies, procedures, technical issues, and problems within their areas of expertise. Certain specialists are granted staff authority because of their position or specialized knowledge. People who hold staff positions do not issue orders or directives except within their own staff departments. Rather, staff people assist other members of the organization whenever the need arises for specialized help. For example, human resources specialists often screen applicants for line managers and recommend only the most qualified candidates for line managers to interview. While the human resources managers can direct the work of employees within their own department (line authority), they can only advise managers in other departments in human resources matters (staff authority). Staff authority is not inferior to line authority; it is just different. The objectives of staff groups ultimately are the same as those of the line departments, namely, the achievement of overall organizational objectives.

Staff supervisors primarily provide guidance, counsel, advice, and service in their specialty to those who request it. Typically they also have the responsibility to see that certain policies and procedures are being carried out by line departments. However, staff supervisors do not have the direct authority to order line people to conform to policies and procedures; they can only persuade, counsel, and advise. Line supervisors can accept the staff person's advice, alter it, or reject it; but since the staff person is usually the expert in the field, line supervisors usually accept and even welcome the advice of the staff person.

It does not matter whether a particular department is a line or staff department. Supervisors are line managers with direct authority over the employees in

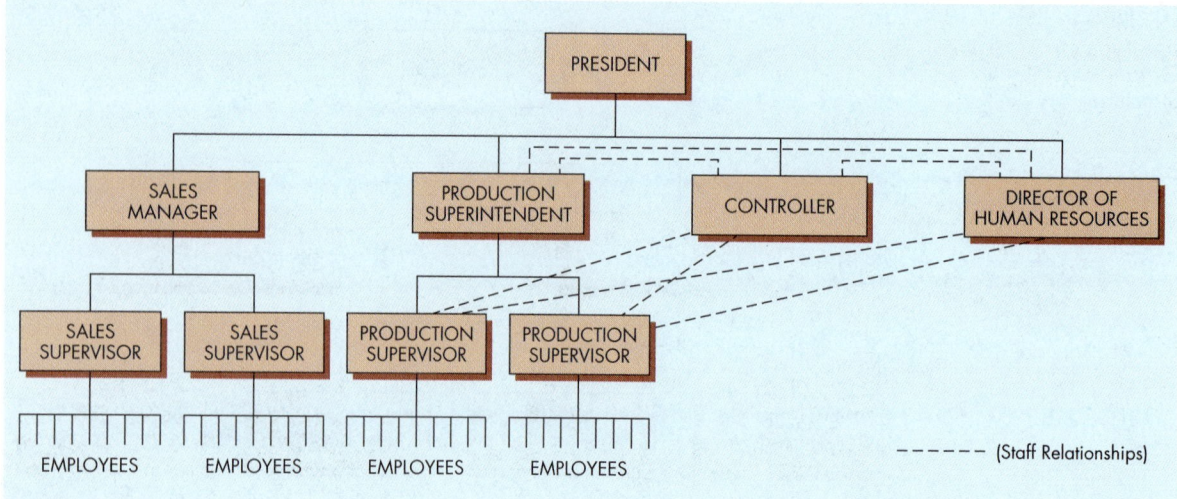

FIGURE 9-5
Line-and-Staff Type
of Organizational
Structure

Line department
Department whose
responsibilities are
directly related to
making, selling, or
distributing the
company's product or
service.

Staff department
Specialized
department
responsible for
supporting line
departments and
providing specialized
advice and services.

Line-and-staff-type
organizational
structure
Structure that
combines line and staff
departments.

their departments, regardless of whether their departments serve the organization in a staff or line capacity. For example, human resources managers can tell their direct reports to put a job ad in the paper. However, they can only advise line managers about how to conduct interviews.

As previously defined, "line" and "staff" refer to different types of authority. In practice, however, these terms also refer to departmental responsibilities within an organizational structure. In this context, **line departments** are those directly involved in making, selling, or distributing the company's product or service. **Staff departments** are specialized departments that support the line departments. Most organizations of appreciable size use a **line-and-staff-type-organizational structure,** which is a combination of these two types of departments. For example, certain departments, such as human resources (personnel), legal, or accounting, usually are classified as staff since they mainly support other departments. This is illustrated by Figure 9-5, which shows the controller and director of human resources as staff. These staff relationships are illustrated with dashed lines. However, these positions and departments are not always staff. As stated before, line and staff are characteristics of authority relationships and not necessarily of functions. Nor does a person's title indicate line or staff. For example, in manufacturing organizations it is common to find a vice-president of production, a vice-president of sales, a vice-president of human resources, and so on. Merely looking at an organization chart is not sufficient to identify staff relationships, because most positions on a chart are shown only as small rectangular boxes with solid lines showing line relationships.

In most organizations the director of human resources and the human resources department operate in a staff capacity. The human resources department, often called the "personnel department," usually exists to provide advice and service to all departments concerning employment matters, such as recruiting, screening, and testing applicants; maintaining personnel records; providing for wage and salary administration; advising line managers on problems of discipline and required fair employment practices; and providing other services and assistance. If line supervisors have difficult employee problems, the human resources department is available for assistance. Staff managers in the human resources department are qualified to furnish advice and current information, since this is their expertise and specialty. Most staff managers prefer to offer suggestions to line supervisors, who in turn must decide whether to accept, alter, or reject those suggestions or recommendations. If a line supervisor feels that a suggestion of the human resources manager is not feasible, the supervisor will make his or her own decision. We will discuss relationships between line supervisors and the human resources department staff in greater detail in Chapter 13.

In most situations, line supervisors will accept the recommendations of staff people because the staff individuals are experts on problems in their areas. Thus, staff authority lies primarily in knowledge and expertise in dealing with special problems. Staff people "sell" their ideas based on the authority derived from their expertise, but they cannot tell others what to do. If a suggestion of the staff person is carried out, it is carried out as a line directive under the name and responsibility of the line supervisor, not that of the staff person.

THE ROLE OF FUNCTIONAL AUTHORITY

6 Describe how functional authority may be granted to specialized staff for certain purposes.

Principle of compulsory staff advice (service) Situation in which supervisors are required by policy to consult with specialized staff before making certain types of decisions.

Functional authority The right granted to specialized staff people to give directives concerning matters within their expertise.

Generally, in a line-and-staff organization, staff managers provide counsel and advice to line managers but do not have the right to give them direct orders. This arrangement maintains the principle of unity of command. However, there are exceptions to this generalization. For example, if an organizational policy requires a supervisor to consult with a staff person before making a certain type of decision, this is known as following the **principle of compulsory staff advice** (or **compulsory staff service**). The supervisor still may accept or reject the staff person's advice, unless functional authority is granted to the staff person.

Functional authority (or "functional staff authority") is a special right given by higher-level management to certain staff people to direct other members of the organization about certain matters within the staff person's specialized field. For example, assume that a company president wants to be sure that the grievance procedures in the labor agreement are interpreted uniformly. Therefore, the president decides to confer sole authority to the labor relations director for the final settlement of grievances—a function that otherwise might belong to line managers. The labor relations director is part of the human resources department, which is a staff department. By giving sole authority for the final adjustment of grievances to the labor relations director, the company president confers authority for this function on someone who ordinarily would not hold this authority. Now the labor relations director has this authority, and it no longer belongs to the line supervisors.

Another example of functional authority is the common case in which a human resources department is given full authority to maintain legal compliance with wage and hour laws, equal employment opportunity laws, and the like. The decisions of line supervisors in these matters must conform to the stipulations of the human resources department. (In a large company, the human resources department itself may rely on advice it receives from the company's legal department or from an outside attorney.)

Because functional authority may be an extension of staff authority conferred upon certain staff specialists, in practice it may be difficult to clearly distinguish between these in some situations. In general, however, the use of functional authority violates the principle of unity of command, since it introduces a second source of authority for certain decisions. But in numerous situations, functional authority is advantageous because it facilitates a more effective use of staff specialists. It is up to top-level management to weigh the advantages and disadvantages of granting functional authority to staff specialists before conferring it.

THE MATRIX-TYPE ORGANIZATIONAL STRUCTURE

7 Discuss applications of matrix-type organizational structure.

In many organizations the need to coordinate activities across department lines has contributed to the development of the **matrix-type of organizational structure.** The matrix form of organization is also called "project structure," "product management structure," or "grid," among other designations. The matrix arrangement is superimposed on the line-staff organization. It adds horizontal dimensions to the

FIGURE 9-6
Basic Matrix Type of
Organizational
Structure

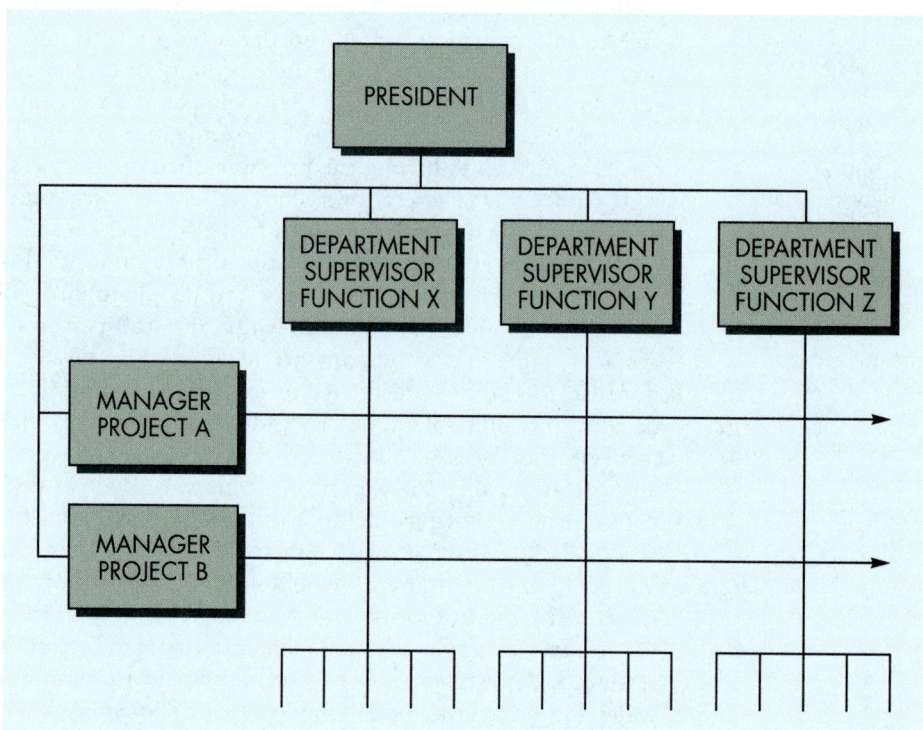

FIGURE 9-7
A disadvantage of the matrix form of organization is that it violates the principle of unity of command.

Matrix-type organizational structure
A hybrid structure in which regular functional departments co-exist with project teams made up of people from different departments.

normal vertical (top-down) orientation of the organizational structure. It is a hybrid arrangement in which both regular (functional) line and staff departments co-exist with project teams or group assignments across departmental lines.

Many high-tech firms employ project (matrix) structures in order to focus special talents from different departments on specific projects for certain periods. Project structure enables managers to undertake several projects simultaneously, some of which may be of relatively short duration. Each project is assigned to a project manager who manages the project from inception to completion. Employees from different functional departments are assigned to work on each project as needed, either part time or full time.

Although the complexity of matrix structure varies, a basic matrix form might resemble the chart shown in Figure 9-6. This chart illustrates how some managers have been given responsibility for specific projects within the firm, while departmental supervisors primarily have the responsibility for supervising employees within their regular departments. The type of arrangement shown in Figure 9-6 might apply to an engineering or architectural firm. The project managers (A and B) are responsible for coordinating activities on their designated projects. However, the project managers must work closely with the departmental supervisors of functions X, Y, and Z. The employees who work in these departments report directly (functionally) to the departmental supervisors, but their services are utilized under the authority and responsibility of the project managers to whom they are assigned for varying periods of time.

There are several problems associated with the matrix organizational structure. The most frequent problem is the question of direct accountability. Like functional authority, the matrix structure violates the principle of unity of command, since departmental employees are accountable to both a departmental supervisor and a

CONTEMPORARY ISSUE
The Virtual Corporation: Organization of the Future in the Age of Agility?

According to a number of business forecasters, the corporate organization of the future eventually will be the ultimate in adaptability. Labeled as the "virtual corporation," it has been described as consisting of a temporary network of independent companies, such as suppliers, customers, and even competitors, who would be linked by information technology and share skills, employees, costs, and access to each other's markets to exploit fast-changing opportunities. The virtual corporation would have no organizational chart, hierarchy, or vertical integration.[1] In a sense, the virtual corporation might be the ultimate project-type organization. At the end of their collaboration in a project or task, partners in a virtual corporation would separate, with no continuing permanent relationship to hold them together.

In recent years, a number of companies already have been involved in certain types of joint ventures, which involve collaboration with various partners to achieve competitive advantages. Although some management theorists believe that the virtual corporation is inevitable, others believe that it is only a business "buzz" phrase that is meaningless in actual application. It would require companies to build networks with other companies in whom they had a high level of trust and collaboration. Each partner would bring its core competence to the overall collaborative effort, but there is the major concern that each partner could lose certain control over its own operations.[2]

Roger Nagel, a prominent authority in the field of manufacturing competitiveness, believes that the virtual corporation is necessary to meet the requirements of competition in an "age of agility." He states, "If virtual companies are to succeed, we need to move toward an era of trust and ethics that did not exist before. It's like a marriage. We are being forced into a trusting culture by the need for cooperation. But it's a change, and people are having trouble with it."[3]

Source: [1,2] "The Virtual Corporation," *Business Week* (February 8, 1993), pp. 98–99; 100–103. [3]*Challenges* (Volume 6, Number 6, June 1993), p. 4. (Published by the Council on Competitiveness.)

project manager. Other problems involve priorities of scheduling for individual employees who are assigned to work on several projects. These problems can be avoided, or at least minimized, by proper planning and clarification of authority relationships by the top-level manager prior to the start of a project.

Despite such problems, the matrix structure is widely used because organizations find it advantageous. The success of a matrix arrangement depends primarily on the willingness of both the project managers and the departmental supervisors and their employees to coordinate various activities and responsibilities in working toward completion of each project. Such coordination is vital in the scheduling of work, and it is imperative in the performance appraisal of employees. Employees must recognize that they remain directly accountable to their departmental supervisor, who will rely to a great extent on the project managers' evaluations of the employees' work when the departmental supervisor conducts the performance appraisals and salary reviews. These are discussed at length in Chapter 15.

ORGANIZATIONAL PRINCIPLES SHOULD SURVIVE MOST ORGANIZATIONAL DOWNSIZING

8 Define downsizing and its implications for organizational principles.

Among the most publicized aspects of corporate business during the 1980s and continuing into the early 1990s has been the large-scale reduction and permanent elimination of thousands of job positions in many major companies. This has been accomplished by plant and office closings, sales of divisions, extensive employee layoffs, attrition and early retirements, and the like. As a result, many companies have eliminated large segments of their workforce; this has been referred to as **downsizing, restructuring,** or **right-sizing.** Typically management downsizes to reduce costs, streamline operations, and become more efficient and competitive. A major organizational impact is a reduction in the number of middle-level managers and the removal of a layer or more of organizational levels. The span of management is usually widened for first-line supervisors and other managers who survive the downsizing. Many supervisors are stretched by being required to add unfamiliar departments or functions to their previous departmental operation.[2]

Some middle-level management and staff positions have been eliminated because information technology has made it possible for higher-level managers to acquire data and information quickly and to keep in close touch with operations without the need for as many information gatherers, blenders, and disseminators. As a result, remaining supervisors and employees usually have to become more widely knowledgeable about numerous aspects of operations than they were in the past.

Studies of the pros and cons of downsizing have revealed a mixed pattern of results. The forecasted economic returns often are not realized as expected, and the impact upon organizational morale and productivity often is negative or detrimental to efficiency efforts. However, the firms that have downsized most effectively appear to be those that have planned for it systematically and have tried to harmonize (insofar as possible) the previous organizational structures and operations with the newer realities in a way that is compatible and acceptable to those who remain. Typically, ideas about authority and the use of authority must be reshaped to give supervisors and employees greater decision-making responsibility.[3]

Some organizational theorists predict that downsizing will continue indefinitely, and that in some firms there will be a "radical restructuring." This could result in organizational structures and practices that conflict with time-honored organizational principles. The concept of **re-engineering** has been offered by some theorists to suggest that firms should restructure on the basis of processes (e.g., meeting customer orders and requirements) rather than on the basis of departments or functions (e.g., sales and production). Such an approach would require supervisors and employees to directly focus on customer needs and services rather than on their own functions and specialties. Focusing on the customer might enhance a firm's efforts to be more efficient and competitive in the marketplace.[4] This could also mean a blurring of line and staff functions and roles. Some authorities have suggested that re-engineering will require an emergence of "process managers," who will manage key processes and whose broadened responsibilities will cut across line and staff functions and levels of an organization.[5] A number of major corporations already have restructured parts of their organizations along customer–process dimensions. If carried out throughout a firm, this would create what has been referred to as the "horizontal corporation," in which organizational structures would become quite flattened and managerial authority relationships would be minimal.[6]

Downsizing (restructuring, right-sizing)
Large-scale reduction and elimination of jobs in a company that usually results in reduction of middle-level managers, removal of organizational levels, and a widened span of management for remaining supervisors.

Re-engineering
Concept of restructuring a firm on the basis of processes and customer needs and services, rather than by departments and functions.

Whether or not radical restructurings will become commonplace in the future is speculative. Moreover, it is not clear that re-engineering differs significantly from what most firms try to do either before or after downsizing. What does seem likely, however, is that the application of organizational principles will always be part of the supervisory position, and that any type of organizational change will require that supervisors understand how to apply and adapt organizational principles to their situations. Applying organizational principles is the primary subject of Chapter 10.

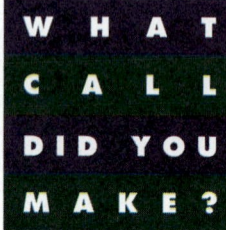

WHAT CALL DID YOU MAKE?

As Alice Austin in the chapter-opening vignette, you must review and apply the basic organizational principles that were discussed in this chapter. Probably the most important is to take steps to restore the unity of command principle in your department. All direct work requests must be communicated through you, and you must not be bypassed, if you are going to retain work control. It may be that your span of supervision is too wide. Perhaps you need to identify one or two lead persons who can serve in your absence in order to have a proper chain of command. Although there are many approaches that you can take, you probably should first discuss this with your manager, the dean of administration, in order to get support to rectify the situation. All parties who use your services need to be informed again of the proper workflow procedures. Furthermore, you need to instruct your employees that they are to accept no direct work requests unless they have your approval to do so, or the approval of a lead person if you decide to appoint such an individual.

SUMMARY

1 Identify the organizing function of management.

The organizing function of management is to design a structural framework, that is, to group and assign activities to specific work areas so as to achieve the desired objectives. Organizing includes establishing authority relationships among managers, supervisors, and departments.

2 Explain the unity of command principle and its applications.

An organization normally should adhere to the principle of unity of command. This principle requires that everyone be directly accountable to only one supervisor and that formal communications should normally flow through the chain of command.

3 Define the span of management principle and the factors that influence its application.

In assigning the number of employees reporting to one supervisor, the principle of span of management should be observed. Also known as the span of supervision or span of control, this principle recognizes that there is an upper limit to the number of individuals a supervisor can manage effectively. The actual span of management is determined by factors such as the competence of the supervisor, the previous training and experience of employees, and the amount and nature of work to be performed. Other things being equal, the smaller the span of management, the more levels of management will be needed; the broader the span of management, the fewer levels will be required.

4 Describe departmentation and alternative approaches for grouping activities and assigning work.

Departmentation is the process of grouping activities and people into distinct organizational units. The most widely used basis of departmentation is to group activities according to functions. Other bases include departmentalizing along geographic lines, by product or service, by customer, by process and equipment, or by time. Rather than designing new departments, supervisors most often will be faced with the task of assigning activities and employees within an existing department for maximum efficiency.

5 Explain the meaning of line and staff authority and how these relate to organizational structures.

Every supervisor is attached to an organization in either a line or a staff capacity. Within their own departments, all supervisors are line managers with line authority to direct their employees. If a person is in a staff authority position, his or her normal role is to furnish counsel, guidance, advice, and service in a specialized field.

A line-type organizational structure has only line authority relationships in a direct chain-of-command arrangement. This is commonplace in very small firms. As organizations increase in size, they usually adopt a line-and-staff type structure. This enables the use of staff people whose specialized knowledge and skills support line managers and others throughout the organization. In the usual line-and-staff structure, a line supervisor may accept or reject the staff's advice.

6 Describe how functional authority may be granted to specialized staff for certain purposes.

When higher-level management grants functional authority to a specialized staff person, this person has the right to issue directives about certain matters within his or her expertise. When a staff person has been granted functional authority over a specialized area, line supervisors are not free to reject the advice or directives that this person may give.

7 Discuss applications of matrix-type organizational structure.

A matrix (project) type of organizational structure places certain managers in charge of project teams whose members are drawn from different departments. At the same time, line supervisors manage the employees in regular departments.

This structure facilitates more efficient use of employees on multiple projects without disrupting the regular departmental arrangements. However, a matrix structure may create problems of priority scheduling and accountability of employees both to a departmental supervisor and project managers.

8 Define downsizing and its implications for organizational principles.

Downsizing usually involves the elimination of job positions and a level (or levels) of management. Supervisors who survive a downsizing have to adapt organizational principles to the changes that have occurred. This usually includes a widened span of management and the need to provide more latitude to employees in sharing in decision making.

KEY TERMS

Organizing (page 238)

Organization (page 238)

Span of management (page 239)

Lead person (page 241)

Division of work (specialization) (page 243)

Departmentation (page 243)

Department (page 243)

Principle of organizational stability (page 246)

Line authority (page 248)

Line-type organizational structure (page 248)

Staff authority (page 248)

Line department (page 250)

Staff department (page 250)

Line-and-staff type organizational structure (page 250)

Principle of compulsory staff advice (service) (page 251)

Functional authority (page 251)

Matrix-type organizational structure (page 253)

Downsizing (restructuring, right-sizing) (page 255)

Re-engineering (page 255)

QUESTIONS FOR DISCUSSION

1. Define the managerial organizing function.

2. What is meant by unity of command? Is this principle realistic in today's large, complex organizations?

3. Define the span of management principle. What are some of the major factors that influence a supervisor's span of management?

4. Explain the trade-off between the number of levels of management and the span of management. How does this problem typically affect a first-line supervisor?

5. Define departmentation. Why is the functional approach the most widely adopted approach to departmentation? Discuss other approaches to departmentation and how these often overlap.

6. How does fair assignment of work activities involve both quantity and quality of work? Why is this important for the stability of a department's operation?

7. Define line authority and staff authority. What is the difference between a line type of organization and a line-and-staff type of organization?

8. Discuss the functions of staff personnel. Does the relationship between a line supervisor and a staff person (from whom the line supervisor seeks advice or counsel) violate the concept of unity of command? Why or why not?

9. Identify the departments in organizations that are most likely to function in a staff capacity. Can you tell from looking at an organizational chart or from a person's title whether that individual is line or staff? Why or why not?

10. Discuss the concept of functional authority. Give several examples of how organizations have used this concept. Does the use of functional authority (or functional staff authority) violate the principle of unity of command? Discuss.

11. Does the matrix organization violate the unity-of-command principle? Discuss. What are the advantages of the matrix structure?

12. What is meant by downsizing (restructuring)? Is it likely that organizational principles will be rendered obsolete by future downsizing and radical restructuring efforts? Discuss.

SKILLS APPLICATIONS

Skills Application 9-1: Organizational Principles and Concepts

1. Identify from this chapter what you believe to be the most important concepts concerning the organizing function of management that a supervisor should understand.

2. After you have developed your list, try it out with someone who is a supervisor to determine how many of the concepts that person is familiar with.

3. If the supervisor is not familiar with the majority of the concepts on your list, does this mean that he or she is not effective? Why or why not?

Skills Application 9-2: Organization Chart Analysis

Review the following organization chart for an insurance company and answer the questions that follow.

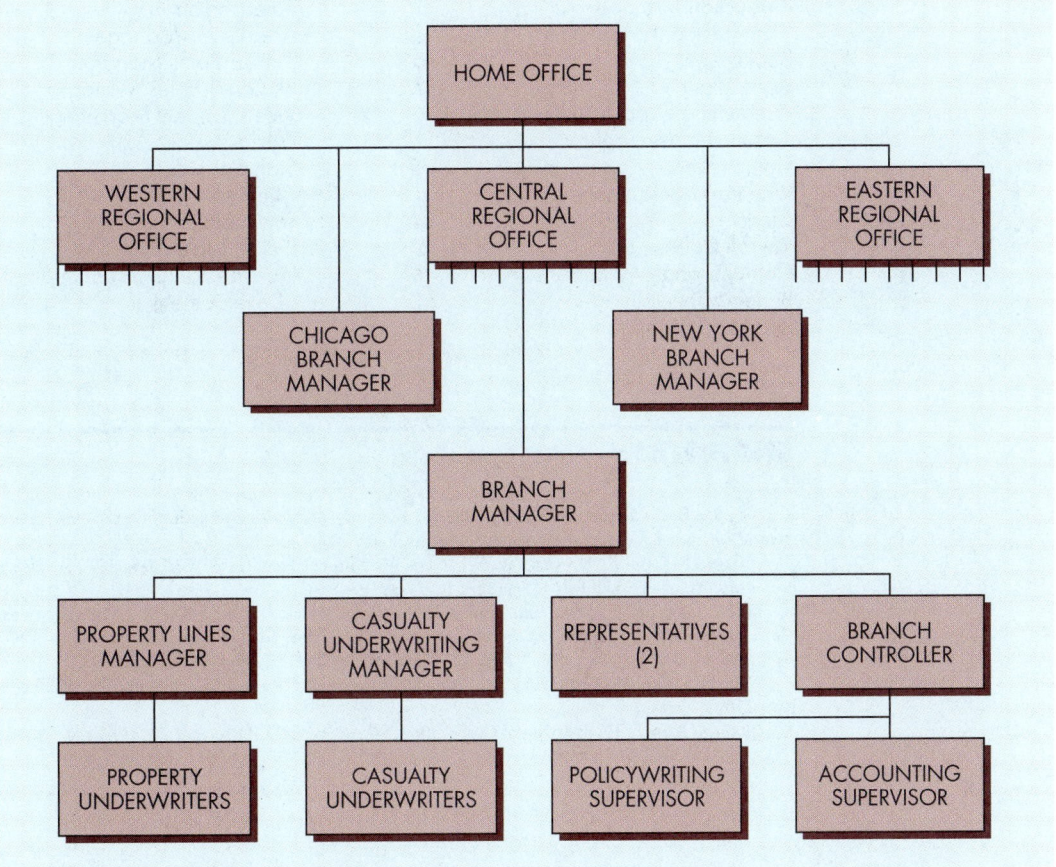

1. Identify the departmentation options that appear in the chart.

2. How would the chart change if the level immediately below the home office were changed to a product/service form of departmentation?

3. What would be some reasons for having only the regional offices report to the home office?

Skills Application 9-3: Organizing a Company

Following is a list of all job titles for an organization as well as the number of people in each position. From this information, construct an organization chart. You may eliminate or change job titles, but you cannot reduce the number of people working for the company.

The company produces and sells a variety of freeze-dried products throughout the United States and Canada. Sales have been growing at about 5 percent a year, slightly above the inflation rate. As a result of the slow growth, projections reveal no new job openings except for replacement.

Job Title	Number of Employees	Job Title	Number of Employees
Production Worker	60	Vice President-Human Resources	1
Production Supervisor	6	Salesperson	100
Production Manager	1	Area Sales Manager	8
Vice President-Production	1	District Sales Manager	8
Bookkeeper	6	Regional Sales Manager	6
Accountant	3	Vice President-Marketing	1
Accounting Supervisor	6	President	1
Accounting Manager	2	Staff Specialist	6
Comptroller	1	Chemists	3
Vice President-Finance	1	Technicians	6
Clerk	4	R & D Supervisor	2
Payroll Coordinator	2	Vice President-Research & Development	1
Compensation Manager	1		
Benefits Specialist	1		
Personnel Manager	1		

ENDNOTES

1.   See Exodus, Chapter 18, in the Bible for the story of Moses and Jethro. Jethro has been referred to as the "world's first management and organization consultant."

2.   Wayne F. Cascio, "Downsizing: What Do We Know? What Have We Learned?" *Academy of Management Executive* (Volume 7, Number 1, February 1993), pp. 95–104.

3.   K.S. Cameron, S.J. Freeman, and A.K. Mishra, "Best Practices in White Collar Downsizing: Managing Contradictions," *Academy of Management Executive* (Volume 5, Number 3, August 1991), pp. 57–73.

4.   "Management's New Gurus," *Business Week* (August 31, 1992), pp. 44–47 and 50–52.

5.   Robert B. Blaha, "Forget Functions, Manage Processes," *HR Magazine* (Volume 38, Number 6, June 1993), pp. 109–110.

6.   John A. Byrne, "The Horizontal Corporation," *Business Week* (December 20, 1993), pp. 76–81.

10

Supervisory Organizing at the Departmental Level

LEARNING OBJECTIVES

After studying this chapter, you will be able to:

1 Discuss how supervisors can organize to empower employees and describe the resulting benefits for the firm and the employees.

2 Explain the importance of delegating and decentralizing authority and identify when recentralizing is appropriate.

3 Describe why and how to develop supervisory understudies.

4 Determine how a supervisor should plan for an "ideal" departmental structure and work toward this objective.

5 Define and discuss organizational tools that are useful in supervisory organizing efforts.

6 Discuss the impact of informal organization and informal group leaders and how supervisors should deal with them.

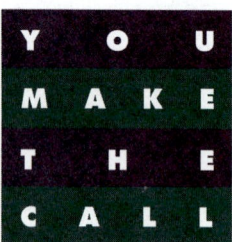

You are Gary Rodriguez, controller of the Rollings Paint Company. You are concerned about one of your supervisors, Walter Grant, who supervises the accounting and payroll department. Walter Grant started with the company over 25 years ago. He began as a one-person accounting department, and he now has 10 employees in his department. He was known as a loyal and hardworking supervisor, but one who preferred to do as many things as possible himself instead of delegating duties to his employees.

In recent years, numerous complaints about the accounting and payroll department have become more frequent and serious. Other company supervisors have complained that the department is "bogged down." Delays in getting up-to-date figures have been increas-

ing, and there have also been more errors in payroll checks and in other vital areas. Just last week, a major computer programming mistake attributed to Grant caused a week's delay and brought numerous complaints about payroll checks that had been computed in error.

Several department employees have spoken with you privately about Grant. Although they like him personally, they are concerned that Grant is behind the times, and that he will not listen to their suggestions and ideas for improvement.

You know that much of the problem in the department centers on Walter Grant. You occasionally have urged him to assign more duties to employees and to delegate authority to them. You have tried to impress upon him the need for new procedures and the importance of listening to ideas from employees. Until now, Grant has not gotten the message and he has been doing nothing to change. In the meantime, things in the accounting and payroll department are getting worse. You are reluctant to fire Grant, because he is 60 years old and a close personal friend. You know that you have to do something, and the sooner the better. What should you do? **YOU MAKE THE CALL.**

SUPERVISORY ORGANIZING FOR EMPLOYEE EMPOWERMENT

1 Discuss how supervisors can organize to empower employees and describe the resulting benefits for the firm and the employees.

Advocates of organizational downsizing (discussed in the previous chapter) have stressed the adoption and application of empowerment. As discussed in Chapter 1, "empowerment" means giving employees the authority and responsibility to accomplish organizational objectives. Organizations that embrace the concept of empowerment have also been called "high-involvement" or "high-performance" workplaces. Organizations with an empowerment policy make a conscious effort to delegate authority to employees at lower levels, allowing them to participate in or make decisions that affect their jobs. Empowerment also usually means a sharing of resources and information with supervisors and employees (or work teams) that previously would have been retained by middle- or top-level managers.[1] In essence, an empowerment policy means that participative management is a commitment throughout the organization.

To empower their employees, effective supervisors structure their departments so that they can delegate more to them and take advantage of their ideas and experience. Workers who are actually doing a job can contribute excellent ideas about how to solve problems concerning the job. Involving employees in decision making can result in better decisions. Also, since most people like to have a voice in decisions that affect them, such participation can result in more satisfied employees.

Most departmental supervisors are not involved in major decisions concerning the design of the overall organizational structure of their firms. Supervisors primarily are involved in decisions about the structure of their own departments. Before we discuss organizing at the departmental level, let's review the importance of delegating and decentralizing authority and the occasional need for recentralizing.

DELEGATION, DECENTRALIZATION, AND RECENTRALIZATION

2 Explain the importance of delegating and decentralizing authority and identify when recentralizing is appropriate.

In Chapter 4, we emphasized that the supervisor's main strategy for getting work done in an organization is the delegation of authority (commensurate with responsibility). There can be no organization without delegation of authority. It is not a question of whether to delegate authority, but rather how much and in what forms authority should be delegated to subordinates at different levels. As discussed in

Chapter 4, the extent to which authority is delegated determines the degree of organizational decentralization. When authority has been widely delegated downward and throughout levels of a firm, the firm has decentralized its decision-making authority. Decentralization, therefore, is a major component of supervisory and employee empowerment.

If delegation of authority is to be effective, a sincere desire and effort to delegate must permeate the entire management team. Top-level managers must believe in delegation. Yet even though top-level managers may intend it, the desired degree of decentralization may not be achieved. Somewhere along the line there may be an authority "hoarder" who refuses to delegate further. Some supervisors are afraid or unwilling to delegate because they fear they may lose control of their departments.

Achieving Decentralization

There are several ways to achieve the desired degree of decentralization. Some organizations make great efforts to indoctrinate their entire management team in the philosophy of decentralization. Managers are made to understand that by carefully delegating authority they neither lose status nor absolve themselves of their responsibilities. One way to accomplish decentralization is to organize so that each manager has a fairly large number of subordinate supervisors. By stretching the span of management, the manager has little choice but to delegate.

Another means that some organizations use is to establish a policy that managers cannot be promoted if they have not developed subordinates who can take over their positions. This policy provides incentive to delegate authority and develop junior supervisors to assume additional responsibilities.

When Recentralization Is Necessary

From time to time, top-level management will take a look at a firm's organizational structure—checking, questioning, and appraising whether it is sound. There may be a need for changes due to technological advances, changes in the environment, changes in the enterprise itself, and other reasons. Reorganization may be needed to overcome perceived shortcomings. Consequently, management may decide to realign, "tighten up," or recentralize. Management may feel that it has lost control over certain activities, perhaps because established controls were not effective. **Recentralization** is the process of reducing or revoking delegated authority in connection with realigning functions or responsibilities. For example, in recent years many companies have centralized their budgetary and financial departments in order to have better financial control over certain production and sales operations that otherwise have been decentralized. A periodic review of the amount of delegated authority is both advisable and necessary in any organization. This also applies to any authority that the supervisor has delegated to employees.

Whenever recentralization takes place, there are apt to be tensions and resistance among members of the organization whose authority is lessened. Feelings of

Recentralization
Reducing or revoking delegated authority when realigning functions or responsibilities.

CONTEMPORARY ISSUE
Decentralization: A Reality or a Sham?

Long-term proponents of decentralization have received considerable encouragement from recent efforts at organizational downsizing, total quality management (TQM), and the like, which have fostered the concept of empowerment. Empowerment is being widely touted as the appropriate style of management by which lower-level employees and supervisors assume greater responsibility and authority for making decisions and responding quickly to organizational and other needs. Many company managers proclaim that they are decentralized, that their organizational structures are different, and that their personnel have been empowered. However, some observers believe that "the more things change, the more they stay the same." Tom Peters, author of *In Search of Excellence,* believes that most decentralization and empowerment claims are more form than substance. According to Peters, "The average decentralized corporation is not decentralized. It is a sham, a sick joke." Peters asserts that organizations must change fundamentally. Managers and supervisors must "act more like consultants than bosses" and "create projects and challenging norms" for which their employees may strive. Peters gives seminars and speeches on the subject. He claims that many managers do not really understand the meaning of decentralization, and they are not willing to really change their organizational approaches, despite the many problems that today's organizations face.

Source: From "Ever in Search of a New Take on Excellence," *Business Week* (August 31, 1992), p. 52.

discouragement, mistrust, suspicion, and insecurity will be common. To ease these feelings, higher-level managers should explain thoroughly to subordinate managers the reasons for the recentralization. Similarly, if a supervisor decides to revoke certain authority that has been delegated to an employee, the supervisor should discuss the reasons for this decision with the employee, as well as with others who may be affected. For example, a housekeeping supervisor of a local motel might decide that employees who previously had wide latitude to determine the order of their tasks now must follow a written daily work schedule to meet the changing priorities of the motel manager. The supervisor may be able to lessen the resulting resentment by discussing the reasons for the change and encouraging the employees to suggest ways to improve the work scheduling process. Generally, recentralization is a difficult process. Careful decentralization of authority in the first place is the best way to avoid the need to recentralize.

DEVELOPING UNDERSTUDIES AS A WAY OF DELEGATING

3 Describe why and how to develop supervisory understudies.

In Chapter 4 we discussed a supervisor's delegation of authority in the daily work situation and the manner in which a supervisor exercises authority. We suggested the *general supervision* approach, which places employees on their own as much as possible. It usually is a better way to use supervisory authority than the close and autocratic exercise of power. In Chapter 16, we will further elaborate upon this approach for leading and motivating employees. In this chapter, our concern is with the supervisor's delegation of authority as a means of building an organizational structure within the department. If the supervisor is away or removed from the scene, operations must go on in an orderly fashion. This usually means that a supervisor has selected and developed an understudy to whom authority and responsibility can be delegated.

The Need for an Understudy

In many situations the number of employees within a supervisor's department will be rather small, and the supervisor may wonder whether it is really necessary to delegate authority. Regardless of the size of the department, however, every supervisor needs someone who can assist and even be able to run the department if the supervisor should have to leave temporarily. This person can be called an **understudy**. Terminology varies in many organizations; for example, an understudy may also be identified as a "lead person," "working supervisor," "foreman," or "supervisory assistant." Regardless of the designation, every department should have someone who can take over when the supervisor has to be away from the job for sickness, meetings, vacations, or other reasons. As mentioned before, a supervisor personally may miss a promotion if no one is capable of taking over the department. Sooner or later, every supervisor needs an understudy. (See Figure 10-1.)

There are several advantages that supervisors will discover if they decide to select, train, and develop understudies. Training understudies usually forces supervisors to formulate a much clearer view of their own duties, departmental operations, and ways to arrange jobs more efficiently. The supervisor will also learn more effective ways of delegating authority to subordinates.

Selecting an Understudy

The first step in developing an understudy is to select the right person for the position. (In this section we assume that the supervisor is not restricted in choosing an understudy, as might be the case in a unionized firm with seniority criteria.) The supervisor usually knows which employees are the most capable. The individual selected preferably should be someone to whom other employees turn in case of questions—a person who is regarded by fellow workers as a leader. This employee should be an individual who knows how to do the job and handle problems as they arise, does not get into arguments, and is respected by other employees. A potential understudy should have demonstrated good judgment in carrying out assignments and in approaching, analyzing, and solving problems. This person should be interested in developing himself or herself for a better position. Without ambition to advance, even the best training will not achieve the desired results. Also, this employee must have shown dependability and a willingness to accept responsibility. Even though he or she has not had the opportunity to display all of these qualities, whatever latent attributes exist usually will be discovered during the training and development process.

Understudy
Someone who can assist the supervisor and is able to run the department in the supervisor's absence.

FIGURE 10-1
Every supervisor needs
an understudy.

If the supervisor has two or three equally good employees as potential understudies in the department, it may be desirable to train all of them. This provides the supervisor with even more backup leadership. It also gives the supervisor more information and greater opportunities to observe potential understudies in action before making the selection.

Developing the Understudy

Although the word "training" frequently is used to denote the educational process for a supervisory understudy, it is not a totally fitting term. Rather, it should be a matter of developing or "bringing along" an employee—an experience of *self-development* on the understudy's part. Understudies must indicate their eagerness to develop themselves and have the initiative to be self-starters. Bringing understudies to the point where they can assume considerable authority may be a slow and tedious process, but it is worth the effort.

Since no two people are alike, no exact procedures or time schedules can be outlined that will work in every case. However, there are some common steps in the development process that seem to work well in most situations. Gradually, supervisors should bring understudies in on the detailed workings of the department. For example, supervisors should show them departmental reports and explain where, when, and how information is provided. They should tell the understudies why such reports are necessary and what is done with them. They should introduce the understudies to other supervisors, staff members, and personnel with whom they must associate, and have them contact these people as time goes on. It is advisable to permit understudies to attend supervisory meetings after they have had a chance to learn general aspects of the supervisory job. Supervisors should show them how the work of each department is related to that of other departments. As daily problems arise, supervisors should encourage the understudies to try to solve some of them on their own. As understudies develop their own solutions, supervisors will have a chance to see how they analyze situations and approach decision making. Supervisors can teach the understudies the steps of decision making, pointing out guidelines to be followed and pitfalls to be avoided (such as those discussed in Chapter 6).

In time, supervisors should give the understudies responsibility for some activities, in other words, delegate more duties and commensurate authority to the understudies. This relationship requires an atmosphere of confidence and trust, with the supervisor recognized by the understudy as a *coach* and *mentor*. In an eagerness to develop understudies as rapidly as possible, supervisors should not overload them or pass on problems that are beyond their capabilities; it may take some time for understudies to be able to handle complex problems. Moreover, supervisors must be aware that sooner or later the understudies will expect some tangible rewards to compensate for the additional duties.

This process may take much effort and many supervisory hours. Often about the time that the understudy can be of major help, he or she may be transferred to another job outside of the supervisor's department or promoted. This may be discouraging for the moment, but the supervisor can be confident that higher-level managers will appreciate the supervisor's efforts and success in the development of a competent understudy. Furthermore, having a part in the development or advancement of an employee is one of the most satisfying personal feelings that a supervisor can experience.

Encouraging the Reluctant Understudy

The development of an understudy and delegation of authority involve a two-sided relationship. Although the supervisor may be willing to delegate authority, a subordinate may be reluctant to accept it. Some employees are unsure of themselves and feel that they may not be able to tackle the job. Or they fear having additional responsibilities that may add to the burden of their daily work. Some employees do not want to move up, since they are reluctant to leave the security of their peer group—for example, if they are part of a labor union or have several friends in their work group. Merely telling a potential understudy to have more self-confidence, or "pull yourself together," will have little effect. However, the supervisor can contribute to a potential understudy's self-confidence by gradually coaching and training the person to undertake additional and more difficult assignments. Employees who have a high sense of responsibility often underrate themselves. Yet these may be the very employees who will develop into excellent understudies if they are encouraged and assisted to accept the challenge. (See Figure 10-2.)

FIGURE 10-2
Although the supervisor may be ready and willing to delegate authority, an employee may be reluctant to accept it.

To delegate effectively, the supervisor must develop a personal relationship with the understudy. This often will be a growing and shifting relationship that becomes more meaningful with the passage of time. At some point, the understudy should be able to take over the complete supervision of the department. When that happens, the supervisor truly will have organized a department that will carry on even if he or she should leave the position.

The same process will hold true if only one understudy is developed, or if the size of the department should warrant a number of assistants. Of course, with increased responsibilities should come positive incentives for supervisory assistants, such as pay increases, appropriate titles, recognized status within the organization, and other tangible or intangible rewards.

PLANNING THE "IDEAL" DEPARTMENTAL STRUCTURE

4 Determine how a supervisor should plan for an "ideal" departmental structure and work toward this objective.

Although some supervisors will have an opportunity to structure a totally new department, most supervisors are placed in charge of existing departments. In either case, all supervisors should think of an *ideal departmental structure*—a structure that the supervisor believes can best achieve the department's objectives. It is not essential that the supervisor's plans for the department appear beautiful on paper or that the organization chart look symmetrical and well balanced. Nor should an "ideal" structure be thought of as being in the distant future. Rather, it should be a goal or standard by which the supervisor can assess the present organizational arrangement and which should serve as a guide for rearrangements and for long-range plans for the department.

The supervisor should plan the departmental structure on the basis of sound organizational principles, not around personalities. If the organization is planned primarily to accommodate current or available individuals, existing shortcomings probably will be perpetuated. If a department is structured around personalities, serious problems can occur when key employees are promoted or resign. But if the departmental organization is planned on the basis of the necessary activities and functions to be performed, then qualified people can be found to fill the positions. For example, if a supervisor relies heavily on one or two key employees who are "Jacks of all trades," then the department will be disrupted if one or both of these employees leave. Conversely, if a number of weak employees do not carry their share of the load, the supervisor may assign too many employees to certain activities to compensate for poorly performing individuals. Therefore, a structure must be designed that will best serve the objectives of the department. Then the available employees should be matched with the tasks to be performed.

This is easier said than done. It frequently happens, particularly in smaller departments, that available employees do not fit well in the planned "ideal" structure. In most situations the supervisor will be placed in charge of an existing department without having had the chance to decide its structure or to choose the employees. In these circumstances the supervisor can gradually adjust to the capacities of the available employees. Then, as time goes on, the supervisor can make changes that will move the department toward the supervisor's "ideal" structure.

ORGANIZATIONAL TOOLS AND THEIR APPLICATION

5 Define and discuss organizational tools that are useful in supervisory organizing efforts.

Some managers, supervisors, and employees do not understand how their positions and responsibilities fit in with the positions and responsibilities of other employees. Organization charts and manuals, job descriptions, and job specifications can reduce the confusion. These tools clarify the organization's structure and assist supervisors in understanding their positions and the relationships between various departments throughout the enterprise. The obligation to prepare a firm's overall organization chart and manual rests with top-level management. However, supervisors will usually develop these tools for their departments and also keep them up to date.

Organization Charts

Organization chart
Graphic portrayal of a company's authority and responsibility relationships.

The **organization chart** is a means of graphically portraying organizational authority and responsibility relationships. An organization chart primarily depicts managerial and supervisory positions as rectangular boxes. (Some organization charts use lines, circles, or other artistic designs to depict organizational positions.) Each box represents one position category, although several employees may be included in the position category. For example, Figure 10-3 shows a position called "Day Nurses." This is one position, although there may be several day nurses. The boxes

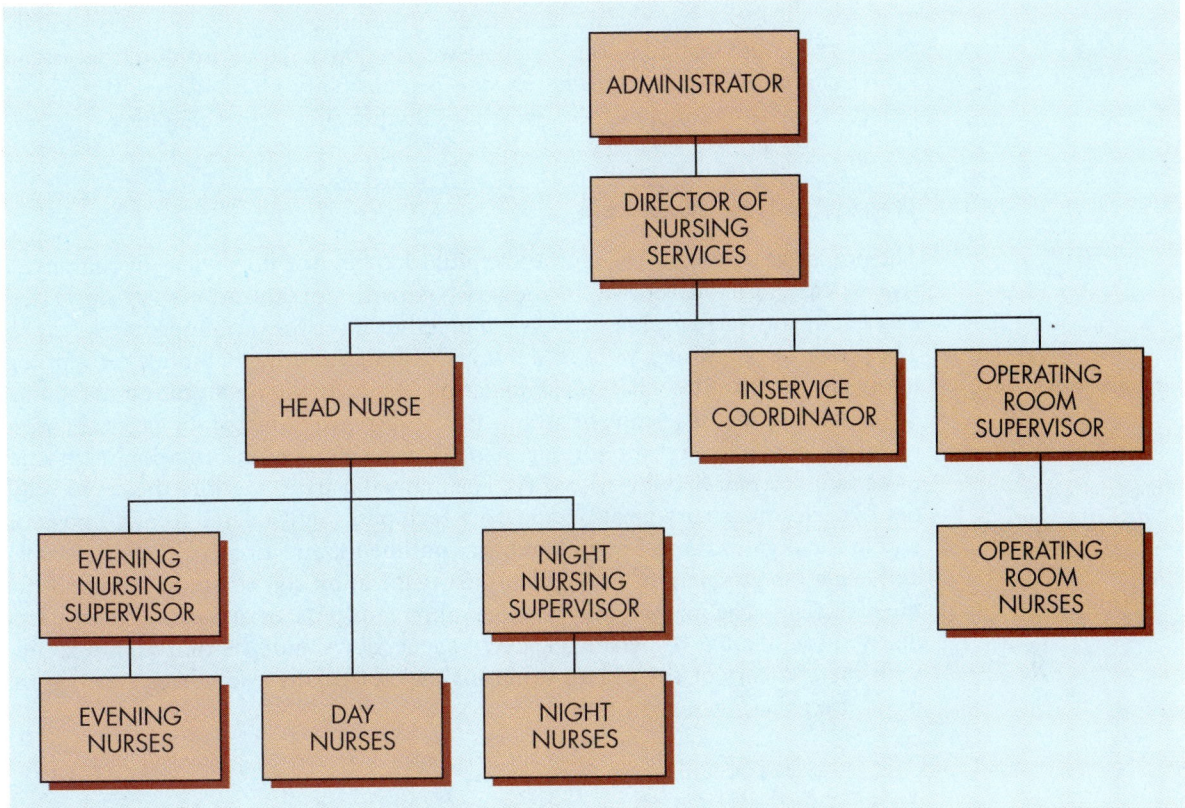

FIGURE 10-3
Organization Chart
for Nursing Services
Department of a
Hospital

are usually interconnected to show the grouping of activities that make up a department, division, or section. By studying the vertical relationships between boxes, anyone can readily determine who reports to whom. Although different types of organization charts are used, the vast majority are constructed vertically and show levels of organization arranged in the shape of a pyramid (see Figure 10-3).

A supervisor will gain a number of advantages from establishing and maintaining an organization chart of the department. It requires, first of all, a careful study and analysis of the departmental structure. Preparing the chart might reveal duplication of efforts or inconsistencies in certain functions or activities. A chart may enable the supervisor to spot where dual reporting relationships exist (that is, where one employee is reporting to two supervisors) or where there are overlapping positions. The chart may also suggest whether the span of management is too wide or too narrow.

Organization charts are a convenient way to acquaint new employees with the structure of the department and the entire enterprise. Most employees want to know where they stand and where their supervisor stands relative to higher-level managers. Of course, there are limitations to charts, especially if they are not kept up to date. All changes should be recorded promptly, since failure to do so makes the chart as outdated and useless as last week's newspaper. Also note that organization charts show formal authority and responsibility relationships; they do not reflect the informal organization, which we discuss later in this chapter.

Organization Manuals

Organization manual
Written description of the authority and responsibilities of managerial and supervisory positions as well as formal channels, major objectives, and policies and procedures.

The organization manual is another helpful tool, because it provides in comprehensive written form the decisions about a company's organizational structure. Not every company has an organization manual, but most firms of appreciable size do. They may be identified by any number of designations, including terminology unique to the firm. By whatever designation, typically the **organization manual** defines and describes the scope of authority and responsibilities of managerial and supervisory positions and the formal channels for obtaining information, assistance, or certain decision-making authority. The manual usually specifies the responsibilities of each supervisory position and how each position is related to other positions within the organization. The manual may outline the functions of each department and explain how relationships within the organization contribute to accomplishing the objectives. The manual may also contain major policies and procedures, particularly those relating to personnel. Every supervisor should be thoroughly familiar with the contents of the organization manual, especially with those sections that most affect their own department.

Job Descriptions and Job Specifications

Job description
Written description of the principal duties and responsibilities of a job.

Job descriptions often are included in an organization manual or can be obtained from the human resources department. A **job description,** sometimes called a "position description," identifies the principal elements, duties, and scope of authority and responsibility involved in a job. Some job descriptions are brief; others are lengthy. Job descriptions often are based substantially on information obtained from employees who actually perform the jobs and from their supervisors.

Some firms include certain expectations—such as the availability to work evenings or to travel—as part of the job descriptions. Some even indicate specific productivity or quality performance standards that must be attained after a training period.[2]

For supervisory and managerial positions, many firms prefer to use the term "position guide" or something other than "job description" in identifying the duties, responsibilities, and results expected for supervisors and managers.

Job specification
Written description of the personal qualifications necessary to perform a job adequately.

In practice, there is some overlap in the use of the terms "job description" and "job specification." Generally speaking, a job description describes the major duties of a position, whereas a **job specification** refers to the skills, capacities and qualities—personal qualifications—that are necessary to perform the job adequately. Many organization manuals include the job specification as part of each job description. Figure 10-4 is an example of a combined job description and speci-

FIGURE 10-4
Job Description and
Specification for
Insurance Company
Senior Terminal
Operator

JOB TITLE	JOB CODE	POSITION STATUS
Senior Terminal Operator	0408	_____ Exempt XX Nonexempt

ORGANIZATIONAL UNIT LOCATION

Administration   XX Home Office   XX Region

SUMMARY STATEMENT (A brief statement of the purpose of this position)

Performs routine and nonroutine input functions on computer terminal under moderate supervision. Provides clerical support as directed by supervisor. In certain regional offices, individual works under an activity standard.

RESPONSIBLE TO: Administration Manager/Supervisor

POSITION DUTIES AND RESPONSIBILITIES (Listed in order of importance to performance in this position. Developed from Job Analysis Questionnaire completed 1/92.)

WEIGHT	DUTIES/RESPONSIBILITIES
60%	1. Key input to system according to established procedures, meeting established time constraints. Review all displays to verify accuracy of input.
10%	2. Assemble material received daily; prioritize material to establish the day's work flow. Review material for accurate completion and send back to source if unable to ascertain correct information. When appropriate, maintain activity records according to established procedures.
10%	3. Perform necessary clerical tasks as directed by supervisor if system is not functioning; notify supervisor of system problems.
10%	4. May analyze information to determine whether original material is incomplete and may obtain information from original material for input directly into the system, without prior review by established resources.
5%	5. Produce various reports according to an established routine and time constraints.
5%	6. Render clerical support to unit staff as directed by supervisor.
100%	

** IMPORTANT **

The above-listed duties and responsibilities are not totally inclusive, but are intended to represent the principal elements of this position.

PLACEMENT CRITERIA (Minimum educational, skill and/or experience requirements as of September 1992.)

1. Light typing skills and/or familiarity with the operation of a computer terminal and keyboard.
2. Knowledge of general clerical functions as normally acquired through a high school education and/or related experience.
3. Knowledge and general understanding of the basics of the line of insurance for which individual is to be responsible, as normally acquired through one (1) year of work experience.

FIGURE 10-4
(continued)

4. Ability to prioritize work flow and organize diverse material.
5. Ability to perform effectively according to an established quota and/or production system with moderate supervision and within established time limits and ongoing deadlines.

WORKING CONDITIONS: Normal office environment. Incumbent will be seated at a computer terminal for the majority of the work day.

EXCEPTIONS TO THE ABOVE HIRING CRITERIA must be approved in writing by Home Office Human Resources.

fication. Note that the requirements to fill the job are called "placement criteria" on this form.

If a department does not have job descriptions and job specifications for existing jobs, or if new jobs are to be created, the supervisor should see to it that they are developed and written up. If help is needed, the supervisor should ask the human resources department, which usually has the necessary experience and know-how to facilitate this task. We will discuss this more in Chapter 13.

INFORMAL ORGANIZATION

6 Discuss the impact of informal organization and informal group leaders and how supervisors should deal with them.

Every enterprise is affected by a social subsystem known as the **informal organization** (sometimes referred to as the "invisible organization"). The informal organization reflects the spontaneous efforts of individuals and groups to influence the conditions of their environment. Whenever people work together, social relationships and informal work groups inevitably will come into being. Informal organization develops when people are in frequent contact with each other, although their relationships are not necessarily a part of formal organizational arrangements. Their contacts may be a part of or incidental to their jobs, or they may primarily stem from the desire to be accepted as a member of a group.

Informal organization
Informal groupings of people, apart from the formal organization structure, that satisfy members' social needs.

At the heart of informal organization are people and their relationships, whereas the formal organization primarily represents the organization's structure and the flow of authority. Supervisors can create and rescind formal organizations that they have designed; they cannot eliminate an informal organization, since they did not establish it.

Informal groups come into existence in order to satisfy needs and desires of their members that the formal organization does not satisfy. Informal organization particularly satisfies the members' social needs by providing recognition, close personal contacts, status, companionship, and other aspects of emotional satisfaction. Groups also offer other benefits to their members, such as protection, security, and

The workings of the informal organization are often evident in the lunchroom.

support. They further provide convenient access to the informal communications network or grapevine (discussed in Chapter 3). The grapevine provides a channel of communication and facilitates satisfaction of the members' desires to know what is going on. Informal organization also influences the behavior of individuals within the group. For example, an informal group may exert pressure on individuals to conform to certain standards of performance agreed upon by the majority of the group. This phenomenon may occur in any department or at any level in the organization.

The Informal Organization and the Supervisor

At times the informal organization may make the job of the supervisor either easier or more difficult. Because of their mutual interdependence, the attitudes, behavior, and customs of informal work groups affect the formal organization. Every organization operates in part through informal work groups, which can exert either a constructive or a negative force on the operations and accomplishments of a department.

Numerous research studies have demonstrated that informal groups can influence employees to either strive for high work performance targets or restrict production; either cooperate with supervisors or make life miserable for them, even to the point of having them removed. Supervisors must be aware that informal groups can be very strong and can even shape the behavior of employees to an extent that interferes with supervision. Pressures from informal groups can frustrate the supervisor in getting the results that higher-level managers expect the supervisor to achieve.

To influence the informal organization to play a positive role, the supervisor first must accept and understand it. The supervisor should group employees so that those most likely to comprise harmonious teams will be working together on the same assignments. Moreover, the supervisor should avoid activities that would unnecessarily disrupt those informal groups whose interests and behavior patterns support the department's overall objectives. Conversely, if an informal group is influencing employees in a negative direction to the extent that there is a serious threat to the department's functioning, a supervisor may have to take action (for example, redistributing work assignments or adjusting work schedules).

Supervising and Informal Work Group Leaders

Most informal work groups develop their own leadership. An informal leader may be chosen by the group or may just assume the reins of leadership by being a spokesperson for the group. Work group leaders play significant roles in both the formal and informal organizations; without their cooperation, the supervisor may have difficulty controlling the performance of the department. A sensitive supervisor, therefore, will make every effort to gain the cooperation and goodwill of informal leaders of different groups and will solicit their cooperation in furthering departmental objectives. If properly approached, an informal leader can be helpful to the supervisor, especially as a channel of communication. An informal leader may even be a viable candidate for the supervisor's understudy, if that person would accept such a position. However, it is questionable whether this person can still function as an informal leader once he or she has been designated as an understudy.

Instead of viewing informal leaders as "ringleaders," supervisors should consider them as employees who have influence and who are "in the know," and then try to work with them. For example, in an effort to build good relationships with informal leaders, a supervisor periodically may provide information to them before anyone else or ask their advice on certain problems. However, the supervisor must be careful to avoid having informal leaders lose status within their groups, because the leaders' close association with the supervisor certainly is being observed and could be interpreted negatively by employees. Similarly, the supervisor should not extend unwarranted favors to informal leaders as this could undermine their leadership roles. Rather, the supervisor should look for subtle approaches to have informal groups and their leaders dovetail their special interests with the department's activities. We will discuss this and other aspects of work groups in Chapter 17.

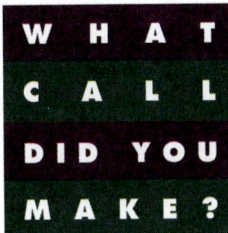

WHAT CALL DID YOU MAKE?

The situation of Walter Grant is all too familiar in many firms. He typifies the hardworking individual who is reluctant to change with the times and his department. Being a one-person accounting department is quite different from being a supervisor involved in managing and coordinating the work of others. Grant finds it difficult to supervise, and he is more comfortable doing what he did as an accountant than managing.

Since in the past you have not been able to convince Grant to change his style of supervision, it is unlikely that just talking with him will accomplish anything. You might, therefore, require him to select an understudy as discussed in this chapter. This would force him to delegate some of his departmental duties to the understudy, who would be groomed for additional responsibilities. This could be part of a plan for Grant to retire in the near future, or to move him to another position where his accounting talents could be utilized.

However, if you feel that Grant must be replaced immediately, you might decide to hire a new supervisor for the department. Grant could be transferred to a staff accounting position at no loss in salary. Before making any move, you should consult with the director of human resources to make sure that whatever action is taken will not lead to charges by Grant that he was discriminated against because of his age.

SUMMARY

1 Discuss how supervisors can organize to empower employees and describe the resulting benefits for the firm and the employees.

An empowerment policy means a company-wide commitment to delegating authority and responsibility to employees at lower levels, so that they can participate in decision making. To empower employees, supervisors should structure their departments to allow more employee participation. Employees actually doing the job can then help solve problems that affect their jobs. This can result in better decisions and more satisfied employees.

2 Explain the importance of delegating and decentralizing authority and identify when recentralizing is appropriate.

Delegation and decentralization of authority are vital if empowerment is to be a reality and there is to be a broad sharing of decision making throughout the enterprise. Decentralization of authority is not achieved easily, because some managers and supervisors are unwilling to delegate. At times, recentralization of authority is appropriate due to organizational realignment or the necessity to tighten up certain operations.

3 Describe why and how to develop supervisory understudies.

At the departmental level, supervisory delegation can be fostered through the selection, training, and development of understudies. Unless the supervisor develops someone to be an understudy and grants authority to this person, the department may be hampered seriously if the supervisor is absent for extended periods.

4 Determine how a supervisor should plan for an "ideal" departmental structure and work toward this objective.

In designing the organizational framework of a department, the supervisor should conceptualize an "ideal" arrangement based on the assumption that all required and qualified employees would be available. Since seldom are there people available with the exact qualifications desired, employees who are available must be fitted into the structure, deviating from the "ideal" where necessary.

5 Define and discuss organizational tools that are useful in supervisory organizing efforts.

The organization chart shows a graphic picture of organizational authority and responsibility relationships. Organization manuals contain statements of objectives, policies, and procedures; identify the authority and responsibilities of managerial and supervisory positions; and describe formal channels for obtaining information, assistance, or certain decision-making authority. The manual also may contain job descriptions, which identify major elements in each job position, and job specifications, which identify personal requirements to qualify for a job position.

6 Discuss the impact of informal organization and informal group leaders and how supervisors should deal with them.

The informal organization interacts with, yet is apart from, the formal organization structure. It can have either a constructive or a negative influence on departmental work performance. In order to make positive use of the informal organization, supervisors should become familiar with the workings of the informal groups and their leaders and determine how to enlist their cooperation to promote accomplishment of departmental objectives.

KEY TERMS

Recentralization (page 264)

Understudy (page 266)

Organization chart (page 270)

Organization manual (page 272)

Job description (page 272)

Job specification (page 272)

Informal organization (page 274)

QUESTIONS FOR DISCUSSION

1. Define "empowerment" ("high involvement") as this term has been utilized in recent years. Why is empowerment essentially a current emphasis upon participative management and part of a continuing challenge to organizations to delegate authority and decentralize? Why should supervisors empower their employees?

2. Why are delegation of authority and decentralization highly interrelated concepts? Is it proper to say that delegation of authority is necessary in order to have an organization? Discuss.

3. Why does top-level management sometimes resort to recentralization? Will a supervisor have occasions to revoke authority (i.e., recentralize)? Discuss.

4. What are the major issues involved in the selection and development of an understudy at the supervisory level?

5. Why do some employees resist opportunities to accept an understudy assignment? What can the supervisor do to encourage capable employees to seek advancement within the organization?

6. Discuss the issues involved in the question of whether a supervisor should organize on an "ideal" basis or on a "real" basis.

7. Define and discuss the application of the following organizational tools at the supervisory level:

- **a.** organization charts
- **b.** organization manuals
- **c.** job descriptions
- **d.** job specifications

8. What is meant by informal organization? How does the informal organization affect the formal organization? Discuss approaches by which the supervisor can foster cooperation with informal groups and their leaders.

SKILLS APPLICATIONS

Skills Application 10-1: Departmental Organization Chart Development

To complete this project, refer to Figure 10-3, which shows an organization chart for a department of a hospital. Recognize that Figure 10-3 was simplified for demonstration purposes.

Develop a departmental organization chart for a department of a firm, or for any enterprise for which you can obtain the required information and assistance. If you are currently employed, ask your supervisor for permission and help in this project.

Use rectangular boxes to show either an organizational unit or a position. Place the title of each position in the box. The title should be descriptive and show the function (e.g., sales manager). Vertical lines of authority should enter at the top center of a box and leave at the bottom center. An exception to this might be where there is a supervisory assistant and a horizontal relationship is involved. Vertical and horizontal solid lines should show the flow of line authority. Dotted or broken lines should show the flow of functional authority, if this is needed.

Keep the chart as simple as possible. Include comments to explain any special aspects.

Skills Application 10-2: The Informal Work Group

Using your current or most recent job, answer the following questions.

1. What informal groups exist, and why do they exist?

2. What pressures, if any, do they exert or can they exert on the supervisor?

3. Do the informal groups affect job performance at any time? If so, how and why? Who are the informal group leaders, and how do they influence job performance?

4. If you are the supervisor, what can you do to influence the groups in a desired direction?

Skills Application 10-3: Supervisory Organizing Applications

1.   Identify from this chapter a list of what you believe to be the most important principles/concepts that a supervisor should apply at the departmental level in order to supervise effectively.

2.   Next, think of the best and worst supervisors you have known or worked for. To what degree did they practice or not practice each of the items on your list?

ENDNOTES

1.   James A. F. Stoner and R. Edward Freeman, *Management* (5th ed.; Englewood Cliffs, N.J.: Prentice-Hall, 1992), p. 358.
2.   See J. E. Osborne, "Job Descriptions Do More Than Describe Duties," *Supervisory Management* (February 1992), p. 8.

11

Meetings, Committees, and Leading Meetings

LEARNING OBJECTIVES

After studying this chapter, you will be able to:

1 Explain why meetings, committees, and leading meetings are important components of supervision.

2 Identify the major types of meetings, their purposes and benefits, and their limitations.

3 Discuss the major types of committees and suggest guidelines for determining the composition and size of a committee.

4 Identify the major factors contributing to effective meetings, including the chairperson's leadership role.

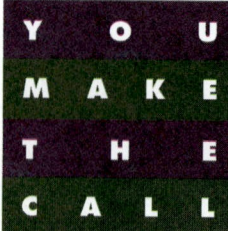

You are Martha Boxerman, a district supervisor for seven retail outlets of the Sheldon Shoe Stores in a metropolitan area. Each of your stores is headed by a store supervisor who has a supervisory assistant. The store supervisors report directly to you.

You used to schedule periodic meetings with your store supervisors and sometimes with their assistants. These meetings usually were held in your district office. The meetings primarily were to present information about sales items and marketing promotions, deal with customer problems, and discuss other issues of mutual interest. However, these meetings were difficult to schedule because of pressing business, vacations and absences, and other activities. At times only a few supervisors would show up for the scheduled meeting. This caused difficulties in

trying to inform those who were not present concerning what had been discussed and decided. Also, you received complaints from your supervisors that some meetings had been a waste of time, including the travel time. Responding to their complaints, you agreed to install an electronic message system between the district office and the stores whereby you could send messages and information to all stores. Each store would receive the same information at the same time, and store supervisors could read the message when they had time to do so.

The electronic message system has been in operation for about six months. Although it has been useful in sending out information, you sense something is missing in the process. You rarely get feedback from the store supervisors concerning information that you have dis-seminated. In several instances, store supervisors claimed that they had not received a message. Moreover, you recognize that the store supervisors now seldom see each other to share experiences and to discuss and decide upon certain problems that you would like them to handle. What should you do?

YOU MAKE THE CALL.

ROLES OF SUPERVISORS IN MEETINGS, COMMITTEES, AND LEADING MEETINGS

1 Explain why meetings, committees, and leading meetings are important components of supervision.

Electronic mail, facsimile transmission, teleconferencing—these and other "high-tech" communication methods have become commonplace in many organizations. Messages flow continuously upward, downward, and sideways through most orga-nizations to the degree that many individuals complain about an information over-load. Yet, with all this flow of messages, gaps and misunderstandings in communi-cation still occur, and they often harm personal relationships and job performance.

Also, job specialization and increasing complexity of functions in most organi-zations require coordination of efforts. To achieve this, there still is no substitute for bringing together the people who are responsible for dealing with the problem at hand. In other words, it still is necessary to call meetings or form committees. Without meetings and committees, it would be impossible for most organizations to operate. Of course, there are other ways to supply information that people need to perform their jobs and to receive their ideas and opinions. However, holding a meeting is often the most effective way to achieve these objectives.

We have included this chapter under the organizing function of management because committees and meetings are an integral part of organization life. For the most part, however, they are not shown on organization charts or identified in or-ganization manuals, since many are temporary. Nevertheless, meetings and com-mittees are a vital part of the organizational network of any firm. All of the con-cepts and principles discussed in Chapter 3 on communication can be applied to committee and meeting situations.

TYPES OF MEETINGS

2 Identify the major types of meetings, their purposes and benefits, and their limitations.

Informational meeting People gathered together to hear the group leader present information.

Most group meetings may be described as being either informational, discussional, or decisional in nature. In the **informational meeting,** the group leader does most of the talking, and the purpose of the meeting is to present information and facts. For example, a supervisor may call a meeting to announce a new job scheduling system as a substitute for posting a notice or speaking to each employee separately. Such a meeting enables everyone in the department to be notified at the same time. It also

Many organizations now use teleconferencing to hold meetings among people in geographically dispersed locations.

provides employees with a chance to ask questions about the meaning and consequences of the announcement.

In a **discussional meeting,** the group leader encourages the participation of group members in order to secure their ideas and opinions. For example, instead of asking employees individually for their suggestions on how to solve a problem, the supervisor could call a meeting for the same purpose. A number of suggestions may be offered and discussed in the meeting. Typically, the implementation of an idea that was suggested and discussed will receive more employee support, since the employees have participated in the solution.

A **decisional meeting** takes place when a discussional group has been delegated authority to make decisions on a particular problem or task. Just as a supervisor can delegate authority to an individual employee to make a decision, a supervisor can call a meeting and delegate authority to a group. For example, if a group of grocery store clerks are concerned about the allocation of overtime and they ask the supervisor to make a decision, the supervisor might prefer that the employees themselves find a solution. The supervisor therefore empowers the clerks to decide for themselves how overtime will be allotted. If the majority of the group make a decision, the solution probably will be more acceptable to the employees. Even if the group's solution is not the very best, it may be better for the supervisor to have an adequate solution that is implemented by the group than to impose a supervisory decision that they resist.

Discussional meeting
People gathered together to participate in a discussion with the group leader by offering their opinions, suggestions, or recommendations.

Decisional meeting
People gathered together to make decisions on a particular problem or task for which the group has been granted decision-making authority.

A supervisor may not be concerned with the detailed solution of a problem as long as the solution remains within certain limits. Such limits must be clearly stated when the problem is submitted to a group for a decision. For example, if the group is to decide on the allocation of overtime, the number of hours available must be stated. Also, the supervisor may need to point out that no one should work for more than a certain number of hours a day, and so forth. When feasible, it is desirable to let the group decide for themselves what should be done within stated guidelines.

Benefits from Meetings

A group of individuals exchanging information, opinions, and experiences usually will develop a better solution to a problem than could any one person who thinks through a problem alone. People bring to a meeting a range of experiences, backgrounds, and abilities, which rarely would be available if the same subject had been assigned to one person alone. Many problems are so complicated that one person could not possibly have all the knowledge, background, and experience needed to arrive at proper solutions. An open interchange of ideas can stimulate and clarify thinking. Solutions or recommendations that a group reaches will tend to be better than those that any single member of the group would have selected.

Group deliberation also can promote cooperation. Suggestions from members of a group are likely to be carried out more willingly than suggestions that come from only one person. When people have participated in the formulation of a plan, they tend to be more motivated toward its implementation than if they have not been consulted. It matters less how much they have actually contributed to the plan, so long as they were part of the meeting. Thus group meetings are advantageous in promoting cooperation and motivation.

Meetings can also be an opportunity for employees to demonstrate their creativity and problem-solving ability, and perhaps get noticed as candidates for promotion. Also, if meetings are conducted in an atmosphere of mutual respect, members will feel responsible for achieving a successful outcome.

Limitations of Meetings

Despite its benefits, the meeting device often is abused. A common complaint of supervisors is that there are too many meetings in their organizations. Another complaint is that many meetings are too time consuming. This complaint usually surfaces when each person at a meeting wants to have a major say and uses up a great amount of time to convince the others of his or her particular point of view. Meetings can also waste time if the agenda is not clearly focused on the problem at hand, the group leader or the members are not well prepared, or the leader allows the group to wander off the subject too much.

Another shortcoming of meetings is the concept of divided responsibility. When a matter is assigned to a group for deliberation, responsibility does not weigh as heavily on the individual members as it does if the matter is assigned to one person.

FIGURE 11-1
Several people
exchanging ideas can
create better solutions
than one person
alone.

The problem becomes everybody's responsibility, which really means it is nobody's responsibility. Although the group leader technically is responsible for the action or inaction of the group, this person can hardly be held accountable for the group's decision. Similarly, it is difficult to criticize the group as a whole or its individual members if each member can hide behind the responsibility of the total group. This thinning out of responsibility is natural, and there is no way to avoid it when a problem is referred to a committee for a decision.

Still another possible shortcoming is the phenomenon of **groupthink.** This occurs when the group's desire for consensus becomes paramount over its desire to reach the best possible decision. Deliberations become dominated by efforts to avoid conflict within the group, and therefore individuals do not express dissenting views that might be helpful in realistically appraising alternative choices of action.[1]

The supervisory problem is to weigh the many advantages emanating from group deliberation against the shortcomings of holding a meeting. Fortunately, the advantages usually exceed the disadvantages. If group members are carefully selected and if meetings are led and managed well, most meetings will become a vital, contributing part of any organization.

Groupthink
Phenomenon that occurs in meetings when group members do not express dissenting views in order to avoid conflict rather than realistically appraise alternatives.

3 Discuss the major types of committees and suggest guidelines for determining the composition and size of a committee.

COMMITTEES: TYPES, COMPOSITION, AND SIZE

A **committee** can be defined as a group of people drawn together to solve a problem or complete a task. We will use this term to include other designations, such as *commission, team, task force, board,* and the like. Supervisors should be familiar with the workings of meetings and committees, because they are frequently members. Moreover, supervisors themselves often conduct meetings, and thus they need to develop their ability to lead a meeting.[2] Members of a committee normally have

Committee
Group of people drawn together to solve a problem or complete a task.

CONTEMPORARY ISSUE
The Electronic Meeting

New technology such as computers and digital audio-visual tools have created a new way for people to meet, called the "electronic meeting." Computer systems that make the electronic meeting possible are often known as "group decision support software" (GDSS). Electronic meetings enable individuals at various locations to meet, discuss, and decide issues without actually getting together in a group setting. Proponents claim that electronic meetings help bring about a more focused effort on achieving the objectives at hand; there are fewer distractions; and the individuals involved can input through anonymous voting systems where this is applicable.

Many people find that the new technology is intrusive, complicated, distracting, and inhuman.

However, proponents of electronic meetings counter that they strip the group of some of the human dynamics that can paralyze open communication. They argue that in regular group meetings, certain individuals—especially managers—often dominate the meeting and discourage disagreement. With an electronic meeting, communication and voting are depersonalized by focusing attention on information on the video screen. Furthermore, it is easier to convey complaints to managers in an anonymous way electronically than to do so in person. The potential for GDSS systems appears to be enormous, provided that people learn to deal with and recognize the shortcomings of the approach.

Source: Adapted from Michael Finley, "Welcome to the Electronic Meeting," *Training* (Volume 28, Number 7, July 1991), pp. 28–32. See also Michael Schrage, "Robert's Electronic Rules of Order," *The Wall Street Journal* (November 29, 1993), p. A12.

other, full-time jobs, and their committee work is an additional duty or corollary assignment.

Permanent (Standing) Committees

Permanent (standing) committee
Group that meets on a more or less permanent basis to deal with recurring issues or problems.

A **permanent** (or **standing**) **committee** usually has an official, even permanent place in an organization. Its members are appointed by someone in higher-level management—or they are elected or nominated in some fashion—to deal with certain recurring issues or problems. Members of a standing committee are expected to serve either for a stated period of time or indefinitely. Usually they are drawn from various departments and represent supervisors, employees, and specialist personnel. Some common examples of permanent standing committees are a plant's safety committee, a university's affirmative-action monitoring committee, an employees' credit union committee, and the like.

Temporary (Ad Hoc) Committees

Temporary (ad hoc) committee
Group that meets only for a limited time and for a specific purpose.

A **temporary** (or **ad hoc**) **committee** is a group that meets only for a certain time period and usually for a limited, specific purpose. When the work of the temporary committee is finished, the group usually is disbanded. Ad hoc committees can discuss almost any type of organizational issue that is not already assigned to a permanent committee. Many of the group meetings that supervisors conduct within their own departments and with other departmental supervisors are of an ad hoc nature.

Membership and Size of a Committee

The membership (or composition) of a committee is important to its success. For far-reaching issues, the committee should bring together representatives from each group affected by the committee's decisions. If specialists from different departments are to be brought together, affected groups should have adequate representation in order to have balanced group deliberation. This allows the interests of departmental personnel to be heard and considered. Although this consideration is important, the supervisor who is appointing the committee should not carry it to extremes. It is more important to have capable members serve on a committee than to have representatives from every group that may be affected. Committees with decision-making responsibility should be composed of people who bring knowledge and experience related to the issue. Individuals selected should be able to express and support their opinions, but they also should be open to other points of view. It is advisable that they be independent of each other (i.e., not in a direct authority-reporting relationship).

There is no optimal committee size. Some authorities have suggested that up to a dozen or so members is near the upper limit for effectiveness. In any event, a committee should be large enough to provide for broad sources of information and thorough group deliberation. However, it should not be so large that it will be unwieldy. If the nature of the subject requires a very large committee, then subcommittees may be needed. For example, a large managerial committee formed to discuss a major program consisting of manufacturing and marketing a new product may find it advantageous to divide into subcommittees. The subcommittees meet separately to consider detailed aspects of the program, such as design, production, advertising, and distribution. After the subcommittees have deliberated, the committee meets as a whole to hear reports from each subcommittee and then proceeds accordingly.

LEADING EFFECTIVE MEETINGS

4 Identify the major factors contributing to effective meetings, including the chairperson's leadership role.

Meetings should be called only when necessary. If a matter can be handled by a telephone call or personal discussion, there is no need to call a meeting. If a supervisor decides that a meeting is necessary, then the topic should be communicated to the meeting participants, and the participants' role should be clarified. It must be clear whether the meeting is to serve an informational, discussional, or decisional purpose. If the supervisor is forming a temporary committee, members should be selected appropriately, and their numbers should be reasonable. However, as previously mentioned, more important than the number of committee members are their qualifications and their willingness to tackle the problems at hand.

FIGURE 11-2
A committee will be
more effective if
affected groups are
properly represented.

FIGURE 11-2
A committee will be more effective if affected groups are properly represented.

Most meetings—especially at the supervisory level—are of a problem-solving nature. These typically are discussional and decisional types of meetings in which a group is asked to grapple with problems and may or may not have delegated authority to implement solutions. In this regard, when a problem is assigned to a committee to make a decision and carry it out, the committee has been given line authority. However, if the charge to the committee is only to deliberate, debate, advise, and make recommendations, then the committee acts in a staff role.

For a meeting involving problem solving to be successful, the goals should be reasonable and achievable. Generally, the goals of the meeting should be (a) to come up with the best feasible solution to the problem, (b) to do this with unanimity or a majority consensus, and (c) to accomplish this in a short period of time.

The Chairperson and Teamwork

The success of any meeting depends largely on the group leader's skills in guiding the meeting toward its stated goals. The leader is often called a "chairperson." A chairperson may be appointed formally or informally. In many situations supervisors serve as chairpersons, especially in meetings held with their own employees.

A chairperson should recognize that participants bring to a meeting unique points of view and behavior patterns. It is human nature for participants to think first of how a topic, issue, or proposal will affect themselves, their jobs, their departments, and their own work environments. These thoughts can easily lead to friction. The chairperson should approach the members in such a way as to fuse individual viewpoints to promote teamwork.

A frequent observation about meetings is that the problems on the table are not as difficult to deal with as the people around the table. Individuals at a meeting often react to each other more than they do to issues or ideas. For instance, whatever Sam Jones suggests might be rejected because he talks too much. Tania Smith

FIGURE 11-3
The autocratic
chairperson may have
difficulty in getting
members to
participate.

FIGURE 11-3
The autocratic chairperson may have difficulty in getting members to participate.

might oppose whatever the group is for. Gloria Sanchez might keep her mouth shut most of the time. The chairperson's patience and skill can reduce such difficulties, so that participants eventually start concentrating on the issues and not just on the individuals around the table. For a meeting to be successful, the chairperson should encourage participants to set aside personalities and outside allegiances and to work as a team to arrive at a workable solution.

Conducting Meetings: The Role of the Chairperson

The role of a chairperson is a demanding one. As stated before, the goal of a problem-solving meeting is to develop a good solution with as much unanimity as can be gained in a short period of time. However, the quality of a group's decision may depend in part on the amount of time spent. A hasty meeting may not produce the most desirable solution. On the other hand, meetings should have a time limit. If a meeting drags on too long, participants become bored and frustrated. It is the chairperson's role to offer members a chance to participate fully and to voice suggestions and opinions. The chairperson may have to persuade a minority to go along with the decision of the majority. On other occasions the chairperson will have to persuade the majority to make concessions to the minority. This takes time, and it may result in a compromise that does not necessarily represent the optimum solution, but at least it is an acceptable one.

Variations in the chairperson's role can run anywhere from one extreme of being very directive to the other extreme of being very democratic. At times, a normally democratic chairperson may have to control a meeting more tightly; at other times only the loosest control is needed. For example, if the purpose of the meeting is to gather as many creative ideas as possible for a new advertising campaign, then the chairperson should foster a loose, freewheeling atmosphere to promote creative thinking. However, if the purpose of the meeting is to make a final decision for an imminent deadline, the chairperson should focus the participants' thinking more tightly on a few feasible alternatives.

The Chairperson's Personal Opinions. A chairperson generally should strive to assist meeting participants in reaching their own decisions by encouraging them to offer and consider different ideas and alternatives. If the chairperson expresses too many personal views, participants may hesitate to disagree. This is especially true if the leader is the manager or part of top-level management. Yet there are occasions when it would be unwise and unrealistic for the chairperson not to express any views. He or she may possess relevant facts or opinions, and the value of the group's deliberations would be lessened without these contributions.

On the whole, therefore, a leader should express opinions, but at the same time must clearly state that those opinions are open to constructive criticisms and suggestions of the group. Silence on the part of a chairperson, especially when the chairperson is the manager or the highest-ranking member of the group, may be interpreted to mean that the chairperson cannot make decisions or does not want to do so for fear of assuming responsibility. Thus the chairperson must use good judgment in determining when and to what extent personal opinions are relevant or needed.

Some organizations deliberately avoid having supervisors and managers chair meetings when their subordinates are participants so as to encourage an atmosphere conducive to open discussion. Whoever is selected as chairperson should be chosen for his or her ability to manage the meeting and not because of other considerations.

Meeting Structure. If participants are well motivated, formality may not be necessary. Normally, however, meetings need some structure and leadership from the chairperson, who is responsible for keeping the meeting moving with orderly discussion directed toward an efficient conclusion. Here, too, sensitive judgment on the chairperson's part is required to maintain an appropriate balance of formal structure with the necessary amount of informality that encourages active participation by all members.

The Agenda. A useful technique for keeping a meeting from wandering off into time-consuming discussion of irrelevant matters is a well-prepared agenda. Before the meeting, the chairperson should outline the overall meeting plan with an agenda. Topics to be discussed should be listed in sequence and should include a tentative time limit for the meeting. The chairperson may even have in mind a general timetable for discussing each item on the agenda, although this should be for general guidance only and not be strictly enforced in the meeting. The actual agenda should be distributed in ample time for participants to prepare themselves for the meeting. The chairperson should emphasize that the meeting will begin promptly at the time indicated on the agenda.

Although an agenda outlines the meeting plan, it must not be so rigid that there is no means for adjusting it. The chairperson should plan and apply the agenda with a degree of flexibility, so that if a particular subject requires more attention than originally anticipated, time allocated to other topics can be adjusted. Although staying close to an agenda will help reduce irrelevant discussion, the chairperson must not be too quick to cut off discussion. What seems trivial to the chairperson may be important to some of the participants. In fact, some irrelevant discussion actually may contribute to a more relaxed atmosphere and relieve tension.

Since the chairperson's role is to keep the meeting moving toward its goals, he or she should pause periodically during the meeting to consult the agenda and remind the group what has been accomplished and what remains to be discussed. Astute leaders learn to sense when the opportune time has arrived to summarize one point and move on to the next item on the agenda. If experience tells them that their meetings have a tendency to run overtime, it might be advisable to schedule them shortly before the lunch break or just before quitting time. This tends to speed up meetings, since no one wants a meeting to cut into personal time.

Encouraging Full Participation. After a few introductory remarks and social pleasantries, the chairperson should make an initial statement of the matter(s) to be discussed. All members should be encouraged to participate in the discussion and to bring out information that is important to them. There are usually some participants who talk too much and others who do not talk enough. One of the chairperson's most important roles is to encourage the latter to speak up and to keep those who talk too much from doing so. This does not mean that all members of a meeting must participate equally. There will be some who know more about a given subject than others, and some will have stronger feelings about an issue than others. The chairperson should strive to stimulate as much overall participation as possible. (See Figure 11-4.)

The chairperson's general approach is of crucial importance. Initially everyone's contribution should be accepted without judgment, and everyone should feel free to participate. The chairperson may have to ask controversial questions in order to get discussion and participation started. This is sometimes done by asking provocative, open-ended questions that ask who, what, why, where, and when. Questions that can be answered with a simple "yes" or "no" should be avoided. Another technique is to start at one side of the conference table and ask each member in turn to express his or her thoughts on the problem. Although this approach forces everyone to participate, it discourages spontaneous participation and allows the rest of the group to sit back and wait until called on. This approach may also cause some individuals to take a stand on an issue before they are mentally prepared to do so.

A chairperson may be so anxious to have everyone say something that there is considerable aimless discussion just for discussion's sake. The chairperson should

FIGURE 11-4
Encouraging everyone
to contribute is an
important task of the
meeting leader.

observe facial expressions for clues as to whether someone has an idea but is reluctant to speak up. This is particularly important when talkative members of the group dominate the meeting while other participants have to struggle to contribute their comments. There are several techniques the chairperson can use to cope with the member who talks too much. After the talkative member has had sufficient opportunity to express opinions, the chairperson can conveniently overlook that person, calling on other participants to speak. Or the chairperson may ask the talkative member to please keep any additional remarks brief so that others may contribute. Most of the time, however, other members of the meeting will find subtle ways of "censoring" those who have too much to say.

If a meeting is made up of a large number of participants, it may be advisable to divide it into smaller groups. Each of the small subgroups reports back to the overall meeting after a specified period of time. This is similar to the subcommittee approach mentioned previously, and it encourages those who hesitate to say anything in a larger group to be more comfortable and willing to offer their opinions.

Guiding the Group to a Decision. Once a problem is identified and is generally understood by members of the group, the relevant facts should be presented in a logical, organized manner. After the facts have been discussed and evaluated, the next appropriate step for the group is to suggest alternative solutions for the problem. From this point, the chairperson should guide the group through the remaining steps of the decision-making process, as outlined in Chapter 6.

A chairperson should always realize that the best solution will only be as good as the best alternative considered. Accordingly, the chairperson should strive to make certain that no realistic solution is overlooked, and participants should be urged to propose as many alternatives as they can develop. The next step is to evaluate alternative solutions and to discuss the advantages and disadvantages of each proposal. Discussion eventually will narrow down to several alternatives on which general agreement can be reached. It then may be advisable to eliminate all other alternatives by unanimous consent. Those alternatives that remain should be evaluated thoroughly in order to arrive at a solution.

The chairperson may have to play the role of a mediator by proposing an overall solution that would be acceptable to most members of the group, possibly even convincing some members that their opinions are not as persuasive as others. Preferably, the final solution will be a synthesis of the desirable outcomes of the few remaining alternatives. By a process of integration, the most important points are incorporated into the most desirable solution. The chairperson also has the sensitive job of helping those holding minority viewpoints to accept the group's decision. It is easier to achieve this if the final decision can incorporate something of each person's ideas so that everyone has contributed. Of course, this can be a long and tedious process, and a compromise may not result in the strongest solution.

The chairperson may be confronted by a group that is hostile to virtually every proposal. In such a situation, it is necessary to find out what is bothering the group, to bring their opposition into the open, and to discuss it frankly and objectively. When confronted with a new idea, participants often concentrate on the objectionable features rather than on the desirable results that may be gained. Objections thus have to be clarified and discussed. If open discussion does not reduce the real and unwarranted fears and objections, it may be appropriate to adjourn the meeting and try again at a later time.

Taking a Vote. A chairperson must decide whether or not to take a vote. Although voting is a democratic way to make decisions, at times it actually accentuates differences among members of a group. Once individuals publicly commit themselves to a position, it becomes difficult for them to change positions. If they are members of the losing minority, they may not carry out the majority decision with enthusiasm. Therefore, whenever possible, it is better not to take an early formal vote but to work toward unanimous or near-unanimous agreement.

A major disadvantage of working toward total agreement is that such a process can take a long time, and unanimity may cause serious delay. Also, for the price of unanimity, the solution may be reduced to a common denominator that is not as ingenious, bold, or imaginative as it would have been otherwise. Whether the chairperson should seek unanimity in a solution or not depends on the situation and the magnitude of the problem.

The skilled chairperson usually can sense the feeling of the meeting. A remark such as, "It seems to me that the consensus of the group is that 'such and such' is our solution," may be appropriate. This type of summary statement can avoid a formal vote. If this is not possible, a vote should be taken in order to reach a decision. In a small group, a show of hands or secret written ballot is adequate. For large group meetings, the observance of normal voting procedures can save time and keep the meeting from becoming unwieldy. The form of the voting procedure

FIGURE 11-5
Summary of
Guidelines for Leading
a Meeting

1. Select participants who will bring knowledge and expertise to the meeting.
2. Notify participants well in advance of the meeting.
3. Have a plan and a prepared agenda.
4. Begin the meeting on time.
5. Present the problems and issues to be discussed and the meeting's objectives.
6. Encourage all group members to participate fully in the discussion.
7. Allow sufficient time for participants to offer information and discuss alternative proposals.
8. Strive to find consensus and areas of agreement before voting on proposals.
9. Try to stay on the subject and adjourn on time, but make adjustments as necessary.
10. Follow up, including distribution of a summary of the meeting (minutes) and actions to be taken.

may be less important than whether the participants understand the issue involved, believe that a fair hearing has been held in the meeting, and are ready to vote.

Importance of Follow Up. As a general rule, the chairperson should appoint someone to record and summarize what happened during the meeting. Subsequently, the chairperson should see to it that the written summary, called "minutes," is provided to every participant. This is a useful device to review what actually took place or what was decided at the meeting. For certain decisions, the summary may serve as a permanent policy guideline for future situations involving similar problems. If some matters are left undecided, the summary can provide a review of the alternatives that were discussed and help to crystallize the thinking of the participants. It may even be advisable to use this opportunity to announce when the group will next meet to take up unsolved problems and to consider new issues.

Leading effective meetings is an important supervisory responsibility. Skillful leadership can guide meetings toward meaningful results. Figure 11-5 provides some practical guidelines for leading effective meetings.

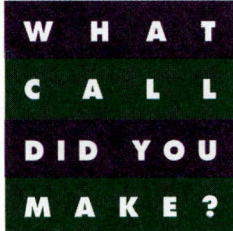
WHAT CALL DID YOU MAKE?

As Martha Boxerman, you have discovered that an electronic message system is not a substitute for holding a meeting. The message system is useful as a one-way flow of communication. However, holding a meeting in which communication flows forward, backward, and sideways between participants is a more vital way for communicating and understanding information. Meetings enable discussion, debate, and decisions that can build commitment among those who participate.

You probably should decide to reinstate scheduled meetings of your store supervisors on some predetermined basis. For example, you might decide that there will be a regular meeting held on the first Tuesday of each month at 9:00 A.M. You must impress upon your store supervisors that this will be a priority claim on their time and that they are expected to attend. Then, it will be important that you master the skills for conducting meetings as described in this chapter. A desirable part of your strategy would be to have the store supervisors participate in suggesting meeting agenda items. You should actively approach your supervisors for their input concerning discussion topics and how to make the meetings more productive and relevant to their needs.

SUMMARY

1 Explain why meetings, committees, and leading meetings are important components of supervision.

Supervisors are involved in meetings and committees either as members, organizers, or chairpersons. Meetings usually are called to disseminate information or to discuss or solve problems. There is no real substitute for bringing together the people who are responsible for dealing with a problem.

2 Identify the major types of meetings, their purposes and benefits, and their limitations.

Informational meetings are primarily for the purpose of presenting information and facts by the group leader. In discussional meetings, participants offer opinions and suggestions. In a decisional meeting, the group has been delegated authority to make decisions on a problem or task.

Group deliberations often produce more satisfactory and acceptable conclusions than those that might be reached by an individual. Major complaints about meetings are that there are too many of them, they are time consuming, and they divide responsibility.

3 Discuss the major types of committees and suggest guidelines for determining the composition and size of a committee.

The function of standing committees is to deal with recurring problems or issues. Ad hoc or temporary committees usually are appointed to serve for a limited time and for a specific task.

In selecting the membership of a committee, groups most affected by the committee's decisions should be represented. Members should be people who bring knowledge and experience related to the issue. They should be willing to present their views, but also be open to other ideas. The size of a committee should be large enough to permit thorough deliberations, but not so large as to make it cumbersome.

4 Identify the major factors contributing to effective meetings, including the chairperson's leadership role.

The success of any meeting depends largely on effective leadership. For discussional and decisional meetings, the chairperson's task is to obtain an optimal solution in a minimal amount of time with the greatest amount of unanimity. The chairperson constantly is faced with the problem of how directive or democratic to be. The chairperson should strive for full group participation that has just enough structure to arrive at an effective and efficient conclusion.

KEY TERMS

Informational meeting (page 283)   Committee (page 286)
Discussional meeting (page 284)   Permanent (standing) committee (page 287)
Decisional meeting (page 284)   Temporary (ad hoc) committee (page 287)
Group think (page 286)

QUESTIONS FOR DISCUSSION

1.   Why are meetings, committees, and leading meetings important aspects of supervisory management?

2.   Discuss the distinctions between (a) an informational meeting, (b) a discussional meeting, and (c) a decisional meeting. Are these distinctions always clear?

3.   Is it advisable for a supervisor to delegate authority to a group of employees? If so, in what form? Discuss. If a supervisor delegates decision-making authority to a group, can he or she escape accountability for the decision that is reached? Why or why not?

4.   Discuss and evaluate the benefits and limitations of a group discussion of problems requiring a departmental decision. Why is the lack of fixed responsibility both an advantage and disadvantage of referring problems to a group?

5.   Is the supervisory complaint that "there are too many meetings and they take up too much time" valid? How should meetings be viewed by the supervisor in relationship to his or her managerial role?

6.   Define and discuss the major differences between a standing committee and an ad hoc committee. Give several examples (other than those given in the text) of each type of committee in various types of organizations.

7.   What are some of the major factors to be considered in deciding on the composition of a committee? Is there an "optimal size" committee? Discuss.

8.   Discuss and evaluate each of the following in reference to meetings involving problem solving and the chairperson's leadership role.
   a.   The usual goals of such a meeting.
   b.   Personalities of the group members.
   c.   Whether the chairperson should express opinions in a meeting; if so, how.
   d.   A flexible or inflexible agenda.
   e.   Achieving participation from all participants.
   f.   Discussion of alternatives in the group decision-making process.
   g.   Whether to take a vote on an issue.
   h.   The need for follow-up after adjournment.

9.   Why is the ability to hold, lead, or participate in meetings an important skill for a supervisor to develop? What steps can supervisors take to ensure that meetings they participate in or chair will be successful?

SKILLS APPLICATIONS

Skills Application 11-1: Rate a Meeting

1. Identify a group meeting you attended recently. Then rate the meeting, applying the following rating scale to each statement.

Strongly Agree	Agree	Undecided	Disagree	Strongly Disagree
1	2	3	4	5

Scoring

_____ 1. The meeting started on time and ended on time.

_____ 2. The meeting seldom drifted off the agenda and identified topics of discussion.

_____ 3. In the meeting, all members participated.

_____ 4. I really felt like I was part of the meeting.

_____ 5. Participants openly communicated disagreements with others' viewpoints and with the chairperson.

_____ 6. I benefited from my participation in the meeting.

_____ 7. No one expressed interest in quitting the group.

_____ 8. If I could, I would volunteer to continue meeting with this group.

_____ TOTAL

2. Add up your scores and compare your total with the following:

8–12	Meeting was very effective and very important to you.
13–20	Meeting was generally effective and your participation was useful.
21–30	Meeting was marginally effective and a source of some frustration for you.
31–40	Meeting was rather ineffective, and your participation created stress for you.

Do you agree with the results? Why or why not?

3. What were the beneficial aspects of your participation in the meeting?

4. What limited the effectiveness of the meeting?

Skills Application 11-2: A Planning Committee

Assume that you are a middle-level manager. You have scheduled a one-day supervisory management workshop for 30 first-line supervisors representing 8 different departments. The workshop will take place in 30 days. The agenda has not been determined except that it is to focus upon improvement of supervisory management skills. You believe that a planning committee to assist you in developing the agenda might be desirable.

1. Why would a planning committee be beneficial to you? What might be its drawbacks?

2. Assuming you were to form a planning committee, what factors would you consider to determine the membership composition?

3. As chairperson of the planning committee, outline how you would structure and handle the first meeting.

Skills Application 11-3: Characteristics of a Good Chairperson

1. Think of the best meeting leader you have observed. Make a list of the characteristics you felt made that person effective in this role.

2. Then compare your list with the concepts presented in this chapter. To what degree do they coincide and/or differ?

ENDNOTES

1.   See Virginia Johnson, "The Groupthink Trap," *Successful Meetings* (Volume 41, Number 10, September 1992), pp. 145–146.

2.   For more comprehensive sources on leading meetings, see Arthur H. Bell, *Mastering the Meeting Maze* (Reading, Mass.: Addison-Wesley Publishing Co., 1990); Clyde W. Burleson, *Effective Meetings: The Complete Guide* (New York: John Wiley & Sons, 1990); and Milo O. Frank, *How to Have a Successful Meeting in Half the Time,* ed. Julie Rubenstein (New York: Pocket Books, 1990).

12

The Labor Union and the Supervisor

LEARNING OBJECTIVES

After studying this chapter, you will be able to:

1 Recognize why and how labor unions continue to affect the organization and the supervisory position.

2 Identify aspects of good management that are likely to deter a union organizer's appeal.

3 Outline procedures for supervisors to follow if confronted with a union-organizing effort.

4 Discuss the importance of good union–management relationships and the supervisor's key role in maintaining them.

5 Discuss the limited but important role of the supervisor in negotiating the labor agreement.

6 Discuss the major role of the supervisor in the interpretation and application of the labor agreement at the departmental level.

7 Describe the nature and importance of a good relationship between a supervisor and the union shop steward.

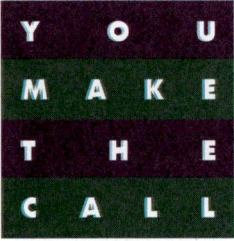

You are Leslie Brown, supervisor of housekeeping services at the Benevolent General Hospital, a 300-bed hospital located in a small city. You are responsible for the overall housekeeping services. You have several assistants (working supervisors) who report to you. There are about 80 full- and part-time employees in your department.

In recent weeks, rumors have been circulating about a major organizational campaign being undertaken by the Service Workers National Union. There have been union organizers reported at several of the hospitals in the city, but you have not noticed any union organizers at your own hospital. This morning, however, Tom Mayes, one of your best employees, who has worked for you for seven years, comes into your office. This is what he says:

"Leslie, I need your advice. Several of my co-workers have cornered me on three occasions, trying to get me to sign union authorization cards. They're trying to organize all of the housekeeping employees into a union bargaining unit. They are saying we're being treated unfairly, both in wages and benefits, and we need a union to get a fair shake. They really are putting the pressure on me and others to sign. They even have been going after me and others while we're trying to get our work done in the hospital. Perhaps we do need a union here. I really don't know whom to believe. I know the names of most of the individuals who want the union here in the hospital.

Perhaps you could talk to them to see if you can resolve some of their complaints. What should I do in the meantime?"

You know that you must respond to Tom. What should you say and do? **YOU MAKE THE CALL.**

LABOR UNIONS ARE PART OF SUPERVISORY ORGANIZATIONAL CONCERNS

1 Recognize why and how labor unions continue to affect the organization and the supervisory position.

Labor union
Legally recognized organization that represents employees and negotiates and administers a labor agreement with an employer.

Labor agreement
Negotiated document between union and employer that covers terms and conditions of employment for the represented employees.

Although membership in labor unions has declined considerably in recent years, labor unions nevertheless continue to be a major organizational consideration for supervisors. As of 1994, about 16 percent of the labor force in the United States was represented by labor unions and employee associations. Although there may be a technical distinction between a "labor union" and an "employee association," in this text we will use the terms **labor union** and "labor organization" interchangeably to describe any legally recognized organization that exists for the purpose of representing a group (or "bargaining unit") of employees and that negotiates and administers a labor agreement with an employer. A **labor agreement,** also called a "union contract," is the negotiated document between the union and the employer that covers terms and conditions of employment for the represented employees.

Historically, labor unions most often were identified with so-called blue-collar employees. In recent years labor organizations have made gains in obtaining representational rights for white-collar employees, such as office workers, salespeople, nurses, teachers, and even engineers. Many government employees, who generally do not have a legal right to strike and whose bargaining rights are somewhat limited, have achieved the right to form and join labor organizations. In fact, the public sector of the workforce in the United States has been one of the few growing segments of the labor movement in recent decades. In 1993, over one third of public-sector workers belonged to a union or association that represented them collectively.

Although many unions have lost members since the late 1970s and the percentage of workers in labor organizations has declined significantly, labor unions remain an important element of the workforce that supervisors should know about and be prepared to deal with appropriately. This is especially true where employees are represented by a labor union and supervisors must abide by the requirements of a labor agreement.

It is beyond the scope of this text to cover the history of labor relations or to discuss the federal and state labor laws that govern union–management relations.[1] Rather, this chapter discusses the organizational considerations, obligations, and rights of supervisors who are confronted with (a) employee attempts to unionize or (b) union activities in a firm whose employees are already represented by a union. In Chapter 20 we will further discuss the handling of grievances under a union contract's grievance procedure.

Those supervisors who are not part of management—such as working supervisors and lead persons—may join the same labor union as their fellow employees. However, most supervisors who are part of management do not have legal protection to join and be represented by labor unions themselves. As management's first-line representatives, supervisors play a major role in determining whether or not a group of employees will turn to a labor union to try to improve their conditions of employment.

UNDERSTANDING EMPLOYEE EFFORTS TO UNIONIZE

2 Identify aspects of good management that are likely to deter a union organizer's appeal.

A major union official once made the following comment to one of the authors of this text: "Labor unions don't just happen; they're caused. And it's the management, not the unions, that causes them!" This labor official was quite candid about his opinion that labor unions were a direct response to failures of management to respond to employee needs. Further, he implied that the sentiments of workers are usually determined more by the conditions existing in their work situations than by a union organizer's campaign. Many studies of employee and labor relations have generally verified the opinion of this union official. These studies recognize that good management and supervision, particularly as exemplified by positive human relations approaches, are usually the most important determinants in preventing the unionization of a work group.

Numerous aspects of good management that contribute to a climate that deters unionizing efforts have been discussed previously throughout this text. Factors rooted in good employee relations make it more difficult for a union organizer's appeal to succeed. These factors include the following:

1. Wages and benefits that are good and reasonably comparable to those offered by other companies.
2. Personal facilities for employees that are generally satisfactory or improving.
3. A stable employment pattern (that is, no severe ups and downs in hiring and layoffs of large numbers of employees).
4. Supervisors who communicate well with their employees and treat them with dignity and respect.
5. Employees who have been well trained and see opportunities for advancement to higher-paying or upgraded positions. This is especially important for employees in low-level jobs who do not like to feel that they will be in "dead-end" positions forever.
6. Supervisors who demonstrate a participative approach to management that encourages employees to share in making decisions about their jobs.
7. Employees who feel that they are treated fairly by being given an opportunity to resolve their complaints through a complaint procedure.

For the most part, the economic conditions surrounding wages, benefits, and employment patterns are not within a supervisor's direct control. However, the supervisor has a significant role in most of the other factors that may cause employees either to join or not to join a labor union.

It does happen that some employees turn to a labor union even though their employer has worked diligently to develop and implement policies and procedures consistent with those listed. Employees may join a labor union primarily to achieve economic objectives such as higher wages and greater benefits. Or they may join to satisfy objectives of a psychological or sociological nature. For example, some employees feel that membership in a labor union provides them with greater security and better control over their jobs through a seniority system. Other employees feel that it is important for a union to be present in processing grievances and complaints in order to get a fairer settlement of their disputes. Still others find a greater sense of identity when they are part of a labor union.

Union shop
A labor agreement provision in which employees are required to join the union as a condition of employment, usually after 30 days.

If a union already is in place, employees may have to join it as a requirement under a **union shop** provision of the labor agreement. A union shop provision in a labor agreement requires an employee to join the union as a condition of employment after a certain period of time, usually 30 days. Even though such employees initially are required to join the union through the union shop provision, eventually most of them become loyal to the union because they believe that they can achieve more collectively than they would individually.

As of 1994, 21 states had so-called "right-to-work" laws, which prohibit the union shop. Also, labor organizations representing employees within the federal government are not permitted to have a union shop. Nevertheless, in organizations that do not have a union shop requirement, all or most of the employees may belong to the union because they want to be part of the overall, combined group effort of promoting employees' rights and interests.

UNION-ORGANIZING EFFORTS AND THE SUPERVISOR

3 Outline procedures for supervisors to follow if confronted with a union-organizing effort.

Union-organizing efforts can take place both outside and within a firm. If a supervisor notices that union-organizing activities are taking place among employees, the supervisor should report what he or she observes to higher-level managers or to the human resources department. This must be done so that the company's response to the union-organizing efforts can be planned. In the meantime, the supervisor should be very careful not to violate—by either actions or statements—the labor laws governing union-organizing activities. Since these labor laws are quite complicated, many companies hire a consultant or attorney to advise higher-level managers and supervisory personnel about what they should and should not do under these circumstances.

The following guidelines, although not comprehensive, are recommended for supervisors during a union-organizing period:

1. Supervisors should not question employees either publicly or privately about union-organizing activities in the department or elsewhere in the company.

CONTEMPORARY ISSUE
Labor Unions in the 1990's

Some observers believe that labor unions are no longer relevant to the needs of American workers. They cite statistics showing that union representation in the U.S. labor force in the early 1990s stood at about 16 percent, down from about 35 percent in the 1970s. Observers further point to the large body of employment laws that have addressed many areas of employee concern, thereby perhaps decreasing the need for employees to have union representation.

Not so, say labor union leaders. In fact, organized labor plans major organizing drives in the 1990s that will focus particularly on the white-collar labor force. A report presented to a major conference of the American Federation of Labor-Congress of Industrial Organizations (AFL-CIO) indicated that white-collar membership in unions was increasing as a percentage of the U.S. labor force and also in actual numbers. Almost 60 percent of working Americans are in white-collar occupations, and about 2 out of 3 individuals entering the workforce in the 1990s will be women. A

major union officer asserted, "We know what unions can mean for women workers. In 1990, the median annual wage for full-time unionized working women was $24,296, while their nonunion counterparts earned $16,952." This same union official indicated that unions increasingly would direct their priorities to issues of interest to women, such as the "glass ceiling," job design, nonexistent career ladders, and sex discrimination.

Another union officer said that unions will use their creative efforts to organize "the contingent workforce—those with part-time or temporary jobs." He, too, stated that the labor movement will be making major efforts to reach out to white-collar workers. "All workers want to connect with an organization that offers them a voice," stated this union official. He emphasized that unions will use new techniques of organizing, such as employee polling, videos, and other forms of electronic communication.

Source: Adapted from "Challenge, Opportunity Seen in White Collar Boom," *AFL-CIO News* (December 21, 1992), p. 4.

Doing this—even merely out of curiosity—can violate labor laws, which provide employees the right to choose a union to represent them without interference or discrimination by the employer.

2. Supervisors should not make any threats or promises related to the possibility of unionization. Any statement that can be construed as a threat (for example, loss of job or loss of privileges if the union succeeds) or a promise (for example, some favor or benefit to the employee if the union fails) is a violation of federal labor law.

3. Supervisors should respond in a neutral manner when employees ask for their opinions on the subject of unionization.

4. Supervisors have the right to prohibit union-organizing activities in work areas if these take place during work hours and interfere with normal work operations. Supervisors may also prohibit outside union organizers from coming into the department to distribute union bulletins and information. However, employees who support the union have the right to distribute these materials to other employees during lunch and break periods, so long as this does not interfere with work operations. If in doubt about what can be done to control union-organizing activities within the department, supervisors should first consult higher-level managers or the human resources department.

5. Supervisors should not look at union authorization cards that employees may have signed. This, too, is considered illegal interference with the employees' rights to organize.
6. Supervisors should continue to do the best supervisory management job possible.

A union-organizing campaign often results in a representational election conducted by the National Labor Relations Board or some other government agency. If the majority of the employees vote for the union, the union becomes the exclusive bargaining representative for these employees. If the union loses the representational election, this means only that the employees will not have a union for the immediate future—perhaps for a minimum of one year. Many companies have found that employees, after having rejected a union in previous elections, later vote it in. (The "Contemporary Issue" in Chapter 17 will discuss two 1993 decisions of the National Labor Relations Board related to employee work group committees during a union representational campaign and when a union already represented employees.)

THE SUPERVISOR'S INVOLVEMENT IN UNION-MANAGEMENT RELATIONSHIPS

4 Discuss the importance of good union–management relationships and the supervisor's key role in maintaining them.

Labor unions are a permanent part of our free-enterprise economy. A union, just like any other institution, has the potential for either advancing or interfering with the common efforts of an organization. Thus, it is in management's self-interest to develop a union–management climate that is conducive to constructive relationships. However, there are no simple formulas for fostering such a climate overnight. It takes patience, sensitivity, and hard work for all managers in an organization to show in their day-to-day relationships that the union is accepted as the official and responsible bargaining representative for the employees.

In any mutual efforts to maintain a constructive relationship between management and the union, often the most important link is the supervisor. It is the supervisor's daily relationships with employees and union representatives that make the labor agreement a living document for better or for worse. This is why it is essential that supervisors be trained in the fundamentals of collective bargaining and be knowledgeable about the labor agreement. For the most part, the supervisor's involvement in union-management relations consists of two phases: (1) a limited role in negotiating the labor agreement and (2) a major role in applying the terms of the agreement on a day-to-day basis.

5 Discuss the limited but important role of the supervisor in negotiating the labor agreement.

The Supervisor's Limited Role in Labor Agreement Negotiations

Labor agreement negotiations, also called "collective bargaining," means the process of discussion and compromise among representatives from labor and man-

United Auto Workers leaders at a bargaining council meeting. Labor agreements often take months to negotiate.

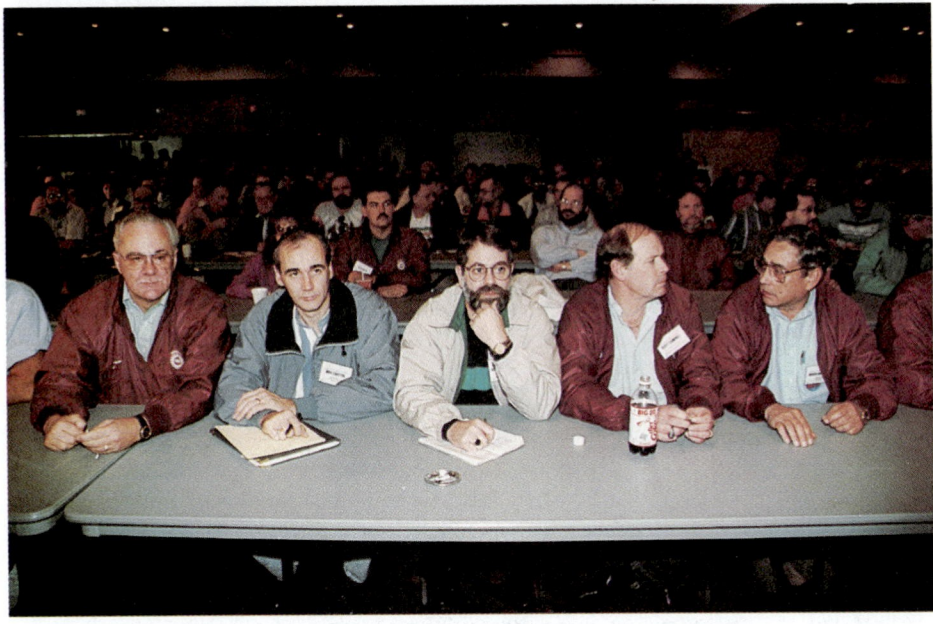

Labor agreement negotiations
The process of discussion and compromise among representatives from labor and management leading to an agreement governing wages, hours, and working conditions for union employees.

agement leading to an agreement governing wages, hours, and working conditions for union employees. Negotiations often involve meetings between the parties extending over months' duration. On occasion, a union may call a work stoppage in an attempt to pressure the employer to agree to certain proposals or make concessions. Because collective bargaining can be complicated, an employer may hire an attorney or consultant to work with human resources department staff and management to develop and carry out its negotiating strategy.

Labor negotiations in a previously nonunionized company may be a trying experience for employees, supervisors, and higher-level managers. Usually emotions run high, and the grapevine is active with rumors and speculation. Because of this climate, negotiations between management and union representatives are usually held away from the company premises, perhaps at a lawyer's office or a conference room in a hotel. If a committee of union employees is participating in the negotiations, a line of communication with the other employees will be established. Supervisors usually are excluded from this line of communication, although higher-level managers may keep them informed.

Most labor agreements cover a period of two, three, or more years. As time goes on and new agreements are negotiated, the supervisor's role becomes an increasingly important one. Most supervisors do not sit at the negotiating table, but it is desirable for higher-level managers to consult with them about (a) how provisions of the existing agreement have worked out and (b) what changes they would like to see in the next agreement. This exchange of information between higher-level managers and supervisors is essential prior to negotiations, and at times it even may be needed as negotiations proceed.

Supervisors should have some influence on negotiations, because they bear a major responsibility for carrying out provisions of the agreement in day-to-day operations of their departments. Many issues discussed during contract negotiations stem from relationships that the supervisors have experienced with their employees. For example, problems concerning work assignments between job classifications, work-shift schedules, seniority rights, working conditions, and transfer and promotion of employees can become important issues for negotiation. Therefore, it is to the supervisors' as well as the firm's advantage that provisions in the agreement be written in such a way that supervisors have as much flexibility as possible in running their departments.

To supply relevant information, supervisors should be keenly aware of what has been going on in their departments. Their views will be considered more credible if they have facts available to substantiate their observations. This again highlights the importance of keeping ample records of prior grievances, productivity, and disciplinary problems. Supervisors should discuss with higher-level managers and the human resources department problems that management should consider in developing an overall bargaining strategy. Thus, even though the primary responsibility of negotiating a labor agreement rests with higher-level managers, supervisors should be prepared to provide relevant input to the negotiations. Supervisors must be willing to express their opinions and substantiate them with documents and examples, so that management's representatives can negotiate desirable changes in the agreement at the bargaining table.

The Supervisor's Major Role in Applying the Labor Agreement

6 Discuss the major role of the supervisor in the interpretation and application of the labor agreement at the departmental level.

The labor agreement that has been agreed upon by representatives of management and the union becomes the document under which both parties will operate during the life of the agreement. Although no two labor agreements are exactly alike, most agreements cover wages, benefits, working conditions, hours of work, overtime, holidays, vacations, leaves of absence, seniority, grievance procedures, and numerous other matters.

A labor agreement outlines union–management relationships. In essence, it is a policy manual that provides rules, procedures, and guidelines—as well as limitations—for both management and the union. To make it a positive instrument for fostering constructive relationships, the agreement must be applied with appropriate and intelligent supervisory decisions. The best written labor agreement will be of little value if it is poorly applied by the supervisor.

Compliance with the Labor Agreement. All supervisors are obliged to manage their departments within the framework of the labor agreement. This means that supervisors should know the provisions of the agreement and also how to interpret them. One way to accomplish this is for higher-level managers or the human resources department to hold meetings with supervisors to brief them on the contents of the agreement and to answer questions about any provisions that

FIGURE 12-1
The supervisor must know what the provisions of the labor agreement are and how to interpret them.

they do not understand. Copies of the contract and clarifications of various provisions should be furnished to the supervisors so that they know what they can and cannot do while managing their departments. (See Figure 12-1.)

Supervisors should recognize that a labor agreement has been negotiated, agreed upon, and signed by both management and union representatives. Even if a provision in the agreement causes a supervisor problems, the supervisor should not try to circumvent the contract in the hope of doing the firm a favor. For example, assume that a provision specifies that work assignments must be made primarily on the basis of seniority. Although this provision may limit the supervisor in assigning the most qualified workers to certain jobs, the supervisor should comply with it or be prepared to face probable conflict with the union. If a labor agreement provision is clear and specific, the supervisor should not attempt to ignore what it requires. If supervisors are not clear about certain provisions, they should ask someone in higher-level management or the human resources department to explain before they attempt to apply the provisions that they do not understand.

Adjustments for the Union. A labor agreement does not fundamentally change a supervisor's position as a manager. Supervisors still must accomplish their objectives by planning, organizing, staffing, leading, and controlling. Supervisors retain the right to require subordinates to comply with instructions and to get the jobs done in their departments. The major adjustment required when a union is present is that supervisors must perform their managerial duties within the framework of the labor agreement. For example, a labor agreement may spell out some limitations to the supervisor's authority, especially in areas of disciplinary action, job transfers, and assignments. Or the labor agreement may specify procedures concerning the seniority rights of employees with regard to shift assignments, holidays, and vacations. Supervisors may not like these provisions. However, they must manage within them and learn to minimize the effects of contractually imposed requirements or restrictions by making sound decisions and relying on their own managerial abilities.

As members of management, supervisors have the right and duty to make decisions. A labor agreement does not take away that right. However, it does give a union the right to challenge a supervisor's decision that the union believes to be a violation of the labor agreement. For example, virtually all labor agreements specify that management has the right to discipline and discharge for "just" (or "proper") cause. Thus taking disciplinary action remains a managerial responsibility and right, but it must meet the just-cause standard. Since a challenge from the union may occur, the supervisor should have a sound case before taking disciplinary action. If a supervisor believes that disciplinary action is called for when an employee breaks a rule, the supervisor should examine thoroughly all aspects of the problem, take the required preliminary steps, and think through the appropriateness of any action. In other words, unless there is a contractual requirement to the contrary, the supervisor normally will carry out the disciplinary action independently of union involvement. However, some labor agreements require that a supervisor notify a union representative prior to imposing discipline or that a union representative be present when the disciplinary action is administered. In Chapter 19, we will discuss in depth the handling of disciplinary matters in both union and nonunion work environments.

Supervisory Decision Making and the Labor Agreement. In practice, the supervisor frequently clarifies provisions of the labor agreement by decisions that interpret and apply them to specific situations. By so doing, the supervisor may establish precedents that arbitrators may consider when deciding grievances.

A **grievance** is a complaint that has been formally presented by the union to management and that alleges a violation of the labor agreement. Most labor agreements specify several steps as part of a grievance procedure before a grievance goes to arbitration. An **arbitrator** is someone who is selected by the union and management to render a final and binding decision concerning a grievance when the union and management are unable to settle the grievance themselves. Procedures for arbitrating grievances are included in most labor agreements. See Figure 20-1 in Chapter 20 for an example of a typical grievance-arbitration provision in a labor agreement.

It would be impossible for management and the union to negotiate an agreement that specified how to solve every possible situation that could occur in union–management relations. Therefore, the supervisor's judgment becomes paramount in applying the agreement to actual situations. Since the supervisor is part of management, an error in the supervisor's decisions becomes management's error. By interpretation and application, a supervisor's decisions may take on dimensions that go well beyond the department itself. A decision involving interpretation of the labor agreement may be long lasting in its impact. The decision may set a

Grievance
A formal complaint presented by the union to management that alleges a violation of the labor agreement.

Arbitrator
Person selected by the union and management to render a final and binding decision concerning a grievance.

precedent that could become binding on both management and the union in the future. Supervisors should bear in mind that unions often base their claims on precedents, and arbitrators often base their decisions on previous decisions made by both sides.

A labor agreement usually contains provisions that state specifically how certain situations should be handled. Examples are provisions associated with work schedules, distribution of overtime, transfers, promotions or demotions, and other recurring matters. Usually the labor agreement specifies certain limits or procedures for handling these types of issues. For example, many agreements have provisions that require the supervisor to consider both seniority and ability in decisions that involve promotion, transfer, and layoff. In these situations the supervisor's personal judgment of the abilities of the employees involved becomes vitally important. Often the opinion of the union will be at odds with the opinion of a supervisor concerning certain contractual meanings. A supervisor should not be afraid to risk the possibility that the union will file a grievance, so long as the supervisor believes that he or she understands the provisions and is complying with them.

Labor agreements also contain broadly stated clauses, such as those associated with the assignment of work between various job classifications, nondiscrimination, management rights, and disciplinary or discharge actions for just cause. In these areas supervisors often encounter difficulty in applying a general statement in the agreement when the situation requires a specific interpretation. If the supervisor has doubts about the meaning of a broadly stated provision, he or she should first consult higher-level managers or the human resources department. Even though the supervisor may be well versed in the content of the labor agreement, problems can develop that necessitate an interpretation beyond the supervisory level.

Maintaining Employees' Compliance with the Labor Agreement. It is also the supervisor's duty to take action whenever employees do not comply with provisions of the labor agreement. Employees may interpret lack of action to mean that the provisions are unimportant or not to be enforced. For example, if a provision specifies that employees are entitled to a 15-minute rest period at designated times during a work shift, the supervisor should see to it that the employees take a 15-minute rest period—no more and no less—during the designated times. Supervisors should make certain that employees observe the provisions of the labor agreement just as supervisors themselves must operate within the agreement. Inaction on the supervisor's part could set a precedent or be interpreted to mean that the provision has been set aside.

7 Describe the nature and importance of a good relationship between a supervisor and the union shop steward.

THE SHOP STEWARD AND THE SUPERVISOR

Supervisors probably will have most of their union contacts with the union shop steward. A **shop steward,** also called a "shop committeeman" or "shop committee-

Shop Steward
Employee elected or appointed to represent employees at the departmental level, particularly in grievance processing.

Union business representative
Paid official of the local or national union who may be involved in grievance processing.

woman," usually is a full-time employee who is elected or appointed to represent the employees at the departmental level, particularly in processing of their grievances. Supervisors may also have to discuss certain issues and grievances with a **union business representative** or "business agent." This person is a paid, full-time official of the local or national union. Some shop stewards prefer to have the business agent present when discussing union-related problems with the supervisor.

For the most part, a shop steward is recognized by fellow employees to be their official spokesperson to management and for the union. This can be a difficult position, since the shop steward must serve two masters. As an employee, the shop steward is expected to perform satisfactory work for the employer by following rules. As a union representative, the shop steward has responsibilities to other employees and to the union. The supervisor must understand this dual role of the shop steward, because a good relationship with the shop steward can create an effective link between the supervisor and the employees.

The Shop Steward's Rights and Duties

Unless the labor agreement contains special provisions pertaining to the shop steward's position, the shop steward is subject to the same standards and regulations for work performance and conduct as every other employee of the department. The labor agreement may specify how much company time the shop steward can devote to union matters, such as meetings or discussions with members, collection of dues, and grievance handling. The labor agreement may also grant the shop steward the right to take time off to attend union conventions and handle other union matters.

A major responsibility of the shop steward is to process complaints and grievances on behalf of employees. The shop steward will communicate these to the supervisor, who then must work with the shop steward to settle the complaints. Labor agreements describe in great detail the procedures for handling complaints and grievances, and the shop steward and the supervisor are obligated to follow those prescribed steps. We will discuss the handling of complaints and grievances in detail in Chapter 20.

Supervisory Relations with the Shop Steward

Some shop stewards are unassuming; others are overbearing. Some are helpful and courteous; others are aggressive and militant. Some take advantage of their position to do as little work as possible; others perform an excellent day's work in addition to their union duties. In other words, the day-to-day behavior of the shop steward depends considerably on his or her individual personality and approach.

At times the supervisor may feel that the shop steward processes petty grievances in order to harass management. This may happen because the shop steward has a political assignment and may feel it necessary to assure workers that the union is working on their behalf. However, an experienced shop steward knows that normally there are enough valid grievances to be settled that it is not necessary to submit shallow complaints that rightfully will be turned down by the supervisor.

Supervisors should bear in mind that the shop steward, as the official union representative, learns quickly what the employees are thinking and what is being communicated through the grapevine. Moreover, the national or local union will train the shop steward to be informed about the content of the labor agreement, management's prerogatives, and employee rights. The local union will expect the shop steward to submit grievances in such a way that they can be carried to a successful conclusion. Before submitting a grievance, the shop steward will ascertain which provisions of the labor agreement allegedly have been violated, whether the company acted unfairly, or whether the employee's health or safety was jeopardized. Once a grievance has been formally submitted, the shop steward will try to win it. In most grievance matters the union is "on the offensive" and the supervisor must be prepared to respond. If the shop steward challenges a supervisor's decision or action, the supervisor must be ready to justify what he or she did or otherwise develop a remedy and resolve the grievance.

Since shop stewards are necessarily interested in satisfying the union members, their behavior may at times antagonize supervisors. It may even become difficult for supervisors to keep a sense of humor or to hold their tempers. A supervisor may not care to discuss issues with the shop steward on an ongoing basis since, in the normal working situation, the shop steward is a subordinate in the department. But a shop steward is the designated representative of union members and should be treated as an equal by a supervisor in matters pertaining to the union. If a sound relationship is developed, the shop steward will keep the supervisor alert and literally force the supervisor to be a better manager!

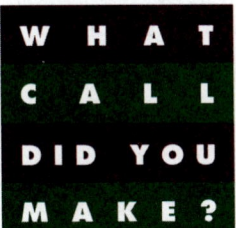

WHAT CALL DID YOU MAKE?

As Leslie Brown, your best response at this point is to tell Tom Mayes that you really don't know how to advise him until after you have checked out his questions with the human resources director and your own manager. Under no circumstances should you ask Tom or anyone else to provide you with the names of the employees who are involved in the union-organizing efforts or who favor the union. Doing this would be a probable violation of labor laws. After adjourning your meeting with Tom, you should immediately report your conversation to the human resources director and your manager for guidance. They most likely will counsel you along the lines of the concepts and principles presented in this chapter. In particular, you should continue to treat all employees fairly, have them participate in some departmental decisions, and be willing to listen to and act upon their legitimate complaints. You should not question, threaten, or interfere with your employees' efforts to organize. However, you should inform all of them that union-organizing efforts cannot take place in hospital working areas during regular work times. Hospital management may or may not decide to conduct a countercampaign; if they decide to do so, you will receive additional instructions about what and what not to do and say.

SUMMARY

1 Recognize why and how labor unions continue
to affect the organization and the supervisory position.

About one in every six employees in the United States is represented by a labor union. Unions continue in their efforts to organize, especially among white-collar and public-sector employees. Supervisors need to know how to respond to employee efforts to unionize and how to manage if departmental employees are represented by a union.

2 Identify aspects of good management
that are likely to deter a union organizer's appeal.

Good management practices can help prevent a labor union from gaining representational rights. Employees may turn to a labor union for representation if they see the union as a vehicle for satisfying certain needs, including economic gains and fair treatment of their concerns. If management addresses employees' needs, then employees are less likely to feel the need for a union to promote their interests.

3 Outline procedures for supervisors to follow if confronted with a union-organizing effort.

Confronted with a union-organizing campaign, the supervisor should report the campaign to higher-level managers or the human resources department. The supervisor must not interfere with or threaten employees or promise any benefits in an effort to influence their choice of whether or not to join the union. The supervisor does have the right to prohibit activities that directly interfere with job performance during working hours and in work areas.

4 Discuss the importance of good union–management
relationships and the supervisor's key role in maintaining them.

Unions are a fact of business life in our society, and they can either advance or interfere with the goals of the organization. Thus, good union–management relations are essential to the organization. The supervisor is the key to good relations, since the supervisor applies the labor agreement in day-to-day contact with employees.

5 Discuss the limited but important role of
the supervisor in negotiating the labor agreement.

Most supervisors do not participate in labor agreement negotiations. Yet many demands that a union presents during negotiations stem from issues that supervisors have encountered with the union and departmental employees. Therefore, supervisors should make their opinions and suggestions known to higher-level managers so that management can attempt to negotiate needed changes in the labor agreement.

6 Discuss the major role of the supervisor in the interpretation
and application of the labor agreement at the departmental level.

The supervisor's major role in union–management relations lies in the day-to-day interpretation and application of the labor agreement. Although a labor agreement does not in itself change a supervisor's job as a manager, it does give a union the right to challenge a supervisor's decision. The supervisor still must carry out managerial duties within the terms of the labor agreement. It is to the supervisor's advantage to seek advice from higher-level managers or the human resources department in interpreting certain clauses of the agreement. The supervisor's actions can set precedents that bind management and the union in the future.

7 Describe the nature and importance of a good relationship between a supervisor and the union shop steward.

Supervisors have most of their union contacts with the union shop steward who represents employees at the departmental level. The shop steward is an employee as well as a union spokesperson for processing employee grievances. The shop steward should be treated as an "equal" by the supervisor in matters relating to the labor agreement. If a proper relationship is developed, a shop steward primarily will challenge only those actions of the supervisor that seem to be unfair or in violation of the agreement. In effect, this will force the supervisor to do a better job of managing the department.

KEY TERMS

Labor union (page 302)
Labor agreement (page 302)
Union shop (page 304)
Labor agreement negotiations (page 307)

Grievance (page 310)
Arbitrator (page 310)
Shop steward (page 312)
Union business representative (page 312)

QUESTIONS FOR DISCUSSION

1. What is the magnitude of labor union and employee representation in the United States? Although labor unions have declined in membership in recent years, why should they still be a major organizational consideration for supervisors?

2. What are some of the major factors that typically are crucial in preventing the formation of a labor union? Over which of these does a supervisor have the most direct control?

3. What are some of the principal reasons why employees join labor unions?

4. Discuss the proper role of the supervisor regarding union-organizing activities. Why should a supervisor generally be neutral in responding to employees' questions about the union-organizing effort?

5. Evaluate the following statement: "The best guideline a supervisor can follow during a union-organizing campaign is to continue to do the best management job possible."

6. What is the supervisor's role in labor agreement negotiations? What input should a supervisor have in the negotiating process?

7. Discuss why the supervisor should not attempt to ignore the labor agreement or circumvent it even if it seems like the smart thing to do.

8. Why should supervisors consult higher-level managers or the human resources department when they need interpretation of a clause in the labor agreement?

9. Evaluate the following statement: "A labor agreement does not fundamentally change a supervisor's position as a manager." Relate this question to the "You Make the Call" situation of Leslie Brown. If the union succeeds in organizing the hospital employees, would Leslie Brown's supervisory position be affected by unionization?

10. How does a labor agreement complicate a supervisor's job?

11. Why does a supervisor retain the right to take action whenever employees do not comply with provisions of the labor agreement?

12. Discuss the role of the shop steward within a department. Why is this person in a key position of influence?

13. Why should the shop steward be treated as an equal by the supervisor in matters relating to the union?

SKILLS APPLICATIONS

Skills Application 12-1: Attitudes About Labor Unions

1.   The following are statements pro and con about labor unions. Respond to each statement, applying the following rating scale.

Strongly Disagree	*Disagree*	*Undecided*	*Agree*	*Strongly Agree*
1	2	3	4	5

Scoring

_____   1. Unions are necessary to protect employees from job favoritism and discrimination.

_____   2. Job seniority is the fairest way to reward employees for their services with a firm.

_____   3. Unions are needed to ensure that workers are paid good wages and receive adequate benefits.

_____   4. Without a labor union, employees have little chance to have their complaints handled fairly.

_____   5. Every employee who benefits from the union should be required to join and support the union (i.e., a union shop).

_____   6. Most employees join a labor union because they want to join and they agree with the union's objectives.

_____   7. The best form of employee job participation occurs when a union can negotiate a labor agreement with an employer to cover terms and conditions of employment.

_____   8. Stronger unions and wider representation of employees by unions are needed in the 1990s to counter corporate greed and management's indifference toward workers.

_____   TOTAL

2.   Add up your scores and compare your total with the following:

10–20	You generally do not agree with or approve of labor unions.
21–30	You have mixed attitudes about labor unions.
31–40	You generally support unions and their objectives.

Do you agree with the results? Why or why not?

Skills Application 12-2: Management and Union Views in a Unionized Work Location

1.   Supervisors and managers often differ in their viewpoints concerning what a labor union does for its members. Visit a plant or office that is unionized. Interview a supervisor, manager, or director of human resources using the first set of questions. Then interview a shop steward or union member using the second set of questions. (Interview several managers and union people if permission to do so is granted.)

    a. *Management Questions*

        (1) How would you describe overall relations between the ＿＿＿＿＿(name of)＿＿＿＿＿ Union and management in this company?

        (2) In general, what things would you say the union members like most here? Least?

        (3) What in your opinion should be improved in the union-management relationship?

        (4) What would you do differently if the union did not exist?

    b. *Union Questions*

        (1) How would you describe the overall relations between your union and management in this company?

        (2) In general, what things would you say your members like most here, and what things do they like least?

        (3) What in your opinion most needs to be improved in the union-management relationship?

        (4) If the union did not exist, what do you think management would do differently?

2.   **a.** What similarities and differences between the responses to each question were the most significant? Most surprising?

    b. Were any of your prior viewpoints about labor unions changed or influenced as a result of these interviews?

Skills Application 12-3: The Supervisor and the Shop Steward

1. From the principles and concepts presented in this chapter—and from your own observations and experiences, if applicable—make a list of what you consider to be the most desirable qualities and approaches that a supervisor should have in order to have a good working relationship with a union shop steward.

2. Discuss your list with a supervisor who has dealt with—or who currently is dealing with—a union shop steward.

    a. To what degree did the supervisor agree with your list?

    b. What additions and/or changes to the list did the supervisor suggest?

    c. How might the personal characteristics of the union shop steward influence how the supervisor would deal with this person?

ENDNOTE

1.   For an introductory overview concerning labor relations laws, processes, and issues in the United States, see Mollie H. Bowers and David A. DeCenzo, *Essentials of Labor Relations* (Englewood Cliffs, N.J.: Prentice-Hall, 1992). For more extensive texts, see John H. Fossum, *Labor Relations: Development, Structure, Process* (5th ed.; Homewood, Ill.: Richard D. Irwin, 1992); and Michael Ballot, *Labor-Management Relations in a Changing Environment* (New York: John Wiley & Sons, 1992).

CASE 3-1
The Customer's Son

Jack Wilder was a principal buyer for Amber Hardware Stores, a large hardware company in Metro City. In this capacity he was an important customer of the Faulkner Metal Co. Annually, Wilder bought hundreds of thousands of dollars worth of metal garden furniture from Faulkner representing about 20 percent of Faulkner's sales volume. When Sarah Freund, sales manager of Faulkner, was making a call on Wilder, Wilder asked her to check with Faulkner's president to see whether she could find a job for Wilder's son Mark, who had dropped out of college and wanted to find work in industry. Freund assured Wilder that she would do her best and would let him know soon.

After a brief discussion and after considering the importance of the account, Harry Faulkner, the company president, agreed to have Mark Wilder come to his office for an interview. Mark was hired and was given the position of assistant to Phil Sullivan, Faulkner's plant superintendent. Sullivan had been appraised of the customer connection, but he was not given any choice in the decision to hire and place Mark Wilder. Mark's job duties essentially consisted of doing the things Phil Sullivan chose to delegate to him; that is, he had a personal assistant position.

Initially, Sullivan was impressed with Mark's willingness to learn, astuteness, and efforts. After a number of weeks, Sullivan told Harry Faulkner "how well young Wilder is coming along." This information was reported to Jack Wilder the next time Sarah Freund, the sales manager, called on him. All went smoothly for a few months, and the orders from Amber Hardware Stores increased at a growing rate. There was no way to judge whether this increase was due to the good news about Mark, or to a business upturn, or whether it constituted preferential treatment.

However, after about six months of work, Mark Wilder's job performance took a turn for the worse. His initial enthusiasm seemed to decrease, his attitude left much to be desired, and he seemed to care less and less about how he was doing his job. Phil Sullivan had a friendly talk with Mark. During this conversation, Mark told Sullivan, "I can always work in my old man's firm if this job doesn't work out. But I can't predict how he'll feel about it and what he'll do if you guys decide to get rid of me." After this meeting with Mark Wilder, Phil Sullivan pondered what he should do next.

Questions for Discussion

1.   Was it a prudent decision on the part of Faulkner management to hire Mark Wilder in the first place? Was the assignment of Mark Wilder to a personal assistant position for Phil Sullivan a particularly sensitive one in this type of situation?

2.   Should Sullivan inform Jack Wilder that Mark Wilder's recent job performance has been lacking? Why or why not?

3.   What should Phil Sullivan and/or Harry Faulkner do?

4.   What are the ethical and business implications of this case?

CASE 3-2
The Interfering Administrative Assistant

Christine Moreno was vice-president of manufacturing at the Coyle Chemical Company. She had direct line authority over Ed McCane, plant superintendent; Charles Evans, chief engineer; Diane Purcell, purchasing and supplies supervisor; Ron Weaver, supervisor of maintenance; and Carol Shiften, supervisor of the shipping department.

Two years ago, Moreno hired Bernice Billings as a secretary. Billings was diligent, capable, and efficient. She quickly won the admiration and confidence of her boss. Moreno felt fortunate to have such a capable secretary, since Billings willingly assumed numerous duties that allowed Moreno to devote more time to her broad responsibility over the five departments. Moreno therefore changed Billings's job title to "administrative assistant" and increased her salary. After receiving this elevation in status, Billings began to do even more than she had previously. For example, at times Moreno's supervisors received written instructions in the form of memos that clearly originated with Billings, but came to them with Moreno's initials. Billings also took it upon herself from time to time to give oral directives to the supervisors. For example, several times she went to the plant superintendent, Ed McCane, and gave him instructions concerning plant scheduling problems. At times she went directly to the production floor and asked employees to rush orders along or made other requests of this sort without seeing McCane first. She often told maintenance employees to do various projects, which, she said, "Ms. Moreno would like you to do." Similar occurrences took place in the shipping department, where she frequently left instructions for special treatment of some customers' orders.

In most of these situations, Moreno was not aware that Billings had taken it upon herself to communicate directly with subordinates to solve problems that had come to her attention. Some individuals grumbled that these directives should have come from either Moreno or the appropriate departmental supervisor. In most cases, however, everyone concerned realized that Billings had the best interests of the firm in mind, and they normally complied with her requests.

However, as time went on, the supervisors began to feel that Billings was interfering more than she was helping. In several instances some of the employees on the production floor did not check with Ed McCane but went directly to Billings for instructions. Similar incidents took place in other departments. One day, over a cup of coffee, Ed McCane, Carol Shiften, and Ron Weaver angrily poured out their concerns to each other. At the outset, they had looked upon Billings favorably, but now they considered her to be a disrupting factor who was undermining their supervisory positions.

Questions for Discussion

1. Why would Bernice Billings take it upon herself to communicate directly with supervisors and employees to solve plant problems? Is this procedure to be admired or condemned? Discuss.
2. Why did various plant personnel comply with Billings's requests and orders, even though they were not sure that these had come from Moreno? Can informal authority be just as powerful as direct line authority?
3. What should the supervisors do? What alternatives are open to them?

CASE 3-3
Unwanted Help

Eureka Medical Center was a large hospital in a southern city. The purchasing department consisted of six buyers, two clerical employees, and one supervisor. It was responsible for all hospital supplies.

Pat House was the newest buyer in the department. Included in her responsibilities were purchasing and inventory monitoring of vouchers, syringes, needles, and I.V. solutions that the hospital used on a daily basis. The hospital's material requirements planning system (MRP) generated weekly reports for Pat House and the other buyers. These reports identified items that needed to be re-ordered.

House was instructed by a fellow-buyer to review this report at the beginning of each week, and place the necessary orders before the end of the week.

John Davies had been promoted about six months previously from buyer to supervisor of the purchasing department. One of his first decisions had been to hire Pat House as his replacement. Davies had worked as a buyer for almost 10 years, and he knew the system inside and out. As supervisor, he reviewed the MRP reports of all the buyers each week to ensure that his buyers would stay on top of the hospital's needs. Shortages in certain supplies could be life threatening.

It was a Wednesday several months after Pat House had been hired. While reviewing the MRP reports, Davies noticed that certain necessary supplies for which House was responsible had not been ordered. Since Davies was very familiar with the needed supplies and the corresponding suppliers, he decided to place some orders to expedite them and also to convey to House that he was willing to help her when she was busy.

On Friday of that week, when House started placing orders that the MRP report had called for, her suppliers questioned her. They asked her if she really needed to double the amount that she usually ordered, since earlier in the week John Davies had placed orders for similar amounts. House was infuriated that Davies had placed orders with her suppliers without informing her. When she confronted Davies about it, he apologized and said he was only trying to help. Davies explained that he thought she had been extremely busy and wanted to reduce her workload.

House thought the problem had been resolved. But as time progressed, Davies continued placing some of her orders, although he always informed her of what he had done. She didn't say anything about this to any of the other buyers, because she was afraid of what they might think. House grew more distressed, because she didn't know how to tell her supervisor to let her do her job without causing hard feelings. House became increasingly concerned that Davies didn't have any confidence in her abilities and that he was unwilling to tell her what he wanted done differently. Her six-month performance appraisal was scheduled for the next week. She wasn't comfortable with her situation, and she worried that her days with the hospital might be numbered. House pondered whether she should quit now or first see the director of human resources or Davies's boss (the hospital's associate administrator) to discuss what she should do.

Questions for Discussion

1. Should a supervisor do the work of an employee to assist the employee or reduce the workload? Discuss.
2. Why would John Davies continue to do some of Pat House's job duties?
3. Why do employees (such as Pat House) often resent it when a supervisor performs some of their job duties, even if this is well intentioned?
4. If you were Pat House, what would you do? Consider alternatives.

CASE 3-4
Turnover on the Third Floor

The following people were employed in various positions at Grove Hospital and are the main characters in this case:

Edna Drombowski, associate administrator

John Davis, director of human resources

Jean Murphy, director of nursing services

Georgia Yamada, supervisor of the third floor

Ted McGuire, a newly hired nurse

John Davis had been working at his new job for about a week when Jean Murphy came to see him. Murphy explained that she needed more registered nurses on the third floor, since that floor was presently understaffed and three more nurses had just submitted their resignations. She added that she hoped he would do a better job of hiring nurses to fill vacancies than the previous human resources director. Davis said that he would take care of the matter.

Realizing that the problem might be more than just a matter of hiring additional nurses, John Davis started checking the personnel records of nurses on the third floor. To his surprise he found that the third floor had a much higher turnover rate for registered nurses than any other floor in the hospital. In fact, only one nurse currently working on the third floor had been at the hospital for more than a year. Davis therefore decided that it was time to see Edna Drombowski about the problem. After explaining the problem to Drombowski, Davis called Jean Murphy in. The three of them agreed to investigate the third floor to see whether any clues to the turnover problem might be discovered.

A week later Drombowski called a meeting to see what progress had been made on the investigation. Murphy reported that she had met with Georgia Yamada to discuss the problem. According to Murphy, it was Yamada's opinion—with which Drombowski concurred—that the high turnover rate on the third floor probably was a matter of coincidence. Yamada indicated that no real problems existed except for the constant lack of nurses, which was the major irritant to people working on the third floor. Yamada said that the work got done and that the type and number of nurses' complaints on the third floor were no different from those on other floors.

Davis then gave his report, but those findings were quite different from Murphy's. First, he had examined the personnel records of all nurses to see whether different patterns existed on the third floor with regard to age, race, marital status, number and age of children, previous experience, and length of employment. Since he could not find any differences, Davis had concluded that the general hiring practices could not be blamed for the high turnover on the third floor.

Davis then decided to examine all the exit interviews involving nurses on the third floor that had been conducted within the last year to see whether these would shed any light on the problem. Although a variety of reasons had been given for leaving the hospital, he noticed that rarely did any of the exit interviews include a reason that was under the hospital's control. Most of the reasons concerned outside factors, such as pregnancy, husband leaving the community, going back to school, no baby sitter available, and the like. Since the past exit interviews, which had been conducted by the previous director of human resources, did not seem to reveal the true reasons for leaving, Davis decided to conduct exit interviews with the three nurses who were about to quit the third floor.

The results of the three exit interviews comprised the most informative portion of Davis's report. By some skillful probing, he discovered the real reasons why the three nurses were quitting Grove Hospital and learned what they felt were major problems on the third floor. These nurses explained that, until about 10 months ago, the third floor had a full-time evening nurse and a full-time night nurse. This meant that the nurses who worked days (the majority of nurses on the floor) were seldom required to rotate to the evening or night shifts. When they rotated, it was usually only once or twice a month. Then, when the two full-time nurses quit due to outside factors, they were not replaced by full-time evening and night nurses. As a result, the day-shift nurses started rotating to the other shifts on a much more regular basis. This upset them. Furthermore, the increased rotation led to other scheduling problems, such as working an evening shift and then doubling back to the day shift the next morning. Because the third floor was shorthanded, the nurses often did not get off work in the evening until midnight or later. And returning to work before seven o'clock the next morning put a real strain on them.

Another major problem as seen by the three nurses was the lack of clear lines of authority on the third floor. The two head nurses who assisted Georgia Yamada on the third floor had quit three months ago but had not yet been formally replaced. It was rumored that recently hired Ted McGuire was eventually going to be one of the head nurses, although Yamada had made no mention of it to the other nurses. Since McGuire often assumed the duties of a head nurse, the other nurses on the floor were perplexed. They didn't know whether they should assume that McGuire had the authority of a head nurse or whether they should receive their instructions from Yamada only.

Finally, the problem of being shorthanded was not minor in the eyes of the three nurses. They felt that they could not do their jobs properly since they spent most of their time on routine tasks, such as passing out medication, carrying out physicians' orders, charting, and so forth. Often they found themselves brushing off conversation with their patients because they had so much to do. They were quite dissatisfied, since their expectations of their roles as nurses were not being met.

After hearing all these reports, Edna Drombowski, John Davis, and Jean Murphy agreed that they had a real problem. They decided to meet a week later to discuss possible solutions.

Questions for Discussion

1.   Make a list of the problems that you can identify in this case. Classify them as major or minor.

2.   Why would the third-floor supervisor and the director of nursing services believe that the high turnover rate on the third floor was "a matter of coincidence"?

3.   Develop a series of recommendations that you feel would address the problems you have defined in this case.

CASE 3-5
Trick or Treat?

The customer relations department of a midwestern utility employed about 100 people whose primary function was to answer customer telephone complaints, problems, and inquiries. The department did not have face-to-face contact with the customers. It was open 24 hours a day, every day. During peak hours, 65 to 70 employees worked in the department.

One October 30, which happened to be the day before Halloween, a group of 12 day-shift female employees decided to dress up as "ladies of the evening" for Halloween. None of the employees consulted her supervisor or the department manager. The next day—Halloween—the group appeared in full dress, including ribbons, extra makeup, and leather miniskirts. When several of the supervisors and the department manager noticed the women, they gave no indication of a negative response. In fact, two of the supervisors laughed at the group's attire and commended them on their originality. Most of the group's co-workers thought that the attire was humorous, although a few employees said that the costumes were "a bit much!"

Approximately an hour after the women had reported for work, one of the supervisors, Sheila Brookings, went into the department manager's office. Brookings was visibly upset. She said that she was outraged at the costumes, and she demanded that the employees be sent home for the day without pay. Brookings commented that in all her 15 years as a supervisor, "I've never been so offended as I am today!" She continued angrily, "This is a business, not a place for partying. Further, I find their dress to be personally offensive to me and my religious values!"

The department manager, Brenda Crampton, knew that this would be one of the busiest days of the year in the department and that she could not afford to send 15 to 20 percent of the staff home and still give proper, prompt service to customers. Crampton also considered the fact that none of the women in the group had had a serious disciplinary problem. Crampton pondered what if any action should be taken against the employees and how to respond to Brookings. Crampton knew that if she suspended or disciplined the employees, many of the office employees would become extremely upset. Crampton feared that she might find the total office disrupted if she took disciplinary action. At the same time, she also felt that she had to be sensitive in responding to Brookings's complaint.

Questions for Discussion

1.   Was management's position compromised since no action was taken when the women reported to work? Discuss.

2.   Did Sheila Brookings overreact, or was she justified in complaining to Crampton?

3.   Should the women be sent home and/or disciplined? What alternatives are open to Brenda Crampton?

4.   What might be done in the future to support employee activities on the job without violating certain individuals' personal values?

CASE 3-6
Sanders Supermarkets Store #32: Why Have Another Meeting?

Sanders Supermarkets operated over 50 stores in a major metropolitan area. In an attempt to improve its market share, the company embarked on a new program in regard to the merchandising and pricing of meat products. A company-wide meeting of all district managers and store supervisors was held.

At the meeting the company president stressed the important points of the new meat program, one of which was that each store supervisor should have a store meeting to explain the program to all the store's employees.

On a follow-up later that same week, Dick Barton, district manager, went into Store #32 to evaluate the progress of the program. Dan Rolan was its store supervisor. The following dialogue took place:

District Manager: Dan, I just walked the store and talked with your bakery, deli, and meat department heads. It seems that there wasn't a store meeting here this week. Why not?

Store Supervisor: I didn't think we needed to have another meeting. I did talk to every one of my department heads about the new meat program, if that's what you're referring to.

District Manager: That's exactly what I was referring to. You know that you were told by the president to have a meeting in the store. Also, you received a bulletin from the sales department explaining the new program, didn't you? And at the bottom of the first page, it said, "Have a store meeting."

Store Supervisor: Dick, do you expect me to have a store meeting every time the sales department writes that on a bulletin? If so, then I'll probably be having a store meeting every other day. When will I find time to manage this store? Besides, how long should such a meeting take? I've never had any training or instructions about holding meetings. Most of the meetings I have with my employees in the store seem to accomplish very little other than to waste my time and theirs.

District Manager: Oh, come now, Dan, it doesn't take any special training to hold meetings. And what are you saying? Do you really mean that "Have a store meeting" appears on quite a few company bulletins?

Store Supervisor: Absolutely, and not only that, Dick. What about all the company mail I receive daily that I have to read? Usually in the middle of the page it says "All Stores Except—." Do you realize just how much store mail comes in every day? And the bad part is that most company bulletins either don't apply to my store or are so redundant that they put me to sleep.

District Manager: Okay, Dan, but why didn't you complain about this before if it's a problem?

Store Supervisor: Frankly, I didn't think it would make any difference if I did complain. There are too many people in our organization who think that communication means just writing memos and having more meetings, even if they're not needed.

District Manager: Well, at any rate, I want you to have a store meeting on the meat program right away. I don't want my boss complaining to me that one of my stores didn't follow through on instructions.

Store Supervisor: Okay, I'll have the meeting, but I think it will be a waste of time. My employees already are well informed on this program.

District Manager: Dan, I understand your feelings, but we all have to follow orders. It seems to me that our discussion today has high-lighted several problems. Think about them, and when I see you again in a few days perhaps we can discuss what we can do to attack them.

Questions for Discussion

1.   Identify the problems of meetings and other communication issues that are apparent in this case.

2.   If a store supervisor is to receive training or instructions about holding meetings, how could this best be accomplished?

3.   Outline a number of suggestions for improving communications among all parties in this organizational setting. Would you recommend that some type of electronic meeting—see the "Contemporary Issue" box in Chapter 11—be utilized for certain types of meetings?

CASE 3-7
Can the Company Avoid Unionization?

The family-owned Royal Furniture Company manufactured and assembled office furniture in a small community in a southern state. It employed about 100 people and was operated by the principal owner, Oliver Thomas. The relationship between management and the workers had been very good in a rather paternalistic way. Wages were competitive, and the employees had numerous extra benefits, which management provided whenever the need arose. For example, wages were advanced if an employee needed money for an emergency; court fines were paid by the company if the employee did not have the funds to do so; and when a worker could not meet a monthly installment obligation, the company usually would advance the amount needed. Several times, union organizers had tried to approach the factory employees to organize them, but each time the union was unsuccessful in getting enough support.

However, in recent years the company had been experiencing more difficult economic times. Wages had not kept pace with inflation, and the company was becoming less generous in giving employees various benefits. Employees were becoming more and more dissatisfied, and a union organizer was again observed passing out union literature outside the plant.

Thomas had stated publicly on several occasions to his supervisors and some employees that, if a union were to win an election, he would either sell the company or close the plant. He did not want to go through union negotiations, and he did not want his managerial prerogatives diminished.

One of the company's office supervisors, Harriet Toole, recently took a human resources management course at a local community college, where she studied labor unions and union-organizing campaigns. She became concerned that Thomas's approach to the situation at the Royal Furniture Company could lead to unionization of the plant and that he might even be violating the law. Toole wondered what she should do.

Questions for Discussion

1. Is a paternalistic management approach a desirable one? Can it work in a small company to a better degree than in a large company? Discuss.

2. Why would Thomas vow to sell his company or close his plant if the union organized his workers? Is this a threat, or just rhetoric designed to discourage unionization? Discuss.

3. How could Harriet Toole influence Oliver Thomas to develop a program of positive employee relations that might improve the situation at the Royal Furniture Company? Discuss alternatives open to her.

4. Why would Oliver Thomas be well advised to seek the advice of an attorney or consultant who is an expert in union–management matters?

CASE 3-8
What Is "Reasonable Time" for the Shop Steward?

Sandra Whitworth supervised a group of 20 employees in the communication services division of a major state university. All employees in this division were represented by a local chapter of the Public Employees Office and Professional Union.

One day Whitworth called Eleanor Kane into her office. Kane was a technical specialist who served as union shop steward. "Elly," said Whitworth, "it's time that we had a showdown about the amount of time you've been spending on union matters in this office. For the last two weeks you've averaged over 2 hours each day away from your job, allegedly to handle union grievances. This is entirely too much. I won't tolerate this anymore!"

"What do you mean, too much?" responded Kane. "The union contract says I'm allowed a reasonable time to handle union grievances, and it does not specify an upper time limit. I take only the time necessary to do my job as union steward. And lately there's been a flock of complaints and grievances which have come to my attention."

"I don't care about your union affairs," replied Whitworth. "You've got a job to do, and being away from your job this much time is unreasonable by any standards. From now on, if you're gone more than one hour each day on union matters, I'm going to dock your pay accordingly."

"Sandra," snapped Kane, "if you do that, I'll file a grievance right away and will fight you all the way to arbitration if necessary. You haven't got a leg to stand on, and you know it. Go see Larry Niland, your director of human resources. He'll tell you the same thing. In the meantime, I'm going to report this harassment to our union business agent at the local union office!" With that, she left Whitworth's office.

Whitworth pondered what her next move, if any, should be. She also reviewed Article 3, Section 1, of the current labor agreement, which in part stated as follows:

A Union shop steward shall be permitted reasonable time to investigate, present, and process grievances on the Employer's property without loss of time or pay during regular working hours, provided that the steward obtains permission from his or her supervisor prior to such absence from assigned duties. Such time spent in handling grievances during the steward's regular working hours shall be considered working hours in computing daily or weekly overtime if within the regular schedule of the steward.

Questions for Discussion

1.   Whose responsibility is it to determine what is meant by the word "reasonable" in Article 3, Section 1 of the labor agreement? Does this have to be negotiated with the union in more specific terms? Discuss.
2.   Should Sandra Whitworth attempt to handle this problem on her own, or should she refer it to Larry Niland, the director of human resources? Why?
3.   Outline a series of recommendations for Whitworth and/or Niland in order to reach a satisfactory resolution of the problem.

CASE 3-9
Different Hours and Rules for
Union and Nonunion Employees

Oscar Pratt, superintendent of the unionized warehouse department of the Ashley Department Stores, was discussing a serious problem with Harmon Ashley, president of the company. According to Pratt, his foremen and the union were complaining about the different treatment of union employees from nonunion employees. For example, only union warehouse workers were docked 15 minutes' pay for 5 minutes of tardiness, while nonunion employees were seen walking in and out of the company buildings at all times. Pratt said, "Apparently the nonunion employees can arrive at any time they care to, and they don't have to comply with regular hours like the unionized warehouse workers do!"

The unionized warehouse workers also told Pratt that nonunion employees could be found in the company cafeteria at all hours of the day and were apparently not restricted to certain regular times or to 15-minute coffee breaks as were the warehouse workers. Pratt pointed out to Ashley that he had handled several formal grievances over this issue and expected even more complaints after the labor agreement expired in about a year.

Pratt urged Ashley to take steps to correct the situation so that working hours and regulations would be more uniform for both union and nonunion employees. Pratt believed that Ashley should have a serious discussion with Gail Massen, the sales manager, and Eric Engel, the assistant store manager, to bring about the desired results.

Ashley was sympathetic to Pratt's concerns. Ashley was known to believe in running a "tight" operation. As president, he reported to his desk before seven o'-clock in the morning and remained until after the official quitting hour. He rarely took a coffee break himself. As he pondered what steps to take, his first reaction was to call Massen and Engel into his office and simply tell them that he wanted the nonunion employees also to put in a regular eight-hour day, to report to work on time, and to limit their break periods. But, on second thought, he realized that this would not always be possible. He was aware of the special problems of sales-people, who often had to work irregular hours to handle peak customer periods in the stores. Some sales representatives might return home late the night before from a business meeting or from entertaining a customer. Similarly, other nonunion personnel such as those in the office, advertising, and purchasing departments, including supervisors, were known to prefer some flexibility in their work schedules. They claimed that this flexibility was necessary in relation to their duties and that it contributed to good work performance and morale.

Harmon Ashley left a telephone message with Marcia Bush, the director of human resources, to come and discuss the situation with him.

Questions for Discussion

1. Should the same policies and rules be in place and enforced for all categories of employees? Why or why not?

2. What should Harmon Ashley, president of the company, do in this situation?

3. What should Marcia Bush, director of human resources, advise Ashley to do?

4. What would be your reaction if you were: (a) Oscar Pratt, the warehouse superintendent, (b) Eric Engel, the assistant store manager, or (c) Gail Massen, the sales manager?

CASE 3-10
Mistaken Overtime Work

Central Container Company manufactured various types of metal container products on a three-shift basis. One of the maintenance employees, Art Glenn, reported for work at 11:00 P.M. on a Friday night shift through an error on his part. He had not been scheduled to work and he had not been called in, although a small crew was scheduled to work this shift.

At about midnight, Glenn's regular supervisor, Gerry Fresno, entered the plant on a trouble call and questioned Glenn regarding his presence in the plant. After some discussion, both realized that Glenn had reported in error.

However, Fresno told Glenn that he could finish the shift. Glenn worked eight hours. This was Glenn's sixth consecutive day of work, and by union contract as well as by law, Glenn was to be paid at a rate of time and one half for this shift.

The next day, however, another maintenance employee, Willie Flanders, filed a grievance because Glenn had worked on a sixth day, although Glenn was junior to Flanders in seniority. Flanders claimed equal pay for the time Glenn worked (eight hours at time and one half, i.e., 12 hours of pay). Flanders and his union steward claimed that in accordance with a well-established practice at the company, overtime had to be offered first to employees in accordance with their seniority and their ability to perform the work.

Several days later, at a grievance meeting held in Fresno's office, Ann Marshall, the union business representative, argued that if Fresno had sent Glenn home after he found him working, no grievance would have been filed. However, since the past practice had been and still was to let the most senior employees work overtime, the union should be upheld in this case, and Flanders should be paid for all time at the appropriate rate that the junior employee (Glenn) was paid.

Fresno responded that the company should not be required to pay 12 hours of pay to another employee. Out of consideration for the employee who reported by mistake, Fresno had allowed Glenn to work the full shift instead of sending him home with one hour's pay. The claim of the union was unjust and inequitable. No union employee, neither Flanders nor anyone else, suffered any loss of work or income because Fresno had acted in a considerate manner. If Glenn had not erroneously reported for work, no one would have worked in that job. Fresno claimed that his decision to allow Glenn to continue to work after he was discovered in the plant should be commended and not criticized.

Ann Marshall ended the meeting with this comment, "If that's your decision, we'll have to pursue this case further, even to arbitration if necessary. You goofed on this one, and you ought to recognize it right now!"

After Marshall left his office, Gerry Fresno decided that he had better take up the grievance with his manager and the director of human resources.

Questions for Discussion

1. If Art Glenn had worked the entire Friday evening shift in error without having met his supervisor, would Glenn have been entitled to payment for the unscheduled work on his part? Why or why not?

2. Should Willie Flanders be entitled to overtime pay under the practice of offering overtime to employees in accordance with their seniority and ability? Why or why not?

3. Evaluate Gerry Fresno's statement that the claim of the union was unjust and inequitable. Evaluate his contention that no union employee, including Flanders, had suffered any loss of work or income because he had acted in a considerate manner.

4. Should the company grant the union grievance and pay Flanders, or should the company deny the grievance and go to arbitration, if necessary?

CASE 3-11
The Paper Chase and Efforts to Reorganize Health Care

Organizing, or reorganizing, is a normal response of firms seeking to find better ways to carry out their objectives. Such reorganization may be spurred on by the need to provide better customer service or to streamline a production process. Whatever the reason, the common denominator is almost always a desire to reduce costs and increase profitability. With its rising costs, an ever-increasing demand for services, and a nationwide desire to change its operational structure, America's health-care system is coming under increasing pressure to reshape the way it does business. Although improved patient care is not unimportant to those who would like to be leaders in this effort, the rapidly rising costs to both patients and firms that pay for their employees' medical insurance coverage are of paramount concern. Add to that President Clinton's campaign promise to make high-quality health care available to all Americans, and you have an industry that is destined to make significant changes in the way it does business.

The annual costs of health care in the United States are staggering. Nationwide, spending on health care in 1992 reached a record $838.5 billion, equivalent to 14 percent of the nation's total economic output. The purchase of health plans by businesses accounts for approximately one-third of the total health care expenditures, a situation that has some companies, such as Chrysler Corp., seeking ways to get out of the health-benefits business by turning the responsibility over to a consolidated provider.

Some people believe that there may be no American industry that could benefit more from the use of total quality management (TQM) techniques than the health care industry. Experts say that a large portion of the nation's annual health-care expenditures can be attributed to waste and inefficiency. "The waste is astronomical," says A. Blanton Godfrey, chairman and CEO of the Juran Institute, a consulting firm. TQM advocates say that using its principles would improve the process of delivering high-quality health-care services, often with the added benefit of cutting costs. George Washington University Medical Center, for example, has already applied TQM techniques to deal with loss or delay in getting prescriptions from a patient's chart to the hospital's pharmacy and to reduce patient waiting time for elective chemotherapy treatment.

Stating that "Most health-care company executives don't run their companies like businesses," Donald Amaral has taken his training as an accountant to the health-care profession. As a Medicaid auditor, he found that most health-care providers seemed interested only in maximizing insurance reimbursements. Believing that this was the wrong approach, Mr. Amaral convinced Burbank, California-based Summit Health Ltd. that they should specialize and compete on quality and cost, not on price. Through a process of reorganization, focusing on what Summit could provide and what services were most needed, he helped management earn $18.6 million on revenues of $510 million in 1993, or 56 cents a share, up from the previous 40 cents a share.

Reorganizing by using existing knowledge and technology has made Atlanta-based First Financial Management Corp. the second-largest independent processor of health-care claims. Using the concept of "consolidate, automate, and dominate," First Financial has expanded its credit card processing operation to include health-care claims processing. In one month alone it paid $116 million for Salt Lake City-based Alta Health Strategies, the largest processor of health-care claims for companies that self-insure.

Perhaps the largest reorganization will come as a result of President and Mrs. Clinton's desire to reform the U.S. health-care system. The system adopted by Xerox Corporation may serve as a model for what is often referred to as "managed health care." With annual health-care premiums rising at a rate of 20 percent a year, Xerox began pegging its contributions to the costs of the most efficient health maintenance organizations (HMOs). Employees who want more expensive coverage are required to pay the difference. The savings have been significant as many employees have switched to the HMOs whose average premiums increased by only 7.7 percent in 1992 and 5.5 percent in 1993. To help reinforce this type of managed health care, some leaders support a proposal that would disallow tax deductions for employer health-care expenses beyond a basic benefits package. They would also tax workers who opt for the more generous coverage packages. The American Hospital Association supports managed-care networks that provide all of the patient's care at a fixed rate, and some physician groups back national spending targets.

Summarizing the trend that seems destined to lead to a reorganization of the entire health care profession, CIGNA Executive Vice-President Robert O'Brien says, "I think there is going to be a huge consolidation" [among health-care providers and insurers]. "We're ready for fundamental change."

References

D. J. Brailer and L. Van Horn, "Health and the Welfare of U.S. Business," *Harvard Business Review* (March–April 1993), pp. 125–132.

E. Faltermayer, "Yes, the Market Can Curb Health Costs," *Fortune* (December 25, 1992), pp. 84–88.

Michele Galen, et al., "Can the Poor Afford Health-Care Reform?" *Business Week* (October 4, 1993), pp. 31–32.

S. B. Garland and T. Smart, "Suddenly, Health-Care Players Are Ready to Talk," *Business Week* (December 28, 1992), pp. 36–37.

Toddi Gunter, "Vertical Integration," *Forbes* (August 30, 1993), pp. 49–50.

Nancy A. Nichols, "Profits with a Purpose: An Interview with Tom Chapman," *Harvard Business Review* (November–December 1992), pp. 87–95.

Christopher Plameri, "Feel the Volume," *Forbes* (May 25, 1992), pp. 98–100.

Elaine Zablocki, "Quality Management Targets Health Care," *Nation's Business* (February 1993), pp. 40–42.

Questions for Discussion

1. What types of organizational problems do you see in the way the U.S. health-care system is currently structured?

2. What are the potential rewards and dangers of trying to reorganize the way health-care services are delivered in the United States?

3. In the video, an explanation is given of how paperwork sometimes flows in our health-care system. What can be done to eliminate or streamline the claims process? What would be the advantages of doing so?

4. How is reorganizing the health-care industry different from reorganizing a business such as General Motors or Pepsi? What groups must be involved in this reorganization? Who should provide the leadership?

PART 4

STAFFING

13

Employee Selection and the Human Resources Department

LEARNING OBJECTIVES

After studying this chapter, you will be able to:

 Discuss the staffing function and describe the roles of the human resources staff and supervisors.

2 Explain how the supervisor prepares to fill job openings and why job descriptions and job specifications are critical to this task.

3 Discuss the selection process and the use of directive and nondirective interviewing in the process.

4 Describe how the supervisor should prepare for and conduct an effective selection interview.

5 Explain the hiring decision and the importance of documentation.

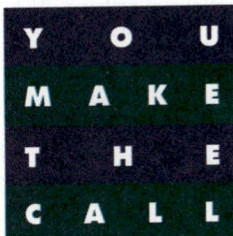

You are Kori Stephens, office supervisor for Medi-Quick. Medi-Quick has 17 satellite medical facilities located throughout Northern Florida. Carrie Webster was hired a little over a year ago for an accounting position at the Ocala facility.

The knowledge and skills required for the job indicated that the employee should have at least three years of job-related experience and a college degree. Carrie's most recent performance appraisal showed that she is an above-average performer.

You learn through the grapevine that Carrie is currently going to school at night to get the degree she claimed to have. You review Carrie's application form. She did cite a baccalaureate degree in business from the University of Central Florida, but did not mention a completion date. Upon further investigation, you discover that Carrie does not have a college degree and barely has enough hours to qualify as a senior. Before she was hired, the human resources department had verified her past employment record and found it to be very good. Apparently, no one had bothered to check her educational background.

You know that if Carrie is dismissed, it will take several months of orientation and training before her replacement can perform at Carrie's level. What should you do to rectify the situation? What safeguards should be installed to prevent the situation from recurring?
YOU MAKE THE CALL.

THE STAFFING FUNCTION AND
THE HUMAN RESOURCES DEPARTMENT

1 Discuss the
staffing function and
describe the roles of
the human resources
staff and supervisors.

Human resources
management (HRM)
Organizational
philosophies, policies,
and practices that
strive for the effective
use of employees.

In a broad sense, **human resources management (HRM)** is the philosophy, policies, procedures, and practices related to the management of people within an organization. To perform the activities necessary to accomplish its goals, not only must the organization have the necessary human resources, but supervisors must find ways to use them effectively. The management of human resources is the supervisor's most important activity, and it begins with staffing.

As was defined in Chapter 2, staffing is the recruitment, selection, placement, orientation, and training of employees. These activities are part of every supervisor's responsibilities, although in large organizations staff specialists provide help and support. The supervisory staffing function also includes evaluation of employee performance and input into how employees are to be rewarded based on their performance.

Not every organization has a human resources (personnel) department. Very small firms, for example, usually do not need or cannot afford to have specialized staff personnel. In these firms, supervisors, in consultation with their managers, carry out staffing tasks. As an organization grows, at some point top-level managers will likely hire a human resources director and staff specialists to assist in carrying out the staffing function. For most organizations, the role and size of the typical human resources department have expanded considerably in recent decades. On the other hand, some organizations have found it to be cost effective to contract out, or "outsource," some of the human resources activities. Concerned over the costs associated with recruiting and selection, increasing numbers of firms are finding other firms to do some of the work they used to do. For an example of an innovative method for solving staffing needs, see the "Contemporary Issue" box in this chapter.

In the discussion to follow, we assume that the enterprise has a human resources (HR) department within its organizational structure and that it is a staff department as discussed in Chapter 9. In some organizations this department is called the personnel department, the industrial relations division, the employee relations section, or by some other name. In very large organizations, specialists in areas such as selection, career development, appraisal, compensation and benefits, organizational design, and communication keep abreast of current developments in their field and provide expertise to managerial personnel. Even in very small organizations, someone is responsible for the hiring and the recordkeeping functions. This person generally shares these responsibilities with other managerial personnel.

Regardless of its official name, the usefulness and effectiveness of any human resources department depends on its ability to develop close working relationships with managers. The quality of these line–staff relationships, in turn, depends on how clearly top-level managers have defined the scope of activities and authority of the human resources department.[1]

CONTEMPORARY ISSUE
The Contingent Workforce

Susan has worked steadily at Aztec Corporation since January. She works 40 hours a week at a variety of tasks for the computer parts maker. She inspects and cleans parts and adjusts wiring on circuits. For this work, Susan receives a regular paycheck. If she works at Aztec long enough, she will be eligible for paid vacation days and holidays. She is covered by a group health insurance plan from her employer.

Susan is not, however, a permanent employee of Aztec. She is a member of the contingency workforce—people hired by firms to cope with unexpected or temporary needs. Susan receives her paycheck not from Aztec, but from a temporary-employment agency. If Susan's job at Aztec ends, she will likely be placed at one of the agency's other client firms.

Aztec supplements its 20 permanent core employees with temporaries during peak periods. When a permanent opening occurs, it is filled by an employee selected from the pool of temps. Aztec has always used temps to fill in for secretaries or clerks on sick leave or vacation. But now the firm also uses temps for light manufacturing tasks. Aztec uses temps to smooth out the peaks and valleys in employment demand. By doing so, the firm avoids hiring permanent workers to meet peak demands only to lay them off when de-mand drops. By having a contingent pool of workers, Aztec can quickly adjust its payroll costs in economic downturns.

Aztec also uses temporary-employment agencies to find, test, and try out employees. In effect, these agencies are taking over many of the functions that used to be done internally by the human resources department.

The number of people working for temporary-placement firms such as Manpower, Kelly Services, and Olsten Staffing Services has increased tremendously in recent years. Estimates of the size of the contingent workforce range from 13 percent to 33 percent of all workers. Olsten, for example, a network of approximately 700 offices located throughout North America, employs over 400,000 assignment employees and caregivers. Manpower, the biggest of the nation's temp agencies, is now the nation's biggest private employer, with roughly 600,000 people on its payroll.

According to a Fortune 500 poll, companies report that they rely more on contingent workers now than they did five years ago. A large percentage (44%) of the surveyed employers "expect to employ still more here-today, gone-tomorrow workers five years from now."[1]

Source: [1] Jaclyn Fierman, "The Contingency Work Force," *Fortune* (January 24, 1994), p. 32.

Balancing Authority

Along with the gradual adoption of the name "human resources department" over the last several decades, most organizations have tried to achieve a proper balance of influence and authority between line supervisors and human resources staff. Line supervisors and human resources staff must work together because their activities are interdependent. Their primary roles and areas of authority should not shift substantially. The human resources department should focus primarily on advising and assisting line supervisors who need their help in certain areas. Line supervisors should take full advantage of the human resources department's expert assistance, while supervising their own departments within the framework of the organization's personnel policies and procedures and any union contract that may exist. As a first step in this direction, supervisors should have a major role in defining employee qualifications and describing job requirements for their own departments.

Assistance in Recruitment and Selection. When supervisors have positions open in their departments, they normally request the human resources department to recruit qualified applicants. Whether a particular job vacancy will be filled by someone from within the organization or someone from outside, the human resources department usually knows where to look to find qualified applicants. Most organizations try to fill job openings above entry-level positions through promotions and transfers. Promotions reward employees for past accomplishments; transfers can protect them from layoff or broaden their job knowledge. Internal applicants already know the organization, and the costs of recruitment, orientation, and training are usually less than for an external applicant.

Generally, internal applicants can be found through the use of computerized skills inventories or job posting and bidding.[2] Information on every employee's skills, educational background, work history, and other pertinent data can be stored in a database that can be reviewed to quickly determine whether any employees qualify for a particular job opening. This procedure helps ensure that every employee who has the necessary qualifications is identified and considered. Most organizations communicate information about job openings by posting vacancy notices on bulletin boards or in newsletters. Interested employees apply or "bid" for the vacant position by submitting applications to the human resources office with a copy to the supervisor. Job posting creates a greater openness in the organization by making all employees aware of job opportunities.

The outside sources of job applicants will vary, depending on the type of job to be filled. In all likelihood, a data entry clerk will not be recruited from the same source as a medical technologist. Advertising, public or private employment agencies, educational institutions, employee referrals, walk-ins, and contract or temporary help agencies are some of the sources that may be used.

To select from among job seekers, usually the human resources department has applicants fill out employment application forms and conducts preliminary interviews to determine whether the applicants' qualifications match the requirements for positions available. The HR department also makes reference checks of the applicants' previous employment and background (see Figure 13-1). For certain positions the department may administer one or more tests to determine whether applicants have the necessary skills and aptitudes. This may mean conducting statistical studies of tests that are used to determine whether they validly predict how an employee will perform on the job.[3] Eventually, applicants who do not have the required qualifications are screened out. Those who do have the qualifications are referred to the supervisor of the department where the job is open.

Supervisors Interview and Decide. After the human resources department has screened and selected qualified applicants for a job opening, the departmental supervisor normally interviews each candidate before any decision is made. The supervisor should make—or at least have the most say in making—the final decision to hire any candidate for a job within his or her department. Of course, the supervisor must follow the same guidelines used by the human resources department to ensure that any selection decision is nondiscriminatory. There may be occasions

FIGURE 13-1
The human resources department makes the necessary reference checks of previous employment and past records of applicants.

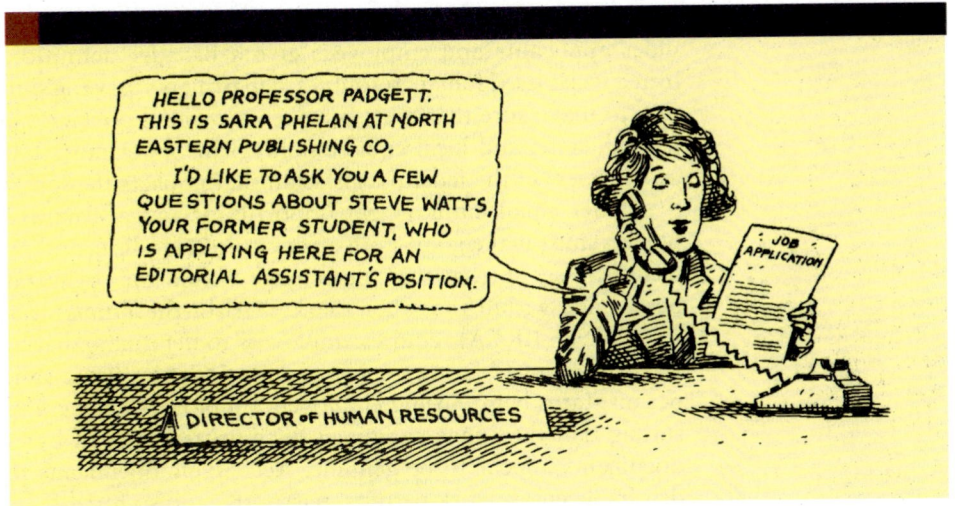

when the supervisor will have to compromise because of affirmative action or other programs mandated by organizational directives. But, in general, the supervisor is the person who should make the decision to hire or not to hire.

In recent years corporate restructuring or downsizing—the temporary or indefinite removal of employees from the organization—has created serious staffing concerns. Supervisors are being asked to do more with fewer employees. The consolidation of various job activities may not be a decision that the supervisor makes, but it is one that he or she must live with. Employees may be transferred from one job to another, or additional responsibilities may be added to the existing ones. Some employees may even be involuntarily demoted from supervisory or staff positions. Unfortunately, supervisors may sometimes find themselves with little or no authority in staffing decisions.

Regardless of who makes the final hiring decision, selection criteria must be developed. **Selection criteria** are the factors that will be used to differentiate among the various applicants. Education, knowledge, previous experience, test scores, application blanks, background investigations, and interpersonal skills often serve as selection criteria.

Selection criteria
Factors used to choose among applicants who apply for a job.

Compliance with Equal Employment Opportunity and Other Laws.
Probably the most pervasive influence that currently affects the staffing function is government laws and regulations. It is easy to understand why supervisors are confused by the numerous laws, executive orders, regulations, and guidelines they may have heard or read about. Title VII of the Civil Rights Act of 1964 prohibits discrimination in employment. The Equal Employment Opportunity Commission (EEOC) was created to increase job opportunities for women and minorities and to enforce the law. The law prohibits employment practices that discriminate on the basis of race, gender, color, religion, and national origin. Laws protecting people

who have physical and mental disabilities, Vietnam-era and other veterans, and older applicants and employees give a broader definition to the so-called "protected" classes. Human resources departments have assumed the primary obligation to make sure that their firms' employment policies and practices comply with federal, state, and local equal employment opportunity laws. Appendix I provides an overview of the federal legislation that impacts the supervisor's authority.

Under equal employment opportunity and affirmative action programs, employers must make good-faith efforts to recruit, hire, and promote members of protected classes so that their percentage within the organization approximates their percentage within the labor market. Also, the Immigration Reform and Control Act of 1986 (IRCA) requires employers to determine that anyone they hire is a citizen of the United States, or is a legal resident, or has a valid immigration or work-permit status before being employed. Employers must complete a special form (I-9) stating that they have examined documents provided by employees and that such documents appear to be genuine. Acceptable documents include birth certificates, drivers' licenses, work permits, passports, and so forth.[4]

Supervisors should not make staffing decisions without considering the legal ramifications of their decisions. While it is difficult to be current on all aspects of the law, effective supervisors should acquaint themselves with the Uniform Guidelines on Employee Selection Procedures because they apply to all aspects of supervisors' staffing responsibilities.[5] In Chapter 18 we discuss the need for supervisors to give special consideration to protected categories of people who are covered by equal employment opportunity laws.

Human Resources Staff Advice and Supervisory Decisions

Because employee problems arise continually, supervisors often consult with human resources department staff for assistance, information, and advice. At times, without even realizing it, supervisors may concede much of their authority and responsibility to that department unnecessarily. The following example illustrates how blurred the distinction can become between the human resources department's function of providing advice and the supervisor's decision-making responsibility.

An office supervisor wants to recommend a starting salary for a newly created data entry clerk position and inquires of the salary administrator in the human resources department about current wage levels for data entry clerks. If the salary administrator states that the average current market rate in the community for experienced data entry clerks is $1,400 per month, he or she is simply providing information without injecting an opinion. However, if the salary administrator states that starting the data entry clerk at the rate of $1,400 per month might be inequitable and cause problems among other experienced employees who are making less than that amount, the salary administrator is providing information and advice. By selecting facts and phrasing comments carefully, the salary administrator may sway the supervisor's decision one way or the other. For example, the administrator may even suggest starting the data entry clerk at a monthly salary of $1,300. Thus, without even being consciously aware of it, the supervisor may allow information to become advice and advice to become a decision. This happens not because the human resources staff person desires to reduce the supervisor's authority, but because the supervisor has willingly encouraged this type of staff influence.

Of course, in this example, it probably would be appropriate for the supervisor to accept the salary administrator's advice. Whenever a member of the human resources staff has expertise and knowledge directly related to a decision, supervisors are well advised to follow that person's advice and recommendations.

Some supervisors readily welcome the human resources staff's willingness to make certain decisions for them so that they will not have to solve difficult employee problems in their own departments. These supervisors reason that their own departmental tasks are more important than dealing with issues that the human resources staff can handle just as well or better than they can. Other supervisors may accept the staff's decision based on the premise that if the decision later proves to be wrong, they can say, "It wasn't my choice; human resources made the decision—not me!" For them it is a relief to rely on the staff's advice and consider it a decision. By so doing, these supervisors defer to the human resources department in the hope they will not be held accountable for the outcome of the decision. However, even when supervisors follow the human resources staff's advice, they are still accountable for the outcomes of their decisions.

Although it is easy to understand why some supervisors are reluctant to reject a human resources staff person's advice, they should recognize that the staff person may see only a part of the entire picture. The director of human resources is not responsible for the performance of a supervisor's department. Usually there are many unique factors that are better understood by each departmental supervisor than by anyone else.

PREPARING TO FILL STAFFING NEEDS

2 Explain how the supervisor prepares to fill job openings and why job descriptions and job specifications are critical to this task.

The staffing function is an ongoing process for the supervisor; it is not something that is done only when a department is first established. It is more realistic to think of staffing in the typical situation in which a supervisor is placed in charge of an existing department. Although it has a nucleus of employees, changes in the department's makeup take place due to employee separations from the workforce, changes in operations, growth, or other reasons. Since supervisors depend on employees for results, they must make certain that there are enough well-trained employees available to fill all positions.

Determining the Need for Employees

A continuous aspect of the supervisory staffing function is that of determining the department's need for employees, both in number and job positions. Supervisors should become familiar with departmental jobs and functions and consult the organization chart or manual if one is available. For example, the supervisor of a maintenance department may have direct reports who are painters, electricians, carpenters, and other employees, each with different skills. The supervisor should study each of these job categories to determine how many positions are needed to get the work done and how employees should work together. The supervisor may have to compromise by adjusting a preferred arrangement to existing realities or by combining several positions into one if there is not enough work for one employee to perform a single function. By carefully studying the organization of the department, the supervisor can reasonably determine how many employees and what skills are needed to accomplish the various work assignments.

Developing Job Descriptions

After determining the number of positions and types of skills needed, the supervisor's next step is to match the jobs available with individuals to perform them. This usually is done with the aid of job descriptions, (as discussed in Chapter 10), which indicate the duties and responsibilities involved in each job. A supervisor may have access to existing job descriptions; if such descriptions are not available, they can be developed with the assistance of higher-level managers or human resources staff. Similarly, if a new job is created, the supervisor should determine its duties and responsibilities and develop an appropriate job description.

The supervisor may find it helpful to ask departmental employees to write down the tasks they perform during a given time period—say, a day or a week. This will provide the supervisor with considerable information from which to develop the content of a job description. Although the final form of the job description may be written by a human resources staff person, it is the supervisor's responsibility to determine what actually goes into it. Figure 13-2 is a step-by-step approach to developing a job description for the position of housekeeper that was developed by an assistant administrator and the personnel director of a hospital. The steps suggested would be adaptable to many other types of jobs.

A supervisor should periodically (at least annually) compare each job description with what each employee does. As job descriptions become outdated, they may no longer fit the actual job duties and should be corrected. The supervisor may find that some of the duties assigned to a job no longer belong to it. They should be deleted or assigned elsewhere. Supervisors should not take the preparation of job descriptions lightly, because they can be used to explain to applicants the duties and responsibilities of a particular job. Job descriptions that describe the jobs accurately are useful in providing a realistic job preview, developing performance standards, conducting performance appraisals, and other staffing functions.

Developing Job Specifications

When the content of each job has been determined or reevaluated, a supervisor next should identify the knowledge and skills that are required of employees who are to perform the job. As discussed in Chapter 10, a written statement of required

FIGURE 13-2
How to Develop Job
Descriptions

The following steps were developed for the preparation of a job description for the position of housekeeper in a hospital:

Step 1. Prepare a questionnaire to be sent to housekeeping employees and their supervisors, asking them to list what they feel are the major functions and subfunctions that must be performed to do their job effectively.

Step 2. Have several higher-level managers who are interested in housekeeping list what functions they feel should and should not be performed by housekeepers.

Step 3. Find out from others in the organization what they believe should be and should not be the functions of a housekeeper.

Step 4. Tabulate the results of each of the three sources given above.

Step 5. Reconcile the differences of the above three viewpoints with the objectives of your organization, and prepare a detailed list of activities to be performed.

Step 6. Classify activities as major and minor activities.

Step 7. Determine what each housekeeper needs to know, what qualifications are necessary to perform designated activities, and specifically why each activity is to be performed.

Step 8. Submit the results of Steps 5 to 7 to a committee of housekeepers and supervisors for their discussion and recommendations. At this point you may find that you have been asking employees to do more than could possibly be accomplished reasonably. Revise and finalize the job description and job specification as appropriate.

Step 9. Periodically—at least annually—review and revise the job description, following the eight steps listed above, when you feel that changes in products, equipment, the economic climate, or service demands necessitate a change in the job to be performed.

knowledge, skills, and abilities is referred to as a job specification. Some firms prefer to use the term "job qualifications," or some similar designation. The approach for determining what an employee needs to know is found in Figure 13-2, step 7. Typically, the job description and job specification are combined into one document. (See Figure 10-4 in Chapter 10.)

For most jobs, an employee must possess certain skills, in addition to previous education or job knowledge, to perform the job adequately. For example, a data entry clerk must be able to use certain software programs and have command of a certain level of keyboarding skills. Job specifications for data entry clerks usually indicate the knowledge and skills required. The supervisor is usually in the best position to describe what skills are wanted, but should avoid the temptation to ask for higher skill levels than are necessary. One way to avoid requiring unnecessarily high levels of knowledge and job skills is to periodically check the job specification against the qualifications of employees who are doing the same or similar kinds of work. For example, investigation may reveal that a college education is not essential for a certain job. Or the supervisor may discover that it is not realistic (or legal) to employ only young men to perform heavy-duty warehouse work when an older man or a woman in good physical condition can do this work. As mentioned previously, equal employment opportunity laws require that job specifications be job related and not discriminate against certain categories of people. A supervisor who does not understand the ramifications of nondiscriminatory employment policies should consult the human resources department for clarification and guidance. In fact, many human resources departments have assumed much of the responsibility for writing job specifications because of concerns about compliance with such laws.

If job specifications are set unrealistically high, the task of finding people to meet them becomes more difficult and costly. Moreover, if the specifications are set too high and people are hired whose abilities are at a much higher level than the job demands, it is likely that these employees will be bored and become troublesome. By the same token, it is just as ill advised to ask for less than is necessary. An employee without sufficient knowledge or skill will probably not be satisfactory. Most of these difficulties can be minimized if the supervisor analyzes each job's content and then realistically and clearly specifies the knowledge and skills required.

Job descriptions and job specifications usually are maintained by the human resources staff as well as by the supervisor. Thus, when a departmental job is open, the supervisor simply notifies the human resources department. The human resources department will recruit suitable applicants based on the job specifications and will screen out applicants who do not have the knowledge, skills, or other requirements. The applicants who best meet all of the requirements will be referred to the supervisor for an interview and the final decision.

Determining How Many to Hire

Supervisors are not frequently confronted with a situation in which large numbers of employees have to be hired at the same time. This situation occurs when a new department is created or when a major expansion takes place. The more usual pattern is to hire one or a few employees as the need arises. Of course, some supervisors constantly request additional employees because they feel pressured to get their work done on time. In many cases, however, a supervisor's problems are not solved by getting more help. In fact, the situation may become worse. Instead of problems being reduced, new problems may arise due to inefficiencies that accompany overstaffing.

Normally, a supervisor will need to hire a replacement when a regular employee leaves the department due to promotion, transfer, resignation, dismissal, retirement, or some other reason. There is little question then that the job must be filled. However, if major technological changes or a downsizing are anticipated, a replacement may not be needed. There are other situations in which additional employees have to be hired. For example, if new functions are to be added to the department and no one in the department possesses the required knowledge and skills, it may be necessary to go into the labor market and recruit new employees. Sometimes a supervisor will ask for additional help because the workload has increased substantially and the department is under extreme pressure. Before requesting additional help, the supervisor should make certain that the employees currently in the department are being utilized fully and that any additional help is absolutely necessary and within the budget.

THE SELECTION PROCESS

3 Discuss the selection process and the use of directive and nondirective interviewing in the process.

Selection is the process of screening applicants to choose the best person for a particular job. Once job applicants have been located, the next step is to gather information that will help determine who should be hired. Usually, the human resources staff or the supervisor reviews résumés or application forms to determine which applicants meet the general qualifications of the position. Then, qualified applicants may be given tests, reference or background checks, and interviews to further narrow the pool of applicants.

Selection
Process of choosing the best applicants to fill open positions.

For supervisors, the most frequently used selection criterion—and often the most important part of the selection process—is the employee selection interview.[6] It is difficult to make an accurate appraisal of a person's strengths and potential from a brief interview. If there are several applicants for a position, the supervisor must ascertain which one is most qualified. This means trying to determine which applicant is most likely to perform best on the job and to stay with the company for the long term.

Interviewing is much more than a technique; it is an art that every supervisor must learn. Although our focus in this chapter is on the employee selection interview, over time every supervisor will conduct or be involved in other types of interviews that occur during the normal course of events. Among these are appraisal and counseling interviews, interviews regarding complaints and grievances, interviews regarding disciplinary measures or discharge, and exit interviews when employees quit voluntarily. The basic techniques, however, are generally common to all interviewing situations.

Basic Approaches to Interviewing

There are two basic approaches to interviewing: directive and nondirective. These approaches are classified primarily according to the amount of structure imposed on the interview by the interviewer.

Directive interview
Interview approach in which the interviewer guides the discussion along a predetermined course.

Directive Interview. In a **directive interview** the interviewer guides the course of the discussion with a predetermined outline and objectives in mind. This approach is sometimes called a "patterned" or "structured" interview. Using an outline helps the interviewer ask specific questions to cover each topic on which infor-

Interviewing job applicants is an important part of the selection process; thus, supervisors need to learn effective interviewing techniques.

mation is wanted. It also allows the interviewer to question and expand on related areas. For example, if a supervisor asks about the applicant's previous work experience, this may lead to questions about what the applicant liked and did not like about previous jobs. The supervisor guides and controls the interview but does not make it a rigid, impersonal experience. As a result of equal employment opportunity requirements, organizations are increasingly asking all applicants the same questions. This approach makes it easier to compare applicants, since all have responded to the same questions.

Nondirective Interview. The purpose of a **nondirective interview** is to encourage interviewees to talk freely and in depth. The applicant has maximum freedom in determining the course of the discussion. Rather than asking specific questions, the supervisor may stimulate the discussion by asking broad, open-ended questions, such as "Tell me about your work in the computer field." Generally, the supervisor will develop a list of possible topics to cover and, depending on how the interview proceeds, may or may not ask them. This unstructured approach to interviewing allows for great flexibility, but it generally is more difficult and time consuming to conduct than are directive interviews. For this reason, it is rarely used in its pure form.

Nondirective interview
Interview approach in which the interviewer asks open-ended questions that allow the applicant greater latitude in responding.

Blending Directive and Nondirective Approaches. Ultimately, the purpose of any interview is to promote mutual understanding—to help the interviewer and interviewee understand each other better through open and full communication. In employee selection interviews, the directive approach is used most often, since supervisors find it convenient to obtain information by asking the same direct questions of all applicants. However, at times supervisors should strive to blend both directive and nondirective techniques to obtain additional information that might be helpful in reaching a decision. Often, interviewers use situational questions to assess what the applicant would do in a certain situation. All applicants are given a specific situation to respond to. For example, the question "How would you assign daily work when two employees are absent?" allows the applicants to organize and express their thoughts about a realistic work situation. The supervisor may gain deeper insights about applicants' abilities to think and solve problems that could make the difference in choosing which applicant to hire.

Regardless of the approach used, development of relevant job-related questions is essential. For example, questions such as "Explain how you trained other employees in the use of the new software package." or "What are the steps involved in replacing a laser printer cartridge?" allow the applicants to reveal their knowledge and skills more clearly than could be ascertained from other sources. The supervisor should avoid using judgmental questions, such as "I believe that unions are a detriment to the employee welfare. What do you think?" Also, answers to questions that require a yes or no response, such as "Do you like to work with figures?" reveal very little about the applicant's ability to perform a particular job. It is better for the supervisor to ask why the applicant does or does not like to work with figures.

Preparation for an Employee Selection Interview

4 Describe how the supervisor should prepare for and conduct an effective selection interview.

Since the purpose of an employee selection interview is to collect information and arrive at a decision concerning a job applicant, the supervisor should prepare carefully for the interview. The supervisor must know what information is needed from the applicant, how to get this information, and how to interpret it.

As stated earlier, the directive interview is the most common approach used in selecting employees. Although most supervisors develop their own questions, some organizations have forms and procedures to guide supervisors in selection interviewing. For example, some firms require supervisors to fill out a detailed form on all applicants who are interviewed. Others use a standard interview form that more or less limits supervisors to asking only the questions that are included on the form. These interview forms sometimes are used to prevent supervisors from asking questions that might be considered discriminatory and in violation of government laws and regulations. Therefore, in preparing for an employee selection interview the supervisor must know what can be and what should not be asked of job applicants during the interview.

Influence of Equal Employment Opportunity Laws. Legislation on equal employment opportunity has placed restrictions on the questions employers ask job applicants. The overriding principle to follow in employee selection interviews is to ask job-related questions. Questions about topics not related to a person's ability to perform the job for which he or she has applied should be avoided. For example, asking an applicant for a position as data entry clerk about previous keyboarding experience would be directly job related. However, asking this applicant about owning or renting a home is of questionable purpose. Employee selection procedures also must ensure that legally protected groups such as minorities and women are treated fairly. Information that would adversely affect members of protected groups can be used only if it is directly job related. For example, the question "Who cares for your children?" is potentially discriminatory, because traditionally it has adversely affected women more than men.

Table 13-1 lists some of the most common areas of illegal and potentially illegal inquiry. The guidelines in Table 13-1 apply to all phases and criteria used in the selection process. Application forms, tests, interviews, reference checks, and physical examinations must all be nondiscriminatory and focus upon job-related requirements.

To determine whether or not a selection criterion is appropriate and complies with the law, one consulting firm has suggested the "OUCH" test.[7] OUCH is a four-letter acronym that represents the following:

<u>O</u>: Objective

<u>U</u>: Uniform in application

<u>C</u>: Consistent in effect

<u>H</u>: Has job relatedness

A selection criterion is objective if it systematically measures an attribute without being distorted by personal feelings. Examples of objective criteria include typing-test scores, number of years of education, degrees, and length of service in previous positions. Examples of subjective criteria include a supervisor's general impression about a person's interest in a job, or feelings that a person is "sharp."

A selection criterion is uniform in application if it is applied consistently to all job candidates. Asking different interview questions of male and female applicants would not be uniform in application.

A selection criterion is consistent in effect if it has the same proportional impact on protected groups as it does on others. For example, criteria such as possessing a high school diploma or living in a certain area of town may be objective and uniformly applied to all job candidates, but they could screen out proportionately more members of minority groups. When a selection criterion is not consistent in effect, the burden of proof is on the employer to demonstrate that it is job related.

A selection criterion has job relatedness if it can be demonstrated that it is necessary in performing the job. For example, in most cases it would be extremely difficult to prove that a selection criterion such as marital status is job related. Job-related criteria should stress skills required to perform the job.

Supervisors may not always understand the reasons for some of the restrictions imposed on them by the equal employment opportunity policies of their organiza-

TABLE 13-1
Areas of Illegal or
Potentially Illegal
Inquiry in Application
Forms and
Employment Interviews

Subject of Inquiry	Illegal or Potentially Illegal Questions
Applicant's name	1. Maiden name 2. Original name (if legally changed)
Civil and family status	1. Marital status. 2. Number and ages of applicant's children. 3. Child-care arrangements. 4. Is applicant pregnant or does she contemplate pregnancy?
Address	1. Foreign addresses that would indicate applicant's national origin.
Age	1. Before hiring, requests for birth certificate, baptismal certificate, or statement of age.
Birthplace (national origin)	1. Birthplace of applicant. 2. Birthplace of applicant's spouse, if any, and parents. 3. Lineage, ancestry, nationality.
Race or color	1. Any question that would indicate applicant's race or color.
Citizenship*	1. Country of citizenship if not United States. 2. Does the applicant intend to become a U.S. citizen? 3. Citizenship of spouse, if any, and of parents.
Disabilities	1. Preemployment physical examinations or questions about an applicant's physical or mental condition.
Religion	1. Religious denomination. 2. Clergyperson's recommendation or reference. 3. Any inquiry into willingness to work a particular religious holiday.
Arrests and convictions	1. Numbers and kinds of arrests experienced.
Education	1. Nationality, race, or religious affiliation of schools attended. 2. Native tongue, or how foreign language skills were acquired.
Organizations	1. Is applicant a member of any association other than a union and/or a professional or trade organization?
Military experience	1. Type of discharge from the U.S. Armed Forces. 2. Did the applicant have military experience with governments other than the U.S. government?
Relatives	1. Names and/or addresses of any relatives.

*However, the Immigration Reform and Control Act of 1986 requires that employers determine that anyone they hire is a U.S. citizen or has a legal residency status.

tions. They should not hesitate to consult with specialists in the human resources department for explanations and guidance in this regard.

Reviewing the Applicant's Background. Before interviewing a job applicant, the supervisor should review all available background information that has been gathered by the human resources office. By studying whatever is available, the supervisor can develop in advance a mental impression of the general qualifications of the job applicant. The application form will supply information concerning the applicant's schooling, experience, and other items that may be relevant.

When studying the completed application form, the supervisor should always keep in mind the job for which the applicant will be interviewed. If questions come to mind, the supervisor should write them down to remember them. For example, if an applicant shows a gap of a year in employment history, the supervisor should plan to ask the applicant about this gap and why it occurred.

A supervisor should also review the results of any employment tests the applicant took.[8] More and more organizations are administering job performance, integrity/honesty, and drug tests prior to the interview stage. Tests should be validated before they are actually used to assist in making hiring decisions. The potential value of preemployment testing was illustrated in a study of 5,000 applicants for the U.S. Postal Service. Applicants who tested positive for drug use had a 59 percent higher absenteeism rate and a 47 percent higher involuntary turnover rate than applicants who had not tested positive.[9] The selection criterion of preemployment drug testing was validated by the study—that is, the selection criterion bears a direct relationship to job success.

Human resources departments often administer job performance tests that measure skill and aptitude for a particular job as part of their normal procedures to screen out unqualified applicants. The human resources department must be able to document that these tests are valid, job related, and nondiscriminatory. This typically involves studies and statistical analyses by staff specialists—procedures that normally are beyond the scope of a supervisor's concern. Applicants whose test scores and other credentials appear to be acceptable are referred to the departmental supervisor for further interviewing. It is essential for the supervisor to understand what a test score represents and how meaningful it is in predicting an applicant's job performance. By consulting human resources department staff, the supervisor can become more familiar with the tests that are used and learn to interpret the meaning of test scores.

An additional source of information is references. Generally, telephone checks are preferable because they save time and allow for greater feedback. For the most part, information obtained from personal sources such as friends or character references will be positively slanted, because applicants tend to list only people who will give them good references. Information from previous supervisors who were in a position to evaluate the applicant's work performance are best. However, because of emerging personal privacy regulations and potential damage claims, an employment background investigation is best conducted by human resources department specialists. If possible, job references should be obtained in writing, should deal with job-related areas, and should be gathered with the knowledge and permission of the applicant. After reviewing all available background information, the supervisor should be able to identify areas in which little or no information is available and areas that require expansion or clarification.

Failure to Check Adequately Can Be Costly. It has been estimated that 85 percent of U.S. companies do not conduct any or do only minimal reference checks prior to hiring. This negligence has led applicants to omit or creatively explain the less positive aspects of their background. Robert LoPresto, facilitator at the Society for Human Resources Management's 1993 Annual Conference, stated that the assertion that "people will lie, cheat and steal to get a job" was never as true as it is in today's job market.[10]

The importance of verifying reference or application form data cannot be overemphasized. Various organizations have been charged with negligently hiring employees who later commit crimes. Typically, the lawsuits charge that the organization has failed to adequately check references, criminal records, or general background information that would have shown the employee's propensity for deviant behavior. At the time of this writing, the U.S. Supreme Court has agreed to review a fraud case involving "after-hire acquired evidence." Some lower courts have ruled that a significant lie or omission on an employee's résumé or application—even if discovered after the employee is fired—prohibits the employee from receiving damages from any wrongful discharge claim, including discrimination. Others have decided otherwise. The rulings in these cases, which range from theft to homicide, should make employers more aware of the need to check applicant references thoroughly. It is suggested that the organization include on the job application a statement to be signed by the applicant stating that all information presented during the entire selection process is truthful and accurate. The statement generally notes that any falsehood is grounds for refusal to hire or for termination.[11]

Preparing Key Questions. In preparing for the interview, the supervisor should develop a list of questions, which may include both directive and nondirective components. Preferably, the supervisor should develop a list of key questions—perhaps six to ten—that are vital to the selection decision and are job related. It is important that all applicants be asked the same core set of key questions, so that responses can be compared and evaluated. For example, the supervisor may want to know technical information about an applicant's previous work experience, why the applicant left a previous employer, and whether the applicant can work alternative shift schedules and overtime without difficulty. By planning to ask such questions in advance, the supervisor can devote more attention to listening to and observing the applicant, instead of having to think about what else should be asked. A thorough plan for the employment interview is well worth the time spent preparing it.

Conducive Physical Setting. Privacy and some degree of comfort are important components of a good interview setting. If a private room is not available to conduct an interview, then the supervisor should at least create an atmosphere of semiprivacy by speaking to the applicant in a place where other employees are not within hearing distance. This much privacy, at least, is necessary.

Conducting the Employee Selection Interview

The employee selection interview is not just a one-way questioning process, since the applicant also will want to know more about the company and the potential job. The interview should enable the job seeker to learn enough to help him or her decide whether or not to accept the position if it is offered. The supervisor must conduct the interview professionally by opening the interview effectively, explaining the job requirements, and using good questioning and note-taking techniques.

Opening the Interview. The experience of applying for a job often is filled with tension for an applicant. It is to the supervisor's advantage to relieve this tension. Some supervisors try to create a feeling of informality by starting the interview with social conversation about the weather, the heavy city traffic, the World Series, or some other topic of broad interest. The supervisor may offer a cup of coffee or make some other appropriate social gesture. An informal opening can be helpful in reducing an applicant's tensions; however, it should be brief, and the discussion should move quickly to job-related matters.

Many supervisors begin the employee selection interview with a question that is nonthreatening and is easily answered by the applicant, but also contains job-related information that the supervisor might need. An example is "How did you learn about this job opening?"

The supervisor should avoid excessive informal conversation, because studies of employee selection interviews have revealed that frequently an interviewer makes a favorable or unfavorable decision after the first five minutes of the interview. If the first ten minutes are spent discussing items not related to the job, then the supervisor may be basing the selection decision primarily on irrelevant information.

Realistic
organizational preview
(ROP)
Sharing of information
by an interviewer with
a job applicant
concerning the
mission, values, and
future direction of the
organization.

Explaining the Job. During the interview, the supervisor should discuss details of the job, working conditions, wages, benefits, and other relevant factors in a realistic way. A **realistic organizational preview (ROP)** includes sharing complete information about the organization: its mission, philosophy, opportunities for the future, and other information that gives applicants a good idea where the job under consideration will fit in and its importance. In discussing the job itself, a **realistic job preview (RJP)** informs applicants about the desirable as well as the undesirable aspects of the job. Because of eagerness to make a job look as attractive as possible, the supervisor may be tempted to describe conditions in terms that make it more attractive than it actually is. For example, a supervisor might "oversell" a job by describing in glowing terms what really is available only for exceptional employees. If the applicant is hired and turns out to be an average worker, this could lead to disappointment and frustration. Applicants who are given realistic information are more likely to remain on the job because they will encounter few unpleasant surprises.[12]

Realistic job preview
(RJP)
Information given by
an interviewer to a job
applicant that provides
an honest view of both
the positive and the
negative aspects of the
job.

Effective Questioning. Even though the supervisor will have some knowledge of the applicant's background from the completed application form and from information that the applicant volunteers, the need still exists to determine the applicant's specific qualifications for the job opening. The supervisor should not ask the applicant to repeat information already provided on the application form. Instead, questions should be rephrased to probe for additional details. For example, the question "What was your last job?" is likely to be answered on the application form. This question could be expanded as follows: "As a data entry clerk at Omega, what type of computer system did you operate?"

Some questions that may not appear to be directly job related nevertheless may be appropriate. For example, it may be important to know what an individual considers to be an acceptable income level. The salary limits of a position for which an applicant is interested may make it impossible for that person to meet existing financial obligations. This could force the individual to seek an additional part-time job to supplement income, thereby taking away some energy from the primary job. Or, in order to meet immediate financial needs, the applicant might accept a low-paying position in which he or she would be unhappy and continue to look for a higher-paying position with another firm. Problems of this nature, although not directly connected with job requirements, are relevant to the work situation and may be part of a selection decision.

A supervisor must use judgment and tact when questioning applicants. The supervisor should avoid "trick" or "leading" questions such as "Do you daydream frequently?" or "Do you have difficulty getting along with other people?" Questions such as these are sometimes used by interviewers to see how an applicant responds to difficult personal questions. However, these questions may antagonize the applicant. By no means should the supervisor pry into personal affairs that are irrelevant or removed from the work situation.

Taking Notes. In their efforts to make better selection decisions, many supervisors take notes during or immediately after the interview. Having written information is especially important if a supervisor interviews a number of applicants. Trying to remember what several applicants said during their interviews, and exactly who said what, is virtually impossible.

The supervisor should avoid writing while an applicant is answering a question. Instead, the supervisor should jot down brief summaries of responses after the applicant has finished talking. This is more courteous and useful. Although the supervisor does not have to take notes on everything said in the interview, key facts that might aid in choosing one applicant over the others should be noted.

Avoiding Pitfalls in Selection Interviewing and Evaluation

The chief problem in employee selection usually lies in interpreting the applicant's background, personal history, and other pertinent information. As normal human beings, supervisors are unable to eliminate their personal preferences and prejudices, but they should face up to their biases and make efforts to avoid or control them. Supervisors should particularly avoid making judgments too quickly during interviews with job applicants. Although it is difficult not to form an early impression, the supervisor should complete the interview before making any decision and should strive to avoid the numerous pitfalls that can occur both during and after an interview.

Halo or Horns Effect. The situation in which a supervisor generalizes from one aspect of a person's behavior to all aspects of the person's behavior is known as the "halo" or "horns" effect. In practice, this means basing one's overall impression of an individual on only partial information about that individual and using this limited impression as a primary influence in rating all the other factors. This may work either favorably (the **halo effect**) or unfavorably (the **horns effect**), but in either case it is improper. For example, the halo effect occurs when a supervisor assumes that if an applicant has superior interpersonal skills, he or she will also be good at keyboarding, working with little direction, and so forth. On the other hand, if a supervisor judges an applicant with a hearing impairment as being low on communication skills and allows this to serve as a basis for low ratings on other dimensions, the horns effect prevails.

Halo effect
The tendency to allow one favorable aspect of a person's behavior to positively influence judgment on all other aspects.

Horns effect
The tendency to allow one negative aspect of a person's behavior to negatively influence judgment on all other aspects.

Overgeneralization. Another common pitfall is overgeneralization. A supervisor should not assume that when an applicant responds in a certain manner during an interview, he or she will behave the same way in all other situations. For example, there may be a special reason why the applicant answers a question in an evasive manner. It would be wrong to conclude from evasiveness in answering one question that the applicant is underhanded and not trustworthy. Or an applicant may be dressed in rather old clothing and may not present a neat appearance. The supervisor should not generalize from this that the applicant will be sloppy and disinterested in good work habits and work performance. Unfortunately, many supervisors are apt to generalize too quickly.

Comparison with Current Employees. Sometimes a supervisor may judge an applicant by comparison with others who currently are working in the department. The supervisor may feel that any applicant who is considerably different from most current employees is undesirable. This kind of thinking can be detrimental, since it tends to breed uniformity and conformity. Carried to the extreme, it could contribute to mediocrity. This should not be interpreted to mean that the supervisor should deliberately look for people who would not fit into the department.[13] However, the fact that an individual does not exactly fit into the same mold as other employees is no reason to conclude that he or she would not make an excellent employee.

Excessive Qualifications. Being eager to get the best talent available, a supervisor may look for qualifications that far exceed the requirements of the job. Although an applicant should be qualified, there is no need to expect qualifications in excess of actual job requirements (see Figure 13-3). In fact, overqualified applicants may make poor employees, because they often become frustrated in jobs that are not sufficiently challenging to them. They also may spread dissatisfaction among co-workers, either by visibly showing unhappiness in the work situation or by demonstrating a superior attitude.

FIGURE 13-3
An overqualified applicant usually makes a poor employee.

Closing the Interview

At the conclusion of the employee selection interview, the supervisor likely will have a choice among several alternatives, ranging from hiring the applicant, deferring the decision until later, or rejecting the applicant. What the supervisor decides will be guided by the policies and procedures of the organization. Some supervisors have the authority to make selection decisions independently; others are required to check with either their managers or the human resources department. Still others may have the authority only to recommend which applicant should be hired. For purposes of brevity, we assume in the following discussion that the supervisor has the authority to make the final selection decision. Under these circumstances, the supervisor can decide to hire an applicant on the spot. All the supervisor has to do is tell the applicant when to report for work and provide any additional instructions that are pertinent.

If the supervisor wishes to defer the decision until several other candidates for the job have been interviewed, the applicant should be informed that he or she will be notified later. The supervisor should indicate a time frame within which the decision will be made. However, it is unfair to use this tactic to avoid the unpleasant task of telling an applicant that he or she is not acceptable. By telling the applicant that a decision is being deferred, the supervisor gives the applicant false hope. While waiting for the supervisor's decision, the applicant might not apply for other jobs, thereby letting opportunities slip by. Therefore, if a supervisor has made the decision not to hire an applicant, the supervisor should tell the applicant tactfully. Some supervisors deem it best to turn down the job seeker in a general way without stating specific reasons. This is often accomplished by merely saying that there was not a sufficient "match" between the needs of the job and the qualifications of the applicant.

The supervisor should keep in mind that an employment interview is an excellent opportunity to build a good reputation for the employer. The applicant realizes that other candidates probably have applied for the job and that not everyone can be selected. The last contact an applicant may ever have with the organization is with the supervisor during the employment interview. Therefore, even if the applicant does not get the job, the supervisor should recognize that the way the interview was handled will make either a good or a negative impression, sometimes a permanent one. Regardless of its outcome, an applicant should leave the interview feeling that he or she has been treated fairly and courteously. It is every supervisor's managerial duty to build as much goodwill as possible, since it is in the organization's self-interest to maintain a good image.

The Hiring Decision

5 Explain the hiring decision and the importance of documentation.

The decision to hire can be challenging when the supervisor has interviewed several applicants and all of them appear to be qualified for the job. There are no definite guidelines that a supervisor can always utilize to select the best-suited individual. At times, information from the application forms, tests, and interviews will indicate which of the applicants should be hired. However, there will be other times when available information is not convincing or perhaps is even conflicting. For example, an applicant's aptitude test score for a sales job may be relatively low, but the person has favorably impressed the supervisor in the interview by showing an enthusiastic interest in the job and a selling career.

This is where supervisory judgment and experience come into play. The supervisor must select employees who are most likely to contribute to good departmental performance. The supervisor may consult with human resources staff for their evaluations, but in the final analysis, it should be the supervisor's responsibility to choose. Before the final decision is made, the supervisor should evaluate each applicant against the selection criteria. By carefully analyzing all of the information available and keeping in mind previous successes and failures in selecting employees, the supervisor should be able to select applicants who are most likely to succeed.

Of course, hiring decisions always involve uncertainties. There are no exact ways to predict how individuals will perform until they actually are placed on the job. However, a supervisor who approaches the hiring decision in a thorough, careful, and professional manner is likely to consistently select applicants who will become excellent employees.

Employee Involvement in the Hiring Decision. The degree to which employees are involved in the selection process differs among organizations. Generally, subordinates, peers, or work team members meet with the applicant and give their impression to the ultimate decision maker. Members of employee work teams, for example, are generally most knowledgeable about particular job responsibilities and challenges. They can offer valuable insight into the employee selection process. Even without formal teams, some organizations allow employees to fulfill various roles, from assisting with the definition of job responsibilities to having a direct say in the final hiring decision. General Motors's Saturn Corporation allows groups of 5 to 15 workers to perform various staffing tasks, such as hiring.[14]

Documentation. In recent years, many supervisors have been asked by higher-level managers and human resources staff to document the reasons for their decisions to hire particular individuals from among the applicants interviewed. Documentation is necessary to ensure that a supervisor's decision to accept or reject an applicant is based on job-related factors and is not discriminatory. At times, a supervisor's hiring decision will be challenged; the supervisor must be able to justify that decision or risk being reversed by higher-level managers. Similarly, supervisors sometimes will be strongly encouraged by higher-level managers or human resources staff to give preferential hiring considerations to minority or female applicants, especially if the organization is actively seeking such employees. Some supervisors resent this type of pressure, but they should recognize that the organization may be obligated under various laws to meet certain hiring goals. In general, if supervisors follow the approaches suggested in this chapter, they should be able to distinguish the most qualified people from among the applicants and also be prepared to justify their employment selections.

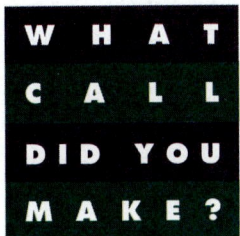

WHAT CALL DID YOU MAKE?

It is vitally important for supervisors like Kori Stephens to verify references and confirm the accuracy of the information provided by applicants. Generally, human resources departments do this for the organization. The reluctance of firms to take the time to do reference checks has fueled applicant dishonesty.

You, as Kori Stephens, should double check the job description and job specifications for the accounting position. Carrie Webster is an above-average performer, and thus a college degree does not appear to be a necessary job qualification. You are right to assume that the human resources department advertised the position, screened initial applicants, and determined that their qualifications matched the job requirements. While this omission or falsification by Carrie Webster is not as bad as some possibilities (e.g., a fast-food restaurant hired a convicted child molester who later assaulted children in the restrooms), the position is that of an accountant, and Carrie did falsify her application to get the job. It has been said that in today's labor market "people will lie, cheat and steal to get a job."

What do you do with Carrie? In practice, each supervisor will apply his or her own set of experiences and values to make the decision. Some supervisors will take the comfortable route; Carrie is doing a good job, and the time and cost involved in replacing her are not worth the effort.

Others may rationalize that "everyone is doing it," while still others believe that if a person is dishonest in one aspect of the job, it will spill over into other aspects.

This "You Make the Call" asks you to develop safeguards to prevent the situation from recurring. You should begin by developing a cooperative arrangement with the human resources department. Review the job descriptions and job specifications for all of your positions. Make certain that the necessary background checks are made. Require written verification of work and educational experiences. Try to recall the selection interview that you had with Carrie to ascertain the types of questions you asked. (If you took notes, this task will be easier.) It is often easy for people to place the blame on others, but you had responsibility for conducting the employment interview. Did you ask the kinds of questions that would have enabled you to detect the omissions or falsifications? You should remember to apply the "OUCH" test. The questions you ask should be related to the job.

SUMMARY

1 Discuss the staffing function and describe the roles of the human resources staff and supervisors.

Managing human resources is the supervisor's most important activity. In fulfilling responsibilities for staffing, the supervisor can be substantially aided by the human resources department. Some organizations are using firms that supply temporary workers to do some of the staffing work.

There must be a balance of authority between line supervisors and human resources staff in staffing policies and decisions. Usually, the human resources department aids in recruitment—advertising the opening, recruiting a pool of applicants, screening, testing, checking background, and the like. The departmental supervisor then interviews applicants and either makes or has most of the say in the final hiring decision.

The pervasive presence of equal opportunity employment laws and regulations has resulted in the human resources staff's assuming much of the responsibility to ensure that an organization's employment policies and practices comply with these laws. Sometimes human resources departments take primary responsibility for hiring, interpreting policy, determining selection criteria, writing job descriptions and specifications, testing applicants, and the like. Supervisors should not release these staffing areas totally to human resources, although at times it might seem expedient to do so. A supervisor remains accountable for decisions, even when relying on the advice of the human resources staff.

2 Explain how the supervisor prepares to fill job openings and why job descriptions and job specifications are critical to this task.

An ongoing process of the staffing function is determining how many employees and what skills are needed to accomplish various work assignments. Job descriptions indicate the duties and responsibilities of the job and must be reviewed periodically. Job descriptions that accurately describe the job are useful in providing a realistic job preview, developing performance standards, conducting performance appraisals, and other staffing functions.

Job specifications detail the knowledge, skills, and abilities an employee should have to perform a job adequately. Applicants are recruited and screened out based on the job specifications.

Supervisors need to ascertain how current employees are being utilized before they make requests for additional help. If new functions are added to the department or the workload increases substantially, supervisors need to determine the number and types of employees needed.

3 Discuss the selection process and the use of directive and nondirective interviewing in the process.

Selection is the process of choosing the best applicant to fill a particular job. After job applicants are located, information must be gathered to help in determining who should be hired.

Supervisors are most likely to be involved in employee selection interviews. Two basic approaches are the directive interview and the nondirective interview. The directive interview is highly structured; the supervisor asks specific questions of each applicant and guides the course of the discussion. In the nondirective interview, the supervisor allows the applicant much freedom in determining the course of the discussion.

Regardless of the approach used, supervisors must develop job-related questions. Situational questions may be used to assess how the applicant would act in a given situation. Judgmental questions and questions that can be answered with a simple yes or no should be avoided.

4 Describe how the supervisor should prepare for and conduct an effective selection interview.

It is vital for a supervisor to thoroughly prepare for the selection interview. A supervisor should be aware of equal employment opportunity concerns and applicable guidelines. Job-related questions that foster nondiscriminatory treatment should be used. Selection criteria should be objective, uniform in application, consistent in effect, and job related. Before conducting the interview, the supervisor should review the applicant's application form, test scores, and other available background materials. By having a list of key questions to ask, the supervisor should be able to cover the most important areas in which more information is wanted.

The supervisor may open the employee selection interview by using an approach that reduces tension, such as asking a question that is easily answered. The supervisor should explain the job, use effective questioning techniques, and take appropriate notes.

When evaluating an applicant, the supervisor should avoid such common pitfalls as the halo effect or horns effect, overgeneralization, comparing the applicant only with current employees, and looking for qualifications that far exceed the requirements of the job. At the conclusion of the interview, the supervisor should remember that the applicant is entitled to a decision just as soon as possible. The supervisor should strive to have the applicant leave with an impression of fair and courteous treatment.

5 Explain the hiring decision and the importance of documentation.

The supervisor wants to select employees who will contribute to excellent department performance. A review of the selection criteria is critical in determining the best applicant. Depending on the organization, subordinates, peers, or team members may have a say in determining who is ultimately hired. This involvement varies from assistance in defining job duties to having a say in the final decision.

Documentation of the selection process is critical in helping to demonstrate that the process is based on job-related factors and is not discriminatory.

KEY TERMS

Human resources management (HRM) (page 338)

Selection criteria (page 341)

Selection (page 347)

Directive interview (page 347)

Nondirective interview (page 348)

Realistic organizational preview (ROP) (page 354)

Realistic job preview (RJP) (page 354)

Halo effect (page 356)

Horns effect (page 356)

QUESTIONS FOR DISCUSSION

1. What are some of the major activities of the human resources department that can assist the line supervisor in the staffing function? What should be the primary responsibility of human resources staff and of line supervisors for various employment and other staffing activities? Is there a clear dividing line of responsibility? Discuss.

2. Define some of the major laws and regulations that govern equal employment opportunity. Why have many organizations assigned to the human resources department the primary responsibility for making sure that their employment policies and practices are in compliance?

3. What is meant by a job description and a job specification? How are they interrelated and useful in staffing decisions?

4. Outline some of the steps a supervisor might take to develop departmental job descriptions and job specifications.

5. Discuss the differences between a directive interview and a nondirective interview. Does the employee selection interview tend to be directive or nondirective in nature or both? Why?

6. Discuss how adequate supervisory preparation for an employee selection interview can be crucial to the interview's success.

7. Discuss each of the following aspects of conducting an employee selection interview:
  a. Opening the interview.
  b. Explaining the job.
  c. Using effective questioning techniques.
  d. Taking notes.
  e. Concluding the interview.

8. Identify several pitfalls that supervisors may encounter in evaluating job applicants, both during and after an interview.

9. What guidelines can be suggested to improve a supervisor's decision making when hiring job applicants?

10. Why are supervisors and many employers now required to document why they did or did not hire applicants they have interviewed?

SKILLS APPLICATIONS

Skills Application 13-1: Job Specifications and Descriptions

1. Visit the job placement office at your college or the local employment office. Select a job at a firm that you might be interested in.

a. What are the specifications for the job to be filled?

b. Is there a job description? If so, what does it convey?

c. Do you believe that the job specification and job description provide a realistic job preview? Why or why not?

Skills Application 13-2: First Impressions in the Selection Process

You may have heard people say, "I know a good person when I see one." Look around the classroom and identify one person whom you do not know.

1. Based on your first impression—just by observing the person—make a list of what you like about him or her.

2. Assume that you would be interviewing this person for the job that you selected in Skills Application 13-1. Jot down a few key questions you would ask.

3. Ask the person whether you may interview him or her for about three to five minutes. A note of caution: Remember to ask the person whether this is a convenient time. Use the questions you developed as the outline for the interview.

4. How did your interview evaluation of the person compare with your first impression?

5. Were you initially influenced by past experiences with people who reminded you of this person?

6. Summarize in 25 words or less what you learned from this skills application.

Skills Application 13-3: The Choice

You are the newly appointed manager of the Wizards baseball team. During spring training, two players, Koss and Rivera, are vying for one open spot on the team—utility infielder. Their physical attributes are very similar. Player Koss has 10 hits in 39 at-bats against left-handed pitchers, for a .256 batting average, and 30 hits in 90 at-bats against right-handers, for a .333 percentage. The corresponding figures for Rivera are 16 for 60, or .266, against southpaws, and 20 for 58, or .345, against right-handed pitchers.

1. You are only going to be able to choose one of the two players to keep on the squad. Who should it be? Why?

2. What other attributes, besides batting averages, should you consider?

3. Compare your ideas with that of another student. Why are there differences?

ENDNOTES

1.   "ASPA-BNS Survey No. 53, Personnel Activities, Budgets, and Staffs: 1988–1989," *Bulletin to Management* (Washington, D.C.: The Bureau of National Affairs, Inc., June 22, 1989), p. 1. Also, see Margaret Magnus, "Personnel's Increasing Management Role," *Personnel Journal* (Volume 68, February 1989), p. 6.

2.   For information on locating qualified internal candidates by computerized record systems, job posting and bidding, and the like see Arthur W. Sherman, Jr., and George W. Bohlander, *Managing Human Resources* (9th ed.; Cincinnati: South-Western Publishing Co., 1992), pp. 149–151.

3.   The resurgence of selection testing can be attributed in part to the positive results of the validity testing program of the U.S. Employment Service. See "Is Preemployment Testing a Good Idea?" *Training and Development* (September 1993), p. 26; Stephen L. Gunn, "Gain Competitive Advantage Through Employment Testing," *HR Focus* (Volume 70, Number 9, September 1993), p. 15; James A. Douglas, Daniel E. Feld, and Nancy Asquith, *Employment Testing Manual* (Boston: Warren, Gorham & Lambert, 1989 and 1991 Supplement), pp. 11–13; and Robert M. Madigan, K. Dow Scott, Diana L. Deadrick, and Jil A. Stoddard, "Employment Testing: The U.S. Service Is Spearheading a Revolution," *Personnel Administrator* (Volume 31, September 1986), p. 102.

4.   The verification procedure applies to all employers, regardless of size, and for all employees. When employers require more or different documents than those required by the Act or demonstrate a preference for one document over another, they are engaging in "document abuse."

5. The Uniform Guidelines on Employee Selection Procedures, first published in 1970, presents the standard of determining the proper use of tests and other selection procedures. See the *Federal Register* (Volume 44, Number 3, March 2, 1979), pp. 11996–12009. For a comprehensive discussion of equal employment opportunity compliance, see David P. Twomey, *Equal Employment Opportunity Law* (2nd ed.; Cincinnati: South-Western Publishing Co., 1990).

6. For additional information on the preemployment interview, see Robert L. Dipboye, *Selection Interviews: Process Perspectives* (Cincinnati: South-Western Publishing Co., 1992); Diane Arthur, *Recruiting, Interviewing, Selecting and Orienting New Employees* (2nd ed.; New York: AMACOM, 1991); Robert W. Eder and Gerald Ferris, eds., *The Employment Interview: Theory, Research, and Practice* (Newbury Park, CA: Sage Publications, 1989); and James M. Jenks and Brian L. P. Zevnik, "ABC's of Job Interviewing," *Harvard Business Review* (Volume 67, July–August 1989), pp. 38–42.

7. This concept was part of a training program developed by Jagerson Associates, Inc., for the Life Office Management Association.

8. Tests can be used as one selection criterion. For a discussion of job relatedness, see Gene Carmean, "Tie Medical Screening to the Job," *HR Magazine* (Volume 37, July 1992), pp. 85–87; and Jonathan A. Segal, "Pre-Employment Physicals Under the ADA," *HR Magazine* (Volume 71, October 1992), pp. 103–107. The 1991 report of the American Psychological Association cautioned employers to avoid honesty tests that lack validity documentation. See Tori DeAngelis, "Honesty Tests Weigh in with Improved Ratings," *The APA Monitor* (Volume 22, June 1991), p. 7.

9. Jacques Normand, Stephen D. Salyards, and John J. Mahoney, "An Evaluation of Preemployment Drug Testing," *Journal of Applied Psychology* (December 1990), pp. 629–639.

10. "Reference Checking Limits Employers' Liability for Negligent Hiring," *Human Resources Management Issues & Trends* (Number 304, June 23, 1993), pp. 102–103.

11. See Robert L. Brady, "High Court to Hear Résumé Fraud Case," *HR Focus* (Volume 70, Number 9, September 1993), p. 11. For further discussion of reference screening, see "College Checks Applicant's Police Records," (Raleigh, N.C.: Associated Press, November 22, 1993); and "Firms Face Lawsuits for Hiring People Who Then Commit Crimes," *The Wall Street Journal* (April 30, 1987), p. 29.

12. John P. Wanous, "Installing a Realistic Job Preview: Ten Tough Choices," *Personnel Psychology* (Volume 42, Number 1, Spring 1989), pp. 117–133.

13. To increase the chances of success, change is essential. Tom Peters has advocated that "Rule #1: ... There are no rules. The key to business success is to do the opposite of what everyone else is doing. Hire "malcontents'—and encourage them to stay that way." See "Tom Peters on Necessary Disorganization: Cutting Edge Business Ideas for the Nanosecond '90s." (forty-minute video available from *Inc.* magazine.)

14. Aaron Bernstein, "Making Teamwork Work—And Appeasing Uncle Sam," *Business Week* (January 25, 1993), p. 101.

Orientation, Training, Promotion, and Compensation

LEARNING OBJECTIVES

After studying this chapter, you will be able to:

1 Identify the characteristics of an effective orientation program.

2 Explain approaches to training and the supervisor's role in employee development.

3 Identify why organizations should apply a policy of promotion from within whenever possible.

4 Describe the criteria and procedures commonly used for making promotion decisions.

5 Discuss the supervisor's role in employee compensation and outline the goals of an effective compensation program.

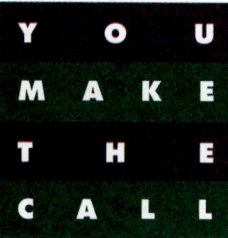

You are Charlotte Kelly, administrative services supervisor for Pine Village Hospital. Pine Village Hospital is a 240-bed facility located 70 miles from the nearest competitor.

You are supervisor of all non-medical-related patient matters from the time the patients are admitted until they are discharged. The admissions, accounting, billing, computer services, switchboard, housekeeping, food service, and other such departments are among your areas of responsibility. Your duties were recently broadened to include overseeing patient financial counseling, coordinating volunteers, helping to negotiate managed health care contracts, and serving as facilitator of the quality assurance team.

Because you believe that the demands of managed health care, combined with the pressures of cost cutting and downsizing, will result in a need for front-line employees who can fill a variety of roles, you undertook a massive training effort during the past year. All of your people were trained and retrained. All employees received extensive computer training. All employees added at least one additional functional area to their skill base. The training process included detailed explanations of how each employee's job impacts patient care and interrelates with the functioning of the total hospital.

The training led to an increase in accuracy and an improvement in staff morale. Employees liked the training; it made them feel more important. The training of the admitting staff to work interchangeably in all departments and vice versa has made the staff more valuable. Jay, for example, works with patient records from preadmitting straight through to discharge, and many times he does the follow-up for insurance or payment after the patient has left the hospital. This cross-functional approach means that an employee works with a group of patients from the beginning to the end of their stay. When patients come back in, they remember the associate, and if there is a problem, they call that associate back. This makes the system more personal.

You are perceived by your staff as an excellent role model and a good listener. Another employee speaks for the staff when she describes you as a firm leader who expects a lot and gets results because you expect no less from yourself.

You encourage your staff to get involved and make a difference. Even before Kevin, a new employee, arrives, you have assigned Aimee, an outstanding performer, to help in the orientation process. Kevin will "shadow" Aimee for the first few weeks on the job.

You recently presented Ahmed Riaz, vice-president for administration, with information on pay-for-performance and skill-based pay plans. In the long run, you believe that your actions will be an advantage to the hospital. You feel that the changes will enable the hospital staff to better serve the customers.

Looking back on the past year, you wonder what else you could have done.

YOU MAKE THE CALL.

ORIENTATION OF NEW EMPLOYEES

1 Identify the characteristics of an effective orientation program.

When new employees report for work the first day, the manner in which the supervisor welcomes them and introduces them to other employees in the department may have a lasting effect on their future performance. The first days on the job for most new employees are disturbing and anxious. They typically feel like strangers in new surroundings among people whom they have just met. It is the supervisor's responsibility to make the transition as smooth as possible and to lead new employees in the desired directions. This initial phase is called "orientation."[1] **Orientation** is a process designed to help new employees become acquainted with the organization and understand the expectations the organization has for them. In short, orientation helps the employee develop a sense of belonging to the organization and become productive as soon as possible.

Orientation
The process for smoothing the transition of new employees into the organization.

There are several approaches that a supervisor can use in departmental orientation of new employees. The supervisor may choose personally to escort the new employees around the department, showing them equipment and facilities and introducing them to other employees. Or the supervisor may prefer to assign new employees to an experienced, capable employee and have this person do all of the orienting, perhaps including instructing new employees on how to perform their jobs.

Using a Checklist

A useful technique to ensure that new employees are well oriented is to use a checklist. When developing an orientation checklist, the supervisor should strive to identify all the things that a new employee ought to know. Without some type of checklist, the supervisor is apt to skip some important item. Figure 14-1 shows an orientation checklist prepared by an insurance company human resources department for use by supervisors.

Discussing the Organization

It usually is a good idea for the supervisor to sit down with new employees on the first day in some quiet area to discuss the department, the organization, and its policies and regulations. In some firms the human resources department provides booklets that give general information about the firm, including benefits, policies, and procedures. There may even be a formal class that provides this type of information to employees and takes them on a tour of the firm's facilities. In small firms, it may be appropriate to introduce new employees to the owner or top-level managers. In larger firms, this is not practical, so sometimes these firms videotape an interview with the chief executive officer or other members of top-level management in which the managers present the vision for the future, corporate philosophy, market and product development, and the like. Employees should receive an explanation of what they can expect from the organization. As discussed in Chapter 13, realistic organization and job previews should clarify employee expectations. The key is that the information must be accurate and that all employees must receive the same information.

A common mistake made by some supervisors when orienting new employees is to give them too much information on the first day. Presenting too many items in a very short time may result in information overload. A new employee is not likely to remember many details if they are all presented in the first two hours of the first day. Consequently, the supervisor should spread different aspects of orientation over a new employee's first few days or weeks. Also, the supervisor should schedule a review session several days or weeks later to discuss any problems or questions the new employee might have.

Being Supportive

More important than the actual techniques used in orienting new employees are the attitudes and behavior of the supervisor. If a supervisor conveys a sincerity in trying to make the transition period a pleasurable experience and tells new employees that they should not hesitate to ask questions, this in itself will smooth their early days on the job. Even when the human resources department provides formal orientation, it remains the supervisor's responsibility to assist each new person to quickly become an accepted member of the departmental work team and a contributing, productive employee.

FIGURE 14-1
Orientation Checklist
of an Insurance
Company

☐   <u>Welcome the new employee.</u> When the new employee arrives, go to the reception area and greet the person cordially. On the new employee's first day, try to make him or her feel at ease.

☐   <u>Show the workplace.</u> Briefly describe the group's work.

☐   <u>Introduce the new employee to co-workers.</u>

☐   <u>Give a tour of the company.</u> This can be done by one of your experienced employees. Show the coat closet, cafeteria, time clock, restroom facilities, and the other departments that will be pertinent to the new employee's job.

☐   <u>Take the new employee to the human resources department.</u> After a tour of the company, take the new employee to the human resources department to fill out the necessary employment papers.

☐   <u>Explain the telephone system.</u> Take the new employee to the reception area, where a switchboard operator will explain the telephone system.

☐   <u>Make sure the new employee understands the following:</u>
• Use of the time clock.
• Starting and stopping times.
• Proper work clothes.
• Parking facilities.
• Lunch period and break period.
• Rate of pay and how it is figured.
• Overtime pay.
• Pay deductions.
• What to do about errors in paycheck.
• Probation period of 30 days.
• Job evaluation.
• Reporting of absences.

☐   <u>Remind the new employee to come to you for information and assistance.</u>

Setting the Stage. Supervisory responsibility goes beyond passing out the employee handbook and distributing department work rules. The supervisor should inform the other employees that someone new is joining the group and let them know something positive about the new person. Imagine how difficult it would be for a person to be received into the work group if the employees had been told "we had to hire this person." The supervisor needs to set the stage for the new employee's arrival, so that he or she is properly socialized into the work group.

Organizations that use work teams believe in pushing authority, responsibility, and accountability downward throughout the organization. For many employees this has meant learning to work more closely with others as team members and depend on each other for the completion of assigned tasks. Over a period of time, effective teams develop openness in communication and relationships. New employees need to understand the purpose of the work group, its goals, why the job is important, where it fits in, and so forth. They also need to understand the roles that various members fulfill. Supervisors must make certain that members of the work team understand it is their responsibility to communicate and contribute to this understanding.

Part of the orientation process is to shape the new employee's behavior in a positive manner. Since people observe and imitate others' behavior, it is not enough for a supervisor to simply state what is expected of the employee. People tend to act—both productively and counterproductively—like those with whom they closely identify. Effective work team members will model positive norms for the new employee. An effective technique is to place the new employee with an outstanding performer, who acts as a coach or mentor. The reason for placing the new employee with an outstanding performer is to perpetuate excellent performance. Finally, as discussed in Chapter 5, *all* employees need positive feedback on performance, and an effective supervisor reinforces the new employee's early successes by giving sincere praise.

Mentoring
The guiding of a newer employee by an experienced employee in areas concerning job and career.

Mentoring. Since the classic *Harvard Business Review* article "Everyone Who Makes It Has a Mentor," research during the past two decades has explored the role that mentors or sponsors play in an employee's development.[2] **Mentoring,** the process of having a more experienced person provide guidance, coaching, or counseling to a less experienced person, is deeply rooted in history, as illustrated by the story of Odysseus turning over the care and development of his young son, Telemachus, to Mentor. In the Middle Ages, guild masters were responsible for their protégés' social, religious, and personal, as well as professional, skills. Broadly defined, the mentor teaches "the tricks of the trade," gives the protégé all the responsibility he or she can handle, thrusts the protégé into new areas, directs and shapes the protégé's performance, suggests how things are to be done, and provides protection.[3]

Mentoring should be looked upon as one way to smooth the transition of new employees into the organization and develop them into productive employees. New employees can build a network of people who can collectively provide the many benefits of a mentor. The supervisor can also fulfill this role by adding to the new employees' knowledge base.

2 Explain approaches to training and the supervisor's role in employee development.

TRAINING AND DEVELOPMENT

In most job situations, new employees require both general and specific training. If skilled workers are hired, the primary training need may be in the area of company and departmental methods and procedures. If unskilled or semiskilled workers are

A mentor provides guidance, coaching, and counseling to a new employee, helping to shape his protégé's future in the firm.

hired, they will have to be taught specific job skills to make them productive within a short period of time. Methods of formal training vary among organizations and depend on the unique circumstances involved in each situation. At the departmental level, helping employees improve their knowledge, skills, and abilities to perform both current and future jobs is an ongoing responsibility of the supervisor.[4]

On-the-Job Training

Most training at the departmental level takes the form of on-the-job training. The supervisor may prefer to do as much of the training personally as time will permit. This has the advantage of helping the supervisor get to know the new employees while they are being trained in the proper methods and standards of performing the job. It also ensures uniform training, since the same person is training everyone. If the supervisor does not have the time or the technical skills to do the training, then the training should be performed by one of the best current employees. The supervisor should give the training task only to experienced employees who enjoy this additional assignment and are qualified to do so. The supervisor should make periodic follow-up visits to see how each new employee is progressing.

Off-the-Job Training

There are many training programs for new as well as existing employees, that are conducted outside of the immediate work area. Some of these may be coordinated or taught by human resources staff or training departments. For skilled crafts involving, for example, electricians, machinists, or toolmakers, a formal apprenticeship training program may be established. Usually this requires the employee to be away from the job for formal schooling and work part of the time.

Increasingly, business firms are initiating college-campus-based programs for training their employees. Generally, college representatives and the firm's supervisors work together to develop a curriculum for employees. Employees attend classes on the campus during nonworking hours. Tuition is paid by the firm, and employees receive credit for taking classes related specifically to their jobs. One example is an apprentice training program developed by representatives of a steel company and a community college. Employees were divided into two groups, each of which receives 640 hours of on-campus lecture and laboratory training pertinent to their craft. The groups alternate every four weeks, with one group assigned to the plant for hands-on experience while the other group receives classroom training. A continual process of curriculum review and assessment of employee on-the-job performance ensures that the program meets the firm's needs.

There also may be programs offered within the firm during or outside of working hours. For example, safety training meetings and seminars are commonly scheduled during working hours for supervisors and employees alike.

Ongoing Development of Employees

Supervisors should assess the skills and potential of employees and provide opportunities for ongoing development of their skills, so that they can perform better both now and in the future. If a supervisor believes that training is needed that cannot be provided at the departmental level, the supervisor should go to a higher-level manager or to the human resources department to see whether there are existing courses outside the organization that can meet training needs.

Many organizations have tuition-aid programs to help employees further their education. A supervisor should be aware of available course offerings at nearby educational institutions and encourage employees to take advantage of all the educational avenues open to them. These learning experiences can help them develop knowledge, abilities, and skills that improve their performance and prepare them for more demanding responsibilities.

The Supervisory Role in Employee Development

The impetus for a training program can come from many directions, as illustrated in Figure 14-2. Generally, operating problems and nonaccomplishment of organizational objectives may highlight the need for training. The entire training activity

FIGURE 14-2
Factors to Consider in
Determining Training
Needs

must be based on the identification of the combined needs of the organization and the employees.

Training must be viewed as an ongoing developmental process, not a simple bandage for a short-term problem. Therefore, training must be relevant, informative, interesting, and applicable to the job, and it must actively involve the trainee in the process. As Confucius put it:

> *I hear and I forget*
> *I see and I remember*
> *I do and I understand.*

Skills that employees need to perform the essential departmental tasks should be the initial training focus. However, in the current business environment, cross-training is becoming essential. Whether "reengineering," "reinventing the organization," "rightsizing," "downsizing," or whatever term is used, reductions in force (RIFs) have left hundreds of thousands of employees wondering what the future holds. Consolidation of job duties suggests that supervisors will need to identify jobs that are important to the ongoing performance of their departments and that can be learned by other employees. Employees will need to learn new skills that will make them more valuable to their organizations. Cross-trained employees will be called on to assume additional responsibilities.

In formulating an employee development program, supervisors should seek answers to the following questions:[5]

1. Who, if anyone, needs training?
2. What training do they need?

3. What are the purposes of the training?
4. What are the instructional objectives that need to be incorporated into the training program? (Instructional objectives are basically what the employee will know or be able to do upon completion of the training.)
5. What training and development programs best meet the instructional objectives?
6. What are the anticipated benefits to be derived from the training?
7. What will the program cost?
8. When and where will the training take place?
9. Who will conduct the training?
10. How will the training effort be evaluated?

Efficient and effective training should contribute to the achievement of organizational objectives. Development of instructional objectives is essential to the formulation of an evaluation plan. Training and development expert Donald Kirkpatrick formulated four levels of evaluation that can be used to measure the benefits of training: (1) employees' reactions to the training program, (2) their learning, (3) their application of learning to the job, and (4) the training's business results.[6] An illustration of how one company makes training pay is found in the "Contemporary Issue" box in this chapter.

Supervisory Training and Career Development

The need for training and development is not limited to departmental employees. Supervisors also need training and development to avoid obsolescence or status-quo thinking. By expanding their own perspectives, supervisors are more likely to encourage employees to improve their knowledge and abilities and to keep up to date.

Most supervisors will probably attend a number of supervisory management training and development programs, as well as courses in technical aspects of company and departmental operations. Supervisors may want to belong to one or more professional or technical associations whose members meet periodically to discuss problems and topics of current interest and share common experiences. In addition, they should subscribe to technical and managerial publications and read articles of professional interest.

Supervisors also should give some thought to their own long-term career development. The ambitious supervisor will find it helpful to formulate a career plan, writing down definite goals he or she would like to achieve during the next 5 to 10 years. Such a plan includes both a preferred pattern of future assignments and job positions and a listing of educational and training activities that will be needed as part of career progression.[7]

Some companies expect their supervisors to periodically indicate their personal training and development needs and objectives on an official company form. This is particularly true if the company uses management by objectives (MBO), as discussed in Chapter 7.

CONTEMPORARY ISSUE
Does Training Pay? The Motorola Experience

Total corporate dedication to key quality initiatives led Motorola to become the first Malcolm Baldrige Award winner. Some of the best training takes place at Motorola. Its factory workers study the fundamentals of computer-aided design, robotics, and customized manufacturing not solely by reading manuals or attending lectures, but by inventing and building their own plastic knickknacks as well. The company runs its worldwide training programs from Motorola University, a collection of computer-equipped classrooms and laboratories at corporate headquarters in Schaumburg, Illinois. In 1992, Motorola University, which includes regional campuses in Phoenix and Austin, Texas, delivered 102,000 days of training to employees, suppliers, and customers.

The school relies on a cadre of outside consultants—engineers, scientists, and former managers—to teach most of its courses. Their role is to prod, guide, and orchestrate, not to pontificate. In a class on reducing manufacturing-cycle time, for example, senior managers break into teams to devise new ways to get a product to market faster.

While most organizations purport that employees are their most valuable resource, Motorola demonstrates it by spending 3.6 percent of payroll on education. This is more than twice as much as the goal of 1.5 percent that President Clinton advocated during his campaign. Motorola calculates that every $1 it spends on training delivers $30 in productivity gains within three years. Since 1987 the company has cut costs by $3.3 billion—not by decreasing the size of the workforce, but by training its employees to simplify processes and reduce waste. Sales per employee have doubled in the past five years, and profits have increased by 47 percent.

William Wiggenhorn, president of Motorola University, stated: "When you buy a piece of equipment, you set aside a percentage for maintenance. Shouldn't you do the same for people?"

Source: Ronald Henkoff, "Companies That Train Best," *Fortune* (March 22, 1993), pp. 62–74.

PROMOTING EMPLOYEES

3 Identify why organizations should apply a policy of promotion from within whenever possible.

Given the proper encouragement, many employees strive to improve their performance and eventually be promoted. A promotion usually means advancement to a job with more responsibility, more privileges, higher status, greater potential, and higher pay.

Although the majority of employees want to improve or advance, this is not true of everyone. Some employees have no desire to advance any further. They may feel that an increase in responsibility would demand too much of their time and energy—which they prefer to devote to other interests—or they may be content with their security in their present positions. But employees who do not want to improve or advance tend to be in the minority. Most employees want promotions. For them, starting at the bottom and rising in status and income over time is part of a normal way of life.

Promotion from Within

Most organizations have policies for promoting employees. The policy of promotion from within is widely practiced, and it is important to both an organization and its employees. For the organization, it means a steady source of trained personnel for higher positions; for employees, it is a major incentive to perform better. If employees have worked for an organization for a long time, more is usually known about them than even the best selection processes and interviews could reveal about outside applicants for the same job. Supervisors should know their own people well, but they do not know individuals hired from the outside until those individuals have worked for them awhile.

Occasionally a supervisor might want to bypass an employee for promotion because the productivity of the department would suffer until a replacement had been found and trained. This kind of thinking is short sighted. It is better for the organization in the long run to have the best-qualified people in high positions, where they can make the greatest contribution to the organization's success.

Similarly, there would be little reason for employees to improve themselves if they believed that the better and higher-paying jobs were reserved for outsiders. Additional job satisfaction results when employees know that stronger efforts on their part may lead to more interesting and challenging work, higher pay and status, and better working conditions. Most employees are better motivated if they see a link between excellent performance and promotion.

In considering promotion for an employee, the supervisor should recognize that what management considers a promotion may not always be perceived as such by the employee. For example, an engineer may believe that a promotion to administrative work is a hardship, not an advancement. The engineer may feel that administrative activities are less interesting or more difficult than technical duties and may be concerned about losing or diluting professional engineering skills. Such an attitude is understandable, and the supervisor should try to suggest promotional opportunities that do not require unacceptable compromises.

Also, the supervisor should be sensitive to employees who appear to be satisfied in their present positions. They may prefer to stay with their fellow employees, and retain responsibilities with which they are familiar and comfortable. These employees should not be pressured by the supervisor to accept higher-level positions. However, if the supervisor believes that such an employee has excellent qualifications for promotion, the supervisor should offer encouragement and counsel which may make a promotion attractive to the employee for either current or future consideration.

Modifying a Promotion-from-Within Policy

Generally, it is preferable to apply a policy of promotion from within whenever possible. However, situations will arise in which strict adherence to this policy would not be sensible and might even be harmful to a firm. If there are no qualified internal candidates for a position, then someone from the outside has to be recruited. For example, if an experienced computer programmer is needed and no existing employee has programming expertise, the departmental supervisor will have to hire one from outside the organization.

At times, bringing a new employee into a department may be desirable, since this person brings different ideas and fresh perspectives to the job. Another reason for recruiting employees from the outside is that an organization may not be in a position to train its own employees in the necessary skills. A particular position may require long, specialized, or expensive training, and the organization may be unable either to offer or to afford such training. Thus, to cover these types of contingencies, an absolute promotion-from-within policy must be modified as appropriate to the situation. This is why most written policy statements concerning promotion from within include a qualifying clause such as "whenever possible" or "whenever feasible."

Criteria for Promotion from Within

4 Describe the criteria and procedures commonly used for making promotion decisions.

Typically, more employees are interested in being promoted than there are openings available. Since promotions should serve as an incentive for employees to perform better, some supervisors believe that employees who have the best records of production, quality, and cooperation are the ones who should be promoted. In some situations, however, it is difficult to measure such aspects of employee performance accurately or objectively, even when there has been a conscientious effort by supervisors in the form of merit ratings or performance appraisals.

Seniority
An employee's length of service within a department or organization.

Seniority. One easily measured and objective criterion that has been applied extensively in an effort to reduce favoritism and discrimination is seniority. **Seniority** is an employee's length of service within the department or organization. Labor unions have emphasized seniority as a major promotion criterion, and its use is also widespread among organizations that are not unionized and for jobs that are not covered by union agreements. Many supervisors are comfortable with the concept of seniority as a basis for promotion. Some supervisors feel that an employee's loyalty, as expressed by length of service, deserves to be rewarded. Basing promotion on seniority also assumes that an employee's abilities tend to increase with service. Although this assumption is not always accurate, it is likely that with continued service an employee's skills and knowledge do improve. If promotion is to be based largely on seniority, then the initial selection procedure for new employees must be careful, and each new employee should receive considerable training in various positions.

Probably the most serious drawback of using seniority as the major criterion for promotion is that it discourages younger employees—that is, those with less seniority. Younger employees may believe that they cannot advance until they, too, have accumulated years of service on the job. Consequently, they may lose enthusiasm and perform at only an average level, since they feel that no matter what they do, they will not be promoted for a long time. Another serious drawback is that the best performer is not always the most senior. If seniority is the only criterion, then there is no incentive to perform well. Employees can be promoted for simply sticking around.

Merit and Ability. Although labor unions have stressed the seniority criterion in promotion, seniority alone does not guarantee that an individual either deserves promotion or is capable of advancing to a higher-level job. In fact, some employees with high seniority may lack the necessary educational or skill levels needed for advancement. Consequently, most unions understand that length of service cannot be the only criterion for promotion. They agree that promotion should be based on seniority combined with merit and ability, and this type of provision is included in many union contracts.

Merit
The quality of an employee's job performance.

Ability
An employee's potential to perform assigned tasks.

Merit usually refers to the quality of an employee's job performance. **Ability** means an employee's capability or potential to perform, or to be trained to perform, a higher-level job. Supervisors often are in the best position to determine the degree to which merit and ability are necessary to compensate for less seniority. However, seniority is frequently the decisive criterion when merit and ability are relatively equal among several candidates seeking a promotion.

Balancing the Criteria. Good supervisory practice attempts to attain a workable balance between the concepts of merit and ability on the one hand and seniority on the other. In selecting from among the most qualified candidates available, the supervisor may decide to choose essentially on the basis of seniority. Or, the supervisor may decide that, to be promoted, the employee who is most capable but who has less seniority will have to be far better than those with more seniority. Otherwise, the supervisor will promote the qualified employee with the greatest seniority, at least on a trial basis.

Because promotion decisions can have great significance, the preferred solution would be to apply all criteria equally. However, promotion decisions often involve so-called "gray" areas or subjective considerations that can lead rejected employees to be dissatisfied and file grievances. Realistically, unless there are unusual circumstances involved, it is unlikely that a supervisor will choose to promote an employee over other eligible candidates solely on the basis of merit and ability, without giving some thought to seniority.

THE SUPERVISOR'S ROLE IN COMPENSATION

5 Discuss the supervisor's role in employee compensation and outline the goals of an effective compensation program.

Although it is not always recognized as such, a supervisor's staffing function includes helping to determine the relative worth of a job. Typically, of course, wage rates and salary schedules are formulated by higher-level management, by the human resources department, by union contract, or by government legislation or regulation. In this respect, the supervisor's authority is limited. Nevertheless, within such limitations the supervisor is responsible for determining appropriate compensation for departmental employees.

The question of how much to pay employees has posed a problem for many companies. It is possible, however, to establish a compensation program that is objective, fair, and relatively easy to administer. The objectives of a compensation program should be to:

- Eliminate pay inequities to minimize dissatisfaction and complaints among employees.
- Establish and/or maintain sufficiently attractive pay rates so that qualified employees are attracted to and retained by the company.
- Conduct periodic employee merit ratings to provide the basis for comparative performance rewards.
- Control labor costs with respect to gains in productivity and government economic or social legislation.
- Reward employees for outstanding performance or the acquisition of additional skills or knowledge.

Every supervisor has some responsibility in establishing standards for compensation that will attract and retain competent employees. Too often wage rate schedules simply follow historical patterns, or they are formulated haphazardly. At the departmental level, wage rate inequities often develop over time due to changes in jobs, changes in personnel, and different supervisors who use varying standards for administering compensation. However, when inequitable wage situations arise, they should not be tolerated. It is part of the supervisor's role to make sure that wages paid in the department are properly aligned both externally and internally.

External Wage Alignment and Compensation Surveys

External wage alignment means that the wages offered for a job compare favorably with going rates for similar jobs at other firms in the community. In effect, firms compete with each other for skilled workers. If wages within the present compensation structure are not externally aligned, the supervisor can expect eventually to lose some competent employees and to experience difficulty in attracting adequate replacements. Of course, external wage alignment implies that a firm's compensation policies are in accord with state and federal laws governing minimum wages, overtime hours, overtime premiums, and the like. These considerations usually are handled by the human resources department, although supervisors, too, should be informed about them and their application to departmental jobs.

To determine whether the compensation rates offered by a department are comparable to those of similar jobs in the area, the supervisor should request the human resources department to gather information from compensation surveys. These surveys provide data on wages and salaries paid by other organizations for similar jobs within an area, as, for example, a wage and salary survey of all retail department store clerks in the area. Normally wage and salary information can be obtained readily from governmental, trade, industrial, or local associations. A comparison of the wages paid at other establishments for similar jobs is vital to the supervisor in determining whether departmental wages are properly aligned externally. At the least, the supervisor may wish to scan the "Help Wanted" section of a local newspaper to get some general idea of the range of wages and salaries that other organizations are offering for various jobs.

Internal Wage Alignment and Job Evaluation

Internal wage alignment means that jobs within a department are paid according to what they are worth relative to each other. Unless there are extreme differences, most employees do not become as upset about questionable external wage alignment as they do about poor internal wage alignment. In part, this is because employees may not really understand how to compare their compensation with wages in other firms. But employees do have a good idea of the relative values of jobs within their own immediate working areas. They are more likely to become disturbed if jobs requiring less skill in the department (or in nearby departments) pay more than their own jobs, which involve more difficult work. Because poor internal wage alignment can lower employee morale, it is important that supervisors eliminate inequities in departmental pay rates.

Job evaluation

The formal process of determining the relative worth of a job.

In order to establish pay scales for jobs within a department according to what the jobs are relatively worth, it is necessary for the human resources staff, an outside consultant, or someone in management to conduct a job evaluation. **Job evaluation** is the formal process of determining the relative worth of a job. It involves rating jobs according to various factors upon which an appropriate wage rate schedule can be based. The procedure is used to answer questions such as the following: Will secretaries be paid more than data entry clerks? If so, how much more? Will computer technicians be paid more than secretaries, or should both groups receive the same pay? Job evaluation is the basis on which these decisions are made. If it has not been done recently, say, within a year or so, the supervisor should request the human resources staff to undertake or assist in a job evaluation for the department.

There are several job evaluation techniques. Among the most frequently used techniques are the following:

- Job ranking: comparing one job against another. This is the system most commonly used in smaller organizations. Jobs are ranked from the simplest to the most challenging. For pay purposes, there is no assurance that the differences between jobs are equal.
- Classification system: comparing a job against an objective or standard and placing it into its proper classification. Groups of jobs are evaluated on their level of difficulty.
- Point rating and factor comparison: quantitative approaches for evaluating the relative worth of jobs in an organization. Most job evaluation plans use the point system. Each job is evaluated on various aspects—education, experience, complexity, relationships with others, working conditions, responsibility, physical effort, and so forth—and points are assigned. Because not all aspects of a job are equal, many firms use a weighted point system. In factor comparison, each job is compared against a benchmark of key points.

The supervisor should rely upon the expertise of the human resources department to conduct an evaluation of the relative values of jobs in the department and throughout the organization. If assistance from a human resources department is not available, the supervisor should request higher-level managers to arrange for a job evaluation, perhaps by employing outside consultants who are knowledgeable in this field.[8]

After completion of the job evaluation, the pay-structure process is completed by establishing pay grades, rate ranges, and job classifications. A **pay grade** is a grouping of a variety of jobs that are similar in terms of skill, work responsibility, and effort. Although it is possible for a pay grade to have a single rate of pay, a range of pays is more likely.

Pay grade
Grouping of jobs that
are similar in
requirements into a
pay range.

The Supervisor's Role in Compensation Decisions

Although a sound and equitable compensation structure should be of great concern to everyone in management, it is an area in which supervisors typically have little direct authority. However, supervisors should make an effort to make higher-level managers aware of serious compensation inequities at the departmental level. This can often be done when supervisors make their recommendations for wage and salary adjustments for individual employees.

Recommending Wage Adjustments. Most supervisors make recommendations to the human resources department or higher-level managers for wage and salary adjustments for departmental employees at various time intervals. Unfortunately, too often supervisors automatically recommend full wage increases rather than seriously considering whether each employee deserves such a raise. Here is where employee performance evaluation becomes crucial. If an employee's work has been satisfactory, then the employee deserves the normal increase. But if the employee has performed at an unsatisfactory level, the supervisor should suspend the recommendation for an increase and discuss this decision with the employee. The supervisor might outline specific targets for job improvement that the employee must meet before the supervisor will recommend a wage increase at a future date. If an employee has performed at an outstanding level, the supervisor should not hesitate to recommend a generous, more-than-average wage increase, if this can be done within the current wage structure. Such a tangible reward will encourage the outstanding employee to continue striving for excellence.

Challenges for the Supervisor. The popular press is full of stories about firms asking their employees to make wage and benefit concessions. The concept of pay comparisons is very important. It is common for employees to refer to their own compensation relative to that of others. This becomes a serious motivational problem for the supervisor when the organization has to lower wages or benefits. As mentioned in Chapter 1, increasing numbers of employees are holding more than one job.

Two-tier wage systems and the use of contract employees are additional challenges for the supervisor in trying to maintain a perception of fairness. Increasing numbers of organizations are implementing two-tier wage systems as a means of lowering their labor costs. Simply stated, newly hired employees are paid less than present employees performing the same or similar jobs. The U.S. Postal Service operates under a two-tier wage system, and Ford Motor Company and the United Auto Workers have negotiated such a plan. Unfortunately, lower-paid employees can have feelings of inequity when working under these systems. Regardless of the compensation system used, employees must perceive that the program is fair. The supervisor must understand the total compensation program and be able to answer employee questions.

Pay for Performance. In recent years, many organizations have adopted a number of bonus arrangements to better reward those who perform in a superior fashion. These approaches have collectively been referred to as **pay for performance,** or "variable pay," which is defined as any pay that is given strictly on the basis of achieving employee or corporate performance goals. Among these approaches are special cash awards, bonuses for meeting performance targets, team (departmental) incentive bonuses, profit sharing, and gain sharing for meeting production or cost-saving goals. **Gain-sharing plans** are group incentive plans. Employees share the monetary benefits (gains) of improved productivity, cost reductions, or improvements in quality or customer service. Most plans use an easy-to-understand formula to calculate productivity gains and the resulting bonus. One heralded gain-sharing program is that of the Lincoln Electric Company, which is profiled in Figure 14-3.

Although the specific formulas for pay-for-performance plans reflect the unique characteristics of each firm, supervisors play an important role in their implementation, especially in determining which individuals or work teams are most deserving of special awards. The supervisor must thoroughly understand any pay-for-performance plan that affects his or her department and be able to explain to employees how the plan works in order to provide the incentives and obtain the intended results.[9]

Skill-Based Pay. A **skill-based pay** or knowledge-based pay system rewards employees for acquiring additional skills or knowledge within the same job category. It does not reward the individual employee for the job he or she does. Employees are rotated through a variety of tasks associated with the job until they learn them all. The rewards are based on acquisition and proficiency in new skills, regardless of the employee's length of service.[10] Employees are rewarded in accordance with the number of skills they have mastered. Skill-based pay has become popular as a way to reward employees when promotional opportunities are scarce.

Skill-based pay is most successful in organizations in which a participatory management philosophy prevails. The supervisor is usually the key to the success of a skill-based pay plan. Other attributes of a skill-based pay system are:

1. The need for deep commitment to training to achieve success.
2. The necessary use of job rotation.
3. The fact that the choice of plan is tied to business needs.
4. The support of supervisors.
5. The fact that it is not for every company.[11]

Pay for performance Compensation, other than base wages, that is given for achieving employee or corporate goals.

Gain-sharing plans Group incentive plans that have employees share in the benefits from improved performance.

Skill-based pay System that rewards employees for acquiring new skills or knowledge.

FIGURE 14-3
Example of a Gain-sharing Plan—Lincoln Electric Company

THE LINCOLN ELECTRIC INCENTIVE COMPENSATION PLAN[12]

From humble beginnings in 1906, Lincoln Electric Company has become the world's largest manufacturer of welding equipment. Lincoln employs about 2,700 in the Cleveland, Ohio, area and approximately 600 in factories located outside the United States.

The company claims that its impressive sales stem from an inspired workforce and entrepreneurial management ideas. Employees have responsibility for hiring replacements for their work group. The company basically subcontracts the work to the work group, using past performance and time studies as standards of performance. When these standards are beaten, the employees share generously in the rewards.

Employees work together on productivity committees to explore ways to lower costs and increase profitability. Each employee is rated twice a year by supervisors on four factors—dependability, quality, production output, and ideas and cooperation—and a bonus is calculated accordingly. How well the individual works with others as a team and his or her willingness to share knowledge with others is important in calculating the merit rating. Lincoln implements approximately 50 suggestions per month. Suggestions affect the employee's merit rating.

Lincoln Electric's profits are divided three ways. The company retains a certain percentage for capital improvements and financial security. Stockholders receive a dividend of approximately 6 to 8 percent of book value of company stock. Employees receive their year-end bonus based on all remaining profits.

As a result, the typical worker's take-home pay is about double that for similar jobs in competitive industries. In recent years the annual bonus has ranged from a low of 55 percent to a high of 115 percent of an employee's annual wage. Lincoln employees must pay for their own health care insurance. The cost is deducted from the employee's year-end bonus.

In 1992, Lincoln recorded its first-ever net loss. The company could have avoided the loss had it not paid year-end bonuses. CEO Donald Hastings said the bonuses were paid because management did not feel it was right to penalize employees for decisions that management made. In December 1993, 2,700 Lincoln employees split approximately $48 million.

Incentive management by itself may not be the answer to the problems facing U.S. business. The answer may lie in gaining employees' commitment by tapping into their heads and hearts while at the same time providing financial rewards.

For a skill-based pay plan to succeed, the company must require and directly benefit from the skills it pays for. A closed-end questionnaire is used by employees to identify the activities, skills, knowledge, and abilities required by their jobs. All jobs are assigned a pay grade based on the value of their required activities, skills, and knowledge.[13] All employees now know what they must be able to do in order to be eligible for a promotion or a lateral transfer.

Suggestion Plans. In earlier chapters, we discussed the fact that employees may be motivated by the sense of achievement that comes from seeing their ideas implemented. Suggestion plans are one way to solicit employee ideas; typically employees are paid based on the value of their suggestions. Suggestion systems, however, may fail if they are evaluated on the basis of the savings alone.[14]

Employee Benefits. In addition to monetary compensation, most organizations provide supplementary benefits for employees, such as vacations with pay, holidays, retirement plans, insurance and health programs, tuition-aid programs, and numerous other services. On the average, the additional cost of supplementary benefits—often called "fringe benefits"—is between 30 and 40 percent of wages and salaries paid to manufacturing employees. Percentages for service and office workers are usually less.[15] In general, benefits are considered part of an employee's overall compensation, and they, too, are provided to stimulate employee motivation and job performance. Most supplementary benefits are established by higher-level management, by law, and by union contracts. Supervisors have little involvement in establishing benefits, but they are obligated to see that departmental employees understand how their benefits operate and that each employee receives his or her fair share.

When employees have questions about benefits, supervisors should consult with human resources staff or higher-level managers. For example, a supervisor often has to make decisions involving employee benefits, as, for example, in scheduling departmental vacations and work shifts during holidays. In these circumstances, the supervisor must be sure that what is done at the departmental level is consistent with the organization's overall policies, as well as with laws, union contract provisions, and the like.

In recent years, many companies have made numerous changes in their benefit programs. Employee stock ownership plans, changes in medical and hospitalization plans, certain forms of child-care support, and other innovations are widespread. Some companies have adopted a **cafeteria** or **flexible benefit plan,** in which employees are permitted to choose—within cost and other limits—which benefits they will receive.[16] Again, supervisors should make every effort to stay informed about their firms' benefit programs and should consult the human resources or benefits office when questions arise. Moreover, supervisors should permit and even encourage employees to visit the human resources department—or the appropriate manager—for advice and assistance concerning benefits. This is particularly desirable when individual employees have personal problems or questions about sensitive areas such as medical and other health benefits and retirement and insurance programs.

Cafeteria (flexible) benefit plan
System that allows employees some choice in determining their benefits.

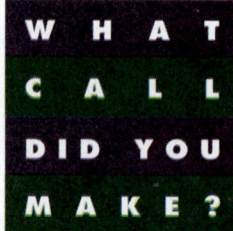 WHAT CALL DID YOU MAKE?

The popular press extols the virtues of being the best in whatever you do. You, as Charlotte Kelly, administrative services supervisor in the "You Make the Call" opening situation, realize that improvements in the quality of patient care are the result of commitment by all employees and health care providers throughout the hospital to provide the highest-quality experience to patients.

Even though the chapter only briefly discussed evaluation of training programs, you should recognize the need to develop a way to measure the effectiveness of your training and development activities. Your proactive leadership has had a positive impact on your employees. When hiring new employees, you should establish as selection standards commitment to patient quality and willingness to become cross-functionally trained. You appear to make sure that each employee—new or experienced—fully understands the importance of his or her job. If you haven't done so, you should develop an orientation checklist that includes the behaviors you want to perpetuate. You identified Aimee as an employee who can model the desired behavior for other employees.

You can use the 10 questions posed in this chapter as your guide for future training. Once you identify additional training needs, you can arrange on-site and/or off-site training programs. If you have not done so, you may want to develop a formal suggestion program to elicit additional employee ideas.

You recognize that employees should be promoted and rewarded, in part, on the basis of their performance gains and skills acquired. They can be promoted and rewarded for teaching skills to other employees. You have investigated various skill-based pay or gain-sharing systems and made recommendations to Ahmed Riaz, your immediate supervisor. You understand that in lean times employees may not have many opportunities for promotion into higher pay grades. Thus, a skill-based pay system should be explored. In the event that hospital revenues decrease, a gain-sharing program could be developed to reward employees.

You should take pride that your employees view you with confidence and pride. You epitomize excellence as a supervisor and should serve as a role model for others. You are to be commended.

SUMMARY

1 Identify the characteristics of an effective orientation program.

Effective orientation of new employees is a top supervisory responsibility. Orientation means helping new employees become acquainted with the organization and understand what is expected in the way of job duties. An orientation checklist can ensure that each new employee receives the same information. In most large organizations, the human resources department helps the supervisor with orientation. Effective orientation programs avoid information overload and generally look at orientation as a process rather than just the first day on the job. The supervisor's supportive attitude and the involvement of other employees is critical. Effective orientation shapes the new employee's behavior in a positive manner. Positive role models, coaches, or mentors should be used to perpetuate excellent performance standards.

2 Explain approaches to training and the supervisor's role in employee development.

On-the-job training is one of the supervisor's major responsibilities. When a supervisor lacks the time or technical skills to do the training personally, she or he can delegate the task to an excellent-performing, experienced employee. Off-the-job training programs can also help employees perform better. Training and development is a continual process, not just a one-time effort.

Supervisors need to determine the skills employees need to do their jobs better. Factors such as failure to meet organizational objectives, operating problems, introduction of new machines and equipment, addition of new job responsibilities to a position, and the like can help the supervisor pinpoint training needs. The supervisor should constantly monitor who needs training and what training each person needs. Development of instructional objectives and a procedure for evaluating the effectiveness of training are critical.

Also, supervisors must recognize the need for their own training and development, and they should utilize whatever opportunities for career development are available to them. Supervisors should also consider having career plans to help them chart and monitor their long-term career progression.

3 Identify why organizations should apply a policy of promotion from within whenever possible.

Most employees want to improve and advance in the organization. Promotion from within is a widely practiced personnel policy that is beneficial to the organization and to the morale of employees. Supervisors know their employees' strengths and abilities; they do not know as much about individuals hired from the outside. If employees know that they have a good chance of advancement, they will have an incentive to improve their job performance. In short, promotion from within rewards employees for their good performance and serves notice to other employees that good performance will lead to advancement.

Strict adherence to a promotion-from-within policy would not be sensible. If internal employees have not received the necessary training, an external candidate may be preferred. Sometimes, an outsider may be needed to inject new and different ideas. However, organizations should promote from within whenever possible.

4 Describe the criteria and procedures commonly used for making promotion decisions.

Since promotions should serve as an incentive for employees to perform better, it is generally believed that employees who have the best performance records should be promoted. Nevertheless, seniority still serves as a basis for many promotions. Seniority is easily understood and withstands charges of favoritism and discrimination. However, a promotional system based solely on seniority removes the incentive for junior employees who want to advance. Although it is difficult to specify exactly what should be the basis for employee promotion, there should be appropriate consideration of ability and merit on the one hand and length of service on the other.

5 Discuss the supervisor's role in employee compensation and outline the goals of an effective compensation program.

The supervisor's staffing function includes making certain that employees of a department are properly compensated. Many compensation considerations are not within the direct domain of a supervisor. Nevertheless, the supervisor should attempt to ascertain whether departmental wages are in reasonable external alignment. Even more important, a supervisor should make certain that job evaluations are conducted to ensure a proper internal wage alignment.

Tangible monetary rewards serve, in part, to meet the needs of employees who perform at an outstanding level. Supervisors must become aware of other compensation arrangements that may better meet their employees' needs. Pay for performance, skill-based pay, suggestion systems, and other benefit plans could be considered.

Since supervisory responsibility and authority are limited in these areas, supervisors should work closely with the human resources staff to maintain equitable compensation offerings and to ensure that departmental employees are informed and fairly treated in regard to benefits and any bonus plans that may be available.

KEY TERMS

Orientation (page 367)

Mentoring (page 370)

Seniority (page 377)

Merit (page 378)

Ability (page 378)

Job evaluation (page 380)

Pay grade (page 381)

Pay for performance (page 382)

Gain-sharing plans (page 382)

Skill-based pay (page 382)

Cafeteria (flexible) benefit plan (page 384)

QUESTIONS FOR DISCUSSION

1. How is orientation of a new employee related to future performance? Discuss approaches that a supervisor may take in orienting a new employee.

2. What is mentoring? Discuss the advantages and disadvantages from the perspective of the person being mentored.

3. Why is on-the-job training most likely to be the type of training utilized at the departmental level? Enumerate other approaches for training and development that may be available.

4. Why should training programs be evaluated?

5. Discuss the need for supervisors to have their own personal training and development programs. Is a supervisor's long-term career plan more likely to aid in career progression or be a source of frustration and disappointment? Discuss.

6. Why do some firms try to maintain a policy of promotion from within whenever feasible? Do most firms adhere strictly to this policy? Why or why not?

7. Discuss and evaluate the issues related to promotion based on seniority on the one hand and merit and ability on the other. Are there clear guidelines that a supervisor can use to ensure a workable balance between these criteria?

8. Define the concepts of external alignment and internal alignment of wage rates. Which of these is usually of the most concern to the first-line supervisor? Why?

9. Define job evaluation. Discuss the supervisor's role, if any, in a firm's job evaluation program.

10. What are the reasons for success of gain-sharing plans?

SKILLS APPLICATIONS

Skills Application 14-1: The First Day on the Job

1. Ask your favorite professor to reflect back to his or her first day on the job.

2. How was the orientation conducted? Was it effective? Why or why not?

3. Were the expectations clearly stated? Did they accurately reflect what is expected of a college professor?

4. What should the college have done to make orientation a more valuable experience?

5. Compare the results of your investigation with that of another student. What recommendations would you make for the orientation of new faculty?

Skills Application 14-2: Career Planning

Broadly defined, the term "career" means the general course one follows during his or her working life. Students are often asked, "What do you want to be when you grow up?"

1. As students, you can find considerable information and personal assistance about careers in your library, student center, or placement office. If you have a primary area of interest, collect information on careers in that field. (If you are undecided, find information on more than one career that interests you.)

    a. What skills, knowledge, and ability should a supervisor in this field possess?

    b. Write a brief paragraph describing one of your accomplishments.

    c. Put the paragraph aside. Then come back to it later and carefully read it to uncover the specific skills, knowledge, and ability you used in that accomplishment. These are the strengths you have.

    d. Match your skills, knowledge, and ability identified in part (c) with those needed, as identified in part (a). What skills, knowledge, and ability do you need to improve?

    e. What can you do to overcome your shortcomings? Establish a timetable for alleviating one weakness.

2. [Optional skill application for the career field selected in item 1.]

    a. Identify a practitioner in your chosen field.

    b. Ask that person the following questions:

        (1) Why must a supervisor in this field stay current?

        (2) How do you anticipate and plan for change?

        (3) What are the difficulties in accepting constructive criticism?

        (4) How do you keep expanding your inventory of personal skills?

        (5) Have you made a contingency plan for the future?

        (6) Why should someone in this field make use of all available resources to advance?

    c. To be successful, a person should enjoy and value the tasks required by the job. It makes sense, then, for most people to select a line of work that provides such satisfaction. What is there in your chosen field that will provide the satisfaction you desire?

Skills Application 14-3: What Is
The Right Way to Pay Employees?

Most colleges and universities pay employees based on a combination of seniority and merit.

1. Would an incentive system be appropriate for college employees? Why or why not?

2. Brainstorm with a group of your classmates the following:

    a. If an incentive program would be appropriate, should there be more than one plan?

    b. What should be the basis of incentive payments?

    c. What kinds of incentives should be included?

3. Why is it important for employees to be compensated on some basis other than seniority?

4. Compare your responses with those of others. What common views do you have? What are areas of difference? Discuss the basis for your differences.

ENDNOTES

1.   For an expanded discussion of employee orientation, see Arthur W. Sherman, Jr., and George W. Bohlander, *Managing Human Resources* (9th ed., Cincinnati: South-Western Publishing Co., 1992), pp. 207–211. Also see Paul Froiland, "Reproducing Star Performers," Training (Volume 30, Number 9, September 1993), pp. 33–37.

2.   Franklin J. Lunding, "Everyone Who Makes It Has a Mentor," *Harvard Business Review* (July–August 1978), pp. 91–100.

3.   Edwin C. Leonard, Jr., John B. Knight, and John L. Vollmer, "Mentoring: A New Look at an Old 'HRM' Intervention," *Proceedings of the Midwest Society for Human Resources/Industrial Relations* (Chicago: 1994), pp. 229–236.

4.   For an expanded discussion of employee training and development, see Kenneth N. Wexley and Gary P. Latham, *Developing and Training Human Resources in Organizations* (2nd ed.; New York: HarperCollins Publishers, 1991). For a discussion of the role of training in continuous improvement, see Alan G. Robinson and Dean M. Schroeder, "Training, Continuous Improvement, and Human Relations: The U.S. TWI Programs and the Japanese Management Style," *California Management Review* (Volume 35, Number 2, Winter 1993), pp. 35–57.

5.   The questions were adapted from a list introduced in Edwin C. Leonard, Jr., *Assessment of Training Needs* (Chicago: Midwest Intergovernmental Training Committee, U.S. Civil Service Commission, 1975), p. 36.

6.   George Kimmerling, "How Is Training Regarded and Practiced in Top-Ranked U.S. Companies?" *Training and Development* (September 1993), pp. 29–36. For a detailed discussion of training program evaluation, see Donald L. Kirkpatrick, *Evaluating Training Programs* (Washington, D.C.: American Society for Training and Development, 1975); and "Four Steps to Measuring Training Effectiveness," *Personnel Administrator* (November 1983), pp. 57–62.

7.   For an expanded discussion of career development, see Sherman and Bohlander, pp. 237–267.

8.   For an expanded discussion of conducting job evaluations, see Richard Henderson, *Compensation Management* (5th ed.; Englewood Cliffs, N.J.: Prentice-Hall, 1989), pp. 168–207. Also see Mary A. Hopkinson, "After the Merger, Paying for Keeps," *Personnel Journal* (Volume 70, August 1991), pp. 29–31.

9.   A 1989 survey indicated that three-fourths of the major firms surveyed had a variable-pay plan in effect. See "Pegging Payroll to Performance," *Management Review* (September 1989), p. 8; Donald Brookes, "Merit Pay: Does It Help or Hinder Productivity?" Hrfocus (Volume 70, January 1993), p. 13; and Edward J. Ost, "Team-Based Pay: New Wave Strategic Incentives," Sloan Management Review (Volume 31, Spring 1990), pp. 19–27.

10.   Paul M. Schafer and Michael B. Jones, "Skill-based Approaches to Secretarial Pay," *Journal of Compensation and Benefits* (Volume 5, Number 1, July–August 1989), pp. 42–45. See also George E. Ledford, Jr., "Three Case Studies on Skill-based Pay: An Overview," *Compensation Review* (Volume 23, March–April 1991), pp. 11–23; and Richard L. Bunning, "Models for Skill-based Plans," *HR Magazine* (Volume 37, February 1991), pp. 62–64.

11.   Nina Gupta, Timothy P. Schweizer, and Douglas Jenkins, Jr., "Pay-for-Knowledge Compensation Plans: Hypotheses and Survey Results," *Monthly Labor Review* (Volume 110, Number 10, October 1987), pp. 40–43.

12.   Much has been written about the Lincoln Electric Company's successful system. See Carolyn Wiley, "Incentive Plan Pushes Production," *Personnel Journal* (Volume 72, August 1993), pp. 86–91; Charles R. Day, Jr., "It's Elitism, Stupid," *Industry Week* (April 5, 1993), p. 7; Harry Handlin, "The Company Built Upon the Golden Rule: Lincoln Electric," *Journal of Organizational Behavior* (Volume 12, Number 1, 1992), pp. 151–163; Gene Epstein, "Inspire Your Team," *Success* (Volume 36, Number 8, October 1989), p. 12; A. D. Sharplin, "Lincoln Electric's Unique Policies," *Personnel Administrator* (Volume 28, June 1983), pp. 8–10; and James Lincoln, A *New Approach to Industrial Economics* (New York: The Devin-Adair Company, 1961).

13.   R. Bradley Hill, "How to Design a Pay-for-Skills-Used Program," *Journal of Compensation and Benefits* (Volume 9, Number 2, September–October 1993), pp. 32–38.

14.   John Allen, "Suggestion Systems and Problem-Solving: One and the Same," *Quality Circles Journal* (Volume 10, Number 1, March 1987), pp. 2–5.

15.   Employee benefits—in particular, employer-provided health care benefits—have gained much attention in recent years. For a discussion of the importance of supplemental compensation; see Kevin Anderson, "Workers Staying Put for Benefits," *USA Today* (September 27, 1991), p. 4B; and *Compensation Personnel Policy and Practice Series* (Washington, D.C.: The Bureau of National Affairs, Inc., 1993).

16.   For information on flexible benefit programs, see Betty A. Iseri and Robert R. Cangemi, "Flexible Benefits: A Growing Option," *Personnel* (Volume 67, Number 3, March 1990), pp. 30–32; Carolyn A. Baker, "Flex Your Benefits," *Personnel Journal* (Volume 67, Number 5, May 1988), pp. 54–61; and Richard J. Anthony, "A Communication Program Model for Flexible Benefits: Keeping Employees Informed Takes Time, Effort, and Planning," *Personnel Administrator* (June 1986), p. 65.

15

Performance Appraisal and Coaching

LEARNING OBJECTIVES

After studying this chapter, you will be able to:

1 Define performance appraisal and clarify the supervisor's role in the process.

2 Explain how often performance feedback should be provided.

3 Discuss the advantages of a formal performance appraisal system.

4 Explain the concepts and techniques in using a written employee appraisal form.

5 Discuss the process of conducting a sound appraisal meeting.

6 Discuss coaching as a follow-up to performance appraisal.

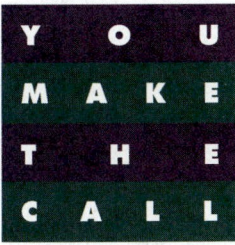

You are Shane Wilson, the distribution center supervisor for Zimmer Wholesale Clubs. All of Zimmer's 36 stores are located east of the Mississippi River. The wholesale club concept of merchandising is very competitive.

You are 42 years old and have been with Zimmer for the past 12 years. When you were promoted to supervisor six years ago, there was no resentment on the part of your employees, because they liked you and realized that you were the best person for the job. The employees still hold tremendous respect for you and your ability to provide the distribution center with positive leadership. There is little possibility for advancement beyond your present position. A lateral move within Zimmer might be possible, but you would hate to uproot your family.

Zimmer has just instituted a formal performance appraisal system. Three weeks from today, you will have to conduct a performance appraisal for all of your employees. You look forward to doing them with one exception—the one for Cheryl Iberra.

Cheryl was promoted to assistant supervisor about two years ago. Cheryl is 33 years old and is regarded as an effective supervisor. She is knowledgeable about the technical aspects of her job. She is a perfectionist about having the work done right. She gets along well with everyone and gets the work done in a timely fashion.

Cheryl will receive her degree from a local college at the end of this term, and you know that she expects to advance in the organization. She is the first person from her family to graduate from college, and she looks forward to the future.

Generally, her employees get the work done in an exceptional manner. She communicates extremely well with all her subordinates. She shares her technical knowledge with them and does a very good job of delegating. However, on occasions, she sides with the employees and openly complains about some of Zimmer's compensation and benefit policies.

Zimmer's sales have not been increasing. People in other area industries have been laid off. Zimmer does not want to lay off people but will reduce employment costs through normal attrition. The consolidation of duties has forced managers and supervisors to find creative solutions to problems and do more with fewer resources. You know that Cheryl's performance stands out above the rest and that she very much wants to become a supervisor. In the near term, there is little likelihood that a position will be open. Even though it appears that supervisory opportunities are in short supply everywhere, you are afraid that Cheryl will leave Zimmer. How will you approach her performance appraisal? **YOU MAKE THE CALL.**

EMPLOYEE PERFORMANCE APPRAISAL

1 Define performance appraisal and clarify the supervisor's role in the process.

Performance appraisal
A systematic assessment of how well employees are performing their jobs, and the communication of that assessment to them.

From the time employees begin their employment with a firm, the supervisor is responsible for evaluating their job performance. **Performance appraisal** is a systematic assessment of how well employees are performing their jobs and the communication of that assessment to them. As discussed in earlier chapters, supervisors establish performance standards or targets that subordinates are expected to achieve. Performance appraisal includes comparing the employee's performance with the standards. Effective supervisors provide their subordinates with day-to-day feedback on performance. Regular feedback on performance is essential to improve employee performance and to provide recognition that will motivate employees to sustain satisfactory performance (see Figure 15-1).

Most organizations also require supervisors to evaluate their employees' performance formally. These evaluations become part of an employee's permanent record and play an important role in management's decisions involving promoting, transferring, retaining, and compensating employees.

Supervisors should approach the appraisal process from the perspective that it is an extension of the planning, organizing, and leading functions. When employees understand what is expected of them and the criteria upon which they will be evaluated, and they believe the process is fairly administered, performance appraisal serves as a powerful motivational tool. While performance appraisals are most frequently used in determining compensation, supervisors also use information from performance appraisals to provide feedback to employees, so that they know where they stand and what they can do to improve performance and develop their full potential.

FIGURE 15-1
The effective
supervisor avoids
these comments by
providing regular
positive feedback on
performance.

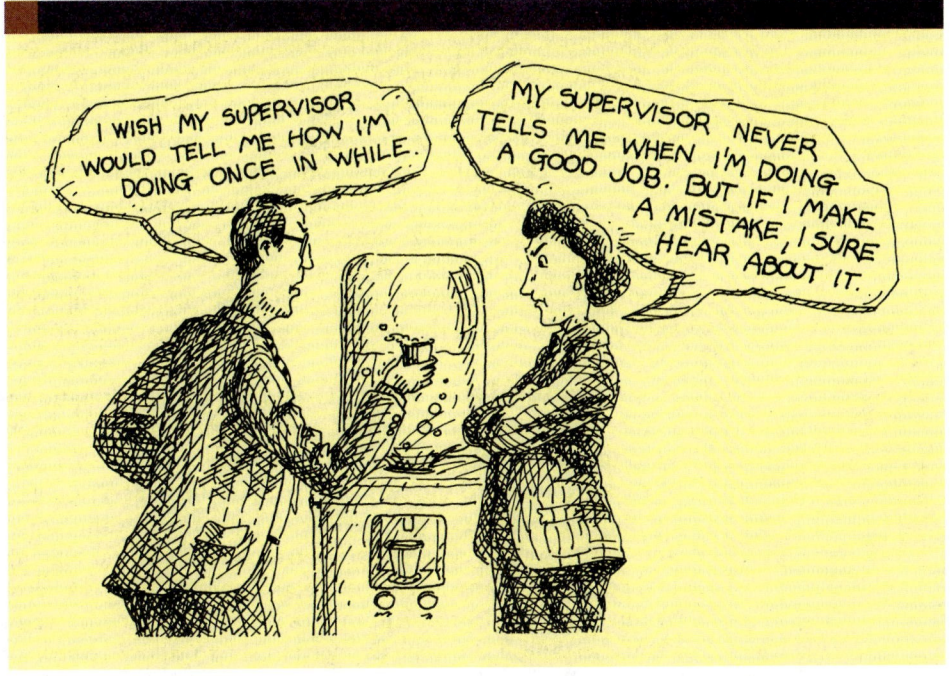

Another reason that supervisors need to keep accurate records of employee performance is to document fulfillment of equal employment opportunity regulations. The importance of documentation of personnel decisions cannot be overemphasized. It is becoming increasingly important for organizations to maintain accurate records to protect themselves against possible charges of discrimination in connection with promotion, compensation, and termination.

Although appraisal of employee performance is a daily, ongoing aspect of the supervisor's job, the focus of this chapter is on the formal system of performance appraisal. The purpose of the formal system is to evaluate, document, and communicate in understandable and objective terms the job achievements and the direct and secondary results of employee effort compared with the job expectations. This is done by taking into consideration factors such as the job description, performance standards, specific objectives, and critical incidents for the evaluation period. The evaluation is based on direct observation of the employee's work over a period of time.[1]

The Supervisor's Responsibility for Performance Appraisal

A performance appraisal should be done by an employee's immediate supervisor, who is usually in the best position to observe and judge how well the employee has performed on the job. There are some situations in which a "consensus" or "pooled" type of appraisal may be done by a group of supervisors. An example of this would be if an employee works for several supervisors because of rotating work-shift schedules, a matrix organizational structure, or for other reasons. Some organizations have implemented work team concepts that expand the supervisor's span of control, and some have become leaner and eliminated middle-level management positions. It is not practical for a supervisor to track the performance of 20, 30, or even 50 workers and evaluate their performance objectively. This restructuring of authority and responsibility could lead to grave inequities in the performance appraisal system. To ensure that employees feel that the appraisal process is fair and just, each evaluator must understand what is necessary for successful job performance and be able to apply the standards uniformly. Supervisors should be trained in the use of the appraisal instrument.

Peer evaluation
The evaluation of an employee's performance by other employees of relatively equal rank.

Peer Evaluations. A **peer evaluation** is the evaluation of an employee's performance by other employees of relatively equal rank. Peers usually have a closer working relationship with each other and are more knowledgeable of an individual's contribution to the team effort than the supervisor. However, safeguards must be built in to ensure that peers are basing their evaluations on performance factors and not on bias, prejudice, or personality conflicts. Having an individual's performance evaluated by a team of peers anonymously is one way to encourage candid evaluation. To protect appraisees from prejudice or vendettas, the organization should establish an appeals mechanism to allow review of ratings by upper-level managers.

Generally, employees work cooperatively to achieve common goals. Consider the situation in which members of work teams evaluate other team members' performance. On one hand, since a peer rating system uses a number of independent judgments, peer evaluations have the potential to be more reliable than supervisory evaluations. But on the other hand, when employees are forced to criticize their teammates via the performance appraisal system, their appraisals could have undesirable consequences for the cooperative culture and defeat the purposes of teamwork. Imagine what could happen to morale and esprit among team members when one worker gets a low evaluation from an unknown co-worker and wonders who was responsible. To safeguard the peer rating process, supervisors can incorporate the input from all peers into a single composite evaluation. Thus, ratings that may be high because of friendship or low due to bias will cancel each other out. Safeguards to ensure confidentiality and minimize the potentiality of bias are critical to the effective use of peer evaluations.[2]

As the concepts of total quality management and self-directed work teams expand, performance appraisals are expected to take on a different role. Some speculate that appraisals will focus more on the future rather than the past and will include input from a wide variety of sources. John F. Welch, CEO of General Electric, has developed a corporate culture that depends on shared values. Welch has stated that:

When you make a value like teamwork important, you shape behavior. If you can't operate as a team player, no matter how valuable you've been, you really don't belong at GE.

To embed our values, we give our people 360-degree evaluations, with input from superiors, peers, and subordinates. They are the roughest evaluations you can get, because people hear things about themselves they've never heard before.

But they get the input they need, and then have the chance to improve. If they don't improve, they have to go.[3]

Increasing, although still few, numbers of organizations are using some form of 360-degree evaluation. A **360-degree evaluation** is based on evaluative feedback regarding the employee's performance collected from all around the employee—from customers, vendors, supervisors, peers, subordinates, and others. These 360-degree evaluations provide employees with feedback on their ability, skills, knowledge, and job-related effectiveness from sources who see different aspects of their work.[4] This approach provides employees with a complete picture of what they do well and where they need to improve from various perspectives.

Self-Evaluations. Many effective supervisors find it appropriate to supplement their own judgments with self-rating from the subordinate. About a week prior to the scheduled performance review, the employee is given a blank evaluation form to be used as a self-evaluation. Surprisingly, research has revealed that employees usually rate their own work less favorably than do their supervisors.[5] The supervisor compares the two evaluations to make sure to discuss all important performance specifics in the appraisal meeting. As mentioned previously, if the supervisor has provided ongoing feedback to the employee, the employee's self-ratings should be very close to the supervisor's ratings. Widely divergent ratings could mean that the supervisor is not giving enough feedback throughout the year for the employee to have a clear picture of how well he or she is doing. Ideally, in a system of participatory management, the formal appraisal should hold no surprises for the employee.

Regardless of the approach used, the ultimate responsibility for completing the appraisal form and conducting the appraisal meeting lies with the immediate supervisor. If peer evaluations are used, the supervisor must still reconcile the appraisals and communicate the information to the employee. Remember: The formal appraisal meeting takes place at a set time each year and should summarize what the supervisor has discussed with the employee throughout the year.

Timing of Appraisals

Upper-level management decides who should appraise and how often formal appraisals should be done. Most organizations require supervisors to conduct formal appraisals of all employees at least once a year. Traditionally, this has been considered long enough to develop a reasonably accurate record of the employee's performance and short enough to provide current, useful information. However, if an employee has just started or if the employee has been transferred to a new and perhaps more responsible position, it is advisable to conduct an appraisal within the first three to six months.

In the case of an employee who is new to the organization, the supervisor may

---

360-degree evaluation Performance appraisal based on data collected from all around the employee—from customers, vendors, supervisors, peers, subordinates, etc.

2 Explain how often performance feedback should be provided.

have to do an appraisal at the end of the employee's probationary period. This appraisal usually determines whether or not the employee will be retained as a regular employee. The performance evaluation of the probationary employee is critical. Employees are usually on their best behavior during the probationary period, and if their performance is less than acceptable, the organization should not make a long-term commitment to them. Consider the following illustration. A supervisor tolerated a probationary employee whose attendance record was not acceptable. Extensive efforts to develop better attendance habits failed. Even so, the supervisor felt that if the employee was terminated, the position might go unfilled and be lost. The supervisor's theory of "half an employee is better than none" cost the company dearly in the long run. The employee never became a satisfactory performer, and he eventually had to be terminated after the company had invested significantly in his training.

After the probationary period, the timing of appraisals varies. In some organizations, appraisals are done on the anniversary of the date when the employee started; in others, appraisals are done once or twice a year on fixed dates.

Any time an employee exhibits a performance problem during the evaluation period, the supervisor should schedule an immediate meeting with the employee. This meeting should be followed by another formal evaluation within 30 days to review the employee's progress. If the performance deficiency is severe, the supervisor should conduct regular appraisals to completely document the performance deficiency and the supervisor's efforts to help the employee.

As stated before, performance evaluation should be a normal part of the day-to-day relationship between a supervisor and employees. If an employee is given ongoing feedback, then the annual appraisal should contain no surprises. The supervisor who frequently communicates with employees concerning how they are doing will find that the annual appraisal primarily is a matter of reviewing much of what has been discussed during the year. Figure 15-2 illustrates how regular feedback can reduce the natural apprehension surrounding performance appraisals by removing the uncertainty.

Ongoing feedback throughout the year, both positive and negative, rewards good performance and guides improvement. Over time, ongoing feedback, as well as formal appraisals, can become an important influence on employee motivation and morale. Appraisals reaffirm the supervisor's genuine interest in employees' growth and development. Most employees would rather be told how they are doing—even if it involves some criticism—than receive no feedback from their supervisor.

ADVANTAGES OF A FORMAL APPRAISAL SYSTEM

3 Discuss the advantages of a formal performance appraisal system.

A formal appraisal system provides a framework to help the supervisor evaluate performance systematically. It forces the supervisor to scrutinize the work of employees from the standpoint of how well they are meeting previously established standards and to identify areas needing improvement.

FIGURE 15-2
Regular feedback reduces the natural apprehension about appraisals.

Most large firms in the United States use some type of formal appraisal system. Management scholar Douglas McGregor identified the reasons for using performance appraisal systems as follows:

1. Performance appraisals provide systematic judgments to support salary increases, promotions, transfers, layoffs, demotions, and terminations.
2. Performance appraisals are a means of telling subordinates how they are doing and of suggesting needed changes in behavior, attitudes, skills, or job knowledge. They let subordinates know where they stand with the supervisors.
3. Performance appraisals are used as a basis for coaching and counseling of employees by supervisors.[6]

Organizations that view their employees as a long-term asset worthy of development adopt the philosophy that all employees can improve their current level of performance.

Employees have the right to know how well they are doing and what they can do to improve. Most employees want to know what their supervisors think of their work. This desire can stem from different reasons. For example, some employees realize that they are doing a relatively poor job, but they hope that the supervisor is not too critical and they are anxious to be assured of this. Other employees feel that they are doing an outstanding job and want to make certain that the supervisor recognizes and appreciates their services.

Regular formal appraisals can be an important incentive, particularly to employees of a large organization. Many employees feel that due to the size of the organization and the great amount of job specialization, individual employees and their contributions are forgotten. Formal, scheduled appraisals provide employees with some assurance that they are not overlooked and that the supervisor and the organization do know and care about them.

Formal appraisals usually become part of an employee's permanent employment record. These appraisals serve as documents that are likely to be reviewed and even relied on in future decisions concerning promotion, compensation, training, disciplinary action, and even termination. Performance appraisals can generate answers to questions such as the following:

- Who should be promoted to department supervisor when the incumbent retires?
- Who should get merit raises this year?
- What should be the raise differential between employees?
- Who, if anyone, needs training?
- What training do they need?
- I see this behavior has happened before. Does the employee need additional coaching, or is it serious enough for disciplinary action?
- An employee is appealing his termination. Do we have adequate documentation?

A formal appraisal system serves another important purpose. An employee's poor performance and failure to improve may be due in part to the supervisor's inadequate supervision. Thus, a formal appraisal system also provides clues to the supervisor's own performance and may suggest where the supervisor needs to improve.

Even when designed and implemented with the best intentions, performance appraisal systems are often a source of anxiety for employee and supervisor alike. Formal performance appraisal systems can be misused as disciplinary devices rather than being used as constructive feedback aimed at rewarding good performance and helping employees improve. This chapter's "Contemporary Issue" box presents recent refinements that some organizations are using to make appraisals more effective.

4 Explain the concepts and techniques in using a written employee appraisal form.

THE PERFORMANCE APPRAISAL PROCESS

Typically a formal employee performance appraisal by a supervisor involves (a) completing a written appraisal form and (b) conducting an appraisal interview.

CONTEMPORARY ISSUE
How to Make Performance Appraisals More Effective

Various studies indicate that the level of dissatisfaction with current performance appraisal systems is increasing.

POINT: Performance ratings may not be linked to achievement of organizational objectives or business results.

SUGGESTION: Performance Targeting. What an employee has accomplished in the past has limited value for improving future performance. Performance targeting, a concept that embraces an orientation toward the future and a strategic perspective, is one way of improving the process.

Performance targeting shifts the focus from documenting and evaluating an employee's work to assessing the partnership between a subordinate and a supervisor. Supervisors and subordinates share the responsibility for attaining desired results. Working together cooperatively is essential for the achievement of organizational goals. From this viewpoint, it makes little sense to assess performance that occurred as much as 12 months previously. The annual performance appraisal should be replaced by a process that focuses on development rather than evaluation. The supervisor should focus on the employee's future achievement.[1]

POINT: Supervisors need to offer constructive criticism that results in higher job performance.

SUGGESTION: LMVE Program. One author who has studied performance appraisal has suggested that:

one way to improve the evaluation process is through the least-most valuable employee (LMVE) program. The program quantifies the elements of job performance such that employees know how they stack up against their peers. Specific skills and areas of task performance that need improvement are identified. This provides the basis for constructive criticism, training, or coaching. LMVE works by asking supervisors to list the skills and tasks that a given group of employees need to master in order to perform their jobs successfully, and, asking every manager or supervisor who is familiar with the group's work to rank the skills of each employee in the group or department numerically from one to five. Results are then tabulated and employees are told where they stand.[2]

Sources: [1]Arie Halachmi, "From Performance Appraisal to Performance Targeting," *Public Personnel Management* (Volume 22, Number 2, 1993), pp. 323–344. [2]Fred Schlissel, "How to Get the Best from Your Worst Employees," *Human Resources Professional* (Volume 5, Number 3, Winter 1993), pp. 39–41.

Completing a Written Appraisal Form

To facilitate the appraisal process and make it more uniform, most organizations use performance appraisal forms. There are numerous types of forms for employee evaluation. These rating forms are usually prepared by the human resources department with input from employees and supervisors. Once the forms are in place, the human resources department usually trains supervisors and employees in their proper use. Often supervisors are responsible for informing new employees about the performance appraisal process as part of their orientation.

Factors in Measuring Performance. Most forms include factors that serve as criteria for measuring job performance, skills, knowledge, and abilities. The following are some of the factors that most frequently are included on employee appraisal rating forms:

Job knowledge	Job attitude
Quantity of work	Suggestions and ideas
Quality of work	Conduct
Timeliness of output	Cooperation (effectiveness in dealing with others)
Effectiveness in use of resources	
Positive and negative effects of effort	Safety
	Customer service orientation
Ability to learn	Aptitude
Dependability (absenteeism, tardiness, work done on time)	Judgment
	Adaptability
Amount of supervision required (initiative)	Appearance
	Ability to work with others

Regardless of the factors used, they must be relevant to the employee's actual job. Factors that enable the supervisor to make performance evaluations rather than personality judgments should be used whenever possible. For each of these factors, the supervisor may be provided with a "check-the-box" choice or a place to fill in the achievement of the employee. Some appraisal forms offer a series of descriptive sentences, phrases, or adjectives to assist the supervisor in understanding how to judge the rating factors. Generally, the "check-the-box" forms are somewhat easier and less time consuming for supervisors to complete. Ideally, the supervisor must write a narrative to justify the evaluation. There should be no shortcuts to performance appraisal. Supervisors should give it as much time as it needs.

Figure 15-3 is an example of a typical appraisal form. The supervisor reads each item and checks the appropriate box. The supervisor identifies the outstanding aspects of the employee's work as well as specific performance characteristics that need improvement (weaknesses) and suggests several things that might be done to improve performance. The form provides space for additional comments about the various aspects of an employee's performance.

If the system calls for employee self-appraisal, the employee's form is usually identical to the regular appraisal form, except that it is labeled as a self-appraisal. Self-appraisals give employees an opportunity to think about their own specific achievements and to prepare for the appraisal meeting.

Problems with Appraisal Forms. Despite the uncomplicated design of most performance appraisal forms, supervisors encounter a number of problems when filling them out. For one thing, not all raters agree on the meaning of such terms as "exceptional," "very good," "satisfactory," "fair," and "unsatisfactory." Descriptive phrases or sentences added to each of these adjectives are helpful in choosing the level that best describes the employee. Even so, the choice of an appraisal term or level depends mostly on the rater's perceptions, and this may be an inaccurate measure of actual performance.

FIGURE 15-3
A "Check-the-Box"
Type of Performance
Appraisal Form

SANDERS SUPERMARKETS

EMPLOYEE APPRAISAL FORM

Employee's Name: _____

Occupation: _____

The following general definitions apply to each factor rated below.

SATISFACTORY: The employee's performance with respect to a factor meets the full job requirements as the job is defined at the time of rating. A satisfactory rating means good performance. THIS IS THE BASIC STANDARD FOR RATING ANY FACTOR BELOW.

FAIR: The employee's performance with respect to a factor is below the requirements for the job and must improve to be satisfactory.

VERY GOOD: The employee's performance with respect to a factor is beyond the requirements for satisfactory performance for the job.

UNSATISFACTORY: The employee's performance with respect to a factor is deficient enough to justify release from present job unless improvement is made.

EXCEPTIONAL: The employee's performance with respect to a factor is extraordinary, approaching the best possible for the job.

RATE ON FACTORS BELOW	UNSATISFACTORY	FAIR	SATISFACTORY	VERY GOOD	EXCEPTIONAL
PERSONAL EFFICIENCY: Speed and effectiveness in performing duties assigned.	Efficiency too poor to retain in job without improvement.	Efficiency below job requirements in some respects.	Personal efficiency fully satisfies job requirements.	Super efficiency.	Extraordinary degree of personal efficiency.
JOB KNOWLEDGE: Extent of job information and understanding possessed by employee.	Knowledge inadequate to retain in job without improvement.	Lacks some required knowledge.	Knowledge fully satisfies job requirements.	Very well informed on all phases of work.	Extraordinary. Beyond scope which present job can fully utilize.
JUDGMENT: Extent to which decisions and actions are based on sound reasoning and weighing of outcome.	Judgment too poor to retain in job without improvement.	Decisions not entirely adequate to meet demands of job.	Makes good decisions in various situations arising in job.	Superior in determining correct decisions and actions.	Extraordinary. Beyond that which present job can fully utilize.
INITIATIVE: Extent to which employee is a "self-starter" in attaining objectives of job.	Lacks sufficient initiative to retain in job without improvement.	Lacks initiative in some respects.	Exercises full amount of initiative required by the job.	Exercises initiative beyond job requirements.	Extraordinary. Beyond that which present job can fully utilize.
JOB ATTITUDE: Amount of interest and enthusiasm shown in work.	Attitude too poor to retain in job without improvement.	Attitude needs improvement to be satisfactory.	Favorable attitude.	High degree of enthusiasm and interest.	Extraordinary degree of enthusiasm and interest.
DEPENDABILITY: Extent to which employee can be counted on to carry out instructions, be on the job, and fulfill responsibilities.	Too unreliable to retain in job without improvement.	Dependability not fully satisfactory.	Fully satisfies dependability demands of job.	Superior to normal job demands.	Extraordinary dependability in all respects.
OVERALL EVALUATION OF EMPLOYEE PERFORMANCE:	Performance inadequate to retain. in present job.	Does not fully meet requirements of the job.	Good performance. Fully competent.	Superior. Beyond satisfactory fulfillment of job requirements.	Extraordinary. Performance approaching the best possible for the job.

(OVER)

FIGURE 15-3
(continued)

USE THIS ITEM ONLY IF THE EMPLOYEE IS STILL IN THE LEARNING STAGE ON THE JOB

EVALUATION OF TRAINEE PERFORMANCE:	UNSATISFACTORY	FAIR	SATISFACTORY	VERY GOOD	EXCEPTIONAL
Considering the length of time on the job, how do you evaluate the employee's performance so far?	Progress too slow to retain job.	Progressing but not as rapidly as required.	Making good progress.	Progressing very rapidly.	Doing exceptionally well. Outstanding rate of development.
	☐	☐	☐	☐	☐

1. Outstanding abilities and accomplishments.

2. Weaknesses.

Recommendations for Improvement:

3. General remarks concerning employee's performance.

4. Specific suggestions for further development.

Rated by: Date

Reviewed by: Date

TO RATER: Initial and date this space when you have discussed this rating with the employee.

_____
                        SUPERVISOR

*Signature of
Employee _____

*This signature merely verifies that this evaluation has been discussed with the employee, and it does not express approval or disapproval of the above.

Another problem is that one supervisor may be more severe than another in the appraisal of employees. A supervisor who gives lower ratings than other supervisors for the same performance is likely to damage the morale of employees, who feel they have been judged unfairly. One such supervisor stated that since no one is perfect, no one should ever be evaluated above average. Another supervisor felt that if he rated his employees too highly, someone would consider them for a promotion elsewhere in the organization and they would be lost to his department. Since he did not want to lose his people, he rated their performance much lower than it actually was. In the long run, the supervisor lost the employees' trust and respect and/or lost them to other firms.

Leniency error
Supervisors give employees higher ratings than they deserve.

On the other hand, some supervisors tend to be overly generous or lenient in their ratings.[7] The **leniency error** occurs when supervisors give employees higher ratings than they deserve. Some supervisors give high ratings because they believe that poor evaluations may reflect negatively on their own performance, suggesting that they have not been able to elicit good performance from the employees. Other supervisors do not give low ratings because they are afraid that they will antagonize the employees and thus make them less cooperative. Some supervisors are so eager to be liked by their employees that they give out only high ratings, even when such ratings are undeserved.

Supervisors also should be aware of the problem of the "halo effect" or "horns effect" (described in Chapter 13), which causes a rating on one factor to result in similar ratings on other factors. One way to avoid the halo or horns effect is for the supervisor to rate all employees on only one factor at a time and then go on to the next factor for all employees, and so on. This suggestion works only if the supervisor is rating several employees at the same time. If that is not the case, then the supervisor should pause and ask, "How does this employee compare on this factor with other employees?" The supervisor must rate each employee in relation either to a standard or to another employee on each factor.

The supervisor should ask what conditions exist when the job is done well. These conditions are performance standards. They should be described in terms of "how much," "how well," "when," and "in what manner." Effectiveness and efficiency measures are part of these standards. The positive and negative effects of performance should also be considered. Consider, for example, the most prolific salesperson in a store. His product knowledge and selling ability are second to none. However, he always expects the cashiers to set other orders aside and ring up his sales first. The cashiers are frustrated, and the other salespeople are not as able to give good service. In addition, he always has the stockroom personnel running errands for him. The salesperson receives accolades on selling, but every one of his sales is a rush project, and others are expected to juggle their schedules to accommodate him. While the salesperson is proficient in his own job performance, in the process of getting his job done, he creates negative impacts elsewhere in the organization. The supervisor needs to broaden the performance standards to include more than product knowledge and selling.

Appraisal Should Be Job Based. Every appraisal should be made within the context of each employee's particular job, and every rating should be based on the total performance of the employee. It would be unfair to appraise an employee on the basis of one assignment that had been done recently, done particularly well, or done very poorly. Random impressions should not influence a supervisor's judgment. The appraisal should be based on an employee's total record for the appraisal period. All relevant factors need to be considered. Moreover, the supervisor must continuously strive to exclude personal biases for or against individuals, which can be a serious pitfall in appraisal.

Although results of performance appraisal are by no means perfect, they can be fairly objective and serve as a positive force in influencing an employee's future performance.

The Appraisal Meeting

5 Discuss the process of conducting a sound appraisal meeting.

The second major part of the appraisal process is the evaluation or appraisal meeting. After the supervisor has completed the rating form, she or he arranges a time to meet with the employee to review the ratings. Since this meeting is the most vital part of the appraisal process, the supervisor should develop a general plan for carrying out the appraisal discussion. If poorly handled, this meeting can lead to considerable resentment and misunderstanding. The conflict that develops may not be repairable.

Unfortunately, some supervisors shy away from the appraisal meeting. They simply fill out an appraisal form and turn it in to their manager or the human resources department. But the entire appraisal process loses its effectiveness if the appraisal meeting does not take place or is handled poorly. Supervisors who avoid the meeting may rationalize that there is no need to discuss annual performance ratings with their employees, since they are in daily contact with them and are always available to discuss problems with them. This, however, is not enough. Supervisors must provide regular feedback and reinforcement for performance.

Employees usually know that appraisal forms will be (or have been) turned in, and they want firsthand reports on how they were evaluated. Employees also may have things on their minds that they do not want to discuss or cannot discuss in everyday contacts with their supervisor. The appraisal meeting gives them the opportunity to discuss such matters.

The Right Purpose. The primary purpose of the appraisal meeting is to let the employee know how he or she is doing. The supervisor formally praises the employee for his or her past and current good performance in the interest of maintaining the employee's good behaviors. The appraisal meeting is also used by the supervisor to help the employee develop good future performance. Emphasizing the strengths on which the employee can build complements the employee's career plans. The supervisor can explain the opportunities for growth that exist within the organization and encourage the employee to develop the skills needed. Finally, the supervisor uses the appraisal meeting to explain past behavior that needs correcting and the need for improvement. Even when improvement is needed, the supervisor

The appraisal meeting is the most important part of the appraisal process, and the supervisor should plan for it carefully.

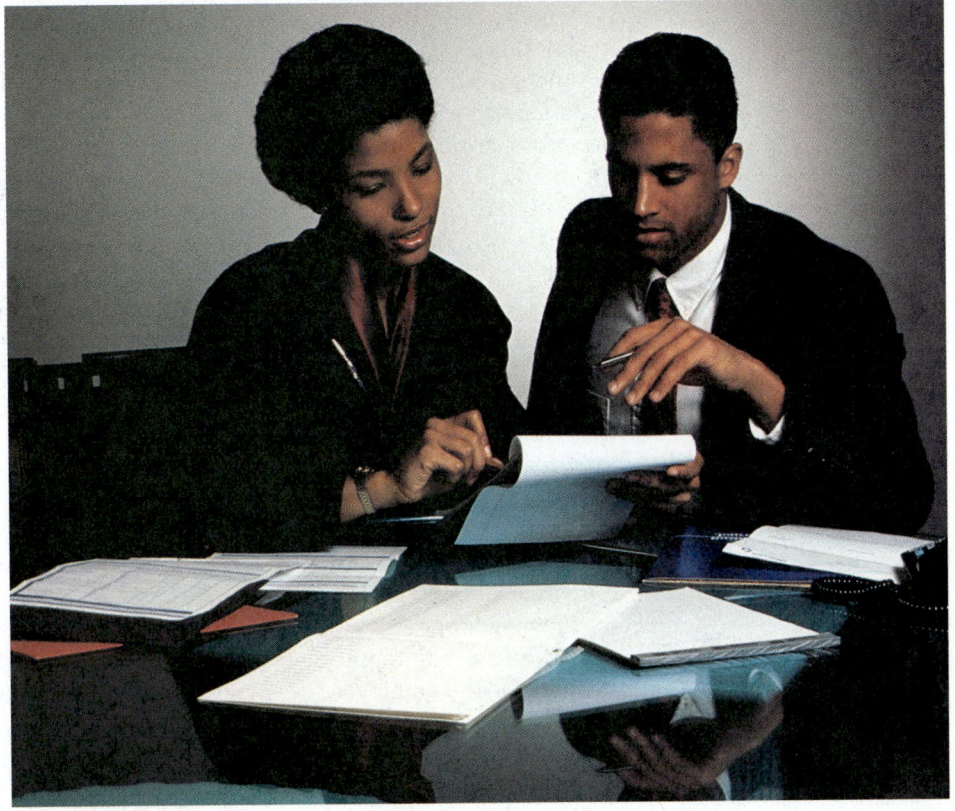

should take the positive approach that he or she believes in the employee's ability to improve and will do everything possible to help. It is important that the supervisor have the right purpose for the appraisal meeting.

The Right Time and Place. Appraisal meetings should be held shortly after the performance rating form has been completed, preferably in a private setting. It is a good idea for the supervisor to complete the rating form several days in advance, and then review it a day or two before the meeting to analyze it objectively and to ensure that it accurately reflects the employee's performance. Privacy and confidentiality should be assured, since this discussion could include criticism, personal feelings, and expressions of opinion.

The supervisor should make the appointment with the employee several days in advance. This enables the employee to be prepared for the appraisal meeting and to consider in advance what he or she would like to discuss.

Conducting the Appraisal Meeting. Most of the discussion of interviewing included in Chapter 13 also applies to the appraisal meeting. Although appraisal meetings tend to be directive, in many situations an appraisal meeting can take on characteristics of a nondirective interview, since the employee may bring up issues that the supervisor did not expect or was not aware of. It is easy for most supervisors to communicate positive aspects of job performance, but it is difficult to communicate major criticisms without generating resentment and defensiveness. There is a limit to how much criticism an individual can absorb in one session. If there is a lot of criticism to impart, dividing the appraisal meeting into several sessions may ease the stress.

The manner in which the supervisor conducts the meeting influences how the employee reacts. After a brief informal opening, the supervisor should state that the purpose of the meeting is to assess the employee's performance in objective terms. During this warm-up period, the supervisor should state that the purpose of the performance appraisal is to congratulate the employee on his or her achievements and to help the employee improve performance, if necessary. The supervisor should review the employee's achievements during the review period, compliment the employee on those accomplishments, identify the employee's strengths, and then proceed to the areas that need improvement. A secret of success is to get the employee to agree upon the strengths that he or she brings to the workplace, because it is easier to build on strengths.

Unfortunately, not every employee performs at the expected level. Limiting criticism to just a few major points, rather than dumping a "laundry list" of minor transgressions on the employee, draws attention to the major areas that need improvement without overwhelming him or her. The supervisor must get the employee to agree upon the areas that need correction or improvement. If there is agreement, then the supervisor and employee can use a problem-solving approach to jointly determine ways that the employee can improve performance. When dealing with an employee who is performing at substandard levels, the supervisor must clearly communicate to the employee that the deficiencies are serious and that substantial improvement must be made. The supervisor should mix in some positive observations so that the employee knows that he or she is doing some things right. The supervisor works with the employee to create an action plan for improvement, with expectations and progress checkpoints along the way. It is important that the employee leave the meeting feeling capable of meeting the expectations.

Performance appraisals have been increasingly scrutinized by the legal system in recent years. It is essential that organizations ensure that their performance appraisal systems are legally defensible. Employees often disagree with negative aspects of the performance appraisal, because the ratings affect their jobs later on. The supervisor must be certain that each employee fully understands the standards of performance that serve as the basis for appraisal. Also, the appraisal must accurately represent the employee's performance and be free of bias. The employee must know that the review is fair, is based on job performance factors, and is supported by proper documentation.

Most mature employees are able to handle deserved, fair criticism. By the same token, those who merit praise want to hear it. Figure 15-4 offers suggestions for relieving the uncertainty of the performance appraisal process.

FIGURE 15-4
Checklist for
Alleviating Fear and
Trembling at
Performance Appraisal
Time

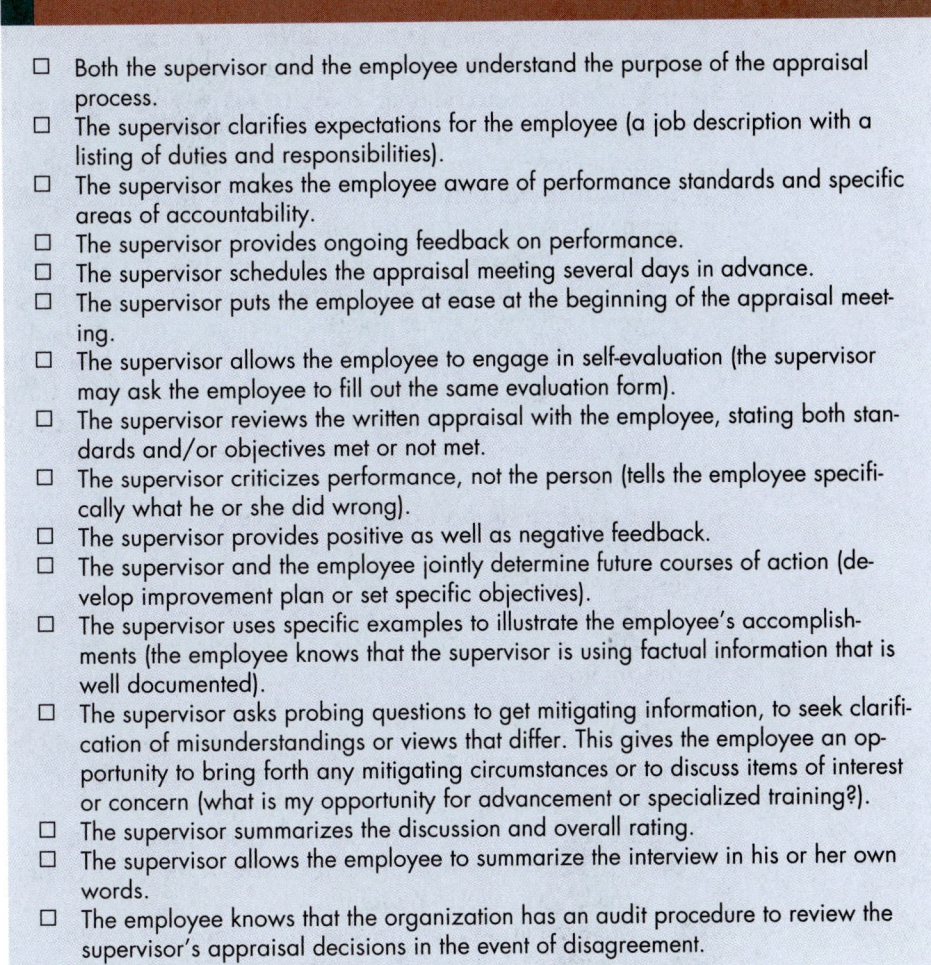

☐ Both the supervisor and the employee understand the purpose of the appraisal process.
☐ The supervisor clarifies expectations for the employee (a job description with a listing of duties and responsibilities).
☐ The supervisor makes the employee aware of performance standards and specific areas of accountability.
☐ The supervisor provides ongoing feedback on performance.
☐ The supervisor schedules the appraisal meeting several days in advance.
☐ The supervisor puts the employee at ease at the beginning of the appraisal meeting.
☐ The supervisor allows the employee to engage in self-evaluation (the supervisor may ask the employee to fill out the same evaluation form).
☐ The supervisor reviews the written appraisal with the employee, stating both standards and/or objectives met or not met.
☐ The supervisor criticizes performance, not the person (tells the employee specifically what he or she did wrong).
☐ The supervisor provides positive as well as negative feedback.
☐ The supervisor and the employee jointly determine future courses of action (develop improvement plan or set specific objectives).
☐ The supervisor uses specific examples to illustrate the employee's accomplishments (the employee knows that the supervisor is using factual information that is well documented).
☐ The supervisor asks probing questions to get mitigating information, to seek clarification of misunderstandings or views that differ. This gives the employee an opportunity to bring forth any mitigating circumstances or to discuss items of interest or concern (what is my opportunity for advancement or specialized training?).
☐ The supervisor summarizes the discussion and overall rating.
☐ The supervisor allows the employee to summarize the interview in his or her own words.
☐ The employee knows that the organization has an audit procedure to review the supervisor's appraisal decisions in the event of disagreement.

During the appraisal meeting, the supervisor should emphasize that everybody in the same job in the same department is evaluated using the same standards and that no one is singled out for special scrutiny. The supervisor must be prepared to support or document ratings by citing specific illustrations and actual instances of good or poor performance. In particular, the supervisor should indicate how the employee performed or behaved in certain situations that were especially crucial or significant to the performance of the department. This is sometimes referred to as the "critical incident method." To use this method, the supervisor must keep a file during the appraisal period of written notes describing situations when employees performed in outstanding fashion and when their work was clearly unsatisfactory. An example of a positive critical incident would be the following. Shortly before closing on October 22, an employee realized that a customer had received an item of lesser value than she had paid for. The employee called the customer to verify that a mistake had been made, apologized for the error, and offered to either credit the customer's account or come to her residence to make the proper exchange. Identification and correction of the problem enabled the store to maintain customer confidence and develop a system to prevent recurrence. When the critical incidents method is used, employees know that the supervisor has a factual record upon which to assess performance.

If the supervisor has chosen to use the employee self-rating approach mentioned earlier, the discussion primarily centers on the differences between the employee's self-ratings and those of the supervisor. This may involve considerable back-and-forth discussion, especially if there are major differences of opinion regarding various parts of the appraisal form. Typically, however, this is not a major difficulty unless the employee has an exaggerated notion of his or her ability or feels that the supervisor's ratings were unjustified. The current spate of downsizing and the shrinking job market may lead to greater disagreement over performance appraisal than in previous years, since there are now more people competing for fewer jobs. Conflict will be particularly likely if the employee perceives that the supervisor's appraisal may jeopardize his or her job.

Regardless of the way the supervisor approaches the meeting, he or she must include a discussion about plans for improvement and possible opportunities for the employee's future. The supervisor should mention any educational or training plans that may be available. The goal of every employer should be to have a better-skilled workforce. This means that the supervisor should be familiar with advancement opportunities open to employees, requirements of future jobs, and each employee's personal ambitions and qualifications. In discussing the future, the supervisor should be careful not to make any promises for training or promotion that are not certain to materialize in the foreseeable future. Making false promises is a quick way to lose credibility.

The evaluation meeting also should provide the employee with an opportunity to ask questions, and the supervisor should answer them as fully as possible. If the supervisor is uncertain about the answer, it is better to say, "I don't know but I'll find out and get back to you with an answer tomorrow." Employees lose trust in supervisors who evade the subject, are not truthful, and do not get back with answers in a timely fashion. In the final analysis, the value of an evaluation meeting depends on the employee's ability to recognize the need for self-improvement and the supervisor's ability to stimulate in the employee a desire to improve. It takes sensitivity and skill for a supervisor to accomplish this, and it is frequently necessary for the supervisor to adapt what is said to each employee's reactions as they surface during the meeting.

Hard Times During the Appraisal Meeting. Many supervisors try to avoid conducting appraisals. They believe the only thing they need to do is to fill out the form. With the increased demands placed on supervisors to do more with less, to increase productivity, and to find ways to continuously improve quality,

FIGURE 15-5
Difficult Responses the
Supervisor May
Encounter

1. "You hired me; therefore, how can I be so bad?"
2. "You're just out to get me!"
3. "You don't like my lifestyle. This has nothing to do with my on-the-job performance."
4. "This evaluation is not fair!"
5. "I didn't know that was important. You never told me that."
6. "Look, my job depends on getting good-quality material from others. I can't turn out quality work because I have to constantly inspect their work first."
7. "You never say anything nice to me. You just make me feel so bad."
8. The employee fails to comprehend what you've said.
9. The employee refuses to talk about it, sits silently by, or fails to respond to your open-ended questions.
10. The employee breaks into tears or rambles off the subject.
11. The employee explodes and vents deep-seated hostilities toward you, his or her spouse, a parent, a co-worker, etc.
12. The employee accuses you of gender, racial, religious, age, or other bias.

many supervisors fail to find adequate time to evaluate the performance of their employees properly. As one manager recently stated, "We don't have time to evaluate around here. As you can see, we're up to our neck in things to do." However, supervisors *must* evaluate their employees' performance.

People react to performance appraisals in different ways. Figure 15-5 lists some of the responses that have been encountered by supervisors conducting performance meetings. Previous discussions regarding communication, interviewing, and conflict resolution should be reviewed for ideas on how to cope with such behaviors. Difficult responses can cause headaches for a supervisor, but they should not cause the supervisor to ignore or short circuit the appraisal process.

Closing the Appraisal Meeting. In closing the appraisal meeting, the supervisor should be certain that the employee has a clear understanding of his or her performance rating. Where applicable, the supervisor and employee should agree on some mutual goals in areas in which the employee needs improvement. The supervisor should set a date with the employee—perhaps in a few months—to discuss progress toward meeting the new goals. This reinforces the supervisor's stated intent to help the employee improve and gives the supervisor an opportunity to praise the employee for progress made.

Many organizations request employees to sign their performance appraisal form after the meeting. If a signature is requested as proof that the supervisor actually held the appraisal meeting, the supervisor should so inform the employee. The supervisor should make sure the employee understands that signing the form does not necessarily indicate agreement with the ratings on the form. Otherwise, the employee may be reluctant to sign the form, especially if he or she disagrees with some of the contents of the appraisal. Some appraisal forms have a line above or below the employee's signature stating that the signature only confirms that the appraisal meeting has taken place, and that the employee does not necessarily agree or disagree with any statements made during the appraisal.

Some organizations require the supervisor to discuss employee appraisals with a manager or the human resources department before the appraisal documents are placed in the individual's permanent employment record. A supervisor may be challenged to justify certain ratings—if, for example, he or she has given very high or very low evaluations to the majority of departmental employees. For the most part, if the supervisor has appraised employees carefully and conscientiously, such challenges will be infrequent.

The employer should have an audit or review process to review supervisors' appraisal decisions. The purposes of this audit are to ensure that evaluations are done fairly and to provide employees with a means of resolving conflicts arising from the appraisal process.

MANAGING THE OUTCOMES OF PERFORMANCE APPRAISAL: COACHING

6 Discuss coaching as a follow-up to performance appraisal.

Coaching
The frequent activity of the supervisor to provide employees with information, instruction, and suggestions relating to their job assignments and performance.

Effective supervisors use periodic performance evaluations as a way to develop their employees' competence. **Coaching** is the frequent activity of the supervisor to provide employees with information, instructions, and suggestions relating to their job assignments and performance. The supervisor must be a coach, a cheerleader, and a facilitator to guide an employee's behaviors toward the desired results.[8] In this role the supervisor must reinforce the employee's positive behaviors and correct the negative behaviors in a positive way.

The supervisor's follow-up role in performance appraisal varies with the assessment. As a rule, supervisors use a coaching approach to help superior employees prepare for greater responsibility as well as to improve the performance of all employees. In both cases, the purpose of coaching is to help the employee become more productive by developing an action plan. Even though a plan may be jointly determined with the employee, the supervisor is ultimately responsible for providing the plan and the necessary instructions for carrying it out. The questions presented in Figure 15-6 may serve as guidelines for the supervisor's coaching effort.

Effective supervisors recognize that ongoing employee skill development is critical to the organization's success. Instruction, practice, and feedback are essential elements of development. Imagine playing golf without first receiving instruction and having a chance to practice the newly learned techniques. Most golfers seek instruction because they want to improve their game. Athletes like Jack Nicklaus, for example, are gifted with fundamental ability; yet they continually seek advice from their coaches.

In business, as in sports, employees benefit from coaching. The coach observes the employee's current performance and communicates what went well and what specifically needs to be done to improve. The plan for improvement usually in-

FIGURE 15-6
Guidelines for
Coaching

The effective supervisor should use the following guidelines to help the employee improve performance.

1. Identify the specific area of performance that needs improvement.
2. Is it worth your time and effort to help the employee improve?
3. Does the employee know that his or her performance needs improvement?
4. Does he or she know what is expected (standards of performance)?
5. Are there barriers beyond the employee's control that influence the current performance?
6. Does the employee know how to do the job?
7. Could the employee do the job if his or her life depended upon it? (If not, then training is necessary.)
8. What happens when the employee does the job well?
9. What do you do when performance is deficient?
10. Have you obtained agreement from the employee that improvement is needed?
11. Have you considered alternative courses of action?
12. Have you and the employee mutually agreed on a course of action to follow?
13. Have you provided information, instruction, and suggestions?
14. What follow-up measures will you use and how will you measure the improvements?
15. How will you reward and reinforce improvement?

cludes defining the expected level of performance, recommending specific steps for improvement, and observing performance. After developing the plan, the coach instructs the employee, allows time to practice the skills, and then observes the employee's performance, providing feedback about the effectiveness of the performance and offering further instruction and encouragement, if needed.

Generally, the employees who benefit most from coaching are the average performers, not the superstars. The former need to develop their skills and learn the fundamentals. The coach must provide constructive feedback on an ongoing basis. Remember, improvement does not occur overnight. Thus, the supervisor should be patient with the employee in the skill development process.

Employee performance usually improves when specific improvement goals are established during the performance appraisal. It is important that the supervisor realize his or her responsibility for improving the performance of a deficient employee. The supervisor must remember that an employee cannot improve performance unless he or she knows exactly what is expected. The supervisor should maintain close contact with the employee and provide instruction when needed. Supervisors also provide suggestions for improvement and serve as mentors. Performance improvements should be supported by positive feedback and reinforcement.

In rare circumstances when the action plan does not result in improved performance and unsatisfactory performance continues, termination may be necessary.

Replacement of an employee is a very expensive proposition. Good coaching can avoid termination in many cases. The role of the supervisor in the positive discipline of less proficient employees is discussed in Chapter 19.

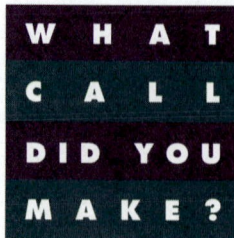

WHAT CALL DID YOU MAKE?

As Shane Wilson, distribution center supervisor for Zimmer Wholesale Clubs, informal appraisals of employees such as Cheryl Iberra have probably been an accepted part of your normal supervisory routine. As an effective supervisor, you provide your employees with frequent feedback on performance.

Zimmer's new system will cause some employees to wonder, "Why are they instituting this system? Will it have something to do with who stays with the organization?" You are well respected by your employees, and to retain that respect, you must have honest answers to any questions that arise during the performance appraisal process. You recognize that the success of Zimmer's newly inaugurated formal appraisal system will depend, in part, on how well you communicate the new system to your employees and how effectively you use it.

Hopefully, Zimmer will have training programs to clarify the new system and discuss the process so that it is employed consistently across and within departments. In communicating the new system to employees, begin by putting yourself in each employee's shoes and try to anticipate the questions he or she might ask you. Try to convey that the formalized system will make it easier for management to make important personnel decisions (e.g., compensation, training, promotion, retention, etc.).

In conducting the formal appraisals, remember to focus on job performance factors. Review the job descriptions, performance standards, and specific objectives that have been previously communicated to your employees. You will want to avoid making any of the various rating errors mentioned in this chapter. Focus on the job the employee is currently doing. Since you have provided your employees with regular feedback on performance, there will be no surprises with the new system. Positive feedback on performance is an effective tool for developing employees. Most of Cheryl's performance is very good. You should focus your attention on those factors. However, it appears that she sometimes displays an "antimanagement" attitude when it comes to company policy and compensation issues. You will need to address this area. If Cheryl believes that several policies are unfair, you can encourage her to develop a proposal and strategy for changing them. She may be correct; the policies might need revision. You want to get her to react in a proactive manner and make suggestions on how they can be changed.

The toughest part of the appraisal meeting will be when Cheryl asks you about the advancement opportunities at Zimmer. Since you have anticipated this question, you will have checked all possibilities with higher-level managers. Above all, you must be honest with Cheryl about the opportunity for advancement. If there are no openings anticipated at Zimmer, you must tell her so. As discussed in the previous chapter, some organizations are adopting a pay-for-skills program when advancement opportunities are limited. You may want to check with management about possibly setting up such a program to help retain good people like Cheryl. On the other hand, you might try to redesign her work in such a way that other rewards become more important than money and title. Certainly, you would hate to lose a good assistant. However, if Cheryl expects to be rewarded with a supervisory position upon completion of her degree and there are none at Zimmer, you might have to resign yourself to the fact that she will be happier working somewhere else.

SUMMARY

1 Define performance appraisal and clarify the supervisor's role in the process.

A formal performance appraisal system is the process of periodically rating an employee's performance against standards and communicating this feedback to the employee. Supervisors are responsible for appraising employee performance both on an informal, day-to-day basis and formally at predetermined intervals. Supervisors need to keep accurate records of employee performance.

To ensure that employees feel that the appraisal process is fair, each evaluator must understand what is necessary for successful job performance. Peer evaluations and 360-degree performance evaluations are ways to provide performance feedback from other perspectives besides the supervisor's, and they can contribute to a more complete performance picture. Including self-rating in the process can facilitate open discussion of an employee's own perceptions of his or her strengths and weaknesses.

2 Explain how often performance feedback should be provided.

Most organizations require formal performance appraisals at least once each year. In addition to formal appraisals, supervisors should provide their employees with frequent feedback on performance throughout the year. Because the decision to retain or not retain a new employee is critical, performance assessment of probationary employees should be done at the end of the probationary period. Anytime there is a performance problem, the supervisor should provide immediate feedback. However, ongoing feedback, both positive and negative, should be a regular part of the supervisor's routine. If the employee is given ongoing feedback, then the annual appraisal should contain no surprises. It should be a review of what the supervisor and employee have discussed during the year.

3 Discuss the advantages of a formal performance appraisal system.

If properly done, formal performance appraisals benefit both the organization and the employee. Organizations use performance appraisals as a basis for making important decisions concerning promotion, raises, terminations, and the like. Performance appraisals reward employees' good performance and inform them about how they can become more productive.

The major advantage of a formal system is that it provides a framework to help the supervisor systematically evaluate performance and communicate to the employees how they are doing. Formal appraisals can be an incentive to employees. They get positive feedback about their performance, and they know that the formal system provides documentation of their performance.

Much of the criticism of performance appraisals dwells on the fact that they often focus only on past accomplishments or deficiencies. Supervisors can overcome this criticism by emphasizing the developmental aspects of performance appraisal.

4 Explain the concepts and techniques in using a written employee appraisal form.

Appraisal forms may vary in format and approach, but they should all allow supervisors to identify the outstanding aspects of the employee's work, specify performance areas that need improvement, and suggest ways to improve performance.

Supervisors should be consistent in applying the terms used to describe an employee's performance. Not all supervisors judge employees' performance accurately, and sometimes a supervisor can damage an employee's morale by giving lower ratings than the employee deserves. Additional perceptual errors include the leniency error, the "halo" and "horns" effects, and other personal biases.

When filling out the appraisal form, the supervisor should focus on the employee's accomplishments. The results should be described in terms of "how much," "how well," and "in what manner." Whatever the choice of appraisal form, it is important that every appraisal be made within the context of the employee's particular job and be based on the employee's total performance.

5 Discuss the process of conducting a sound appraisal meeting.

Although the appraisal meeting may be a trying situation, the entire employee performance appraisal system is of no use if this aspect is ignored or is carried out improperly. The supervisor should begin by stating that the overall purpose of the appraisal meeting is to let the employee know how he or she is doing. The supervisor should give positive strokes for good performance, emphasize strengths that the employee can build upon, and identify performance aspects that need improvement.

The meeting should be conducted shortly after the form is completed, and in private. How the supervisor conducts the meeting depends to a large extent on the employee's performance. Supervisors should direct criticisms to those areas that need correction or improvement. An employee performing at a substandard level must clearly understand that the deficiencies are serious and that substantial improvement is needed. An employee is more likely to agree with the appraisal when he or she understands the standards of performance and recognizes that the appraisal is free of bias.

The supervisor should emphasize that all employees in the same job are evaluated using the same standards and process. Supervisors may use a critical incident method for documenting employee performance that is very good or unsatisfactory. Employees should be given an opportunity to ask questions, and the supervisor should answer them honestly. The supervisor should anticipate questions, potential areas of disagreement, and difficult responses that may arise during the appraisal meeting.

The employee should clearly understand his or her evaluation. New objectives should be set and areas for improvement identified. Generally, the employee is asked to sign the appraisal form to prove that the meeting took place. Organizations should have an audit process to resolve conflicts arising from the appraisal.

6 Discuss coaching as a follow-up to performance appraisal.

All supervisors should fulfill the role of coach in the conduct of their daily activities. During the performance appraisal process, supervisors provide employees with information, instruction, and suggestions relating to their job assignments and performance.

Supervisors can use a coaching approach to prepare superior employees for greater responsibility as well as to improve the performance of all employees. Ongoing employee skill development is essential. Based on the performance appraisal, the coach develops a plan for improvement. Specific improvement goals are set. The employee receives instruction and is given an opportunity to practice. The coach provides feedback and encouragement.

KEY TERMS

Performance appraisal (page 392)
Peer evaluation (page 394)
360-degree evaluation (page 395)

Leniency error (page 403)
Coaching (page 410)

QUESTIONS FOR DISCUSSION

1. Why should supervisors be responsible for performance appraisal?

2. What are the benefits of using peer ratings, 360-degree evaluations, or an employee self-rating approach?

3. What are the major purposes of performance appraisal, and in what ways might they be contradictory?

4. What are some of the factors that most frequently are included on employee performance appraisal forms? Why should most performance appraisal forms include space for supervisors to write comments about the employee being evaluated?

5. How should the organization deal with a supervisor who constantly rates employees much below their deserved outstanding rating? Rates them above their deserved rating?

6. Outline the major aspects of conducting an appraisal meeting. What are some of the major difficulties associated with this meeting?

7. How should supervisors cope with the various employee behaviors they may encounter during appraisal meetings?

8. What can a supervisor do to feel more comfortable in conducting performance appraisals?

9. How would you appraise an above-average performer with high potential for advancement under the following circumstances?

   a. There is a roadblock ahead of the employee that will be with the organization for at least another 12 years.

   b. The organization is downsizing and the employee will be lucky to retain his or her current job.

   c. There are several opportunities for advancement in the organization, but they require either a relocation or substantial overnight travel (both undesirable alternatives from the employee's perspective).

10. Outline a coaching program for an employee who exhibits unsatisfactory behaviors. How will your program meet the needs of both the organization and the employee?

SKILLS APPLICATIONS

Skills Application 15-1: Effective Guidelines for Appraisal

1. Select a person who is currently employed and ask him or her the following questions:

a. Briefly describe the circumstances under which a performance appraisal had positive effects on your morale or development.

b. If you were a supervisor and had to conduct a performance appraisal of your employees, what one thing would you do to ensure that the appraisal has a positive impact on employee morale or development?

2. Compare your findings with those of several classmates. To what extent are your findings comparable?

Skills Application 15-2: Build on Strengths or Deal with Weaknesses

1. Think of the best college professor you have known. Make a list of his or her strengths. Should these become standards for all professors?

2. Think of the college professor you have least preferred. If you were that professor's immediate supervisor, how easy would it be for you to openly discuss performance deficiencies with him or her? Why do you think so?

3. Would it be appropriate to develop a coaching strategy for either of the two professors? Why or why not?

Skills Application 15-3: Role Play Exercise

1. Select a fellow student to play the role of your least-preferred professor. Assume that you are the professor's department chairperson, and briefly conduct a performance appraisal meeting.

2. At the conclusion of the meeting, evaluate your own performance using the following guidelines:

a. Did you state the purpose of the appraisal?

b. Did you inform the professor of the process of the appraisal discussion?

c. Did you put the professor at ease?

d. Did you review performance standards—specifically what is expected in the way of performance?

e. Did you get the professor to engage in self-evaluation?

f. Did you present specific performance examples?

g. Did you focus on the professor's performance, rather than personality?

h. Did you probe for additional information from the professor?

i. Did you provide positive feedback for what the professor does well?

j. Did you clarify specific examples of how and when the professor did not meet standards?

k. Did you leave the professor feeling good about himself or herself and the organization?

l. Did you and the professor develop a specific plan for the future?

3. In what areas of the performance discussion do you need to sharpen your own skills? Identify specific actions you can take to improve.

ENDNOTES

1. For an expanded discussion of performance appraisal, see Arthur W. Sherman, Jr., and George W. Bolander, *Managing Human Resources* (9th ed.; Cincinnati: South-Western Publishing Co.), Chapter 9, for information on various types of appraisal instruments; Robert D. Bretz, Jr., George T. Milkovich, and Walter Read, "The Current State of Performance Appraisal Research and Practice: Concerns, Directions, and Implications," *Journal of Management* (Volume 18, Number 2, June 1992), pp. 321–352; Yitzhak Fried, Robert B. Tiegs, and Alphonso R. Bellamy, "Personal and Interpersonal Predictors of Supervisors' Avoidance of Evaluating Subordinates," *Journal of Applied Psychology* (Volume 77, Number 4, August 1992), pp. 462–468; and Ron Sorenson and Geralyn McClure Franklin, "Teamwork Developed a Successful Appraisal System," *HR Focus* (Volume 69, Number 2, August 1992), pp. 3–4.

2. For a discussion of peer appraisals, see G. M. McEvoy, P. F. Buller, and S. R. Roghaar, "A Jury of One's Peers," *Personnel Administrator* (May 1988), pp. 94–98. For a discussion of the team approach to appraisals, see Carol A. Norman and Robert A. Zawacki, "Team Appraisals—Team Approach," *Personnel Journal* (Volume 70, September 1991), pp. 101–104.

3. Stratford Sherman, "A Master Class in Radical Change," Fortune (December 13, 1993), p. 83.

4. Kenneth M. Nowack, "360-Degree Feedback: The Whole Story," *Training & Development* (January 1993), pp. 69–72. Also, see Catherine Romano, "Fear of Feedback," *Management Review* (December 1993), pp. 38–41.

5. Patricia J. Hewitt, "The Rating Game," *Incentive* (Volume 167, Number 8, August 1993), p. 39–41. Also see Michael Rigg, "Reasons for Removing Employee Evaluations from Management's Control," *Industrial Engineering* (Volume 28, Number 8, August 1992), p. 17.

6. Douglas McGregor, "An Uneasy Look at Performance Appraisal," *Harvard Business Review* (September–October 1972), pp. 133–134. For an expanded discussion on how supervisors can make more effective use of performance appraisals, see Wally Bock, "How Am I Gonna Tell Him?" *Supervisory Management* (March 1993), p. 7; Roger J. and Sandra J. Planchy, "Focus on Results, Not Behavior," *Personnel Journal* (March 1993), p. 28; James McAlister, "Appraisal Interviews: Do's and Don'ts," *Supervisory Management* (April 1993), p. 12; and James Goodale, "Seven Ways to Improve Performance Appraisals," HR Magazine (May 1993), pp. 77–80.

7. Barbara Holmes, "The Lenient Evaluator's Hurting Your Organization," *HR Magazine* (June 1993), pp. 75–77.

8. For an interesting discussion of the supervisor's role as coach, see Bill Halson, "Teaching Supervisors to Coach," *Personnel Management* (March 1990), pp. 36–53; and Roger D. Evered and James C. Selman, "Coaching and the Act of Management," *Organizational Dynamics* (Autumn 1989), pp. 16–31.

CASE 4-1
An Ethical Selection Dilemma

Charles Holmes was a supervisor in charge of pet foods production for a food processing firm located in the southeastern United States. In Holmes's earlier years at the company plant, he had relied on a fellow supervisor, Ellis Duvall, for assistance in learning many aspects of production and quality control and in meeting deadlines. Duvall subsequently became plant manager, and he now was Holmes's immediate boss.

Holmes was facing a difficult dilemma. Ellis Duvall had called, saying that his nephew, Rob Ling, had just graduated from college and was looking for a job. Duvall knew that Holmes's department had an opening for a quality control inspector. Holmes interviewed Rob Ling and found him to be a reasonably intelligent young man, but Ling had absolutely no experience to do the kind of work that Holmes required in an important area. To complicate the matter further, Holmes had found out that Rob Ling's father was a buyer for a large food store chain that was a major customer of the company.

Prior to meeting with Ling, Holmes had interviewed several applicants for the position, who had been referred to him by the human resources department. Three of the applicants were far more qualified than Rob Ling. The best qualified individual was a young woman, Susan Wilson, who had excellent credentials and several years of experience as a quality control inspector. Holmes had almost hired Wilson on the spot, and now he wished he had.

Holmes decided to talk with Arleen Hunter, the human resources manager, about his dilemma. Hunter was not very helpful, stating that "I've seen jobs given as favors over and over again; you have to make up your own mind on this one. However, I would point out that your boss, Ellis Duvall, is on the management review committee, which currently is studying different ways of reducing supervisory and other managerial personnel. I think you've got a difficult choice to make."

As Charles Holmes left Arleen Hunter's office, he primarily wondered whether his job would be eliminated if he failed to hire Rob Ling.

Questions for Discussion

1. Could Charles Holmes lose his job by refusing to hire Rob Ling? Discuss.

2. What alternatives does Holmes have if he doesn't hire Ling?

3. Is it possible to do what's right for the company and what's right for yourself at the same time?

4. If Ling is hired and Susan Wilson discovers what has happened, could she file sex discrimination charges? What is the likelihood that she would win a sex discrimination case?

CASE 4-2
The Stress Interview Approach

Bradley Distributors, Inc., employed 500 employees in its warehouse and retail outlets. Sterling Durbin, the director of human resources, had held this position for the past 17 years. He prided himself on his ability to conduct interviews effectively. When Patricia Sutton was hired as a new assistant human resources manager, Durbin took great pleasure in "breaking in" this recent college graduate on the practical aspects of effective interviewing.

"I can size anyone up in 10 minutes or less in an interview. My record shows how good I am at this, and I'll give you a few tips," Durbin told his new assistant. "We don't use written tests anymore because of EEOC hassles with them. It's just as well, because I didn't put much faith in what those tests showed anyway. As for personal interviews, we use several interviewers for important positions to get the effect of a group interview. All of the interviewers ask the questions that they feel are important, and they report to me anything outstanding or particularly negative that turns up. My interview with a prospective employee is the one that usually counts the most, though. I'm looking for 'hard drivers' and people who I think will succeed around here. In just a few minutes, I can tell by the way they look at me, the kind of clothes they wear, and their general confidence in themselves whether or not they're likely to be good employees. For example, you can tell a lot about a man by the kind of shoes he wears and how well they are polished. Also, I put a lot of stock in whether or not the applicants have finished the education they began, whether it's high school, junior college, or university. It shows that they can finish things and can stick to their tasks."

Durbin continued, "The best technique I've found to separate the poor applicants from those with real promise is to ask them how they would handle the following situation. I give them two alternatives to stop employees from arguing constantly with each other. First, the employees could be told either to work it out
among themselves or to get a transfer out of the department. Second, the supervisor could sit down with the employees and work out the difficulties together.
Whichever approach the applicant picks, I tell them that they are wrong. If they select the first method, I tell them that their job is to develop and help employees to
perform better. If they select the second, I tell them they have more important
things to do than to work out personal problems between employees. By doing
this, I see how applicants handle stress and find out what they're made of. Good
potential employees will stick by their guns and give me some good reasons why
their approach should be followed. With all this information, I can usually make a
good decision in a pretty short time. I've found that I am seldom wrong."

Questions for Discussion

1.   Evaluate Sterling Durbin's interview techniques. What are the strengths and weaknesses of Durbin's system?
2.   Is it possible to do an adequate job of interviewing in so short a time? Discuss.
3.   How valid is the stress aspect of the interview?
4.   What recommendations, if any, would you make to Durbin in regard to his interviewing?
5.   What recommendations, if any, would you make to the new assistant, Patricia Sutton,
concerning whether or not she should adopt the same interviewing approach as that of her
supervisor?

CASE 4-3
From Part Time to Full Time?

Alice Tumser was supervisor of the clerical staff in the medical records department
of a community hospital. She had the authority to hire and fire for her department,
and she was not affected by a union contract since the hospital had no union. She
had seven employees working for her full time. Whenever a regular clerical employee did not show up, she called Helen Drew, who worked as a relief person on
a part-time basis.

Recently, Drew told Tumser that she would like to work full time, since she
needed the income and was now in a position to leave her two small children with
a babysitter. This request came as something of a surprise and a problem to
Tumser. She had observed that whenever Drew came in to help out, there seemed
to be friction. Apparently Drew did not get along well with the rest of the employees, most of whom were young, unmarried people in their early twenties. Tumser
did not know whose fault it was, but there were numerous complaints about Drew

from the other employees. Drew's work was of high quality, however; Tumser was certain of this.

Shortly after Helen Drew had asked to be considered for a permanent position, a full-time job opened up in the department. Alice Tumser pondered whether she should offer this job to Drew. Of course, Drew would be very pleased to get this position, and she knew it was open. But Tumser was concerned about the reaction of the other employees in the department.

Questions for Discussion

1. When considering hiring a full-time employee, which is more important: (a) the work performance of the potential employee or (b) the way the individual will fit in with other employees in the department? Why is there seldom a clear answer to this question?

2. Did Tumser's failure to investigate the prior situation between Helen Drew and the other employees contribute to the current problem? Discuss.

3. Alice Tumser has to make an important decision. Should she seek advice of employees in the department, or is this a decision she must make on her own? What should she do? Consider alternatives.

CASE 4-4
Sanders Supermarkets Store #21: Orientation of a New Employee

Max Brown was one of the most promising young applicants Nancy Brewer had interviewed and hired in months. As the employment manager of Sanders Supermarkets, she had instructed him on company policies, pay periods, rate of pay, and so forth, and had given him information about the union. He then left with his referral slip to report to Store #21, located in a suburban shopping center.

Before Brown went to his new job, he stopped at his favorite clothing store and bought new white shirts to conform with the company dress code described by Brewer. He then went to the barber shop for a haircut, his first since graduating from high school several months ago.

Upon arriving at Store #21, Brown introduced himself to Carl Dressel, the store supervisor. Dressel then told Brown to go over to aisle 3 and tell Sean Kelly, the head stock clerk, that he was to work with him. Brown walked into aisle 3, but no one was there. Not knowing what to do next, he just waited for someone to show up. About 20 minutes later, Kelly came into the aisle with a stock truck full of cases. Brown introduced himself and said, "Mr. Dressel told me to come and work with Sean Kelly. Is that you?"

"Yeah," said Kelly, "I was just going to lunch. Here's my case cutter and stock list. You can figure it out. I'll see you in 30 minutes or so."

Kelly then left the aisle with Max Brown standing there rather confused. "Some training program," he thought to himself. Nancy Brewer had said that there would be lockers in the store for his personal items, but he wondered where they were. Brewer had also told him about punching a time card, so he wondered where the time cards were. Since Kelly had an apron on to protect his clothes, Brown tried to figure out where he could get one, too. He thought he might look in the back room to see whether the answers to some of his questions might be back there. Walking into the back room, he introduced himself to a young woman who said that she was Evita Chavez, one of the store's produce department clerks. Brown asked her whether she knew where he could hang his coat, get a time card, and find an apron. Chavez responded, "For the most part, we just throw our coats on top of the overstock; the aprons are in the office, and so are the time cards."

"At last," thought Brown. "Now I'm getting someplace." On his way to the office, he saw several stock clerks working in aisle 1. He had seen four stock clerks so far, and only one wore a tie. Two had on plaid shirts, and the other had hair at least three inches below the collar. "I don't understand why Nancy Brewer was worried about the way I looked," he thought.

Finally, Brown found an apron and a time card. To find the time clock, he went toward the back room again and asked one of the meat cutters where the time clock was. He was given directions to go through the meat department to the other side of the store. He went through the door he was told to go through, which had a sign on it saying "Authorized Personnel Only." He was worried that he might not be an "authorized" person. He finally found the time clock, and, with a little difficulty, he figured out how to clock in. This done, he hurried back to aisle 3, where Carl Dressel stood waiting for him. "Where the hell have you been?" asked Dressel. "And where is Kelly?"

Brown explained that Kelly had gone to lunch and that he himself had been looking for an apron, the time clock, and a place to hang his coat. "You might as well learn right away that your job is putting up the loads of stock—and fast! I don't want to hear any more excuses. Now get to work," said Dressel.

As Brown started to open the top of the first box of cases, he thought to himself, "The only thing I know for sure right now is that Nancy Brewer has never worked in this store!"

Questions for Discussion

1. Identify and discuss several places where Max Brown's experiences in Store #21 could have been improved by proper orientation.

2. Although Carl Dressel's approach is certainly lacking, could some of the blame for Brown's poor orientation be attributed to Nancy Brewer? Why or why not? Discuss.

3. Outline a checklist or approach for orienting new employees in this type of work environment.

CASE 4-5
Feelings of Demotion

Frank Schneider, plant superintendent of Central Metalworks Co., had just been informed that a young man named Kirk Bell had been hired from outside the firm for the position of vice-president of manufacturing, a job that Schneider very much wanted to have. Bell was in his early thirties and had an undergraduate engineering degree, a master's degree in business administration, and some previous working experience.

Schneider was 50 years old. He had been with this firm for almost 30 years, working his way up from the bottom. Starting as a machine operator, he progressed to the positions of leadman, foreman of various departments, assistant superintendent, and his current job, which he had held for seven years. He had no formal education after finishing high school, but he had a well-recognized talent for machines, tools, and anything associated with manufacturing metal parts. He also had an excellent ability to work with people, and he was well liked and respected by the employees.

When the president of the company, R. D. Allen, told Schneider who his new boss would be, Schneider replied, "I don't know whether I can work for a young man 20 years my junior, especially one who never dirtied his hands fixing or running a piece of machinery. What can a fellow like this possibly know about running a manufacturing plant?"

A few days later, Allen met with Bell in his office. "Kirk," said Allen, "I think you may have a serious problem with Frank Schneider. He's a good man, but his feelings are hurt, and he thinks he's been demoted. What would you propose to do to win him over?"

Questions for Discussion

1. Why would the president of the company choose a young man with an engineering degree and a master's degree in business administration over Schneider, who for seven years has been plant superintendent? Was this a prudent choice?
2. Is Schneider being unreasonable in his attitude toward his new boss? Discuss.
3. How should Bell approach the situation with Schneider? Should Allen assist Bell in trying to win Schneider over and soothe his hurt feelings? Consider alternatives open to them.

CASE 4-6
Sanders Supermarkets Store #13:
Who Should Be Promoted to Head Stock Clerk?

Amanda Frazier was the store supervisor for Store #13 of the Sanders Supermarkets. Early one morning Jerry Stiffelman, stock clerk, approached her.

Stock Clerk: Amanda, I hear that Tim Stapleton was promoted to head stock clerk. Why didn't I get a chance at the promotion? I've been working here eight years, and he's only been here six. Doesn't seniority count as long as two people are equally qualified?

Store Supervisor: Jerry, you were considered for the job at one time, but now I don't feel that you are qualified to handle the job. So you were passed over.

Stock Clerk: What do you mean, I'm not qualified? I've done the job several times in the past when other head stock clerks were on vacation. You've never told me before that I couldn't handle it. It was my understanding that I'd get the next promotion on the basis of my seniority. Now you are telling me that I don't have the ability to do what I've already done before.

Store Supervisor: Nevertheless, that's our decision.

Stock Clerk: That may be your decision now, but you'll think differently when the union contacts you. (And with that, Jerry walked away.)

Amanda Frazier started to think about what Jerry Stiffelman had said and remembered certain facts that she would bring out if the union did get involved. She considered Stiffelman a satisfactory stock clerk but certainly not above average. She believed that Stiffelman lacked the ability and dependability to handle the job of head stock clerk. On several occasions that Stiffelman had relieved other head stock clerks, the store had experienced out-of-stocks as a result of his poor job of ordering. Twice Frazier had received telephone calls from the police on the nights that Stiffelman had closed up the store and had accidentally set off the burglar alarm. She further noted that Stiffelman was frequently absent from work. During the previous year, Stiffelman had been absent 18 days, offering illness as the reason for his absences.

Several days later, Frazier was confronted by her boss, Susan Kennedy. As district manager, Kennedy was responsible for seven Sanders stores. The following dialogue took place:

District Manager: Amanda, we have a grievance filed by the union on behalf of Jerry Stiffelman. The union claims that we should let him have the chance to prove he can handle the job. How well has he done as a temporary head stock clerk?

Store Supervisor: Terrible, Susan. The police woke me up two times because Stiffelman bungled the burglar alarm, and we had numerous out-of-stocks from his ordering.

District Manager: Why didn't you tell me about this before? Did you talk to Stiffelman about these things?

Store Supervisor: I thought I did tell you, Susan, didn't I? But I think I did talk to him about it for sure. Customers were driving me crazy because we were out of toilet paper. He caused me a lot of headaches.

District Manager: Well, according to his personnel file, he has never been written up. And as far as I can see, by seniority he was in line for a promotion.

In response to the union grievance, I told the human resources department that we'd consider giving the head stock clerk position to Stiffelman on the basis of his seniority over Tim Stapleton.

Store Supervisor: That's a big mistake, Susan, because Stiffelman cannot handle it. Besides all that, he is absent too often.

District Manager: What do you mean, absent too often?

Store Supervisor: Over the past year he has been "sick" 18 days.

District Manager: There's no mention of any sick pay granted in his file. Was he paid for sick leave?

Store Supervisor: Darned if I know. I don't have time to pay attention to all these paperwork details.

District Manager: Okay, Amanda. I guess we've got a real problem. Take a look at this provision of the union contract. It says that in making promotions we must give preference to the most senior employee, provided merit and ability are equal. What do you think we should do? The union business agent told me that if we don't promote Jerry Stiffelman, the union will take this case all the way to arbitration.

Store Supervisor: I think we should take a stand and stick with our original decision. Stiffelman just doesn't deserve the promotion, and I'll have nothing but trouble if he becomes a head stock clerk.

Questions for Discussion

1. Outline arguments that the union is likely to make in processing its grievance on behalf of Jerry Stiffleman.

2. Outline the arguments that the management of Sanders Supermarkets would take in defending its decision to promote Stapleton over Stiffelman.

3. What should the store's management do? Consider alternatives.

4. If the management should decide to acquiesce to the union grievance and promote Jerry Stiffelman, what should it do to determine that Stiffelman can properly handle the head clerk's job? Consider alternatives.

CASE 4-7
What Do I Say to Him?

Jane McGraw sat at her desk, preparing for an evaluation session with one of her employees. McGraw was the advertising director in the marketing department of a major retail department store chain. She supervised 14 employees in her unit. Several days ago, McGraw had completed a performance appraisal form for Art Gross, a copyediting employee. She was now waiting for Gross to come to her office for his evaluation interview.

McGraw was concerned about what she should say to Gross regarding his evaluation. She expected that there would be problems, because she again had rated Gross as "average" on most of the categories on the appraisal form. Only on "attendance" and "relationships with other employees" had she rated him as being "above average."

McGraw believed that Gross had not performed at anything other than a general or average level in most of his work responsibilities. In reviewing last year's appraisal form, she recognized that this was the same level that she had appraised Gross at that time. During her interview with him last year, Gross had disagreed strongly with her evaluation, because he thought he should have been rated "above average" or "excellent" on most factors. McGraw had tried to explain to him at that time why she had rated Gross as "average" on most categories and that she felt these were proper ratings. He had responded that her evaluation was unfair and that he felt it was discriminatory as compared to other employees. McGraw denied this, and she let the evaluation form stand as she had developed it. Gross refused to sign the form, since he was quite upset about it.

Now another year had gone by. McGraw recognized that she really had not given Art Gross any good specific guidance as to how to improve his job performance. She also recognized that she had had only several conversations with him during the past year, most of which were about certain job situations and did not relate specifically to his performance. McGraw recognized that she should have kept much better records and developed some specific examples to discuss with Gross. But pressures of business and the responsibilities of supervising a large group of employees had kept her from keeping good records.

Now she wondered what would happen this time, and what she should say to him. Jane McGraw was convinced in her own mind that Art Gross was at best an average employee who had not improved over the last year. As she was pondering what she should say, Gross entered her office.

Questions for Discussion

1. Identify the errors made by Jane McGraw that are apparent in this case.
2. Is it possible that Art Gross is a better employee than McGraw believes? Discuss.
3. If you were in Jane McGraw's situation at the end of the case, what would you say to Art Gross in explaining your evaluation of his performance?
4. Outline a series of steps for Jane McGraw to follow in the future to prevent this type of situation from happening again.

CASE 4-8
What Makes for a Successful Supervisor?

The objective of performance appraisals is to determine how well employees are doing with regard to a set of stated objectives for their performance. Sometimes, however, it is just as difficult to know what the performance objectives should be as it is to accurately measure their accomplishment. This seems to be especially true in outlining the expectations for supervisors and then prioritizing those expectations.

In a nationwide survey of 600 supervisors conducted by Personnel Decisions, Inc. (PDI), researchers found that supervisors and their managers generally agree on the qualities that a successful supervisor should have. In the study, supervisors and their managers were requested to describe the most important management skills. The supervisors were then rated on these skills, with the ratings including their own self-assessments. According to a majority of the respondents, *the ability to act with integrity* is the most important management skill. Ranked in their order of importance, other key skills listed were *using sound judgment, providing direction, motivating others, managing execution, demonstrating adaptability, fostering teamwork, driving for results, thinking strategically,* and *focusing on customer needs.* Interestingly, two highly touted skills, *promoting corporate citizenship* and *valuing diversity,* were among the bottom five on the list.

The study found that although the supervisors and their managers ranked the skills similarly, the supervisors' performance on all of the skills met neither their own expectations nor those of their managers. Susan H. Gebelein, PDI vice-president, surmised that "In general, [supervisors] have not yet caught up with the changing demands in the business world. These changes require [supervisors] to exhibit participative—rather than autocratic—leadership, to build trust and influence others without direct challenge, and to champion change. For many, these skills are new, so they are just learning them."

In a related report, Wayne D. Calloway, chairman and CEO of PepsiCo, Inc., and one of the nation's most admired corporate leaders, outlined three reasons supervisors do not reach their full potential. The first reason he called *flawed values.* Specifically, Calloway said that some supervisors, perhaps in their attempts to show confidence, actually become arrogant. Arrogance, he said, is a roadblock to success in a business where teamwork is important. The second failure, according to Calloway, is a *lack of commitment.* He defined this failure as an unwillingness to continue to seek answers to problems after having failed once or twice. Finally, he said, *loyalty* is lacking in some leaders. Loyalty does not mean an unwillingness to question authority; it means a willingness to put the needs of the company ahead of your own, said Calloway. When this type of loyalty is not present, then pettiness, constant complaints and excuses, cutting down co-workers, and efforts to protect one's backside become commonplace in the organization.

What do employees want from their supervisors? Richard A. Moran, the organizational-change practice leader for Sibson & Co., a management consulting firm, met with over 50,000 employees throughout the United States to attempt to find out. He reported eight comments from employees:

1. Although employees believe in the value of change, they want management to prove that it is serious about making changes, then follow through on them.
2. Employees want to have satisfied customers, just as management does, but they need to know what resources are available to them and that supervisors will support them when they exercise personal judgment.

3. When management does not listen to the suggestions of employees, the employees assume that the organization does not care, and they stop speaking up.
4. Employees want to be sure that the money spent on the corporate staff is the best use of the company's financial resources.
5. Employees want to be evaluated using measures that are relevant to their jobs, and they want everyone to be measured using the same system.
6. If management will keep employees informed of the company's strategic destination, they can help reach it.
7. Employees expect supervisors to be truthful in all aspects of the business.
8. Employees want to be given the support they need to be able to make a positive impact in their jobs.

References

Tom Brown, "A Penny Saved . . . ," *Industry Week* (May 20, 1991), p. 22.
"Managers Fall Short of Their Supervisors' Expectations," *HR Focus* (March 1992), p. 22.
Brian S. Moskal, "Arrogance: The Executive Achilles's Heel," *Industry Week* (June 3, 1991), p. 19.
"What Employees Want from Management," *Personnel Journal* (April 1993), pp. 19–22.

Questions for Discussion

1. After reading the case summary and listening to the tape, list what appear to be the most important qualities of the supervisor.

2. Does there appear to be a difference in what top-level managers expect of their supervisors and what supervisors' employees expect of them? Explain.

3. Should a supervisor's employees be given the opportunity to input into the supervisor's performance evaluation? Why or why not? What are the advantages? The disadvantages?

PART 5

LEADING

16

Supervisory Leadership and the Introduction of Change

LEARNING OBJECTIVES

After studying this chapter, you will be able to:

1 Define the leading function of management and discuss the importance of leadership at the supervisory level.

2 Discuss the unity-of-command principle in relation to issuing directives.

3 Identify and discuss major characteristics of a good supervisory directive.

4 Discuss why supervisors should explain the reasons for their directives.

5 Compare autocratic supervision with participative management and general supervision.

6 Suggest approaches for introducing change to employees and for proposing change to higher-level managers.

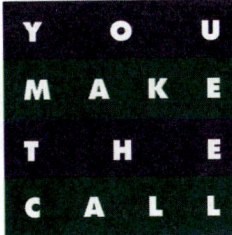

YOU MAKE THE CALL

You are Lee McKenna, supervisor of the receiving and shipping department of a manufacturing plant of Tideway Corporation, a producer of paper products. You have supervised this department for two years after having worked as an employee in the department for about eight years. Fourteen employees report to you; all are members of the plant's labor union.

Because the union shop steward registered a complaint about your supervisory style in a grievance meeting (which included your manager and the director of human resources), you were told to attend a one-week supervisory management seminar sponsored by a local consulting firm. You learned about theories and models of supervisory leadership, especially those urging a participatory approach. You were taught tech-

niques for giving directives to employees that were less authoritative than those you used previously. Participative styles were emphasized as being far more effective than just giving out orders.

It has been four weeks since you attended the seminar, and you have tried to implement what you learned. On a number of occasions you have asked employees—both individually and in groups—for their suggestions and opinions concerning what should be done. You have avoided giving direct orders and have tried to suggest to employees what needed to be done rather than spelling out your own objectives in detail. However, despite your best efforts, nothing seems to have changed. Work performance has not improved, and the employees seem to be going through the motions of their jobs just as be-

431

fore. The department shop steward even told you this morning that she did not think you understood how employees felt and that you had forgotten how it was to be a worker.

You wonder whether there is something wrong with your new approach. Is it just a waste of time? Do the employees resent the fact that you were promoted to a supervisory position? You wonder whether you should just forget about the participative approach to management that you learned and go back to being a firm and authoritative supervisor. What should you do? **YOU MAKE THE CALL.**

THE LEADING FUNCTION OF SUPERVISORY MANAGEMENT

1 Define the leading function of management and discuss the importance of leadership at the supervisory level.

Leading
The managerial function of guiding employees toward accomplishing organizational objectives.

Leadership
The ability to guide, influence, and motivate the opinions and actions of others toward the accomplishment of organizational objectives.

The leading function of management is associated with a number of managerial principles. It often is associated with managerial authority, which we have discussed in several places in previous chapters. As discussed in Chapter 4, leading may be associated with the concept of "power" that can be exerted by individuals because of their personal, positional, or professional relationships to others.[1] For our purposes, we will define **leading** as the managerial function of guiding employees toward accomplishing organizational objectives. Thus, **leadership** is the ability to guide, influence, and motivate the opinions, attitudes, and actions of others toward the accomplishment of organizational objectives. It follows that the real test of supervisory leadership resides in a supervisor's ability to obtain employees' willingness to follow in order to accomplish objectives in a superior fashion.

Since leading is the process that managers use to achieve goal-directed behavior from employees, it can be viewed as the managerial function that initiates action. It primarily means issuing instructions, assignments, and directives, but it also includes building an effective workforce by encouraging employees to work willingly and enthusiastically toward the accomplishment of organizational objectives. Thus leading also has been identified as "directing," "motivating," "activating," or "influencing."

Every manager—a president of a company, a regional sales manager, an administrator of a university, or a departmental supervisor—performs the leading function. However, the time and effort a manager spends in leading will vary, depending upon the manager's level in the organization, the number of employees supervised, and the duties the employees are expected to perform. First-line supervisors normally spend most of their time leading, whereas top-level executives usually spend relatively less time on this function.

The supervisor's leading function is closely related to each of the other managerial functions. Planning, organizing, and staffing can be viewed as preparatory functions, and controlling can be considered a check to see whether or not goals are being achieved. The function that transforms preparation into action toward goal achievement is leading.

Many supervisory activities are included in the leading function. In this chapter, we will focus primarily on supervisory directives and supervisory styles of leadership that influence the way employees respond. We also will discuss introducing change, both downward and upward, as another important aspect of a supervisor's ability to lead.

ISSUING DIRECTIVES AND THE UNITY-OF-COMMAND PRINCIPLE

2 Discuss the unity-of-command principle in relation to issuing directives.

Directive
The communications approach by which a supervisor conveys to employees what, how, and why something is to be accomplished.

Guiding employees effectively is at the heart of a supervisor's leadership style. Employees usually need direction from their supervisor, and the manner by which the supervisor guides them often makes the difference between willing and superior performance or reluctant and marginal performance.

When guiding employees, the supervisor tries to influence them to meet the desired objectives and standards of work. A **directive** can be defined as the communications approach by which a supervisor conveys to employees what, how, and why something is to be accomplished.

Giving directives is a major part of a supervisor's daily routine. Directives are often referred to as "orders," "assignments," "instructions," or by other terms. Although any supervisor can learn to assign work in some fashion, some ways are more effective than others. The experienced supervisor knows that poorly stated directives can upset even the best-laid plans. Instead of coordination of efforts, turmoil can result.

Recall from Chapter 9 that unity of command means that each employee should have only one immediate supervisor, and that directives to an employee normally should be given only by that immediate supervisor—except in an emergency or in unusual circumstances. Employees cannot serve two or more supervisors without confusion and loss of efficiency. Following unity of command provides for a direct line of authority from a supervisor to subordinates.

Unfortunately, the unity-of-command principle is frequently violated. This sometimes occurs when a supervisor is under pressure and needs to communicate with someone who reports to another supervisor. For example, a sales manager may go directly to a shipping department clerk to tell the clerk to rush delivery on a certain order. If the sales manager does not later clear this directive with the shipping department supervisor, it can lead to resentment. The shipping department supervisor will feel by-passed, and his or her departmental authority may be weakened.

To repeat, therefore, directives should come from the employee's immediate supervisor to follow the unity-of-command principle. When this is not possible—for example, in emergencies or in matrix-type organizational structures (as discussed in Chapter 9)—supervisors should be careful to explain the reasons for these exceptions, both to their fellow supervisors and to the affected employees. If necessary, supervisors should seek clarification from higher-level managers to clear up areas of overlap in their departments, so that their direct authority and unity of command can be maintained.

CHARACTERISTICS OF GOOD SUPERVISORY DIRECTIVES

3 Identify and discuss major characteristics of a good supervisory directive.

Some supervisors who "break every rule in the book" when giving directives seem to achieve excellent results. Other supervisors who use the accepted techniques and who phrase their directives in courteous language still get only reluctant compliance. The most appropriate way to give a directive depends on the supervisor's and subordinates' personalities and attitudes, the job situation, and other factors. More important, however, is that the directive itself must be a good one.

Since issuing directives is the primary means for a supervisor to start, modify, or stop employee activities, every supervisor should thoroughly understand the fundamental characteristics of a good, sound directive. Directives should be reasonable, understandable, and specific; have a definite time limit; be compatible with organizational objectives; and be communicated with an appropriate tone and wording.

Reasonable

The first essential characteristic of a good directive is that it must be reasonable. Reasonableness obviously means that no orders should be issued requiring activities that physically cannot be accomplished or that would be personally dangerous to attempt, as, for example, an order to lift a steel bar that weighs 500 pounds. To judge whether a directive can be accomplished reasonably, the supervisor should appraise it from his or her own point of view, as well as the employee's. The supervisor should not issue a directive if the employee receiving it does not have the capability or experience necessary to comply. (See Figure 16-1).

There are occasions when a supervisor may issue unreasonable directives. For example, to please higher-level managers, a supervisor may promise the completion of a job at a particular time. The supervisor proceeds to issue work orders without consulting with the employees who are to do the work and without checking to determine whether other required resources to meet the commitment are available. If the job is not completed on time, the supervisor will have difficulty explaining this failure, and his or her credibility will be seriously tarnished.

Therefore, before issuing directives, supervisors first should mentally place themselves in the position of the employees and thoughtfully consider whether compliance can reasonably be expected. There are some borderline cases in which directives actually are intended to stretch the employees' capabilities a bit beyond what previously has been requested. In such instances the question of reasonableness becomes a matter of degree. Generally speaking, however, a primary requirement of a good directive is that it can be accomplished in the desired manner by the employee to whom the directive is given.

FIGURE 16-1
The effective
supervisor does not
issue unreasonable
directives.

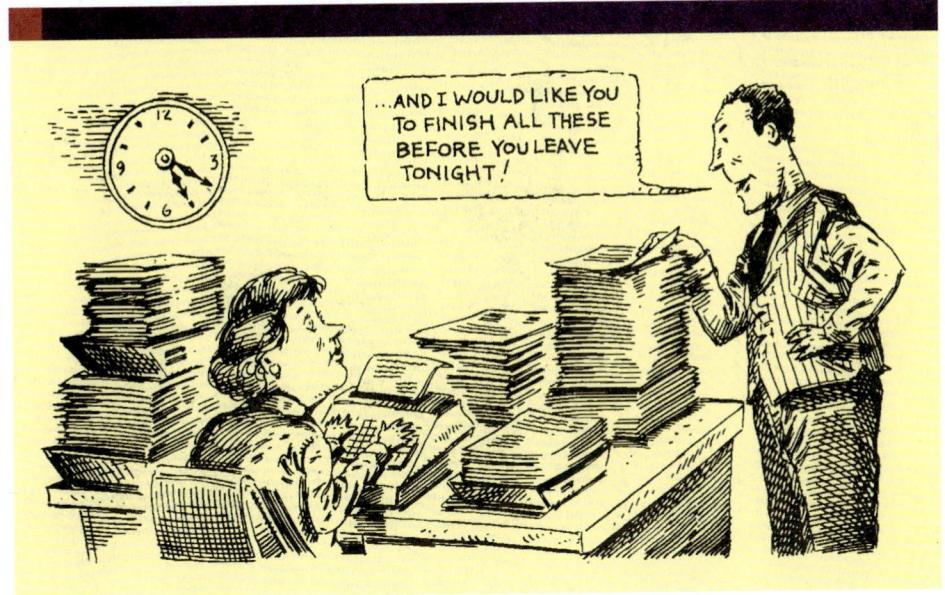

Understandable

A directive should be understandable to those who receive it. This is essentially a matter of communication, as was discussed in Chapter 3. The supervisor should make certain that an employee understands a directive by speaking in words that are familiar to the employee and by using the technique of feedback. Instructions should be clear but not necessarily lengthy. What is clear and complete to the supervisor is not always clear and complete to the employee.

Specific and with a Definite Time Limit

Good directives state specifically what is expected of the employee, especially in terms of quantity and quality of work performance. If a directive contains several steps to be performed, the supervisor may find it desirable to put the directive in writing and then discuss the steps with the employee to clear up possible ambiguities.

A good directive should also specify a time limit within which it should be completed. A reasonable amount of time must be allowed, since the quality of work may depend on the time allotment. When the time factor needs to be agreed on, the supervisor and employee should discuss how the directive can be carried out within a reasonable time. If the supervisor needs to impose a time limit, perhaps this can be done with the understanding that the time limit can be modified if circumstances dictate. It is generally undesirable to simply tell an employee to do something "when you get around to it." A busy employee may never find the time.

FIGURE 16-2
Good supervisory
directives should not
conflict with
organizational
policies.

Compatible with Organizational Objectives

A good directive should be compatible with the objectives of the organization. If it is not, employees may be reluctant to carry it out. For example, assume that the employees of a utility company have been told over and over again that serving customers is the major purpose of the company. Then one day their supervisor, under pressure to reduce costs and avoid overtime work, simply tells them to "stop work and let the customer wait for service until the following day." This directive may conflict with the employees' previous understanding that customer service always had top priority. Therefore, if a supervisor issues a directive that appears to employees to be in conflict with organizational objectives or contrary to what is done normally, the supervisor must explain the reasons why such a directive may be necessary.

Of course, any directive must comply with policies, regulations, and stated ethical standards of the organization (see Figure 16-2). Any directive that would require or permit employees to falsify documents, claim undeserved expenses, and the like is obviously unacceptable. In fact, a supervisor who issues such directives may eventually be found out by higher-level management, and this can be grounds for the supervisor's dismissal.

Appropriate Tone and Wording

The tone and wording of a directive can significantly affect the employees' acceptance and performance. A polite, considerate tone is more likely to encourage willing response and acceptance. Supervisors should avoid using the term "order," and instead should use terms such as "assignment," "request," "instruction," or "suggestion." (An exception to this, however, might be a health-care facility, a military installation, or a government agency where the term "order" is customarily used.) Phrasing a work assignment as a request does not reduce its character as a requirement, but there is usually a difference in the reaction a request inspires as compared to an order or command.

Commands. Some individuals must be told firmly what to do. At times, a direct order to these individuals may be needed to get things done. For example, a supervisor might have to say, "George, we are running behind schedule. You must get five units out today." Everyone remembers commands from parents and school teachers as a part of growing up. Employees are adults and should be treated as such. Therefore, a supervisor should avoid commands and orders whenever possible; in most instances, there are better ways to communicate what is needed.

Requests. A directive may be phrased as a request. For the majority of employees, a request is all that is needed. It is a mature way of stating what needs to be done, especially with employees who have been working for the supervisor for some time and who are familiar with the supervisor and the job. A request usually works better with this kind of employee than a direct command. For example, a supervisor could say, "George, would you see if you can get five units out today? We seem to be behind schedule."

Suggestions. In other instances a directive can be phrased as a suggestion, which is even milder than a request. For example, the preceding directive could be stated, "George, we are five units behind schedule today and we need to get back on track." Suggestions usually accomplish their purpose because responsible employees grasp their meaning. Most employees take the initiative to get the job accomplished when the need is communicated to them. However, suggestive types of directives are not advisable if the supervisor is dealing with new employees who do not have sufficient training and familiarity with the department's routine. Likewise, suggestions generally are not an effective way to give assignments to employees who are incompetent or undependable.

EXPLAINING REASONS FOR DIRECTIVES

4 Discuss why supervisors should explain the reasons for their directives.

Except for routine activities, whenever possible supervisors should explain the reasons behind their directives and why certain things have to be done. It is difficult for a supervisor to issue a directive so completely as to cover all contingencies and leave no room for interpretation or adaptation. But employees who know the purpose and reasons behind a directive usually are better prepared to use good judgment and perform in a manner that will produce the desired results. Without knowing the "why" of directives, employees may experience stress, particularly if they encounter unforeseen circumstances. They will not have enough information to decide how to adjust to the situation.

There is an old story that illustrates the importance of explaining the reasons behind directives. A supervisor instructed a crew of workers to dig holes at random in the factory yard. During the morning, each time two workers had dug a hole four feet deep, the supervisor came over to inspect the hole and then ordered the workers to fill it up again. After the lunch break, the work crew threatened to quit doing the job, since they thought it was useless and stupid. At this point the supervisor told them that the blueprints for an old water main had been lost and that they were searching for this water main. Having heard the explanation, the workers were content to resume their job. Obviously, the supervisor could have avoided this conflict by explaining the reason for the job right at the beginning. Moreover, as each hole was dug, the workers themselves could have searched for the water main, and the supervisor would not have had to inspect each hole.

In explaining reasons behind directives, a supervisor may overdo a good thing. Explanations should include enough information to give employees sufficient background without overwhelming them. If a directive involves only a minor activity and time is limited, the explanation should be brief. For example, a data entry clerk might ask the supervisor to explain why a completely new data record must be entered into the computerized payroll system because of a minor change in state tax rates. All the supervisor needs to explain is the how and why of the task, rather than launching into a 20-minute discussion of computers and the theory of taxation! Furthermore, the supervisor should avoid using detailed technical language in trying to explain the meaning of each data record entry or the clerk might become even more confused.

Supervisors must use good judgment in deciding how far to go in explaining the reasons for their directives. Much will depend on factors such as the content of the directive, the supervisor's attitude, the time available, the employee's capacity to understand, and the employee's previous training.

APPROACHES TO SUPERVISION

5 Compare autocratic supervision with participative management and general supervision.

In Chapter 5 we discussed employee motivation and the concept of a hierarchy of human needs, along with Theory X, Theory Y, and other approaches to management that reflect different assumptions about motivation in relation to these needs. In other chapters we introduced concepts of broad and narrow delegation of authority and participative decision making. We expand these concepts in this chapter to relate them to a supervisor's day-to-day approaches to leading employees.

As discussed in Chapter 4, the basic styles of supervision range from autocratic supervision (based on Theory X assumptions) to general supervision (based on Theory Y assumptions). In a textbook discussion, these two styles can be presented as extremes. However, in practice the supervisor usually blends these approaches.

The proportions will vary depending on the supervisor's skill and experience, the employees involved, the situation at hand, and other factors. No one style of supervision is correct in all situations. Every supervisor should be sensitive to the needs of each situation and adjust his or her style as necessary to accomplish the objectives.

Autocratic Supervision

Autocratic supervision means close control of employees. Autocratic supervisors issue direct orders with detailed instructions to subordinates. Employees have little room for initiative. Autocratic supervisors delegate as little authority as possible. They believe that they know how to do the job better than any of their employees, and that employees are not paid to think but to follow directions. These supervisors further believe that since they have been put in charge and are being paid for it, they should do the planning and decision making. Since they are quite explicit in telling employees exactly how and in what sequence things are to be done, they follow through with close supervision.

Some autocratic supervisors do not necessarily distrust their employees; they firmly believe that without detailed instructions, employees could not do the job well. Some autocratic supervisors assume that the average employee does not want to do the job; therefore, close supervision and threats of loss of job or income are required to get employees to work (Theory X). These supervisors feel that if they are not on the scene watching their employees closely, the employees will stop working.

Probably the major advantages of autocratic supervision are that it is quick and easy to apply and that it usually gets rapid results in the short run. It may be appropriate when employees are new and inexperienced, especially if the supervisor is under major time pressures. However, the autocratic method of supervision is not conducive to developing employee talents, and it tends to frustrate employees who have ambition and potential.

Effects of Autocratic Supervision.
For most employees the consequences of autocratic supervision are negative. They lose interest and initiative; they stop thinking for themselves because there is little need for independent thought. They may be obedient, but it is difficult for them to remain loyal to the organization and the supervisor. Given an alternative, ambitious employees will not remain in positions in which the supervisor is not willing to delegate some degree of authority. Any employee who is willing to learn and who wants to progress will resent constant, detailed instructions.

In some cases employees may become hostile toward an autocratic supervisor and even resist carrying out the supervisor's directives. The resistance may not even be apparent to the supervisor when it takes the form of slow work, mistakes, and poor quality of work. If the supervisor makes a mistake, these employees secretly rejoice over it!

When Autocratic Supervision Is Appropriate. Under certain circumstances and with some employees, autocratic supervision is both logical and appropriate. Some employees do not want to think for themselves; they prefer to receive orders. Others lack ambition and do not wish to become much involved in their daily jobs. This is often the case when jobs are very structured, highly mechanized, automated, or routinized, so that employees may prefer a supervisor who mainly issues orders to them and otherwise leaves them alone.

There are also employees who have been reared by authoritarian parents or in authoritarian environments, and who expect a supervisor to be firm and totally in charge. However, these types of employees usually are in the minority. In the American culture, most men and women have been reared in a democratic society from their early school days, and they view order-giving by autocratic bosses as being contrary to the democratic way of life.

Participative Management and General Supervision

In Chapter 5, "participative management" was discussed as being synonymous with employee participation in decision making. Chapter 4 explained "general supervision" as a style that allows employees to make some decisions about how to do their jobs. Both operate from the premises of Theory Y and can be practiced simultaneously by the supervisor.

The Meaning of Participative Management. The supervisor who uses a participative approach discusses with employees the feasibility, workability, extent, and content of a problem before making a decision and issuing a directive. A participatory style does not lessen a supervisor's authority; the right to decide remains with the supervisor, and the employees' suggestions can be rejected. Participation means that a supervisor expresses personal opinions in a manner that indicates to employees that these opinions are subject to critical appraisal. It also means sharing of ideas and information between supervisor and employees and thorough discussion of alternative solutions to a problem, regardless of who originates the solutions.

More important than the exact approach is the supervisor's attitude. Some supervisors are inclined to use a pseudo-participatory approach simply to give employees the feeling that they have been consulted. These supervisors ask for suggestions even though they already have decided on a definite course of action. They use this approach to manipulate employees to do what will be required with or without their consultation. However, employees can sense superficiality and will usually perceive whether a supervisor is genuinely considering their ideas. If employees believe that their participation is fake, the results may be worse than if the supervisor had practiced autocratic supervision.

If participative management is to be successful, not only must the supervisor be in favor of it, but also the employees must want it. If the employees believe that the supervisor knows best and that making decisions is none of their concern, then an opportunity to participate is not likely to induce higher motivation and better

CONTEMPORARY ISSUE
Participative Management Is a Mixed Bag

Many scholars and authorities have urged participative management as being the best approach for boosting employee morale and encouraging employees to become more effective in the workplace. However, what sounds good in theory is often difficult to put into practice, particularly in periods of recession and layoffs. Studies of companies that have tried various participative approaches indicate that unless there is trust on the part of the workers that it is a real change and in their best interest, adoption of some participatory approaches can be more trouble than it is worth.

This particularly appears to be the case with first-line supervisors. First-line supervisors may feel threat-

ened by employee participation in decision making. The entire process may be undermined even though middle- and top-level managers encourage the practice. Many companies have found that it takes trial and error to make participative management a reality. Organizations and managers often become discouraged with their efforts, and they go back to authoritative ways without giving participation the time necessary to make it work. Warren Bennis, author of *On Becoming a Leader*, states: "Participatory management is a matter of necessity. Without it, corporations aren't going to keep the brightest and the best. We must change to survive."

Source: Adapted from Donna Brown, "Why Participative Management Won't Work Here," *Management Review* (June 1992), pp. 42–46.

morale. Furthermore, employees should be consulted only in those areas where they are capable of expressing valid opinions and where they can draw on their own fund of knowledge. The problems involved should be consistent with the employees' experiences and abilities. Asking for participation in areas that are far outside of the employees' scope of competence may make them feel inadequate and frustrated.

Advantages of Participative Management. Perhaps the greatest advantage of participative management is that a supervisor's directive can be changed from an order to a solution that employees themselves have discovered, or at least one in which they have participated. This normally leads employees to cooperate with more enthusiasm in carrying out the directive. Also, employees' morale is apt to be higher when their ideas are valued. Active participation provides an opportunity to make worthwhile contributions. Still another advantage is that participative management permits closer communication between employees and the supervisor, so that they learn to know and respect each other better.

Organized Participative Management Programs. In Chapter 5 we discussed a number of participative management programs adopted by many organizations. These programs have been called "quality circles," "quality-of-work-life programs," "total quality management (TQM)," "employee participation teams," and the like.[2] In essence, all of these efforts employ principles of participative management, and they have most of the same attendant advantages. When such a program is in place, the supervisor by definition is forced to utilize a style of supervision that may go considerably beyond mere consultation. Some of these programs call for active employee involvement in making and implementing decisions. Most are concerned with problems stemming from work operations at the departmental level; however, some of the problems may even involve companywide situations and interdepartmental relationships. We will discuss organized participative management programs further in Chapter 17.

The Meaning of General Supervision.
General supervision means permitting employees—within prescribed limits—to work out the details of their daily tasks and to make many of the decisions about how tasks will be performed. In so doing, the supervisor believes that employees want to do a good job and will find greater satisfaction in making decisions for themselves. The supervisor communicates the desired results, standards, and limits within which the employees can work and then delegates accordingly.

For example, a school maintenance supervisor might assign a group of employees to paint the interior walls of the school. The supervisor tells the group where to get the paint and other materials, and reminds them that they should do the painting without interfering in the normal school operations. Then the supervisor suggests a target date for completing the project and leaves the group to work on their own. The supervisor may say that he or she will occasionally check back with the group to see whether they are encountering any problems or need help.

General supervision is not the same as no supervision. Under general supervision, employees are expected to know the routine of their jobs and what results are expected. But the supervisor avoids giving detailed instructions that specify precisely how results are to be achieved.

General supervision also means that the supervisor, or the supervisor and employees together, should set realistic standards or performance targets. These should be high enough to represent a challenge, but not so high that they cannot be achieved. Such targets sometimes are known as **stretching standards.** Employees know that their efforts are being measured against these standards. If they are unable to accomplish the targeted objectives, they are expected to inform the supervisor so that the standards can be discussed again and perhaps modified.

Stretching standards
Targeted job objectives that present a challenge but are achievable.

Participative Management and General Supervision as a Way of Life.
When practiced simultaneously, participative management and general supervision are a way of life that must be followed over a period of time. A supervisor cannot expect sudden results by introducing these types of supervision into a situation in which employees have been accustomed to autocratic supervision. It may take considerable time and patience before positive results are evident.

Successful implementation of participative management and general supervision requires a continuous effort on a supervisor's part to develop employees beyond their present skills. Employees learn more when they can work out solutions for themselves rather than being given solutions. They learn best from their own successes and failures.

The participative type of supervisor spends considerable time encouraging employees to solve their own problems and to participate in and make decisions. As employees become more competent and self-confident, there is less need for the supervisor to instruct and watch them. A valid way to gauge the effectiveness of a supervisor is to study how employees in the department function when the supervisor is away from the job.

Although a supervisor may use participative management and general supervision whenever possible, from time to time he or she will have to demonstrate authority with employees who require close supervision. Participative managers and general supervisors must be as performance conscious as any other type of supervisor. It is merely the style they use that differentiates them from authoritarian supervisors.

INTRODUCING CHANGE

6 Suggest approaches for introducing change to employees and for proposing change to higher-level managers.

Another challenging aspect of a supervisor's leading function occurs whenever there is a need to introduce change. Change is expected as part of everyday life, and the survival and growth of most enterprises depend on change and innovation. The introduction of change—such as a new work method, a new product, a new work schedule, or a new personnel policy—usually requires implementation at the departmental level. In the final analysis, it is the supervisor who typically has to bring about the change.[3]

Reasons for Resistance to Change

Some supervisors are inclined to discount the existence and magnitude of human resistance to change. What may seem like a trifling change to the supervisor may bring strong reaction from the employees. Supervisors should remember that employees seldom resist change just to be stubborn. They resist because they believe a change threatens their positions socially, psychologically, or economically. Therefore, the supervisor should be familiar with the ways in which resistance to change can be minimized and handled successfully.

Most people pride themselves on being up to date. As consumers, they expect and welcome changes in material things such as new automobiles, homes, clothing, appliances, or gadgets. But as employees, they may resist changes on the job or changes in personal relationships, even though such changes are vital for the operation of the organization. If an organization is to survive, it must be able to react to prevailing conditions by implementing necessary adjustments.

Change disturbs the environment in which people exist. Prior to a change, employees become accustomed to a work environment in which patterns of relationships and behavior have reached a degree of stability. When a change takes place, new ideas and new methods may be perceived as a threat to the security of the work group. Many employees fear change because they cannot predict what the change will mean in terms of their own positions, activities, or abilities (Figure 16-3). It makes no difference whether the change actually has a negative result.

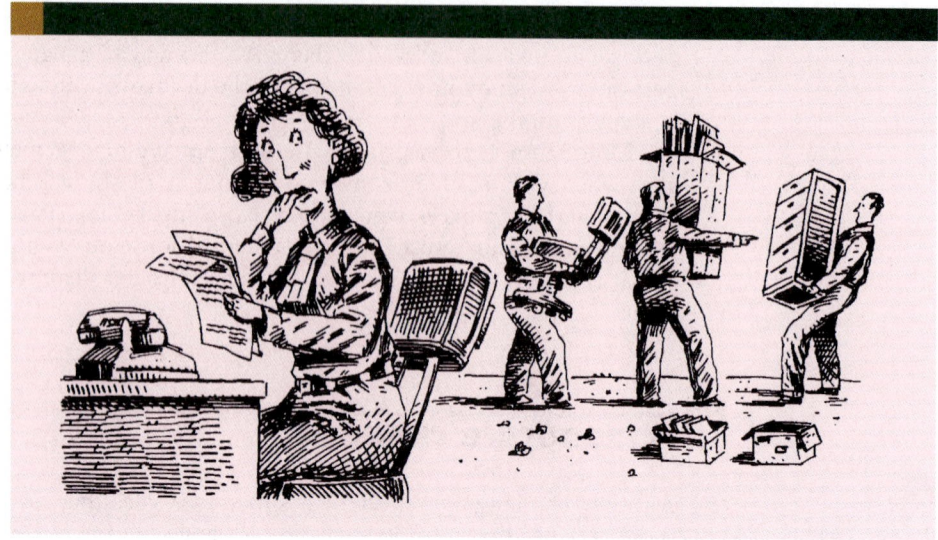

What matters is that the employees believe that the change will cause negative consequences.

For example, the introduction of new equipment is usually accompanied by employee fears of loss of jobs or skills. Even though the supervisor and higher-level managers announce that no employees will be laid off, rumors circulate that layoffs will occur or existing jobs will be downgraded. Employee fears may not subside until months after the change has been in place.

Changes affect individuals in different ways. A change that causes great disturbance to one person may create only a small problem for another. A supervisor must learn to recognize how changes affect different employees and observe how individuals develop patterns of behavior that serve as barriers to accepting change.

Reducing Resistance to Change

Probably the most important factor in gaining employee acceptance of new ideas and methods is the personal relationship that exists between the supervisor who is introducing the change and the employees who are affected by it. If a relationship of confidence and trust exists, the employees are more likely to accept the change with minimal resistance.[4]

Provide Adequate Information. In the final analysis, it is not the change itself that usually leads to resistance. Rather, it is the manner in which the supervisor introduces the change. Thus, resistance to change that comes from fear of the unknown can be minimized by supplying all the information that the employees consciously and subconsciously need to know to minimize their fears.

Whenever possible, a supervisor should explain what will happen, why, and how the employees and the department will be affected by a change. If applicable, the supervisor should emphasize how the change will leave employees no worse off or may even improve their present situation. This information should be communicated to all employees who are directly or indirectly involved, either individually or collectively, and as early as appropriate. Only then can employees assess what a change will mean in terms of their activities. This will be facilitated if the supervisor has tried consistently to give ample background information for all directives.

Employees who are well acquainted with the underlying factors that surround departmental operations usually understand the necessity for change. They probably will ask questions about a change, but they then can adjust to it and go on. When employees have been informed of the reasons for a change, what to expect, and how their jobs will be affected, they usually make reasonable adaptations. Instead of insecurity, they experience feelings of relative confidence and willing compliance.

However, if the change definitely will involve closing certain operations and loss of jobs, this should be explained openly and frankly. It is especially important to discuss which employees are likely to be affected and how the job cuts will be made. If higher-level managers have decided not to identify which individuals will be terminated until it actually happens, the supervisor should explain this as a reality and not try to hide behind vague promises or raise unrealistic expectations.

If a firm has 100 or more employees and it plans to close a plant or lay off major segments of employees, the firm must comply with the notification provisions of the 1988 Worker Adjustment and Retraining Notification Act (WARN). This law requires that employees must be given at least 60 days' prior notice before the closings or layoffs are carried out. There are certain exceptions to this requirement. Compliance with this law is normally the responsibility of the firm's human resources or legal department, but supervisors may become involved in communicating the notifications to employees.

Encourage Participation in Decision Making. Another technique for reducing resistance to change is to permit the employees affected by the change to share in making decisions about it. If several employees are involved in a change, group decision making is an effective way to reduce their fears and objections. When employees have an opportunity to work through new ideas and methods from the beginning, usually they will consider the new directives as something of their own making and give them their support. The group may even apply pressure on those who have reservations about going along with the change, and it is likely that each member of the group will carry out the change once there is agreement on how to proceed.

Group decision making is especially effective in changes in which the supervisor is indifferent about the details, as long as the change is implemented. In these cases, the supervisor must set the limits within which the group can decide. For example, a supervisor may not care how a new departmental work schedule is divided among the group as long as the work is accomplished within a prescribed time, with a given number of employees, and without overtime.

Proposing Change to Higher-Level Managers

In many organizations higher-level managers complain that supervisors are too content with the status quo and are unwilling to suggest new and innovative ways of improving departmental performance. Supervisors, on the other hand, complain that higher-level managers are not receptive to ideas that they have suggested for their departments. There is probably some truth to both complaints.

If supervisors wish to propose changes, it is important that they understand how to present ideas not only to their employees but also to higher-level managers. "Selling" an idea to a manager involves the art of persuasion, much as a good salesperson uses persuasion in selling a product or service to a reluctant customer.

Obtain Needed Information. A supervisor who has a good idea or who wishes to suggest a change should first ask, "What aspects of the idea or change will be of most interest to the boss?" Higher-level managers usually are interested if a change might improve production, increase profits, improve morale, or reduce overhead and other costs. It is important to do considerable homework to see whether a proposed change is feasible and adaptable to the departmental operation. By thinking through the idea carefully and getting as much information as possible, the supervisor will be in a better position to argue strong and weak points of the proposal. In addition, the supervisor should find out whether any other departments or organizations have used the proposed idea—either successfully or unsuccessfully. Doing this will impress the manager that the supervisor has invested time and effort in checking out the idea in other work environments.

Consult with Other Supervisors. To get an idea or proposal beyond the discussion stage, the supervisor should consult with other supervisors and personnel who might be affected and get their reactions to the proposed change. Checking it out with them gives them a chance to think the idea through, offer suggestions and criticisms, and work out some of the problems. Otherwise some supervisors may resist or resent the change if they feel they have been ignored.

If possible, it is helpful to get the tentative commitment of other supervisors. It is not always necessary to obtain their total approval, but higher-level managers will be more inclined to consider an idea if it has been discussed at least in preliminary form with knowledgeable people in the organization.

Formal Written Proposal. At times a supervisor may be asked by the manager to put the proposed idea in writing, so that copies may be forwarded to higher-level managers, other supervisors, or other personnel. This requires effort. The supervisor may have to engage in considerable study outside of normal working hours to obtain all the information needed. Relevant information on costs, prices, productivity data, and the like should be included in the proposal, even if some data are only educated guesses. Highly uncertain estimates should be labeled as tentative, and exaggerated claims and opinions should be avoided. Risks, as well as potential advantages, should be acknowledged in the formal proposal.

This supervisor is making effective use of charts and graphs to enhance her formal presentation.

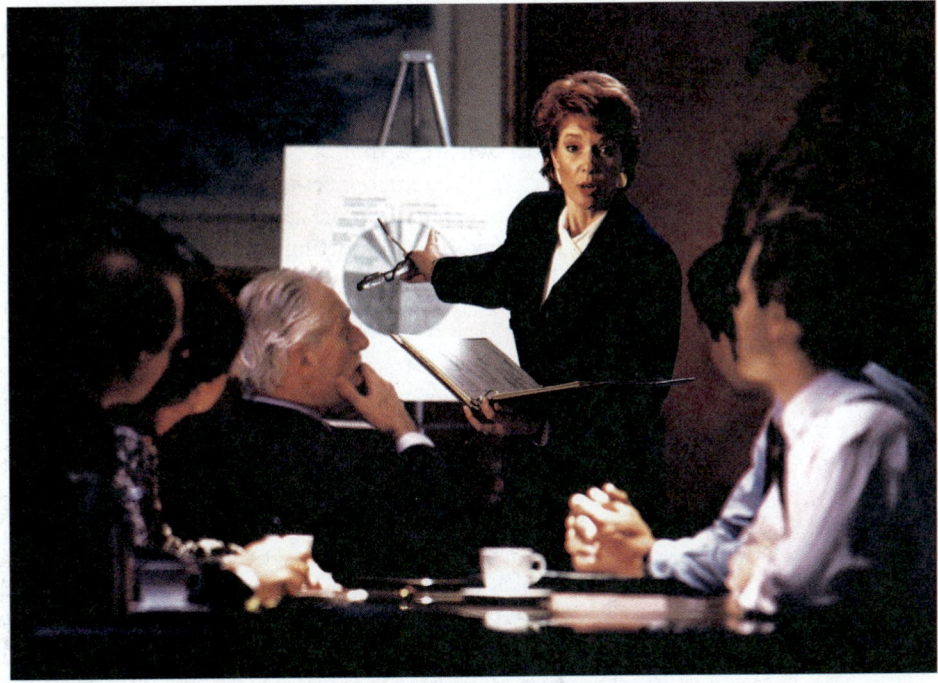

Formal Presentation. If a supervisor is asked to make a formal presentation of the proposal to a committee or at a meeting, ample planning and preparation are required. The presentation should be made thoroughly and in an unhurried fashion, allowing sufficient time for questions and discusion.

A supervisor who has carefully thought through an idea should not be afraid to express it in a firm and convincing manner. The supervisor should be enthusiastic in explaining the idea, but at the same time be patient and empathetic with those who may not agree with it. A helpful technique in a formal presentation is to utilize some type of chart, diagram, or visual aid to dramatize it.

Acceptance or Rejection of Change by Higher-Level Managers

A supervisor who is able to persuade higher-level managers and other supervisors to accept a proposed change will feel inner satisfaction. Of course, any good idea requires careful implementation, follow-up, and refinement. Rarely does a change follow the exact blueprint suggested. Following up and working out the problems with others are important aspects of making any change effective.

Despite a supervisor's best efforts, the idea may be rejected, altered greatly, or shelved. This can be frustrating, particularly to a supervisor who has worked diligently to develop an idea that he or she believes would lead to positive results. The important thing here is to avoid becoming discouraged and developing a negative outlook. There may be valid reasons why the idea was rejected, or the timing may not have been right. A supervisor should resolve to try again, perhaps to further refine and polish the idea for resubmission at a future date.

A supervisor who has developed an idea for change, even if it has not been accepted, usually will find that such efforts were appreciated by higher-level managers. Moreover, the experience of having worked through a proposal for change will make the supervisor a more valuable member of the organizational team, and there will be many other opportunities to work for the introduction of change.

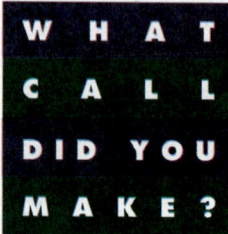

WHAT CALL DID YOU MAKE?

As Lee McKenna, you are discouraged that your new supervisory approach to leading employees is not taking hold the way you had anticipated. This is because you thought it would bring fast improvement. You must recognize that to be an effective supervisor who leads rather than bosses can take a long time, especially if you primarily relied on your authority as a supervisor previously. Your best approach now is to be patient. Keep applying what you have learned, and do not expect changes to be instant or dramatic. For example, you might apply your new participative management style selectively with a few employees who you believe are most likely to welcome this approach. The employees have got to be convinced that your style of supervisory leadership really has changed and that you are serious about making participative management a reality in your department. Review the concepts and principles presented in this chapter. They are sound, and in the long run they will work most of the time for most people. You might also talk with some fellow supervisors and the director of human resources to find out how they give directives and lead their employees.

SUMMARY

1 Define the leading function of management and discuss the importance of leadership at the supervisory level.

The managerial leading function forms the connecting link between planning, organizing, and staffing on the one hand and controlling on the other. Leading primarily involves guiding employees toward accomplishing organizational objectives. Supervisory leadership is the ability of the supervisor to influence and motivate employees to perform willingly and in a superior fashion. Supervisors spend the majority of their time carrying out the leading function.

2 Discuss the unity-of-command principle in relation to issuing directives.

Instructing employees effectively is at the heart of a supervisor's leadership style. Directives are the communications by which a supervisor conveys what, how, and why something is to be accomplished. Directives issued by a supervisor should normally follow the principle of unity of command.

3 Identify and discuss major characteristics of a good supervisory directive.

Good supervisory directives should be: (a) reasonable, (b) understandable, (c) specific and have a definite time limit, (d) compatible with organizational objectives, and (e) appropriate tone and wording.

4 Discuss why supervisors should explain the reasons for their directives.

When employees know the reasons behind a directive, they are better prepared to use good judgment in carrying out their assignments. If they do not understand the reasons for doing something, employees may find it stressful and difficult to determine what to do.

5 Compare autocratic supervision with participative management and general supervision.

A supervisor may use approaches ranging from autocratic supervision at one extreme to general supervision at the other. Autocratic supervision is effective for certain occasions, employees, and conditions. However, for most situations it is better to apply participative management and general supervision techniques. Participative management is particularly adaptable for new job assignments, whereas general supervision is appropriate for routine assignments and daily tasks.

6 Suggest approaches for introducing change to employees and for proposing change to higher-level managers.

To successfully cope with employees' normal resistance to change, supervisors must understand why resistance surfaces and what can be done to help employees adjust and accept necessary changes. A supervisor also should learn the principles of "selling" change to higher-level managers. This typically involves persuading the immediate superior, higher-level managers, and other supervisors that the acceptance of a proposal will benefit them and the total organization.

KEY WORDS

Leading (page 432)
Leadership (page 432)

Directive (page 433)
Stretching standards (page 442)

QUESTIONS FOR DISCUSSION

1. Define the managerial function of leading. Why is leading the function that most involves day-to-day supervisory activities?

2. Why is guiding employees effectively at the heart of a supervisor's leadership style?

3. Should the unity-of-command principle always be followed in issuing directives? Discuss.

4. Review each characteristic of a good supervisory directive, and discuss how these characteristics relate to communication concepts.

5. Distinguish between autocratic supervision on the one hand and participative management and general supervision on the other. What theoretical differences are implied in each of these approaches? (Relate these to concepts concerning delegation of authority and motivation.)

6. Is autocratic supervision always negative in its consequences? Why or why not?

7. Why are employee attitudes and expectations important if participative management is to be successful?

8. What are the advantages of organized participative management programs such as quality circles, TQM, and employee participation teams?

9. How does general supervision differ from "no supervision" in determining targets and standards?

10. Discuss the statement, "When practiced simultaneously, participative management and general supervision are a way of life that must be followed over a period of time."

11. What are some of the advantages to supervisors and employees when participative management and general supervision are practiced?

12. Discuss supervisory approaches for the effective introduction of change to employees. How are these approaches related to some of the common barriers that cause employees to resist change?

13. Discuss the principles of proposing change to higher-level managers. How do these compare with those utilized when introducing change downward to employees?

SKILLS APPLICATIONS

Skills Application 16-1: A Supervisor's Style of Leading

1. Think of a supervisor you have known or observed who had the best abilities to lead employees to achieve superior results. Make a list of the characteristics and techniques you felt made this supervisor effective.

2. Compare your list with the concepts presented in this chapter. To what degree do they coincide or differ?

Skills Application 16-2: Writing Supervisory Directives

You are Travis Smith, a plant production supervisor. You are in your office on Saturday morning, although the rest of the plant is closed for the weekend. You will be leaving this afternoon for a one-week vacation with your family. Several memos are on your desk that require responses from you before you leave the office. Read each of the following memos, and write a brief directive to the appropriate employees about what they should do while you are away.

MEMO 1

To: Travis Smith, Supervisor
From: Mary Zimmer, Quality Control Specialist

Travis,

Mike Barr, one of your operators, has been processing too many units of unacceptable quality. He needs to service his machine every two hours to prevent this. I've told him this several times, but he doesn't seem to listen. Perhaps you need to talk to him.

Mary

MEMO 2

To: Travis Smith, Supervisor
From: Betty Ramirez, Human Resources Manager

Travis,

It has come to my attention that several of your employees have been leaving work early. Although this doesn't appear to be a major problem now, I do want it stopped before it gets out of hand.
See what you can do.

Betty

MEMO 3

To: Travis Smith, Supervisor
From: Tom Borsch, Production Worker

Travis,

Production tends to fall behind toward the end of every week because raw materials are not shipped from our central warehouse on time. It happened again this week. Can you rectify this?

Tom

MEMO 4

To: Travis Smith, Supervisor
From: Carl Winter, Vice-President of Operations

Travis,

For the last two weeks, someone has been parking in my reserved parking spot. Usually I don't mind if I can get a safe parking place. The other day, however, I had to park in Lot C (one block away) and somebody scraped the left side of my car. If I ever catch that employee, he's terminated. Instruct your people not to park in my spot if they value their jobs.

Carl

Skills Application 16-3: Supervisory Styles

After reading each of the following scenarios, identify the type of supervisory style (i.e., autocratic supervision or participative management and general supervision) that you feel would be preferable, and why. Assume that for each scenario, only 10 individuals report directly to you at any one time.

Scenario 1: You are a supervisor in charge of work crews who lay track for a railroad line. Their basic duties are to lay railroad ties and secure the track to the ties.

Scenario 2: You are a supervisor in charge of a cancer research project in a pharmaceutical firm. The duties of your subordinates vary greatly due to the experimental nature of the project. You supervise chemists, biologists, and technicians.

Scenario 3: You supervise a word processing center that provides numerous clerical and other services for a company of 300 employees. The work flow is extremely erratic. Some days there is little work, while others there is an overload.

Scenario 4: You are a drill instructor at a military installation. Your job is to train and educate new recruits.

ENDNOTES

1.   See endnote 2 at the end of Chapter 2 for sources concerning use of power in organizations.

2.   For expanded discussions concerning various types of organized participative management programs such as those mentioned in this chapter, see Arthur W. Sherman, Jr. and George W. Bohlander, *Managing Human Resources* (9th ed.; Cincinnati: South-Western Publishing Co., 1992), pp. 124–131 and 468–476; and John M. Ivancevich, *Human Resource Management* (5th ed.; Homewood, Ill.: Richard D. Irwin, 1992), pp. 757–764.

3.   For expanded discussions concerning introduction of change, see Fred Pomeroy, "Introducing Change in the Workplace," *Business Quarterly* (Volume 56, Number 3, Winter 1992), pp. 127–131; or Donald L. Kirkpatrick, "Riding the Winds of Change," *Training and Development* (Volume 47, Number 2, February 1993), pp. 28–32.

4.   For expanded discussions concerning building trust between supervisors and employees, see Lois P. Frankel and Karen L. Otazo, "Employee Coaching: The Way to Gain Commitment, Not Just Compliance," *Employment Relations Today* (Volume 19, Number 3, Autumn 1992), pp. 311–320; or Parry Pascarella, "Fifteen Ways to Win People's Trust," *Industry Week* (Volume 242, Number 3, February 1, 1993), pp. 47–51.

17

Building Effective Work Teams and Maintaining Morale

LEARNING OBJECTIVES

After studying this chapter, you will be able to:

1 Explain why work groups form and function and their importance.

2 Classify clusters of work groups and their meaning for supervisors.

3 Suggest supervisory approaches for managing work groups that are consistent with the Hawthorne Studies and other behavioral research.

4 Identify principles for building effective work teams that are associated with organized participative management programs.

5 Discuss the importance of employee morale and its relationship to teamwork and productivity.

6 Understand the factors that influence employee morale and the supervisor's role in dealing with both external and internal factors.

7 Identify programs that organizations use to assist employees with personal and work-related problems.

8 Discuss techniques to assess employee morale, including observation and employee attitude surveys.

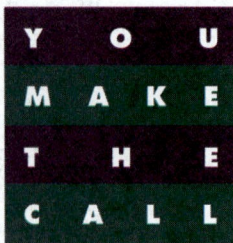

You are Sam Moreno, director of human resources for a small plant that manufactures plastics products. There are approximately 200 employees in the plant. The plant is not unionized.

One of your supervisors, Karen Jacobson, has come to your office for advice. This is what she has to say:

Sam, I just don't quite know how to deal with my departmental employees. I've got 15 men and women in my department, and sometimes I wonder who really is in charge. It seems that every time I give a work order to someone, he or she goes out and talks it over with co-workers. Most of the time they follow my instructions, but it seems as if they refuse to do anything until they check it out with somebody in the department. This goes for simple instructions as well as for more complex problems that we've had. I've had departmental group meetings where I've asked for their help to figure out better ways to do things. They usually don't come up with anything in the meetings or when I'm around, but sometimes they come up with suggestions after they have talked it over themselves.

While I'm at it, Sam, I really don't know how to size up their morale. Some days the employees seem to be as happy as larks, and they go about their jobs as if they don't have a care in the world. On other days, it's just doom and gloom. I've been getting more and more requests from individuals about taking days off because of personal problems they have at home. This is getting to be a real pain. If I start worrying more about what's going on in their personal lives, how will I ever get the departmental work done? I wish you could tell me what I should do. Sometimes I think we would be better off having a union in this place, because then all I would have to do is deal with one shop steward instead of a bunch of individuals and groups who primarily are just looking out for themselves.

As director of human resources, you know that your supervisor needs help. What should you say to her? **YOU MAKE THE CALL.**

UNDERSTANDING WORK GROUPS AND THEIR IMPORTANCE

1 Explain why work groups form and function and their importance.

In Chapter 10 we presented a brief overview of the "informal organization," with particular reference to the supervisor's relationship with informal work groups and their leaders. We mentioned that informal work groups can exert a positive or negative influence on employee motivation and performance. Throughout this book we have emphasized that a supervisor's decisions must be concerned not only with employees as individuals, but also with how they relate to groups both within and outside the supervisor's own department.

An individual's motivations and clues to behavior are often found in the context of the person's associates, colleagues, and peers. On the job, an employee's attitudes and morale can be shaped to a large degree by co-workers, at times even more so than by the supervisor or other factors in the work environment. Therefore, a supervisor should be aware of work groups and how they function. Moreover, a supervisor needs to develop a keen understanding of how morale influences employee performance and what can be done to maintain a high level of morale at the departmental level.

Why Work Groups Form and Function

There are many reasons why work groups form and function in work settings.[1] Among the most commonly identified reasons are:

1. *Companionship and identification.* The work group provides a peer relationship and a sense of belonging, which help satisfy the individual employee's social needs.
2. *Behavior guidelines.* People tend to look to others, especially their peers, for motivational guides to acceptable behavior in the workplace.
3. *Problem solving.* The work group may be instrumental in providing a viable means by which an individual employee may solve a personal problem.
4. *Protection.* The old adage of "strength in numbers" is not lost on employees, who often look to the group for protection from outside pressures, such as those placed by supervisors and higher-level managers.

Much behavioral research has focused on factors that make work groups tightly knit, cohesive, and effective. Work groups are most cohesive when:

1. The group members perceive themselves to have a higher status as compared to other employees, as, for example, in matters of job classification or pay.
2. The group is generally small in size.
3. The group shares similar personal characteristics, such as age, sex, ethnic background, off-the-job interests, and the like.
4. The group is located relatively distant from other employees, such as geographically dispersed work groups or groups located away from the home office.
5. The group has been formed due to outside pressures or for self-protection, such as a layoff or disciplinary action taken by management.
6. Group members can communicate with one another relatively easily.
7. The group has been successful in some previous group effort, which encourages the members to seek new group objectives.

Of course, a supervisor will never be completely aware of the kinds of forces that are most prevalent in the group dynamics of the department. However, a sensitivity to the considerations just described can help the supervisor deal with work groups more effectively.

CLASSIFICATIONS OF WORK GROUPS

2 Classify clusters of work groups and their meaning for supervisors.

Four major clusters of employee work groups exist in most organizations.[2] They can be classified as command groups, task groups, friendship groups, and special-interest groups. Since there is some overlap in these classifications, a supervisor should recognize that individual employees may be members of several such groups simultaneously.

Command group
Grouping of employees according to authority relationships on the formal organization chart.

Command Group. The **command group** is a grouping of employees according to the authority relationships shown on the formal organizational chart. For example, at the departmental level a command group consists of the supervisor and the employees who report to this supervisor. Throughout the organization there will be interrelated departments or divisions of command groups that reflect the formal authority structure.

Task group
Grouping of employees who come together to accomplish a particular task.

Task Group. Consisting of employees from different departments, a **task group** comes together to accomplish a particular task. For example, for a telephone to operate in a customer's home, the telephone company's employees and supervisors from a number of departments—such as customer service, construction, plant installation, central office equipment, accounting, and test center—may come into contact with one another to accomplish the job. Another example would be a hospital, where numerous interdepartmental task relationships and communications take place among hospital personnel from departments such as admitting, nursing, laboratory, dietary, pharmacy, physical therapy, and medical records in order to care for a patient.

Friendship group
Informal grouping of employees based on similar personalities and social interests.

Friendship Group. The **friendship group** is an informal group of people who have similar personalities and social interests. Many friendship groups are related primarily to common factors such as age, sex, ethnic background, outside interests, and marital status. Of course, the presence of command and task groups may be instrumental in bringing clusters of friendship groups together.

Special-interest group
Grouping of employees that exists to accomplish something in a group that individuals do not choose to pursue individually.

Special-Interest Group. The **special-interest group** exists to accomplish in a group something that individuals feel incapable of or unwilling to pursue individually. Such a group can be either temporary or permanent. A temporary special-interest group might be a committee of employees who wish to protest an action taken by a supervisor or management, to promote a charitable undertaking, or to organize an employee picnic. A labor union is an example of a more permanent special-interest group, since it is legally and formally organized. A labor union brings together employees from different departments and divisions to unite them in striving for economic and other objectives.

As stated earlier, an employee may be a member of a number of groups in the workplace, and the supervisor who understands the nature of these different groups is more likely to be in a position to influence them. Some research studies have suggested that a supervisor has a better chance to influence an individual employee's behavior as a member of a work group than to deal with that employee individually (that is, without having the work group's influence in mind). Some concepts in this regard will be presented later in this chapter.

SUPERVISORY APPROACHES FOR MANAGING WORK GROUPS

3 Suggest supervisory approaches for managing work groups that are consistent with the Hawthorne Studies and other behavioral research.

Numerous behavioral studies have been made of work groups and how they function. From these, a number of approaches for managing work groups effectively have been suggested. Although they are by no means certain to produce the desired results, they are consistent with behavioral research findings concerning work group dynamics and group behavior.

Insights from the Hawthorne Studies

Hawthorne Studies
Comprehensive research studies that focused on work-group dynamics as related to employee attitudes and productivity.

The work group studies that probably have had the most lasting influence during this century were conducted in the late 1920s and early 1930s at the Western Electric Company's Hawthorne plant near Chicago, Illinois.[3] Known as the **Hawthorne Studies,** they remain even today a comprehensive and definitive source on the subject of work-group dynamics as related to employee attitudes and productivity.

A brief synopsis of two of the major experiments at the Hawthorne plant is given here. These are the relay assembly room experiment and the bank wiring observation room experiment.

Relay Assembly Room Experiment. In the relay assembly room experiment, a group of six female employees worked on jobs consisting of assembling electrical relay equipment. They were closely observed in a special room while being subjected to varying conditions. For about two years, researchers experimented with a number of scheduling arrangements, such as changes in rest and lunch periods, in workday arrangements, and in the workweek. Regardless of whether the changes instituted were favorable or unfavorable to the group, the outcome was that the employees' performance generally improved. By the end of this experiment, overall productivity had risen to about 30 percent over the pre-experiment level!

The researchers found that the primary reasons for the marked improvement in work performance were the attitudes and morale that had developed the employees into a solid, cohesive group. The employees became involved in the changes that were implemented, and they felt that they were part of a team. The employees said that they felt that their supervision was much more informal and relaxed than they had experienced previously. Equally important was the fact that they considered the experiment to be an important part of a major project in the company. Since their work took on new importance, they developed their own norms for doing their jobs better. The research results clearly showed that a work group can be a positive influence on job performance if the group believes that it is part of a team and that what they are doing is important.

Bank Wiring Observation Room Experiment. A second group research experiment at the Hawthorne plant occurred a little later and lasted for almost a year. It involved 14 male employees whose work was to attach and solder banks of wires to telephone equipment. These employees and an observer were placed in a special room. The purpose of this experiment was to determine the impact of a series of wage incentive plans on employee productivity. The result of this experiment, however, revealed that a work group can have a negative influence on job performance. It turned out that the bank wiring observation room employees, as a group, developed an entirely different approach to their jobs than did the women in the relay assembly room experiment. The men decided to restrict output and keep it at a constant standard (or norm), which they referred to as the "bogey." It was learned from observation and interviews with the men in this group that there was strong pressure on the group members not to do anything more than the standard agreed upon by them. In effect, their approach was to maintain production at a level considered sufficient to keep the company satisfied, but not nearly as much as the employees could do. In fact, the employees believed that if they increased production significantly, it would not mean higher wages but would instead lead to a management "speed-up" without additional compensation, and some employees might be laid off.

In today's businesses, many supervisors complain that their employees would perform at higher levels if it were not for work groups that place considerable pressure on individual employees not to do too much. The ongoing challenge to today's supervisor is to encourage positive attitudes among work groups to perform at superior levels, such as that exhibited many years ago by the relay assembly room group at the Hawthorne plant.

Influencing Work Groups Toward Positive Goals

While no approach will succeed in all situations, the following are some approaches by which supervisors can influence work groups in a positive direction.

Assigning Compatible Employees. Generally, it is preferable for a supervisor to assign employees who are friendly with each other to work together or at adjoining workstations. Human nature is such that trying to force people who dislike each other to work together—or even in close proximity—will usually lead to disruption. A number of studies have shown that employees who like each other tend to perform better as a team than those who are antagonistic toward each other. It may be possible for the supervisor to allow employees to choose from their own work groups for certain tasks. For example, several studies in the construction industry showed that when carpenters and bricklayers were allowed to pick their co-workers on work projects, these teams outproduced comparable groups who were assigned solely by a supervisor. A caution, however, is that the supervisor must see to it that friendship does not lead to too much socializing, which interferes with completion of their jobs.

Counseling the "Loners." Another approach is to be alert for individual employees who seem to be "loners" or who have difficulty adjusting to their co-workers. By having a private counseling session with such an individual, the supervisor may be able to uncover the reasons for this situation and take actions to help the individual gain acceptance by his or her peers. This is especially important if the "loner" is a new employee. As was discussed in Chapter 14, it may be desirable to assign a senior employee to help a new employee get familiar with the new work environment and be brought into the social functioning of the department.

Rotating Assignments. Another technique that can foster a sense of teamwork in the department is to rotate work assignments within a group. This technique can take the form of job rotation, job enlargement, or job enrichment, which were discussed as motivational approaches in Chapter 5. Having employees fill in on different jobs, or do some of the more challenging jobs, often helps provide them with a greater sense of identity with the group. For example, restaurant managers train their servers to help one another in the overall job of serving customers. Even though they may have their own specific table assignments, they help each other by cleaning tables, pouring water, or performing other services. If better service is provided, then these servers should receive more generous tips from appreciative customers.

Maintaining a Managerial Perspective. Regardless of which approach is used, supervisors must maintain their perspective as managers. This means that a supervisor should not become too personally involved in their employees' problems. Becoming too close to any individual or work group within a department may lead a supervisor to lose objectivity in decision making. It may also open a supervisor to criticism for showing favoritism to certain employees. As the old saying goes, "You can't be a buddy and a boss!"

Generally, it is more desirable for supervisors to socialize on the job with other supervisors and members of management, although this may not be comfortable for some supervisors. Ideally, supervisors need to balance loyalty to higher-level management and to their employee work groups. This is not an easy task. But the supervisor who is sensitive to work groups and who maintains a sound managerial perspective can usually figure out ways to manage work groups effectively and, at the same time, have a cordial relationship with them.

BUILDING EFFECTIVE WORK TEAMS THROUGH ORGANIZED PARTICIPATIVE MANAGEMENT PROGRAMS

4 Identify principles for building effective work teams that are associated with organized participative management programs.

In a number of places in this book we have mentioned various types of organized participative management programs. These have been called by many names—most prominently quality circles, employee involvement, and total quality management (TQM). Many firms have developed their own versions, but all have certain characteristics in common. For the most part, they try to build effective work teams that will foster continual improvement of work processes, project tasks, and service to customers. Thus, they are easily classified as "task groups," which were defined earlier in this chapter.

Figure 17-1 is a statement excerpted from a major company training manual that summarizes this firm's commitment to developing teams throughout the organization that will make major contributions toward improvement. Like many other firms, this company has organized teams from all parts of its organization consisting of employees, supervisors, professionals, and others. These teams grapple with and find solutions for problems that cross departmental lines.

Many studies have been made of both effective and ineffective organized participative management programs. One of the most comprehensive was conducted by two management consultants, Jon Katzenbach and Douglas Smith.[4] They interviewed hundreds of team members in dozens of organizations that had utilized teams to address various types of problems. Their research led them to identify principles that were most associated with effective work teams. Among these were the following:

1. The members of the team must be committed to the group and the performance of the group.
2. Teams function better when they are small, usually 10 members or less.
3. Teams should be composed of individuals who have skills that are complementary and sufficient to deal with the problem at hand.
4. The team should be committed to an objective that is specific and realistic.

Not all participative management programs have been successful. In fact, a growing number of firms have abandoned these programs for a variety of reasons. Some problems were procedural or technical, such as cases in which the teams were preoccupied with internal processes rather than focusing on external and tar-

FIGURE 17-1
Excerpts from Policy
Statement Concerning
a Firm's Total Quality
Management Program

ELEMENTS OF A TOTAL QUALITY MANAGEMENT SYSTEM

People—Teams and Partnerships

People are obviously the primary drivers in reaching customer satisfaction. People develop the systems and the processes and in turn use them to perform their jobs.

How can we best work together? In complex operations like ours, we need to bring groups of people together so that they can apply their combined talents to develop and improve processes. As more and more companies are learning, we need to work in teams. Teams enable the company to bring every ounce of intelligence and motivation and experience to bear on a process or problem or opportunity.

Every employee is empowered. This is one of the key elements of our TQM system. All employees have both the responsibility and the authority for performing their work, for the quality of their work, and for improving the way their work is done. They have the responsibility and authority to improve processes, procedures and systems that will improve the way their work is done.

Probably no element of our TQM system is more misunderstood than empowerment. It doesn't mean that employees can act totally independently of their supervisors; employees are empowered within defined boundaries. It doesn't mean that supervisors have no control over their areas of responsibility. Supervisors must still know what's going on and must set directions for the department; and among other duties, they must give people regular and constructive feedback.

Management, employees, union members, suppliers, customers—all are important constituencies for our company, and one of our goals is to build teams among them in order to achieve our goal of total customer satisfaction.

A partnership or team in which all members accept responsibility for their work, a team that gets the kind of support and coaching it needs to accomplish its tasks, is a team that produces impressive results.

geted results. Perhaps the primary reason why some organized participative management programs have failed is that management was looking for a "quick fix." Stating this another way, a program such as TQM will work only to the degree that top-level management gives its full support, effort, and resources over a period of time to make the program a major part of ongoing organizational life.[5]

UNDERSTANDING AND MAINTAINING EMPLOYEE MORALE

5 Discuss the importance of employee morale and its relationship to teamwork and productivity.

Most definitions of morale recognize that it is essentially a state of mind. For example, Webster's dictionary defines the word "morale" as "the mental and emotional condition (as of enthusiasm, spirit, loyalty) of an individual or a group with regard to the function or tasks at hand." For our purposes we will consider **morale** as consisting of the attitudes and feelings of individuals and groups toward their work, their environment, their supervisors, top-level management, and the or-

CONTEMPORARY ISSUE
When Does an Employee Work Group Committee Violate Labor Law?

Two 1993 case decisions decided by the federal agency that interprets the major law governing labor relations in the United States have placed cooperative types of employee work group committees under a legal cloud.

In a decision of the National Labor Relations Board (NLRB) involving Electromation, Inc., of Elkhart, Indiana, the NLRB ruled that worker committees that had been set up by the company to tackle various kinds of problems in the plant were a violation of national labor law. The company had organized worker groups to meet, discuss, and make recommendations concerning certain issues, including absenteeism, smoking policies, pay, and attendance bonuses. These worker committees were established at about the same time the Teamsters Union began an organizing campaign among the plant's workers. The NLRB unanimously held that the worker committees were in violation of the law, because in reality they were "sham unions."

In a second decision, involving a New Jersey plant of the DuPont Corporation, the NLRB held that seven "safety and fitness committees" were "illegal labor organizations." The Board held that these committees were set up, organized, and controlled by plant management and dealt with issues such as incentives and awards for workers when the Chemical Workers

Union already represented plant employees.

In general, management groups have denounced these NLRB decisions as being a major blow to various types of cooperative programs such as quality circles, total quality management (TQM), and the like. Some believe that virtually all types of employee participation programs could conceivably come under legal scrutiny. However, labor unions and other observers believe that the decisions of the National Labor Relations Board were more narrowly drawn from the specific circumstances of the Electromation and DuPont cases.

Both cases may be appealed further in the federal courts. At this time, however, it appears that worker committees that are set up primarily for communications; that offer ideas and suggestions regarding work processes, quality, and the like; and that primarily deal with matters that the employee groups themselves decide, will probably pass the legal test. However, work groups that become involved in handling complaints or grievances, wages, hours of work, and other matters of employment probably will be violations of the law. In cases where a union already is present to represent the employees, worker committees that are set up unilaterally by management probably will be in legal limbo.

Source: See Bob Smith, "Employee Committee or Labor Union?" *Management Review* (Volume 82, Number 4, April 1993), pp. 54–57; and Kevin G. Salwen, "DuPont Is Told It Must Disband Nonunion Panels," *The Wall Street Journal* (June 7, 1993), pp. A2 and A4.

Morale
A composite of feelings and attitudes that individuals and groups have toward their work, their environment, their supervisors, top-level management, and the organization.

ganization. Morale is not a single feeling, but a composite of feelings and attitudes. It affects employee performance and willingness to work, which in turn affect individual and organizational objectives. When employee morale is high, employees usually do what the organization wants them to do; when it is low, the opposite tends to occur.

Recent studies have suggested that today's employees are unhappier with many aspects of their jobs than were employees of earlier decades. Much of this lowered morale is attributed to a belief that many employers do not trust and are not loyal to their employees, and therefore employees do not trust and are not loyal to their employers. Thus, employees are likely to change jobs more frequently than otherwise would be the case.[6]

There should be little doubt that employee morale is an important supervisory consideration. Some supervisors simply believe that morale is something that employees either have or do not have. Actually, morale is always present in some form, and it can be positive (high), negative (low), or a mixture. High morale, of course, is desirable. Employees with high morale find satisfaction in their positions, have confidence in their abilities, and usually work with enthusiasm and to the extent of their abilities. High morale cannot be ordered, but it can be fostered by conditions in the workplace that are favorable to its development. High morale is not the cause of good human relations; it is the result of good human relations. High morale is the result of positive motivation, respect for people, effective supervisory leadership, good communication, participation, counseling, and desirable human relations practices. The state of employee morale reflects to a large degree how effectively a supervisor is performing his or her managerial responsibilities.

Morale Should Be Everyone's Concern

Every manager, from the chief executive down to the supervisor, should be concerned with the morale of the workforce. It should be a priority concern to develop and maintain employee morale at as high a level as possible without sacrificing the company's objectives. The first-line supervisor, probably more than anyone else, influences the level of morale in day-to-day contacts with employees.

Bringing morale to a high level and maintaining it there is a continuous process; it cannot be achieved simply through short-run devices such as pep talks or contests. High morale is slow to develop and difficult to maintain. The level of morale can vary considerably from day to day. Morale is contagious in both directions, because both favorable and unfavorable attitudes spread rapidly among employees. Unfortunately it seems to be human nature that employees quickly forget the good and long remember the bad when it comes to factors influencing their morale.

The supervisor is not alone in desiring high morale. Employees are just as much concerned with morale, since it is paramount to their work satisfaction. High morale helps to make the employee's day at work a pleasure and not a misery. High morale also is important to an organization's customers. They usually can sense whether employees are serving them with enthusiasm or just going through the motions with a "care-less" attitude.

Relationships Among Morale, Teamwork, and Productivity

Teamwork
People working cooperatively to solve problems and achieve goals important to the group.

Teamwork is often associated with morale, but the two terms do not mean the same thing. Morale refers to the attitudes and feelings of employees, whereas **teamwork** means people working cooperatively to solve problems and achieve goals important to the group. Good morale is helpful in achieving teamwork, but teamwork can be high when morale is low. Such a situation might exist in times when jobs are scarce and employees tolerate bad conditions and poor supervision for fear of losing their jobs. On the other hand, teamwork may be absent when morale is high. For example, employees working on a piecework basis or salespeople being paid on a straight commission basis typically are rewarded for individual efforts rather than for group performance.

Many supervisors believe that high morale usually is accompanied by high productivity. Much research has been done to study this assumption. Although there are many ramifications and some contradictions in research results, there is sub-

Teamwork is an
effective way to
achieve organizational
objectives.

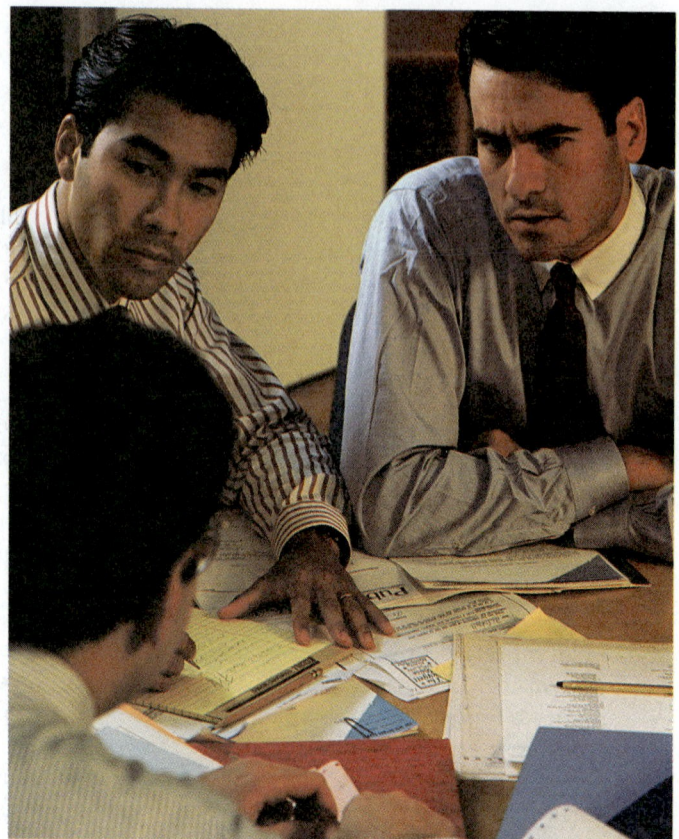

stantial evidence to suggest that in the long run high-producing employees do tend
to have high morale. That is to say, well-motivated, self-disciplined groups of employees tend to do a more satisfactory job than those from whom the supervisor
tries to force such performance. Furthermore, when supervisors are considerate of
their employees and try to foster positive attitudes among them, there tends to be
greater mutual trust, lower absenteeism and turnover, and fewer grievances.[7]
Regardless of its other effects, there is little question that a high level of morale
tends to make work more pleasant, particularly for the supervisor!

6 Understand the
factors that influence
employee morale and
the supervisor's role in
dealing with both
external and internal
factors.

FACTORS INFLUENCING MORALE

Virtually anything can influence the morale of employees either positively or negatively. Some of these are within the control of the supervisor; others are not. These
factors generally can be classified as two broad types: external and internal.

External Factors

Influences outside the organization generally are beyond the supervisor's control. Nevertheless, they may significantly affect the morale of employees at work. Examples of external factors are family relationships, care of children or elderly parents, problems with friends, a breakdown of the car, sickness or death in the family, outside pressures, and the like. What happens at home can change an employee's feelings very quickly. An argument before leaving for work may set an emotional tone for the rest of the day. Even headlines in the morning newspaper may be depressing or uplifting.

Counseling interview
Nondirective interview during which the supervisor listens empathetically and encourages the employee to discuss problems openly and develop solutions.

Because external factors are beyond the supervisor's direct control, the supervisor can only be alert to them, especially when an employee's attendance or good performance is slipping. One way to mitigate the negative effects of an outside occurrence is to meet privately with the employee in a counseling interview. A **counseling interview** is essentially nondirective (as described in Chapter 14); the supervisor primarily serves as an empathetic listener, and the employee is encouraged to discuss his or her problem frankly and to develop solutions.

By being a good listener, the supervisor can find out what happened and may help the employee develop alternatives. For example, an employee is upset because of a sudden financial crisis, and her work performance shows a marked decline. She spends more time thinking about how to solve her financial problems than she does thinking about her work. The supervisor may serve as an empathetic listener by discussing with the employee possible avenues to obtain financial counseling or assistance. The supervisor should not offer specific advice, which might bring unwanted repercussions. If the employee should feel dissatisfied with the results of following a supervisor's advice, she might blame the supervisor for her problems. This would only complicate a difficult situation. If the problem is beyond the supervisor's range of experience, perhaps the supervisor can arrange for the employee to get help from a professional or refer the employee to the human resources department, where assistance may be available. For example, although only a small percentage of employers have their own child-care facilities, many employers provide various forms of assistance and referral services for employees who have child-care and other family-care problems.[8] Many large employers also have employee assistance programs, which will be discussed later in this chapter.

Aside from a private counseling interview or referral of the employee to some source of assistance, there may be little else that the supervisor can do to cope with the outside factors that affect an employee's morale. The supervisor's main role is to help get the employee's performance back to an acceptable level.

If the employee's problem involves a request for a leave of absence because of sickness or because of certain family considerations such as childbirth or care for a seriously ill member of the immediate family, the supervisor normally should refer the request to the human resources department or higher-level managers. Many employers have developed policies for handling such requests. In late 1993, however, the federal Family and Medical Leave Act was enacted. It mandates that employers with 50 or more employees must follow certain requirements in response to

FIGURE 17-2
Major Provisions of the
Family and Medical
Leave Act

THE FAMILY AND MEDICAL LEAVE ACT OF 1993 (FMLA)

The Family and Medical Leave Act of 1993 became effective on August 5, 1993, and it is administered by the U.S. Department of Labor. Major provisions of this Act include the following:

- Employers that have 50 or more employees within a 75-mile radius are covered; coverage applies to businesses and also nonprofit and governmental organizations.
- Employers are required to provide up to 12 weeks of unpaid leave upon the birth, adoption, or serious illness of a child; or to care for a seriously ill spouse or parent; or in case of an employee's own serious illness.
- Health care coverage of employees must be continued during the unpaid leave.
- Employees are guaranteed that they will return either to the same job or to a comparable position upon completion of the leave.
- Certain employees can be exempted. Among these are "key" employees, defined as the highest paid 10 percent of the workforce and whose leave could cause economic harm to the employer; employees who have not worked for a year; and employees who have not worked at least 1,250 hours, or 25 hours a week, in the previous 12 months.
- An employer may require a doctor's certification or a second medical opinion to verify a serious illness.
- An employee's accrued paid leave can be substituted for part of the 12-week period of family leave.
- Employees can be required to provide 30 days' notice for those kinds of leaves that are called "foreseeable," such as for birth, adoption, or planned medical treatment.

requests for leaves for medical and family reasons. Figure 17-2 provides a summary of the principal provisions of this law, which generally requires the employer to grant up to 12 weeks of unpaid leave to workers who request it because of sickness; after childbirth or adoption; or to care for a seriously ill child, spouse, or parent.[9]

Numerous states also have passed their own laws to cover family and medical leaves. In some cases, these laws cover smaller employers, have different eligibility standards, and may require the employer to grant leaves for purposes other than those covered in the federal statute.[10]

Internal Factors and the Supervisor's Influence

Conditions within the company can also influence morale. Examples of internal factors are compensation, job security, the nature of work, relations with co-workers, working conditions, recognition, and so on. These factors are partially or fully within the supervisor's control. For example, when compensation is adequate, other factors may assume a more significant role. But even when wages are good,

FIGURE 17-3
A supervisor's general attitude and behavior can result in good or poor employee morale.

morale can sink quickly if working conditions are neglected. The critical factor here is whether or not the supervisor attempts to improve working conditions. Employees often will perform very well under undesirable conditions and still maintain high morale if they believe that their supervisor is seriously trying to improve conditions.

All aspects of good supervision impact employee morale in relation to conditions on the job. However, as illustrated in Figure 17-3, probably the most significant influence on employee morale is the supervisor's general attitude and behavior in day-to-day relationships. If a supervisor's behavior indicates suspicion about the employees' motives and actions, low morale will likely result. If the supervisor acts worried or depressed, employees tend to follow suit. If the supervisor loses his or her temper, some employees may also lose theirs. Conversely, if the supervisor shows confidence in the employees' work and commends them for good performance, this reinforces their positive outlook.

This does not mean that a supervisor should overlook difficulties that arise from time to time. Rather, it means that if something goes wrong, the supervisor should act as a leader who has the situation in hand. The supervisor should demonstrate an attitude that the employees will be relied on to correct the situation and to do what is necessary to prevent occurrence of a similar situation.

Supervisors should not relax in their efforts to build and maintain high employee morale. However, they should not become discouraged if morale drops from time to time, because many factors beyond their control can cause this. Supervisors can be reasonably satisfied if employee morale is high most of the time.

PROGRAMS FOR ASSISTING EMPLOYEES WITH PERSONAL AND WORK-RELATED PROBLEMS

7 Identify programs that organizations use to assist employees with personal and work-related problems.

As discussed previously, supervisors at times hold counseling interviews with employees who are exhibiting low morale or experiencing personal or work-related problems. By being an empathetic and sincere listener, the supervisor may help such employees work out their own solutions or suggest avenues of professional advice or assistance. Alternatively, the supervisor may refer an employee to the human resources department or some designated management person who will hold the counseling interview and suggest possibilities for help.

In recent years, many organizations—especially large corporations and major government agencies—have adopted **employee assistance programs (EAPs).** These programs typically involve a special department or outside resources retained by the firm to whom supervisors may refer employees with certain types of problems.[11] Additionally, employees may seek help on their own from the EAP, or they may be referred to the EAP by other sources, such as their union. Most employee assistance programs provide help for alcoholism and substance abuse; marriage, child-care, and family problems; financial questions; and other personal, emotional, or psychological problems that may be interfering with job performance. Figure 17-4 is a policy statement included in the EAP booklet provided to employees of a major corporation, which illustrates the typical elements of this type of program.

Employee assistance program (EAP)
Company program to assist employees with certain personal or work-related problems that are interfering with job performance.

The supervisor's role in an EAP is essential for its effectiveness. The supervisor needs to be alert to signs that an employee may be troubled, even though the supervisor has tried to respond to the employee's work performance using normal supervisory procedures. For example, a supervisor may be concerned about an employee's recent poor attendance and low production while at work. The supervisor suspects that something is amiss, perhaps an alcohol-related problem. In talking with the employee, the supervisor should focus primarily on the person's poor or deteriorating job performance and then suggest to the employee the EAP services that might be of some help. Figure 17-5 is a procedural statement excerpted from a supervisory policy manual within a major firm's EAP. The procedural guidelines for supervisors in this policy are representative of types of approaches that most major organizations have adopted in their EAP efforts.

Most EAPs emphasize the confidential nature of the services. Supervisors should discuss this with employees and assure them that no stigma will be associated with their seeking EAP help. However, the supervisor should inform an employee who refuses EAP assistance and whose work performance continues to deteriorate that such a refusal might be a consideration in a termination decision.

Ombudsman
Staff person who serves as a neutral mediator in resolving conflicts on the job.

Another approach for assisting employees with special work-related problems is to use an **ombudsman** (or "corporate ombudsman"). Typically, the ombudsman is a staff person who serves as a neutral mediator in resolving conflicts on the job. Only large companies are likely to have an ombudsman. The person serving in the ombudsman role may or may not be part of an EAP program or human resources staff. In some firms the ombudsman is part of a separate department, which might

FIGURE 17-4
Policy Statement for an
Employee Assistance
Program (EAP)

EMPLOYEE ASSISTANCE PROGRAM

Introduction

The employee assistance program (EAP) was adopted to provide confidential, professional assistance to employees and their families. The program also provides managers and union representatives with a constructive way to help employees and reduce the adverse economic impact to the company that occurs when personal problems interfere with job performance.

How the Program Works

There are essentially four ways that a person may enter the EAP—self-referral, management referral, union referral, or medical referral.

Self-Referral

Any employee or family member may call the EAP office for information or to make an appointment to discuss a personal problem. The contact, as well as what is discussed, is handled in strictest confidence.

Management Referral

Managers and supervisors may suggest to an employee that he or she seek help when there is a noticeable decline in the employee's work performance that is not correctable through usual supervisory procedures or where there are specific on-the-job incidents that indicate the presence of a personal problem.

Union Referral

Official union representatives are encouraged to ask their members to make use of the services provided by the EAP. Union officials may call the EAP office and speak with the counselor or provide the employee or family member with the EAP office telephone number.

Medical Referral

Medical referrals to the EAP will be based either upon the identification of a medical symptom or disorder that is normally associated with a personal problem or upon a request from the employee for advice or assistance regarding a personal problem.

be identified as the "personnel communications department" or the "liaison department." Employees who have work-related problems are encouraged to come to this department to be interviewed confidentially. Often the employee has a conflict with his or her supervisor that the employee is afraid to discuss with the supervisor. Or perhaps the employee is dissatisfied about something that has happened—for example, being passed over for a promotion, being disciplined, being

FIGURE 17-5
One Firm's Procedural
Guidelines for EAP
Case Handling by
Supervisors

SUPERVISORY PROCEDURES FOR EAP CASE HANDLING

The employee assistance program is for all employees—management and occupational—who want help with their personal problems. The EAP is prepared to accept referrals from many sources, including supervisors and union representatives, who believe that personal problems are causing an employee's job performance to deteriorate. Experience has shown that many employees will seek assistance once they realize that help is readily available. But the decision to seek help must always be the employee's, and actual counseling should be left to professionals.

The following procedures generally apply when trying to help an employee improve job performance:

Talk about job performance in an initial discussion with the employee. Only deteriorating job performance should be discussed. Opinions and judgments about possible personal problems should be avoided—leave that to the professional counselor. Specific instances of deteriorating job performance, such as unsatisfactory attendance, quality of work, or productivity, will be the basis for the initial discussion.

Employees who initiate discussion of personal problems with either supervisors or union representatives should be informed of the employee assistance program and encouraged to participate on a voluntary basis.

Describe the employee assistance program after job performance has been discussed. Tell the employee about the service available through the employee assistance program. Stress that EAP contacts are confidential; no information concerning the nature of the problem or the specific treatment will be revealed without the employee's consent. Usually, the employee will not be terminated for the unsatisfactory job performance until an opportunity to use EAP has been offered.

If the employee chooses to accept help, referral will be made directly to the EAP counselor to determine the nature of the problem and develop a course of action.

To help the EAP counselor, any information pertaining to the employee's job performance or behavior should be provided by the supervisor or union representative at the time of referral.

The EAP counselor may determine that outside resources are appropriate. If so, these referrals will be made as necessary.

The employee will be allowed a reasonable period to improve job performance with the aid of counseling and supervisory support.

If the employee rejects the offer of assistance and the job performance problems do not continue or recur, nothing further need be done.

If the offer is rejected by the employee and job performance problems continue or recur, appropriate action may then be taken in accordance with existing company policy and the union agreement for handling problems of deteriorating job performance.

given unfair work assignments or schedules, and the like. The ombudsman listens to the employee's concerns and then may choose to follow a number of alternatives in an effort to resolve the problem. The ombudsman does not have any direct authority, but acts as a "third party" or "neutral service" when, for example, he or she meets with the employee's supervisor to discuss the matter and to see what—if anything—might be done. In this regard, the ombudsman is acting as a communications link, which often becomes the most important aspect of resolving or at least reducing the magnitude of a conflict.[12]

ASSESSING EMPLOYEE MORALE

8 Discuss techniques to assess employee morale, including observation and employee attitude surveys.

Although most firms believe that employee morale is important in the long run if the organization is to be successful, good measurements of employee morale are somewhat elusive. Some firms rely on statistical comparisons to assess the state of their company's morale. They look at data that compare their employees with industry standards for employee attendance, turnover, the use of sick leave, and other broad indicators.[13]

These comparisons are useful, but for supervisors they may or may not be relevant to the departmental situation. Some supervisors pride themselves on their ability to size up morale intuitively. However, most supervisors would be better advised to approach the measurement of morale in a more systematic fashion. Although it may not be possible to measure morale precisely, there are techniques for assessing prevailing levels and trends. The two most frequently used techniques are (1) observation and study and (2) attitude surveys.

Observing and Studying Indicators of Morale

By observing, monitoring, and studying patterns of employee behavior, a supervisor can often discover clues to employee morale. The supervisor should closely monitor such key indicators as job performance levels, tardiness and absenteeism, the amount of waste or scrap, employee complaints, and accident and safety records. Any significant changes in the levels of these indicators should be analyzed, since they often are interrelated. For example, excessive tardiness and absenteeism seriously interfere with job performance. The supervisor should find out why employees are often tardy or absent. If reasons are related to morale, are the causes within the supervisor's control, or should the employee be referred somewhere for counseling or assistance?

It is relatively easy to observe the extremes of high and low morale. However, it is quite difficult to differentiate among intermediate degrees of morale—or to assess when morale is changing. For example, an employee's facial expression or shrug of the shoulder may or may not reflect that person's level of morale. Only an alert supervisor can judge whether this employee is becoming depressed or frustrated. Supervisors must sharpen their powers of observation and be careful not to brush indicators of change conveniently aside.

The closeness of daily working relationships offers numerous opportunities for a supervisor to observe and analyze changes in employee morale. However, many supervisors do not take time to observe, and others do not analyze what they observe. It is only when an extreme, obvious drop in the level of morale has taken place that some supervisors recall the first indications of change. By then, the problems that led to this lowered state of morale probably will have magnified to the point where major corrective actions will be necessary. As so often is the case in supervision, an "ounce of prevention" would have been worth more than a "pound of cure."

Many companies conduct **exit interviews** with individuals leaving their employment. Exit interviews are usually conduced by a human resources staff person, although sometimes, especially in a small firm, the supervisor may fill this role. The interviewer asks questions about why the person is leaving and about conditions within the firm as that person sees them. Results of exit interviews are used to assess the morale in the firm or in certain departments of the firm, as well as to identify reasons for employee turnover.

Exit interview
Interview with individuals who leave a firm to assess morale and reasons for employee turnover.

Employee Attitude Surveys

Attitude survey
Survey of employee opinions about major aspects of organizational life used to assess morale.

Another approach to assessing employee morale is **attitude surveys,** also called "opinion" or "morale" surveys. Employees are asked to express their opinions about major aspects of organizational life, usually in the form of answers to questions printed on a survey form. The survey questionnaire elicits employee opinions about such factors as management and supervision, job conditions, job satisfaction, co-workers, pay and benefits, job security, advancement opportunities, and so on.

Employee attitude surveys are rarely initiated by a supervisor. Usually they are undertaken by top-level management and are prepared with the help of the human resources department or an outside consulting firm. The survey questionnaire should be written in language that is appropriate for most employees.

Attitude surveys, or questionnaires, may be completed on the job or in the privacy of the employee's home. Some organizations prefer to have employees answer these questionnaires on the job, because a high percentage of questionnaires that are mailed out are never returned. On the other hand, a possible advantage of filling out the questionnaire at home is that employees may give more thoughtful and truthful answers. Regardless of where they are completed, questionnaires should not be signed so that they remain anonymous, although some surveys may request employees to indicate their departments.

Many attitude survey forms offer employees the choice of answering questions from a given list of answers. Other forms are not so specific and provide employees the opportunity to answer as freely as they wish. Since some employees may find it difficult to write down their opinions in sentences or to complete started sentences, better results usually are obtained with a survey form on which the employees simply check the printed responses that correspond to their answers.

Follow-Up of Survey Results. The tabulation and analysis of questionnaires usually are assigned to the human resources department or to an outside consulting firm. Survey results are first presented to top-level and middle-level managers and eventually to departmental supervisors. In some organizations, survey results are used as discussion materials during supervisory training, especially when they provide clues about ways to improve employee morale.

Attitude surveys may reveal deficiencies that the supervisor can eliminate. For example, a complaint that there is a lack of soap in the washroom can be resolved easily. But frequently the responses are difficult to evaluate, as, for example, a complaint that communication channels are not open to employees. Such complaints raise more questions than answers and may necessitate a careful study of existing policies and procedures to see whether corrective actions are warranted.

If the attitude survey reveals a correctable problem at the departmental level—perhaps with an individual supervisor—the solution should be developed and implemented by the supervisor involved. On the other hand, a broader problem that requires the attention of higher-level managers should be reported to the appropriate manager for action. If supervisors and higher-level managers do not make needed changes as a result of a survey, the survey was a waste of time and money. In fact, if no changes materialize, or if changes are not communicated to the employees, a decline in morale may occur after the survey. Employees may feel that their problems and suggestions have been ignored. Thus, whenever possible, dissatisfactions expressed in an attitude survey should be addressed promptly by managers and supervisors, or at least employees should be informed that management is aware of the dissatisfactions and what may be done to change things by some future date.

Organizational Development. Many companies follow up their attitude surveys with feedback meetings and conference sessions with groups of employees and supervisors. Typically these meetings are conducted by an outside consultant, or by a staff person from the human resources or some other department. In these meetings, results of attitude surveys are discussed and debated openly. The groups are expected to develop recommendations for improvement, which are forwarded anonymously to higher-level management for consideration and possible implementation.

This approach is often part of a broader concept that also has become widespread in many large enterprises. Usually known as **organizational development (OD)** or "team building," or "conflict resolution," this usually involves having scheduled group meetings under the guidance of a neutral conference leader. The groups may involve just employees, employees and supervisors, just supervisors, just higher-level managers, or whatever composition is appropriate. For the most part, the meetings focus on solving problems that may be hindering effective work performance or causing disruption, poor coordination, fouled-up communications, and strained personal relations. When there is frank discussion in a relatively open and informal atmosphere, individuals tend to open up about what really is on their minds and what might be done to resolve problems and reduce conflict. Organiza-

Organizational development
Meetings with groups under the guidance of a neutral conference leader to solve problems that are hindering organizational effectiveness.

tional development can take numerous forms, which are beyond the scope of this text.[14] Suffice it to say, however, that many supervisors will be involved in organizational development efforts, since these programs can contribute to the improvement of morale and organizational effectiveness.

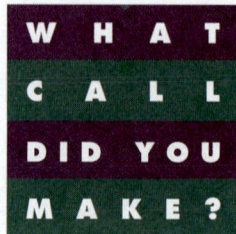

WHAT CALL DID YOU MAKE?

As Sam Moreno, director of human resources, you realize that your supervisor, Karen Jacobson, has some major problems in understanding and supervising her departmental employees. Jacobson has not been able to reach her people in a way that would build effective work teams with a high level of morale. All of the concepts and principles discussed in this chapter are relevant to Jacobson's problems. You should tell her to try to be more sensitive to the dynamics of the overall group and of the subgroups in her department. Counsel her about how to phrase work directives as requests or suggestions, rather than just giving out orders.

She should try to assess whether informal leaders have emerged. Furthermore, caution Jacobson to be patient in her approaches rather than expecting everyone in the department to be agreeable to everything that she has in mind. She should be con-

stantly alert for clues concerning changes in the morale of individuals and groups.

Jacobson also should be informed about the requirements of the Family and Medical Leave Act and your company's policies for accommodating leave requests of employees to deal with family matters. If your company has an assistance program to which employees can be referred, you should make your supervisor aware of the proper procedures to follow.

Finally, it might be appropriate for the human resources department to implement an employee attitude survey. By tabulating response data on a department-by-department basis, you could assess the state of morale in Jacobson's department in comparison to employees in other departments. This, too, could help identify problems and possibly point to areas needing supervisory and management attention.

SUMMARY

1 Explain why work groups form and function and their importance.

Work groups typically are formed to provide companionship and identification, behavior guidelines, problem-solving help, and protection. Various factors can contribute to the cohesiveness and functioning of the work group, such as the group's status, size, personal characteristics, location, and previous success. Work groups can exert significant influences upon employee attitudes and job performance, which supervisors must recognize and be prepared to deal with.

2 Classify clusters of work groups and their meaning for supervisors.

At any time, an employee may be a member of a command group, task group, friendship group, or special-interest group. Command and task groups are formed primarily based on job-related factors; friendship and special-interest groups primarily reflect personal relationships and interests. Supervisors should be sensitive to all of these clusters and how they impact employee members.

3 Suggest supervisory approaches for managing work groups that are consistent with the Hawthorne Studies and other behavioral research.

The Hawthorne research studies demonstrated that work groups can have either a positive or a negative influence on employee performance. To influence work groups in a positive direction, supervisors should consider approaches such as assigning compatible employees to work together, counseling and helping "loners" to adjust and become accepted by the peer group, rotating job assignments, and maintaining the proper supervisory relationship.

4 Identify principles for building effective work teams that are associated with organized participative management programs.

Organized participative management programs, such as total quality management (TQM), primarily involve building effective teams to work on tasks that will improve work performance and customer service. For such a program to be most effective, top-level managers must give their full support over a sufficient time period. The teams should be relatively small, and members must have sufficient skills and be committed to a specific and realistic objective.

5 Discuss the importance of employee morale and its relationship to teamwork and productivity.

Employee morale is a composite of feelings and attitudes of individuals and groups toward their work environment, supervision, and the organization as a whole. Morale can vary from very high to very low and can change considerably from day to day. A concern for morale should be felt by everyone in the organization. Morale and teamwork are not synonymous, but high morale usually contributes to high productivity.

6 Understand the factors that influence employee morale and the supervisor's role in dealing with both external and internal factors.

Morale can be influenced by factors from outside the organization as well as by on-the-job factors. There is relatively little a supervisor can do to change the existence of external factors. The supervisor can be an empathetic listener to the employee's concerns and perhaps refer the employee to a source of assistance. If an employee requests a leave of absence because of sickness or certain types of family considerations, the supervisor should refer this to higher-level management or the human resources department because of legal requirements that must be met. In general, a supervisor's own attitude and behavior can significantly influence employee morale.

Many internal factors associated with the job can influence employee morale. Good supervisory management practices can do much to positively influence these factors. The supervisor's general attitude and behavior in day-to-day relationships with employees will have the most influence on the direction of employee morale.

7 Identify programs that organizations use to
assist employees with personal and work-related problems.

To assist employees with personal and work-related problems that a supervisor would not
be competent to handle, some organizations have employee assistance programs or ombudsmen. EAPs and ombudsmen help employees solve problems that detract from their job performance. The goal is to restore them to their full capabilities to meet acceptable work standards.

8 Discuss techniques to assess employee morale,
including observation and employee attitude surveys.

Astute supervisors can sense a change in the level of morale by observing employee behaviors and key indicators, such as absenteeism and performance trends. Another means of assessing levels of employee morale is to conduct an attitude survey. Supervisors and higher-
level managers should—if possible—correct problems that have been brought to their
attention through the survey. It is also desirable to discuss the results of an attitude survey in
meetings with groups of employees and supervisors and to encourage them to recommend
improvements.

KEY TERMS

Command group (page 456)
Task group (page 456)
Friendship group (page 457)
Special-interest group (page 457)
Hawthorne Studies (page 457)
Morale (page 462)
Teamwork (page 463)
Counseling interview (page 465)

Employee assistance program (EAP) (page
  468)
Ombudsman (page 468)
Exit interview (page 472)
Attitude survey (page 472)
Organizational development (OD) (page
  473)

QUESTIONS FOR DISCUSSION

1.   What are some of the most common reasons for forming work groups? What are some
factors that make a work group cohesive? Is cohesiveness of a work group always desirable?
Discuss.

2.   Define each of the following classifications of work groups:
  a.   Command group.
  b.   Task group.
  c.   Friendship group.
  d.   Special-interest group.

3.   What were the principal aspects and results of the relay assembly room experiment
and the bank wiring observation room experiment conducted as part of the Hawthorne
Studies? Discuss the relevance of these findings to modern supervision.

4. Discuss various approaches that supervisors can implement to influence their work groups in a positive direction.

5. Identify some of the principles for building effective work teams that are associated with organized participative management programs (such as TQM). Why do employers sometimes abandon these efforts?

6. Define the concept of employee morale. Evaluate the statement "High morale is not the cause of good human relations; it is the result of good human relations."

7. Why should employee morale be of concern to everyone in the organization?

8. Discuss the relationships between (a) morale and teamwork and (b) morale and productivity. Is it possible for employees to have low morale and still perform at a high level of work performance? Discuss.

9. Differentiate between external factors and internal factors that influence employee morale. What should a supervisor do to minimize the influence of external factors on an employee's work?

10. What legal requirements must be met if an employee requests a leave of absence for sickness or family care reasons? What should a supervisor do when an employee requests a family or medical leave?

11. Why does the supervisor have a significant influence on employee morale? Should a supervisor make a major effort to be liked by his or her employees? Discuss.

12. Discuss the use of employee assistance programs and ombudsmen, especially in large enterprises. Why would such approaches probably not be cost-effective in small organizations?

13. How can study and observation be a basis for assessing employee morale at the departmental level?

14. Discuss the use of employee attitude surveys in assessing employee morale. Why is follow-up on survey results vital if an attitude survey is to be worth anything? What types of follow-up can managers and supervisors utilize? Discuss.

SKILLS APPLICATIONS

Skills Application 17-1: Policies and Procedures for Employee Personal and Work-Related Problems

1. Contact two human resources department employees who are willing to be interviewed concerning their firms' policies and procedures for handling employee personal and work-related problems. Preferably, one should be with an organization that has a formal employee assistance program (EAP); the other should be with a firm that does not have a formal program. In your interviews, ask these people to respond to the following:

a. What are your policies/procedures for supervisors to follow when they suspect that an employee's personal or work-related problems are hindering job performance?

b. What company and other assistance services are available for referral?

c. What are your policies/procedures regarding the time period and steps to be taken if the employee does not improve?

d. How has the Family and Medical Leave Act of 1993 changed the firm's policies/procedures concerning employee requests for leaves that are covered by this law?

2. Compare the responses of the human resources employees for similarities and differences. Were their policies/procedures more or less in line with the concepts and examples presented in this chapter? Why or why not?

Skills Application 17-2: An Employee Attitude Survey

Below are data from an attitude survey taken among 150 employees in a small industrial plant. There were 15 first-line supervisors in the plant. The question posed to employees was *"What attention or emphasis is given to the following by your supervisor?"*

	Too Much Attention	About Right	Too Little Attention	Does Not Apply
The quality of your work	32 (21%)	98 (65%)	16 (11%)	4 (3%)
Costs involved in your work	68 (45%)	57 (38%)	18 (12%)	7 (5%)
Meeting schedules	54 (36%)	62 (41%)	22 (15%)	12 (8%)
Getting your reactions and suggestions	28 (19%)	39 (26%)	80 (53%)	3 (2%)
Giving you information	24 (16%)	104 (69%)	20 (13%)	2 (1%)
Making full use of your abilities	23 (15%)	47 (31%)	68 (45%)	12 (8%)
Safety and housekeeping	38 (25%)	90 (60%)	12 (8%)	10 (7%)
Development of employees	40 (27%)	57 (38%)	48 (32%)	5 (3%)
Innovations, new ideas	26 (17%)	52 (35%)	70 (47%)	2 (1%)
Effective teamwork among employees	31 (21%)	102 (68%)	12 (8%)	5 (3%)

After reviewing the data, answer the following questions:

1. What overall observations would you make about the style of supervision that generally is in place according to the survey data? Why?

2. What positive factors were revealed by the survey data?

3. What specific actions would you suggest to respond to potential problems revealed by the survey data?

4. What role could a supervisory training and development program play in responding to the survey data?

Skills Application 17-3: The Supervisor and Work Groups

1. From the materials in this chapter, develop a list of the concepts and principles that were presented as being appropriate for supervision of work groups and building effective work teams.

2. Contact two supervisors (or managers) who are willing to be interviewed. One supervisor should be with a firm that has an organized participative management program (e.g., TQM) in place; the other should be with a firm that does not have such a program. Ask the supervisors to identify what they believe to be the five most important considerations and techniques for good supervision of work groups and building of effective work teams.

3. Compare the supervisors' lists with your list. To what degree were these lists similar or different? If there were major differences in the observations of the two supervisors, what do you feel were the reasons for this?

ENDNOTES

1.   For an expanded discussion of group processes in organizations, see Dan L. Costley and Ralph Todd, *Human Relations in Organizations* (4th ed.; St. Paul, Minn.: West Publishing Company, 1991), pp. 257–278.

2.   See David H. Holt, *Management: Principles and Practices* (3rd ed.; Englewood Cliffs, N.J.: Prentice-Hall, 1993), pp. 351–352.

3.   For discussions of the Hawthorne Studies and their impact, see Paul R. Timm, Brent D. Peterson, and Jackson C. Stevens, *People at Work* (3rd ed.; St. Paul, Minn.: West Publishing Company, 1990), pp. 6–12; or Andrew J. DuBrin and R. Duane Ireland, *Management and Organization* (2d ed.; Cincinnati: South-Western Publishing Co., 1993), pp. 39–40.

4.   Jon R. Katzenbach and Douglas K. Smith, *The Wisdom of Teams: Creating the High Performance Organization* (Boston: Harvard Business School Press, 1993).

5.   Oren Harari, "Ten Reasons Why TQM Doesn't Work," *Management Review* (Volume 82, Number 1, January 1993), pp. 33–38.

6.   See Robert Levering, "Can Companies Trust Their Employees?" *Business and Society Review* (Spring 1992), pp. 8–12.

7.   See D. W. Organ and T. S. Bateman, *Organizational Behavior* (4th ed.; Homewood, Ill.: Richard D. Irwin, 1991), pp. 548–550.

8.   See "Work-Family Programs Sound More Inclusive," *The Wall Street Journal* (May 10, 1993), p. B1; and "Employers Try New Ways to Help with Child Care," *The Wall Street Journal* (May 19, 1993), p. B1.

9.   See "Most Small Businesses Appear Prepared to Cope with New Family-Leave Rules," *The Wall Street Journal* (February 8, 1993), pp. B1–B2.

10.   See Warren Gorham Lamont Special Study, *Family and Medical Leaves: The New Federal Statute and State Laws* (New York: Research Institute of America, February 1993).

11.   See Cynthia D. Fischer, Lyle F. Schoenfeldt, and James B. Shaw, *Human Resource Management* (2d ed.; Boston: Houghton-Mifflin, 1993), pp. 653–660.

12.   For an evaluation of the effectiveness of employee problem solving and assistance approaches, see Kenneth M. Wexley and Gary O. Latham, *Developing and Training Human Resources in Organizations* (2d ed.; New York: HarperCollins Publishers, 1991), pp. 295–297.

13.   From "Checking Your Firm's Morale," *Communication Briefings* (Volume 12, Number 6, April 1993), p. 3.

14.   An excellent overall source is Larry Hirschhorn, *Managing in the New Team Environment* (Reading, Mass.: Addison-Wesley Publishing Company, 1991). This book is one in the publisher's series of texts on organizational development. Also, see Edward Glassman, *The Creativity Factor: Understanding the Potential of Your Team* (San Diego: Pfeiffer & Co., 1991).

The Supervisor and Protected Groups

LEARNING OBJECTIVES

After studying this chapter, you will be able to:

1 Identify the major categories of legally protected employees and general guidelines for supervising diversity.

2 Discuss issues involved in the supervision of racial/ethnic minority employees.

3 Discuss factors that are particularly important when supervising women employees.

4 Identify and discuss legal and other considerations involved in supervision of employees with physical and mental disabilities.

5 Discuss considerations involved when supervising older workers, employees of different religious views, and Vietnam-era and other veterans.

6 Recognize several pressures faced by supervisors who themselves are members of protected groups.

7 Discuss the issue of reverse discrimination.

8 Discuss the overriding concern in supervision of all employees.

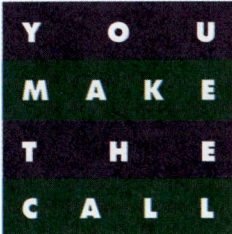

You are Charlie Willow, supervisor in a small printing plant. You have just had two interviews that left you confused. This morning one of your fairly new printing press assistant employees, Cindy Stowe, came into your office and accused her lead person, George Cross, of sexual and other forms of harassment. She claimed that Cross resented her as a woman on his otherwise male work crew, and that he continually criticized her for being unable to do her work in the way that Cross wanted it done. She claimed that Cross had told her that she was "too small and weak" to handle the job; further, Cross had used a number of obscene and sexual words when "yelling" at her to get the job done. Stowe stated that either it had to stop or she would file harassment and discrimination charges against the company.

About an hour later, however, you interviewed George Cross. His version was quite different. He denied ever having used any sexual or obscene words toward Cindy Stowe. He acknowledged that he had not been satisfied with her work since she came to work in the firm several months ago. However, he said he had gone to great lengths to help her whenever he could. Cross did not think that Stowe was able to handle the demands of the job, and he said that she had "a poor attitude." He denied ever having made any reference to her as being physically unable to do her work. Cross claimed that Stowe was simply out to get him in order to save her own job.

You frankly don't know whom to believe. You believe that there may be some merit in the statements of both employees, but you don't

481

know how to determine the truth. You know that your company has a strong policy prohibiting sexual harassment that is similar to the policy statement shown in Figure 18-3 in this chapter. You don't know how to apply the policy in this situation. What should you do? **YOU MAKE THE CALL.**

PROTECTED-GROUP EMPLOYEES AND SUPERVISION OF DIVERSITY

1 Identify the major categories of legally protected employees and general guidelines for supervising diversity.

Throughout this book, we have stressed the fact that employees are individuals shaped by a variety of forces from within and without the organization. In Chapter 17 we discussed how employees form groups and why supervisors should be aware of group dynamics. In this chapter we focus on the need for supervisors to develop a special awareness, sensitivity, and adaptability to protected-group employees, a term that we recognize in a legal sense but that also has many human dimensions.

The identification of employees who have been afforded special legal protection comes primarily from civil rights legislation, equal employment opportunity regulations, and numerous court decisions. Various laws and regulations that govern employment policies and practices are listed in Appendix I. Areas of lawful and potentially unlawful inquiry during the selection process of job applicants were presented in Table 13-1. For our purposes in this chapter, we will use the term **protected-group employees** to identify classes of employees who have been afforded certain legal protections in their employment situations. The underlying legal philosophy is that many individuals within these classes have been unfairly or illegally discriminated against in the past or that they should be afforded special consideration to enhance their opportunities for fair treatment in employment.

Protected-group employees
Classes of employees who have been afforded certain legal protections in their employment situations.

Classifications of Protected-Group Employees

The protected-group employees that we will discuss in this chapter are classified according to their:

- Racial/ethnic origin.
- Sex (i.e., women).
- Physical or mental disability (i.e., disabled, handicapped).
- Age (i.e., over 40).
- Religion.
- Military service (i.e., Vietnam-era or other veterans).

In recent years, much has been written about the management of diversity. As was discussed in Chapter 1, "diversity" in the workforce means that the workforce is quite heterogeneous, with a variety of ethnic, cultural, life-style, age, gender, religious, and other differences represented. Firms should make extra effort to provide channels of opportunity for those who otherwise might not be afforded them.[1]

The supervision of protected-group employees by definition is part of a firm's efforts to manage diversity in a way that will benefit both the firm and the employees. Regardless of personal views, supervisors must be sensitive to possible illegal discriminatory actions and adjust their supervisory practices accordingly. More important, however, is that supervisors recognize the strengths and potential contributions of *all* employees and supervise in ways that will not limit opportunities for development to any employee for inappropriate reasons.

The OUCH Test in Supervision of All Employees

The OUCH test, which we discussed in Chapter 13 as a guideline in selecting employees, also applies to day-to-day supervision. This test should remind supervisors that their actions should be:

O—*Objective,*

U—*Uniform in application,*

C—*Consistently applied,* and

H—*Have job relatedness.*

For example, assume that an organization's policy specifies a disciplinary warning for being tardy three times in one month. The supervisor should give the same warning to *every* employee who is late the third time in one month, regardless of whether the employee is in a protected-group category. This supervisory approach would meet the OUCH test, because the tardiness is an observable behavior that is objectively measured for all employees. The penalty is the same for all employees, is consistently applied, and is clearly job related.

A myth occasionally voiced by some supervisors is that certain categories of employees cannot be disciplined or discharged because of government regulations (Figure 18-1). That view is false. Laws and regulations do not prevent a supervisor from taking disciplinary action against protected-group employees. However, they do require that such employees be treated the same as other employees whenever disciplinary actions are taken. Therefore, it is extremely important that supervisors be careful in meeting the OUCH test and in justifying their actions through adequate documentation. We discuss this in more detail in Chapters 19 and 20.

SUPERVISING RACIAL AND ETHNIC MINORITY EMPLOYEES

2 Discuss issues involved in the supervision of racial/ethnic minority employees.

The most frequently identified racial and ethnic minority populations in the United States are African-Americans (blacks), Hispanics, native Americans, and Asian-Americans. With the passage of major civil rights legislation, most employers have developed nondiscrimination and/or affirmative-action policies or programs for employment of people from racial and ethnic minority groups. A major thrust of these policies and programs is to ensure that minorities, as well as certain other protected-group individuals, receive special consideration in hiring and promotion decisions. The philosophy underlying affirmative-action plans is to overcome the

FIGURE 18-1
One myth occasionally
voiced by some
supervisors is that
protected-group
employees cannot be
disciplined or
discharged.

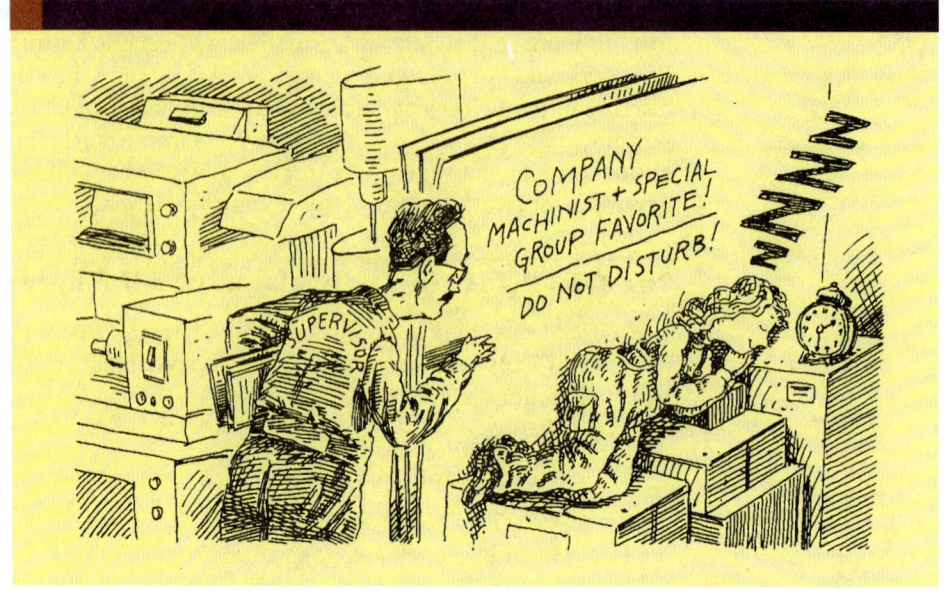

FIGURE 18-1
One myth occasionally voiced by some supervisors is that protected-group employees cannot be disciplined or discharged.

impact of past discriminatory practices and to provide greater opportunities for underrepresented groups to participate more fully throughout the workforce. The long-term goal is to have a fully diversified workforce in which all employees are hired and supervised solely on the basis of their individual capabilities and performance.

Effects of Previous Discrimination

Minority employees who have experienced prejudiced treatment may resent supervisors of different racial/ethnic backgrounds. The most common area of tension continues to be between black employees and white managers. Even though nondiscrimination laws have been in place for several decades, annual data compiled by the federal Equal Employment Opportunity Commission (EEOC) show that minority group members file tens of thousands of complaints about unfair treatment because of their race. Typically, alleged discriminatory discipline and discharge have been the most frequent bases for these complaints.

Since responsibility for initiating discipline and discharge actions usually rests with supervisors, such decisions play a significant role in generating charges of discrimination. Investigations of charges require extensive time, effort, and involvement of supervisors, human resources and legal specialists, and others. Thus supervisors must be sensitive to the feelings of minority employees who may have experienced discriminatory treatment in the past or who believe that they currently have been discriminated against in some way. Supervisors should respond with empathy to minority employees who display lingering resentment and suspicion. More important, supervisors must be fair and considerate when making decisions that affect these employees. By demonstrating that minority employees will be supervised in the same manner as other employees, a supervisor can reduce the negative effects of past discrimination.

Cultural Differences

A continuing debate about human behavior concerns how much heredity, as compared to environment, shapes an individual. Obviously, heredity is a major factor in the physical and ethnic makeup of a person. Moreover, because members of various races or ethnic origins often have different environmental experiences, unique subcultures have developed for each racial/ethnic minority group. For example, the ties that native Americans have to their heritage reflect their subculture. People of Asian descent have distinctive values and traditions that reflect their heritage and cultures.

Unfortunately, differences in cultural backgrounds can contribute to prejudicial attitudes and treatment of minority employees by supervisors. For example, a minority employee's values regarding the importance of work and punctuality may be different from those held by a supervisor. If a minority employee has not grown up in an environment that stresses the importance of being punctual, especially in a work situation, the supervisor must be prepared to spend extra time explaining to that employee the reasons for punctual attendance and the consequences of tardiness and absenteeism. Regardless of what cultural differences exist, it is the supervisor's job to exert special efforts to reduce the effects of these differences so that the minority person can become a fully contributing member of the department.

Language Difficulties

Another consideration in supervising minority employees relates to different languages that may be spoken in a work environment. Some Hispanic Americans and native Mexicans who legally work in the United States may speak Spanish fluently but have difficulty with English. Or a native of Southeast Asia may speak Vietnamese but hardly any English. It has even been observed that some African Americans have unique dialect variations of American English and that they use certain words that are unfamiliar to most white people.

Some employers have held training programs to sensitize supervisors and managers to better understand minority language patterns. For example, one large firm held a series of one-day training sessions for supervisors, managers, and professional staff to make them more knowledgeable about the cultural and language backgrounds of certain minorities. The training program focused on language expressions and speech habits with which people from other racial and ethnic backgrounds are generally not familiar.

The other side of the language problem has been addressed by some employers who sponsor English improvement and business English courses for minority employees. These programs focus on development of writing and speaking skills needed for job improvement and advancement.

At one time, some employers attempted to prevent employees from using their native languages at work. However, such restrictions today are viewed by courts and enforcement agencies with skepticism, unless interpersonal communication is a critical part of the job. For example, a manufacturing company's refusal to hire a Spanish-speaking worker on an assembly line might be ruled as prejudicial, since on this job communication skills may be much less important than manual dexterity skills. However, for a salesperson in a department store, or for a nurse working in an emergency room, adequate interpersonal language skills would be essential. In some parts of the United States, such as Miami, Florida, or San Antonio, Texas, a bilingual (Spanish-English) person would be a valuable asset. The large number of Spanish-speaking people in those areas represents a major pool of potential clients who could be better served by a bilingual person. In summary, supervising racial/ethnic minority employees requires a high degree of sensitivity and even extra fairness when the supervisor is not a member of that minority group.

Fairness in All Supervisory Actions and Decisions

Many minority employees are clustered in entry-level or service positions for which they see little potential for advancement. Others find themselves in job situations where competition is keen for advancement to better-paying and more challenging positions. Tensions between majority and minority employees may be particularly noticeable at those times when a minority employee alleges discrimination or unfair treatment in a job assignment, promotional opportunity, or disciplinary matter.

For all employees—but especially when minority employees are part of the departmental work group—supervisors should strive at all times to be scrupulously fair. In assignment of work, training opportunities, performance appraisals, disciplinary actions—in short, all of their supervisory actions and decisions—supervisors must make every effort to make their decisions on objective and job-related grounds and to avoid any discriminatory treatment. If a minority employee complains of harassment or discriminatory treatment by a fellow-employee or some other person, the supervisor must treat that complaint as a priority concern. In most cases, the supervisor should listen carefully to the nature of the complaint and report it to a higher-level manager or the human resources department for further consideration and direction concerning what to do. In no way should a supervisor retaliate against the minority person, even if the supervisor believes that the discrimination or harassment allegation is without merit. The law protects a minority employee's right to challenge management decisions and actions that the person believes are discriminatory. The supervisor is responsible for making sure that this right is genuinely protected.

3 Discuss factors that are particularly important when supervising women employees.

SUPERVISING WOMEN

Throughout the last several decades, both the number and the percentage of women in the labor force have increased dramatically. There are reasons for this, but some of the reasons mentioned most often are changing values regarding personal fulfillment through work, wider career opportunities, the feminist movement, higher educational levels, growth in single-parent and single-adult households, and economic pressures. As of 1993, women comprised slightly under one-half of the U.S. labor force. By the end of this century, it is estimated that three out of every five working age women will hold paying jobs.

Both men and women supervisors should be aware of a number of important concerns that affect the supervision of women. While not all inclusive, the areas to be discussed here represent a range of issues that supervisors should recognize and deal with appropriately.

Entry of Women into Many Career Fields

The combined effects of antidiscrimination laws, affirmative-action programs, and the increasing number of women in the workforce have led to the movement of women into many jobs that were traditionally dominated by men. For example, in greater numbers than ever before, women are financiers, scientists, engineers, utility repair specialists, sales and technical representatives, accountants, and managers. However, a high percentage of women still work predominantly in clerical and service jobs. Figure 18-2 illustrates these trends, which are expected to continue for the immediate future.

The entry of women into jobs requiring hard physical labor and craft skills has been comparatively limited, but when women do assume craft or other physically demanding jobs, changes often occur. Experiences of a number of firms indicate that some equipment may have to be modified. For example, one utility company found that it had to change the shape of some wrenches and other tools to accommodate the smaller hands of women. Telephone companies have changed the mounting position for ladders on trucks used by outside repair employees to make them easier for women to reach and have bought lightweight ladders that are easier to carry. Also, special clothing and shoes were developed so that women employees could have the proper protective equipment.

Although women have successfully broken down many of the barriers that previously limited their entry into male-dominated positions, there are still problems that occur, especially at the departmental level. One such problem is illustrated in the "You Make the Call" situation at the beginning of this chapter. A common supervisory consideration when a woman takes a job traditionally held by men is the reaction of the current male employees. Some of the men may resent and even openly criticize her. The supervisor should be prepared to deal with such attitudes to enable the woman to perform her job satisfactorily. The supervisor should first inform the men about the starting employment date of the woman so that her presence does not come as a surprise. Then the supervisor should make it clear to the men that disciplinary action will be taken if this woman—or any women employees in the future—is ignored or subjected to abuse or harassment. The supervisor should also make it clear that any woman taking a previously all-male job will be afforded a realistic opportunity to succeed based on her capabilities to perform the job.

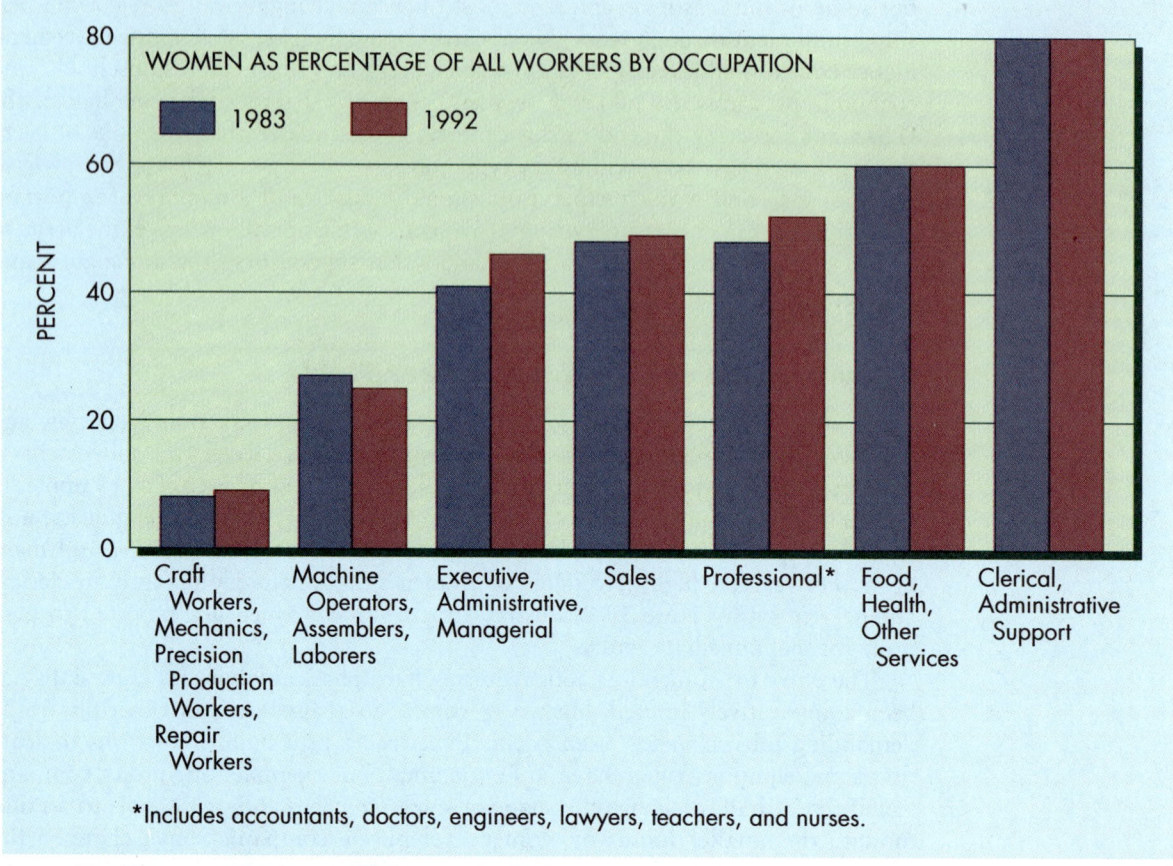

WOMEN AS PERCENTAGE OF ALL WORKERS BY OCCUPATION

*Includes accountants, doctors, engineers, lawyers, teachers, and nurses.

Source of Data: U.S. Department of Labor and U.S. Department of Commerce.

FIGURE 18-2
Women in
Occupational Fields,
1983–1992

Issues of Sexual Harassment and Sexual Stereotyping

A growing number of civil rights and court cases in the United States have dealt with problems of sexual harassment. Sexual harassment usually means situations in which a female employee is subjected to sexual language, touching, or sexual advances by a male employee, male supervisor, or male customer. For example, if a female employee resists or protests such behavior by a male supervisor, she may fear retribution when the supervisor is considering pay raises or promotions. It is important to note that a female supervisor also can be charged with sexual harassment of a male employee, and harassment can also occur when both parties are of the same sex. However, sexual harassment of women by men has been the focus of most of the cases heard by federal agencies and the courts.

Guidelines issued by the Equal Employment Opportunity Commission (EEOC), which enforces the federal Civil Rights Act, define **sexual harassment** as sexual ad-

FIGURE 18-3
No-Harassment Policy
Statement of a Printing
Company

NO-HARASSMENT POLICY

This company does not and will not tolerate harassment of our employees. The term "harassment" includes, but is not limited to, slurs, jokes, and other verbal, graphic, or physical conduct relating to an individual's race, color, sex, religion, national origin, citizenship, age, or handicap. "Harassment" also includes sexual advances; requests for sexual favors; unwelcome or offensive touching; and other verbal, graphic, or physical conduct of a sexual nature.

VIOLATION OF THIS POLICY WILL SUBJECT AN EMPLOYEE TO DISCIPLINARY ACTION, UP TO AND INCLUDING IMMEDIATE DISCHARGE.

If you feel that you are being harassed in any way by another employee or by a customer or vendor, you should make your feelings known to your supervisor immediately. The matter will be thoroughly investigated, and where appropriate, disciplinary action will be taken. If you do not feel that you can discuss the matter with your supervisor or if you are not satisfied with the way your complaint has been handled, please contact either the human resources director or the company president. Your complaint will be kept as confidential as possible, and you will not be penalized in any way for reporting such conduct.

Please do not assume that the company is aware of your problem. It is your responsibility to bring your complaints and concerns to our attention so that we can help resolve them.

Sexual harassment
Unwelcome sexual advances, requests, or conduct when submission to such conduct is tied to the individual's continuing employment or advancement, unreasonably interferes with job performance, or creates a hostile work environment.

vances, requests for sexual favors, and other verbal or physical conduct of a sexual nature when:

- Submission to such conduct is made either explicitly or implicitly as a condition of an individual's employment.
- Submission to or rejection of such conduct by an individual is used as the basis for employment decisions affecting that person.
- Such conduct has the purpose or effect of unreasonably interfering with an individual's work performance or creating an intimidating, hostile, or offensive working environment.

Many firms have developed sexual harassment policy statements.[2] Figure 18-3 is an example of such a statement by a printing company that defines the term "harassment" even beyond gender terms. The statement informs employees what to do if they encounter what they consider to be harassment.

Court decisions have generally held that an employer is liable if sexual harassment of employees is condoned, overlooked, or does not lead to corrective actions by management. Reprimand and discipline of offending employees and supervisors are recommended courses of action. Consequently, supervisors should avoid and discourage sexual language, innuendos, and behavior that are inappropriate in the work environment. Supervisors who use their positions improperly in this regard are engaging in conduct that certainly is unacceptable and could lead to their own dismissal.

Sexual stereotyping means the use of language or judgments to demean someone, usually by men toward women. For example, a department store supervisor may find that women buyers strongly resent being referred to as "the girls." Or a supervisor may imply that women are more emotional, less rational, and less reliable than men.

Many assertions about women employees as compared to men employees are inaccurate. For example, one large firm examined the absenteeism records of both their men and women employees. This firm found no significant difference in absentee rates between the two sexes and that their women employees with children had a lower absentee rate than single men. Thus, the supervisor should not make supervisory decisions based on sexual stereotypes.

Many job titles have been changed to avoid gender implications. For example, the job title "fireman" is now "fire fighter"; a "mailman" is now a "letter carrier"; a "stewardess" is now a "flight attendant"; and so forth.

> **Sexual stereotyping**
> Use of language or judgments that demean someone, usually by men toward women.

Training and Development Opportunities

Women employees should be offered equal access to available training and development activities, and those who have potential should be encouraged to develop their skills. This is especially important with regard to upgrading women to supervisory and other managerial positions.

A number of research studies have found that women employees often benefit from special training and development opportunities that focus on enhancing their self-esteem, communication skills, and career development. For women who already are managers and supervisors, many firms provide programs that include such topics as personal awareness, assertiveness training, managerial barriers to success, time management, delegation, and special problems encountered by women in managerial positions.

Pregnancy and Family Care

Prior to the Civil Rights Act of 1964, many public school systems and other employers prohibited a pregnant woman from working when her pregnant state became obvious. However, such policies are now unlawful.

The Pregnancy Discrimination Act of 1978, which amended the 1964 Civil Rights Act, requires that pregnancy be treated no differently from illnesses or health disabilities if an employer has medical benefits or a disability plan. In addition, many states have laws that require certain pregnancy benefits for employed women. In response, most employers have policies that allow a pregnant employee to work as long as she and her physician certify that it is appropriate. These policies also grant the pregnant employee a leave of absence until she can return to work. To prevent abuse of pregnancy leaves—or any other type of leave for that matter—many employers require a physician's statement to verify a continuing disability.

In Chapter 17, we discussed the Family and Medical Leave Act of 1993. For employers covered by this law, a woman employee must be granted up to 120 days of unpaid leave upon the birth of her child. Health-care coverage must be continued during this period, and she must be returned to her former or a comparable position when she returns to work. Although the law makes these and other stipulations, an employer may go beyond these requirements—for example, by granting paid leave during the period of the employee's pregnancy or after childbirth.

Supervisors must see to it that pregnant employees are treated in a nondiscriminatory manner, although they are not required to give them easier job assignments. A more difficult problem for the supervisor is a pregnant employee's uncertainty about returning to work after her pregnancy leave is over. This affects supervisors in scheduling work and anticipating future staffing needs. Supervisors may have to hire part-time or temporary help, schedule overtime work, or take other temporary actions until the woman definitely decides whether and when she will return to work. This is not an unduly burdensome problem if a supervisor plans well in advance to accommodate the temporary absence of the employee.

One of the well-recognized major problems that have accompanied the growth of women in the labor force has been the conflict between the job demands placed on women and their family responsibilities. Women with children often must cope with demanding responsibilities at home, which are not always shared equally by their husbands. Moreover, many women head single-parent households in which they are the primary provider for their families.

Because of concern over this problem, many employers have adopted flexible policies concerning work schedules, leaves, and other arrangements in order to accommodate employees—especially women—in meeting their obligations. The Family and Medical Leave Act of 1993 now requires employers to grant unpaid leave to cover certain types of family-care situations, i.e., to take care of a seriously ill child, spouse, or parent (see Figure 17-2). There have been legislative proposals that would provide grants to assist in arranging child care for employees who must work and for whom no other care would be available. Regardless of the outcome of legislation, it appears that the tension between family and job responsibilities is one that employers and supervisors will have to address into the next decade. Supervisors should become familiar with their firm's policies regarding family- and child-care assistance and endeavor to resolve whenever possible those conflicts that interfere with the employee's capacity to carry out her or his job responsibilities.

Equity in Compensation

Statistically, the pay received by women employees in the United States workforce generally has been below that of men. Although estimates vary, the aggregate statistical median for women's compensation in the early 1990s was about 70 percent of that for men.[3] This disparity exists even though the Equal Pay Act of 1963 requires that men and women performing equal work must receive equal pay. For example, a female bookkeeper and a male bookkeeper in the same firm who have approximately the same seniority and performance levels must be paid equally.

Although equal pay has not always been interpreted to mean "exactly the same," a firm would probably be in violation of the Equal Pay Act if it paid the female bookkeeper $1.00 an hour less than her male counterpart.

Comparable worth
Concept that jobs should be paid at the same level if they require similar skills or abilities.

A more complex reason for the disparity in the pay of men and women has been the issue of comparable worth. **Comparable worth** is a concept that jobs should draw approximately the same pay if they require similar skills and abilities. The issue arises when jobs that are distinctly different but require similar levels of skills and abilities have different pay scales—especially if one job is predominantly held by men and the other by women. For example, compare the job of medical technologist, which is held predominantly by women, with that of electrician, which is held mainly by men. Both jobs require licensing or certification, but medical technologists typically have more formal education. Now assume that the pay scales for medical technologists in a hospital are about one-third lower than those for electricians working in the same hospital. A comparison of these dissimilar jobs might suggest that unequal pay is being given for jobs of comparable worth.

However, a probable major cause for the difference in such pay scales is the labor market in the area. If unionized electricians are paid $21 per hour by other employers, the hospital would have to set its pay scale at this level in order to compete for electricians. Similarly, if the going rate for nonunionized medical technologists is $14 per hour, the hospital is likely to pay its medical technologists this rate.

Although the concept of comparable worth has received much attention from certain women's groups, it has received little support from most employers and mixed support from government agencies, legislatures, and the courts. The difficulty of determining which jobs are comparable, as well as the role of supply and demand for different jobs, have been the major reasons why employers question this concept. Also, differences in pay may be attributable to numerous factors, including the supply or shortages of women in certain jobs. In the example cited, the reason why the job of electrician is predominantly held by men is that, in the past, few women sought or were permitted to become electricians. Only by providing training and entry opportunities for qualified women to become electricians will the disparity in pay be eliminated. Likewise, men with the appropriate interests and abilities could be encouraged to become medical technologists.

It is important for supervisors to understand the issue of comparable worth if it becomes a major issue in the future. However, it is even more important for supervisors to identify and support qualified women to train and develop for higher-paying jobs that have been held predominantly by men. Supervisors should be willing to encourage, select, and assist these women as they progress into higher-paying positions of greater skill and responsibility.

4 Identify and discuss legal and other considerations involved in supervision of employees with physical and mental disabilities.

SUPERVISING EMPLOYEES WITH DISABILITIES

For decades, many organizations have made special efforts to provide employment opportunities for people with physical and mental disabilities. Many of these efforts were made voluntarily and from the conviction that it was the proper thing to do. However, as a result of a number of laws and government regulations, particularly the Rehabilitation Act of 1973, people with disabilities were identified as a protected group that was to receive special consideration in employment and other organizational areas. The 1973 law used the term "handicapped" in defining individuals with physical or mental impairments, but the preferred usage today is "individuals with disabilities." This law requires certain employers doing business with the federal government and federal agencies to develop an affirmative action program and to make reasonable accommodation for the employment of such persons.

In 1990, the Americans with Disabilities Act (ADA) was passed. It is the most significant legislation dealing with legal protection for a group since the Civil Rights Act of 1964. The ADA identifies coverage for people who have disabilities. Under the ADA, a disabled individual is one who:

1. has a physical or mental impairment that substantially limits one or more of the major life activities of such individual;
2. has a record of such an impairment; or
3. has been regarded as having such an impairment.

The ADA requires that employers provide access to public spaces for people with disabilities and make necessary alterations to public accommodations and commercial facilities for accessibility by people with disabilities.

Many of the details of the ADA are technical and are beyond the scope of this book.[4] Nevertheless, supervisors need to be familiar with the major provisions of the Act, and, more important, its implications for supervision of employees with disabilities.

Who Is a Qualified Disabled Individual?

To be protected under the ADA employment provisions, an individual with a disability must be qualified. A **qualified disabled individual** is someone with a disability who can perform the essential components of a job position with or without a reasonable accommodation on the part of the employer. This means that a person with a disability must have the skills and other qualifications needed for the job to receive employment protection under ADA.

The definition of a disabled person is very broad. By some estimates, about one in six Americans (or roughly about 45 million people) could be considered disabled under the statute's definitions. The law does exempt a number of categories from its definitions of disability, such as those who have an infectious disease and whose job includes food handling; homosexuals; and people who currently use illegal drugs. However, the definition of disability covers most major diseases, including cancer, epilepsy, diabetes, and HIV-positive condition/AIDS.[5] The concept of making a reasonable accommodation for individuals with disabilities was established by the Rehabilitation Act of 1973. **Reasonable accommodation** means altering the usual ways of doing things so that an otherwise qualified disabled person can perform the essential duties of a job, but without creating an undue hardship for the employer. Undue hardship means an alteration that would require a significant ex-

Qualified disabled individual
Defined by the Americans with Disabilities Act as someone with a disability who can perform the essential components of a job with or without reasonable accommodation.

Reasonable accommodation
Altering the usual ways of doing things so that an otherwise qualified disabled person can perform the essential job duties, but without creating an undue hardship for the employer.

pense or an unreasonable change in activities on the part of the employer to accommodate the disabled person.

Complying with the ADA

Various provisions of the Americans with Disabilities Act became effective at different times, beginning in 1992. The employment provisions became effective in 1992 for employers with 25 or more employees; in 1994, the law became effective for employers who have 15 or more employees. Other provisions of the Act involving public accommodations and other considerations have different effective dates.

To comply with the Act, many employers have conducted training programs for supervisors who will carry a significant responsibility in making the necessary adjustments. In the employment process, for example, an employer cannot require a pre-job-offer medical examination to screen out applicants (with the exception of a drug test) or make any type of pre-employment inquiries about the nature of an applicant's disability. Supervisors must be very cautious in talking about the requirements of a job and not bring into a pre-employment interview the possibility of an employee's disability or past medical record. However, an applicant may be given a medical examination after a job offer has been made to determine whether she or he is physically capable of performing the required components of the job. Most employers have reviewed their application forms to make sure that improper questions are not included. Many employers have revised their job descriptions to define the essential functions of each job.

Reasonable accommodation may take any number of forms. It typically means making buildings accessible by building ramps, removing barriers such as steps or curbs, and altering restroom facilities. Reasonable accommodation may mean that the arrangement of desks and widths of aisles have to be altered to allow people in wheelchairs access to job locations. It conceivably could include modifying work schedules, acquiring certain equipment or devices, providing readers or interpreters, and other types of adjustments.

In some situations, job duties can be altered to accommodate people with disabilities. For example, in one company an employee who assembled small component units was also expected to place the completed units in a carton at the end of an assembly process. Several times a day the full carton had to be carried to the shipping area. In order for an employee in a wheelchair to perform the subassembly job, the supervisor arranged for a shipping clerk to pick up completed component units at designated times each day. Thus, the supervisor made a reasonable accommodation so that a physically impaired employee could handle the subassembly job. Another supervisor added a flashing warning light to equipment that already contained a warning buzzer so that an employee with a hearing impairment could be employed safely.

Attitudes of Supervisors and Employees

The Americans with Disabilities Act is aimed at changing perceptions as well as actions in the workplace. The law encourages supervisors and employees to recognize the abilities rather than the disabilities of co-workers and others. As much as anything else, attitudes will play an important role in organizational efforts to accommodate people with disabilities.

Many companies have training programs for their supervisors and employees to familiarize them with the needs of people with disabilities. It is important that they recognize that the ADA is the law and that they believe it is the proper thing to do. Training programs are aimed at allowing an open discussion about different disabilities and opportunities to air questions and feelings of discomfort. Employees should be aware that certain words, although not intentional, may actually carry negative messages. For example, the ADA uses the term "disability" rather than "handicapped" because this is the preference of most people with disabilities. Some training programs have utilized simulated experiences in which nondisabled employees are required to experience certain types of mental, hearing, physical, or visual impairments. This includes sitting in a wheelchair and trying to maneuver through a work area. This type of training helps employees gain a better understanding of what it might be like to experience the difficulties of such a disability.

The type of disability an employee has may even affect the leadership style used by a supervisor. For example, employees who are mentally disabled may require somewhat close and direct supervision. However, a physically disabled employee who uses a wheelchair while working as a proofreader probably should be supervised with a more general and participative style.

Much research has shown that individuals with disabilities can make excellent employees, provided that they are placed in jobs where their abilities can be adapted and utilized appropriately. As in so many other areas, the departmental supervisor is often the primary person to make this happen.

OTHER PROTECTED GROUPS AND THE SUPERVISOR

5 Discuss considerations involved when supervising older workers, employees of different religious views, and Vietnam-era and other veterans.

In addition to racial and ethnic minorities, women, and people with disabilities, there are a number of other protected-group categories with which supervisors should be familiar. A discussion of all the aspects of these categories is beyond the scope of this book. In this section we only highlight some of the additional supervisory considerations applicable to employees who are older; those who have different religious beliefs; and Vietnam-era and other veterans.

Older Employees

As of the early 1990s, approximately two-fifths of the U.S. labor force were 40 years of age and older. This large segment constitutes another legally protected group.

The Age Discrimination in Employment Act, as amended in 1986, prohibits discrimination in employment for most individuals beyond 40 years of age. Consequently, mandatory retirement ages (such as at age 70) no longer are permissible for most employees. Nevertheless, many workers still retire at age 65 or ear-

CONTEMPORARY ISSUE
The Americans with Disabilities Act (ADA): Ambivalence and Apprehension Among Human Resources Managers

A 1992 survey taken among a representative sample of human resources management professionals revealed that most firms were taking the Americans with Disabilities Act very seriously. A substantial majority of human resources management professionals indicated that they had taken necessary steps to comply with ADA, such as upgrading their employment application forms; training supervisors and managers concerning the ADA; and reviewing recruitment methods, selection criteria, and other aspects of their policies and procedures. However, only about half of these professionals responded that they had completed a review of their firms' job descriptions to outline "essential job functions" for all positions. This was described as a task of major proportions that some firms' human resources staff simply had not had time to undertake.

The majority of respondents indicated that the ADA was legislation whose time had come. Over two-thirds of the respondents made comments to the effect that the law will require managers to have greater sensitivity to the abilities of disabled people, and that it will provide opportunities to individuals who previously would not have been employed. A number of respondents indicated that the ADA was morally and humanistically right, and that it would require people to become more open minded in focusing upon capabilities of disabled people rather than holding to old stereotypes.

However, about three-fourths of the respondents saw many serious problems associated with the ADA. Among their major concerns was that "reasonable accommodation" was vaguely and poorly defined. Similarly, the term "disability" was defined in the law in a way that would lead to many interpretations, for example, for individuals who might have AIDS. The biggest problem cited was the fear of litigation. Human resources managers believe that there is a tremendous potential for lawsuits, and that attorneys will seek to exploit the law for their own benefit. Several respondents referred to the ADA as the "attorneys' full-employment law," and they believed that fear of, as well as actual litigation, will drive up costs far beyond what proponents of the ADA estimated. A number of respondents indicated that they were taking a "wait-and-see" attitude about some aspects of the law, since they just did not know how much would be required to comply.

In summary, human resources professionals generally favored the goals of ADA and were making efforts to comply. But they have considerable apprehension about its application, costs, and litigation. If the ADA is to become a positive reality, it appears that human resources professionals and supervisors must maintain a commitment and diligence to make it work as intended. Hopefully, there will be reasonableness in the enforcement and legal process as all parties grapple with the interpretation and application of this law.

Source: Adapted from Raymond L. Hilgert, "Compliance with the Americans with Disabilities Act," *Proceedings of The Midwest Society of Human Resources/Industrial Relations* (March 1993), pp. 112–119.

lier. In part, this is because of the existence of improved retirement programs and pension plans, including plans that allow early retirement. Some early-retirement plans permit employees who have 30 years of service to retire before age 60.

When making decisions to hire, promote, or discharge, supervisors should be aware of the legal protections afforded older workers. For example, selecting a 35-year-old person for a sales position instead of a 55-year-old with more selling experience might result in an age discrimination lawsuit. Laying off a 50-year-old engineer while keeping a 30-year-old engineer on the payroll during a reduction in force might be age discrimination, unless the younger engineer is superior in abilities to the older one.

Making adjustments in workload and encouraging participation in preretirement activities are two ways supervisors can help older employees function on the job and make the transition to retirement more comfortable.

Supervisory decisions to demote or terminate older employees should be documented with sound, objective performance appraisals. Terminating a 62-year-old clerical worker simply for "poor job performance" might be discriminatory if this employee's work performance was not objectively measured and compared with all employees in the department. Some supervisors complain that greater costs and inefficiencies are incurred if they are required to "carry" older workers who no longer can do the job. Whether or not this complaint is valid, the supervisor must appraise the performance of all employees in an impartial, objective way before making decisions that adversely affect older workers. As emphasized in Chapter 15, performance appraisal is a significant part of any supervisor's job, but it is especially important when older workers are in the department.

Supervisors often express concern about older workers who show a decline in physical and mental abilities. While some older people do lose some of their former strengths on the job, they may be able to compensate by using their experience. Even with a decline in physical strength due to age, most firms report that older workers tend to have better quality, safety, and attendance records than do younger employees.

Moreover, it may be possible, within certain limits, for supervisors to make special accommodations for some older employees. Supervisors should not disregard years of dedicated and faithful service. Adjustments in the older employee's workload, scheduling, and the like can be reasonable allowances that others in the work group can understand and accept, particularly those who are themselves advancing in years and who recognize that someday their capabilities might also diminish somewhat.

Older employees who are approaching retirement present another problem that requires sensitivity on the part of supervisors. Some employees who have worked for 30 years or more look forward to retirement as a time to enjoy a greater variety of leisure activities. However, others view retirement with anxieties about the security of a daily routine, steady income, and established social relationships.

Supervisors should be supportive and understanding as older employees near retirement. These employees should be encouraged to take advantage of preretirement planning activities that may be available in the company or through outside agencies. Some companies allow employees nearing retirement to attend retirement-related workshops during working hours without loss of pay. Members of the human resources department or a benefits specialist may spend considerable time with each employee nearing retirement to discuss pensions, insurance, social security, and other financial matters. Supervisors should also encourage recent retirees to attend company social functions and to maintain contact with their former supervisors and co-workers wherever possible. Such contacts are valuable aids in making the transition to retirement more comfortable.

Accommodation for Different Religious Views

Since the passage of the Civil Rights Act of 1964, most employers are required to afford nondiscriminatory treatment to employees who hold different religious views. Although EEOC and court decisions have not always clearly defined religious discrimination, the principle has evolved that employers must make reasonable accommodation for employees who hold differing religious beliefs.

In this regard, work and holiday schedules have been the major focus for employers. For example, employees who follow the orthodox Jewish faith consider Saturday as the day for their religious observance instead of Sunday. Requiring such employees to work on Saturday would be the same as requiring employees who are members of some fundamentalist Christian sects to work on Sundays. A supervisor might be able to accommodate the religious views of such employees by scheduling their workweeks in a way that takes into account their religious preferences. Allowing Jewish employees to take holidays on Rosh Hashana and Yom Kippur instead of Christmas and Easter is another example of accommodation.

Supervisors may be confronted with situations in which it is difficult to accommodate all employees' religious preferences and still schedule the work. If this happens, a supervisor would be well advised to discuss the problem with his or her manager and with the human resources staff to determine whether scheduling alternatives are available that might accommodate the employees and yet not be too costly or disruptive.

Vietnam-Era and Other Veterans

Vietnam-era and other military veterans are another group that has been identified for certain employment protection. After the end of the Vietnam War and with many men and women released from military service in the 1970s, legislators and political leaders felt that Vietnam-era veterans were entitled to assistance to facilitate their reentry into the civilian labor force. The Vietnam-Era Veteran's Readjustment Act of 1974 was passed, which applies primarily to employers who have contracts with the federal government. This law requires employers to have affirmative-action programs for the hiring and advancement of veterans. Other laws and regulations—particularly in public and government employment—provide for preferential hiring policies for veterans, including those who participated in "Operation Desert Storm" in the early 1990s.

Supervision of military veterans usually involves few special considerations in comparison to supervision of other legally protected employees. Except for those veterans who experienced mental or physical impairment and who may continue to show some effects, most veterans cannot be distinguished from nonveterans. Consequently, once they have been employed and have adjusted to the work environment, veterans generally should be supervised just like everyone else. As the years progress, it seems likely that employers will afford this protected group less special consideration than in previous years.

PROTECTED-GROUP SUPERVISORS

6 Recognize several pressures faced by supervisors who themselves are members of protected groups.

Thus far we have discussed how the supervision of legally protected employees requires both awareness and sensitivity to a variety of factors. Additional concerns can arise for supervisors who themselves are members of a legally protected category (e.g., minorities and women) and who may experience resistance and resentment in their supervisory positions.

For example, it is common today to find a woman supervisor whose subordinates primarily are men. Skepticism about the qualifications of the woman supervisor may be voiced in men's comments, such as "She didn't deserve the job" or "She got it because she's female." A woman supervisor in such a situation may feel that she has to accomplish more than a male supervisor might be expected to achieve in a similar job. However, past experiences of many women supervisors indicate that, once they have proven their competence, most of this initial skepticism will fade away.

Another example might be an African-American production supervisor in a manufacturing plant who supervises black employees and who may be faced with a dilemma. Because the supervisor is of the same race, some employees may attempt to take advantage of the situation, perhaps by taking more extended break periods than allowed. On the other hand, the supervisor may put greater pressure on black employees to perform and to obey the rules so that no charge of favoritism can be justified.

Similarly, the woman supervisor who feels obliged to accomplish more than her male counterparts and who wishes to avoid charges of favoritism toward female subordinates may put greater pressure on women employees. This tendency has led some women employees to say that they would rather work for male supervisors, because female supervisors are "tougher" on them than are men.

On the other hand, research studies have suggested that, in general, supervisors tend to be able to communicate better with subordinates who are of the same race or the same sex. For example, an Asian-American supervisor is likely to understand better the culture, speech patterns, and attitudes of Asian-American employees.

Problems such as those cited are not unusual, and they should even be anticipated by supervisors or potential supervisors. It is helpful if such issues are openly discussed in supervisory training and development meetings. In addition, protected-group supervisors—just like all other supervisors—must have performance expectations, policies, and decisions that are applied consistently and uniformly to all employees, regardless of race, gender, age, and other such considerations.

UNDERSTANDING REVERSE DISCRIMINATION

7 Discuss the issue of reverse discrimination.

Reverse discrimination
Preference given to protected-group members in hiring and promotion over more qualified or more experienced workers from nonprotected groups.

The reactions of employees who are not members of a legally protected group to hiring and promotion decisions represent another challenge to supervisors. These employees may view the promotion of a protected-group employee as reverse discrimination. **Reverse discrimination** may be charged when a more senior or qualified person is denied a job opportunity or promotion because preference has been given to a protected-group individual who may be less qualified or junior in seniority.

For example, in a significant U.S. Supreme Court case, a white male with higher seniority was denied admission to a company–union training program because a specific number of openings were designated to be filled by black employees with less seniority. The Supreme Court decided that the white male had not been discriminated against illegally because the company and the labor union had negotiated a voluntary affirmative-action program. Although the court indicated that there were times that such reverse favoritism might be unlawful, it did not identify those instances. Thus, the court upheld the idea of affirmative action but did not clearly rule for or against the issue of reverse discrimination.

Equal employment opportunity and affirmative-action programs most often impact white male employees. Some white males feel that they do not have an equal or fair opportunity to compete for promotions or higher-paying jobs. Furthermore, some interpret the existence of numerical goals in affirmative-action programs as "quotas" that have to be met by hiring and promoting unqualified or less qualified women or minorities.

Supervisors of integrated racial groups and male and female employees may be apprehensive about their situations. For example, supervisors may become reluctant to discipline anyone, so as to avoid charges of favoritism or discrimination. Another difficulty is that conflicts and distrust among these various groups may arise that place stress on interpersonal relationships and may affect the performance of the department. Such problems are not easily overcome. However, communication between the supervisor and all groups of employees is absolutely essential, and the supervisor should try to correct misperceptions about any employee's abilities and qualifications as they occur. Whether reverse discrimination exists is not really important. Rather, what is important is the supervisor's response to the feelings of all groups and individuals in an understanding, empathetic, fair, and objective manner.

GOOD SUPERVISION: THE OVERRIDING CONSIDERATION

8 Discuss the overriding concern in supervision of all employees.

The issues discussed in this chapter will likely concern supervisors for years to come. Additional legislation and court decisions will specify or clarify other considerations for protected-groups that now exist and, perhaps, for other groups to be identified in the future.

Supervisors must adapt their ways of managing their departments to meet the considerations afforded to legally protected employees. In this effort supervisors should always recognize that the best way to manage *all* employees in their departments—protected or not—is to constantly apply the principles of good supervision as presented throughout this book.

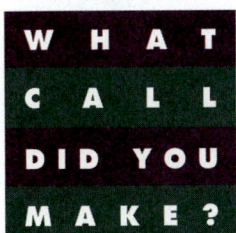

W H A T C A L L D I D Y O U M A K E ?

As supervisor Charlie Willow, you have found that life is complicated and becoming more so. You have just experienced a classic "she said, he said" situation where truth is difficult to ascertain. First interview other employees in the department to see whether or not any of them will back up either Cindy Stowe's allegations or George Cross's denials. In these types of cases, often no one else in the department will have seen or heard anything; or other employees do not want to get involved, so they refuse to say anything. If you are unable to get any further information that would support either version, you should immediately report the case to the human resources department or the manager who is responsible for handling issues of sexual harassment or discrimination. Since this may have serious legal implications,

further handling of the case probably should be left to those individuals.

However, as supervisor, you should again talk to George Cross and warn him to be very careful in what he says and does in relationship to Ms. Stowe. Tell him that you will be watching very closely to make sure that Ms. Stowe is being treated fairly, and that no type of harassment of her will be tolerated. You also should talk to Ms. Stowe to tell her what you have done, but also remind her that she must measure up to the requirements of the job. Assure her that if she needs any help, she should not hesitate to discuss her situation with you. Finally, you should be sure that your future actions are consistent and fair toward all employees regardless of any protected-group status.

SUMMARY

1 Identify the major categories of legally protected
employees and general guidelines for supervising diversity.

The major classifications of protected-group employees are by racial/ethnic origin, sex, age, physical and mental impairment, religion, and military service.

Supervisors need to be aware of legal protections that are afforded to protected groups and understand that this is part of supervising a diversified workforce. All employees should be supervised in a fair and objective manner that focuses upon their talents, abilities, and potential contributions.

2 Discuss issues involved in the supervision of racial/ethnic minority employees.

When supervising racial/ethnic minority employees, supervisors should try to reduce the impact of past discrimination. Awareness of cultural factors and recognition of language differences are important aspects of a supervisor's sensitivities toward minority employees. Being scrupulously fair in all aspects of supervision and striving to prevent any type of discriminatory treatment toward minorities are essential.

3 Discuss factors that are particularly important when supervising women employees.

Supervisors must try to ensure that women are provided fair opportunities as they move into a greater variety of career fields and positions. Avoidance of sexual harassment and stereotyping is mandatory. Human resources policies should stress training and development opportunities for women, nondiscriminatory treatment during pregnancy, flexibility in resolving family-care conflicts and problems, and equity in compensation.

4 Identify and discuss legal and other considerations involved
in supervision of employees with physical and mental disabilities.

The Americans with Disabilities Act prohibits discrimination in employment against individuals who have physical and mental disabilities. This law prohibits making certain pre-employment inquiries and physical examinations of job applicants. It further requires that employers make reasonable accommodations for otherwise qualified disabled individuals who are capable of performing the essential components of a job. People with disabilities who are placed in job positions that are consistent with their capabilities and who are given a fair opportunity to perform by their supervisors typically become excellent employees.

5 Discuss considerations involved when supervising older workers,
employees of different religious views, and Vietnam-era and other veterans.

The Age Discrimination in Employment Act prohibits discrimination against most employees over 40 years of age. Thus, when making decisions concerning older employees, supervisors should appraise their qualifications and performance objectively. Supervisors should try to adjust to reduced abilities of older workers, if possible. Also, supervisors should assist employees who are nearing retirement to prepare for it.

The principle of reasonable accommodation also should be followed when supervising employees of different religious beliefs. Reasonable adjustments in work scheduling should be afforded individuals who have certain religious requirements.

Vietnam-era and other veterans may be afforded special consideration when hiring decisions are made, but they usually require only regular supervision after they have adjusted to their work environment.

6 Recognize several pressures faced by supervisors who themselves are members of protected groups.

The supervisor who is a member of a protected group may encounter pressures from both protected-group and nonprotected-group employees. These typically involve questions about qualifications and fair treatment. The supervisor should see to it that all employees are provided equal treatment and equal performance expectations.

7 Discuss the issue of reverse discrimination.

Supervisors should be sensitive to the feelings of some employees about the issue of reverse discrimination. Employees may accuse the company of reverse discrimination if a protected-group person is hired or promoted over a more experienced or more qualified member of a nonprotected group.

8 Discuss the overriding concern in supervision of all employees.

No matter how future legislation and court decisions affect the issues related to protected groups, the best way to manage will always be to apply the principles of good supervision to *all* employees.

KEY TERMS

Protected-group employees (page 482)
Sexual harassment (page 489)
Sexual stereotyping (page 490)
Comparable worth (page 492)

Qualified disabled individual (page 493)
Reasonable accommodation (page 493)
Reverse discrimination (page 500)

QUESTIONS FOR DISCUSSION

1.   Who are classified as protected-group employees? Does "protected group" mean the same as a "special group" of employees? Discuss.

2.   What are some of the major considerations that supervisors of ethnic/racial minority employees should keep in mind?

3.   Identify a particular racial/ethnic minority (other than the examples given in the text) and discuss some cultural factors, language, and other differences that a supervisor might need to consider in supervising this group.

4.   Discuss why and how employers have given women access to special training and development opportunities and/or moved them into jobs that might require the modification of existing tools or equipment.

5.   What is meant by sexual harassment and sexual stereotyping? Give an example of sexual harassment (other than those given in the text) and describe what a supervisor should do to deal with it.

6.   Discuss how women are affected by pregnancy and family-care situations and employer policies. What legal requirements are imposed, and not imposed, for employers in these areas?

7.   Does equity in compensation for women mean that an employer must apply the principle of comparable worth in compensating all employees? Discuss.

8. How has the Americans with Disabilities Act (ADA) expanded legal protections for individuals with disabilities?

9. Discuss: (a) the ADA's definition of a "disabled" person and (b) what is meant by "reasonable accommodation" for someone with a disability to perform the "essential functions" of a job position. Why will these areas be difficult for supervisors to comply with in certain job situations?

10. What legal protections are afforded most employees who are beyond 40 years of age?

11. Assume that a supervisor has a 60-year-old secretarial assistant whose performance has slipped recently. What considerations should affect the supervisor's actions toward this employee?

12. How does the concept of reasonable accommodation apply to employees of different religious persuasions? Are there limits to reasonable accommodation? Discuss.

13. Why does supervision of military veterans usually require few special considerations once they are employed and have adjusted to the job?

14. "Protected-group supervisors tend to be more demanding of employees who belong to the same protected group." Discuss this statement.

15. What is meant by "reverse discrimination?" Is it a valid concept or a new stereotype or myth? How does it affect the practice of supervisory management?

16. Why should the application of the principles of good supervision be the overriding concern of a supervisor in charge of a department that is racially mixed, has both male and female employees, and has employees who have other legal protections?

SKILLS APPLICATIONS

Skills Application 18-1: Attitudes Toward People with Disabilities and the ADA

Below are a series of statements that relate to attitudes toward disabled people and the Americans with Disabilities Act (ADA). Mark each statement according to how much you agree or disagree with it, using the following scale:

Strongly Agree	Agree	No Opinion	Disagree	Strongly Disagree
(SA)	(A)	(N)	(D)	(SD)

_____ 1. Individuals with severe disabilities are not able to compete for jobs that require demanding physical and mental capabilities.

_____ 2. Under the ADA, an employer can expect just as much from a disabled person as from anyone else.

_____ 3. People with disabilities usually are more conscientious and reliable at work than other employees.

_____ 4. Most people with severe disabilities expect others to show sympathy toward them and provide them extra help to hold a job.

_____ 5. Employers will find that the ADA will be impossible to comply with in many situations without extraordinary costs and efforts.

_____ 6. The ADA will benefit attorneys far more than it will help people with disabilities.

_____   7. Compliance with the ADA will cause considerable resentment toward people with disabilities.

_____   8. The ADA is morally and ethically appropriate and will assist qualified disabled individuals to become more self-sufficient.

_____   9. People with disabilities are usually more cheerful and enthusiastic on the job than other employees.

_____ 10. Reasonable accommodation under the ADA really means that special preferential treatment must be granted to people with disabilities.

After completing this survey, answer the following questions:

1. Why would awareness of attitudes toward people with disabilities and the ADA be important to supervisors?

2. Compare your responses to those of others. What common views do you have? What areas of difference? Discuss the bases for your differences of opinion.

3. If you were (are) a supervisor, how would you deal with negative attitudes toward people with disabilities and/or the ADA that might be held by other employees in a work group that includes a disabled person?

Skills Application 18-2: Sexual Harassment

Various actions may be perceived as sexual harassment, especially if they are objected to by someone of the opposite sex. Virtually everyone has experienced, heard of, or participated in actions that possibly could be viewed as sexual harassment. Respond to the following questions, and then compare and discuss your responses with others who have responded to these same questions.

1. Identify two situations of sexual harassment of which you have personal knowledge. Briefly describe each.

2. How did you and others react to each situation?

3. What could or should be done to prevent similar situations in the future?

Skills Application 18-3: The Supervisor and Protected Groups

1. From the materials in this chapter, develop a list of the requirements and considerations that you believe are essential for appropriate supervision of protected-group employees.

2. Contact two practicing supervisors (or managers) who would be willing to be interviewed. One supervisor should be nonprotected (e.g., a white male under 40 years of age); the other supervisor should be in a protected category (e.g., a minority group member or a woman). Ask the supervisors to identify what they believe to be the five most important requirements for good supervision of protected-group employees within their departments.

3. Compare the supervisors' lists with your list. To what degree were these lists similar or different? If there were major differences, what do you feel is the most likely explanation?

ENDNOTES

1.   For example, see Ann M. Morrison, *The New Leaders: Guidelines on Leadership Diversity in America* (San Francisco: Jossey-Bass Publishers, 1992). See also sources that are included in Endnote 1 at the conclusion of Chapter 1.

2.   See Samuel J. Bressler and Rebecca Thacker, "Four-Point Plan Helps Solve Harassment Problems," *HR Magazine* (Volume 38, Number 5, May 1993), pp. 117–124.

3.   Joan E. Rigdon, "Three Decades After the Equal Pay Act, Women's Wages Remain Far from Parity," *The Wall Street Journal* (June 9, 1993), pp. B1 and B3.

4.   For a concise guide to compliance with the ADA and other laws relative to people with disabilities, see *Accommodating Disabilities: Business Management Guide* (Chicago: Commerce Clearing House, 1991).

5.   For an extensive discussion, see William F. Banta, *AIDS in the Workplace* (Lexington, Mass.: Lexington Books, 1993).

19

Positive

Discipline

LEARNING OBJECTIVES

After studying this chapter, you will be able to:

1 Discuss the basis and importance of positive discipline in an organization.

2 Identify disciplinary situations that violate rules of conduct and discuss the need to confront them appropriately.

3 Discuss the disciplinary process and approaches that ensure disciplinary action for just cause.

4 Define and discuss the application of progressive discipline.

5 Explain the hot stove rule approach for disciplinary actions.

6 Discuss the need to document disciplinary actions and to provide the right of appeal.

7 Explain the discipline without punishment approach as an alternative to progressive discipline.

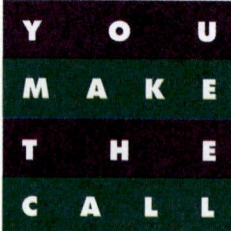

You are Linda Juarez, a departmental supervisor for a major aerospace firm. You currently manage a group of six accountants and financial analysts and a clerk that is responsible for maintaining all contract records for one of the company's aircraft programs. All of the accountants and financial analysts have bachelors' degrees, and most are currently pursuing or have completed requirements for a master's degree. Over the past year, two of your employees left the company. Because the company was facing difficult times, these individuals were not replaced. Consequently, the remaining members of the department had to keep up with heavy workloads. Considerable overtime and Saturday work were necessary. About a month ago, higher-level management agreed to move an available person from another de-

partment to your department. This employee, Scott Stoner, had worked for the company for five years since graduating from college. During this time he completed his master's degree at a local university. He came to the department with excellent credentials, and he had a high recommendation from his previous supervisor in corporate accounting.

Thursday at 5:30 P.M. Kathy Florence, one of your financial analysts, comes into your office. This is what she has to say:

Well I don't really know where to start, Linda, so I guess I'll just jump right in. Quite a few of us in the department are upset with Scott. I don't know if you're aware of the situation or not, but the bottom line is he just doesn't do anything. He's great at reading The Wall Street

Journal and making weekend and evening plans. But when the rest of us are busting our tails to get the job done, it's a bit frustrating to watch him relaxing at his desk. He even went so far as to give out his office telephone number when he listed his car for sale. Then because he was on the phone all the time, most calls went to our department clerk, John. He was really angry, and I don't blame him. He has enough to do just supporting the rest of us. I know Scott's still pretty new in our department, but the job here is not that different from the work he did in cor-porate accounting. Given how short-handed we are, department morale is certainly going to drop further if he continues this way. One last thing. He's called in sick three days this month. None of us believes that he was sick, since all of his absences were on Friday or Monday.

The conversation continues just a bit longer. After Kathy leaves, you wonder how to handle the situation. You have never experienced a problem quite like this in three years of supervising this department. **YOU MAKE THE CALL.**

THE BASIS AND IMPORTANCE OF POSITIVE DISCIPLINE

1 Discuss the basis and importance of positive discipline in an organization.

Discipline
State of orderliness; that is, the degree to which employees act according to expected standards of behavior.

Positive discipline
Condition that exists when employees generally follow the rules and meet the standards of the organization.

Positive self-discipline
Employees regulating their own behavior out of self-interest and their normal desire to meet reasonable standards.

The term "discipline" is used in several different ways. Many supervisors associate it with the use of authority, force, or punishment. In this text, however, we prefer to consider **discipline** as a condition of orderliness, that is, the degree to which members of an organization act properly and observe the expected standards of behavior. **Positive discipline** exists when employees generally follow the rules and meet the standards of the organization. Discipline is negative (or bad) when they follow the rules reluctantly or when they actually disobey regulations and violate the prescribed standards of acceptable behavior.

Discipline is not identical to morale. As discussed in Chapter 17, morale is a state of mind, whereas discipline is primarily a state of affairs. However, there is some correlation between morale and discipline. Normally there are fewer disciplinary problems when morale is high; conversely, low morale is usually accompanied by more disciplinary problems. Yet a high degree of positive discipline could be present in spite of low morale. This could result from insecurity, fear, or sheer force. Nevertheless, it is unlikely that a high degree of positive employee discipline will be maintained indefinitely unless there is an acceptable level of employee morale.

The best type of discipline is **positive self-discipline,** in which employees essentially regulate themselves out of their own self-interest. This is based on the normal human tendency to do what needs to be done, to do one's share, and to follow reasonable standards of acceptable behavior. Even before they start to work, most people accept the idea that following instructions and fair rules of conduct are normal responsibilities in any job.

FIGURE 19-1
Self-discipline must
exist at the supervisory
level before it will exist
at the employee level.

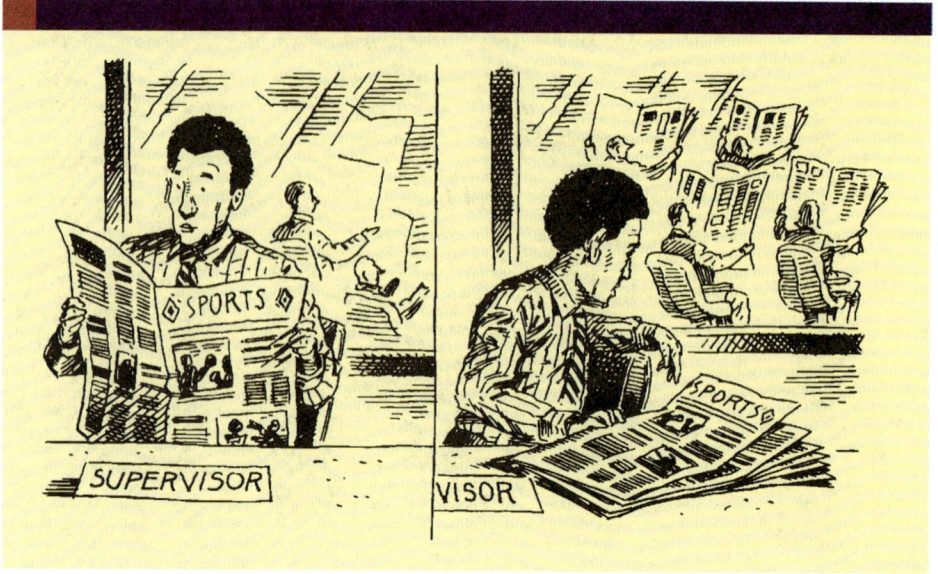

Positive self-discipline relies on the premise that most employees want to do the right thing and can be counted on to exercise self-control. They believe in performing their work properly; coming to work on time; following the supervisor's instructions; and refraining from fighting, using drugs, drinking liquor, or stealing. They know that it is natural to subordinate some of their own personal interests to the needs of the organization. As long as company rules are communicated and are perceived as reasonable, most employees usually will observe the rules.

Unfortunately, there are always some employees who, for one reason or another, fail to observe established rules and standards even after having been informed of them. Employee theft from employers nationwide amounts to billions of dollars of loss annually. When added to other forms of employee dishonesty—including habitual misuse or "stealing" of company time by unwarranted absenteeism, tardiness, doing personal business, and socializing on company time—the cost of employee theft to American businesses has been estimated to be over $200 billion a year.

Despite such unfortunate statistics, supervisors should maintain a balanced perspective that employees at the departmental level will take most of their cues for self-discipline from their supervisors and managers (see Figure 19-1). Ideally, positive self-discipline should exist throughout the entire management team, beginning at the top and extending through all supervisors. Supervisors should not expect their employees to practice positive self-discipline if they themselves do not set a good example. As we have stated several times previously, a supervisor's actions and behavior are easy targets for the employees to either emulate or reject. Further, if the supervisor is able to encourage the vast majority of the employees in the department to show a strong sense of self-discipline, usually these employees will exert group pressure on the dissenters. For example, if a no-smoking rule is introduced in an office, usually someone in the group itself will enforce this rule by reminding smokers to leave the premises before lighting a cigarette. Thus the need for corrective action by the supervisor is reduced when most employees practice positive self-discipline.

IDENTIFYING AND CONFRONTING DISCIPLINARY SITUATIONS

2 Identify disciplinary situations that violate rules of conduct and discuss the need to confront them appropriately.

Because individuals do not always agree on what should be acceptable standards of conduct, top-level managers must define the standards for supervisors and employees. In many companies, standards are defined in statements of ethical codes and rules of conduct.

Ethical Standards and Rules of Conduct

Many organizations have developed statements of ethical standards or ethical codes. These usually outline in broad, philosophical terms the norms and ideals that are supposed to guide everyone within the organization. Figure 19-2 is an example of a code of ethics. The nine principles within this code are expanded upon in a policy manual that provides guidance for employees concerning the meaning of the principles and compliance with them.

Not every organization has a formal code of ethics. However, virtually every large firm has some formal statement or list of rules of behavior to which employees are expected to conform.

In Chapter 7, we discussed the need for policies, procedures, methods, and rules as standing plans that cover many aspects of ongoing operations. These are particularly vital in informing employees of what standards of behavior are expected and what types are not acceptable.

Most organizations provide employees with a written list of rules or codes of conduct. These are sometimes included in an employee handbook; otherwise, they are provided as a separate booklet or as a memorandum posted in each department. The supervisor must ensure that employees read and understand the general and departmental rules, which may include safety and technical regulations, depending upon the activity of a department.

Written rules and regulations provide a common code or standard that should assist the supervisor in encouraging employee self-discipline. Some organizations spell out very detailed lists of rules and infractions, and they may include classifications of the likely penalties for violations. Other organizations—probably the majority—prefer to list their major rules and regulations but without tying down the consequences for violations of various rules. An example of such a list is shown in Figure 19-3. Regardless of what type of list is used, the supervisor is the person most responsible for the consistent application and enforcement of both company

FIGURE 19-2
Code of Ethics

CODE OF ETHICS

Integrity and ethics exist in the individual or they do not exist at all. They must be upheld by individuals or they are not upheld at all. In order for integrity and ethics to be characteristics of the corporation we must strive to be:

- Honest and trustworthy in all our relationships;
- Reliable in carrying out assignments and responsibilities;
- Truthful and accurate in what we say and write;
- Cooperative and constructive in all work undertaken;
- Fair and considerate in our treatment of fellow employees, customers, and all other people;
- Law abiding in all our activities;
- Committed to accomplishing all tasks in a superior way;
- Economical in utilizing company resources; and
- Dedicated in service to our company and to improvement of the quality of life in the world in which we live.

FIGURE 19-3
Partial List of Company
Rules and Regulations

COMPANY RULES AND REGULATIONS

The efficient operation of our plants and the general welfare of our employees require the establishment of certain uniform standards of behavior. Accordingly, the following offenses are considered to be violations of these standards, and employees who refuse to accept this guidance will subject themselves to appropriate disciplinary action.

1. Habitual tardiness and absenteeism.
2. Theft or attempted theft of Company or other employee's property.
3. Fighting or attempting bodily injury upon another employee.
4. Horseplay, malicious mischief, or any other conduct affecting the rights of other employees.
5. Intoxication or drinking on the job; or being in a condition that makes it impossible to perform work in a satisfactory manner.
6. Refusal or failure to perform assigned work; or refusal or failure to comply with supervisory instructions.
7. Inattention to duties; carelessness in performance of duties; loafing on the job, sleeping, or reading papers during working hours.
8. Violation of published safety or health rules.
9. Possessing, consuming, selling, or being under the influence of illegal drugs on the premises.
10. Unauthorized possession of weapons, firearms, or explosives on the premises.
11. Requests for sexual favors, sexual advances, and physical conduct of a sexual nature toward another employee on the premises.

and departmental rules. In fact, the degree to which employees follow the rules in a positive, self-disciplined way is usually more attributable to the supervisor's role than to any other single factor.

Confronting Disciplinary Situations

Despite a supervisor's best efforts to prevent infractions, it is almost inevitable that the supervisor at times will be confronted with situations requiring some type of disciplinary action. Among the most common situations requiring supervisory disciplinary actions are (a) infractions of rules regarding time schedules, rest periods, procedures, safety, and so forth; (b) excessive absenteeism or tardiness; (c) defective or inadequate work performance; and (d) poor attitudes that influence the work of others or damage the firm's public image.

At times a supervisor might experience open insubordination, such as an employee's refusal to carry out a legitimate work assignment. A supervisor may even be confronted with disciplinary problems that stem from employee behavior off the job. For example, an employee may have a drinking problem or may be taking illegal drugs. Whenever an employee's off-the-job conduct has an impact on his or her job performance, the supervisor must be prepared to respond to the problem in an appropriate fashion. In Chapter 17 we discussed a number of approaches by which employees with personal and work-related problems might be assisted.

Situations that call for disciplinary action are not pleasant, but the supervisor must have the courage to deal with them rather than ignoring them, hoping they will go away. If the supervisor does not take responsible action when required, some borderline employees might be encouraged to try similar violations.

A supervisor should not be afraid to draw on some of the authority inherent in the supervisory position, even though the supervisor might prefer to overlook the matter or "pass the buck" to higher-level managers or the human resources department. A supervisor who finds it expedient to ask the human resources department to take over all departmental disciplinary problems is shirking responsibility and undermining his or her own position of authority.

Normally a good supervisor will not have to take disciplinary action frequently. But whenever it becomes necessary, the supervisor should be ready to take the proper action no matter how unpleasant the task may be.

THE DISCIPLINARY PROCESS

3 Discuss the disciplinary process and approaches that ensure disciplinary action for just cause.

Supervisors must initiate any disciplinary action with sensitivity and sound judgment. The purpose of a disciplinary action should not be to punish or seek revenge, but to improve the employees' future behavior. In other words, the primary purpose of a disciplinary action is to prevent similar infractions in the future.

In this chapter we do not consider directly those situations in which union contractual obligations may restrict the supervisor's authority in taking disciplinary action. Special considerations involving labor unions are discussed in Chapters 12

CONTEMPORARY ISSUE
Employees Who Report Wrongdoing May Find Their Jobs in Jeopardy

Employees who are urged to report wrongdoing may find that their own jobs are in peril. Many major firms have established so-called "hot lines" or ethics reporting systems by which employees are encouraged to report questionable situations or individuals whom they believe are acting unethically, improperly, or illegally. Some firms have a corporate ombudsman who investigates the allegations and takes appropriate actions when justified. The person who reported the alleged wrongdoing is supposed to be granted anonymity, and there is supposed to be no retaliation in the event the report is not supportable by facts and evidence. However, sometimes employees who have reported wrongdoing, often known as "whistleblowers," have found that their own jobs are in jeopardy rather than those of the people they reported.

Although companies maintain that their corporate hot lines are helpful in ferreting out fraud and maintaining ethical standards, some are recognized as flawed. Managers investigating the allegations may retaliate against the whistleblower if the allegations are against someone in top-level management. The retaliation can take place in various ways, such as demotion, transfer, or termination. Observers say this is a classic "fox guarding the hen house" type of arrangement. Preferably, investigations of hot line reports should be carried out by a neutral person, such as an ombudsman, or by someone from internal security who will follow through and let the investigation take its proper course.

Another problem that sometimes occurs is when one person falsely accuses a rival to gain some type of revenge or advantage. It is important that false allegations be kept confidential so that the reputation of the person who is falsely accused is not irreparably damaged.

Most authorities believe that a hot line or ethical reporting system requires a top-level management commitment to make the system credible—first, to deal firmly with wrongdoing when it is reported, and second, not to retaliate against the messenger who delivered an unwelcome message.

Source: Adapted from Joan E. Rigdon, "Tipsters Telephoning Ethics Hot Lines Can End Up Sabotaging Their Own Jobs," *The Wall Street Journal* (August 27, 1992), pp. B1–B2; Debra R. Meyer, "More on Whistleblowing," *Management Accounting* (Volume 74, Number 12, June 1993), p. 26; and Marcy Mason, "The Curse of Whistleblowing," *The Wall Street Journal* (March 14, 1994), p. A14.

and 20. Nevertheless, the ideas discussed here are generally applicable in most unionized as well as nonunionized organizations.

Disciplinary Action Should Have Just Cause

Just cause
Standard for disciplinary action requiring tests of fairness and elements of normal due process, such as proper notification, investigation, sufficient evidence, and a penalty commensurate with the nature of the infraction.

Most employers accept the general premise that disciplinary action taken against an employee should be based on "just cause." **Just cause** (or "proper cause") means that the disciplinary action meets certain tests of fairness and elements of normal due process, such as proper notification, investigation, sufficient evidence, and a penalty commensurate with the nature of the infraction. Figure 19-4 is a list of seven questions that arbitrators apply in union/management disciplinary-type grievance matters. A "no" answer to one or more of these questions in a particular case means that the just-cause standard was not fully met, and the arbitrator might then set aside or modify management's disciplinary action.

The overwhelming preponderance of labor union contracts specify a just-cause or proper-cause standard for discipline and discharge. Similarly, many cases decided by government agencies and by the courts have required employers to prove that disciplinary actions taken against legally protected employees (as discussed in Chapter 18) were not discriminatory but were for just cause.

SEVEN TESTS FOR JUST CAUSE

1. Did the company give the employee forewarning or foreknowledge of the possible or probable disciplinary consequences of the employee's conduct?
2. Was the company's rule or managerial order reasonably related to (a) the orderly, efficient, and safe operation of the company's business and (b) the performance that the company might properly expect of the employee?
3. Did the company, before administering discipline to an employee, make an effort to discover whether the employee did in fact violate or disobey a rule or order of management?
4. Was the company's investigation conducted fairly and objectively?
5. At the investigation, was there substantial evidence or proof that the employee was guilty as charged?
6. Has the company applied its rules, orders, and penalties even-handedly and without discrimination to all employees?
7. Was the degree of discipline administered by the company in a particular case reasonably related to (a) the seriousness of the employee's proven offense and (b) the record of the employee's service with the company?

Source: These seven tests for just cause were originally suggested by arbitrator Carroll R. Daugherty. They are included in many texts and arbitral citations. See Raymond L. Hilgert and Sterling H. Schoen, *Cases in Collective Bargaining and Industrial Relations* (7th ed.; Homewood, Ill.: Richard D. Irwin, 1993), pp. 222–223.

Although the ramifications of a just-cause standard for disciplinary action can be rather complicated, the guidelines presented in this chapter are consistent with the principles and requirements necessary to justify any disciplinary or discharge action. The supervisor who follows these guidelines in a conscientious way normally should be able to meet a just-cause standard, irrespective of whether it involves a unionized firm, a nonunionized organization, or a potential area of legal discrimination.[1]

Precautionary Questions and Measures

As a first consideration in any disciplinary situation, a supervisor should guard against undue haste or taking unwarranted action based on emotional response. There are a number of precautionary questions and measures that a supervisor should follow before deciding on any disciplinary action in response to an alleged employee offense.

Investigate the Situation. Before doing anything, the supervisor should investigate what happened and why. The following questions, while not comprehensive, might be used as a checklist as the supervisor considers what should be done.

1. Are all or most of the facts available, and are they reported accurately? That is, can the alleged offense be proved by direct or circumstantial evidence, or is the allegation based merely on suspicion?

2. How serious (minor, major, or intolerable) is the offense? Were others involved
    or affected by it? Were company funds or equipment involved?
3. Did the employee know the rule or standard? Does the employee have a rea-
    sonable excuse, and are there any extenuating circumstances?
4. What is the employee's past disciplinary record, length of service, and perfor-
    mance level? Does the offense indicate carelessness, absentmindedness, loss of
    temper, and so forth? How does this employee react to criticism?
5. Should the employee receive the same treatment others have had for the same
    offense? If not, is it possible to establish a basis for differentiating the present
    alleged offense from past offenses of a similar nature?
6. Is all the necessary documentation available in case the matter leads to outside
    review?

For certain gross violations, such as stealing, illegal substance use, and violence,
an organization may call in law enforcement authorities to conduct an investigation and to take appropriate action. Some firms will employ a consultant to administer a polygraph test in an effort to determine who committed the violations, particularly in matters involving theft. The use of the polygraph, however, has been
restricted as a result of a 1988 federal law. This statute prohibits random polygraph testing, but permits an employer with "reasonable suspicion" of employee
wrongdoing to use a polygraph if certain safeguards are met. Supervisors, for the
most part, do not make the decision to use a polygraph; such a decision is made by
someone in higher-level management, or the human resources staff, after consultation with legal counsel.

When an employee is injured on the job, many firms require the employee to
take a drug and alcohol screening test. Such tests usually are given by a qualified
person in the firm's first-aid room, or by someone at an occupational health clinic
where the employee is treated. Safeguards concerning employee privacy and test-re-
sult validation usually are followed, although the results may be utilized as part of
management's investigation and decision-making process.[2]

Investigatory Interviews. As part of the supervisor's investigation of an alleged infraction, it may be necessary to question the employee involved, as well as
other employees who may have relevant information. In general, such interviews
should be conducted in private and on an individual basis—perhaps with a guarantee of confidentiality. This is usually less threatening to an employee who otherwise
may be reluctant to tell what he or she knows. This also helps to prevent having
what employees say unduly influenced by another's versions and interpretations.

If a union employee is to be interviewed concerning a disciplinary matter, the
employee may request that a union representative or co-worker be present during
the interview. Normally the supervisor should grant such a request. Under interpretations of federal labor laws, a union employee has the right to have a union representative present during an investigatory interview if the employee reasonably believes that the investigation may lead to disciplinary action. However, a representative or co-worker witness cannot disrupt an investigatory interview or answer

questions in place of the employee being interviewed. Of course, if the employee is to have a witness present, the supervisor is well advised to have a fellow supervisor present to serve as a supervisory witness to the interview.

In conducting an investigatory interview, most of the principles of interviewing discussed in Chapter 13 are applicable. The supervisor should ask both directive and nondirective questions that are designed to elicit specific answers concerning what happened and why. Above all, the supervisor should avoid making any final judgments until all the interviews have been held and other relevant information has been assembled.

Maintaining Self-Control. Regardless of the severity of an employee violation, a supervisor must not lose self-control. This does not mean that a supervisor should face a disciplinary situation half-heartedly or indifferently. But if a supervisor feels in danger of losing control of temper or emotions, the supervisor should delay the investigatory interviews and not take any action until he or she calms down. A supervisor's loss of self-control or display of anger could compromise fair and objective judgment.

Generally, a supervisor should never lay a hand on an employee in any way. Except for emergencies, when an employee has been injured or becomes ill, or when employees who are fighting need to be separated, any physical gesture could easily be misunderstood. A supervisor who engages in physical violence, except in self-defense, normally would be subjected to disciplinary action by higher-level management.

Privacy in Disciplining. When a supervisor finally decides on a course of disciplinary action, she or he should communicate the discipline to the offending employee in private. A public reprimand not only humiliates the employee in the eyes of co-workers but also can lead to loss of morale in the department or even a grievance. If in the opinion of the other employees a public disciplinary action is too severe for the violation, the disciplined employee might emerge as a martyr in the view of every employee in the department.

Many union contracts require that employees who are to be disciplined for an infraction have the right to have a union representative present. If this is the case, it is desirable to have more than one management person present—for example, the supervisor, the supervisor's superior, and perhaps the human resources director. Thus both management and the union have witnesses to the disciplinary action, even when it takes place in a private area.

Only under extreme circumstances should disciplinary action be taken in public. For example, a supervisor's authority may be challenged directly and openly by an employee who repeatedly refuses to carry out a reasonable work request. Or an employee may be drunk or fighting on the job. In these cases it is necessary for the supervisor to reach a disciplinary decision quickly—for example, by sending the offending employee home on suspension pending further investigation. The supervisor may even have to do this in the view of other employees in order to regain control of the situation and to maintain their respect.

Disciplinary action should be taken in private to avoid humiliating the employee and damaging departmental morale.

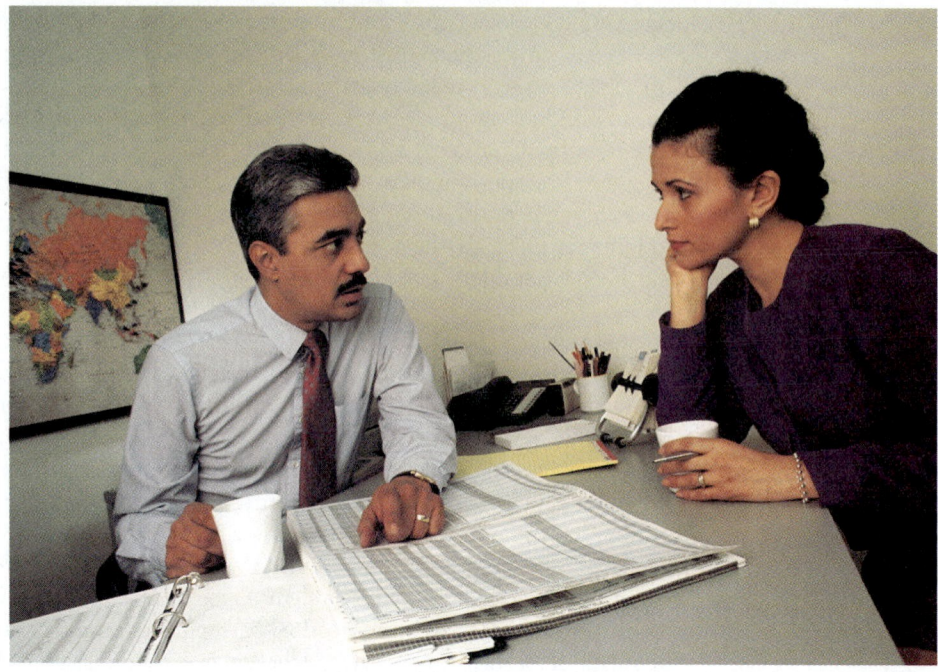

Disciplinary Time Element. When a supervisor decides to impose a disciplinary action, the question arises as to how long the violation should be held against an employee. Generally, it is desirable to disregard minor or intermediate offenses after a year or so has elapsed since they were committed. Thus, an employee with a poor record of defective work might be given a "clean bill of health" by subsequently compiling a good record for six months or one year. Some companies have adopted "point systems" to cover certain infractions—especially absenteeism and tardiness. Employees can have points removed from their records if they have perfect or acceptable attendance during later periods.

There are situations when the time element is of no importance. For example, if an employee is caught brandishing a knife in a heated argument at work, the supervisor need not worry about any time element or previous offenses. This act is serious enough to warrant immediate discharge.

4 Define and discuss the application of progressive discipline.

Progressive discipline
System of disciplinary action that increases the severity of the penalty with each offense.

PRACTICING PROGRESSIVE DISCIPLINE

Unless a serious wrong, such as stealing, physical violence, or gross insubordination, has been committed, the offending employee rarely is discharged for a first offense. Although the type of disciplinary action appropriate to a situation will vary, many organizations practice a system of **progressive discipline,** which provides for

FIGURE 19-5
Progressive
Disciplinary Policy for
a Hospital

HOSPITAL CORRECTIVE ACTION POLICY

Policy

Corrective action shall progress from verbal counseling to written reprimand, suspension, and termination. All actions taken shall include a reference to the specific policy or procedure that has been violated, the adverse consequence resulting from the violation, the type of behavior expected in the future, and the corrective action that will be taken if further violations occur. A copy of a written corrective action form shall be given to the employee. The following are guidelines for corrective action procedure:

A. *Verbal Counseling*—A verbal counseling shall be given for all minor violations of Hospital rules and policies. More than two verbal counselings within the last 12-month period regarding violations of any rules or policies warrants a written reprimand.

B. *Written Reprimands*—Written reprimands shall be given for repeated minor infractions or for first-time occurrences of more serious offenses.

   Written reprimands shall be documented on the Notice of Corrective Action form, which is signed by the department head or supervisor and the employee.

C. *Suspension*—An employee shall be suspended without pay for one to four scheduled working days for a critical or major offense or for repeated minor or serious offenses.

D. *Termination*—An employee may be terminated for repeated violations of Hospital rules and regulations or for first offenses of a critical nature.

an increase in the severity of the penalty with each offense. The following stages comprise a system of progressive disciplinary action: informal talk, oral warning, written warning, disciplinary layoff (suspension), transfer or demotion, and discharge. Figures 19-5 and 19-6 illustrate progressive discipline.

Early Stages in Progressive Discipline

Many disciplinary situations can be handled solely or primarily by the supervisor without escalating into a difficult confrontation. In the early stages of progressive discipline, the supervisor communicates with the employee concerning the problem and how to correct it.

Informal Talk. If the offense is relatively minor and if the employee has had no previous disciplinary record, a friendly and informal talk will clear up the problem in many cases. During this talk, the supervisor should try to determine the underlying reasons for the employee's unacceptable conduct. At the same time, the supervisor should reaffirm the employee's sense of responsibility and acknowledge his or her previous good behavior.

Oral Warning. If a friendly talk does not take care of the situation, the next step is to give the employee an oral warning (sometimes known as "counseling"). Here the supervisor emphasizes the undesirability of the employee's repeated violation in a straightforward manner. Although the supervisor should stress the preventive purpose of discipline, the supervisor should also emphasize that, unless the employee improves, more serious disciplinary action will be taken. In some organizations a record of this oral warning is made in the employee's file. Or the supervisor may simply write a brief note in a supervisory log book to document the fact that an oral warning was given on a particular date. This can be important evidence if the same employee commits another infraction in the future.

If oral warnings are carried out skillfully, many employees will respond and improve at this stage. The oral warning should leave the employee with the feeling that there must be improvement in the future, but that the supervisor believes the employee can improve and stands ready to help the employee do so.

Written Warning. A written warning contains a statement of the violation and the potential consequences of future violations. It is a formal document that becomes a permanent part of the employee's record. The supervisor should review with the employee the nature of this written warning and again stress the necessity for improvement. The employee should be placed on clear notice that future infractions or unacceptable conduct will lead to more serious discipline, such as suspension or discharge.

Written warnings are particularly necessary in unionized organizations, because they can serve as evidence in grievance procedures. Such documentation is also important if the employee is a member of a legally protected group, such as minorities

FIGURE 19-7
Example of a Written
Warning Used by a
Supermarket

EMPLOYEE CORRECTIVE ACTION NOTICE

Employee's Name _____ Date of Notice _____

Store Address _____ Store # ____ Dept. ____ Job Classification _____

This notice is a: First Warning   Second Warning   Third Warning   Final Warning
                         ☐   ☐   ☐   ☐

Reason for Corrective Action: (Check below)

☐ Cooperation/Interest   ☐ Cash register   ☐ Insubordination
                                 discrepancy

☐ Quality/Quantity of   ☐ Dress code   ☐ Time card violation
  work

☐ Tardiness/Absenteeism   ☐ Disregard for safety   ☐ Other causes (Explain)

Explanation must accompany reason checked above:

_____

_____

_____

I HEREBY SIGNIFY THAT I HAVE RECEIVED A FULL EXPLANATION OF MY FAILURE
TO PERFORM AS EXPECTED. THE COMPANY AND I UNDERSTAND THAT FURTHER
FAILURE ON MY PART WILL BE DUE CAUSE FOR DISCIPLINARY ACTION UP TO,
AND INCLUDING, DISCHARGE.

_____   _____   _____   _____
Employee's signature   Date   Supervisor's signature   Date

                                     _____   _____
                                     Store Manager's signature   Date

REFUSAL OF EMPLOYEE TO SIGN THIS NOTICE SHOULD BE SO NOTED HEREON.

Note: Prepare original and three copies. Send original and one copy to the Human
Resources Director. Send one copy to the Store Manager and one copy to the employee.

or women. The employee usually receives a duplicate copy of the written warning,
and another copy is sent to the human resources department. Figure 19-7 is an example of a written warning used by a supermarket chain. The form even provides
space for the supervisor to note if the employee refuses to sign it.

Even at this stage in the disciplinary process, the supervisor should continue to
express to the employee a belief in the employee's ability to improve and the super-

visor's willingness to help in whatever way possible. The primary goal of disciplinary action up until discharge should be to assist the person to improve and become a valuable employee.

Advanced Stages in Progressive Discipline

Unfortunately, not every employee will respond to the counseling and warnings of the supervisor to improve job behavior. In progressive discipline, more serious disciplinary actions may be administered for repeated violations, with discharge being the final step.

Disciplinary Layoff (Suspension). If an employee has committed offenses repeatedly and previous warnings were of no avail, a disciplinary layoff would probably constitute the next disciplinary step. Disciplinary layoffs involve a loss of pay and usually extend from one day to several days or weeks. Because a disciplinary layoff involves a loss of pay, most organizations limit a supervisor's authority at this stage. Most supervisors can only initiate a disciplinary layoff, which then must be approved by higher-level managers after consultation with the human resources department.

Employees who do not respond to oral or written warnings usually find a disciplinary layoff to be a rude awakening. The layoff may restore in them the need to comply with the organization's rules and regulations. However, managers in some organizations seldom apply layoffs as a disciplinary measure. They believe that laying off a trained employee will hurt their own production, especially in times of labor shortages. Further, they reason that the laid-off employee may return in an even more unpleasant frame of mind. Despite this possible reaction, in many employee situations disciplinary layoffs can be an effective disciplinary measure.

Transfer. Transferring an employee to a job in another department typically involves no loss of pay or skill. This disciplinary action is usually taken when an offending employee seems to be experiencing difficulty in working for a particular supervisor, in working at a current job, or in associating with certain other employees. The transfer may bring about a marked improvement if the employee adjusts to the new department and the new supervisor in a positive fashion. If a transfer is made simply to give the employee a last chance to retain a job in the company, the employee should be told that he or she must improve in the new job or else be subject to discharge. Of course, the supervisor who accepts the transferred employee should be informed about the circumstances surrounding the transfer. This will help the supervisor in assisting the transferred employee to make a successful transition.

Demotion. Another disciplinary measure, the value of which is open to serious question, is demotion to a lower-paying job. This course of action is likely to bring about dissatisfaction and discouragement, since losing pay and status over an extended period of time is a form of constant punishment. The dissatisfaction of the demoted employee can also spread to other employees. Therefore, most organizations avoid demotion (or downgrading) as a disciplinary action.

Demotion should be used only in unusual situations in which a disciplinary layoff or a discharge is not a better alternative. For example, a long-service employee may not be maintaining the standards of work performance required in a certain job. In order to retain seniority and other accrued fringe benefits, this employee may accept a demotion as an alternative to discharge.

Discharge (Termination). The most drastic form of disciplinary action is discharge (or termination). The discharged employee loses all seniority standing and may have difficulty obtaining employment elsewhere. Discharge should be reserved only for the most serious offenses and as a last resort.

A discharge involves loss and waste. It means having to train a new employee and disrupting the makeup of the work group, which may affect the morale of other employees. Moreover, in unionized companies management becomes concerned about possible prolonged grievance and arbitration proceedings. Management knows that labor arbitrators are unwilling to sustain discharge except for severe offenses or for a series of violations that cumulatively justify the discharge. If the discharge involves an employee who is a member of a legally protected group, such as minorities and women, management will have to be concerned about meeting appropriate standards for nondiscrimination. Therefore, because of the serious implications and consequences of discharge, many organizations have taken the right to discharge away from supervisors and have reserved it for higher-level managers. Other organizations require that any discharge recommended by a supervisor be reviewed and approved by higher-level managers or the human resources department.

The preceding is true even for employers who traditionally have had the freedom to dismiss employees at will, at any time, and for any reasons except for unlawful discrimination, union activity, and the like, or where there are restrictions imposed by a contract, a policy manual, or some form of employment agreement. This has been called **employment-at-will,** and it still is generally considered applicable from a legal point of view.[3] However, as stated before, most employers recognize that a discharge action should have some basis, such as economic necessity, or should be for just cause. If they follow the principles of progressive disciplinary action coupled with good supervisory practices, employers usually will not have to resort to employment-at-will to decide whether to terminate an employee who has not performed in an acceptable manner.

Employment-at-will
Legal concept that employers can dismiss employees at any time and for any reasons, except unlawful discrimination or contractual or other restrictions.

APPLYING THE HOT STOVE RULE

5 Explain the hot stove rule approach for disciplinary actions.

Taking disciplinary action may place the supervisor in a strained, difficult position. Disciplinary action tends to generate employee resentment, and it is not a pleasant experience. To assist the supervisor in applying the necessary disciplinary measure

Hot stove rule
Guideline for applying
discipline analogous
to touching a hot
stove: advance
warning and con-
sequences that are
immediate, consistent,
and applied with
impersonality.

so that it will be least resented and likely to withstand challenges from various sources, some authorities have advocated the use of the **hot stove rule.** This rule compares touching a hot stove with experiencing discipline. Both contain four elements: advance warning, immediacy, consistency, and impersonality.

Everyone knows what will happen if he or she touches a red-hot stove (*advance warning*). Someone who touches a hot stove gets burned right away, with no questions of cause and effect (*immediacy*). Every time a person touches a hot stove, that person gets burned (*consistency*). Whoever touches a hot stove is burned because of the act of touching the stove, regardless of who the person is (*impersonality*). These four elements of the hot stove rule can be applied by the supervisor when maintaining employee discipline.

Advance Warning

For employees to accept disciplinary action as fair, it is essential that all employees know in advance what is expected of them and what the rules and regulations are. Employees must be informed clearly that certain acts will lead to disciplinary action. Many organizations use orientation sessions, employee handbooks, and bulletin board announcements to inform employees about the rules and how they are to be enforced. In addition, supervisors are responsible for clarifying any questions that arise concerning rules and their enforcement.

Some firms print their rules in an employee handbook, which every new employee receives. As part of orientation, the supervisor should explain to each new employee the departmental rules and the rules that are part of the employee handbook. Some organizations require employees to sign a document stating that they have read and understood the rules and regulations.

Unfortunately, in some organizations there are rules on the books that have not been enforced. For example, there may be a rule prohibiting smoking in a certain area that the supervisor has not previously enforced. Of course, it would be improper for the supervisor to suddenly decide that it is time to enforce this rule strictly and try to make an example by taking disciplinary action against an employee found smoking in this area.

However, the fact that a certain rule has not been enforced in the past does not mean that it can never be enforced. To enforce such a rule, the supervisor must inform and warn the employees that the rule will be strictly enforced from this point on. It is not enough just to post a notice on the bulletin board, since not everyone looks at this board every day. The supervisor must issue a clear, written notice and supplement it with oral communication.

Immediacy

After noticing an offense, the supervisor should take disciplinary action as promptly as possible. At the same time, the supervisor should avoid haste, which might lead to unwarranted reactions. The sooner the discipline is imposed, the more closely it will be connected with the offensive act.

There will be instances when it appears that an employee is guilty of a violation, but the supervisor may be doubtful as to what degree of penalty should be imposed. For example, incidents such as fighting, intoxication, or insubordination often require an immediate response from the supervisor. In these cases the supervisor may place the employee on temporary suspension, which means being suspended pending a final decision. The temporarily suspended employee is advised that he or she will be informed about the ultimate disciplinary decision as soon as possible or at a specific date.

Temporary suspension in itself is not a punishment. It protects both management and the employee. It provides the supervisor with time to make an investigation and an opportunity to cool off. If the ensuing investigation indicates that no disciplinary action is warranted, then the employee is recalled and does not suffer any loss of pay. If a disciplinary layoff eventually is applied, then the time during which the employee was temporarily suspended will constitute part of the disciplinary layoff. The advantage of temporary suspension is that the supervisor can act promptly. However, it should not be used indiscriminately.

Consistency

Appropriate disciplinary action should be taken each time an infraction occurs. The supervisor who feels inclined to be lenient every now and then is, in reality, not doing the employees a favor. Inconsistency in imposing discipline will lead to employee anxiety and create doubts as to what employees can and cannot do. This type of situation can be compared to the relations between a motorist and a traffic police officer in an area where the speed limit is enforced only occasionally. Whenever the motorist exceeds the speed limit, the motorist experiences anxiety because he or she knows that the police officer can enforce the law at any time. Most motorists would agree that it is easier to operate in a location where the police force is consistent in enforcing or not enforcing speed limits. Employees, too, find it easier to work in an environment in which the supervisor is consistent in applying disciplinary action.

However, being consistent in applying disciplinary action does not necessarily mean treating everyone in exactly the same manner. Special considerations surrounding an offense may need to be considered, such as the circumstances, the employee's productivity, job attitudes, length of service, and the like. The extent to which a supervisor can be consistent and yet consider the individual's situation can be illustrated with the following example. Assume that three employees become involved in some kind of horseplay. Employee A just started work a few days ago, Employee B has been warned once before about this, and Employee C has been involved in numerous cases of horseplay. In taking disciplinary action, the supervisor could decide to have a friendly, informal talk with Employee A, give a written warning to Employee B, and impose a two-day disciplinary layoff on Employee C. Thus, each case is considered on its own merits, with the employees being judged according to their work history. Of course, if two of these employees had the same number of previous warnings, their penalties should be identical.

Imposing discipline consistently is one way a supervisor demonstrates a sense of fair play. Yet, this may be easier said than done. There are times when the department is particularly rushed and the supervisor may be inclined to conveniently overlook infractions. Perhaps the supervisor does not wish to upset the workforce or does not wish to lose the output of a valuable employee at a critical time. This type of consideration is paramount, especially when it is difficult to obtain employees with the skill that the offending employee possesses. Most employees, however, will accept an exception as fair if they know why the exception was made and if they consider it justified. However, the employees must feel that any other employee in exactly the same situation would receive similar treatment.

Impersonality

All employees who commit the same or a similar offense should be penalized. Penalties should be connected with the offensive act, not with the person or personality of the employee involved. It should not make any difference whether the employee is white or black, male or female, young or old, or a member of any other group. The same standards of disciplinary expectations and actions should be applied uniformly.

It is only natural for an employee who has been disciplined to feel some resentment. The supervisor can reduce the amount of resentment by making disciplinary action as impersonal as possible. This means that once the disciplinary action has been taken, the supervisor should treat the employee the same as before the infraction, without being apologetic about what had to be done.

DOCUMENTATION AND THE RIGHT TO APPEAL

6 Discuss the need to document disciplinary actions and to provide the right of appeal.

Documentation
Keeping records of memoranda, documents, and meetings that are relevant to a disciplinary action.

Right to appeal
Procedures by which an employee may request higher-level management to review a supervisor's disciplinary action.

Whenever a disciplinary action is taken, the supervisor must keep records of the offense committed and the decision made, including the reasoning involved in the decision. This is called **documentation**, and it may include keeping files of memoranda, documents, minutes of meetings, and the like that were part of the case handling. Documentation is necessary because the supervisor may be asked at some future time to justify the action taken, and the burden of proof is usually on the supervisor. It is not prudent for the supervisor to depend on memory alone. This is particularly true in unionized firms, where grievance-arbitration procedures often result in a challenge to disciplinary actions imposed on employees.

The **right to appeal** means that it should be possible for an employee to request a review of a supervisor's disciplinary action from higher-level management. If the employee belongs to a labor union, this right is part of a grievance procedure. In nonunionized firms, the appeal should be directed to the supervisor's superior, thereby following the chain of command. Many nonunion firms have provided for a hierarchy of several levels of management through which an appeal may be taken. The human resources department may become directly involved in an appeal procedure. Complaint procedures in nonunion firms and grievance procedures in unionized organizations are discussed in Chapter 20.

The right of appeal must be recognized as a real privilege and not merely a formality. Some supervisors tell their employees that they can appeal to higher-level management but that it will be held against them if they do so. This attitude is indicative of a supervisor's own insecurity. Supervisors should not be afraid to encourage their employees to appeal to higher-level management if the employees feel that they have been treated unfairly. Nor should supervisors feel that an appeal threatens or weakens their position as departmental managers. For the most part, a supervisor's manager will be inclined to support the supervisor's original action. If supervisors do not foster an open appeal procedure, employees may enlist aid from outside, such as a union would provide. Management's failure to provide a realistic appeal procedure is one of the reasons why some employees have resorted to unionization.

In the course of an appeal, the disciplinary penalty imposed or recommended by a supervisor may be reduced or reversed by the higher-level manager. The supervisor's decision might be reversed because the supervisor has not been consistent in imposing disciplinary action or has not considered all the necessary facts. Under these circumstances the supervisor may become discouraged and feel that the manager has not backed him or her up. Although this situation is unfortunate, it is better for the supervisor to be disheartened than for an employee to be penalized unjustly. This is not too high a price to pay to provide every employee the right to appeal. Situations such as these can be avoided if supervisors adhere closely to the principles and steps discussed in this chapter before taking disciplinary action.

DISCIPLINE WITHOUT PUNISHMENT

7 Explain the discipline without punishment approach as an alternative to progressive discipline.

Discipline without punishment
Disciplinary approach that uses coaching and counseling as preliminary steps and a paid decision-making leave for employees to decide whether to improve and stay, or quit.

In recent years, a number of companies have adopted disciplinary procedures called **discipline without punishment.** The major thrust of this approach is to stress extensive coaching, counseling, and problem solving and to avoid confrontation. A significant (and controversial) feature is the so-called paid "decision-making leave" in which an employee is sent home for a day or more with pay to decide whether or not he or she is willing to make a commitment to meet the expected standards of performance heretofore not met. If the employee makes a commitment to improve but fails to do so, the employee is then terminated.

In general, this approach replaces warnings and suspensions with coaching sessions and reminders by supervisors of the expected standards. The decision-making leave with pay is posed as a decision to be made by the employee, namely, to improve and stay, or quit.

Organizations that have implemented this approach successfully have reported various benefits, particularly in the area of reduced complaints and grievances and improved employee morale. It is too early to predict whether discipline without punishment programs will be adopted extensively, since it is not clear that these programs are very different in concept and outcome from progressive disciplinary action as discussed in this chapter. It is clear that a discipline without punishment approach requires commitment from all management levels—especially from supervisors—if it is to be carried out successfully.[4]

**W H A T
C A L L
D I D Y O U
M A K E ?**

As Linda Juarez, you recognize that following the principles discussed in this chapter is sometimes easier said than done. The situation in your department first requires investigation before you take action. You should make extra effort to observe Scott Stoner to see if you can verify any of Kathy Florence's allegations. At the same time, you probably should talk with your own manager or the director of human resources for their suggestions as how to proceed. Then you should talk with several other employees in your department to get

their versions of Scott Stoner's behavior to see how they compare with Kathy's report.

If they concur with Kathy's version, you should meet with Scott Stoner to inform him of the allegations and hear his side of the story, even if his explanation is primarily self-serving. If you believe that there is a major disciplinary problem, you should go over the relevant rules of the department with Scott so that he is clear about your expectations concerning the rules, attendance, and work performance. You need to remind him of the importance of good work habits, including a reminder that most personal business should not be performed during work hours. Urge him to establish better relationships with his co-workers, and point out that if he does not, his contributions to the department will be minimal. Try to get him to agree to some specific target objectives for various components of his job which you then can evaluate more directly than otherwise might be the case. Tell Scott that he should consider this discussion as a verbal or informal warning, and that you will be monitoring his performance closely in the weeks to follow.

Tell him that you hope his performance will improve considerably and that his relationships with his co-workers will foster teamwork. At the same time, make sure he understands that if similar complaints continue and his performance is not satisfactory, you will have to consider future disciplinary action. If he asks what such disciplinary action might be, do not be specific, but be sure that he understands that it will be more than a verbal warning and that it even could result in his termination.

Finally, after your interview with Scott, write a memorandum that summarizes the interview. This memorandum should be kept confidential and in a safe place. It could be valuable as documentation if future disciplinary action becomes necessary.

SUMMARY

1 Discuss the basis and importance of positive discipline in an organization.

Employee discipline can be thought of as the degree to which employees act according to expected standards of behavior. It is likely that if employee morale is high, discipline will be positive and there will be less need for the supervisor to take disciplinary action. Supervisors should recognize that most employees want to do the right thing. Positive self-discipline means that employees essentially regulate their own behavior out of self-interest and their normal desire to meet reasonable standards.

2 Identify disciplinary situations that violate rules of conduct and discuss the need to confront them appropriately.

Many employers have codes of ethics that describe in broad terms the ideals of the enterprise. Most organizations have written rules and regulations with definitions of infractions and possible penalties for infractions. Rules of conduct typically address areas of attendance, work scheduling, job performance, safety, improper behavior, and other matters. When infractions do occur, supervisors must take appropriate disciplinary action. If ignored, the problems will not go away.

3 Discuss the disciplinary process and approaches that ensure disciplinary action for just cause.

When infractions occur, the supervisor should take disciplinary action with the objective of improving employees' future behavior. Before disciplining, the supervisor first needs to investigate the situation thoroughly. Any disciplinary action should have just cause. Emotional and physical responses should be avoided. The supervisor should determine whether there is sufficient evidence to conclude that the employee knew about the rule or standard and in fact violated it. The supervisor should consider the severity of the violation, the employee's past service record, and other relevant factors. If a disciplinary action is necessary, it normally should be administered in private.

4 Define and discuss the application of progressive discipline.

A number of progressively severe disciplinary actions, ranging from an informal talk to a warning, a suspension, and discharge, are open to a supervisor as alternative choices, depending on the circumstances and the nature of the infraction. The supervisor's purpose in taking disciplinary action should be to improve the employee's behavior and to maintain proper discipline within the entire department.

5 Explain the hot stove rule approach for disciplinary actions.

Taking disciplinary action usually is an unpleasant experience for both the employee and the supervisor. To reduce the distasteful aspects, each disciplinary action should fulfill as much as possible the requirements of the hot stove rule. These are advance warning, immediacy, consistency, and impersonality.

6 Discuss the need to document disciplinary actions and to provide the right of appeal.

Documentation of a disciplinary action is important in order to substantiate the reasons for the action taken by a supervisor. This is especially important if there is appeal of the disciplinary decision to higher-level management through a grievance or complaint procedure. In the interest of fairness, an appeal procedure provides the employee with a review process by which the supervisor's disciplinary decision may be sustained, modified, or set aside.

7 Explain the discipline without punishment approach as an alternative to progressive discipline.

The discipline without punishment approach utilizes extensive coaching and counseling as preliminary steps. If there is no improvement, a paid decision-making leave may be given to the employee to decide whether he or she will make a commitment to improvement or be terminated.

KEY TERMS

Discipline (page 509)
Positive discipline (page 509)
Positive self-discipline (page 509)
Just cause (page 514)
Progressive discipline (page 518)

Employment-at-will (page 523)
Hot stove rule (page 524)
Documentation (page 527)
Right to appeal (page 527)
Discipline without punishment (page 528)

QUESTIONS FOR DISCUSSION

1.   Define the concept of employee discipline as a part of the working environment in a firm. In this context, differentiate between positive discipline and negative discipline.

2. Discuss the relationship between discipline and morale.

3. Evaluate the following statement: "The best type of discipline is positive self-discipline."

4. What is the difference between a code of ethics and written rules and regulations? What are their purposes?

5. Why should supervisors not be afraid to confront disciplinary situations when they occur?

6. What is meant by the concept that disciplinary action should have just cause?

7. Discuss the importance of each of the following precautionary measures that supervisors must bear in mind when taking disciplinary action:

    a. Careful study and investigation.

    b. Considerations in conducting investigatory interviews.

    c. Avoiding emotional or physical outbursts.

    d. Privacy in administering discipline.

    e. Observing the time element.

8. Define and evaluate each of the following steps of progressive discipline:

    a. Informal talk.

    b. Oral warning or reprimand.

    c. Written warning.

    d. Disciplinary layoff.

    e. Transfer.

    f. Demotion.

    g. Discharge.

    Why is demotion considered to be the least desirable form of disciplinary action?

9. What should be the purpose of any disciplinary action?

10. Define and evaluate each of the following elements of the hot stove rule:

    a. Advance warning.

    b. Immediacy.

    c. Consistency.

    d. Impersonality.

11. Discuss the following statement: "Discipline should be directed against the act and not against the person." Why is this sometimes difficult for a supervisor to accomplish?

12. Why should a supervisor document any disciplinary action that is taken?

13. What is meant by the right to appeal? How can this right be implemented in a nonunion organization? Discuss.

14. Is a discipline without punishment approach significantly different from regular progressive discipline? Discuss.

SKILLS APPLICATIONS

Skills Application 19-1: Employee Dress and Appearance Standards

One of the difficult current areas of discipline involves employee dress and appearance. This concern is especially important when employees deal directly with the public, such as in banks, retail stores, and restaurants. There also is concern about individual rights because of racial/gender/ethnic and other differences that often cause problems or potential issues of favoritism or discrimination.

1. Identify an organization that you are familiar with and write a dress/appearance code for employees as it might appear in an employee handbook.

2. Give at least two examples of attire and appearance for which some disagreements about acceptability could arise, and propose how you would handle such disagreements.

3. How would you propose handling repeated violations of the dress/appearance standards?

4. If possible, obtain the employee handbook for the organization you have used as your model. If this firm does not have a dress/appearance code, try to obtain such a code from another firm whose employees would be performing similar job duties as the one you identified. What were the similarities and differences between your dress/appearance code and your proposals for handling violations, and those of the firm? Can you explain the reasons for these differences?

Skills Application 19-2: Rules of Conduct

Reproduced below is a list of rules of conduct of the Acme Company as it appears in this company's employee handbook. The firm is not unionized. Review these rules and then answer the questions that follow.

RULES OF CONDUCT

Rules and guidelines have been established for the mutual benefit of Acme Co. and all employees. We ask your cooperation in following these rules. Our purpose is not to prohibit your rights but to help you be as productive and effective as possible.

The following list summarizes rule and policy violations subject to disciplinary action:

First Offense—Suspension or Immediate Discharge

1. Absence from work two consecutive days without authorization.
2. Intoxication and/or use of drugs.
3. Theft or unauthorized possession of Acme property.
4. Careless, negligent, or improper use of Acme property.
5. Falsifying employment application.
6. Refusal to work.
7. Abusive or threatening language to staff, supervisors, employees, or customers.
8. Fighting.
9. Falsifying work records or time cards.
10. Punching another employee's time card.
11. Releasing confidential information without proper authority.

First Offense—Verbal and/or Written Warning

1. Insubordination.
2. Unauthorized absence.
3. Excessive absenteeism.
4. Repeated tardiness.
5. Failure to report to work.
6. Failure to maintain satisfactory relationships with other employees.
7. Smoking in unauthorized areas.

8. Failure to punch the time clock.
9. Sleeping on the job.
10. Inefficiency; incompetency.
11. Disregard of personal appearance, dress.
12. Leaving assigned place of work without supervisory permission.

<u>Second and/or Third Offense—Suspension or Immediate Discharge</u>

Any of the above rule violations listed under "First Offense—Verbal and/or Written Warning" that occur a second or third time may result in a disciplinary suspension or immediate discharge.

The above rules of conduct are meant only to serve as a guide. Variations in disciplinary actions taken may depend on the severity and intent of the offense and other circumstances.

1. How does the list of violations illustrate a progressive discipline system?

2. Do you agree that the violations leading to possible immediate discharge after the first offense are appropriate? Why or why not? Which should be dropped, or what should be added?

3. Under a second and/or third offense, why might the vagueness of the process be both an advantage and a potential problem?

4. If you were to rewrite or edit this list of rules, what would you propose?

Skills Application 19-3: Disciplinary Action for Just Cause

1. From the materials in this chapter, develop a list of the requirements and considerations that you believe are the most essential for ensuring that a disciplinary action taken against an employee has a just cause basis.

2. **a.** Contact two practicing supervisors (or managers) who are willing to be interviewed. One supervisor should be in a unionized firm and have departmental employees under a union contract. The other should be in a firm whose employees are not represented by a union. Ask each supervisor to identify what he or she believes to be the five or more most important requirements and considerations when a supervisor takes disciplinary action against an employee. (Note: Do not use the term "just cause" in making your request.)

b. Ask each supervisor to respond to the following hypothetical situation: "You discover an employee sound asleep at his or her work station, which is isolated from the view of other employees. It is 10:00 A.M. How would you proceed?"

3. **a.** Compare the supervisors' lists with your list. To what degree were these lists similar or different? If there were major differences, what do you feel would be the most likely explanation?

b. Compare each supervisor's response to the hypothetical situation posed in question **2b**. If there were major differences, how might they be explained?

ENDNOTES

1.   See Arthur A. Sloane and Fred Witney, *Labor Relations* (7th ed.; Englewood Cliffs, N.J.: Prentice-Hall, 1991), pp. 432–438; or William H. Holly and Kenneth M. Jennings, *The Labor Relations Process* (4th ed.; Chicago: The Dryden Press, 1991), pp. 302–317.

2.   Many companies also conduct random and other drug tests on their employees, especially federal government contractors and employers as mandated by the Drug-Free Workplace Act of 1988. Companies usually have policies and procedures that outline how tests will be taken, safeguards, and possible penalties for violations. See "Testing . . . Testing," *Business Week* (May 2, 1994). p. 6.

3.   See Michael J. Phillips, "Toward a Middle Way in the Polarized Debate Over Employment at Will," *American Business Law Journal* (Volume 30, Number 3, November 1992), pp. 441–483; or Kenneth Gilberg, "Employers Must Protect Against Employee Lawsuits," *Supervision* (Volume 53, Number 11, November 1992), pp. 12–13.

4.   See Chimezie A. B. Osigweh, "To Punish or Not to Punish? Managing Human Resources Through "Positive Discipline,' " *Employee Relations* (Volume 12, Number 3, 1990), pp. 27–32; or Mark Sherman and Al Lucia, "Positive Discipline and Labor Arbitration," *Arbitration Journal* (Volume 47, Number 2, June 1992), pp. 56–58. In these articles, the term "positive discipline" is used synonymously with the discipline without punishment approaches.

20

Handling Complaints and Grievances

LEARNING OBJECTIVES

After studying this chapter, you will be able to:

1 Discuss the handling of employee complaints and grievances as a natural component of supervision.

2 Compare the meaning of a grievance in a unionized situation to a complaint in any work setting.

3 Explain the major differences between grievance procedures in unionized organizations and complaint procedures in nonunionized organizations.

4 Describe the supervisor's role at the initial step in a grievance or complaint procedure, especially the need for open and frank communication.

5 Identify guidelines for supervisors for resolving complaints and grievances in an effective manner.

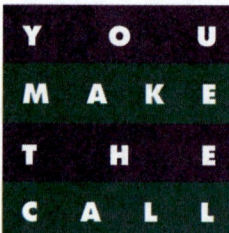

You are Alfred Perry, a department supervisor in a plastics products plant. You have 14 employees in your department, all of whom are represented by the United Plastics Workers Union. You have supervised this department for about six months after having been transferred to this plant from another company plant. In the mail you have just received a written grievance signed by Allison Howard, union shop steward, on behalf of all department employees. The grievance protests the decision that you announced yesterday to stop the preparation of a pot of coffee in the department during working hours. The union grievance states:

The union protests your unfair decision to take away a privilege that has been in place for at least five years. Making coffee in our depart-ment only requires a few minutes time by an employee each day. All costs are borne by the employees. Your decision violates Article 13, Section 3 of our labor–management agreement, which states: "The com-pany shall not take away any privi-leges that are now enjoyed by the employees." We demand that you withdraw your decision, and that the long-established practice of having coffee brewed in our department be restored.

You are not too surprised by the union grievance, but when you made your decision you felt you had the right to do so. You relied on Article 2, Section 1 of the labor–management agreement, which says, "It is the responsibility of com-pany management to maintain disci-pline and efficiency in this plant."

Since becoming supervisor, you had warned the employees several times that making coffee, standing around drinking coffee, and other forms of wasting time in the department could not be tolerated. There are two other departments in the plant. Neither of these departments permits making coffee on company premises during work hours. However, employees can bring their own coffee in thermos bottles and drink it if it does not interfere with work. You felt it was time to put a stop to a practice that the previous supervisor had condoned, because it was interfering with efficiency and production. You wonder how to respond to the union grievance.

YOU MAKE THE CALL.

COMPLAINTS AND GRIEVANCES ARE PART OF SUPERVISION

1 Discuss the handling of employee complaints and grievances as a natural component of supervision.

Many supervisors become irritated and confused when they experience a challenge to their authority in the form of an employee complaint or grievance. Some find it difficult to function because they feel that employee complaints and grievances reflect on their performance, or perhaps that there is something wrong with them as supervisors or people. However, employee complaints and grievances should be viewed as an expected part of the relationship between any manager and employee group. Of course, it is not desirable for supervisors to have a constant flood of employee disagreements, since this would indicate severe problems in the department. Yet, supervisors should understand that as they carry out their managerial responsibilities, it is normal to expect that at times their perspectives and decisions will conflict with those of employees or the labor union. Therefore, a supervisor should recognize that employee complaints and grievances are a natural component of the supervisory position.

In a unionized firm, the number and types of grievances that arise within a department can reflect the state of union–management relations. Of course, grievances can also be related to internal union politics, which usually are beyond a supervisor's control. Whether or not employees are unionized, every supervisor should handle employee complaints and grievances in a systematic and professional manner. It requires skills and efforts that are major indicators of a supervisor's overall managerial capabilities.[1]

2 Compare the meaning of a grievance in a unionized situation to a complaint in any work setting.

Complaint
Any individual or group problem or dissatisfaction that employees can channel upward to management, including discrimination complaints.

DISTINGUISHING BETWEEN COMPLAINTS AND GRIEVANCES

The terms "complaint" and "grievance" are not synonyms. As commonly understood, a **complaint** is any individual or group problem or dissatisfaction that employees can channel upward to management. A complaint normally can be lodged in any work environment, and the term can be used to include legal issues, such as

Grievance
Formal complaint concerning interpretation or application of a union–management labor agreement.

a complaint of racial or sexual discrimination. Typically, a **grievance** is defined more specifically as a formal complaint involving the interpretation or application of the labor agreement in a unionized setting. This usually means that it has been presented to a supervisor or another management representative by a shop steward or some other union official.

In this chapter, we use the terms "complaint" and "grievance" somewhat interchangeably. The underlying principles for handling complaints and grievances are basically the same, even though the procedures for processing them may be different. The approach suggested here should generally be followed regardless of the issue involved or whether the work environment is unionized.

PROCEDURES FOR RESOLVING GRIEVANCES AND COMPLAINTS

3 Explain the major differences between grievance procedures in unionized organizations and complaint procedures in nonunionized organizations.

Although procedures for resolving grievances and complaints are similar, there are important distinctions that supervisors should understand. This section will discuss these distinctions.

Grievance Procedures

Grievance procedure
Negotiated series of steps in a labor agreement for processing grievances, beginning at the supervisory level and ending with arbitration.

Grievances usually result from a misunderstanding, a different interpretation of the labor agreement, or an alleged violation of a provision of the labor agreement. Virtually all labor agreements contain a **grievance procedure**, which is a negotiated series of steps for processing grievances, usually beginning at the departmental level. If a grievance is not settled at the first step, it may be appealed to higher levels of management or the human resources department. The last step typically involves having an arbitrator render a final and binding decision in the matter. Figure 20-1 is an example of a grievance and arbitration procedure included in a labor agreement.

Complaint Procedures

Complaint procedure
A management-designed series of steps for handling employee complaints that usually provides for a number of appeals before a final decision.

Many nonunion organizations have adopted formal problem-solving or complaint procedures to resolve complaints that employees bring to the attention of their supervisors. A **complaint procedure**, which may be called a "problem solving procedure" or by some other designation, is a management-designed procedure for handling employee complaints that usually provides for a number of appeal steps before a final decision is reached. A complaint procedure usually is explained in an employee handbook or a policies-and-procedures manual. Even when no formal system is spelled out, it usually is understood that employees have the right to register a complaint with the possibility of an appeal to higher-level management. A procedure for handling complaints differs from a union grievance procedure pri-

FIGURE 20-1
Grievance and
Arbitration Procedure
in a Labor Agreement
for a Retail Store's
Unionized Employees

ARTICLE 4—GRIEVANCES AND ARBITRATION

4.1 Should any differences, disputes or complaints arise over the interpretation or application of the contents of this Agreement, there shall be an earnest effort made on the part of both parties to settle same promptly through the following steps:

Step 1. By conference between the aggrieved employee, the union steward and/or business agent, or both, and the store manager or owner. Store management shall make its decision known within two (2) working days thereafter. If the matter is not resolved in Step 1, it shall be referred to Step 2 within two (2) working days.

Step 2. By conference between the business agent and the owner or a supervisor of the Employer. The Employer shall make its decision known within three (3) working days thereafter. If the matter is not resolved in Step 2, it shall be reduced to writing and referred within three (3) working days to Step 3.

Step 3. By conference between an official or officials of the Union and a designated representative of the Employer.

Step 4. In the event the last step fails to settle the complaint, it shall be referred within seven (7) working days to arbitration.

4.2 In any case in which an employee is aggrieved and the Union promptly notifies the employee that it does not intend to request arbitration after the Step 3 meeting, the time for requesting arbitration shall be stayed pending the employee's exhaustion of internal union appeals to the Union's Executive Board.

4.3 The Employer and the Union shall mutually agree to an impartial arbitrator to hear said arbitration case; however, if said arbitrator cannot be chosen within three (3) days then the Federal Mediation and Conciliation Service will be requested to furnish a panel of seven (7) names from which the arbitrator may be chosen. The arbitrator will be selected within seven (7) days after the receipt of the panel by alternately striking names. The party striking first will be determined by the flip of a coin. The decision of the arbitrator shall be binding on both parties. The expenses of the arbitrator shall be paid for jointly.
Such arbitrator shall not be empowered to add to, detract from, or alter the terms of this Agreement.

4.4 The Employer may, at any time, discharge any worker for proper cause. The Union or the employee may file a written complaint with the Employer within seven (7) days after the date of discharge asserting that the discharge was improper. Such complaint must be taken up promptly. If the Employer and the Union fail to agree within five (5) days, it shall be referred to arbitration. Should the arbitrator determine that it was an unfair discharge, the Employer shall abide by the decision of the arbitrator.

4.5 Grievances must be taken up promptly. No grievance will be considered, discussed, or become arbitrable which is presented later than seven (7) days after such has happened.

FIGURE 20-1
(continued)

> 4.6 The Employer shall have the right to call a conference with a Union steward or of-
>   ficials of the Union for the purpose of discussing a grievance, criticisms, or other
>   problems.
> 4.7 Grievances will be discussed only through the outlined procedures; except that by
>   mutual agreement between the Union and the Employer, the time limits may be
>   waived.
> 4.8 There shall be no lockout or cessation of work pending the decision of the arbitra-
>   tor.

marily in two respects. First, the employee normally must make the complaint without assistance in presenting or arguing the case; and second, the final decision is usually made by the chief executive or the human resources director rather than by an outside arbitrator.

Figure 20-2 is an edited excerpt of a problem-solving procedure that was established by a firm for its nonunion employees. Note that it involves a series of steps that begins at the supervisory level and ends with the company president or executive vice-president.

In recent years, some companies have offered their employees assistance in processing complaints by providing an ombudsman or counselor to serve in intermediary roles. Numerous companies have adopted complaint procedures for nonunion employees that include a "jury" or "panel" of employees and managers who serve as a form of arbitration board at the final step in their complaint procedures. Some are experimenting with providing a neutral arbitrator at the final step to resolve complaints, primarily in discharge cases. These types of approaches have been labeled as **alternative dispute resolution (ADR)**, which generally means processing and deciding employee complaints internally as an alternative to filing lawsuits to resolve disputes, usually those involving discipline or discharge. The use of alternative dispute resolution approaches is likely to increase, particularly if future legislation requires protection for employees-at-will. The "Contemporary Issue" box in this chapter discusses ADR, including a proposal being considered for uniform adoption by all states.

Alternative dispute resolution (ADR)
Approach for processing and deciding employee complaints internally as an alternative to filing a lawsuit, usually for disputes involving discipline or discharge.

4 Describe the supervisor's role at the initial step in a grievance or complaint procedure, especially the need for open and frank communication.

THE SUPERVISOR AND THE SIGNIFICANT FIRST STEP

As in so many other areas, the supervisor's role in the handling of employee complaints and grievances is often the most crucial part in the eventual determination of the outcome. At the first step in a unionized firm, the departmental shop steward usually will present a grievance to the supervisor, and the aggrieved employee (or employees) may also be present. The supervisor should listen to them very care-

FIGURE 20-2
A Problem-Solving
Procedure for
Complaints

AJAX CORPORATION
PROBLEM-SOLVING PROCEDURE

Objective

It is our purpose to provide employees with an effective means to bring problems to the attention of management and get them resolved. A problem may be any condition of employment an employee feels is unjust or inequitable. Employees are encouraged to air any concern about their treatment or conditions of work over which the company might be expected to exercise some control.

Normal Procedure

Step #1 — The First-Line Supervisor — Problems are best resolved by the people closest to the situation. Employees are thus asked to first discuss their concerns with their immediate supervisor. Supervisors should, of course, seek a satisfactory resolution. If the employee feels that the supervisor is not the right person to solve the problem, he or she can ignore this step.

Step #2 — The District Manager — If the problem is not resolved after discussion with the First-Line Supervisor, the employee should be referred to the District Manager (or Assistant).

Step #3 — Higher-Level Divisional Management — If the problem has not been settled by either the First-Line Supervisor or District Manager, the employee should be referred to Higher-Level Divisional Management.

Step #3 — Alternate — The Human Resources Staff — As an alternative, the employee can discuss his or her problem with a member of the Human Resources staff rather than Higher-Level Divisional Management.

Step #4 — The President — If the matter is not adjusted satisfactorily by any of the foregoing, the employee may request an appointment with the President (or Executive Vice-President), who will see that a decision is finalized.

Policies

1. *Freedom from Retaliation —* Employees should not be discriminated against for exercising their rights to discuss problems. Obviously any retaliation would seriously distort the climate in which our problem-solving procedure is intended to operate.
2. *Prompt Handling —* A problem can become magnified if it isn't dealt with promptly. Supervisors are expected to set aside time to discuss an employee's concerns within one working day of an employee's request. Supervisors should seek to resolve a problem within three working days of a discussion.
3. *Fair Hearing —* Supervisors should concentrate on listening. Often, hearing an employee out can resolve the problem. Supervisors should objectively determine whether the employee has been wronged and, if so, seek a satisfactory remedy.

President's Gripe Box

The President's "Gripe Box" is located on each floor of our Home Office buildings. Employees should feel free to use the "Gripe Box" to get problems to the President's attention expeditiously. Employees may or may not sign gripes. Written responses will be sent for all signed gripes.

CONTEMPORARY ISSUE
Alternative Dispute Resolution: An Approach Whose Time Has Come?

Under the legal concept of employment-at-will, employees who are not covered by some type of contract and who do not have any form of legal protection can be terminated by an employer with or without notice or cause. However, over the last decade or so, thousands of employees have filed lawsuits charging unfair dismissal. These are called "wrongful discharge" lawsuits. Courts in many states have been chipping away at employment-at-will, and a number of large damage awards have been afforded to individuals who successfully pursued their complaints in court.

Primarily as a result of the high costs of litigation, a national legal commission has proposed a new uniform employment statute that would permit terminated employees to take their cases before a neutral arbitrator. This commission, called the National Conference of Commissioners on Uniform State Laws, has proposed a plan that would involve a system of arbitration to cover potentially some 60 million workers in the United States. A number of states are seriously considering adopting this system of arbitration for at-will employees. Some employers favor such a sys-

tem, especially in states where the courts have been particularly willing to erode the employment-at-will concept. Whether this proposal will be widely adopted is a matter of conjecture.

A number of employers already have developed their own alternative dispute resolution (ADR) approaches, some of which contain their own forms of arbitration. In return for an employee signing a waiver of a right to resolve an employment dispute in court, the employer has a procedure in place that provides access for the employee to private arbitration for a final and binding resolution of an employment dispute. Many issues have to be resolved if an employer sets up its own alternative dispute resolution program. Among the most vexing are procedural questions concerning how employers and employees are represented before an arbitrator and who pays the costs of arbitration. If an employer chooses to adopt its own form of alternative dispute resolution, the procedure must be perceived as being a fair one that will protect employee as well as employer interests.

Source: Adapted from "Tell It to the Arbitrator," *Business Week* (November 4, 1991), p. 109; and Edward T. Lynch and Courtney E. Redfern, "Committing Employees to Out-of-Court Resolution," *HR Magazine* (Volume 38, Number 5, May 1993), pp. 97–103.

fully. There is nothing to prohibit the supervisor from speaking directly with the employee in front of the shop steward. In other words, there should be frank and open communication among the parties. If the shop steward does not bring the employee along, the supervisor nonetheless should listen to the shop steward.

It is unusual for an aggrieved employee to present a grievance to a supervisor in the absence of the shop steward. However, if this should happen, it is appropriate for the supervisor to listen to the employee's problem and to determine whether it involves the labor agreement or the shop steward, or whether the union should be involved at all. Under no circumstances should the supervisor give the impression that he or she is trying to undermine the shop steward's authority or relationship with the employee. If the labor agreement or union interests are involved, then the supervisor should notify the shop steward concerning the employee's presentation of the problem.

If a grievance is not settled at the first step and if the shop steward believes that the grievance is justified, the grievance will proceed to the next step. The shop steward may carry the grievance further with some other objective in mind. In

Chapter 12 we mentioned that the shop steward usually is an elected representative of the employees, is familiar with the labor agreement, and is knowledgeable in submitting a grievance. The shop steward may be eager to receive credit for filing a grievance. By making a good showing or by winning as much as possible for the employees, his or her chances of being reelected as shop steward at the next union election are enhanced.

If the firm is not unionized, some employees may be afraid to bring their legitimate complaints to their supervisor. They fear that complaining may be held against them, and possibly that there may be retaliation if they dare to challenge a supervisor's decision. At the other extreme are employees who resent supervisory authority and take every opportunity to gripe about matters that they do not like in the department. They even relish making the supervisor uncomfortable by bringing complaints to his or her attention. Since they do not have union representation, they may approach the supervisor as a group, believing that this approach gives them strength and protection.

The importance of the supervisor's handling of employee complaints at the first step cannot be overemphasized. Open and frank communication between all parties is usually the key element in finding an amicable resolution of the problem. If such communication does not occur, disagreement, resentment, and possibly an appeal to higher levels of management will be the likely outcome.

For the most part, the supervisor should take into account the same general considerations and use the same skills in handling both grievances and complaints. Although grievances and complaints have their own unique factual circumstances, the supervisory process for resolving them should follow the same guidelines.

SUPERVISORY GUIDELINES FOR RESOLVING COMPLAINTS AND GRIEVANCES

5 Identify guidelines for supervisors for resolving complaints and grievances in an effective manner.

Regardless of the nature of an employee complaint or grievance, a supervisor should fully investigate details of the problem and determine whether it can be resolved quickly. It is always better to settle minor issues before they grow into major ones. Although there will be cases that have to be referred to higher-level managers, the supervisor for the most part should endeavor to settle a grievance or complaint at the first step. If many go beyond the first step, the supervisor probably is not carrying out his or her duties appropriately. Unless circumstances are beyond the supervisor's control, complaints and grievances should be handled within reasonable time limits and brought to a fair conclusion within the pattern of supervisory considerations discussed in the sections that follow.

Make Time Available

The supervisor should find time to hear a complaint or grievance as soon as possible. This does not mean that the supervisor must drop everything to meet immediately with the employee or shop steward. Rather, it means making every effort to set a time for an initial hearing. If the supervisor makes it difficult for a complaining employee to have a hearing as expeditiously as possible under the circumstances, the employee could become frustrated and feel resentful. A long delay could be interpreted to mean that the supervisor does not consider the problem important. Or it could even be interpreted as stalling and indifference on the part of management.

Listen Patiently and with an Open Mind

Often supervisors become preoccupied with defending themselves and trying to justify their own positions without giving the shop steward and/or the complaining employee ample time to present their cases. Supervisors should bear in mind that all the principles discussed in the chapters on communication and interviewing are applicable to complaints and grievances. All people involved should be encouraged to say whatever they have on their minds. If they gain the impression that the supervisor is willing to listen to them and wants to provide fair treatment, the problem may not seem as large to them as it did before. Also, the more a person talks, the more likely that person is to make contradictory remarks that weaken the argument. The person may even uncover a solution as he or she talks out the problem. Sometimes, the employee simply wants to vent frustrations, and after this is done the problem may be solved. Thus, by listening empathetically, the supervisor can minimize tensions and even solve some problems in the initial hearing.

Distinguish Facts from Opinions

Distinguishing facts from opinions means being cautious about relying on hearsay and opinionated statements. However, the supervisor should not try to confuse the employee or shop steward. The supervisor should ask factual, pointed questions regarding who or what is involved; when, where, and why the alleged problem took place; and whether there was any connection between this situation and some other problem. Frequently it is impossible to gather all the relevant information at once, making it inappropriate to settle the complaint or grievance immediately. Under such conditions the supervisor should tell the complaining employee or the shop steward that he or she will gather the necessary information within a reasonable time and by a definite date. The supervisor should not postpone a decision with the excuse of needing more facts when the relevant information can be obtained without delay.

Determine the Real Issue

In both union and nonunion work settings, there may be times when an employee complaint represents a symptom of a deeper problem. For example, a complaint about unfair work assignments may really reflect personality clashes among several employees in the department. Or a complaint that newly installed machinery does

When a supervisor listens to complaints and grievances with an open mind, the problem often seems less severe to the employee.

not allow employees to maintain their previous incentive rates may indicate that the employees are actually having a difficult time adjusting to the operation of the new equipment after years of operating old machines. Unless the real issue is clearly defined and settled, complaints of a similar nature are likely to be raised again in the future.

Check and Consult

Checking and consulting are perhaps the most important aspects of a supervisor's role in handling employee complaints and grievances. We cannot emphasize too strongly that the labor agreement, as well as company policies and procedures, must be administered fairly and uniformly. In a unionized setting, the supervisor may not be sure whether the grievance is valid under the existing labor agreement; or provisions of the labor agreement might be unclear in reference to the alleged violation. In no case should the supervisor make a decision until after he or she has carefully reviewed the company's manual on policies and procedures and the labor agreement.

As stated previously, grievances revolve around interpretation of the labor agreement, and complaints in nonunion settings may include questions of employment policies. Furthermore, complaints that involve allegations of discrimination and other aspects of equal employment opportunity have legal implications.

Therefore, whenever a grievance or complaint requires contractual, policy, or legal interpretation, the supervisor should tell the complaining individuals that it will be necessary to look into the matter and that an answer will be given by a definite date. Subsequently, the supervisor should consult with the human resources department and higher-level managers for advice and guidance on these matters.

Seeking assistance from human resources staff or higher-level managers is neither buck-passing nor revealing ignorance. Nor should it be considered by the supervisor as showing weakness, because the supervisor usually is not authorized or qualified to make the policy or legal interpretations necessary to respond to certain employee complaints and grievances.

Avoid Setting Precedents

The supervisor should consult records of previous settlements and make sure that any proposed decision is consistent with established practices. If a particular issue has never been encountered in the past, the supervisor should seek guidance from other supervisors or staff personnel who may have experienced similar but not necessarily identical problems. If circumstances require a departure from previous decisions, the supervisor should explain the reasons why to the employee or the shop steward. They also should be informed about whether any exception will constitute a new precedent.

Unless there is a valid, unique reason or unless the supervisor has received approval from higher-level management or the human resources department, the supervisor should avoid making individual exceptions to a policy. Making an exception is setting a precedent, and precedents often come back to haunt the supervisor and the organization. In labor arbitration issues, most arbitrators believe that precedents can become almost as binding on an organization as if they were negotiated in the labor agreement itself. Thus a supervisor should be very careful about making an individual exception in a union grievance, because a grievance settlement may become part of a future labor agreement.

Exercise Self-Control

Sometimes emotions, arguments, and personality clashes distort the communication between the supervisor and complaining individuals. The worst thing the supervisor can do in these situations is to engage in a shouting match or to "talk down" to the complaining employees. Emotional outbursts usually lead to little constructive thinking. Arguing and shouting may escalate a problem to far more serious proportions. Of course, there are limits to a supervisor's patience. If the employee or the shop steward persists in loud arguments, profanity, or the like, the supervisor should terminate the meeting at that point and schedule another, hoping that the problem can be discussed later in a calm and less emotional manner.

If the complaint or grievance is trivial or not even valid, the supervisor must be careful not to show any personal animosity toward the shop steward or the complaining employee. The supervisor should explain why a grievance has no merit. The supervisor cannot expect the shop steward to do the explaining, since the steward is the employee's official representative.

Sometimes an employee or the shop steward may provoke an argument as a way of deliberately putting the supervisor on the defensive. Even this type of situation should not arouse open hostilities on the supervisor's part. If the supervisor does not know how to handle situations of this sort, he or she should consult with higher-level managers or the human resources department for assistance.

Minimize Delay in Reaching a Decision

Many labor agreements require a definite time period within which a grievance must be answered. The same principle should hold true in nonunion work situations. If an employee has raised a complaint, that employee should be entitled to know—within a reasonable time—exactly when management will make a decision concerning that complaint. If the complaint can be handled immediately and if it is within the supervisor's authority to do so, of course this should be done practically on the spot. But if the complaint involves an issue that requires consultation with higher-level managers or the human resources staff, the supervisor should close the hearing with a definite commitment as to when an answer or decision will be given.

Postponing a decision in the hope that the grievance will disappear can invite trouble and more grievances. However, arriving at a speedy settlement should not outweigh the importance of a sound decision. If delay is necessary, the supervisor should inform the parties and explain why, not leave them thinking they are being ignored. Since waiting for a decision is bothersome to everyone, prompt handling is of utmost importance.

Explain the Decision Clearly and with Sensitivity

The supervisor should make every effort to give a straightforward, clear answer to the complaint or grievance as decided by management (see Figure 20-3). In addition, the supervisor should communicate as specifically as possible the reasons for the decision, especially if it goes against the employee's case. It is frustrating for an employee just to get a "no" without any explanation other than that management "feels" that it does not have to do what the employee requests.

Even when the complaint is not justified, the supervisor should not in any way convey to the employee that the problem is trivial or unnecessary. There are probably good reasons in the employee's mind for raising the complaint. Therefore, the supervisor's response should be sensitive to the employee's perspective.

If a written reply to a grievance is required under the labor agreement, the supervisor should restrict it to the specific grievance and make certain that the response is relevant to the case. References to provisions of the labor agreement or

FIGURE 20-3
The supervisor should
answer a complaint or
grievance in a
straightforward,
reasonable manner.

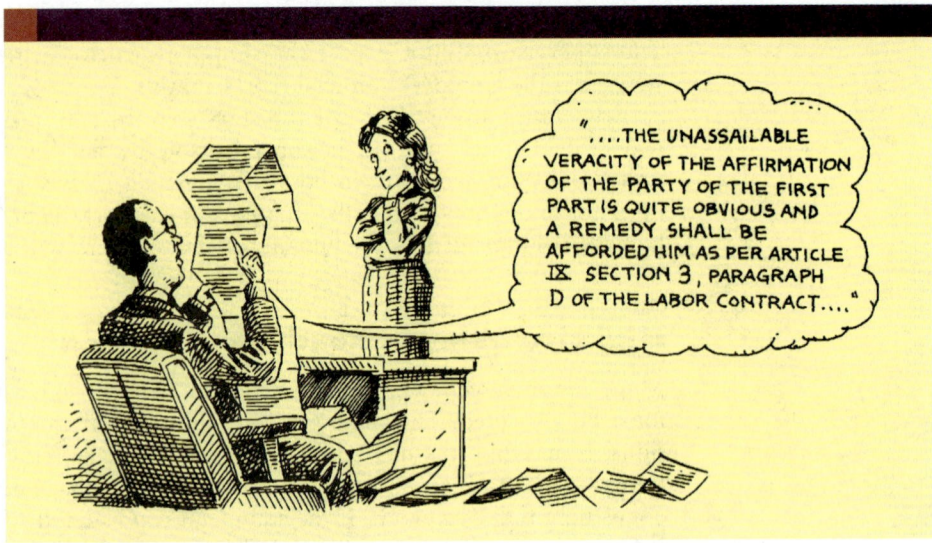

plant rules should be confined to those in question. The supervisor is well advised to first discuss the implications of a written reply with higher-level managers or the human resources department so that it will be worded appropriately.

Keep Records and Documents

Despite good-faith efforts of supervisors or higher-level managers to settle complaints or grievances, an employee may choose to appeal an adverse decision. If the complaint involves discrimination, the employee may file a formal complaint with a government agency for legal processing. If there is a union grievance, it may eventually go all the way to arbitration. In a nonunionized firm, the firm's complaint procedures may provide several steps for appeal. This is why it is important for a supervisor to maintain documentation of all available evidence, discussions, and meetings. In any appeal process, written evidence is generally superior to oral testimony and hearsay.

Keeping good records is especially important when a complaint or grievance is not settled at the supervisory level. The burden of proof is usually on management to justify its position. Therefore, a supervisor should be ready to explain previous actions without having to depend solely on memory. Documentation can be very supportive in this regard.

Do Not Fear a Challenge

A supervisor should make every effort to resolve a complaint or grievance at the first step without sacrificing a fair decision. Unfortunately, supervisors at times are tempted to grant a questionable complaint or grievance because they fear a challenge or want to avoid a hassle. By giving in to an employee or the union just to avoid an argument, the supervisor may invite others to adopt the "squeaky wheel gets the grease" theory. That is, other employees or shop stewards will be encouraged to submit minor complaints because they feel that by complaining often and loudly, they have a better chance of gaining a concession. Thus, a supervisor's "caving in" can establish a perception that may lead to even greater problems.

In efforts to settle a complaint or grievance, there will always be gray areas where a supervisor must use prudent judgment. The supervisor should be willing to admit and rectify mistakes. However, if the supervisor believes that a fair and objective decision was made, he or she should have the courage to hold to a firm decision, even if the employee threatens to appeal. The fact that the employee appeals an adverse decision does not mean that the supervisor is wrong. Even if higher-level managers or an arbitrator should later reverse a supervisor's decision, this in itself does not imply poor handling by the supervisor. There will always be some decisions that will be modified or reversed during the appeal process for reasons that may go beyond the supervisor's responsibility.

Supervisors who generally follow the guidelines discussed in this chapter and who have done their best to reach a fair solution, will be backed up by higher-level management in most cases. At the very least, a supervisor normally should be able to handle a complaint or grievance in a professional manner and avoid having minor issues escalate into major ones.

In summary, handling employee complaints and grievances is another of the many skills of effective supervision. It requires sensitivity, objectivity, and sound analytical judgment—which are the same qualities that are required in most other areas of supervisory management.

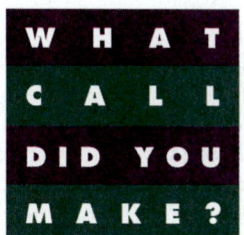

WHAT CALL DID YOU MAKE?

As department supervisor Alfred Perry, you face a common dilemma in interpretation and application of a labor–management agreement, namely, which provision should prevail in determining a proper course of action. The union claims that a coffee-making privilege is protected under the labor–management agreement and cannot be changed unilaterally by a supervisor. However, you feel that the same agreement gives management the right to make necessary decisions to maintain discipline and efficiency. The grievance and the grievance procedure will test which view shall prevail.

Since interpretation of a labor–management agreement is at the heart of this grievance, you should refer it to the director of human resources for guidance. Virtually all of the principles included in this chapter may become applicable in the processing of the case. In particular, you should investigate thoroughly all aspects of the contested issue in your department and document all information that supports your position. Unless there is a settlement or compromise of some sort, the case conceivably could go all the way to arbitration for a final and binding decision.

Throughout the steps of the grievance procedure, you should argue your position in a straightforward manner, but do not attempt to belittle the union members' concern about retaining a privilege that they have had previously. Regardless of the final outcome of the grievance, you should understand that employees have the right to submit grievances, and the grievance procedure will eventually bring about a decision, hopefully in a fair and professional manner.

SUMMARY

1 Discuss the handling of employee complaints and grievances as a natural component of supervision.

As supervisors manage their departments, it is natural that their perspectives and decisions at times will conflict with those of employees and/or the union. Handling employee complaints and grievances is part of each supervisor's job, and the manner of handling them is a major indicator of a supervisor's overall managerial capabilities.

2 Compare the meaning of a grievance in a unionized situation to a complaint in any work setting.

An employee complaint can occur in any work environment. Complaints may involve individual or group dissatisfactions that can be registered with a supervisor and possibly appealed further. A grievance is normally identified as a complaint involving the interpretation and application of a labor agreement where employees are represented by a union.

3 Explain the major differences between grievance procedures in unionized organizations and complaint procedures in nonunionized organizations.

Although both types of procedures usually have a number of steps beginning at the supervisory level, a grievance procedure in a unionized setting and a complaint procedure in a nonunionized setting differ in two major ways. In the nonunionized setting, the employee normally must make a complaint without any assistance; an employee who files a union grievance will have the assistance of a shop steward or some other union representative. Second, the final decision is usually made by the chief executive or the human resources director in a nonunionized firm, and some firms use other ways to resolve complaints. In a union grievance matter, an outside neutral arbitrator may make the final decision.

4 Describe the supervisor's role at the initial step in a grievance or complaint procedure, especially the need for open and frank communication.

During the initial step in handling grievances, there should be open, frank communication between the supervisor and the complaining employee and the shop steward. If the grievance is not settled at this step, the shop steward probably will carry the grievance further, and it may eventually be submitted to an outside arbitrator. The same need for open and frank communication exists in hearing and resolving employee complaints at the supervisory level.

Employee complaints should be settled in an amicable fashion by the supervisor whenever possible, rather than having them appealed and decided at higher levels.

5 Identify guidelines for supervisors for resolving complaints and grievances in an effective manner.

Whether or not employees are represented by a labor union, the supervisor should follow the same general guidelines in resolving complaints or grievances. Among the most important supervisory considerations are the following: (a) make time available; (b) listen patiently and with an open mind; (c) distinguish facts from opinions; (d) determine the real issue; (e) check and consult; (f) avoid setting precedents; (g) exercise self-control; (h) minimize delay in reaching a decision; (i) explain the decision clearly and with sensitivity; (j) keep records and documents; and (k) do not fear a challenge.

KEY TERMS

Complaint (page 537)
Grievance (page 538)
Grievance procedure (page 538)

Complaint procedure (page 538)
Alternative dispute resolution (ADR) (page 540)

QUESTIONS FOR DISCUSSION

1. Why should employee complaints and grievances be considered a natural component of the supervisory position?

2. How is a grievance defined in unionized firms? What are the major distinctions between a union grievance and an employee complaint in a nonunionized firm?

3. Distinguish between a union grievance procedure and a complaint (or problem-solving) procedure. What is meant by alternative dispute resolution (ADR)?

4. Discuss the shop steward's role in the grievance procedure. Why is it generally preferable that the supervisor listen to the shop steward and the complaining employee together?

5. Why is open and frank communication a key element in supervisory handling of a complaint or grievance at the initial meeting?

6. Why should most complaints and grievances be settled by the supervisor at the departmental level? Which should be referred to higher-level managers or human resources staff for decisions? Discuss.

7. Review and discuss each of the 11 guidelines for resolving complaints and grievances. Analyze the interrelationships among them. Why is the satisfactory handling of complaints or grievances a major component of effective supervisory management?

SKILLS APPLICATIONS

Skills Application 20-1: Your Complaint

Everyone who has held a job has had work-related problems. However, many employees do not register complaints in nonunion situations. For this project, remember a situation in which you could have made a complaint to your supervisor but did not. Now is your opportunity.

1. State the nature of your complaint in one or two sentences and provide relevant background information.

2. What do you believe should have been done, assuming you had filed the complaint as part of the firm's complaint procedure?

3. What justification could the supervisor or higher-level managers cite for refusing to make any adjustments because of your complaint?

4. If a union had represented you, would you have filed a grievance in this situation? Why or why not?

5. How could a neutral arbitrator have helped in resolving your complaint?

Skills Application 20-2: The Supervisor and Handling Employee Complaints and Grievances

1. From the materials in this chapter, develop a list of the guidelines and considerations that you believe are the most essential for supervisory handling of employee complaints and grievances in an effective manner.

2. Contact two practicing supervisors (or managers) who are willing to be interviewed. One supervisor should be in a unionized firm and have departmental employees under a union contract. The other supervisor should be in a firm whose employees are not represented by a union. Ask each supervisor to identify what he or she believes to be the most important guidelines and considerations when a supervisor receives an employee complaint or grievance. *Note*: Do not distinguish between a "complaint" and a "grievance" unless the supervisor asks for a clarification or makes a distinction himself or herself.

3. Compare the supervisors' lists with your list. To what degree were these lists similar or different? If there were major differences, what do you feel is the most likely explanation?

Skills Application 20-3: The Discharge and the Union Grievance

The primary decision that usually must be made in a grievance situation is whether or not an action violated provisions of the labor agreement. The short case that follows is an abridged version of one that actually occurred. All names are disguised. Read the case and answer the questions that follow.

CASE

Midwest Meat Packers is located in an agricultural community with a population of 25,000. The plant employees are represented by the International Meat Packers Union. On Monday, October 8, Raymond Sanders left work with a bad toothache. Since he couldn't find his supervisor, he told Joe Teeters, a foreman with a subcontractor doing work at the plant, to notify Sanders's supervisor, Lewis Ranger. On Tuesday, October 9, when Sanders returned to work, he had no time card and he found a replacement working in his department. That day, the plant manager told Sanders he was terminated for violating Company Work Rule #6: "Walking off the job and leaving the plant without permission is a violation that will result in immediate termination of employment."

The union immediately filed a grievance on behalf of Raymond Sanders, claiming that the matter was not handled properly by the company and asking that Sanders be reinstated. The union claimed that the company did not have "just cause" to terminate Sanders as required by the labor–management agreement.

The company's written answer to the union grievance stated that Raymond Sanders had clearly violated Company Work Rule #6 and thus the company had just cause to terminate his employment.

At a grievance hearing held several weeks later, Raymond Sanders acknowledged that on October 8 he had left the plant at about 12:15 P.M. to go to lunch. He did not "clock out," and he did not return to work that afternoon. He did not ask for permission to leave work from any plant supervisor or the plant nurse, nor did he tell any of them that he was leaving. He admitted that it was a violation of the rules to leave work during his work shift without permission, but he stated that he did not think that it was a serious violation considering what had occurred.

Sanders stated that on that day he ate lunch with Joe Teeters, an independent electrical contractor. During lunch his wisdom tooth started hurting, and the pain became quite severe. He told Teeters that he was not going back to work and asked Teeters to tell his plant supervisor, Lewis Ranger, that he had gone home because of a toothache. Sanders claimed that several days later he saw Teeters. Teeters said he had told Dave Lillis, another plant supervisor, about Sanders leaving work.

Lillis was called from the plant to testify at the grievance hearing. Lillis claimed that he had no recollection of seeing or talking to Teeters on October 8; and further, if Teeters had given him a message for Raymond Sanders, he would have immediately passed it on to Lewis Ranger or the plant manager.

1.   Why would the union pursue a grievance over this matter?

2.   How does this case illustrate the importance of a grievance procedure?

3.   What additional details would be useful before management could make a decision to deny the union grievance or to grant the union grievance and reinstate Sanders?

4.   Assume that the case is pursued to arbitration and that you are the arbitrator. What would you decide and why? (Suggestion: Before deciding, review some of the concepts in Chapter 19 regarding the just-cause standard for discipline and discharge.)

ENDNOTE

1.   For expanded discussions concerning the various concepts and guidelines included in this chapter, the following are recommended:

Joseph T. Straub, "Dealing with Complainers, Whiners, and General Malcontents," *Supervisory Management* (Volume 37, Number 7, July 1992), pp. 1–2;

Kenneth A. Ehrman, "Settling Disputes Through Mediation," *Nation's Business* (Volume 80, Number 11, November 1992), pp. 48–49;

David W. Meyer, "Right Approach to Avoiding Wrongful Discharge," *Risk Management* (Volume 37, Number 9, September 1990), pp. 56–62;

Robert Coulson, "Avoiding Litigation with Alternative Dispute Resolution," *Risk Management* (Volume 40, Number 1, January 1993), pp. 20–26.

CASE 5-1
Who Needs TQM?

Merrill Dawe, plant manager of a major food processing plant, had attended a meeting of an industry association in which he had been impressed by several presentations on total quality management (TQM) and labor–management participation teams. Dawe was convinced that such approaches would be very appropriate in his plant, since he felt they could help improve the employee relations climate and perhaps assist in improving productivity and reducing quality problems. Dawe decided to call a number of his supervisors, along with the local union president and several of the plant's union shop stewards, to his office to discuss his plans to implement TQM. At a meeting in his office, Dawe outlined what he proposed to do. He said that he planned to have TQM meetings on a periodic basis, probably once a month, in which various departmental employee groups and committees, along with their supervisors, would discuss production problems, quality problems, and any other problems that needed attention. Dawe emphasized that employees would be paid for the time they spent in these meetings and that any ideas and suggestions would be given open consideration and attention by supervisors and higher-level managers.

After listening patiently to Dawe's presentation, Jerry Bruno, the plant's local union president, responded as follows: "Mr. Dawe, our national and local union have heard about TQM and efforts of this nature. In general, we're skeptical about being part of them. We've heard that many companies simply use these as a way of trying to bypass the union contract and the grievance procedure. We feel that this can be just another tactic to lull employees into thinking that management is concerned about them. Frankly, I'd bet that TQM meetings will be little more than a place where the workers will say what's on their minds, and then company management will continue to ignore their concerns. Unless I'm convinced—and my fellow union representatives are convinced—that any such program in this plant will not be used to ignore the union and our labor agreement, we will not cooperate with you in this effort."

Dawe pondered what his response should be to Bruno's comments and whether he should seriously attempt to implement a TQM program.

Questions for Discussion

1.   Evaluate how Merrill Dawe presented his ideas for a TQM program in the company plant. How might he have approached this in a way that would have gained greater support from the employees and the union? Discuss.

2.   Evaluate the response of Jerry Bruno, the local union president. Why are these objections serious and difficult to overcome in a short period of time?

3.   At the end of the case, what should Merrill Dawe do? On the assumption that Dawe decides to continue with the implementation of a TQM program, outline a series of steps or recommendations that would be helpful in overcoming union and worker opposition and making the program a worthwhile investment of time and management attention.

CASE 5-2
The "Theory Triple X" Manager

Otto Wood was an engineering technologist for the Waite Conveyor Company. He was busy working on the final stages of the installation of a sophisticated computerized conveyor system in the Webster Department Stores. A sales engineer, Warren Clark, was in charge of the overall project from the time it was sold until it would be turned over to the Webster Department Stores. Clark had negotiated a deadline for installation, which was 10 days away. The sales contract provided for a severe price penalty in case of late delivery.

Wood's immediate boss was Will Meyers, head of the Installation and Inspection Department. Last night, Wood phoned Meyers and told him that he was quitting immediately. He had had all he could take from Warren Clark, and he had decided to leave the firm. Wood told Meyers that Clark had been "breathing down his neck" continuously and that he had been pressuring him needlessly to get the job completed. Wood assured Meyers that he had been doing his best but that, in a sophisticated installation of this sort, many things create problems and interfere with getting quick results. Wood said that he didn't attempt to explain the problems to Clark because, in Wood's words, "Mr. Clark knows next to nothing about the intricate nature of the problems involved." The last straw was a threat from

Clark to lock him in the building until the installation was operable, even if he had to bring him his food. Wood said he realized that Clark did not intend to do this; but Clark's threat, after everything else he had done, was too much to take. In Wood's view, Clark was a Theory Triple X manager all the way!

Meyers wondered what to do. He knew that people with Otto Wood's skills were hard to find. Particularly at this stage of the project, it would be next to impossible to get a replacement employee who could come in to pick up the installation where Wood had left off and complete the project on time. Meyers understood the meaning of a penalty for late delivery. The next morning he decided to meet with Warren Clark to discuss the situation.

Questions for Discussion

1. Is Warren Clark a "Theory Triple X" manager, or is he operating in a way that reflects the pressure of the job situation? Discuss.

2. Who should be in charge of meeting an installation deadline in a situation of this sort? Does Clark have the right to issue orders to Wood under the organizational set-up in the Waite Conveyor Company? Discuss.

3. What approach should Will Meyers take in meeting with Clark to discuss the situation? What approach should they both take in working with Wood to finish the project on time?

4. What should be done to avoid future problems of the types illustrated by this case? Consider alternatives.

CASE 5-3
A Group Decision Baffles the Supervisor

Shirley Rice was the supervisor of the Packing Department of the Amcee Novelty Company. She supervised 15 employees, predominantly young workers in their twenties, whose job it was to wrap finished products in tissue paper, put them into cardboard boxes, and then glue labels to the outside of the boxes. She was known as an experienced and firm supervisor. After observing and timing the operations frequently, she had arrived at what she considered to be a fair standard of how many items each employee could box during an eight-hour day. However, this standard was seldom reached. In order to improve the situation, after additional studies she installed a different layout, rearranged the work benches, simplified the procedures, and did all she could to raise the output of the department. But output remained considerably below her expected standard.

As a last resort, Rice decided to try an idea that had greatly impressed her. During the last two months, once a week, the company had made it possible for all supervisors to attend a series of lectures given at a local university. These lectures covered the basics of good supervisory management. During the last lecture, the professor had discussed the advantages of group decision making and group discussion, including the advantages of decisions reached by those who will be concerned with the outcome. The professor stated that, in such cases, the employees usually will do their utmost to carry their decisions through to a successful conclusion. He compared them with decisions handed down unilaterally by supervisors, which employees often only grudgingly complied with.

Rice decided to apply this method and called a meeting of the workers in the department. She told them that the current standard of output was too low and that a new standard of output had to be set. Instead of establishing the new production standard by herself, however, she wanted them to decide as a group what it should be. Of course, she hoped—but she did not say this—that they would arrive at a higher standard than the level at which they had been operating.

Several days later, much to Shirley Rice's amazement, the group arrived at a standard that was significantly lower than the current one. The group claimed that even with the new work arrangements, the current standard was too high. Shirley Rice realized that she now had a more serious problem than before.

Questions for Discussion

1. Analyze Shirley Rice's leadership style throughout this case in terms of (a) McGregor's Theory X–Theory Y and (b) the Leadership (Managerial) Grid. (See Chapter 5 if you need to review these models.)
2. How could Shirley Rice have avoided the outcome of the group's decision by another approach or approaches?
3. Why did the group set a lower rather than a higher production standard?
4. Why does Rice have a more difficult problem of getting group acceptance than she did before?
5. What should Rice do? What alternatives are open to her?

CASE 5-4
Lunches with the Supervisor

Beth Conners was a recent electrical engineering graduate of a major university. She went to work for the Wilcox Engineering Company, and she was assigned to work on projects designing electrical systems for automated and computerized equipment.

Beth was enjoying her work and developing a rapport with other engineers in the firm. The department supervisor was Terry Wells. Terry had been with the firm about six years, and he had been a supervisor for two years. He was 30 years old; like Beth, he was single.

Beth had been with the firm about four months when Terry Wells called her into his office to review her progress. Terry told Beth that she was doing a great job, and he was very pleased with her work performance. He discussed a few suggestions that he felt would further her development technically. When he was finished, he looked at his watch and said, "Wow, it is already lunchtime. Would you like to join me?" Hesitating at first, Beth agreed to have lunch with him at a local restaurant. Terry paid the bill for both of them.

Early the next morning, Beth was working on a computer-aided drawing system, when Terry came into her office to chat. He made a lot of small talk, and then he asked her whether she again would accompany him for lunch. A little uncomfortable, Beth again agreed. Beth thought that this second luncheon offer was unusual, but she passed it off, thinking that maybe she was being overly sensitive.

However, Beth grew very concerned during the next several weeks when the invitations for lunch continued. Furthermore, on several occasions Terry asked her for dates for which she made up excuses to decline. Beth felt that she couldn't refuse the luncheon invitations since Terry was her supervisor. But she didn't want to have any kind of off-the-job relationship with her supervisor, even though she did like him personally.

The situation became very stressful when several of her colleagues told her at a coffee break that she was earning the reputation of getting special treatment from their supervisor. One engineer even asked, "Are you and Terry having an affair?"

Beth became even more distressed when one day Terry came into her office and made the following remark: "Beth, I don't know why you won't let me take you out some evening. I know we hit it off well at lunch, and I know we both are attracted to each other." Beth told Terry that she would think it over and let him know later.

Beth realized that the situation with Terry was getting out of hand, and that she had to do something. She knew the company had a policy on sexual harassment, but she didn't know whether this situation applied. She was concerned that if she reported this matter in confidence to the human resources director or to someone in higher-level management, it might jeopardize her position in the company. She pondered what she should do.

Questions for Discussion

1. Is this a situation of sexual harassment? Why or why not?

2. Should Beth Conners refuse any further luncheon invitations from her supervisor? Should she continue to refuse to date him, even if she genuinely likes him as a person? Discuss.

3. What options are open to Beth Conners? What would you recommend that she do?

CASE 5-5
Resentment Toward the Black Supervisor

"What's the matter with you, coming down so hard on me about my work? Why don't you get off my back and deal with the white employees in this department who are getting away with murder? You're worse than having a white boss!" These words, uttered by Sarah Washington, one of his African-American subordinates, worried the department supervisor, Walter Rawlins. The thought that other minority employees might resent his supervisory management position had disturbed him ever since he took over the department. Although no one had called him an "Uncle Tom" to his face, Rawlins knew that some of the employees thought this of him.

Walter Rawlins had graduated from a small southern college. He received a special fellowship for minority students that enabled him to complete an MBA degree at a midwestern university. Upon receiving his MBA, he accepted a position with a major department store chain in its accounting services division. After a year and a half in several staff positions, he was promoted to supervisor of the customer accounts department. Some 24 employees were in this department. All were women except for two male computer programmers. Eight of the employees were minority persons.

Since he became department supervisor about a year ago, the Human Resources Department had received several complaints from African-American employees about Rawlins's tendency to set higher standards for black employees under his supervision than for white employees. These complaints were passed on to Rawlins by May Carlins, the director of human resources. Rawlins had responded that the charges were not valid. He told Carlins, "I let everyone set their own pace. Some employees are going to come out ahead of others. I reward the ones who come out in front. That's my job."

The manager of accounting services, Rollie Dinkins, believed that Rawlins treated all employees alike. Dinkins evaluated Rawlins's overall performance as very good, and he was of the opinion that one of his strengths was fairness in dealing with employees.

This most recent comment was not the only occasion on which certain employees had suggested to him that the black employees in the department felt that they did not receive the same treatment as whites. These previous comments had involved the grapevine rather than a direct verbal confrontation.

Sarah Washington had begun her employment in the customer accounts department at an entry-level clerical position. Over a period of five years, she advanced through a series of promotions to one of the highest-level clerical positions in the department. Her job was complex, involving the maintenance and adjustment of billing records. The billing system had undergone a major transition to a state-of-the-art computerized system. During this transition a number of intermediate systems had been in use. Sarah Washington was one of the few people in the department who understood the intermediate systems and methods of adjusting records that occurred under each. She occasionally would try to impress Rawlins with her knowledge of adjustments to the billing system by asking him questions for which she knew he would not have the answers. She once asked Rawlins in front of several employees, "How do you expect to know in a few months what it took me five years to learn?"

Washington was an extremely ambitious young woman. On several occasions she had complained to the human resources department about being passed over for promotion into a supervisory position. Rollie Dinkins had passed her over for promotion to supervisor, because he said that she lacked the tact and interpersonal skills needed in a supervisory position.

Walter Rawlins decided that the time had come for some response on his part, but he pondered what it should be. At least, he knew that he must be prepared to respond to Washington's next insinuation.

Questions for Discussion

1. Why is a problem of this nature extremely sensitive for all individuals involved?
2. To what degree, if any, should Rollie Dinkins become involved in this situation? Should the director of human resources become involved?
3. Should Walter Rawlins approach this problem as a disciplinary matter, a racial matter, a performance question, or a work-group situation? Discuss.
4. What would you recommend that Walter Rawlins do?

CASE 5-6
Preferential Treatment

George Mason was foreman of the production department of a small manufacturing company. Most of the time, he supervised eight to ten people. One of his employees was Paula Whisler, an African-American woman who was a widow with five small children. She was a very good worker, but she almost always was late for work in the morning. Mason had spoken to her numerous times about tardiness, but to no avail. She assured him that she tried hard to be at work on time, but she "just did not seem to be able to make it" at 7:30 A.M. since she had to get her children off to school and to the babysitter. She argued that she worked twice as hard as anyone else and that she stayed over in the evening to make up for the time she lost in the mornings. There was little doubt in Mason's mind that Whisler did produce as much as or more than anyone else and that she did stay later in the evening to make up the time she lost by being late in the morning.

One Thursday morning, however, Paula Whisler's tardiness was holding up a job that had to be finished by noon. Regardless of how hard she might work during the morning, it would be difficult to finish the job on time, since the production material had to dry for three hours before it could leave the department. Although some other worker could have performed the operation, George Mason felt that Whisler was most qualified to do it. But should she not come in at all or be quite late, again the entire production schedule would be thrown out of balance. All of this was going through Mason's mind when he heard one of the workers say to a co-worker, "Whisler is getting preferred treatment. Why should a black be given any favors, like she's better than the rest of us?"

Sure enough, Paula Whisler arrived 45 minutes late. George Mason realized that the situation required action on his part, but he didn't know what it should be.

Questions for Discussion

1.   Analyze how the principles of the hot stove rule discussed in Chapter 19 were not properly applied by George Mason in the circumstances of this case.

2.   Should George Mason take into account Paula Whisler's home situation when trying to maintain departmental standards? Why or why not?

3.   Can the conflict between organization demands and personal problems of employees be reconciled and still have the objectives of the organization accomplished? If so, how?

4.   What action should Mason take? What alternatives are open if the problem is not resolved quickly?

CASE 5-7
Sexual Harassment in the Accounting Office

Charlie Gillespie was office manager of a group of accountants and accounting clerks in the corporate budget office of a large publishing company. He was known to be a "happy-go-lucky" supervisor, who found it very difficult to confront inappropriate behavior or take disciplinary action. Charlie normally tried to avoid conflict by looking the other way, pretending that he didn't observe inappropriate conduct.

On a number of occasions, Gillespie had observed one of his accountants, Oliver Olson, making crude and suggestive comments to a group of female accounting clerks in the department. Although Gillespie did not like what he heard and observed, he thought that most of the employees understood Olson for what he was and did not take him seriously.

However, one day an accounting clerk named Julie Lowe came to Gillespie's office. She claimed that Olson's comments were a form of sexual harassment. Lowe stated that she understood the company had a policy prohibiting sexual harassment and that, even though Olson had not made any direct sexual overtures to any of the female employees, his vulgar language and crude questions no longer could be tolerated by the women in the office. Gillespie responded that Olson was just a "good old boy," and that the women should ignore him and the problem would take care of itself.

Several weeks later, Lowe resigned her position with the company without giving an explanation as to why she had resigned. One week after she left her job, the company received a notice that Julie Lowe had filed charges with the Equal Employment Opportunity Commission, claiming that she had been discriminated against because of her sex. In her complaint, she had stated that there was an "atmosphere of sexual harassment in the office"; that because of this continued harassment the "hostile work environment caused her severe tension and distress," which she no longer could tolerate and which forced her to end her employment with the company.

Gillespie had received a copy of Lowe's discrimination and harassment charges from Pamela Richter, the company's director of human resources. Richter requested that Charlie Gillespie come to her office to discuss what the company's response to these charges should be.

Questions for Discussion

1. When do crude and vulgar humor and language become sexual harassment? Discuss.
2. What should Charlie Gillespie have done when he first observed Oliver Olson engaging in the undesirable behavior?
3. What should Charlie Gillespie have done when Julie Lowe complained to him about Oliver Olson? Evaluate his counsel that Olson was a "good old boy" who should be ignored.
4. At the end of the case, what would you recommend that the company's response to the EEOC charges of discrimination and sexual harassment should be? Discuss.

CASE 5-8
Affirmative Action or Reverse Discrimination?

Thompson Machine Company was a job shop that made cylinders. It was a relatively small company with approximately 300 employees. Over 60 percent of its business came from federal government contracts. The company was recently audited by the U.S. Department of Labor concerning affirmative action provisions required of federal government contractors. The Department of Labor informed the Thompson Company that failures to meet previously established targets for employment and promotion of minorities and women could result in the loss of its contracts.

At about the same time, the set-up worker in the lathe shop retired and a replacement was needed. This was the highest-paid job in the shop. Company policy was to promote from within when possible. Fred Saunders, the lathe department supervisor, believed that there were only two candidates to consider. These were Glenn Arbor, a 25-year employee with 16 years on lathes, and Jessica Stanley, a lathe operator with 7 years' experience. Saunders believed that the person with the most job knowledge, experience, and seniority should be selected. Although Saunders felt that Jessica Stanley had sufficient job knowledge and experience, Glenn Arbor had considerably more and he was the most senior employee by far. Therefore, Saunders thought this was an easy decision, and he contacted Brenda Moore in human resources to give her his recommendation.

After reviewing the situation, Brenda Moore felt that Fred Saunders hadn't considered the Department of Labor pressures. She called Saunders to her office for a meeting. Moore told Saunders about the affirmative action requirements, and she told him that top-level management had decided that Jessica Stanley should be awarded the position since she was an African-American woman. Moore explained that she knew it was a difficult situation, but she felt that Jessica Stanley was qualified for the position and a failure to promote Stanley could potentially result in major loss of business.

Fred Saunders informed Glenn Arbor and Jessica Stanley of the decision, and he then gathered the department together for the formal announcement. The news didn't sit well with most of the employees and particularly with Glenn Arbor. Arbor went to see Brenda Moore in human resources. He asserted that the only reason that he didn't get the position was because he was a white male. He said this was obvious reverse discrimination. Further, he said that if the Thompson Machine Company had been unionized, the union wouldn't allow this because he had far more qualifications and seniority. Brenda Moore tried to explain the situation, but Glenn Arbor was still upset when he left her office.

Glenn Arbor continued working at Thompson, but with considerable resentment. The problem wasn't so much what he said and did; it was more what he didn't say and didn't do. He refused to assist Jessica Stanley whenever she asked for help, even to the point of allowing her to make errors that could have been avoided with his help. His negative attitude began to spread throughout the department. Jessica Stanley was finding it difficult to get the cooperation she needed from other employees for the efficient operation of the department. She brought the problem to Fred Saunders's attention. When Saunders told her it was her problem to solve, Jessica Stanley became angry. She told Saunders that it was his problem; if he didn't resolve it, she would resign and file sex and race discrimination charges against the Thompson firm.

Fred Saunders pondered what he should do next.

Questions for Discussion

1.   Was management's decision to promote Jessica Stanley reverse discrimination, or was it a prudent economic decision made to preserve its business? Discuss.

2.   Evaluate Glenn Arbor's assertion that this would not have occurred if a labor union represented the employees.

3.   What should Fred Saunders do?

4.   What should top-level management do?

CASE 5-9
The Problem Employee

Phyllis Walker, human resources manager at Marsh Electric Company, looked through her in-basket for a memo Steve Coster had mentioned briefly to her that morning. Steve, the contracts manager, was a relatively new, inexperienced supervisor, who had only been with the office for a few months. Happy that Steve had asked for guidance on how to handle what he had referred to as a touchy situation, Phyllis located the memo and read it immediately.

TO: Phyllis Walker, HRM Manager
FROM: Steve Coster, Contracts Manager
SUBJECT: Stephanie Barkwell—Problem Employee

We've got a problem, Phyllis, and I need some advice on how to handle it. One of my department secretaries, Stephanie Barkwell, is beginning to act up. For the last couple of months she has been late to work almost a third of the time, and she regularly takes 45 minutes or more for lunch when the allotted time is only half an hour. Her frequent absences are disrupting office efficiency. Her 13-year-old boy is her usual excuse.

However, there are some recent unfavorable rumors that I've heard circulating through the department. I'm a bit uncomfortable mentioning them to you, although I have a gut feeling they might be true. The Tuesday before last, Stephanie called me at home around 9:30 at night, and she told me that she had some personal business to take care of and probably wouldn't be in the following day. She wasn't; nor did she show up at the office on Wednesday or Thursday. Friday she called and said she was too emotional to function at work, but she would be in on Monday.

On Monday she told me that her son was having trouble with the police. However, the rumor mill has it that Stephanie herself was arrested and held on drug charges. I've not discussed the issue with her; I would like your input first.

As a single parent, perhaps she has to deal with problems you and I don't face. However, we have a job to do here at Marsh, and people depend on Stephanie for secretarial support. When at work, Stephanie is very productive and pleasant to work with. Her prior work record apparently has been excellent. We're already shorthanded, and her recent absences and tardiness are now affecting the overall performance of my department. I've tried to be tolerant, but it is becoming a continuing problem. I've been getting complaints from her co-workers.

Let's sit down and talk about this soon, before I approach Stephanie. Please call me when you have had a chance to review her file, and we'll figure out the best way to handle this situation.

"Steve was not kidding," thought Phyllis as she completed her review of Stephanie's file. "It's a shame that this firm doesn't have an employee assistance program; in this case it might have been just the ticket."

Phyllis pondered the situation and wondered what the best course of action would be.

Questions for Discussion

1. If you were Phyllis Walker, what advice would you offer Steve Coster about how to proceed?

2. If Steve Coster determined that Stephanie Barkwell had a drug problem or some other type of serious personal problem, would the company be obligated to offer some form of personal assistance to her? Why or why not?

3. Once Steve Coster is fully aware of Stephanie's situation, how much information should he share with her co-workers?

4. Would you try to retain Stephanie Barkwell as an employee? Would it make a difference if the police are indeed involved in this situation?

5. If you decided to keep her at this time, what steps would you take to ensure that her work performance improved?

CASE 5-10
Under the Influence?

Carl Kloski had been employed as a laborer for eight years in the warehouse division of a wholesale appliance distributor. His record over the years indicated the following disciplinary actions:

1. Three written reprimands for unexcused absences.
2. One one-day suspension for reporting to work under the influence of alcohol.
3. One five-day suspension for reporting to work under the influence of alcohol.
4. One one-day suspension for failure to report to work.

On a Friday morning, Kloski reported to work at about 7:30 A.M. Sometime prior to the beginning of the shift, Kloski's lead person, George Ramsey, noticed that Kloski appeared to be under the influence of alcohol, since he was talking loudly and walking about in a confused manner. Ramsey reported this to his boss, the warehouse supervisor Steven Bell. Bell sent Ramsey and the rest of the crew out to perform their normal duties, but he ordered Kloski to stay behind to do clean-up work in the employee lunch room. About an hour or so later, Bell noticed that Kloski had done very little clean-up work. Bell approached Kloski and asked him why he had not followed his instructions. Kloski objected to this questioning, and he continued in a loud manner that the supervisor was always "picking on him" and "being discriminatory."

In response to these accusations, Bell took Kloski into his office to review his file for past performance appraisals and disciplinary actions. A lengthy discussion followed in which Kloski continued talking in a loud and angry manner. Both Bell and the office clerk, Marilyn O'Toole, believed that they could smell liquor on Kloski's breath.

Finally, Bell said, "Carl, I think you're under the influence of alcohol again, and with your past record, I ought to terminate you immediately!"

Kloski exploded, "What in the hell do you mean 'under the influence?' You assigned me to work over an hour ago, and you've got no proof whatsoever. You're just mad because I don't jump when you say, 'Jump!' "

Steven Bell pondered what his next response would be.

Questions for Discussion

1. What should Ramsey or Bell have done when they first believed that Carl Kloski might have been under the influence of alcohol? Discuss alternatives.

2. Was the decision to assign Kloski work to do, even though it was not his normal work, a questionable decision? Why or why not?

3. Discuss the response of Kloski to Bell to the effect that the company had no proof whatsoever that he was under the influence of alcohol.

4. To what degree is Kloski's past disciplinary record relevant to the decision Bell will have to make at the end of the case?

5. What should Steven Bell do? Consider alternatives.

CASE 5-11
Go Home, Bob

Maria Martinez was a supervisor in a claims processing department of a state welfare agency. Martinez supervised 12 employees who worked on various aspects of processing and accounting for payments of dependent benefit claims.

One day Martinez received a report from several of her employees that Bob Turner, a clerk in the department, had a severe cold and cough and was disturbing other employees in the department. The employees told Martinez that Turner's "wheezing and coughing" were annoying and that they feared catching his cold. Subsequently, Martinez approached Turner and suggested that he go home and get some rest to improve his condition. Turner replied, "I'm not ill; I've got a little cough, but that's all." At this point Martinez stated, "Bob, I think you should go home, because other employees are complaining about your condition." Turner replied, "You can't make me go home. I'm not ill. Besides, I've used up all my allowed sick leave days for this year, and you'll probably discipline me for being off again if I go home today." Martinez replied, "Are you telling me, Bob, that you won't go home like I've told you to do?" Turner responded, "If you try to force me out of here, I'll go to human resources and the agency's executive director about this, because it just wouldn't be right for you to send me home! You're always complaining about people being off from work, and here I'm at work and you're making a big issue over a little cough." Martinez pondered what she should say and do next.

Questions for Discussion

1. What options are open to Maria Martinez if Bob Turner continues to refuse to go home as requested?

2. Evaluate Bob Turner's reasons for not going home. Which are most persuasive? Least persuasive?

3. If Turner is disciplined in this case—either for insubordination or for excessive sick days—and he complains to the human resources department or higher-level management, how should higher-level management or the human resources department respond to such a complaint? Discuss.

CASE 5-12
Locker Room Theft

For a number of months, Charlie Blair, the supervisor of a large warehouse servicing a major retail food distributor, had been concerned about reports of missing valuables from the lockers of employees in the employee dressing room in the warehouse. The company provided metal lockers for employees to use, but they had no locks. Employees shared these lockers on a rotating-shift basis, and the company never considered it necessary to assign lockers to individuals. The lockers were provided mainly for the convenience of employees to leave their clothing and other items while they were working in the warehouse.

Blair had reminded employees on a number of occasions about not leaving valuables in the lockers. He told the employees that the company assumed no responsibility for any loss, and he also told them that anyone found guilty of stealing a valuable that belonged to another employee would be immediately terminated for theft. This was in accordance with posted company rules in the warehouse.

However, for the last several months Blair had received reports of numerous items missing from employees' lockers. These reports included items such as a sweater, a lunchbox, food from several lunchboxes, and a baseball glove.

For a number of reasons, including several rumors that had been circulated to Blair, he was suspicious of a fairly new warehouse employee named Eric Raleigh. Raleigh was a young warehouse worker who operated a tow truck. He was about 22, and he had been employed by the company about six months previously. Coincidentally, the reports of missing items from the locker room seemed to have become more frequent the last several months.

On a Tuesday morning, Blair received a report from a warehouse employee named Willie Jeffries that a small transistor radio was missing from his locker. Jeffries stated that he had placed it in his locker when he reported to work at 7:30 A.M., and he noticed it missing when he came to his locker during his morning coffee break.

Upon receiving this report, Blair decided to conduct a search of Raleigh's locker while all the employees were in the warehouse working. At about 11:00 A.M., Charlie Blair went into the locker room and searched the locker where Raleigh had his clothing and lunchbox. At the bottom of the locker, underneath a number of magazines, Blair found a transistor radio. Blair returned to the office and summoned Jeffries to identify the radio. Jeffries identified the radio as his own; Blair did not disclose to Jeffries where he had found it.

Shortly thereafter, Charlie Blair asked Eric Raleigh to come to his office. Blair explained to Raleigh the nature of the report he had received, what he had done, and how he had found the missing radio in Raleigh's locker. Charlie Blair did not directly accuse Raleigh of theft; but he suggested that perhaps Raleigh might want to consider resigning from the firm because of the suspicions that had been circulating about his connection to the other missing items in the lockers.

At this point Raleigh became very angry. He stated that he would not resign because he was innocent; he felt that someone else had been stealing the items from the employee lockers and that whoever it was had planted the radio in his locker in order to place the blame on him. Raleigh insisted he was innocent, and he said that he would be willing to take a polygraph (lie detector) test to prove his innocence. He told Blair, "If the company decides to fire me for this, I'll get the union and a lawyer to sue the company for everything it has for false accusation and unjust termination." With that, Eric Raleigh left Charlie Blair's office and returned to his job.

Blair was somewhat taken aback by Raleigh's adamant denial of any involvement in locker room theft. Blair was not sure what he should do in this situation. He recognized that the union contract for employees in the warehouse required that any disciplinary action must be for "just cause." Charlie Blair decided that he would discuss the situation with Elaine Haas, the company's director of human resources.

Questions for Discussion

1. Evaluate the search of the locker by Charlie Blair. Was this an advisable course on his part?
2. What alternatives might Charlie Blair have utilized other than confronting Eric Raleigh in his office? Discuss.
3. Should Blair have suggested to Raleigh that he consider resignation? Why or why not?
4. At the end of the case, what should the company do?

CASE 5-13
The Unsafe Pole

Henry Floyd was supervisor of a construction crew for Municipal Power and Light Company. The crew consisted of Roy McMillan, Howard Bierman, and Mel Shostak.

One morning, while out on the job, Floyd directed Bierman and Shostak to climb a pole and remove a number of tree limbs that had fallen on a main power line carrying some 7,000 to 8,000 volts. Senior lineman Roy McMillan said, "Henry, I don't believe it's safe to climb that pole with the wind blowing the way it is. You never can tell what will happen when you have broken limbs on a power line."

Floyd responded, "Oh, come on, Roy, we've done jobs like this on many occasions and we've never had any problems." Floyd proceeded to outline how McMillan should do the job to avoid an accident. McMillan then went back to the truck, where Bierman and Shostak were gathering their tools. Shortly afterward the three of them approached Floyd.

McMillan said, "Henry, we're not going to climb that pole. We think it's unsafe. Either we do it another day or we've got to have more men on the job in order to do it safely."

Floyd replied, "Now listen, fellows, we've been through this many times before. It's the supervisor who ultimately makes the decision whether or not a job is safe. We've done many jobs far more dangerous than this one without any problems."

McMillan went on, "We checked our union agreement, and the safety clause in it gives us the right to determine whether or not a job is safe." Floyd looked at the contract clause, which McMillan showed him. It read:

All employees have the responsibility for the safety of their fellow employees and others who are affected by their work. Safety engineering and other support personnel are responsible for assisting supervisors with their safety responsibilities.

All employees have the final responsibility for their own safety. They have the final control over their actions and the last possible chance of being aware of what can injure them and of doing their best to see that it does not. This is one of the job requirements for every employee of Municipal Power and Light Company.

Floyd said, "Yeah, but you're overlooking the fact that there's a clause that precedes it saying that supervisors have the direct responsibility!" With that he read the following clause:

Supervisors have the direct responsibility for safety. This means managers, superintendents, engineers, section heads, division managers, department heads, officers, and all supervisors are responsible for safety in their areas. This includes carrying out safety activities appropriate for their operations.

They continued to discuss the issue. Finally, Roy McMillan said, "Henry, we're simply not going to climb that pole. You can't make us. You can send us home if you want, but if you do we're going to file a grievance and we're also going to file an OSHA complaint for the company's failure to maintain safety standards!"

With that Henry Floyd pondered what he should do.

Questions for Discussion

1. Should the union and/or employees have the right to determine whether a job is safe or not? Should the safety of a job be the sole responsibility of management? Discuss.

2. If the union and management disagree concerning the safety of a particular job, should a neutral or third party be brought in to decide whether the job is safe? Discuss. What is the role of OSHA in this type of situation?

3. Suppose that Floyd ordered an employee to climb a pole that the employee felt was unsafe and the employee subsequently was injured. What are the ramifications of a supervisor's decision under such circumstances?

4. Why does a case of this sort have implications involving the ultimate authority of a supervisor to manage the department?

CASE 5-14
Discharge for Striking a Student

Gino Barsanti was employed as a maintenance worker at Midwest University, located in a small town in a midwestern state. Barsanti was considered to be a handyman who did every type of assignment ranging from manual labor to skilled carpentry and electrical work. He had been employed by the university for six years, and his work record was excellent. He had never received a reprimand, suspension, or any other type of disciplinary action during his six years of service at the university.

One day, Barsanti and two other employees were working on a broken fence adjacent to the baseball field. They were engaged in a heated discussion about religion and politics. Barsanti particularly was arguing that abortion was a terrible sin, to be condemned. Several students happened to be passing by and heard some of the comments being made by the employees. One of the students, Sidney Rose, decided that he would join in the conversation. Eventually Rose made several derogatory remarks about religion in general and the abortion issue in particular. Barsanti became angry that a student had entered into the conversation. Barsanti stated to him, "Who asked you to join in this discussion? Get out of here." At this point Rose responded, "There's no use trying to reason with a rigid religious nut!" Barsanti became enraged. He took two steps toward the student and hit him squarely on the jaw. Rose was bleeding from the mouth when he and his fellow students left the area.

Shortly thereafter, Barsanti was summoned to the office of the maintenance superintendent, Alex Higgins. Rose had reported what had happened, and Barsanti did not deny that he had struck the student. Barsanti was sent home for the rest of the day. The next morning Barsanti was notified by Higgins that the university had decided to terminate him for striking a student, which Higgins felt was in violation of the university's strict "no fighting" policy for employees while on campus and during work hours.

On the day following Barsanti's termination, the union business representative, William Kelford, filed a grievance on behalf of Barsanti, claiming that Barsanti's termination did not meet the requirement of "just cause" in the labor agreement for a discharge action to be taken against an employee. Kelford spoke with Higgins about the grievance and told him that no employee should be required to take the kind of abuse from a student to which Barsanti had been subjected. Further, in view of the fact that Barsanti had never had a previous disciplinary action against him and that no specific rule covered this type of event, Kelford argued that Barsanti should be reinstated immediately. Kelford also contended that the university's no-fighting policy for employees was never intended to be applied to circumstances like the situation that confronted Barsanti, and therefore discharge was extreme and not justified.

Alex Higgins told William Kelford that he would study the union grievance and make a decision within the next two days.

Questions for Discussion

1. Instead of striking the student as he did, what alternatives might Gino Barsanti have pursued in regard to the offensive remarks of the student Sidney Rose?
2. Given all of the circumstances of the case, was the university justified in discharging Gino Barsanti? Discuss.
3. At the end of the case, what should the university do? Consider this question from the standpoint of an arbitrator being asked to decide the case if the university refuses to rescind Barsanti's discharge and the union pursues the case to arbitration.

CASE 5-15
Can Saturn's Leaders Continue the Success Story?

After 10 years and a $4.5 billion investment in what may be called the U.S. auto industry's most innovative venture, The Saturn Division of General Motors finally broke into the black in mid-1993. However, the demand for Saturn cars still outstrips the company's ability to produce them at its Spring Hill, Tennessee, plant. Saturn president Richard G. (Skip) LeFauve estimates that Saturn could sell another 200,000 cars each year, and GM is seeking ways to make that happen. Nonetheless, this seemingly good news for Saturn's management is beginning to cause problems for GM's newest member. The management style upon which the Saturn division was originally built may be in jeopardy, partly due to the overwhelming success of its product.

According to James L. Lewandowski, Saturn's founding vice-president of human resources, and William P. MacKinnon, GM's personnel vice-president during Saturn's formation, there were several important human relations decisions that were made when the Saturn project began. One of these was a site-selection process that focused on people issues as well as financial ones. Giving consideration to the attractiveness of the location, its proximity to high-quality educational opportunities, and the availability of employee training facilities and resources received a high priority. The importance of the latter factor is evidenced by the fact that the first Saturn employees received some 700 hours of initial schooling. Much of this training was used to instill an emphasis on participative teamwork. Lewandowski and MacKinnon believe that this initial investment in training paid enormous dividends. A collaborative style of management called for a different type of union involvement as well, so the UAW was involved from the very beginning of the project.

Another innovation at the new Saturn plant was the removal of the white-collar and blue-collar distinctions common to all other GM facilities. Saturn employees became "team members," free to wear a multiple-item wardrobe bearing the company logo or to continue to wear their non-Saturn wardrobes. Finally, Saturn made a commitment to preserving the environment of the surrounding community, and in 1990 it was awarded the "Take Pride in America" award from the U.S. Department of the Interior.

On January 13, 1993, Saturn received a jolt to its short-lived history of labor–management cooperation when 5,000 union workers voted in a key referendum on the company's innovative labor system. Although a majority of the workers voted to keep the current step-up, a surprising 29 percent backed a shift toward the traditional, more adversarial labor–management relations. Several factors are credited with causing this seeming shift in worker beliefs. One is that the recently hired workers are often less committed to Saturn's employee-participation ideals. Many of the dissenters are workers who were laid off at other GM plants. This problem seems to be compounded by the fact that the new employees now receive only 175 hours of initial schooling, most of which is job specific rather than in skills needed to learn to work in teams. Company officials now say that additional training is a luxury that they cannot afford.

Another problem confronting Saturn employees is the 50-hour and up work-weeks. Included in this rigorous schedule is the president of Saturn's UAW Local 1853, who has begun to question his ability to continue his seven-day workweeks. There is also a growing distrust of the union's close ties with Saturn's management and anger at the lack of elections for key union posts on the shop floor. Currently, the UAW and company officials appoint the shop-floor union leaders, who act as middle-level managers. Saying that the appointees sometimes ignore members' gripes and focus on what's best for the company, some union members want the officials to be elected. Others believe that such elections would undermine the part-nerships union appointees have with their jointly appointed management counter-parts.

Thus far the Saturn project, which former GM Chairman Roger B. Smith con-ceived as a laboratory in which to reinvent his company, has been an undisputed success. Will GM and its workers recognize the reasons for Saturn's being where it is today, or will they fall prey to their successes when the going becomes difficult?

References

"Saturn: GM Finally Has a Real Winner. But Success Is Bringing a Fresh Batch of Problems," Kathleen Kerwin, *Business Week* (August 17, 1992), pp. 86–91.

"Viewpoint: What We Learned at Saturn," James L. Lewandowski and William P. MacKinnon, *Personnel Journal* (December 1992), pp. 30–32.

"Saturn at 10: Happy Birthday?" Frank Washington, *Newsweek* (December 6, 1993), p. 43.

"Saturn: Labor's Love Lost?" David Woodruff, *Business Week* (February 8, 1993), pp. 122–124.

Questions for Discussion

1.   Former General Motors chairman Roger B. Smith referred to the Saturn project as a laboratory in which to reinvent the company. What do you think he meant by that? What types of changes was he trying to make at GM?

2.   One of the key components of the Saturn Division was the use of teamwork. Discuss what steps were taken to help the workers at all levels learn to work as teams. How does this approach differ from the traditional style of management?

3.   Although the Saturn is a well-built automobile that is much in demand, and the jobs of all members of the Saturn workforce appear to be secure, there are signs of problems among the workforce. What has management done that may have led to these problems? What can be done to begin to solve them?

4.   What are the complaints of the members of the union at the Saturn plant? How can they be handled without destroying the concepts involved in teamwork?

PART 6

CONTROLLING

21

Fundamentals of Controlling

LEARNING OBJECTIVES

After studying this chapter, you will be able to:

1 Describe the nature and importance of the managerial controlling function.

2 Identify three types of control mechanisms based on time.

3 Explain the essential characteristics of effective controls.

4 Describe the essential steps in the control process.

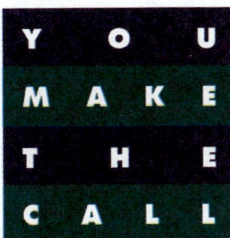

You are Larry Edwards, owner of Edwards' Homecenter and Lumber Company. The business began 36 years ago and has been profitable. Shortly after opening, you affiliated with Hardware Wholesalers Inc. (HWI). You are one of 3,000 HWI members located throughout North America.

Unfortunately, the floor plan of your facility has hindered the work flow, increasing costs and causing delivery backlogs. You charged your floor supervisor, Susan Edwards, with working out a program to control the backlogs. After initially planning the steps that should be taken, she called upon HWI's home office for consultation. They analyzed the store, the flow of inventory, work processes, and the like.

Collaboratively, they devised certain layout changes. Then Susan consulted with an industrial engineer and accountant to familiarize herself with times and costs in critical labor steps. After discussing these ideas with your key personnel, she developed a plan. Standards were set for each of the areas, and strategic control points were established. Unfortunately, some deliveries were delayed and orders mixed up during the implementation process, but within 30 days customer complaints declined significantly.

Six months later, material handling costs have been reduced, service quality has been enhanced, and profitability has increased. What else could you have done? **YOU MAKE THE CALL.**

THE SUPERVISOR'S ROLE IN CONTROLLING

Although the word "control" often elicits negative reactions, control is a normal part of daily life. At home, at work, and in the community everyone is affected by a variety of controls, such as alarm clocks, thermostats, fuel and electronic gauges, traffic lights, and police officers directing traffic. Controls also play an important role in all organizations. Controls assure that results match what was planned. Every manager—from the chief executive down to the supervisor—must develop and apply controls that regulate the organization's activities to achieve the desired results.

Controlling
The managerial function aimed at determining whether actual performance conforms to expected standards and taking corrective action when it does not conform.

The managerial function of **controlling** consists of checking to determine whether operations are adhering to established plans, ascertaining whether proper progress is being made toward objectives, and taking appropriate actions where necessary to correct any deviations from established plans. In other words, the supervisor takes action to make things happen the way they were planned. Controlling is essential whenever a supervisor assigns duties to employees, because the supervisor remains responsible for assigned work. If all plans set in motion proceeded according to design without interference, there would be no need for the controlling function. As every supervisor knows, this is not the case in real life. Thus, it is part of the supervisor's job to keep activities in line and, where necessary, to get them back on track. This is done by controlling.

Nature of the Controlling Function

Controlling is one of the five primary managerial functions. It is so closely related to the others that a line of demarcation between controlling and the other functions is not always clear. However, the controlling function is most closely related to the planning function. In planning, the supervisor sets objectives, and in turn these objectives become standards against which performance is appraised. If there are deviations between performance and standards, the supervisor must carry out the controlling function by taking corrective action, which may involve establishing new plans and different standards.

Since controlling is the last managerial function discussed in this book, it might be perceived as something that the supervisor performs after all other functions have been executed. This might lead to the impression that controlling is concerned only with events after they have happened. It is true that the need for controlling is evident after a mistake has been made. However, it is much better to view controlling as a function that goes on simultaneously with the other managerial functions. As we discuss later in this chapter, there are control mechanisms that are utilized before, during, and after an activity.

Employee Responses to Controls

Employees often view controls negatively, because the amount of control that exists within their department may determine how much freedom of action they have in performing their jobs. Yet most employees understand that a certain amount of control is essential to regulate performance. They know that, without controls, confusion, inefficiency, and even chaos would result.

In a behavioral sense, controls and on-the-job freedom seem to conflict. However, when controls are well designed and properly implemented, they can be a positive influence on employee motivation and behavior. The supervisor should try to design and apply control systems that employees will accept without resentment, but that also will be effective in monitoring performance in the department.

Controlling Should Be Forward Looking

There is nothing a supervisor can do about the past. For example, if work assigned to an employee for the day has not been accomplished, controlling cannot correct the day's results. Yet some supervisors believe that the main purpose of controlling is to blame someone who is responsible for mistakes. This attitude is not sound, since supervisors primarily should look forward rather than backward. Of course, supervisors should study the past to learn what and why something happened and then take steps so that future activities will not lead to the same mistakes.

Since supervisors should be forward looking while controlling, it is essential that they discover any deviations from established standards as quickly as possible. Setting up controls within a process or within an activity's established timeframe—rather than at its end—will enable the supervisor to take prompt corrective action. For example, instead of waiting until the day is over, the supervisor could check at midday to see whether a job is progressing satisfactorily. Even though the morning is past and nothing can change what has already happened, there may be time to correct a problem before the damage becomes excessive.

Controlling and Closeness of Supervision

Supervisors need to know how closely to monitor employees' work. The closeness of supervisory follow-up is based on such factors as an employee's experience, initiative, dependability, and resourcefulness. Permitting an employee to work on an assignment without close supervision is both a challenge and a test of a supervisor's ability to delegate. This does not mean that the supervisor should leave the employee completely alone until it is time to inspect the final results. It does mean that the supervisor should avoid watching every detail of every employee's work. By becoming familiar with each employee's abilities, the supervisor can develop a sensitivity as to how much leeway to give and how closely to follow up and control.

TIME FACTOR CONTROL MECHANISMS

2 Identify three types of control mechanisms based on time.

Before we discuss the steps of the controlling process, it is important to distinguish among three types of control mechanisms. These are classified according to time as (a) feedforward (or preliminary, preventive, anticipatory) controls, (b) concurrent (or in-process) controls, and (c) feedback (or after-the-process) controls.

Feedforward (Preliminary, Preventive, Anticipatory) Controls

Feedforward control
Anticipatory action taken to ensure that problems do not occur.

Since controlling has forward-looking aspects, the purpose of a **feedforward control** is to anticipate and prevent potential sources of deviation from standards by considering in advance the possibility of any malfunction or undesirable outcomes. A preventive maintenance program, designed so that equipment will not break down at the height of production, is an example of a feedforward control. The produce clerk who checks samples of bananas to ensure their acceptability is another example. The clerk selects a sample from the crates before the crates are unloaded and the merchandise is placed on display. Requiring assemblers to ascertain the quality of components prior to installation and to signify that they have done so is becoming increasingly commonplace. Other examples of feedforward controls include devices such as safety posters; fire drills; disciplinary rules; checklists to follow before starting up certain equipment; and the policies, procedures, and methods drawn up by managers when planning operations. Everyone uses feedforward control at one time or another. For example, a person who checks tires, oil, and gas gauge before beginning a trip is using feedforward control.

Concurrent (In-Process) Controls

Concurrent control
Corrective action taken during the production or delivery process to ensure that standards are being met.

A control that is applied while operations are going on and that spots problems as they occur is called a **concurrent control**. The traveler who notices that the fuel gauge is below half full or that the fuel warning light has just come on and pulls into the next gas station for a fill-up is using concurrent control. Examples of concurrent control mechanisms are on-line computer systems, numerical counters, automatic switches, gauges, and warning signals. To illustrate, suppose a retail store optically scans customers' purchases. The customer gets a printout of what was purchased and the price paid (the sales receipt). At the same time, the store's count of the number of items in inventory is automatically decreased by the number just sold. The store's computer records the items purchased and stores the information. The computer has been programmed either to alert the purchasing supervisor or to automatically place a purchase order when the store's inventory reaches a specified level. Thus, the stock is replenished as needed and the store does not risk running out. Where these types of aids are not in place, supervisors monitor activities by observation, often with the assistance of departmental employees.

Even though feedforward controls have been set up, concurrent controls are still necessary to catch problems that feedforward controls were not able to anticipate. Consider the situation of the traveler who filled the fuel tank prior to the trip and estimated, based on past experience, that she should be able to travel the 300 miles to her destination without having to refuel. Unexpectedly, the weather turns unseasonably warm, and the traveler experiences a lengthy delay due to a highway accident. For the convenience of the passengers, the traveler allows the car to run with the air conditioner on while they are tied up in traffic. The expected six-hour

Using concurrent controls to monitor packaging film production.

trip takes longer due to the delay, and the unexpected need for the air conditioner increases fuel consumption. Unless the traveler periodically checks the fuel gauge or is alerted by the low fuel warning light (concurrent controls), she will run out of fuel before she reaches her destination.

Feedback (After-the-Process) Controls

Feedback control
Action taken after the activity, product, or service has been completed to prevent future problems.

The purpose of a **feedback control** is to evaluate the results of a process or operation when it is finished to determine ways to prevent future deviations from standard. The traveler who calculates average miles per gallon and uses that feedback when planning the budget for the next trip is using feedback control. Other examples of feedback controls include measurements of the quality and quantity of units produced, various kinds of statistical information, accounting reports, and visual inspections. Since these controls are applied after a task, process, service, or product is finished, they are the least desirable control mechanisms if damage or mistakes have occurred. If no damage or mistakes took place, feedback controls are used as a basis for further improvement of the process or the finished product. Feedback controls are probably the most widely used category of controls at the supervisory level. Too often, however, they are used primarily to determine what went wrong and where to fix blame, rather than to prevent recurrence of the problem in the future.

CHARACTERISTICS OF EFFECTIVE CONTROLS

3 Explain the essential characteristics of effective controls.

For control mechanisms to work effectively, they should be understandable, timely, suitable and economical, indicational, and flexible. These characteristics are required of the controls used in all supervisory jobs—in manufacturing, retailing, office work, health care, government service, banks, and other services. Because there is such a diversity of activities in different departments, these characteristics will be discussed only in a general way here. Supervisors have to tailor control mechanisms to the particular activities, circumstances, and needs of their departments.

Understandable

All control mechanisms—feedforward, concurrent, and feedback—must be understood by the managers, supervisors, and employees who are to use them. At higher management levels, control mechanisms may be rather sophisticated and based on management information systems, mathematical formulas, complex charts and graphs, and detailed reports. At the top levels, such controls should be understandable to all of the managers who utilize them. However, controls should be much less complicated at the departmental level. For example, a supervisor might use a brief, one-page report as a control device. In a dry cleaning store, this report might show the number of different types of clothes cleaned and the number of employee hours worked on a given day. It is uncomplicated, straightforward, and understandable. If the control mechanisms in use are confusing or too sophisticated for the employees, the supervisor should devise new control systems that will meet departmental needs and be understandable to everyone who uses them.

Timely

Control mechanisms should indicate deviations from standard without delay, and such deviations should be reported to the supervisor promptly, even if they are substantiated only by approximate figures, preliminary estimates, or partial information. It is better for the supervisor to know when things are about to go wrong than to learn later that they already are out of control. The sooner a supervisor is aware of deviations, the more quickly the deviations can be corrected.

For example, assume that a project that requires the installation of equipment must be completed within a tight schedule. The supervisor should have reports on a daily or weekly basis showing where the project stands at that time and how this progress compares to the schedule. Potential roadblocks (e.g., missing parts or absences from work) that might delay the completion of the project should be included in these reports. The supervisor needs this type of information early in order to take corrective steps before the situation gets out of hand. This does not mean that the supervisor should jump to conclusions and resort to drastic action hastily. Generally, the supervisor's experience and familiarity with the job will be helpful in sensing when a job is not progressing the way it should.

Suitable and Economical

Controls must be suitable for the activity to be watched. A complex information system control approach that is necessary for a large corporation would not be applicable in a small department. The need for control exists in the small department, but the magnitude of the control system will be different. Whatever controls the supervisor applies, it is essential that they be suitable and economical for the job involved. There is no need to control a minor assignment as elaborately as a manager would control a major capital investment project.

For example, the head nurse in a hospital will usually control the supply of narcotics with greater care and frequency than the number of bandages on hand. Or, in a small company with three clerical employees, it would be inappropriate and uneconomical to have someone assigned full time to check their work for clerical mistakes. It is better to make each employee responsible for checking his or her own work or, possibly, to make employees responsible for checking each other's work. However, in a large department involving the work of several hundred employees who are mass producing a small-unit product, it makes considerable sense to employ full-time inspectors or quality control specialists to check the results. Typically, this is done on a sampling basis, since it is impossible to check every item that goes through the production process. There are many in-between situations in which supervisors must use good judgment as to the suitability of the controls utilized.

Controls also must be economical; that is, they must be worth their expense, even though it may be difficult to determine how much a control system costs and how much it is worth. In such a situation, it is advisable to consider the consequences that could result if controls were not in place. For example, think of the value of an elaborate, expensive control system in a company producing pharmaceuticals as compared to an enterprise manufacturing rubber bands. Defective rubber bands would be an inconvenience, but defective drugs could kill people! The risks for the pharmaceutical company make elaborate controls worth the expense.

Indicational

It is not enough for controls just to expose deviations as they occur. A control mechanism should also indicate who is responsible for the deviation and where the deviation occurred. If several subassemblies or successive operations are involved in a work process, it may be necessary for the supervisor to check performance after each step has been accomplished and before the work moves on to the next workstation. Otherwise, if end results are not up to standards, the supervisor may not know where to take corrective action.

Flexible

Since work operations occur in a dynamic setting, unforeseen circumstances can play havoc with even the best-laid plans and systems. Therefore, controls should be

FIGURE 21-1
Steps in the Control
Process

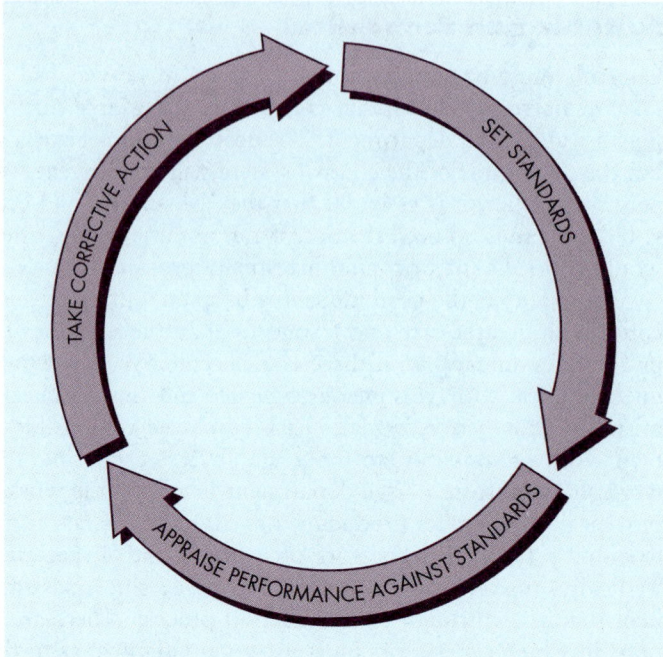

flexible enough to cope with unanticipated changing patterns and problems. Control mechanisms must permit changes when such changes are required. For example, if an employee encounters significant changes in conditions early in a work assignment—such as an equipment failure or a shortage of materials—the supervisor must recognize this and adjust the plans and standards accordingly. If these difficulties are due to conditions beyond the employee's control, the supervisor also must adjust the criteria by which the employee's performance will be appraised.

STEPS IN THE CONTROL PROCESS

4 Describe the essential steps in the control process.

The control process involves three sequential steps. The first step (which usually is part of the planning function) begins with the setting of appropriate standards for what should be accomplished. Next, actual performance must be measured against these standards. If performance does not meet the standards, the third step is to take corrective action. These three steps must be followed in the sequence presented if controlling is to achieve the desired results. (See Figure 21-1.)

Standards
Units of measurement or specific criteria against which to evaluate results.

Setting Standards

Standards may be defined as units of measurement or specific criteria against which to judge performance or results. Standards indicate the targets that should

CONTEMPORARY ISSUE

"P.R.I.D.E."—A Commitment to Exceed Customer Expectations

Shambaugh & Son, Inc., National Contractor of the Year, 1989, developed a "commitment to excellence" program to help achieve its mission to deliver the industry's leading levels of quality and productivity at a competitive price. The contracting-engineering firm has existed since 1926. It is among the 10 largest design/build contractors in the United States. Top-level management commitment and employee training and development are the foundations of the firm's commitment to excellence.

"P.R.I.D.E.," the foundation of Shambaugh's program, was formally kicked off in January 1992. P.R.I.D.E. stands for:

Productivity

Responsiveness

Innovation

Dedication

Enthusiasm

According to President Mark Shambaugh, "These are quality attributes which we want our clients to hold us responsible for on each and every project. It's one thing to promise quality—it's quite another thing to deliver it. Shambaugh & Son is committed to being our industry leader in both quality and productivity and will be involving our clients in this commitment through our 'quality report card,' which will be distributed to our clients on every project."[1]

Shambaugh and the client establish standards of excellence prior to the beginning of the project. The construction crew chief for each project meets with the client daily to gain feedback on performance. The report is reviewed and, if necessary, corrective action is taken. The "quality report card" asks the client to rate Shambaugh on the following 10 "P.R.I.D.E." principles:

1. Develop partnerships with its customers.
2. Do what it says it's going to do, when it says it's going to do it.
3. Produce the industry's highest level of quality services and productivity.

4. Continue to be the industry's leader in on-time, on-schedule completion.
5. Be flexible, responsive, and enthusiastic in servicing the customer.
6. Enlist all available Shambaugh & Son resources, expertise, and experience.
7. Provide innovative alternatives in engineering, design, construction, and service.
8. Promote a highly visible and effective safety program.
9. Keep customers proactively informed to the degree that they will never have to call to learn the status of their project or service call.
10. Discover the customer's needs, recognizing that the burden of communication rests with Shambaugh & Son.

Shambaugh & Son views the providing of customer service as a continuous process, beginning with the understanding of the customer's needs and expectations and ending with the customer's satisfaction. Shambaugh uses a variety of control mechanisms to reinforce the objectives. What is learned on one project is transferred to the next one.

According to one estimate, the typical organization spends between 20 and 25 percent of its operating budget on finding and fixing mistakes.[2] At Shambaugh, the emphasis is on doing the job right the first time. All employees know what the customer expects. In order for the work process to undergo continuous improvement, Shambaugh actively manages the process. The feedback gained on a daily basis serves as a useful tool to help Shambaugh improve work-site productivity, not only on a particular project, but also on others. All construction crew chiefs are taught how to work toward error-free performance. The "commitment to excellence" program was built on the principles of control—setting appropriate standards for what should be accomplished, measuring actual performance against these standards, taking corrective action in a timely manner, and sharing the results of the feedback with others. Shambaugh's success, in part, lies in its ability to use feedforward, concurrent, and feedback control.

Sources: [1]From Mark Shambaugh, president, Shambaugh & Son, Inc. (Fort Wayne, Indiana, January 1992).

[2]Otis Port, "The Push for Quality," *Business Week* (June 8, 1987), pp. 130–136. Kerry O'Brien, of K. E. O'Brien & Associates Inc., reported that the average construction tradesman is only involved in direct on-site productivity 32 percent of the day (September 19, 1992, presentation in Fort Wayne, Indiana).

be achieved; they are criteria against which performance will be compared for exercising control. Standards must be set before any meaningful evaluations can be made about a person's work, a finished product, or a service. In Chapter 7, we described visioning and the establishment of objectives as the foundation of planning. Objectives give specific targets for employees to aim for. However, just having specific targets does not mean they will be attained. The effective supervisor needs to follow up to ensure that the actions that are supposed to be taken are, indeed, being taken and that the objectives are being achieved. This chapter's "Contemporary Issue" box highlights one successful company's use of standards as part of its "commitment to excellence" program.

Tangible standards
Standards for performance results that are identifiable and measurable.

Intangible standards
Standards for performance results that are difficult to measure and often relate to human characteristics (e.g., attitude, morale, satisfaction, etc.).

Many types of standards can be established, depending on the areas of performance or results that need to be measured. **Tangible standards** are performance targets for results that are identifiable and measurable. For example, tangible standards can be set to measure such things as quantity of output, quality of output, labor costs, overhead expenses, time spent in producing a unit or providing the service, market share, and the like. (Tangible standards included on employee appraisal rating forms were identified in Chapter 15.) **Intangible standards** are targets for results that have no physical form; they may cover such areas as an organization's reputation, employee morale, and the quality of humane, loving care of patients in a health-care center or nursing home. It is usually more difficult to establish intangible standards in numerical or precise terms.

The most frequent tangible standards that supervisors determine (or must follow) pertain to the operations of their departments. For example, in a production department, standards can be set for the number of units to be produced; the labor hours per unit; and the quality of the product in terms of durability, finish, and closeness of dimensions. In a sales department, standards might be set for the number of customers contacted, the sales dollars realized, and the number and types of customer complaints.

In setting standards, a supervisor can be guided by experience and knowledge of the jobs to be performed. Through experience and observation, most supervisors have a general idea of how much time it takes to perform certain jobs, the different resources required, and what constitutes good or poor quality. By study and analysis of previous budgets, past production, and other departmental records, supervisors should be able to develop workable standards of performance for most aspects of their departments' operations.

Motion study
An analysis of work activities to determine how to make the job easier and quicker to do.

Time study
A technique for analyzing jobs to determine the standard time needed to complete them.

Motion and Time Studies. A more thorough and systematic way to establish standards for the amount of work employees should accomplish within a given period is to have industrial engineers perform motion and time studies. A **motion study** is an analysis of how a job currently is performed with a view to improving, eliminating, changing, or combining steps to make the job easier and quicker to perform. After a thorough analysis of the work motions and layout, the industrial engineer will develop what he or she considers to be the best current method for doing this job.

Once the best current method has been designed, a **time study** is performed to determine a time standard for the job. This is accomplished in a systematic and largely quantitative manner by selecting certain employees for observation; observing the times used to accomplish various parts of the job; applying correction factors; and making allowances for fatigue, personal needs, and unavoidable delays. When all these factors are combined properly, a time standard for performing the job is the result.

Although this approach attempts to be objective, considerable judgment and approximations are part of the established time standard. A time standard determined by motion and time study is neither wholly scientific nor beyond dispute, but it does provide a sound basis on which a supervisor can set realistic standards.[1] Standards developed by motion and time studies can help the supervisor distribute work more evenly and judge each employee's performance fairly. Such standards also assist the supervisor in predicting the number of employees required and the probable cost of a job to be done.

Most supervisors work in organizations without industrial engineers. When a new job is to be performed in the department, the supervisor can set tentative standards based on similar operations in this or other departments. When no comparison standard is readily available, the supervisor should identify the key tasks necessary to accomplish the job, and then directly observe the employees or ask them to record the time required to complete the tasks. From these data a reasonable standard can be calculated.

To illustrate, suppose a shift supervisor in a fast-food restaurant needs to determine how long it takes employees to prepare a new menu item. The supervisor lists all the steps necessary to complete the job. Then the supervisor can perform the task under several different circumstances and record the required time. The supervisor can also select several employees to perform the task under a variety of conditions. From among the several observations, the supervisor can determine the average time required to complete the task. Not only will realistic standards be established, but such an approach might also uncover better ways of doing the job.

Employee Participation. Some employees resent standards, especially those arrived at through motion and time studies. This resentment is part of a longstanding fear that so-called "efficiency experts" and supervisors use motion and time studies primarily to speed up the workers' output. However, the main purpose for setting performance standards should be to create realistic targets—that is, objectives that can be achieved and that are considered fair by both the supervisor and the employees. Workers are more apt to accept standards as reasonable and fair if they have played an active role in the formulation of those standards.

One technique for having employees participate in establishing standards is to form a committee of workers to assist the supervisor and/or industrial engineer in carrying out a work measurement program. The employees selected for this committee should be those who, in the supervisor's judgment, consistently do a fair day's work.

In addition, the supervisor and industrial engineer should explain to all employees what is involved in motion and time studies, including areas in which judgment is involved. Employees should be given opportunities to challenge any standard that they consider to be unfair, perhaps even to have a job restudied and retimed if necessary. Most workers will accept performance standards if they feel that the supervisor has sincerely tried to help them understand the basis for the standards and has been willing to reconsider and adjust standards that appear to be unreasonable.

Strategic Control Points. The number of standards needed to determine the quantity and quality of performance may become larger as the department expands. As operations become more complex and as functions of a department increase, it becomes time consuming and impractical for the supervisor to constantly check against every conceivable standard. Therefore, the supervisor should concentrate on certain strategic control points against which overall performance can be monitored. **Strategic control points,** or strategic standards, consist of a limited number of key indicators that give the supervisor a good sampling of overall performance. There are no specific rules on how to select strategic control points. Because the nature of the department and the makeup of the supervisor and employees are different in each situation, only general guidelines can be suggested.

A major consideration in choosing one standard as being more strategic than another is its timeliness. Time is essential in control; therefore, the sooner a deviation can be discovered, the better it can be corrected. A supervisor needs to recognize at what critical step operations should be checked during a given process. For example, a strategic control point might be established when a subassembly operation is finished but before the product is put together with other parts and spray painted. A similar approach can be applied in the process of dry cleaning a soiled party dress for a customer. A strategic control point is established shortly after the stain remover is applied. Imagine the costs incurred if all other operations had been completed and the stain was still present.

A supervisor should be careful that the selection of a strategic control point does not have a significant adverse effect on another important standard. For example, excessive control to increase the quantity of production might have an adverse effect on the quality of the product. Likewise, if labor expenses are selected as a strategic control point, supervisors might try to hold down wage expenses by not hiring enough workers, causing both quality and quantity standards to deteriorate. To illustrate, a laundry department supervisor in a nursing home must not sacrifice the high standards set to prevent infections simply to achieve a goal of reducing the cost of laundering linen to a certain price per pound. Thus, decisions about strategic control points depend to some extent on the nature of the work performed. What serves well as a strategic control point in one department will not necessarily apply in another.

Another example of applying the concept of strategic control points is the supervisor who wishes to assess the quality of departmental employee relations. The supervisor might decide to use the following indicators as strategic control standards:

- Number of employees' voluntary resignations and requests for transfer.
- Levels of absenteeism, tardiness, and turnover.
- Accident frequency and severity rates.

Strategic control points
Performance criteria chosen for assessment because they are key indicators of overall performance.

- Number and types of grievances and complaints.
- Amount of scrap, rejects, or customer complaints.

By closely watching trends and changes in these indicators, the supervisor should be able to spot problems requiring corrective action. If the trend of most or all of these selected indicators is unfavorable, major supervisory attention is needed.

Consider the example of a wire manufacturer that used simple statistics to track the productivity of machine operators. It was noted that during the preceding hour, scrap exceeded the acceptable standard by 10 percent. Using strategic control points in a timely fashion, the supervisor working with the operators and the maintenance department knew it was time to check the production process. A check of the diamond dies, pressure settings, and quality of the raw stock led to action so that scrap rates did not increase further and could be returned to their previous lower levels.[2] Strategic control points should be established so that corrective action can be taken early in the production process.

As mentioned previously, there are also areas of an intangible nature that should be monitored closely, even though it is difficult to set precise standards for them. For example, the state of employee morale is typically an important element of departmental operations that a supervisor may decide to appraise and assess as a strategic control standard. Techniques for measurement and evaluation of employee morale were discussed extensively in Chapter 16.

Checking Performance Against Standards

The second major step in the control process is to check actual performance against established standards. This is an ongoing activity for every supervisor. The primary ways for a supervisor to do this are by observing, studying oral and written reports, making spot checks, and using statistical sampling techniques. Figure 21-2 takes a lighthearted look at tracking performance.

Personal Observation. For monitoring employee performance, there is no substitute for direct observation and personal contact by a supervisor. The opportunity for inspection and close personal observation of employee performance is an advantage the supervisor has over top-level managers. This is because the farther removed a manager is from where the employees actually carry out the organization's work, the more the manager will have to depend on reports from others. The supervisor, however, has ample opportunity for direct observation all day long.

When supervisors find deviations from expected standards, they should assume a questioning attitude, but not necessarily a fault-finding one. It is possible that the problem is due to something outside of the employees' control, such as a malfunctioning machine or faulty raw materials. Supervisors should raise questions about mistakes in a positive, helpful manner. For example, instead of just criticizing what happened, a supervisor first should ask what caused the problem and whether there is any way in which he or she can help the employees do their jobs more easily, safely, or efficiently. Supervisors also should elicit suggestions from employees concerning what should be done to correct existing problems. When standards are

FIGURE 21-2
After developing
performance
standards, the
supervisor must be
alert for any deviations
from these standards.

stated primarily in general terms, supervisors should look for specific unsatisfactory conditions, such as inadequate output, sloppy work, or unsafe practices. It is not enough just to tell an employee that his or her work is "unacceptable" or "not satisfactory." If the supervisor can point to specific instances or cite actual recent examples, the employee is more likely to acknowledge the deficiencies that must be corrected.

Also, supervisors can use personal observation and questioning to turn up causes of poor performance that are not the employees' fault, such as inadequate training, problems with work-flow design, or an unusual increase in workload. For example, if a retail store supervisor discovers that customers are not being processed through the cashier quickly enough, the reason may be that an unusually large number of customers entered the store at one time. Instead of chastising employees, the proper corrective action may be to open up another checkout lane. Also, the supervisor may need to find a better way to predict customer traffic or hire a backup cashier. The supervisor may build alternative ways of doing the job into future plans. Employees may have valuable ideas on how to prevent the problem from recurring.

Checking employee performance through personal observation does have limitations. It is time consuming, and it may require the supervisor to spend hours away from his or her desk. Also, it may not be possible to observe some important activities at critical times. There always will be some employees who perform well while being observed but revert to poorer, less diligent habits when the supervisor is not around. Nevertheless, personal observation still is the most widely used and probably the best method of checking employee performance at the supervisory level.

Oral and Written Reports. If a department is large, operates in different locations, or works around the clock, oral and written reports are necessary. For example, if a department operates around the clock and its supervisor has the overall responsibility for more than one shift, the supervisor must depend on reports submitted by employees to appraise the performance of shifts that occur when the supervisor is not present. When a department operates multiple shifts and different supervisors are in charge on different shifts, each supervisor should arrive early to get a firsthand report from the supervisor who is completing the previous shift.

Whenever reports are required, the supervisor should insist that they be clear, complete but concise, and correct. If possible, written reports should be submitted along with an oral presentation. Reports are more effective when they are substantiated with statistical data.

Most employees submit reasonably accurate reports, even when they contain unfavorable outcomes. Report accuracy depends a great deal on the supervisor's reaction to reports and his or her existing relations with employees. If the supervisor handles adverse reports in a constructive and helpful manner, appreciating honesty instead of just giving demerits, employees will be encouraged to submit accurate reports even if the reports show them in an unfavorable light.

In checking reports, supervisors usually find that many activities have been performed according to standards and can be passed over quickly. As a result, many supervisors use the **exception principle** by concentrating on those areas in which performance is significantly above or below standard. Supervisors may even request employees to forego reporting on activities that have for the most part attained the established standards and to report only on activities that are exceptionally below or above standard. If performance is significantly below standard, the supervisor will have to move to the third stage of the control process, taking corrective action. If performance is significantly above standard, the supervisor should praise the employees and study how such exceptional performance was achieved to determine whether what was done can be repeated in the future.

Exception principle
Concept that supervisors should concentrate their investigations on activities that deviate substantially from the standard.

Spot Checks. If the employees' work routine does not lend itself to reports, the supervisor may have to rely on periodic spot checks. For example, a data systems supervisor who is responsible for a centralized computer department that works around the clock six days a week should occasionally come to work at varying times to see what goes on in the department during the different shifts. Supervisors who have little or no opportunity to perform spot checks usually have to depend on reports.

Sampling Techniques. Sampling techniques are really supplements to strategic control points and spot checks. In some firms, each part or product is inspected to determine whether it meets the prescribed standards. Inspecting every item is a time consuming and costly process. While a detailed discussion is beyond the scope of this book, it is becoming increasingly crucial for supervisors, particularly in production facilities, to acquaint themselves with statistical quality control (SQC). SQC is a method to help supervisors determine not only which products, product components, or services to inspect, but also how many of each to inspect.[3]

Sampling
The technique of evaluating some number of items from a larger group to determine whether the group meets acceptable quality standards.

Sampling is the process of inspecting some predetermined number of products from a batch to determine whether the batch is acceptable or unacceptable. To illustrate, suppose that a store manager has been concerned with the quality of produce received from a distributor. The store manager and the produce manager use SQC to determine how many of an incoming shipment should be inspected. Rather than inspecting the entire lot of produce, they compare random samples against a predetermined acceptable quality standard. If a certain number of the samples do not meet the standard, then they reject the entire lot. Note that if the distributor used this technique prior to shipping the produce, it would be feedback control. The same process used by the store manager would be feedforward control. While SQC saves time and money in inspection costs, the supervisor must ensure that the units inspected accurately represent the quality of all the units.

Taking Corrective Action

When no deviations from established standards occur, the process of control is fulfilled by the first two steps—setting standards and checking actual performance against the standards. But if discrepancies or deviations have been noted through personal observation, reports, or spot checks, then the supervisor must take the third step of taking corrective action to bring performance back into line.

Prior to taking specific corrective action, the supervisor should bear in mind that there are various reasons why discrepancies or deviations from standards can occur in any job. Among these are the following:

1. The standards could not be achieved because they were based on faulty forecasts or assumptions or because an unforeseen problem arose that distorted the anticipated results.
2. Failure already occurred in some other job (or activity) that preceded the job in question.
3. The employee who performed the job either was unqualified or was not given adequate directions or instructions.
4. The employee who performed the job was negligent or did not follow required directions or procedures.

Therefore, before taking corrective action, the supervisor should analyze the facts of the situation to determine the specific causes for the deviation. Only after identifying the specific causes can the supervisor decide what remedial actions are necessary to obtain better results in the future. For example, if the reason for the deviation lies in the standards themselves, the supervisor must revise the standards accordingly. If the employee who performed the job was not qualified, additional training and closer supervision might be the answer. Or if the employee was not given the proper instructions, then the supervisor should accept the blame and improve his or her own techniques for giving directives. In the case of sheer negligence or insubordination on the part of the employee, corrective action may consist of a discussion with the employee or a verbal or written reprimand. At times, more serious forms of disciplinary action may have to be taken, including suspending or replacing the employee. Under such circumstances, the disciplinary procedures discussed in Chapter 19 should be followed.

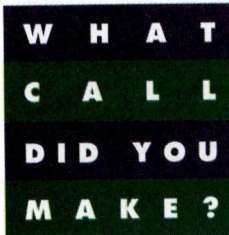

WHAT CALL DID YOU MAKE?

You, Larry Edwards, were correct in identifying the problems that your store was experiencing. The notion that continuous improvement begins and ends with the customer appears to be the driving force for your business. The various backlogs in delivery gave you cause for concern. But wait a minute. Did the problem just develop overnight or did symptoms occur previously? Organizations such as yours should have specific objectives for customer delivery. Before you began the changes, did you and your floor supervisor, Susan Edwards, ascertain the extent of the delivery backlogs? Remember, there is always some variance in performance. What is the industry standard for delivery time? What are your customers' expectations for delivery?

The sad part about this "You Make the Call" scenario is that, with better controls, it could have been handled much sooner. Susan was charged with the responsibility of working out a program to minimize the backlogs. Hopefully, you also gave her responsibility for establishing standards for delivery time (if they do not already exist) or reviewing them to see that they are consistent with customer expectations.

Susan did many things right. She worked through the problem and secured the advice of key personnel and outside experts to devise corrective action. The solution appears to be working. You and Susan should sit down and identify other key indicators that reflect organizational performance. These strategic control points should be identified and monitored in a timely fashion. The earlier a problem is discovered, the sooner it can be corrected. Since the opening scenario is mute on the point, did you assume that Susan failed to solicit employee or customer input? This is the one area where Susan could have added value to the redesign process. As discussed throughout this book, employees are an excellent source of ideas. Any control system or restructuring should involve employees in order to gather as many good ideas as possible and to increase employee acceptance of the process. Involving employees who are affected by the process could result in their making other suggestions to improve customer service, reduce costs, and so forth.

On one hand, Susan fulfilled the needs of the customers. But on the other, was she effective in fulfilling employees' needs to participate and see their suggestions put into effect? Hopefully, even though the customers were temporarily inconvenienced during the restructuring, the company's growing reputation for high-quality customer service will help it gain new business in the future.

SUMMARY

1 Describe the nature and importance of the managerial controlling function.

Controlling is the managerial function that determines whether or not plans are being followed and performance conforms to standards. Every manager must develop and apply controls that regulate the organization's activities to achieve the desired results. The controlling function is most closely related to the planning function. Supervisors set objectives and, in turn, these objectives become standards against which performance is checked. Well-designed controls can be a positive influence on employee motivation. Control should be forward looking, since nothing can be done about the past. The closeness of supervisory control depends, in part, on the employees' experience, initiative, dependability, and resourcefulness.

2 Identify three types of control mechanisms based on time.

Control mechanisms can be categorized as feedforward, concurrent, and feedback, based on when they are implemented in the process. Feedforward, or preliminary, controls are used to anticipate and prevent undesirable outcomes. The person who checks the tires, oil, gas gauge, and the like before beginning a trip is using feedforward control. The traveler who notices that the fuel gauge is below half full or that the fuel warning light has just come on and pulls into the next gas station for a fill-up is using concurrent control. Feedback controls are employed after the fact—they are used as a basis for further improvement. The traveler who calculates average miles per gallon and uses that information when planning the budget for the next trip is using feedback control. Generally, effective supervisors rely on all three types of control mechanisms to improve the process or prevent recurrence of a problem in the future.

3 Explain the essential characteristics of effective controls.

To be effective, controls must be understandable to everyone who uses them and must yield timely information, so that problems can be corrected before the situation gets out of hand. Also, controls should be suitable and economical for the situation. The more serious the consequences of mistakes, the tighter the controls should be, despite the expense. Finally, controls should indicate where the trouble lies in the process and be flexible enough to adjust to changing conditions.

4 Describe the essential steps in the control process.

In performing the controlling function, a supervisor should follow three basic steps: setting standards, checking actual performance against standards, and taking corrective action if necessary. Standards may be set for both tangible and intangible areas. A supervisor's own experience and knowledge can serve to develop certain performance standards. More precise work standards can be accomplished through motion and time studies and the use of work-flow charts. Employee participation in setting standards is crucial to their acceptance. Many supervisors focus their control efforts on selected strategic control points (or strategic standards) that provide major indicators of performance.

The supervisor should check performance against the established standards. In some instances the supervisor has to depend on reports, but in most cases personal observation and inspection are appropriate for checking employee performance. At times, the supervisor may apply the exception principle, which means concentrating on areas where performance is significantly below or above the expected standards. Sampling can be used to help the supervisor determine whether or not products meet prescribed standards. When discrepancies from standards are revealed, the supervisor must take the necessary corrective actions to bring the performance back in line and to prevent future deviations.

KEY TERMS

Controlling (page 576)
Feedforward control (page 578)
Concurrent control (page 578)
Feedback control (page 579)
Standards (page 582)
Tangible standards (page 584)

Intangible standards (page 584)
Motion study (page 584)
Time study (page 584)
Strategic control points (page 586)
Exception principle (page 589)
Sampling (page 590)

QUESTIONS FOR DISCUSSION

1.   Define the managerial function of controlling and discuss its relationship to the other managerial functions.

2.   Why do many people view controls negatively?

3.   If control should be forward looking, does this mean that looking backward is improper in the controlling process? Discuss.

4.   Evaluate the statement "Permitting an employee to work on an assignment without close supervision is both a challenge and a test of delegation."

5.   Define and give examples of each of the following:
   a.   feedforward controls
   b.   concurrent controls
   c.   feedback controls

6.   In your experience, how bad is the problem of absenteeism? What should be done to control it?

7.   How can supervisors use the exception principle to control absenteeism?

8.   Define and discuss each of the primary steps in the control process:
   a.   setting standards
   b.   checking actual performance against standards
   c.   taking corrective action

9.   To maintain high-quality service in a fast-food restaurant, how should standards be set?

10. What guidelines would you recommend to supervisors using control as a form of discipline?

SKILLS APPLICATIONS

Skills Application 21-1: Analysis of Examination Results

Think about your most recent test in the context of Figure 21-1. The test gave you a chance to appraise your performance.

1.   What standards of performance did you set for yourself in the course?

2. Did the test results reflect your knowledge? Why or why not?

3. Look over the learning objectives (standards) listed in the textbook or presented by your professor. Did the test adequately cover the standards? Why or why not?

4. What corrective action might be indicated by the test results?

Skills Application 21-2: Quality Control

An article in the November 1992 issue of *Industrial Engineering* detailed how Raychem Corporation's facility in Menlo Park, California, is building quality control checks into an increasingly automated production process. The Menlo Park facility is portrayed as an innovative, high-volume manufacturing facility. Raychem's purpose is to meet the challenges of high-volume, high-quality output.

1. Find a recent article (one written in the past year) that discusses Raychem. Is it a successful organization today? If so, is there any indication that its success is, at least in part, due to the implementation of quality control techniques?

2. What can you learn from reviewing the strategies of successful organizations?

Skills Application 21-3: Effective Controls

You are the supervisory intern at the Sycamore Hamburger and Shake Palace. At certain times during the day, there are varying backlogs in the burger prep area. As a result, the flow of work slows down, waste increases, and customers complain about the wait or that their orders are not evenly warmed. Your assignment is to design a control system to deal with the problem.

1. List the steps you would take to complete the assignment.

2. What one thing should you do to ensure that your completed project is acceptable?

3. Compare your responses with those of another student. Is there a single recommendation (feedback) that the two of you could make to Sycamore? If so, what would it be?

4. Summarize, in 25 words or less, what you learned from this skill application.

ENDNOTES

1. For a more detailed description of work measurement techniques, see Donald Fogarty, Thomas Hoffmann, and Peter Stonebraker, *Production and Operations Management* (Cincinnati: South-Western Publishing Co., 1989), pp. 332–369.

2. For additional information on productivity measurement, see Robert O. Brinkerhoff and Dennis E. Dressler, *Productivity Measurement: A Guide for Managers and Evaluators* (Newbury Park, CA: Sage Publications, Applied Social Research Methods Series, Volume 19, 1990).

3. For a detailed discussion of SQC, see Eugene Richman and William Zachary, "Quality and Reliability Management: A Review and Update," *Industrial Management* (Volume 35, Number 4, July/August 1993), pp. 8–11; Erwin M. Saniga, "Decision Support and Statistical Quality Control," *International Journal of Quality and Reliability Management* (Volume 10, Number 2, 1993), pp. 9–17; Douglas C. Montgomery, *Introduction to Statistical Quality Control* (2nd ed.; New York: John Wiley & Sons, 1991); Gary S. Vasilash, "TQM/SPC: Get a Buy-In or Watch Them Bug-Out," *Production* (Volume 105, Number 10, October 1993), p. 54; Keki R. Bhote, *World Class Quality: Using Design of Experiments to Make It Happen* (New York: Amacom, 1991); and William H. McNeese, *Statistical Methods for Process Industries* (Milwaukee: ASQC Quality Press, 1991).

22

Financial Reports, Budgets, and Other Controls

LEARNING OBJECTIVES

After studying this chapter, you will be able to:

1 Define accounting and discuss several accounting tools with which supervisors should be familiar.

2 Explain the role of financial analysis in interpreting accounting information.

3 Discuss budgets and the supervisor's role in creating budgets and controlling through them.

4 Discuss the supervisor's role in maintaining cost consciousness and in responding to higher-level managers' orders to reduce costs.

5 Identify additional control areas and show how the controlling function is closely related to the other managerial functions.

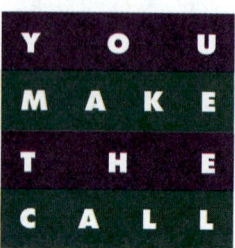

You are David Adams, owner-manager of David's Gift Shoppe. The shop operates from a single location and has been very successful catering to a variety of customer needs. The store is located in a strip mall on the outskirts of a medium-sized city. Ease of entry and exit, ample free parking, a good variety of high-quality merchandise, and a customer-oriented group of employees help to give the Gift Shoppe a competitive advantage. Your marketing orientation consists of finding a need and filling it.

You loved your college marketing classes, and after working for a national chain for several years you began your entrepreneurial career by co-owning a small franchise operation in the mall. In 1989, your Aunt Matilda died and left you $50,000 to start your own business. You spent the better part of a year visiting stores in various parts of the country, getting ideas on what they did exceptionally well. You networked with several of your old college friends to find a variety of offshore suppliers.

Your marketing efforts focus on satisfying consumer needs not currently met by other businesses, training employees in customer service, and making a profit. Your employees are a close-knit group, and none is full time. Several school teachers work for you evenings and weekends. Your wife, Sharon, helps out three afternoons each week and during the holiday season.

It appears that you are successful, but you are not certain that you are making the best use of your money. You never did like to work with numbers, and you did not do well in your college accounting and finance courses. Thus, you rely heavily on the advice of Daniel Kennedy, your accountant. Your wife, Sharon, claims that she and your two children were better off when you were working for someone else. She recently gave you an excerpt of an article in which management consultant Paul Parish said that growing companies get blindsided by two common mistakes:

1. Failure to invest in financial systems. Firms get into trouble because they skimp on salaries of office managers and buy the cheapest computer systems. That means that they cannot keep track of their own growth or identify accounting problems until it is too late.

2. Lack of accounting supervision. Firms should get regular experienced help to verify the accuracy of every aspect of the accounting system.[1]

How can an improved knowledge of accounting and financial tools help you?
YOU MAKE THE CALL.

ACCOUNTING TOOLS FOR CONTROL

1 Define accounting and discuss several accounting tools with which supervisors should be familiar.

Sooner or later, and certainly in the final analysis, all of the activities that an organization undertakes will be reflected in monetary terms. Consequently, not-for-profit, as well as profit-seeking, organizations must establish financial controls through accounting and budgeting processes. The purpose of this chapter is not to discuss the technical and legal framework of accounting statements or budgets, since these aspects usually are not the responsibility of first-line supervisors. Rather, the aim is to provide an overview of basic accounting and financial controls and other control areas as they affect supervisors. We will also review briefly several aspects of the controlling function that have been discussed in different contexts in other chapters of this text.

Financial information about an organization must be expressed in accounting terms. **Accounting** is the system of recording, classifying, and summarizing business transactions and interpreting the summarized information for use in decision making.

Accounting
The system of recording, classifying, summarizing, and interpreting financial data for use in decision making.

To keep accurate and detailed cost summaries of the economic transactions of an organization, the accounting department or controller's office establishes a number of accounts in which the dollar amounts of various business transactions are recorded. Each of these accounts is given a title and a number. For example, the business transaction of purchasing office supplies might be charged to the account "715—Office Supplies." Other transactions, such as purchases of raw materials, wages and salaries, and payment for utilities, will be recorded in different accounts, each with its own number and title. Thus, when keeping departmental records that may eventually be submitted to the accounting department, supervisors must know to which particular account(s) they should charge each expenditure.

Financial information prepared by the accounting department is usually summarized in the form of financial statements. The most common financial statements that supervisors may come in contact with are the income statement, balance sheet, and statement of cash flows.

Income Statement

Income statement
The firm's financial summary of income, expenses, and profit or loss over a stated period of time.

The **income statement** lists revenue and expenses of the organization for a stated period of time, such as a year, six months, a quarter, or a month. In not-for-profit organizations, such as hospitals, educational institutions, and government agencies, the term "operating statement" is used. The profit (surplus) or loss (deficit) is the difference between income (sales and other sources of revenue, if any) and expenses (the cost of doing business). When the income statement shows losses or low earnings, top-level managers will frequently press supervisors to reduce costs in their departments.

Sales
Dollar amount charged to customers for goods and services provided.

Net income
Profit after all expenses have been subtracted from sales.

Expenses
Costs incurred by the business.

Cost of goods sold
The sum of all product-related expenses, such as acquiring, transporting, and packaging an item sold.

Figure 22-1 is an example of an income statement for David's Gift Shoppe. The **sales** figure at the top of the income statement is the dollar amount charged to customers for goods and services provided. An income statement starts with sales, then subtracts all expenses to arrive at **net income**, which is the company's profit. **Expenses** are the costs incurred by the business. The **cost of goods sold** is the sum of all expenses, that is, costs incurred in obtaining the goods that have been sold to customers. Cost of goods sold is usually the major expense of a merchandising company.

If David Adams sells an animated Christmas display to a customer for $400, this amount would be the sales, or revenue. The amount of money David paid to buy the display from the manufacturer ($180) is the purchase cost of the item sold. The amount David makes from the sale ($220) is called gross profit ($400 – $180). But David has all kinds of other expenses, including advertising, rent, utilities, payroll, supplies, and so on. These expenses, called "operating expenses," are costs of providing goods to customers, and they must be subtracted from gross profit to determine whether or not David made a profit. Gross profit less operating expenses gives net income (or loss) from operations and indicates whether or not David's business made a profit from providing goods to customers.

Other revenues and expenses on the income statement are revenues earned and expenses incurred from operations that are not directly related to providing goods and services to customers. In our example, if David Adams rented part of his building to a friend as an office, the rental income would be "other revenue" on his income statement, since this income has nothing to do with his main business of selling gift items. "Net income" at the bottom of the income statement is David's profit after all expenses have been subtracted.

Balance Sheet

Balance sheet
Statement of a firm's financial condition at a certain point in time.

The **balance sheet**, such as the one shown in Figure 22-2, is a statement of an organization's financial condition at a particular point in time. Although the format of

FIGURE 22-1
Income Statement

David's Gift Shoppe Income Statement For the Years Ended December 31, 1992, 1993, and 1994 (in thousands)			
	1994	**1993**	**1992**
Sales	$1,450	$1,167	$1,100
Cost of Goods Sold			
Beginning inventory	$ 165	$ 176	$ 166
Purchases	1,180	851	833
Freight in	31	18	23
Goods available	$1,376	$1,045	$1,022
Ending inventory	(172)	(165)	(176)
Cost of Goods Sold	$1,204	$ 880	$ 846
Gross Profit	$ 246	$ 287	$ 254
Operating Expenses			
Payroll	$ 121	$ 113	$ 112
Rent, utilities	27	25	25
Advertising	26	8	7
Other operating expenses	49	45	42
Total Operating Expenses	$ 223	$ 191	$ 186
Net Income from Operations	$ 23	$ 96	$ 68
Other Revenues and Expenses	20	14	13
Income Before Income Taxes	$ 43	$ 110	$ 81
Income Tax Expense	(13)	(36)	(26)
Net Income	$ 30	$ 74	$ 55

Assets
The resources owned by a firm, such as cash, accounts receivable, inventory, land, and equipment.

Liabilities
The organization's debts.

Owners' equity
The value of the owners' investment in the company.

this statement varies from one organization to another, it consists of two main sections: (a) assets and (b) liabilities and owners' equity. **Assets** represent the items that the organization owns, such as cash, accounts receivable, inventory, land, buildings, and equipment. Current assets are "liquid" assets that the firm expects to use or turn into cash within one year, such as customers' charge account balances. Long-term assets are resources expected to provide benefits to the company for more than one year, such as buildings and equipment. **Liabilities** consist of the debts of the organization, such as notes payable and accounts payable (loan payments), and other debts. Current liabilities are debts that must be paid within one year. Long-term liabilities must be paid at some time later than one year. **Owners' equity** is the value of the owners' investment in the business. Stockholders are the owners of corporations, so the different kinds of stock represent the owners' investment. "Retained earnings" on the balance sheet are the profits of the company that have been reinvested in the business rather than paid to the owners as dividends.

FIGURE 22-2
Balance Sheet.

David's Gift Shoppe
Balance Sheet
December 31, 1992, 1993, and 1994
(in thousands)

	1994	1993	1992
ASSETS			
Current Assets			
Cash	$ 66	$ 79	$ 73
Accounts receivable	203	155	132
Notes receivable	25	13	3
Inventory	172	165	176
Prepaid expenses	5	8	8
Total Current Assets	$ 471	$ 420	$ 392
Long-Term Assets			
Equipment and fixtures	$ 413	$ 375	$ 290
Less: Accumulated depreciation	(126)	(99)	(81)
Land held for expansion	0	17	0
Total Long-Term Assets	$ 287	$ 293	$ 209
Total Assets	$ 758	$ 713	$ 601
LIABILITIES AND OWNERS' EQUITY			
Current Liabilities			
Accounts payable	$ 152	$ 139	$ 117
Notes and loans payable	122	97	89
Accrued expenses	5	4	6
Current portion of mortgage	6	5	5
Total Current Liabilities	$ 285	$ 245	$ 217
Long-Term Debt			
Mortgage notes	$ 136	$ 144	$ 151
Total Liabilities	$ 421	$ 389	$ 368
Owners' Equity			
Capital stock	$ 10	$ 10	$ 10
Retained earnings	327	314	223
Total Owners' Equity	$ 337	324	233
Total Liabilities and Owners' Equity	$ 758	$ 713	$ 601

On a balance sheet, as Figure 22-2 shows, the total assets always equal the total of the liabilities and owners' equity. Thus, the financial position of a firm can be expressed in equation form, as follows:

$$\text{Assets} = \text{Liabilities} + \text{Owners' Equity}$$

This is often referred to as the "accounting equation." The accounting equation serves as the basis for recording the transactions of a firm in the financial accounting system and for providing information about the firm in the financial statements.

Statement of Cash Flows

In addition to the income statement and the balance sheet, many firms prepare another accounting statement, called a "statement of cash flows." All firms listed on organized stock exchanges are required to prepare a statement of cash flows to include with the income statement and balance sheet as part of their annual registration information. In addition, major lenders often require it.

Statement of cash flows
Financial statement showing the movement of cash into and out of the business.

The **statement of cash flows** shows the movement of cash into and out of the firm during a specified period of time. The statement of cash flows, such as the one shown in Figure 22-3, is divided into three sections. "Cash flows from operating activities" indicates the cash generated by the firm's main business of providing goods and services to customers. Basically, this includes the cash generated by sales reported on the income statement and the cash used for the various expenses incurred by the firm. "Cash flows from investing activities" indicates how much cash was invested in the firm's plant and equipment. "Cash flows from financing activities" details the cash flows that resulted from transactions with owners and other suppliers of financing.

Figure 22-3 presents the projected statement of cash flows for David's Gift Shoppe. The preparation and scrutiny of this type of statement help firms determine their ability to pay bills from their cash resources. Profitable firms have been forced into bankruptcy because they did not have the cash needed to continue day-to-day operations. Firms can have increasing sales and profits yet still have negative cash flows due, in part, to excessive inventories and unpaid customer charge accounts. Businesses cannot pay their bills with products sitting in their warehouses—they need cash. A review of the Gift Shoppe's financial statements indicates that David Adams should be concerned. While sales increased $283,000 from 1993 to 1994, as shown in Figure 22-1, and total assets increased $45,000, as shown in Figure 22-2, David's cash position declined by $13,000 (16%, as shown in Figure 22-3). It appears that he may be putting too much of his cash from sales into purchasing assets, so that he may not have enough cash to pay his bills.

Opening Up the Books for Employees to See

From his examination of 20 top U.S. firms, author Robert Levering concludes that any manager can turn a bad workplace into a good one by granting employees more responsibility for their jobs. "Management's new approach involves establishing a partnership with employees rather than acting as adversaries."[2] In forging a partnership with its employees, a firm must be willing to share financial information with them. Information sharing is becoming common in small, as well as large, firms.

An example of one such firm is Springfield Remanufacturing Company, a privately held engine rebuilder in Springfield, Missouri, that shares all of its financial information with employees. Since 1983, employees have been provided with weekly information on all aspects of the business, from revenue and purchasing

FIGURE 22-3
Statement of Cash
Flows

David's Gift Shoppe
Statement of Cash Flows
For the Years Ended December 31, 1993 and 1994
(in thousands)

	1994	1993
Cash Flows from Operating Activities		
Cash collected from customers	$1,395	$1,148
Cash paid to suppliers	(1,198)	(847)
Cash paid to employees	(120)	(115)
Cash paid for other expenses	(72)	(60)
Cash paid for taxes	(13)	(36)
Net Cash Provided (Used) by Operating Activities	$ (8)	$ 90
Cash Flows from Investing Activities		
Purchase of equipment	$ (55)	$ (68)
Purchase of land for expansion		(17)
Proceeds of sale of land held for expansion	32	0
Net Cash Used in Investing Activities	$ (23)	$ (85)
Cash Flows from Financing Activities		
Proceeds of short-term borrowing, net of repayments	$ 25	$ 8
Repayment of long-term debt	(7)	(7)
Net Cash Provided by Financing Activities	$ 18	1
Net Increase (Decrease) in Cash	$ (13)	$ 6
Cash at Beginning of Year	79	73
Cash at End of Year	$ 66	$ 79

costs to labor and management expenses. It seems to be a good way to involve employees in the organization. Its revenues have grown from $16 million in 1983 to $82.7 million in 1993 and are projected to be $90 million in 1994.[3] However it is not enough for a firm to simply share financial information with employees. Employees must have an understanding of what the financial data mean and a basis for comparing their firm's current financial information with that of previous years and competitors.

USE OF FINANCIAL STATEMENTS[4]

[2] Explain the role of financial analysis in interpreting accounting information.

Once accounting data is collected about the individual transactions of the business and financial statements have been produced, they must be interpreted. Generally, accountants will gather, record, report, and interpret financial information. The

FIGURE 22-4
Illustration of Vertical
Analysis

Percentage of Net Sales for David's Gift Shoppe
For the Years Ended December 31, 1992, 1993, 1994

	1994	1993	1992
Sales	100.0	100.0	100.0
Cost of Goods Sold	83.0	75.4	76.9
Gross Profit	17.0	24.6	23.1
Payroll expense	8.3	9.7	10.2
Rent, utilities	1.9	2.1	2.3
Advertising	1.8	0.7	0.6
Other	3.4	3.9	3.8
Total Operating Expense	15.4	16.4	16.9
Net Income from Operations	1.6	8.2	6.2
Net Income	2.1	6.3	5.0

owners of the business will rely on the information to determine how well the business is doing. Managers are the major users of the information, which aids them in planning and assessing the day-to-day operations. Potential investors use accounting information to help them decide whether to invest in the business.

Three techniques to aid management in planning and assessing the day-to-day operations are horizontal analysis, vertical analysis, and ratio analysis. **Horizontal analysis** is a comparison of the firm's financial statements over time to uncover trends. Each income statement and balance sheet item is expressed as a percentage change from the preceding period. **Vertical analysis** expresses various income statement items as a percentage of sales or balance sheet items as a percentage of total assets. Such an analysis helps firms see where they are spending their income. Figure 22-4 reveals how David's Gift Shoppe's income statement can be converted into a percentage of sales using vertical analysis. As you can see, David is spending a disproportionate amount on cost of goods sold. From this analysis, David may decide to try to cut costs in an area that seems inappropriately high. Cost and expense items shown in percentage form can quickly be compared with those of previous periods or with other firms in the industry to note trends.

Horizontal analysis
Financial analysis that
compares financial
statements over time to
uncover trends.

Vertical analysis
Financial statements
that show income
statement items as a
percentage of sales
and balance sheet
items as a percentage
of total assets.

Ratio Analysis

What is particularly helpful to financial analysis is the use of percentages or ratios to measure a firm's economic health. Most people are familiar with ratios; they are used all the time to measure productivity. For example, the number of miles driven divided by the number of gallons of fuel used gives a useful ratio—miles per gallon (mpg). But mpg is but one measure of a car's efficiency. More information is needed. Like mpg, accounting numbers are not very meaningful in and of themselves, but they become useful when compared with other numbers.

The income statement and the balance sheet provide the data necessary to express the accounting information as a ratio. Four categories of ratios are useful in interpreting financial statements: liquidity ratios, activity ratios, profitability ratios, and debt ratios.

Liquidity Ratios. Liquidity ratios provide information about the firm's ability to pay its current bills. Two common types are the current ratio and the quick ratio.

The current ratio compares current assets with current liabilities. David's ability to pay his current debts as they come due is measured as:

$$\text{Current Ratio} = \frac{\text{Current Assets}}{\text{Current Liabilities}} = \frac{\$471}{\$285} = 1.65 \text{ to } 1$$

This means that David has $1.65 of current assets for every $1 of current liabilities. Traditionally, a current ratio of 2 to 1 was considered to be acceptable. However, in a sample of firms similar to David's, it was found that only 3 of 24 firms had an average current ratio greater than 2 to 1 during the 1988–1992 time frame. David should also compare this ratio of 1.65 to previous operating periods to determine its appropriateness. David's current ratio of 1.65 to 1 has improved slightly over the past year.

Quick ratios measure the firm's ability to meet its current debt on short notice. It does not include inventory or prepaid expenses; only highly liquid assets are considered. David's current balance sheet (Figure 22-2) lists the following liquid assets: cash ($66), accounts receivable ($203), and notes receivable ($25). The quick ratio is computed as:

$$\text{Quick Ratio} = \frac{\text{Cash} + \text{Receivables}}{\text{Current Liabilities}} = \frac{\$294}{\$285} = 1.03 \text{ to } 1$$

Because the traditional rule of thumb for an adequate quick ratio is 1 to 1, David appears to be in a good short-term credit position. The sample of comparative firms revealed that only 5 of the 24 had an average quick ratio greater than 1 to 1 from 1988 to 1992. Comparing David's quick ratio with previous operating periods indicates that he is now better able to meet current debt on short notice.

Activity Ratios. Activity ratios provide information about the effectiveness of the firm's use of resources. The most frequently used activity ratio is the inventory turnover ratio, which indicates how fast inventory is sold. It is calculated by dividing the cost of goods sold by the average amount of inventory. If the amount of inventory varies substantially from month to month, all 12 of the end-of-month inventories should be totaled and divided by 12 to determine the average inventory for the year. Since David's inventory is relatively consistent throughout the year, average inventory is determined by adding the January 1 beginning inventory of $165,000 and the December 31 ending inventory of $172,000 (as shown on the income statement, Figure 21-1) and dividing by two. The average inventory of $168,500 is then divided into the cost of goods sold using the following equation:

$$\text{Inventory Turnover Ratio} = \frac{\text{Cost of Goods Sold}}{\text{Average Inventory}} = \frac{\$1,204,000}{\$168,500} = 7.1$$

Generally, the higher the inventory turnover ratio, the more efficiently inventory assets are being used. But the figure itself is meaningless. It has to be compared with industry standards. A turnover rate of 7.1 times would be inadequate for a supermarket, for which a turnover rate of 18 times is considered adequate. For furniture stores, the average turnover rate of 1.5 times is about average, while for a business like David's a turnover rate of 4.8 is average. David's higher than average ratio may indicate that he is carrying too little inventory. David should look into the situation carefully.

Profitability Ratios. Profitability ratios are used to indicate how successful a firm is in terms of its earning power as compared with sales or investment. Return on sales is a financial ratio that measures profitability by comparing net income and sales. For David's Gift Shoppe, the ratio is computed as:

$$\text{Return on Sales} = \frac{\text{Net Income}}{\text{Sales}} = \frac{\$30,000}{\$1,450,000} = .021, \text{ or } 2.1 \text{ percent}$$

This figure indicates that David made a profit of 2.1 cents for every dollar of sales. This ratio varies widely among business firms. Generally, retail firms average a 5 percent return on sales. However, when David compares the ratio of 2.1 percent with past performance, it becomes evident that the firm's profit picture has declined substantially over the past two years. One way to increase the ratio is to increase prices, but if David is in a highly competitive market, he may want to keep prices low.

Return on equity tells the owners of a firm specifically how much they are earning on their investment. It is the ratio between net income and owners' equity. Data from both the income statement and the balance sheet are necessary to calculate this ratio:

$$\text{Return on Equity} = \frac{\text{Net Income}}{\text{Owners' Equity}} = \frac{\$30,000}{\$377,000} = .089, \text{ or } 8.9 \text{ percent}$$

While David's return of almost 9 percent on equity may appear to be satisfactory, owners use this ratio to compare whether their funds invested in the business are generating a greater return on their money than if they did something else with the money, such as depositing it in a bank or buying stock in another company.

Debt Ratios. Debt ratios provide information about the capital structure of the firm—that is, the relative importance of debt and equity in providing resources for the firm. The debt ratio is calculated as:

$$\text{Debt Ratio} = \frac{\text{Total Liabilities}}{\text{Total Assets}} = \frac{\$421,000}{\$758,000} = 0.56$$

The debt to owners' equity ratio indicates the amount of funds contributed by creditors as compared with the total funds provided. The ratio for David's is computed as:

$$\text{Debt to Equity Ratio} = \frac{\text{Total Liabilities}}{\text{Total Equity}} = \frac{\$421,000}{\$337,000} = 1.25$$

David's debt-to-equity ratio of 1.25 indicates that the firm is relying more on debt financing than on owners' equity. Other things being equal, a business with a lower debt ratio and lower debt-to-equity ratio will be better able to meet its obligations when they come due. Lenders are less likely to extend credit to firms with high debt-to-equity ratios.

Remember: Ratios only give the supervisor a "snapshot" of the financial health of the organization at a given point in time. A ratio, in and of itself, is meaningless unless the supervisor has something to compare it with. Ratios are only useful when compared with the ratios of the same company over time, with other companies in the same line of business, and with industry averages. The information provided by ratios can be misleading without a basis for comparison.

BUDGETARY CONTROL

3 Discuss budgets and the supervisor's role in creating budgets and controlling through them.

Budget
A financial plan that projects expected revenues and expenditures during a stated period of time.

Operating budget
The projection of dollar allocations to various costs and expenses needed to run the business, based on expected revenue.

Among the tools for financial control, the budget usually is the one with which supervisors have the most frequent contact. A **budget** is a written plan expressed in numerical terms that projects anticipated resources and expenditures for a period of time, such as a month, a quarter, six months, or a year. Firms usually prepare a variety of budgets. Supervisors are most familiar with the operating budget. The **operating budget** is the projection of dollar amounts of various costs and expenses needed to run the business, given projected revenues. David, for example, will develop an operating budget like that shown in Figure 22-5 to show how much he expects to spend on inventory, salaries, supplies, travel, rent, utilities, advertising, and other expenses.

Some organizations develop capital budgets to determine how much they will spend on assets such as property, building, and equipment. They also prepare cash budgets to project the cash balance at the end of a given period, and master budgets to tie all budgets together and summarize the proposed financial activity of the firm.

At times it is convenient to express budgets in terms other than dollars. Budgets pertaining to employment requirements, for example, may be expressed in numbers of employee-hours allocated for certain activities or numbers of workers needed for each job classification. Eventually, however, the various nonfinancial budgets are converted into monetary figures—an operating budget—which is a statement by which the organization's overall activities are summarized and

FIGURE 22-5
Operating Budget for
David's Gift Shoppe

Period: January, 1995

	Estimate	Actual
Cash on Hand (beginning of the month)	$ 66,000	
Sales	$138,000	
Other revenues	$ 4,000	
TOTAL CASH AVAILABLE	$208,000	
Expenses (cash paid out)		
Purchases (merchandise)	$ 84,000	
Freight in	$ 3,500	
Payroll expenses	$ 11,600	
Rent	$ 1,200	
Telephone	$ 200	
Utilities	$ 1,000	
Advertising	$ 1,500	
Outside services (cleaning)	$ 1,000	
Supplies (office & operating)	$ 500	
Repair and maintenance	$ 500	
Car, delivery, travel	$ 1,200	
Accounting and legal	$ 500	
Insurance	$ 500	
Taxes (nonemployee)	$ 1,500	
Interest	$ 700	
Miscellaneous	$ 500	
SUBTOTAL	$109,900	
Loan principal payment	$ 1,000	
Capital Purchases	$ 2,500	
Accounts payable	$ 35,000	
Owners' withdrawals	$ 1,000	
TOTAL CASH PAID OUT	$149,400	
Cash Position	$ 58,600	

Note: In preparing his budget, David projects his cash funds available and anticipated expenses. In actual practice each of the expense items will have an account number (e.g., 715—Supplies). At the end of the month, he compares actual expenses with budgeted expenses.

through which managers can plan and control the use of financial and other resources.[5]

All managers, from the chief executive officer down to the supervisors, must learn how to plan budgets, live within their limitations, and use them for control purposes. The term "budgetary control" refers to the use of budgets by supervisors and higher-level managers to control operations so that they will comply with the standards established by the organization in making the budgets.

Preparing the Budget

Preparing a budget, whether it is expressed in monetary or other terms, requires the budget maker to quantify estimates about the future by attaching numerical values to each budgeted item. The numerical figures in the final overall budget become the desired financial standards of the organization. Similarly, the numerical figures in the final departmental budgets become the standards to be met by each department and departmental supervisors.

Incremental budgeting
A technique for making revenue and expense projections based on previous history.

Zero-base budgeting
The process of assessing all activities to justify their existence on a benefit and cost basis.

Most annual budgets are projections for the following year based on the previous year's budget. This approach for making a budget is known as **incremental budgeting**. Another approach, which has gained some acceptance in recent years, is zero-base budgeting. If an organization practices **zero-base budgeting**, all budgets must begin "from scratch," and each budget item must be justified and substantiated. In zero-base budgeting, the previous budget does not constitute a valid basis for a budget being prepared for a future period. The advantage of zero-base budgeting, sometimes called "zero-base review," is that all ongoing programs, activities, projects, products, and the like are reassessed by management in terms of their benefits and costs to the organization. This avoids the tendency of simply continuing expenditures from a previous budget period without much consideration. The disadvantage of zero-base budgeting is that it involves a large amount of paperwork and is very time consuming. Moreover, in actual practice it is difficult to apply the concept to some departments and types of operations.[6]

Supervisory Participation in Budget Making

The budget that most concerns supervisors is usually the departmental expense budget, which covers the variety of expenditures to be incurred in the department. In the discussion that follows, we presume that a firm uses incremental budgeting practices. To many supervisors, budgets have a negative connotation of arbitrariness, inflexibility, conflicts, and problems. If the budget is perceived in this manner, it will tend to breed resentment. To facilitate acceptance, expense budgets should be determined with the participation and cooperation of those responsible for executing them. Preferably, supervisors should have an opportunity to participate in making their own departmental budgets. When they are allowed to do this, supervisors must be familiar with both general and detailed aspects of budget preparation. Even when a budget is just handed down to supervisors by higher-level management, supervisors must still understand the budget and the reasoning behind each budget figure.

To participate successfully in budget making, supervisors have to demonstrate the actual need for each amount they request and document their requests with historical data wherever possible. Frequently the final budget will contain lower figures than those first submitted. A supervisor should not consider this as a personal rejection, because other supervisors also are making budget requests and having them cut. It is rarely possible for higher-level management to grant everyone's requests. Much will depend on how realistic the supervisors have been and how well

FIGURE 22-6
A Departmental
Monthly Cost
Summary

Models Assembled In Dept. 4	No. of Units	Materials		Labor		Overhead	
		Budget Standard Per Unit	Budgeted Total Materials Costs	Budget Standard Per Unit	Budgeted Total Labor Costs	Budget Standard Per Unit	Budgeted Total Overhead Costs
Model 101	10	$315	$3,150	$462	$4,620	$462	$9,240
109	8	420	3,360	368	2,944	368	5,888
113	11	641	7,051	441	4,851	441	9,702
154	20	199	3,980	407	8,140	407	$16,280
Total	49		$17,541		$20,555		$41,110
Actual costs in November			17,152		21,063		42,225
Variances from budget Standard			$+389		$-508		$-1,115

their budget needs are documented or substantiated. Supervisors can only hope that the final budget will be close to what they requested and will give them sufficient resources to operate their departments efficiently.

Budgetary Control by Supervisors

Budget making falls under the managerial function of planning, but carrying out the budget—or living within the budget—is part of the controlling function. Supervisors must manage their departments within budget limits and refer to their budgets to monitor their expenditures during the operating period. When a budget is approved by higher-level management, the supervisor is allocated specific amounts of money for each item in the budget. Expenditures in the supervisor's department must be charged against various budget accounts. At regular intervals (e.g., monthly), the supervisor must review the budgeted figures and compare them with the actual expenses incurred. This comparison is usually reported to the supervisor by the accounting department. Figure 22-6 is an example of a departmental monthly cost summary prepared by the accounting department. Most firms utilize computer-based cost and financial control systems. Income and cost projections and reports are produced in the form of computer printouts, which may be prepared and distributed by the information systems department.

If the supervisor notes that actual expenditures for a specific item greatly exceed the budgeted amount, he or she must find out what happened. Investigation could reveal a logical explanation for the discrepancy. For example, if the amount spent on labor in a manufacturing department exceeded the budgeted amount, this could be due to an unanticipated demand for the firm's product, which required working overtime to meet it. If the excessive deviation from the budgeted amount

FIGURE 22-7
Budget flexibility
means that the budget
figures are not "carved
in stone."

cannot be justified, the supervisor must take whatever actions are necessary to bring the out-of-control expenditures back to where they should be, at least from that point on. Excessive deviations usually have to be explained by the supervisor to higher-level managers or the accounting department. To avoid this unpleasant task, a supervisor is well advised to make regular comparisons of actual expenditures with budgeted amounts and to keep expenses close to the budget.

Budget Flexibility

Budgets should not be so detailed that they become cumbersome. Rather, they should allow the supervisor some freedom to accomplish departmental objectives with a reasonable degree of latitude. Flexibility does not mean that the supervisor can change budget figures unilaterally or take them lightly. Rather, it means that the supervisor should not be led to believe that budget figures are carved in stone (see Figure 22-7). Budgets are guides for management decisions, not substitutes for good judgment.

Sometimes certain expenses can be charged to more than one account. For example, assume that the expense of attending a seminar out of town can be charged to either the travel expense account or the educational expense account. Knowing the status of both of these accounts can help the supervisor determine where to charge the expense of attending the seminar. If the travel expense account is already exhausted and the educational expense account is not, the astute supervisor may take advantage of the flexibility of the budget and charge the expense to the latter account.

To prevent a budget from becoming a straitjacket, most organizations provide for regular budget reviews by supervisors together with higher-level managers. These reviews should take place about every three months—or at least every six months—to ensure a proper degree of flexibility. If operating conditions have changed appreciably since the budget was established, or if there are valid indications that the budget cannot be followed in the future, a revision is in order. For example, unexpected price increases or major fluctuations in the general economic climate might be reasons for revising the budget. Usually there is enough flexibility built into a budget to permit common-sense departures to accomplish the objectives of the department and the total organization.

COST CONTROL AND THE SUPERVISOR

4 Discuss the supervisor's role in maintaining cost consciousness and in responding to higher-level managers' orders to reduce costs.

Competition from domestic companies and from abroad and the changing economic environment require most organizations to strive continuously to control their costs. Sooner or later most supervisors become involved in some way with cost control, because higher-level managers expect supervisors to control costs at the department level to help meet organizational cost goals. Thus, cost consciousness should be an ongoing concern of supervisors. Sporadic efforts to curtail costs, crash programs, and economy drives seldom have lasting benefits. Although many large organizations employ consultants trained in work efficiency and cost control, in the final analysis it remains the supervisor's duty to look at cost consciousness as a permanent part of the managerial job.

Maintaining Cost Awareness

Because cost consciousness is of ongoing concern to the supervisor, plans should be made for achieving cost awareness throughout the department. Here is where planning and controlling again become closely interrelated. By setting objectives and defining specific results to be achieved within a certain time frame, cost priorities can be set.

In setting cost objectives, the supervisor should involve the employees who are in positions that will be most affected. Employees often can make valuable contributions. The supervisor should fully communicate cost-reducing objectives to employees and get as much input from them as possible. The more employees contribute to a cost-control program, the more committed they will be to meeting objectives. It may also be advisable to point out to employees that eventually everyone benefits from continuous cost awareness. Supervisors should help employees see cost containment as part of their jobs and as being in their own long-term interest. Firms that do not control costs cannot remain competitive, which could mean loss of jobs. Most employees will try to do the right thing and seek to reduce waste and costs if their supervisors approach them in a positive way.

Responding to a Cost-Cutting Order

Reducing costs is a natural concern of most organizations, and it is frequently brought on by competition. It is likely that within an enterprise, at one time or another, an order will come from top-level managers to cut all costs across the board by a certain percentage. At first glance such a blanket order could be considered fair and just; however, this may not be so, since it could affect some supervisors much more severely than others. Some supervisors are continuously aware of costs and operate their departments efficiently, while others are lax and perhaps even wasteful. How should a supervisor react to such a blanket order?

There are some supervisors who will read the order to mean that everything possible should be done immediately to bring about the desired percentage of cost reduction. They might hold "pep rallies" with employees or, at the other extreme, engage in harsh criticism of employees and others. Some supervisors might stop buying supplies, leading eventually to work delays. Others might eliminate preventive maintenance work, even though this eventually could lead to equipment breakdowns and interruptions of the work flow. Although these actions might bring about some cost reductions, they could be more expensive in the long run.

Other supervisors will merely follow the cost-cutting directive halfheartedly. They will make minimal efforts here and there to give the appearance that they are doing something about costs. Such efforts are not likely to impress the employees, who in turn will also make only a halfhearted effort. This type of supervisory response will not contribute adequately to a cost-control program.

An across-the-board cost-reduction order may present a hardship to the diligent, cost-conscious supervisor whose department is working efficiently. Nevertheless, this supervisor will strive to take some action by looking again at areas where there is still room to reduce expenses. This supervisor will call for suggestions from employees, because they are the ones who can bring about results. For example, there may be some paperwork that can be postponed indefinitely. Or there may be certain operations that are not absolutely necessary, even if they are performed efficiently. The supervisor should point out to the employees which are the most expensive operations and let them know what these actually cost. An employee might suggest a less expensive way of doing a job; if so, the supervisor should welcome the suggestion. The supervisor should be committed to the cost-reduction campaign and should set a good personal example whenever possible. Although it may be difficult for such a supervisor to come up with large savings, at least he or she will have made a diligent effort to support the organization's cost-cutting drive.

While supervisors play a key role in cost reduction, they cannot succeed without employee commitment. The "Contemporary Issue" box provides an example of a hospital that initiated a creative cost-saving program that involved employees as the key to success.

Elimination of things that cost money is one way to save money. Effective supervisors are constantly on the lookout for ways to eliminate excess costs by questioning the necessity of everything that is done in their department.

Even if an organization does not have a formal suggestion program, supervisors

CONTEMPORARY ISSUE
A BAD Program That Worked

Pine Valley Community Hospital (PVCH) was faced with escalating costs and fewer patients. The other two area hospitals had announced merger plans. The vice-president of administrative services and an employee group worked together with a consultant to develop an employee suggestion program. The objective was to find ways to eliminate at least $50,000 in costs. While some organizations would eliminate jobs or not fill positions as people retired or quit, PVCH's management did not want to eliminate jobs. PVCH had been involved in a cooperative purchasing effort for about 15 years, and thus the purchasing area was not one that could generate cost savings.

The program was dubbed the BAD program ("buck a day"). Each employee was given a new dollar bill and told to look for ways to reduce costs by that much each day. Coffee cups, tee-shirts, and prominently located posters all promoted the BAD program. PVCH's employees could easily identify with the "buck" (most people cannot comprehend $50,000), and they readily began looking for ways to save. Department supervisors explained the suggestion program to employees. The program was straightforward and easily understood. BAD checklists were developed along with constant reminders to employees to be on the lookout for things that cost money. Items on the checklist included the following:

1. Look at each process through the eyes of a stranger.

- Why is it necessary?
- Is it needed?
- Could certain operations be simplified, combined, or eliminated?

2. Analyze each procedure to determine whether or not costs associated with the procedure are necessary.
3. Look for ways to:

- Eliminate idle time.
- Eliminate handling time.
- Eliminate indirect costs.
- Eliminate costs by simplifying, combining, or eliminating operations.
- Eliminate unused inventory, machinery, equipment, or tools.
- Eliminate overtime or extra-cost operations.

4. Analyze the work flow.

- Would better coordination improve work flow?
- What can we do to improve communication?
- How can scheduling be more efficient?

5. Can we make better use of employees?

- Are we using more employees on a job than are actually needed?
- Are there occasions when not having enough employees on a job results in unnecessary overtime?
- Are we using highly paid, skilled employees on jobs that lower-paid employees can do?
- Do we fail to use skilled employees in their specialties for reasons of day-to-day expediency?
- Are employees lacking in job knowledge because of our failure to provide on-the-job training?
- Are some department supervisors not policing overtime?
- Are we using our employees to their fullest potential?

Awards were given for each suggestion. In addition, each employee submitting a suggestion was entered in a drawing for a grand prize—a trip to the Indianapolis 500. Each time someone won an award, supervisors used the occasion to highlight the idea that suggestions pay off.

Review committees evaluated each suggestion and championed those ideas that were worthy of implementation. The net result was that employees suggested ways to eliminate over $100,000 in expenses.

Source: Edwin C. Leonard, Jr. (1994). The name of the hospital has been changed to preserve anonymity.

can establish a climate of mutual trust and respect that encourages suggestions from their employees. The supervisor can use formal and informal encouragement during departmental meetings to emphasize the value of making suggestions. In the Chapter 15 "You Make the Call" scenario, Cheryl Iberra, the assistant supervisor, complained about the company's compensation and benefits. Shane Wilson, the supervisor, effectively handled the situation by saying, "Why don't you do something about it? Maybe we need a change. Think of a better way and we'll take it to top management. Any credit for the idea will be yours."

Whether for changing policies or controlling costs, employee suggestions can be a valuable source of ideas. Employees like to see their ideas put into effect and are more committed to goals they helped to set.

OTHER CONTROLS

5 Identify additional control areas and show how the controlling function is closely related to the other managerial functions.

In addition to accounting and budgetary controls, other areas of management control exist in many organizations. Typically these control areas are supervised by specialized departments and are outside the realm of most supervisors' direct authority and responsibility. Nevertheless, supervisors should be aware of these control areas, and, if necessary, should familiarize themselves with the methods employed by the specialists who perform these control activities. Often such specialists are attached to the organization in staff positions.

Specialized Controls

Inventory control is concerned with keeping watch over raw materials, supplies, work in process, finished goods, and the like. Maintaining sufficient but not excessive inventory on hand, keeping status records of all inventory, ordering economic lot sizes, and many other problems connected with inventory policy are part of inventory control.

Quality control consists of maintaining the quality standards set by a firm for its products or services. These must be continually tested to make certain that quality is maintained. Quality control of products is often accomplished by testing randomly selected samples to determine whether or not quality standards are being met.

Production control usually consists of a number of activities to maintain overall operations on schedule. It involves routing of operations, scheduling, and, if necessary, expediting of the work flow. Elaborate charts and network analyses may be utilized. For example, the production control department may start with a Gantt chart, which is a diagram or pictorial representation of the progress and status of various jobs in production. If practical, this can lead to a computerized network analysis. Two of the most widely used analyses, PERT (program evaluation review technique) and CPM (critical path method), were discussed in Chapter 7.

Controlling and the Other Managerial Functions

Throughout this book, we have discussed numerous aspects of effective managerial controls from different perspectives. At this point we will review several of them as they relate to the controlling function.

Testing randomly selected samples is one way to accomplish quality control.

In Chapters 5 and 7, we discussed the system of MBO (management by objectives) in connection with motivation and planning. The MBO process involves setting objectives and standards, evaluating results, following up, and revising previous objectives if necessary. Evaluation of results, follow up, and establishment of new objectives are elements of control.

In Chapter 7, we also discussed standing (repeat-use) plans, such as policies, procedures, methods, and rules, primarily in regard to managerial planning. However, when standing plans are not working or are not followed, the supervisor must take the necessary corrective actions to bring the department's operations back in line. Thus these types of standing plans may be seen as forward-looking control devices.

Performance appraisal, which we discussed under the staffing function in Chapter 15, also has a place as a control mechanism. During a performance appraisal meeting, the supervisor evaluates an employee's performance against predetermined objectives and standards. At the same time, the supervisor and the employee may agree on steps for corrective action, as well as new objectives and standards. The element of supervisory control can be detected throughout a performance appraisal cycle.

In Chapter 19 we treated the subject of maintaining employee discipline as part of the leading function of management. If a supervisor takes disciplinary measures when established rules are not followed by employees, such measures serve as control techniques.

These managerial activities show how intrinsically related the controlling function is to all the other managerial functions. As stated previously, controlling typically is performed simultaneously with the other managerial functions. The better the supervisor plans, organizes, staffs, and leads, the better will be his or her ability to control the activities and employees in the department. Thus, controlling takes a forward-looking view, even though it has been discussed as the "final" managerial function in this book.

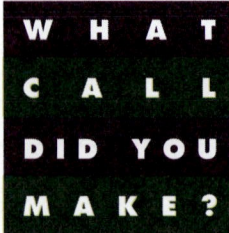

WHAT CALL DID YOU MAKE?

As David Adams in the "You Make the Call" scenario, you need to understand accounting tools so that you can forecast objectives and assess results. All the things your business does will be reflected in monetary terms. It is essential that you or your employees be able to keep accurate and detailed revenue and cost data.

While your accountant may do a good job of preparing the income statement and balance sheet, you need to fully appreciate how you can use the information to do a better job of managing your business. A review of Figure 22-1 shows that your net income from operations is down sharply from previous years, and that it appears that during the year you made a decision to increase advertising expenditures drastically. Cost of goods sold increased approximately 50 percent. Thus, you may want to analyze your previous markup and your decisions as to type of inventory stocked. Figure 22-3, the statement of cash flows, shows that less cash is available to start the year than in previous years. You must have an understanding of what the financial data mean and a basis for comparing your company's current financial information with that of previous years and your competitors.

You need to compare the various financial ratios to get a better picture of your company's health. You must learn how to develop a budget for your shop, live within that budget, and develop strategies for increasing revenues. You may want to consider using a zero-base budgeting concept and look at each aspect of your operation through the eyes of a stranger. You need to develop plans to achieve cost awareness among all your employees.

You need to recognize that the decisions you make and the plans you formulate are tied to the bottom line. Thus, not only do you need to have an adequate knowledge of accounting and finance, but you should also be concerned with inventory control and quality control.

SUMMARY

1 Define accounting and discuss several accounting tools with which supervisors should be familiar.

Accounting is the system of recording, classifying, and summarizing business transactions and interpreting the summarized information. Supervisors need to be familiar with the various accounting controls their organizations have in place. Supervisors must know the accounts to which they will charge various expenses. They may also come in contact with financial statements prepared by the accounting department—the income statement, balance sheet, and statement of cash flows.

The income statement summarizes revenues and expenses of an organization for a stated period of time. It shows whether the organization has made a profit or not.

The balance sheet is the statement of an organization's financial condition at a given point in time. It records all the assets the firm owns and its liabilities (debts). The sum of all assets must always equal the sum of all liabilities and owners' equity on the balance sheet. The accounting equation, assets = liabilities + owners' equity, serves as the basis for recording the firm's transactions in its financial accounting system.

The statement of cash flows shows the movement of cash into and out of the business. Firms need sufficient cash to pay for day-to-day operations.

2 Explain the role of financial analysis in interpreting accounting information.

Two types of analysis, horizontal and vertical, provide interpretation of a firm's cost and expense data. These techniques also enable analysis of the firm's revenue data and provide an indication of how the firm's financial position has changed over time. Horizontal analysis is a comparison of the firm's financial data from year to year. Vertical analysis expresses various items as a percentage of either net sales or total assets.

Liquidity ratios, activity ratios, profitability ratios, and debt ratios are useful in measuring a firm's performance. Industry ratios are used as a comparative measure. It is also beneficial to compare the firm's current performance with that of previous time periods.

3 Discuss budgets and the supervisor's role in creating budgets and controlling through them.

The most widely used financial control device is the budget. The preparation of a budget is primarily a planning function. However, applying, supervising, and living within the budget are part of the controlling function. Supervisors should have an opportunity to participate in preparing budgets for their departments, regardless of whether the enterprise practices traditional or zero-base budgeting. Virtually all budgets need some built-in flexibility to allow for adjustments when necessary. When significant deviations from the budget occur, the supervisor must investigate and take whatever actions are appropriate to bring expenditures back in line.

4 Discuss the supervisor's role in maintaining cost consciousness and in responding to higher-level managers' orders to reduce costs.

Cost control and cost consciousness should be a continuing concern of all supervisors. When top-level managers issue cost-cutting orders, supervisors should avoid taking extreme measures that may in the long run be more costly than the reductions themselves.

Involving employees in cost reduction efforts is one way that the effective supervisor can create cost awareness. Suggestion programs can be used to solicit ideas for potential areas of cost reduction. The supervisor should constantly be on the lookout for ways to eliminate excess costs. Periodically, the supervisor should look at the department through the eyes of a stranger and question the necessity of everything that is done in the department.

5 Identify additional control areas and show how the controlling function is closely related to the other managerial functions.

Many organizations have specialists who concentrate on inventory control, quality control, and production control. These types of control systems usually are not under the direct authority of most departmental supervisors but are handled by staff specialists. Other managerial concepts, techniques, and approaches used by departmental supervisors contain aspects of the controlling function. Among these are MBO, use of standing plans, maintenance of discipline, and employee performance appraisal. Thus, controlling is intimately interrelated with all the other managerial functions.

KEY TERMS

Accounting (page 597)
Income statement (page 598)
Sales (page 598)
Net income (page 598)
Expenses (page 598)
Cost of goods sold (page 598)
Balance sheet (page 598)
Assets (page 599)
Liabilities (page 599)

Owners' equity (page 599)
Statement of cash flows (page 601)
Horizontal analysis (page 603)
Vertical analysis (page 603)
Budget (page 606)
Operating budget (page 606)
Incremental budgeting (page 608)
Zero-base budgeting (page 608)

QUESTIONS FOR DISCUSSION

1. Define and discuss the importance of the following to supervisors:
    a. Account numbers and titles
    b. Income statement
    c. Balance sheet
    d. Statement of cash flows

2. Identify the major components of the balance sheet and income statement and explain the purpose of each component.

3. Explain the purposes of the statement of cash flows.

4. Financial ratios can be categorized into four basic categories. Identify these categories and identify specific ratios in each.

5. Why can a budget be described as a "projected financial statement"?

6. What is meant by zero-base budgeting? How realistic is this approach in today's operating environment?

7. To what degree should supervisors be permitted to participate in the budget-making process? Employees? Discuss.

8. Discuss the supervisor's duty to take appropriate action when accounting reports indicate that actual expenditures are significantly above or below budget allocations.

9. Why should cost consciousness be of major concern to a supervisor?

10. How should effective supervisors develop cost-reduction strategies?

SKILLS APPLICATIONS

Skills Application 22-1: Income Statement Analysis

The Utopia Toy Company prepared the following comparative income statements for the years ended December 31, 1993 and 1994:

UTOPIA TOY COMPANY
Comparative Income Statements
For Years Ended December 31, 1993 and 1994

	1994		1993	
	Amount	Percent	Amount	Percent
Sales	$367,650	100	$350,250	100
Sales Returns	(23,000)	6.3	(25,000)	7.1
Sales (net)	$344,650	93.7	$325,250	92.9
Cost of goods sold	(192,450)	53.3	(178,000)	50.8
Gross profit	$152,200	41.4	$147,250	42.0
Selling expenses	(38,675)	10.5	(37,250)	10.6
General expenses	(46,150)	12.6	(56,500)	16.1
Operating income	$ 67,375	18.3	$ 53,500	15.3
Interest expense	(5,775)	1.6	(2,000)	0.6
Income before income taxes	$ 61,600	16.8	$ 51,500	14.7
Income tax expense	(30,800)	8.4	(25,750)	7.4
Net Income	$ 30,800	8.4	$ 25,750	7.4

1. What are the advantages of showing values for various items on Utopia's income statement in percentages based upon sales?

2. To what do you attribute Utopia's increase in net income in 1994?

3. What financial ratios would you use to understand whether or not Utopia Toy Company is really successful? Why would you use those rather than others?

4. Suppose that Utopia's top-level managers want to increase net income to 10 percent of sales next year. If you were a supervisor at Utopia, what specific recommendations would you make to help achieve the objective? Why?

5. Compare your responses with those of another student. What similarities exist in your responses?

6. (Optional assignment) Calculate appropriate financial ratios to demonstrate the financial condition of Utopia Toy Company.

7. (Optional assignment) Visit the library and secure comparable information on toy retailers. How does Utopia compare?

Skills Application 22-2: Preparing Budgets

Budgets are both planning and controlling tools. They help managers and supervisors determine the best use of available funds and control spending.

1. Identify and list your major expense categories—for example, tuition, books and supplies, transportation, lodging, food, and the like.

2. Estimate your expenditures in each of these categories for the next three months.

3. Identify your sources of revenue for the next three months.

4. Will you need to secure additional sources of cash or reduce expenses? Why or why not?

5. Keep a log of revenue and expenses for the next three months.

    a. How accurate do you expect your budget to be?

    b. Why might deviations occur?

6. Compare your budget categories with those of another student. Did you fail to include some possible expenses? If so, why?

Skills Application 22-3: Cost-Cutting Exercise

Assume that your college tuition has increased dramatically over the past years. You have just been elected president of the student body or to membership on the governing board. Students are concerned about the increasing costs of higher education.

1. Design a cost-consciousness program to instill in members of the academic community the need to minimize costs.

2. Assume that your college needs to reduce costs by 15 percent over the next two years. You are asked to advise the president on areas where costs can be reduced. What would be your recommendations?

3. Compare your responses with those of another student. What are areas of similarity? Differences? Why?

ENDNOTES

Professor David Gotlob, assistant professor of accounting, Indiana University-Purdue University at Fort Wayne, aided in the development of the financial data for David's Gift Shoppe. He also collaborated with the authors in the development of the Skills Applications for this chapter.

1. Jill Andresky Fraser, "Financial Strategies: Accounting—Penny Wise," *Inc.* (September 1993), p. 40.

2. Beth Brophy, "Nice Guys (and Workshops) Finish First," *U.S. News and World Report* (August 22, 1988), p. 44.

3. See Timothy L. O'Brien, "Company Wins Workers' Loyalty by Opening Its Books," *The Wall Street Journal* (December 20, 1993), pp. B1, B2. Financial information provided by Springfield Remanufacturing Company Vice President Thomas R. Samsel (telephone interview, May 10, 1994). Some companies are providing training in accounting and financial concepts to all their employees so that they may better understand how their individual and departmental decisions affect profitability. See Willard I. Zangwill, "Focusing All Eyes on the Bottom Line," *The Wall Street Journal* (March 21, 1994), p. A12.

4. Basic discussions of horizontal analysis, common-size financial statements, and financial ratios are provided in most accounting textbooks. For detailed information, see Chapter 16, "Financial Reporting and Analysis in Perspective," in Michael H. Granof, Philip W. Bell, and Bruce R. Neumann, *Accounting for Managers and Investors* (Englewood Cliffs, N.J.: Prentice-Hall, 1993).

5. For a brief overview of the cash budget, see Marilyn A. Schwartz, "Cash Budgeting," *National Public Accountant* (December 1991), pp. 6, 23. For a broader discussion of the problems, benefits, and complexities of the budgeting process, see Glenn A. Welsch, Ronald W. Hilton, and Paul N. Gordon, *Budgeting: Profit Planning and Control* (Englewood Cliffs, N.J.: Prentice-Hall, 1988) or Douglas Gorbutt, *How to Budget and Control Cash* (Brookfield, Vt.: Gower, 1985).

6. For additional discussion of zero-base budgeting, see Charles T. Horngren and George Foster, *Cost Accounting: A Managerial Emphasis* (6th ed.; Englewood Cliffs, N.J.: Prentice-Hall, 1987), pp. 382–383; or Robert Anthony and James Reece, *Accounting* (8th ed.; Homewood, Ill.: Richard D. Irwin, 1989), pp. 896–897.

CASE 6-1
Sanders Supermarkets Store #16:
What Happened to Control?

Juan Sanchez was store supervisor at Store #16 of Sanders Supermarkets. For about three months he had been talking to his district manager, Sandra Greenberg, about a major renovation for the grocery section in the store. At last, Greenberg called Sanchez to tell him that a meeting at the corporate main office would be held to discuss the renovation project for Store #16.

The meeting was attended by supervisors from the sales department and the construction department, several district managers, and the corporate operations manager. By the end of the meeting, it was generally agreed that Store #16 should be reorganized (called "reset" in the language of the company), including relocating several main aisles. The supervisor of the reset crew and the construction supervisor were to submit final plans and a cost estimate at the next meeting of the group, which was scheduled for a week later.

During her next visit to Store #16, Greenberg told Sanchez about the meeting. Greenberg informed Sanchez about the plans for Store #16, although she added that nothing was finalized yet. She failed to mention that part of the reset would include moving some of the aisles.

The next week, completed plans and costs were submitted to and given a final approval by the corporate operations manager. Since new shelving had to be ordered and schedules made, the supervisor of the reset crew and the construction supervisor were assigned the job of putting the necessary paperwork into motion. Greenberg then called Sanchez and said, "The reset project for your store has been okayed. I'll let you know more as soon as I hear."

One month later, as Sanchez was driving to work, he made a mental note to call Greenberg to ask about the reset project. However, when Sanchez arrived at Store #16, he soon forgot about this plan. He walked into the store to find three major problems: the frozen food case had broken down, the floor scrubber was malfunctioning, and the grinder in the meat department had quit working. After some checking, he found that no maintenance calls had been made, because each of his two assistant supervisors, Jane Oliver and Wally Withers, had thought the other was going to do it. The floor scrubber had not worked well for three days, the frozen food case had broken down the previous afternoon, and the meat grinder had just conked out.

"It just doesn't pay to take a day off," Sanchez muttered to himself as he headed for the telephone. He called the maintenance department, explained what had happened, and requested immediate service. While waiting for the maintenance person, Sanchez called Jane Oliver and Wally Withers to talk to them about letting him and each other know about these kinds of problems and how to control them. "All it takes," he said, "is working together, communication, and follow-through to ensure that our customers get the best service available. We can't be out of merchandise, especially frozen food. And we have to make sure that when we are busy, as we will be this week, our customers aren't stepping over workers in the aisles."

At about that time, Sanchez was called to his office. When he arrived, he was greeted by five carpenters and laborers. "We just wanted to tell you we're here, and we'll get started right away," said the carpenter in charge.

"How come it takes this many people to fix a frozen food case?" asked Sanchez.

"We're not here to fix a frozen food case," said the carpenter. "We're here to move the shelving in the aisles and to reset the store."

"Today?" replied Sanchez. "Nobody told me that you guys were doing this today. I can't have you moving aisles during the day. What are my customers going to do?"

Sanchez then called Greenberg. "Sandy, did you know that they were going to start the reset project in the store today?"

"No," said Sandy, "I wasn't notified either."

"Why wasn't I consulted on this?" exclaimed Sanchez. "First of all, the first week of the month is always too busy a time for laborers to be working in the aisles. Second, this type of work must be done at night. Maybe other stores can handle this in the daytime, but my customers will not tolerate that kind of inconvenience."

"OK," said Greenberg, "it sounds like things are really out of control at your store right now. What are you going to do about it?"

"Sandy, don't you mean, what are *we* going to do about it?"

Questions for Discussion

1.   Define various places where the managers did not plan in specific terms and then failed to follow through on their responsibilities.

2.   Analyze Juan Sanchez's discussion with his two assistants, especially when he said that "All it takes is working together, communication, and follow-through." Are these factors the essence of supervision, or does good supervision require something more? Discuss.

3.   What should Greenberg and Sanchez do in regard to the immediate problem of the carpenters in the store?

4.   Develop a series of general recommendations to improve planning and control procedures in the Sanders company.

CASE 6-2
Resistance to a Work Sampling Program

Debbie Quarter, a new staff engineer for the C. W. S. Manufacturing Company, had been assigned the responsibility of administering the plant's work sampling program. This was the first assignment of this nature in her career. Her only knowledge of the program until this time came in the form of comments from friends working as plant foremen or supervisors. She recalled that they referred to the work sampling program as "bird dogging." They seemed universally to regard the program as unfair, a waste of time, and a personal affront. She realized that only the line superintendents supported the program, and even some of them regarded it as a necessary evil.

Details of the Program

The work sampling program, or ratio-delay as it was sometimes called, involved the statistical sampling of the activities of hourly production and maintenance department employees, which included approximately two-thirds of the plant's 2,000 employees. The sampling was conducted on a continuous basis by a full-time observer who walked through the plant via a series of randomly selected, predetermined routes. The observer's job was to record the activity of each worker as the worker was first observed. An activity could fall into one of seven categories, which in turn were subclasses of either "working," "traveling," or "nonworking." The data were compiled monthly, and results were charted for each group and sent to the various supervisors and superintendents.

The program had been in effect for about five years at the plant. At the time it was initiated, management stated the purpose of the program as threefold: (1) It was to be used as an indication of supervisory effectiveness; (2) it was to be of help in identifying problems interfering with work performance; and (3) it was to be a control measure of the effect of changes in work methods, equipment, facilities, or supervision.

Meetings on the Program

Realizing the widespread resistance to the program, Debbie Quarter began immediately to conduct informational meetings for all line foremen and supervisors. In these sessions she discussed the purpose of the program and the mechanics of conducting it. She also attempted to answer any questions raised. The foremen and supervisors were most vocal in expressing their negative opinions about the program, and after a few meetings she noted that certain comments were being repeated in some form by almost every group.

Most supervisory groups identified some particular aspects of the sampling program that they thought biased its results against them. The most common complaint of this type was that the sampling was too often conducted during periods when work was normally lightest, that is, during coffee breaks and early or late in the day. Since the method of scheduling visits was quite complex, efforts to explain the concept of randomness and how fairness was ensured had never been accepted. Some basic statistical training had been attempted in the past but with little success—especially among the foremen who had traditionally come up through the ranks and had little technical background.

Another frequently repeated complaint was that activities normally considered as work were not recorded as such. Examples of this were going for tools or carrying materials. The reason for this, as had been explained to the foremen, was to allow identification of those factors not directly accomplishing work, since these were the areas where improvements could be made.

Several maintenance foremen complained that results were repeatedly used to pressure them to "ride" their workers. When they would tighten down, these foremen said, the workers would resist, and less was accomplished than before. One foreman quoted his boss as saying, "These figures (work sampling results) better be up next month, or I'm going to have three new foremen in here!" It was general knowledge that the superintendents placed quite a bit of emphasis on these results when appraising the supervisors and foremen.

Virtually no one at any level of supervision had a good understanding of how results could be affected by sample size. Small groups with few samples said they had experienced wide fluctuations in results that "just couldn't happen." This, of course, reinforced their distrust of sampling methods.

There had been few, if any, changes initiated by first-line supervisors as a result of work sampling results. Several staff projects had been generated—some of which were quite popular with the workers (for example, motorized personnel carriers)—but these were not generally associated with work sampling results.

After the first few sessions, Debbie Quarter wondered whether her meetings with the foremen and supervisors were perhaps doing more harm than good. The meetings seemed to get everyone upset, and anything that was learned was probably lost in the emotional discussion. She pondered what she should do next.

Questions for Discussion

1. Evaluate the work sampling program as described in this case.
2. Evaluate the work sampling program in view of the principles of a sound control system as outlined in Chapter 21.
3. Outline a course of action for Debbie Quarter.

CASE 6-3
Who's Telling the Truth about Quality Control?

Bartholomew Equipment Co. was a major manufacturer of complex electronic data processing equipment. The company had very strict delivery schedules, which had to be kept in order to preserve its good image with its customers. Currently, the company was involved in designing an extremely high-cost computer with specific data characteristics, which was to be submitted to one of Bartholomew's largest customers, the Kee Corporation.

Preparation of the Data Package

The project manager for the company, Ray Edwards, was responsible for gathering all the necessary data that would be incorporated into the final design data packages for various computers. Edwards had an engineer, Stan Neil, to whom he had assigned major responsibility for the Kee project. Neil had been with the company for only six months, but he had steadily gained knowledge of data packages and had carefully tried to understand what was required.

During the collection of various data, representatives of the Kee Corporation visited the Bartholomew plant to check on the progress of the data package. The representatives held meetings with Neil and Edwards, explaining what they wanted and various changes they required. Neil believed that these meetings had developed the full requirements for this customer's data package.

Inspection by Quality Control

Neil continued to gather the data in a timely manner. The deadline was drawing near, and some items were not complete. He felt that a major obstacle to completion on time could be the quality control department, which had the reputation of having been unable to meet scheduled inspection deadlines on other projects. To get the quality control people to recognize the urgency for meeting deadlines on the Kee project, he thought it might be beneficial to provide them with a portion of the data package that was already complete. He went to the quality control department to meet with Rebecca Chang, one of the inspectors. Chang accepted the drawings and data after being informed of the urgent requirements for the package. Chang said she would do all she could to expedite the matter.

Conflict Between the Departments

Neil went back to Edwards and told him that the quality control department would be entirely too slow in doing its work. He stated, "Rebecca Chang wants us to do work that the customer has not said is necessary. We'll never meet the delivery date if she continues to delay the inspection and approval of the data package!"

Edwards, who had not had a good working relationship with the quality control people in the past, took Neil at his word. Edwards complained to the company president about quality control's position and slow work. As a result, the company president, Marcus Finley, decided to call a meeting with Edwards, Neil, and Vic Johnson, the supervisor of the quality control department. These three people were notified to attend a meeting in Finley's office, although Finley did not inform them as to what the meeting would cover.

At the meeting, the trend of the conversation was directly aimed at quality control. Marcus Finley told Vic Johnson that his department was delaying the important Kee project, and this had to stop. Johnson became very defensive and told Finley, "I have no idea what is going on. I don't know who is responsible for this job or what the status of it is. You did not tell me what this meeting was going to cover. I feel very concerned about the way this meeting is being handled. I will not make any statements until I talk to my people about this job." At this point Johnson asked to be excused. He said he could be of more help after he had more of the facts.

Marcus Finley and Vic Johnson had a private meeting that afternoon. Finley apologized for the way the meeting was handled and asked Johnson to check into the problem.

Two days later, the Kee data package was approved by Rebecca Chang in quality control. However, Johnson sent a memo to Finley stating, "The engineering done on this data package was horrible." Johnson added that his department was not furnished the proper or complete drawings and data and that Edwards and Neil had been most uncooperative. He also mentioned Edwards and Neil specifically as having "very poor customer attitudes."

When Ray Edwards received a copy of this memo, he was beside himself. He considered whether he should write his own "poison pen" letter to tell his side of the story.

Questions for Discussion

1. Evaluate Neil's approach in trying to get the data package approved. Why did Neil report back to his manager, Ray Edwards, that the quality control department would hold up the project?

2. Evaluate whether Ray Edwards, the project manager for the company, was well advised to bring the president of the company into this problem situation. How might he have handled the situation otherwise?

3. Why would Vic Johnson send the memo to Finley complaining about the engineering on the data package and also complaining about Edwards and Neil? Was this a prudent move on his part?

4.   If you were Edwards, what would you do?

CASE 6-4
Intolerable Working Conditions

At 10:00 A.M., Dan Michaels, production supervisor of calcium phosphates at Monarch Chemical Company's Bromwich plant, received a phone call from Rose Stern, president of Local 35 of the National Chemical Workers Union. Stern requested that a meeting be set up immediately to include herself, Dan, and John Casten, a shift operator in the raw material preparation department of the plant.

The hourly workforce in this department had 80 workers who performed operating, packing, and manual labor jobs. The entire plant had undergone a series of automation projects that had reduced the number of required operating personnel by 33 percent in four years. The automation projects had created several air-conditioned control centers throughout the plant from which employees performed their new functions.

The Department Operation

The raw material preparation department (one of six major operating units) consisted of a five-story building composed of two operating sections and two control center areas. Its function was to receive the rock-like raw material, and by a series of crushing, mixing, heating, and adjusting steps, prepare this material in slurry form for use by the remaining production units in the plant. The department had been among the first to be automated, and the resultant job combinations reduced the staffing from two to one worker per shift.

It was the operator's duty to make sure all equipment and instruments were functioning properly, to run frequent checks on product quality, and to adjust the prepared raw material as required by these checks. In addition, the operator was required to spend at least 30 minutes per shift cleaning up the area; this was the only manual labor involved in the job. The operator was responsible for the entire five-story building and was the only person in the building. The operator was provided with an elevator and was to use telephone contact with a central plant shift foreman's office whenever troubles occurred in the area.

The job was generally pleasant except in the summer, when heat and humidity conditions often raised temperatures to 105 to 110 degrees in some areas. During periods of major breakdowns (about once every two weeks), severe dusting occurred for periods of up to an hour. This made it necessary for anyone working in the building to wear a dust mask in order to breathe without irritation. The building's control centers had not been air conditioned during the automation project, since it was felt that the operator's job required continual movement through the building.

The raw material used in the department had just been changed to one that cost 70 percent of the cost of the former material used. It was slightly harder to handle than the original raw material and involved use of more preparation equipment. The plant was set up to operate on an interim basis with this raw material. Plans were being formulated to install permanent handling facilities for the new raw material.

The Issue

The meeting of Rose Stern, Dan Michaels, and John Casten was held at 10:30 the following morning on the lower floor of the building. Casten opened the meeting, obviously upset, with the statement that the "dust, heat, and noise conditions of the fifth floor were intolerable," and that he felt that he and the other shift operators had a right to refuse to work under such conditions. A discussion was then conducted on each of these complaints.

With regard to dust conditions, Casten felt that there were several dust sources in the building. Another major dusting area was pointed out by Rose Stern. At this point, Dan Michaels stated that it was management's intention to install a dust-collecting device to control major dusting in this area within the next six weeks.

About the noise, the complaint was voiced by Casten that the equipment was extremely loud and annoying, and he felt the noise level could be harmful. Dan asked whether the noise was worse than in the past. Casten answered, "Yes, it sure is worse, especially on the fifth floor! Why don't you try it out for a while yourself?"

Concerning the heat, Casten stated that all the operators felt the heat on the fifth floor was excessive. He complained that the exhaust fans on that floor had not worked for several days, and that this had been reported to the shift foreman, but nothing had been done to fix the fans. Although the heat probably was no worse than at some occasions in the past, Casten felt it was a severe problem that had been "lived with, but just because the country boys put up with the heat for years is no reason I have to. I'm a city boy! Besides, times have changed, and I don't have to work in a 'sweat shop' anymore."

The meeting continued with further questions and discussion as to why this issue of working conditions had arisen at this time. John Casten said that the operators had gotten together and discussed their problems, and they felt that "all the other operating employees, with the exception of one other group, now have air-conditioned control centers in which to spend all or part of their time. Further, Monarch is going to save a lot of money in the next few years by using a different type of raw material, so why can't the raw material unit operators have an air-conditioned room built on the fifth floor in which to cool-off? Besides, we have plenty of time to spend in it."

The meeting then adjourned, with Dan Michaels promising to present management's answer to Rose Stern within a week. Six days later, Rose and Dan held another meeting on the subject. Dan stated that all the dust leaks had been fixed except the worst one on the third floor, which was scheduled to be completed soon.

A noise survey had indicated that no serious problem existed on the fifth floor. The exhaust fans had been fixed, and a heat survey would be taken during the summer months to determine whether a serious problem truly existed. Michaels further said that the plant's safety engineer had made several spot checks of the areas and the company's safety equipment (including ear plugs). The company was in compliance with federal (OSHA) and state safety standards. Stern replied that the raw material unit operators needed an air-conditioned room, and that if management would not give them one, the union would have to file a formal grievance and, if necessary, take it to arbitration in order to obtain one. Stern said that the problem was both a human needs and a safety issue. She cited a provision in the parties' labor-management agreement that included a statement to the effect that the company acknowledged its responsibility to provide safe working conditions in the plant consistent with the necessity for efficient operation.

The meeting adjourned with this statement. Dan Michaels pondered his next move.

Questions for Discussion

1. Do you feel that the union's complaint is a human needs and safety issue? Why or why not?

2. Was management wise in not providing an air-conditioned center for the raw material preparation department? Why or why not?

3. Define "intolerable working conditions." Why is this difficult to define and respond to?

4. Consider the alternatives open to Dan Michaels. Even ignoring cost factors involved in providing an air-conditioned room, what other problems might be associated with granting the union its request?

5. Do you feel that the union is likely to file a grievance and take it to arbitration if the company refuses to grant its request?

CASE 6-5
The Speedy Stock Clerk

Gary Powell, age 19, had recently been hired as a stock clerk for a major discount department store in an urban center. Powell was African-American, and this was his first full-time job after graduation from high school. He was excited about being hired, since he felt that the job offered potential for future advancement if he did good work in his entry-level position.

Powell was assigned to work from 11:00 P.M. to 7:00 A.M., the so-called "graveyard" shift, as part of a group of some six other stock clerks. These stock clerks reported to a supervisor, Sylvia Prater. They were responsible primarily for replenishing and arranging merchandise throughout the store.

One evening about three weeks after Gary Powell had begun his job, he asked if he could talk with Sylvia Prater in her office. "Sylvia," said Gary, "I'm really upset about what has happened the last few evenings on the job. I've had several of my fellow employees tell me that I was working too fast, filling too many of the store's aisles, and that I was making the rest of them look bad. One employee even told me that if I didn't slow down that 'something might happen' that I wouldn't like, especially if I kept on making the rest of the clerks look bad."

"Why that's terrible," replied Sylvia Prater. "Give me the names of the employees who talked to you in this fashion, and I'll put a stop to it immediately.

"Oh, I can't do that," replied Gary Powell, "because then I'm sure that no one would have anything to do with me. I'm the only black stock clerk, you know, and it's tough enough trying to be accepted by my fellow employees as it is without giving you names of the ones who have been pressuring me to slow down. In fact, I'm sort of worried about coming to you with this in the first place. If the word gets back to the rest of the group that I've complained to you, things may get worse rather than better."

Prater realized that she had a problem. Powell seemed to be a conscientious employee who was being pressured by his fellow clerks about his good work performance. Yet she realized that she would have to be very careful in how she approached the problem so as not to make it worse than it already was.

"Thank you, Gary, for coming to me with your concerns," said Sylvia Prater. "I'll think about it and see what I can do to straighten this problem out. In the meantime, Gary, keep working as you have been doing, the best you know how. And if someone says something to you again, just try to laugh it off and kid them about it rather than make an issue of it." With that, Gary Powell left Sylvia Prater's office.

Questions for Discussion

1. Should Gary Powell have told his supervisor his problem without being willing to reveal the names of the employees who were pressuring him? Discuss.
2. Evaluate the advice that Sylvia Prater gave to Gary Powell as to how he should handle the situation. What other advice might Prater have given to Powell in response to his complaint?
3. Outline a series of recommendations concerning how Sylvia Prater should approach the problem that has been presented to her by Gary Powell. Consider alternatives.

CASE 6-6
Long Lunch Periods and the Senior Employee

Ries Company was a food processor that sold its product lines throughout the United States. One of the company's six plants was located in a large midwestern city, and it produced four of the eight major Ries products. In addition, it served as a warehouse and distribution point for an area that included most of the central United States.

The materials handling and shipping department had the task of storing products manufactured in the plant, as well as creating temporary storage facilities for products imported from other plants. Because of somewhat limited space in the warehouse, the supervisors in this department were under constant pressure to make maximum use of available space. To accomplish this, the department was responsible for loading as many boxcars each day as required to meet the company's shipping and space necessities.

The Supervisor's Problem

Tanya Rube was hired by the Ries Company after she received a business administration degree from a midwestern university. She was working as a trainee foreman in the materials handling and shipping department in order to obtain experience at the "grass roots" of the company. She hoped to advance to a department head position either at this plant or at one of the other company plants.

Since Rube believed that her advancement would hinge on how well she performed at her present job, she was now grappling with a serious problem concerning her work group of 15 people. The workers had been leaving for their lunch periods from five to ten minutes early each day. This disturbed her because she had always been quite liberal in enforcing the time allowed for lunch. Although the union contract provided a paid 30-minute lunch period, Rube and the other shift supervisors had always allowed the workers an extra ten minutes. The supervisors figured that this extra time was needed by the workers to get to the lunch room from their workstations and back.

A quick investigation revealed that one of the older workers, Mike Lange, usually left for his lunch period 15 to 30 minutes early. Since the other employees (most of whom were younger) observed this, they thought that they could do the same.

Lange had been employed continuously by the Ries Company for 28 years. He started to work at the plant after graduating from high school. He unquestionably was the hardest working and most productive person in Rube's work group. Lange knew only one way to work—and that was to drive himself every minute he was on the job. He was very critical of most of the younger employees, often telling Rube that "the younger kids these days are lazy and would never have lasted in the old days."

Diana Royse, the director of human resources, told Rube of an incident that had taken place some years ago. In Lange's zest to complete a job in the shortest time possible, he drove his towmotor at rather reckless speeds around the warehouse. When the plant supervisor sternly reprimanded Lange about his work habits, Lange responded by organizing a work slowdown. As a result, everyone in the department worked at half speed for an entire week so that their output for that week was an all-time low in the department. The slowdown caused the warehouse to become so clogged that products from other plants could not be unloaded. This situation had brought considerable criticism from the home office.

From discussions with several older supervisors, Rube also learned that the slightest criticism could cause Mike Lange to become very upset. Lange invariably would state that "management didn't know how fortunate they were to have a person of his abilities still around."

The Supervisor's Alternatives

Rube felt that the output of the average worker in the department was already below standards. If she tried to force Mike Lange to observe the proper time to leave for lunch, she might lose Lange's extraordinary productive ability. Furthermore, Rube did not wish to contend with a work slowdown that Lange might instigate again.

On the other hand, Rube could allow the lunch period situation to continue in order to avoid alienating anyone. This action, however, would mean the continued loss of considerable work time.

Could Rube appeal to the union? She thought this action might be futile because Lange's seniority placed him in a privileged class among the union membership.

Rube preferred not to discuss this problem with her department head, as this might imply that she could not handle the job. She pondered what to do.

Questions for Discussion

1. Identify the problems in this situation that have contributed to Tanya Rube's loss of control.

2. Should a showdown with Mike Lange take place at this point?

3. Is Rube's attitude of not wanting to discuss the situation with her department head understandable? Is it desirable under the circumstances?

4. What alternatives are open to Rube? What should she do?

CASE 6-7
The Airlines Have Their Ups and Downs

Speaking of the future of the megacarriers in the airlines business, one analyst bluntly states, "They have to change if they are to survive." Such a forecast is based not only on the fact that in the last three years American, United, and Delta Airlines have had losses totaling $10 billion, but also the emergence of new, leaner competitors. Revising operating plans that forecasted continued growth and prosperity, the major airlines now are planning some fairly radical new strategies in order to survive the coming changes.

Management–Union Conflicts

Possibly one of the key battles will be between management and its employees' unions. The airlines are seeking higher levels of productivity and changes in some of the unions' hard-earned rights that now may be too costly for the more mature airlines to bear. In fact, some airline executives are close to predicting the demise of their businesses unless labor costs are reduced and passenger miles increase. Both Delta and American began reducing their staffs in 1993, with Delta planning to reduce its pilot crews by 600 and American planning to lay off 500 pilots, 400 maintenance employees, and an unstated number of flight attendants. The furlough at Delta was the first in 35 years.

In response to the layoffs, Delta's pilots' group proposed an immediate 5 percent wage cut. The cut would be reversed after Delta had one year of operating profits, or when the union and Delta made proposals to reopen the current contract. The contract was scheduled to be negotiated on October 31, 1994. The union estimated that the cuts would be worth $90 million. In addition, the union offered to agree to proposed revisions to vacation and health benefits. In exchange, union negotiators asked for revisions to their contract's job security provisions, expanded jumpseat rights, and modifications to crew-scheduling practices. Delta management shunned the offer, however, stating that the pilots were not accepting the same level of concessions made by every other employee group, including management. Delta's only union is the one that represents its pilots.

In addition to these cost-cutting efforts, Delta is to return two leased McDonnell Douglas MD-11 airplanes used to provide nonstop service between Los Angeles and Tokyo. The reason is that the McDonnell Douglas airplanes use General Electric powerplants rather than the Pratt & Whitney PW4000 engines that power the Delta-owned MD-11s. This difference required Delta to maintain a separate set of spare parts and tooling. Delta will, however, take delivery of two McDonnell Douglas MD-11s and will continue to offer all of its trans-Pacific flights.

Increased Competition

The second threat to the major airlines is tougher competition from the reemerging second-tier carriers. Flight attendants and mechanics at Northwest Airlines agreed to accept stock ownership for concessions. USAir's merger with British Airways has improved its cash position. Continental Airlines, after only recently emerging from bankruptcy, has the lowest seat-mile cost among the majors. In the words of Candace Browning, first vice-president, Merrill Lynch, "Threatened by low-cost competition and a changed marketplace, megacarriers are in danger of becoming corporate dinosaurs." She goes on to say that the megacarriers will adapt to the ever-changing deregulated airline environment without the help of the unions. Toward that end, Stephen M. Wolf, chairman and chief executive officer of United Airlines, predicted, "We can expect more change in the next two to three years than we have experienced in the last 15. The right way would be to join together to find ways of reducing costs."

Other than the actions just mentioned, the airlines have begun to take several other steps to stop their money drains. The three major carriers have deferred delivery of 371 aircraft. Delta and American have grounded approximately 56 airplanes and deemphasized short-haul flying, where they cannot be competitive with low-cost operators. They are also reviewing the possibility of selling some airline-owned operations and evaluating outside contracts for food, cabin, and maintenance services.

With these and other cost-controlling measures, can the major airlines reorganize and survive? According to Alan R. Bender, assistant professor of aeronautical science at Embry-Riddle Aeronautical University, "Major U.S. carriers are still wasteful and inefficient, overcharging for ineffectual service and amenities in order to subsidize outmoded labor, management, and operating practices. The U.S. airline industry is one of the U.S.'s last corporate vestiges of union sloth and management complacency and incompetence." He concludes that "in the 1990's David may defeat the Goliaths; there is already some evidence that upstarts like Kiwi International have learned the hard lessons of the early 1980's. The big boys, on the other hand, apparently have learned next to nothing as they slash payrolls, fleets, and routes willy-nilly rather than face their only viable long-term solution: restructure from the ground up."

References

Alan R. Bender, "Majors' Inefficiency May Benefit Upstarts," *Aviation Week & Space Technology* (June 14, 1993), p. 97.

"Don't Bury the Airlines," *Newsweek* (May 24, 1993), p. 44.

"Maintenance Charges Bare Labor Strife at USAir," *Aviation Week & Space Technology* (April 5, 1993), p. 22.

James T. McKenna, "Delta, Pilots Union Concession Talks Stalled," *Aviation Week & Space Technology* (May 10, 1993), p. 34.

James Ott, "Airlines Fight Labor for Survival," *Aviation Week & Space Technology* (April 5, 1993), pp. 20–21.

James Ott, "Big Three Seek Loan Guarantees; Northwest Eyes Tax Relief," *Aviation Week & Space Technology* (April 5, 1993), pp. 21–22.

James Ott, "New Market Reshapes Embattled Big Three," *Aviation Week & Space Technology* (May 10, 1993), pp. 31–32.

Anthony L. Velocci, Jr., "Capital Crunch May Stall Airline Fleet Upgrades," *Aviation Week & Space Technology* (May 31, 1993), pp. 92–94.

Questions for Discussion

1. What indications do the airlines have that they need to employ the controlling function?

2. What types of controls have Delta and other airlines employed?

3. Do you think that the controls that have been employed are forward looking or short-term stopgap measures? Explain.

4. Do you think that more attention to one or more of the other managerial functions could have reduced the necessity for some of the controlling actions that are now being taken? If so, which ones? Explain.

Appendix I

Partial

Listing of

Federal

Employment

Legislation

That Impacts

Supervisors

1992 *Family and Medical Leave Act.* Provides for up to 12 weeks of unpaid leave for certain personal and family health-related circumstances.

1991 *Civil Rights Act.* Amended five existing civil rights laws to extend their coverage and protection in employment situations. Increased damage awards to victims of discrimination up to $300,000 for corporations with over 500 employees. Reversed or responded to nine Supreme Court decisions.

1990 *Americans with Disabilities Act (ADA).* Prohibits discrimination based on physical or mental disabilities in places of employment and public accommodation. Modeled after the Rehabilitation Act of 1973 but applies to state and local governments, employment agencies, and labor unions, as well as private employers with 15 or more employees. In effect, employment discrimination is prohibited against "qualified individuals with disabilities."

1988 *Worker Adjustment and Retraining Act (WARN).* Requires firms employing 100 or more workers to provide 60 days advance notice to employees before shutting down or conducting substantial layoffs.

1988 *Drug-Free Workplace Act.* Requires companies receiving $25,000 or more in federal contracts to maintain a "drug-free workplace," including establishing and communicating policies to achieve this objective.

1988 *Employee Polygraph Protection Act.* Prohibits use of the lie detector in most employment decisions.

1986 *Consolidated Omnibus Budget Reconciliation Act (COBRA).* Requires that employers with more than 20 employees offer continuation of health care coverage for 18 to 36 months after an employee is fired, quits, or is laid off. Amended in 1989.

1978 *Civil Service Reform Act (Title VII).* Provides representation and collective bargaining rights to federal government employees.

1978 *Pregnancy Discrimination Act.* Requires employers to treat pregnancy, childbirth, or related medical conditions the same as any other medical disability.

1974 *Vietnam Era Veterans Readjustment Assistance Act.* Requires affirmative action among federal subcontractors for military veterans.

1974 *Employment Retirement Income Security Act (ERISA), as amended.* Covers most pension benefit plans of private employers; provides for vesting of pension benefits after certain years of service.

1973 *Rehabilitation Act, Section 503.* Prohibits job discrimination because of a disability. Employers holding $2,500 or more in federal contracts or subcontracts must set up affirmative action program. Enforced by Office of Federal Contract Compliance Programs (OFCCP).

1972 *Equal Employment Opportunity Act.* Extended coverage of Title VII of the Civil Rights Act to government employees, local employers, and educational institutions.

1970 *Occupational Safety and Health Act (OSHA).* Designed to protect the safety and health of employees. Employers are responsible for providing workplaces free from safety and health hazards. Created Occupational Safety and Health Administration to carry out provisions of the Act.

1967 *Age Discrimination in Employment Act, as amended.* Prohibits discrimination in employment on the basis of age to most employees over age 40.

1964 *Title VII of the Civil Rights Act, as amended.* Prohibits discrimination in hiring, promotion, discharge, pay, benefits, and other aspects of employment on the basis of race, color, religion, sex, or national origin. Equal Employment Opportunity Commission (EEOC) has authority to bring lawsuits against employers in the federal courts.

1963 *Equal Pay Act.* Requires equal payment of wages to women and men who perform substantially equal work.

1947 *Labor Management Relations Act (Taft-Hartley).* Amended the National Labor Relations Act (Wagner Act); specified unfair labor union practices, provided for Federal Mediation and Conciliation Service (FMCS) to assist in resolving labor-management disputes, and more clearly identified requirements for bargaining in good faith.

1938 *Fair Labor Standards Act (FLSA) as amended.* Established that employers covered by Act must pay an employee (1) at least a minimum wage, and (2) time and a half for all hours worked in excess of 40 in a given week. Classified a person working in a job that is not subject to the provisions of the Act as "exempt" from the overtime pay provisions. Most supervisors, professional staff, and outside salespersons fall in this category.

1935 *National Labor Relations Act (Wagner Act).* Gave workers the right to unionize and bargain collectively over hours, wages, and other terms and conditions of employment. Specified five unfair management practices. Created National Labor Relations Board (NLRB) to (1) certify labor unions as the sole bargaining representative of employees and (2) investigate unfair labor practices.

1935 *Social Security Act, as amended.* Provided for old age and survivors insurance (pensions) and later established medical/hospitalization insurance for elderly.

As discussed in Chapter 5, The Managerial Grid proposed five different styles of leadership. Figures II-1 and II-2 present the 1991 modifications.

FIGURE II-1
Seven Leadership
Styles

1,1   **Impoverished management,** often referred to as laissez-faire leadership. Leaders in this position have little concern for people or productivity, avoid taking sides, and stay out of conflicts. They do just enough to get by.

1,9   **Country Club management.** Managers in this position have great concern for people and little concern for production. They try to avoid conflicts and concentrate on being well liked. To them the task is less important than good interpersonal relations. Their goal is to keep people happy. (This is a soft Theory X approach and not a sound human relations approach.)

9,1   **Authority-Obedience.** Managers in this position have great concern for production and little concern for people. They desire tight control in order to get tasks done efficiently. They consider creativity and human relations to be unnecessary.

5,5   **Organization Man management,** often termed middle-of-the-road leadership. Leaders in this position have medium concern for people and production. They attempt to balance their concern for both people and production, but are not committed to either.

9+9   **Paternalistic "father knows best" management,** a style in which reward is promised for compliance and punishment threatened for non-compliance.

Opp   **Opportunistic "what's in it for me" management,** in which the style utilized depends on which style the leader feels will return him or her the greatest self-benefit.

9,9   **Team management.** This style of leadership is considered to be ideal. Such managers have great concern for both people and production. They work to motivate employees to reach their highest levels of accomplishment. They are flexible and responsive to change, and they understand the need to change.

Source: Robert R. Blake and Jane S. Mouton. *The Managerial Grid III* (Houston: Gulf Publishing Company, copyright © 1985), chaps. 1–7 as modified here. Reproduced by permission of the owners.

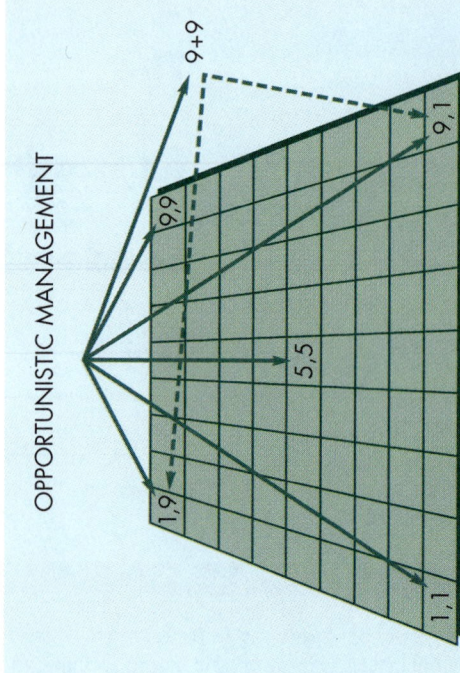

OPPORTUNISTIC MANAGEMENT

In opportunistic management organization performance occurs according to a system of exchanges, whereby effort is given only for an equivalent measure of the same. People adapt to the situation to gain maximum advantage of it.

FIGURE II-3

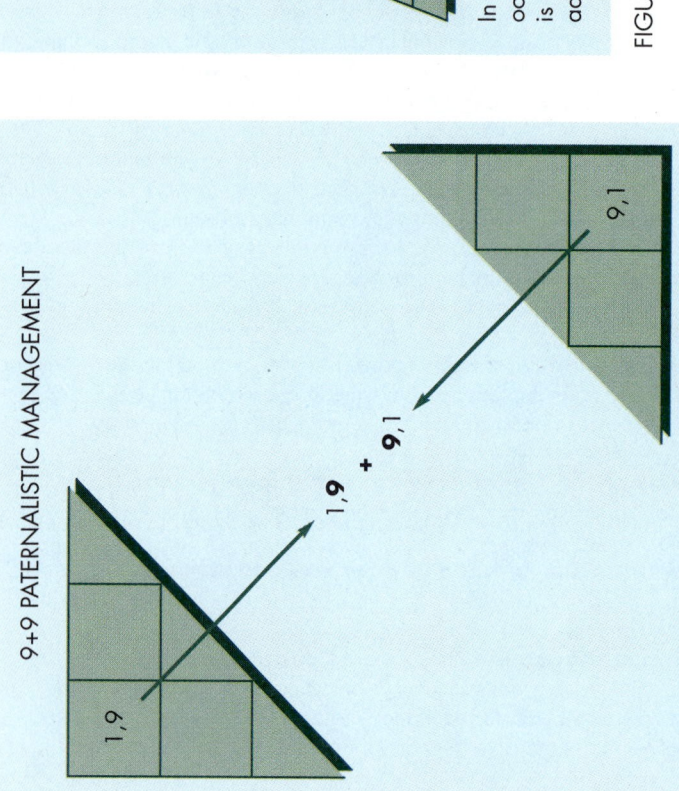

9+9 PATERNALISTIC MANAGEMENT

In 9+9 paternalistic management, reward and approval are granted to people in return for loyalty and obedience; failure to comply leads to punishment.

Source: The Paternalistic Figure from *Leadership Dilemmas—Grid Solutions*, by Robert R. Blake and Anne Adams McCanse, Houston: Gulf Publishing Company, p. 30. Copyright © 1991, by Scientific Methods, Inc. Reproduced by permission of the owners.

FIGURE II-2   Paternalistic Management

A

Ability An employee's potential to perform assigned tasks. (page 378)

Acceptance theory of authority Theory that holds that the manager only possesses authority when the employee accepts it. (page 81)

Accountability The expectation that employees will accept credit or blame for the results achieved in performing assigned tasks. (page 84)

Accounting The system of recording, classifying, summarizing, and interpreting financial data for use in decision making. (page 597)

Administrative skills The ability to plan, organize, and coordinate activities. (page 32)

Alternative dispute resolution (ADR) Approach for processing and deciding employee complaints internally as an alternative to filing a lawsuit, usually for disputes involving discipline or discharge. (page 540)

Arbitrator Person selected by the union and management to render a final and binding decision concerning a grievance. (page 310)

Assets The resources owned by a firm, such as cash, accounts receivable, inventory, land, and equipment. (page 599)

Attitude survey Survey of employee opinions about major aspects of organizational life used to assess morale. (page 472)

Authority The legitimate right to lead others. (page 39)

Autocratic supervision The supervisory style that relies on formal authority, threats, pressure, and close control. (page 94)

B

Balance sheet Statement of a firm's financial condition at a certain point in time. (page 598)

Benchmarking The process of identifying and improving upon the practices of the leaders. (page 173)

Biological needs The basic physical needs, such as food, rest, shelter, and recreation. (page 107)

Body language All observable actions of either the sender or the receiver. (page 59)

Brainstorming A free flow of ideas within a group, while suspending judgment, aimed at developing many alternative solutions to a problem. (page 153)

Budget A financial plan that projects expected revenues and expenditures during a stated period of time. (pages 186, 606)

C

Cafeteria (flexible) benefit plan System that allows employees some choice in determining their benefits. (page 384)

Centralized authority The organizational approach to delegation that places most decision-making responsibility with upper-level managers. (page 88)

Coaching The frequent activity of the supervisor to provide employees with information, instruction, and suggestions relating to their job assignments and performance. (page 410)

Command group Grouping of employees according to authority relationships on the formal organization chart. (page 456)

Committee Group of people drawn together to solve a problem or complete a task. (page 286)

Communication The process of transmitting information and understanding. (page 52)

Comparable worth Concept that jobs should be paid at the same level if they require similar skills or abilities. (page 492)

Complaint Any individual or group problem or dissatisfaction that employees can channel upward to management, including discrimination complaints. (page 537)

Complaint procedure A management-designed series of steps for handling employee complaints that usually provides for a number of appeals before a final decision. (page 538)

Conceptual skills The ability to obtain, interpret, and apply information. (page 32)

Concurrent control Corrective action taken during the production or delivery process to ensure that standards are being met. (page 578)

Contingency-style leadership Models that hold that no one leadership style is best; the appropriate style depends on the situation. (page 119)

Contract employees Workers supplied by an external agency for a specified period of time and for a fee. (page 17)

Controlling The management function aimed at determining whether actual performance conforms to expected standards and taking corrective action when it does not conform. (pages 37, 576)

Cooperation The willingness of individuals to work with and help one another. (page 42)

Coordination The synchronization of employees' efforts and the organization's resources toward achieving goals. (page 42)

Corporate culture Set of shared purposes, values, and beliefs that employees hold about their organization. (page 18)

Cost of goods sold The sum of all product-related expenses, such as acquiring, transporting, and packaging an item sold. (page 598)

Counseling interview Nondirective interview during which the supervisor listens empathetically and encourages the employee to discuss problems openly and develop solutions. (page 465)

Critical path The path of activities in the PERT network that will take the longest time to complete. (page 190)

D

Decentralized authority The organizational approach to delegation that disperses authority and decision making to the lowest feasible level in the organization. (page 88)

Decision criteria Standards to use in evaluating alternatives. (page 151)

Decision making Making a choice between two or more alternatives. (page 146)

Decision-making process A systematic, step-by-step process to aid in choosing the best alternative. (page 149)

Decisional meeting People gathered together to make decisions on a particular problem or task for which the group has been granted decision-making authority. (page 284)

Delegation The process of entrusting duties and related authority to subordinates. (page 41)

Department An organizational unit for which a supervisor has responsibility and authority. (page 243)

Departmentation The process of grouping activities and people into distinct organizational units. (page 243)

Directive The communications approach by which a supervisor conveys to employees what, how, and why something is to be accomplished. (page 433)

Directive interview Interview approach in which the interviewer guides the discussion along a predetermined course. (page 347)

Discipline State of orderliness; that is, the degree to which employees act according to expected standards of behavior. (page 509)

Discipline without punishment Disciplinary approach that uses coaching and counseling as preliminary steps and a paid decision-making leave for employees to decide whether to improve and stay, or quit. (page 528)

Discussional meeting People gathered together to participate in a discussion with the group leader by offering their opinions, suggestions, or recommendations. (page 284)

Diversity The cultural, ethnic, gender, age, educational level, racial, and life-style differences among employees. (page 10)

Division of work (specialization) Dividing work into smaller components and specialized tasks to improve efficiency and output. (page 243)

Documentation Keeping records of memoranda, documents, and meetings that are relevant to a disciplinary action. (page 527)

Downsizing (restructuring, rightsizing) Large-scale reduction and elimination of jobs in a company that usually results in reduction of middle-level managers, removal of organizational levels, and a widened span of management for remaining supervisors. (page 255)

E

Employee assistance program (EAP) Company program to assist employees with certain personal or work-related problems that are interfering with job performance. (page 468)

Employment-at-will Legal concept that employers can dismiss employees at any time and for any reasons, except unlawful discrimination or contractual or other restrictions. (page 523)

Empowerment Giving employees the authority and responsibility to accomplish organizational objectives. (page 20)

Exception principle Concept that supervisors should concentrate their investigations on activities that deviate substantially from the standard. (page 589)

Exit interview Interview with individuals who leave a firm to assess morale and reasons for employee turnover. (page 472)

Expectancy theory Theory of motivation that holds that employees will perform better if they believe such efforts will lead to desired rewards. (page 112)

Expenses Costs incurred by the business. (page 598)

External stressors Causes of stress that arise from outside the individual, such as job pressures, responsibilities, and work itself. (page 213)

F

Feedback control Action taken after the activity, product, or service has been completed to prevent future problems. (page 579)

Feedback The receiver's verbal or nonverbal response to a message. (page 66)

Feedforward control Anticipatory action taken to ensure that problems do not occur. (page 578)

Filtering The process of omitting or softening unpleasant details. (page 64)

Flextime Policy that allows employees to choose their work hours within stated limits. (page 12)

Forecasts Predictions of future events. (page 200)

Friendship group Informal grouping of employees based on similar personalities and social interests. (page 457)

Functional approach School of management thought that asserts that managers apply various functions in doing their jobs, e.g., planning, organizing, staffing, leading, and controlling. (page 8)

Functional authority The right granted to specialized staff people to give directives concerning matters within their expertise. (page 251)

G

Gain-sharing plans Group incentive plans that have employees share in the benefits from improved performance. (page 382)

Gantt chart A graphic scheduling technique that shows the activity to be scheduled on the vertical axis and necessary completion dates on the horizontal axis. (page 188)

General supervision The style of supervision in which the supervisor sets goals and limits but allows employees to decide how to achieve the goals. (page 92)

Glass ceiling Invisible barrier that limits advancement of women and minorities. (page 14)

Glass walls Invisible barriers that compartmentalize or segregate women and minorities into certain occupational classes. (page 14)

Grapevine The informal, unofficial communication channel. (page 56)

Grievance A formal complaint presented by the union to

management that alleges a violation of the labor agreement. (pages 310, 538)

Grievance procedure Negotiated series of steps in a labor agreement for processing grievances, beginning at the supervisory level and ending with arbitration. (page 538)

Groupthink Phenomenon that occurs in meetings when group members do not express dissenting views in order to avoid conflict rather than realistically appraise alternatives. (page 286)

H

Halo effect The tendency to allow one favorable aspect of a person's behavior to positively influence judgment on all other aspects. (page 356)

Hawthorne effect The mere fact that interest is shown in people causes them to behave differently. (page 9)

Hawthorne Studies Comprehensive research studies that focused on work-group dynamics as related to employee attitudes and productivity. (page 457)

Hierarchy of needs (Maslow) Maslow's theory of motivation, which suggests that employee needs are arranged in priority order such that lower-order needs must be satisfied before higher-order needs become motivating. (page 106)

Horizontal analysis Financial analysis that compares financial statements over time to uncover trends. (page 603)

Horns effect The tendency to allow one negative aspect of a person's behavior to negatively influence judgment on all other aspects. (page 356)

Hot stove rule Guideline for applying discipline analogous to touching a hot stove: advance warning and consequences that are immediate, consistent, and applied with impersonality. (page 524)

Human relations movement/behavioral science approach Approach to management that focuses on the behavior of people in the work environment. (page 9)

Human relations skills The ability to work with and through people. (page 32)

Human resources management (HRM) Organizational philosophies, policies, and practices that strive for the effective use of employees. (page 338)

Hygiene factors Elements in the work environment that, if positive, reduce dissatisfaction but do not tend to motivate. (page 111)

I

Income statement The firm's financial summary of income, expenses, and profit or loss over a stated period of time. (page 598)

Incremental budgeting A technique for making revenue and expense projections based on previous history. (page 608)

Informal organization Informal groupings of people, apart from the formal organization structure, that satisfy members' social needs. (page 274)

Informational meeting People gathered together to hear the group leader present information. (page 283)

Innovative duties Creative activities aimed at finding a better way to do something. (page 215)

Intangible standards Standards for performance results that are difficult to measure and often relate to human characteristics (e.g., attitude, morale, satisfaction, etc.). (page 584)

Internal stressors Pressures that people put on themselves, such as feeling a need to be perfect. (page 213)

ISO 9000 A rigorous series of quality standards created by the International Organization for Standardization. (page 174)

J

Jargon The use of words that are peculiar to a particular occupation or specialty. (page 62)

Job description Written description of the principal duties of a job. (page 272)

Job enlargement Increasing the number of tasks an individual performs. (page 120)

Job enrichment Job design that helps fulfill employees' high-level needs by giving them more challenging tasks and more decision-making responsibility for their jobs. (page 120)

Job evaluation The formal process of determining the relative worth of a job. (page 380)

Job rotation The process of switching job tasks among employees in the work group. (page 120)

Job sharing Policy that allows two or more employees to perform a job normally done by one full-time employee. (page 12)

Job specification Written description of the personal qualifications necessary to perform a job adequately. (page 272)

Just cause Standard for disciplinary action requiring tests of fairness and elements of normal due process, such as proper notification, investigation, sufficient evidence, and a penalty commensurate with the nature of the infraction. (page 514)

Just-in-time (JIT) inventory control system A system for scheduling materials to arrive precisely when they are needed in the production process. (page 188)

K

Kanban Another name for a just-in-time inventory control system. (page 188)

L

Labor agreement Negotiated document between union and employer that covers terms and conditions of employment for the represented employees. (page 302)

Labor agreement negotiations The process of discussion and compromise among representatives from labor and management leading to an agreement governing wages, hours, and working conditions for union employees. (page 307)

Labor union Legally recognized organization that represents employees and negotiates and administers a labor agreement with an employer. (page 302)

Lead person Employee placed in charge of other employees who performs limited managerial functions but is not considered part of management. (page 241)

Leadership The ability to guide, influence, and motivate the opinions and actions of others toward the accomplishment of organizational objectives. (page 432)

Leading The managerial function of guiding employees toward accomplishing organizational objectives. (pages 36, 432)

Leniency error Supervisors give employees higher ratings than they deserve. (page 403)

Liabilities The organization's debts. (page 599)

Line authority The right to direct others and to require them to conform to decisions, policies, rules, and objectives. (page 248)

Line department Department whose responsibilities are directly related to making, selling, or distributing the company's product or service. (page 250)

Line-and-staff-type organizational structure Structure that combines line and staff departments. (page 250)

Line-type organizational structure A structure that consists entirely of line authority arrangements with a direct chain of authority relationships. (page 248)

M

Management Getting objectives accomplished with and through people. (page 34)

Management by objectives (MBO) A process in which the supervisor and employee jointly set the employee's objectives, and the employee receives rewards based on achievement of these objectives. (pages 124, 176)

Matrix-type organizational structure A hybrid structure in which regular functional departments co-exist with project teams made up of people from different departments. (page 253)

Mentoring The guiding of a newer employee by an experienced employee in areas concerning job and career. (page 370)

Merit The quality of an employee's job performance. (page 378)

Method A standing plan that details exactly how a single operation is to be performed. (page 184)

Morale A composite of feelings and attitudes that individuals and groups have toward their work, their environment, their supervisors, top-level management, and the organization. (page 462)

Motion study An analysis of work activities to determine how to make the job easier and quicker to do. (page 584)

Motivation A willingness to exert effort toward achieving a goal, stimulated by the effort's ability to fulfill an individual need. (page 106)

Motivation factors Elements intrinsic in the job that promote job performance. (page 111)

Motivation-hygiene theory Herzberg's theory that factors in the work environment only influence the degree of job dissatisfaction, while job content factors influence the amount of job satisfaction. (page 111)

N

Net income Profit after all expenses have been subtracted from sales. (page 598)

Networking Individuals or groups linked together by a commitment to shared purpose. (page 43)

Noise Obstacles that distort messages between people. (page 62)

Nondirective interview Interview approach in which the

interviewer asks open-ended questions that allow the applicant greater latitude in responding. (page 348)

Nonprogrammed decisions Solutions to unique problems that require judgment, intuition, and creativity. (page 148)

O

Ombudsman Staff person who serves as a neutral mediator in resolving conflicts on the job. (page 468)

Operating budget The projection of dollar allocations to various costs and expenses needed to run the business, based on expected revenue. (page 606)

Optimizing Selecting the best alternative. (page 155)

Organization Group structured by management to carry out designated functions and accomplish certain objectives. (page 238)

Organization chart Graphic portrayal of a company's authority and responsibility relationships. (page 270)

Organization manual Written description of the authority and responsibilities of managerial and supervisory positions as well as formal channels, major objectives, and policies and procedures. (page 272)

Organizational development (OD) Meetings with groups under the guidance of a neutral conference leader to solve problems that are hindering organizational effectiveness. (page 473)

Organizing Arranging and distributing work among members of the work group to accomplish the organization's goals. (pages 36, 238)

Orientation The process for smoothing the transition of new employees into the organization. (page 367)

Owners' equity The value of the owners' investment in the company. (page 599)

P

Participative management Supervisory approach that gives employees an active role in making decisions about their jobs. (pages 20, 123)

Pay for performance Compensation, other than base wages, that is given for achieving employee or corporate goals. (page 382)

Pay grade Grouping of jobs that are similar in requirements into a pay range. (page 381)

Peer evaluation The evaluation of an employee's performance by other employees of relatively equal rank. (page 394)

Performance appraisal A systematic assessment of how well employees are performing their jobs, and the communication of that assessment to them. (page 392)

Permanent (standing) committee Group that meets on a more or less permanent basis to deal with recurring issues or problems. (page 287)

Personal power Power derived from a person's skill, knowledge, or ability and how others perceive them. (page 83)

Personality The knowledge, attitudes, and attributes that combine to make up the unique human being. (page 104)

PERT activity A specific task to be accomplished. (page 189)

PERT event The beginning and/or ending of an activity. (page 189)

Planning Establishing objectives based on the current situation and forecasts of the future, and determining the actions needed to achieve the objectives. (pages 35, 167)

Policy A standing plan that serves as a guide to thinking in making decisions. (page 180)

Political skills The ability to understand how things get done outside of formal channels. (page 32)

Position power Power derived from the formal rank a person holds in the chain of command. (page 83)

Positive discipline Condition that exists when employees generally follow the rules and meet the standards of the organization. (page 509)

Positive self-discipline Employees regulating their own behavior out of self-interest and their normal desire to meet reasonable standards. (page 509)

Principle of compulsory staff advice (service) Situation in which supervisors are required by policy to consult with specialized staff before making certain types of decisions. (page 251)

Principle of organizational stability Principle that holds that no organization should become overly dependent upon one or several "indispensable" individuals. (page 246)

Procedure A standing plan that defines the sequence of activities to be performed to achieve objectives. (page 183)

Program A comprehensive single-use plan designed to accomplish the organization's objectives. (page 187)

Program evaluation and review technique (PERT) A flowchart for managing large projects, showing the necessary activities with estimates of the time needed to complete each activity and the sequential relationship among them. (page 188)

Programmed decisions Solutions to repetitive and routine problems provided by existing policies, procedures, rules, etc. (page 148)

Progressive discipline System of disciplinary action that increases the severity of the penalty with each offense. (page 518)

Project A single-use plan for accomplishing a specific nonrecurring activity. (page 187)

Protected-group employees Classes of employees who have been afforded certain legal protections in their employment situations. (page 482)

Q

Qualified disabled individual Defined by the Americans with Disabilities Act as someone with a disability who can perform the essential components of a job with or without reasonable accommodation. (page 493)

Quality-of-work-life (QWL) programs Management philosophy that enhances employee dignity, introduces cultural change, and provides opportunity for employee development. (page 124)

Quantitative approach Field of management that uses mathematical modeling as a foundation. (page 9)

R

Re-engineering Concept of restructuring a firm on the basis of processes and customer needs and services, rather than by department and functions. (page 255)

Realistic job preview (RJP) Information given by an interviewer to a job applicant that provides an honest view of both the positive and the negative aspects of the job. (page 354)

Realistic organizational preview (ROP) Sharing of information by an interviewer with a job applicant concerning the mission, values, and future direction of the organization. (page 354)

Reasonable accommodation Altering the usual ways of doing things so that an otherwise qualified disabled person can perform the essential job duties, but without creating an undue hardship for the employer. (page 493)

Recentralization Reducing or revoking delegated authority when realigning functions or responsibilities. (page 264)

Regular duties The essential components of a supervisor's job, such as giving directives and checking performance. (page 215)

Reverse discrimination Preference given to protected-group members in hiring and promotion over more qualified or more experienced workers from nonprotected groups. (page 500)

Right to appeal Procedures by which an employee may request higher-level management to review a supervisor's disciplinary action. (page 527)

Routine duties Minor tasks, done daily, that make a minor contribution to achievement of objectives. (page 214)

Rule A directive that must be applied and enforced consistently. (page 184)

S

Sales Dollar amount charged to customers for goods and services provided. (page 598)

Sampling The technique of evaluating some number of items from a larger group to determine whether the group meets acceptable quality standards. (page 590)

Satisficing Selecting the alternative that minimally meets the decision criteria. (page 155)

Scheduling The process of developing a detailed list of activities, their sequence, and the required resources. (page 188)

Scientific management approach School of management thought that focuses on the "one best way" to achieve production efficiency. (page 7)

Security needs Desire for protection against danger and life's uncertainties. (page 107)

Selection Process of choosing the best applicants to fill open positions. (page 347)

Selection criteria Factors used to choose among applicants who apply for a job. (page 341)

Self-fulfillment needs Desire to use one's abilities to the fullest extent. (page 108)

Self-respect needs Desire for recognition, achievement, status, and a sense of accomplishment. (page 108)

Semantics The multiple meanings of words. (page 63)

Seniority An employee's length of service within a department or organization. (page 377)

Sexual harassment Unwelcome sexual advances, requests, or conduct when submission to such conduct is tied to the individual's continuing employment or advancement, unreasonably interferes with job performance, or creates a hostile work environment. (page 489)

Sexual stereotyping Use of language or judgments that demean someone, usually by men toward women. (page 490)

Shop steward Employee elected or appointed to represent employees at the departmental level, particularly in grievance processing. (page 312)

Single-use plans Plans developed to accomplish a specific objective that, once achieved, most likely will not recur. (page 185)

SKAs Skills, knowledge, and abilities that a person has. (page 14)

Skill-based pay System that rewards employees for acquiring new skills or knowledge. (page 382)

Social needs Desire for love and affection and affiliation with something worthwhile. (page 107)

Span of management The maximum number of subordinates that a supervisor can manage effectively. (page 239)

Special duties Tasks not directly related to the core of the department, such as meetings and committee work. (page 215)

Special-interest group Grouping of employees that exists to accomplish something in a group that individuals do not choose to pursue individually. (page 457)

Staff authority The right to provide counsel, advice, support, and service in a person's areas of expertise. (page 248)

Staff department Specialized department responsible for supporting line departments and providing specialized advice and services. (page 250)

Staffing The tasks of recruiting, selecting, orienting, training, appraising, and evaluating employees. (page 36)

Standards Units of measurement or specific criteria against which to evaluate results. (page 582)

Standing plans Policies, procedures, methods, and rules that can be applied to recurring situations. (page 180)

Statement of cash flows Financial statement showing the movement of cash into and out of the business. (page 601)

Status Attitudes toward a person based on the position he or she occupies. (page 63)

Stereotyping The perception that all people in a certain group share common attitudes, values, and beliefs. (page 65)

Strategic alliances Cooperative ventures between different organizations to build on each other's strengths to accomplish mutual objectives more efficiently. (page 16)

Strategic control points Performance criteria chosen for assessment because they are key indicators of overall performance. (page 586)

Strategic planning The process of making decisions that will enable an organization to achieve its long-term objectives. (page 168)

Stretching standards Targeted job objectives that present a challenge but are achievable. (page 442)

Supervisor First-level manager in charge of entry-level and other departmental employees. (page 4)

T

Tangible standards Standards for performance results that are identifiable and measurable. (page 584)

Task group Grouping of employees who come together to accomplish a particular task. (page 456)

Teamwork People working cooperatively to solve problems and achieve goals important to the group. (page 463)

Technical skills The ability to do the job. (page 32)

Telecommuting Receiving and sending work to the office from home via a computer and modem. (page 12)

Temporary (ad hoc) committee Group that meets only for a limited time and for a specific purpose. (page 287)

Theory X Assumption that employees dislike work, avoid responsibility, and must be coerced to do the job. (page 115)

Theory Y Assumption that employees enjoy work, seek responsibility, and are capable of self-direction. (page 115)

360-degree evaluation Performance appraisal based on data collected from all around the employee—from customers, vendors, supervisors, peers, subordinates, etc. (page 395)

Time study A technique for analyzing jobs to determine the standard time needed to complete them. (page 584)

Total quality management (TQM) An organizational approach involving all employees in the continual improvement of goods and services. (page 173)

Two-tier wage system Paying new employees at a lower rate than more senior employees. (page 17)

U

Underemployment Situation in which people are in jobs that do not utilize their skills, knowledge, and abilities (SKAs). (page 14)

Understudy Someone who can assist the supervisor and is able to run the department in the supervisor's absence. (page 266)

Union business representative Paid official of the local or national union who may be involved in grievance processing (page 312)

Union shop A labor agreement provision in which employees are required to join the union as a condition of employment, usually after 30 days. (page 304)

Unity-of-command principle Principle that holds that each employee should report to only one supervisor. (page 85)

V

Vertical analysis Financial statements that show income statement items as a percentage of sales and balance sheet items as a percentage of total assets. (page 603)

Visioning Management's view of what the company is to become that sets the foundation for other activities. (page 169)

Z

Zero-base budgeting The process of assessing all activities to justify their existence on a benefit and cost basis. (page 608)

A

Ability, 377–378; definition of, 378
Absences, planning for, 210
Accommodation, communication and, 71
Accountability, 86–87; definition of, 84
Accounting: as control mechanism, 597–602; definition of, 597
Action, reinforcing words with, 69
Activities, nature and complexity of, span of management and, 241
Activity ratios, 604
Ad hoc committee. *See* Temporary committee
Administrative skills, definition of, 32
Advance warning, in applying discipline, 524

Advice, decision making and, 157
Age discrimination, 495–497
Agenda, 291–292
Aldag, Ramon, 35, 49*n*
Allen, John, 389*n*
Alternative dispute resolution (ADR), 540–542; definition of, 540
Alternatives: developing, 152–153; evaluating, 154–155; selecting, 155–158
Amaral, Donald, 332
Americans with Disabilities Act (ADA), 493–496; compliance with, 494; supervisor and employee attitudes toward, 494–496
Anderson, Kevin, 389*n*
Anthony, Richard J., 389*n*
Anthony, Robert, 620*n*
Anthony, William P., 223*n*

Arbitrator, definition of, 310
Arthur, Diane, 364*n*
Ash, Stephen, 224*n*
Ashton, David, 197*n*
Asquith, Nancy, 363*n*
Assad, Arjang A., 197*n*
Assets, definition of, 599
Atmosphere, calm, communication and, 67
Attitude survey: definition of, 472; follow up, 473
Austin, M. Jill, 196*n*
Austin, Nancy, 49*n*
Authority: acceptance theory of, 81–82; definition of, 39; delegation of, 41; formal, origins of, 80–81; granting, 85; limitations to, 82–83; managerial, understanding, 80–83
Authority, centralized, 88; definition of, 88
Authority, decentralized:

broad, 88–89; definition of, 88; limited, 88
Authority relationships, line and staff, 247–248
Avolio, Bruce J., 77*n*
Axley, Stephen R., 76*n*

B

Background review: importance of, 352–353; in selection process, 351–352
Bacon, Donald S., 197*n*
Baker, Carolyn A., 389*n*
Balance sheet, 598–601; definition of, 598
Ball, Judith S., 131*n*
Ballot, Michael, 317*n*
Banta, William F., 506*n*
Baron, Robert A., 76*n*–77*n*
Bateman, T.S., 479*n*
Baughman, J., 27*n*
Becker, Gary S., 28*n*

Note: Page numbers followed by *n* indicate a citation from a note.

PHOTO CREDITS